Elementary Data Structures with
PASCAL

Elementary Data Structures
with
PASCAL

ANGELA B. SHIFLET

WOFFORD COLLEGE

West Publishing Company

ST. PAUL · NEW YORK · LOS ANGELES · SAN FRANCISCO

Production Credits
Copyedit: Sheryl Rose
Text design: Paula Schlosser
Composition: G & S Typesetters, Inc.
Text art: G & S Typesetters, Inc.
Cover photo: Michel Tcherevkoff/The Image Bank

COPYRIGHT ©1990   By WEST PUBLISHING COMPANY
50 W. Kellogg Boulevard
P.O. Box 64526
St. Paul, MN 55164-1003

97 96 95 94 93 92 91 90   8 7 6 5 4 3 2 1 0

Library of Congress Cataloging-in-Publication Data

Shiflet, Angela B.
   Elementary data structures with Pascal / Angela B. Shiflet.
      p.   cm.
   ISBN 0-314-66780-6
   1. Pascal (Computer program language)   2. Data structures (Computer science)   I. Title.
QA76.73.P2S524   1990
005.13′3—dc20   89-29442
                                                                            CIP

Dedicated to
my husband,
George,
and my parents,
Isabell and Carroll Buzzett

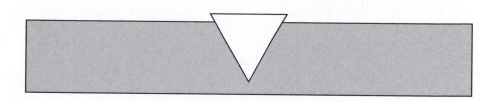

CONTENTS

PREFACE

Elementary Data Structures with Pascal introduces the CS2 or elementary data structures student to the subject in a clear, visual, top-down manner. The text first presents each data structure as an abstract data type (ADT), or a set of data objects and fundamental operations on this set. The use of boldface type emphasizes changes in the structures and the values of the variables. English descriptions and accompanying diagrams, give the student a visual concept of the data structure.

Applications are then developed using pseudocode and ADT operations, often with diagrams to clarify the words of the algorithms. By first considering data structures on a high level without concern for the implementation details, the student obtains a powerful tool which simplifies the process of handling data and extends naturally the concept of structured programming. One of the major goals of data abstraction is to encapsulate the structure so that details of implementation are hidden from the user. With such information hidden, the programmer can consider applications on a higher plane with major operations as opposed to on a lower level where there is the very real danger of becoming lost in a sea of details.

After studying and using the data structure on the abstract data type level, the text examines how the structure is represented and how the operations can be written in Standard Pascal. Appendix B covers important extensions in Turbo Pascal and UCSD Pascal. Often, there are several ways to implement a particular ADT. Advantages and disadvantages of these implementations and the circumstances which make one more desirable than another are also discussed.

For the convenience of the instructor, a disk is available with Standard Pascal implementations of the abstract data types. Use of these files saves time in designing, coding, typing, and testing the Pascal implementations of the abstract data types. This disk, which is described in greater detail under *Supplementary Materials,* may be copied freely for the students.

The text presents many applications in examples, exercises, and programming projects. Each section has a number of exercises with answers to selected problems with italicized numbers in Appendix D. Among other features described below, the *Instructor's Manual* contains answers to all of the remaining exercises. Pascal code in the text, the *Instructor's Manual,* and on the disk of ADT implementations have been computer tested.

A chapter-by-chapter description of the organization of the text and a more detailed description of learning features follows.

Organization

Chapter 1

Sections 1.1 through 1.3 examine the process of developing quality software. These sections provide a good review and enhancement of the programming principles covered in the prerequisite course of Pascal programming. Early discussion of analysis of algorithms (Section 1.4) provides a measure of the efficiency of algorithms to be used throughout the text.

Chapter 2

Recursion is covered early (Section 2.1) in the text. Thus, this powerful technique is employed in the development of a number of procedures and functions. Section 2.2 compares recursion and iteration and discusses how to convert a recursive algorithm to an iterative one. The study of program verification techniques is important to the computer science major. The instructor may decide, however, to postpone its study in Section 2.3 to later in the course. The last section of the chapter introduces the topic of abstract data type, the fundamental approach to data structures employed in the text.

Chapter 3

In this chapter the text continues the study of abstract data types by examining various composite types that are built into Pascal—array, record, file, and set. After defining each as an ADT, the text presents its built-in Standard Pascal implementation along with applications. The discussion of arrays is augmented by a study of the sequential and binary search methods in Section 3.2. Depending on the level of the class, the instructor can treat this chapter as reference material or cover the topics in detail.

Chapter 4

Chapter 4 covers the ADT string along with various array implementations and applications in text editing. After the discussion in Chapter 7, a linked list implementation is considered and compared to the array one (Section 8.2). The instructor again has the option of treating the material of this chapter in a cursory or detailed fashion.

Chapter 5

Section 5.1 gives a conceptual view of a stack, defines stack as an abstract data type, and presents various short applications. The next section discusses an implementation of the ADT stack with arrays, postponing one with linked lists until Chapter 8. Additional applications in Section 5.3 include postfix notation and simulation of recursion using a stack and iteration.

Chapter 6

The format of this chapter parallels that of Chapter 5. The first section covers the abstract data type queue with several short applications, and Section 6.2 presents an array implementation. The last section develops a simulation of a waiting line at a post office with top-down design and pseudocode development of the procedures.

Chapter 7

After studying pointers in Section 7.1, the text devotes the rest of this chapter to the abstract data type linked list. Manipulations of linked lists pictorially (Section 7.2) precede the formal ADT definition (Section 7.3). Section 7.4 covers implementations with dynamic and static memory allocations. Circular, doubly, and multiply linked lists are discussed in the optional, last section along with an application to sparse matrices.

Chapter 8

In Section 8.1 the text discusses various applications of linked lists: memory management with the development of user-defined *New* and *Dispose* operations; arithmetic on very large, nonnegative integers; and a generalized list structure similar to that employed by the language LISP. In Sections 8.2 through 8.4 the text reconsiders the abstract data types of string, stack, and queue, previously implemented statically with arrays, now implemented dynamically with linked lists. For each ADT the advantages and disadvantages of these two implementation techniques are discussed. Faced with a choice in the coding of the abstract data types, in Section 8.5 the text reexamines how the programmer should develop Pascal programs with ADT objects and operations hidden, to be used like they are predefined. The student sees that by using ADT objects and operations in the development of applications, he or she can substitute different implementations of the ADT without changing significantly the code of the application program.

Chapter 9

This chapter examines the ADT table along with five implementations and applications, such as to relational data bases. Section 9.2 compares and contrasts four implementations of the ADT table involving a static memory allocation with ordered and unordered arrays and a dynamic memory allocation with ordered and unordered linked lists. The hash table implementation is presented in the last section.

Chapter 10

The first section of this chapter introduces tree terminology and traversals, while the next defines the abstract data type binary tree. Two binary tree implementations involving pointers are presented in Sections 10.3 and 10.4. With the first of these implementations, many of the algorithms are developed recursively. The instructor may choose to omit the second method, using threaded trees, which illustrates a nonrecursive alternative. Section 10.5 explores binary search trees, while optional Section 10.6 introduces AVL trees. The last of this chapter examines several applications of binary trees: expression trees, decision trees, game trees, and Huffman codes.

Chapter 11

In this chapter the text presents several algorithms for sorting: insertion sort, selection sort, quicksort, heapsort, mergesort, and sorting with a permutation array. This examination of sorting considers the complexities of the various methods and the situations for which they are best suited. The instructor may, however, choose to omit one or more of these techniques, such as the selection sort of Section 11.2. Because this chapter is substantially self-contained, the instructor also has the option of covering the material earlier in the course.

Chapter 12

The abstract data type graph, discussed in Section 12.1, is implemented with adjacency matrices (Section 12.2) and with adjacency lists (Section 12.3). Section 12.4 presents algorithms with accompanying diagrams for depth-first and breadth-first traversals of graphs. In the last section the text covers applications involving mazes, minimal spanning trees, and shortest paths in networks.

Learning Features

Chapter introductions   One to several paragraphs at the beginning of each chapter give an overview of the material in the chapter.

Example operations/applications   Examples help to clarify the material. The organized approach to examples, particularly with accompanying diagrams, aids understanding of the material. Applications illustrate the use of a data structure, demonstrate its importance, and provide interest.

Numerous diagrams with boldface type to emphasize changes   Diagrams help students visualize the actions of operations and algorithms.

Implementations of an ADT presented after the formal definition   Only after students become familiar with a data structure on the higher level of an ADT does the text consider implementation details.

Historical anecdotes   Such anecdotes add interest to the text. Moreover, they often present material that a computer science major should know about the history of the discipline.

Numerous exercises at the end of each section   Exercises are at the end of each section, not just at the end of the chapter. On the average there are 21 exercises per section, 95 per chapter. Exercises include short answer problems, diagrams of the execution of segments, design of procedures and functions using pseudocode and ADT operations, coding of procedures and functions, applications, and questions from the Advanced Placement Examination in Computer Science.

Answers to all exercises   Answers in Appendix D to some exercises (those with italicized numbers) for each section allow students to check their work for immediate reinforcement. The *Instructor's Manual* contains answers to all the remaining exercises.

Programming projects   On the average, there are 6 programming projects per chapter. These are major assignments to be implemented on the computer. By completing such a project, the student implements an application of the data structure and enhances his or her understanding of the material and abilities in software design.

Organized comparison of different implementations of ADTs   These comparisons provide guidelines for the implementations which are best to employ in various situations.

Supplementary Materials

Disk of ADT implementations

A disk with implementations in Pascal of the abstract data types is available to adopters from West upon request. Each ADT implementation appears in two source files on the disk:

1. A text file in the format of a Turbo Pascal unit is ready for compilation in that version of the language. Minor modifications convert this file to one that can be used by other versions of Pascal which permit separate compilation.

2. Another text file contains the implementation as it would appear after a program statement. For appropriate versions of Pascal, this file can be used as an "include" file. If separately compiled units or include files are not available, this text file can be copied for use in a program.

A file, called "Read Me," and documentation in the *Instructor's Manual* describe how to employ these. Since the files are stored as text files, they can be easily edited with an editor or a word processor. The disk is available as a 3½" Macintosh, 3½" IBM, or 5¼" IBM disk. A free site license is issued to any school which adopts the text.

Instructor's Manual

An Instructor's Manual, written by the author and John S. Hinkel, contains all solutions to text exercises that are not provided in the text appendix, answers to at least one project per chapter, and additional test problems with answers. The Pascal code was tested on a Macintosh computer using Turbo Pascal.

Acknowledgements

Many people provided valuable assistance in the completion of this book. John S. Hinkel has been extremely helpful in many ways. As coauthor of the *Instructor's Manual,* among other tasks, he wrote and implemented the programming exercises, projects, and units in Pascal. As problem checker, he carefully verified all examples and answers included in the text, testing operations on the computer where appropriate. As one of the reviewers of the first and second drafts of the manuscript, he provided insightful suggestions for improvements to the book. As a colleague, he gave me another viewpoint concerning issues relative to the text. I truly appreciate his help and friendship.

The administration at Wofford College, especially my chairman, Richard Robinson, has been generous in providing me encouragement and a reduced load to write the book.

Friends at Lawrence Livermore National Laboratory (LLNL), where I have worked for six summers, have given me many opportunities and taught me much which have enhanced this text. Special thanks go to Ted Einwohner, Bob Cralle, George Michael, and John Ranelletti.

Peter Marshall, Executive Editor at West Publishing Company, is a marvelous editor. He provided many good ideas, a clear direction, and valuable assistance. Tamborah Moore, Production Editor, kept the production moving smoothly and on time. My thanks also go to Sheryl Rose for her accurate copy editing; to Paula Schlosser for her nice design; and to Maralene Bates for her assistance in the review stage.

I am grateful to the following reviewers who offered many valuable constructive criticisms:

John Hinkel
Lander College, South Carolina

Andrew Bernat
University of Texas, El Paso

Nancy Wiegand
University of Wisconsin, Madison

Dean Arden
State University of New York, Albany

John Bertani
Oregon State University

Debra Trantina
Arizona State University

Luegina Mounfield
*Louisiana State University,
Baton Rouge*

Krithi Ramamritham
*University of Massachusetts,
Amherst*

Ben Moreland
University of Connecticut, Storrs

Anne Louise Radimsky
*California State University,
Sacramento*

George Strawn
Iowa State University

Paul Schnare
Eastern Kentucky University

Ralph H. Bjork
University of Wisconsin, Platteville

My husband, George W. Shiflet, Jr., has been helpful in so many ways, including proofreading galleys and page proofs.

George and my parents, Isabell and Carroll Buzzett, have given me many years of love and encouragement along with their prayers. Without them this book would not be possible; and so, it is dedicated to those whom I love the most.

CHAPTER 1

Programming Methodology

Introduction

Structures that hold data, operations that manipulate these structures, and algorithms that use these operations are the essence of data structures. Since we will be developing application programs employing data structures, we begin by studying an organized approach to the creation of programs and a measure of the efficiency of the methods we use.

In the first three sections of this chapter we examine the process of developing software with particular emphasis on the design, coding, and testing phases. Careful attention to these areas is essential to the production of good programs and software systems. Usually, we have a choice of techniques to use in the design of different parts, or modules, in a program. In the last section of this chapter we study a measure of the efficiency of algorithms. This measure gives us a basis of comparison so that we can select the most appropriate technique to use in a particular situation.

SECTION 1.1

Program Design

Data structures is a study of the various frameworks for storing data and the algorithms that implement and perform operations on these structures. Undoubtedly, you have already written a number of algorithms. An **algorithm** is a method for accomplishing something in a finite number of steps. The term is derived from the last name of a Persian mathematician, Abu Ja'far Mohammed ibn Mûsâ al-Khowârizmî, who wrote an important arithmetic textbook about 825 A.D. In the prerequisite programming course you covered algorithmic development as well as details of the Pascal language.

Before launching into a study of data structures, we will review the process of problem solving involved in software development. This process, called the **software life cycle**, has five major steps:

1. Analysis

2. Design

3. Coding

4. Testing

5. Maintenance

The first step of the software life cycle is to obtain a clear understanding of the problem through a detailed analysis. Only after a careful and thorough design process should we attempt to translate the solution into a programming language. Such attention to the design phase often will minimize the time needed for debugging. Problems revealed at a stage such as the coding or testing phase may require that we return to an earlier step and repeat part of the life cycle, making necessary changes. Many professional programmers spend a majority of their time maintaining existing systems of programs by correcting and modifying them.

In beginning computer science courses you are usually given the specifications for new problems so that your emphasis is on the design, coding, and testing steps of the software life cycle. Thus, in this chapter we cover suggestions for producing quality work in each of these three phases. The last section of the chapter covers the basis for evaluating and comparing the algorithms we develop.

In 1976 Edsger Dijkstra wrote of the importance of using **structured programming** techniques. Structured programs use only three basic constructs:

1. **Sequential structure,** with steps performed one after another in succession.

2. **Selection structure,** such as implemented with an *if-then-else* or *case* statement.

3. **Repetition structure,** such as implemented with a *for, while*, or *repeat* loop.

Every program can and should be written using only these three constructs. Structured programming has proved to be an effective technique in producing programs that are easier to write, read, test, debug, and maintain.

Another aspect of structured programming is **top-down design** or the development of a solution in a **modular** fashion starting at the highest level with repeated refinement. It is impossible to keep all aspects of a complex program in mind. We can, however, design the major steps of the solution as modules. In turn, each of these steps can be further broken down into more manageable portions or submodules. Within a program the modules are usually realized as procedures or functions with the main program invoking subprograms at the highest level of design. It is best for each subprogram to perform only one major task and usually to have no more than about 30 statements. Each of these modules can be tested and debugged independently. Consider how much easier it would be to find an error in 30 lines of code of a module as opposed to

300 lines in an entire program. In a modular design, only the offending module, as opposed to the entire program, may need to be rewritten. Moreover, with such a design, if we find a better algorithm for performing a particular task—for example, a better method for alphabetizing names—we only need to substitute one module for another. We can also more easily add features, such as a menu-driven display, by inserting new modules.

A **structured diagram** or **hierarchy chart** is a graph of the program modules and their relation to one another. At the highest level a rectangle represents the main program. Below this rectangle are other rectangles with the names of the modules invoked by the main program, listed in order from left to right. Likewise, each of these modules has its submodules displayed in a hierarchical fashion.

Consider the problem of discovering those students who had above average performance on a test. Figure 1.1 displays the structured diagram for a solution.

Figure 1.1

Structured diagram for program to print names of students with above average test scores

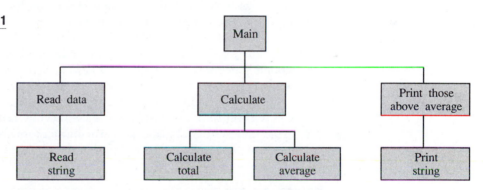

The Read-Data module has the overall task of reading and storing students' names and test scores in an array of records. To perform part of this mission a Read-String module is called to read a string, in this case a name. The corresponding test score is read in the Read-Data module. A **string** is a sequence of characters. In a later chapter we consider a more formal definition of string along with various string operations and two different implementations. In fact, many versions of Pascal, such as Turbo Pascal, have a built-in operation to read strings. The reference manual for the compiler you are using documents how that version handles string operations; also, Appendix B contains an outline of some of the extensions available in two popular versions of the language. We employ a standard implementation in this text and assume you can implement an appropriate procedure to read a string in your version of Pascal. In this chapter we design and implement a Read-String procedure using an array to hold the characters in the string along with a variable, *length*, to store the number of these characters.

After constructing a structured diagram, we write each module in **pseudocode**, a structured English outline of the design. For example, the Read-String module for our design can be written in pseudocode as follows:

length ← 0
Read a character
While the character is supposed to be in the string and
   there is room in the string array do the following:
 Increment *length*
 Put the character into next element of string array
 Read a character
Pad the rest of the string array with blanks
Skip over extra characters in the name that do not fit in the string array

The first line of the algorithm indicates that *length* is initialized with the value of zero. The *read* statement before the loop, called a **priming read,** enables the *while* condition to test that the character is in the string. The indented statements directly below the *while* statement are all included within the loop; in pseudocode designs we use indentation to indicate a *begin-end* block in Pascal. Notice that details of implementation in a particular language are still masked. Thus, at this stage the programmer can concentrate on the design of the solution as opposed to the syntax of the language.

One caution in designing a program is to avoid "clever" solutions that might save a little execution time but are difficult for humans to understand. Such programming contortions are usually hard to debug and even harder for someone else to maintain. Computers have become much faster in recent years so that the programmer's time is now a more important consideration than efficiency issues. Of course, we still want to use significantly faster algorithms and want to avoid unnecessary statements, particularly those embedded deeply in nested statements; but "cute," tricky designs are undesirable.

▽

SECTION 1.1 EXERCISES

The answers to exercises in this text with italicized numbers are given in Appendix D.

Write pseudocode for the modules in Figure 1.1 listed in Exercises 1–7.

1. Main program procedure.

2. Procedure to read data into an array of records. This procedure should handle the interactive prompts for name and test score, should call the Read-String module to read a name, but should read the numeric test score itself.

3. Calculate procedure.

4. Function to calculate the total.

5. Function to calculate the average.

6. Procedure to print the names and scores of those students with above average scores.

7. Procedure to print the first *length* characters in an array of characters.

8. Modify the structured diagram in Figure 1.1 to find the maximum and minimum scores and the names of the students who made those scores.

9. Write pseudocode for the modules added in Exercise 8.

10. Write pseudocode to merge two sorted text files of numbers into one output file.

▽

PROGRAMMING PROJECTS

The following programming projects evolve over three sections. In this section you are asked to design the programs; in the next, to code; and in Section 1.3, to test and debug. For Programming Projects 1–4, draw a structured diagram for the program and then write pseudocode for each of its modules.

1. A professor wants to maintain an interactive system to return students' final letter grades in a course. Students may phone or come by the professor's office during a one-hour period during exams to inquire about their grades. For confidentiality and ease of reading, the professor would like to display only one requesting student's name and grade at a time.

   The program should interactively read names and final letter grades into an array of records. The professor plans to enter the data in alphabetical order by last name. One line of input will contain the student's last name, a comma and a blank, the student's first initial followed by a period, one or more blanks, and then the grade. For example, one student's data could read as follows:

   ```
   Jones, J.    B
   ```

   After placing the class information into the array, the program should repeat the following process until some sentinel or terminating value is read: prompt the professor for a name, read a name, and search the array to return that student's name and grade. A sample of the output is as follows:

   ```
   Student Grade Report for Data Structures
   Name:   Jones, J.              Grade:   B
   ```

   The search for a student's name should be sequential, from one element to the next, and should terminate when the name is found or it becomes obvious that the name is not in the array. The names are in alphabetical order, so there is no need to look for the grade of Jones, J. beyond where the name should appear in the array. If a name is not in the array, the computer should print a message to that effect. The design should have a search function that returns the index of the name or zero if the name is not in the array.

2. Design a program to play craps. In craps someone places a bet and then throws a pair of dice. If the first roll is a 7 or 11, the player wins; if the roll is

2, 3, or 12, the player loses. If any other number appears the player rolls again, perhaps several times. To win, the player must roll the first number again before a 7 appears.

Use a random number generator to simulate the roll of a die. If your version of Pascal does not have such a generator, refer to Appendix A to find one you can write yourself.

Your program should be interactive, asking the player how much to bet. If a win occurs, ask the player if he or she wishes to play again; if so, obtain another bet. If a loss occurs, the person cannot play again. When the game is over, print how much was won or lost. The program should simulate the play for only one person.

3. Design a program for the higher-lower game. In this game the computer picks a random integer between 1 and 100; the player tries to guess the number. With each wrong guess the computer instructs the player to guess a number higher or lower. The player has a fixed number of guesses.

Initially, ask the player his or her name and address the player personally in some of the displays. Also, allow the player to set the degree of difficulty as easy (a maximum of 15 guesses), moderate (8 guesses), or hard (4 guesses), and let him or her play as often as desired. When the player quits, give the final win-loss tally along with the average number of guesses. Refer to Appendix A for a random number generator if one is not predefined in your version of Pascal.

4. Design a banker program that first asks the user the balance in his or her checking and savings accounts and then gives a menu of choices:

   a. Make a deposit.
   b. Make a withdrawal.
   c. Perform an electronic funds transfer.
   d. Display balances.
   e. Quit.

A deposit can be made to the checking or savings account. A withdrawal can be made from either account but carries a 10% penalty from the savings account. An electronic funds transfer has a $0.50 charge and can only be made from the checking account. Allow the user to make any number of transactions. Of course, he or she cannot withdraw or transfer from an account more money than is in the balance. When the user quits, automatically display the balances.

SECTION 1.2

Coding

The process of translating an algorithm into a computer language such as Pascal is called **coding**. The Pascal language is named after Blaise Pascal, the great scientist and mathematician of the 17th century. During his late teens and twenties, he designed and built the first workable automatic calculator to help his father, who was overwhelmed with work as a tax assessor. Pascal suffered from violent headaches all his life and alternated between periods of great scientific achievement and intense religious fervor. Intrigued by the questions of a gambling friend, he helped to establish the mathematical theory of probability. During a period in which he was writing many religious essays, to take his mind off a painful toothache he immersed himself in the study of geometry, working many previously unsolved problems. Blaise Pascal died at the age of 39 in 1662 after suffering a brain hemorrhage.

In coding with the Pascal language, the sequential, selection, and repetition programming constructs should mimic our structured design constructs. Thus, although a *goto* statement is available, by all means resist the temptation to use it. Employing *goto*s often results in "spaghetti code," which is difficult to understand and even harder to debug. One rare situation in which a *goto* statement might be beneficial is in the innermost level of a deep nesting when there is the possibility of calling an error-handling routine and then halting execution. In this case, the most understandable way for the program to abort is for the error procedure to branch unconditionally to the last statement in the program.

Another temptation is to use global variables to excess. The **scope** of a variable, or the area in which it may be referenced, is the block in which it is declared. Variables declared in the main program are **global**, and those declared in a subprogram are **local** to that module. In general, variables that need to be accessed by a module and a submodule should be passed through the argument-parameter list. Thus, the independence of the module is preserved, the structured design is maintained, and errors involving variables are easier to find and correct. The only exception to having local variables is when a variable such as an array or file is accessed in almost every module. In that case, the global declaration is meaningful and more readable.

Parameters that pass values into and out of a procedure are declared as **variable parameters** by beginning their declaration with *var*. When the procedure is called, a copy of an argument is not made for a corresponding variable parameter, but the argument's memory location is made available to that parameter. Thus, a change in the value of a variable parameter within the procedure changes the value of the corresponding argument in the calling routine. If the value only goes into a procedure, declare the variable as a **value parameter** by not using *var*. When the procedure is called or the function is invoked, a memory location is established for the value parameter and the value of the argument is copied into that location; all further communication between the argument and parameter is severed. Functions should return only one scalar value. Thus, to avoid the unintentional side effect of changing another variable's value in a function, make all parameters value parameters. Again, there is an exception: When passing a large array to a function or procedure, use a variable parameter to avoid having the computer take the time and room to copy the entire array.

One useful type of variable parameter for a procedure is a **flag** or boolean variable that indicates the success or failure of a process. For example, suppose a procedure is to read a value into an array. Should the array already be filled, a *success* flag could be returned as *false* to indicate that the addition to the array was not achieved.

Variable names like *success* are meaningful and, therefore, easier to remember. If we use cryptic names such as *X*, the code becomes much more difficult to read. Often, multiple word names are descriptive, particularly when the first letter in each word is capitalized as in *TaxRate*.

Constant identifiers can also enhance readability as well as the universality of the program. For example, suppose the test scores of 35 students are to be read into an array of the type definition

```
score = array [1..35] of integer;
```

Subsequent loop statements might read

```
for i := 1 to 35 do
```

or

```
while i <= 35 do
```

If later the program is to be executed for a class of 40 students, that type definition and every loop terminal value using that 35 must be located and changed to 40. How much easier it would be to have a constant *MaxNumStu* used in the type definition:

```
const
    MaxNumStu = 35;
type
    score = array [1..MaxNumStu] of integer;
```

with loop statements of

```
for i := 1 to MaxNumStu do
```

or

```
while i <= MaxNumStu do
```

Then, to accommodate the additional 5 students, we only need to alter the constant definition:

```
const
    MaxNumStu = 40;
```

We do not need to tamper with every loop or other statement that references the maximum of 35.

Meaningful names for these constant identifiers as well as for variable names help to make the code more **self-documenting** or self-explanatory. Additionally, we should have comments containing descriptions of each variable where it is declared. Internal documentation can also enhance readability and facilitate error checking and maintenance. Each module and major section of code should have a brief introductory comment explaining the purpose of the forthcoming statements. A longer comment at the beginning of the program should contain the following information:

1. Author

2. Date

3. Purpose

4. Input files

5. Output files

6. Assumptions

For example, the program described in Section 1.1 might have the following header comment:

```
{ **********************************************

Author:     Mary Smith
Date:       9/1/92

This program finds the students who scored above average
on a test.

Input:          Standard Input file of names and
                    test scores
Output:         Standard Output file of names and scores
                    of students who scored above average
Assumptions:    There is a maximum class size of 35 and
                a maximum name length of 20.


********************************************** }
```

Because of the number of *begin-end* blocks normally contained in a Pascal program and the necessity of matching each *begin* with an *end*, it is a good idea to place a comment after an *end* statement indicating the block with which it is associated. For example,

```
end { while }
```

or

```
end { ReadStr }
```

could be used to indicate the *end* statement for a *while* loop or for the procedure *ReadStr*, respectively.

The blank lines that make this beginning comment more readable can also make code more readable. Thus, we should surround procedures, functions, and blocks of code with blank lines. A statement, too, is easier to read if there are enough blanks, such as those surrounding operators and the assignment symbol and those after commas.

Figure 1.2

Coding for procedure
ReadStr

```pascal
program AboveAverage (Input, Output);
{ Place header comments here. }
const
    MaxNumStu    = 35;                   {maximum number of students}
    MaxStr       = 20;                   {maximum length of name}

type
    lengthType   = 0..MaxStr;
    GradeType    = 0..100;
    NumStuType   = 0..MaxNumStu;

    StringType   = record
        length   : lengthType;
        str      : array [1..MaxStr] of char
    end;

    elType       = record
        Name     : StringType;
        Grade    : GradeType
    end;

    ArrayType    = array [1..MaxNumStu] of elType;

var
    NameString   : StringType;          {name}
    StudentRec   : ArrayType;           {array of student records}
    NumStu       : NumStuType;          {number of students}
    average      : real;                {average grade}
{ ***********************************************************************
   Procedure to read a string into an array from the standard input
   file. A comma terminates the input string.
   *********************************************************************** }
procedure ReadStr ( var NameString: StringType );
const
    comma = ',';
    blank = ' ';

var
    i       : lengthType;               {index}
    ch      : char;                     {character that is read}
begin          { ReadStr }
    with NameString do
        begin   { with }
            length := 0;
```

Figure 1.2

continued

```
{****** Read characters into string array ******}
read (ch);
while ( ch <> comma ) and ( length < MaxStr ) do
   begin
      length := length + 1;
      str[length] := ch;
      read (ch)
   end;         { while }

{****** Pad end of string array with blanks ****** }
for i := length + 1 to MaxStr do
   str[i] := blank;

{****** Skip over extra characters in the ****** }
{****** name that do not fit in the array ****** }
while ( ch <> comma ) do
   read (ch)

          end    { with }
   end;          { ReadStr }
```

Another beneficial cosmetic feature is indentation. Within a decision statement or any *begin-end* block, we should indent statements three to five spaces. For clarity, make sure that the matching *begin* and *end* line up as do statements in the same level of nesting.

Figure 1.2 illustrates this indentation as well as other coding conventions for the module designed in the last section. Note that we primarily use lowercase with some capital letters for emphasis. You might choose to employ another convention such as capitalizing only reserved words or only user-defined variables. The main criterion should be that the system enhances readability.

In some programs, you may want to detect the end of the string with a comma, semicolon, period, or blank, and in others you may use *eoln* to detect termination of the string with the end-of-line marker. In the former case a set can be useful in the *while* statement with constants *comma, semicolon, period,* and *blank* appropriately defined:

```
while not ( ch in [comma, semicolon, period, blank] )
   and ( length < MaxNumStu ) do
```

In the latter case the *while* statement would read as follows:

```
while not eoln (input) and ( length < MaxNumStu ) do
```

In Exercises 1–9 write Pascal code for the modules designed in the indicated exercises from Section 1.1.

1. Main program from Exercise 1.

2. Procedure from Exercise 2 to read data into an array of records.

3. Calculate procedure from Exercise 3.

4. Function from Exercise 4 to calculate the total.

5. Function from Exercise 5 to calculate the average.

6. Procedure from Exercise 6 to print the names and scores of those students with above average scores.

7. Procedure from Exercise 7 to print a string.

8. Procedures from Exercise 8 and 9 to find the maximum and minimum scores and who made them.

9. Program from Exercise 10 to merge two sorted files of numbers into one output file.

10. Write code for a module to switch the values of two parameters, *X* and *Y*.

11. Write an error-handling procedure that receives an error code, prints an appropriate error message, and halts execution by jumping to the last statement in the program. The error code could be of an enumeration type such as (*DivisionByZero, NoData, IndexOutOfRange, NoGrade, NegativeGrade, Over100Grade, NameTooLong*).

For Programming Projects 1–4, write Pascal code for your design of the corresponding project from Section 1.1.

1. Project 1, to maintain an interactive system to return a student's final letter grade in a course.

2. Project 2, to play craps.

3. Project 3, to play the higher-lower game.

4. Project 4, to produce a banker program.

▽

SECTION 1.3

Testing and Debugging

The origin of the term "bug" goes back to the days of the first electromechanical, general purpose computer, the Mark I, completed during World War II.

The lack of air conditioning meant that the windows were left open on hot summer days. One such day the computer malfunctioned. After hours of testing, the laboratory workers opened the machine. There on one of the relays was the problem—a moth lodged on the contacts was preventing the flow of electricity. Carefully removing the insect and pasting it into the logbook, they wrote in the entry for the day of the "bug" that had been found in the computer. This famous bug is now on display at the Smithsonian Institution.

With testing, we attempt to discover and subsequently correct the bugs in programs. As much as possible, we should test a representative from each category of data so that all branches in the program are exercised. In Chapter 2, we examine techniques to prove that a program is correct. We should also test that the program properly handles exceptional situations such as an empty input file or improper data.

We should not wait until the entire program is entered to begin this testing, but should correct modules one at a time. For example, to test the *ReadStr* procedure from Section 1.2 we could design a short calling program. Using the same definitions and declarations listed in Section 1.2 along with an index *i* declared to be of type *NumStuType* and *choice* to be of type *char,* the main body of the program could read as follows:

```
begin    { AboveAverage to test ReadStr }

    repeat
        writeln('Type a name followed by a comma and return.');
        ReadStr(NameString);
        readln;                    {skip eoln marker}

        write('Name = ');
        for i := 1 to MaxStr do
            write(NameString.str[i]);
        writeln('Length = ', NameString.length);

        writeln;
        write('Press <Q> to quit, any other key to continue. ');
        readln(choice)
    until choice in ['Q', 'q']
end.      { AboveAverage to test ReadStr }
```

As we discuss in the section on arrays, Standard Pascal allows an entire packed array of characters to be written but not read. Because we did not declare *NameString.str* as packed, we print in the same way we read, one character at a time. The test program writes the length on the same line to verify that the padding of the name with blanks has occurred properly. The repeat loop enables us to execute *ReadStr* several times and to test that the procedure operates correctly for various types of data—short names, names of more than 20 characters, and names incorrectly entered with no terminating comma.

During the testing of a module, the complete main or **driver** program can also be entered into the computer and debugged. If a module is to be invoked that has not been entered, it can be recorded as a **stub**. Consisting only of a *write* statement, a stub such as the one that follows helps to trace the flow of a program:

```
procedure AboveAvg (var GradeBook: ArrayType; Average: real);
   begin
      writeln ('AboveAvg procedure executed')
   end; {AboveAvg}
```

Another use of stubs is to check the syntax of declarations and definitions through compilation. For this test, constant and type definitions, variable declarations, and procedure and function headers should be included in the code. Functions must return some artificial value, but descriptive comments can replace all other missing code. A successful compilation of this structure establishes a syntactically correct framework for testing individual modules. Just as the program should be entered and tested one module at a time, this syntax check of declarations and definitions should be compiled in stages of one or several stubs at a time. Nothing is quite so frustrating or seemingly hopeless as to enter an entire program, compile for the first time, and get page after page of syntax errors. One compiler will even send the disheartening message

TOO MANY ERRORS TO PRINT!

after several pages of compile-time errors. Often one syntax error results in countless others because the compiler cannot determine what is meant by the code.

If we cannot discover the source of a semantic or run-time error by quick inspection, we should place *write* statements at strategic locations in the program to indicate the flow of control and the intermediate values of variables. As a procedure or function is entered, the name of the subprogram and all input parameters can be printed as illustrated below:

```
function gcd ( M, N: integer ): integer;
var
   GreatestCommonDivisor : integer;
begin
   writeln ('gcd entered');
   writeln ('M = ', M, ' N = ', N);
```

Upon leaving the subprogram, we repeat the process, printing all output parameters or function values such as:

```
   writeln ('Exit from gcd');
   writeln ('gcd = ', GreatestCommonDivisor)
```

The reading of variables should be **echo printed**; that is, the value of each variable should be written immediately after it is read. Moreover, as each variable changes, its value should be printed again. Though it takes a little time to add these *write* statements and to recompile, examination of the resulting output can save hours of frustration. Check to see if your version of Pascal has a debugger. If so, it may allow you to trace the flow of your program; to step through the execution, one statement at a time; to establish break points where execution stops, awaiting further debugging instructions; and to follow the changing values of variables automatically.

Whatever we do, we should not start making arbitrary changes in the desperate hope of miraculously curing the error. Invariably, such antics result in more errors and a huge mess. Similarly, we should not just patch the program with an *if* statement covering one case without finding the root of the error. Often such a patch does not handle other exceptional situations, but does result in more errors. The rule is first to understand an error so that we can *correct*, not suppress, the problem.

Precautions we take with exceptional situations can avoid errors in future execution of the program. For example, on calculating the average of an array of test scores, does your module handle the empty situation when there are no scores? If not, you could get a division-by-zero error. Whenever there is division, we should consider if division by zero is ever possible; if it is, use an *if* statement to deal with the situation, perhaps as follows:

```
if count = 0 then
   begin
      writeln('No scores. Average not calculated.');
      average := 0
   end    {if}
else
   average := total / count
```

We should handle error situations such as division-by-zero with appropriate diagnostic messages. Otherwise, the program could end abnormally at a location far from the offending statement with little information about the problem. A well-written design handles error conditions appropriately without crashing or producing invalid output.

Special care needs to be taken with interactive programs. Messages at the beginning should tell the user exactly what the program does and how to terminate execution. When input is requested, we need to inform the user of acceptable responses such as:

```
write ('Are you a registered voter (Y/N)? ');
readln (Ans)
```

Then we should handle all reasonable responses such as an upper- or lower case y. Also, we must be sure to deal with responses that do not match reasonable answers. For instance, with the following segment an answer of n or even M would result in "Congratulations" being printed:

```
if Ans = 'N' then
   writeln('Please register')
else
   writeln('Congratulations')
```

As demonstrated below, *repeat* statements can be used to continue prompting for a correct response. Sets can enumerate all legal answers.

```
repeat
    write ('Are you a registered voter (Y/N)? ');
    readln (Ans)
until Ans in [ 'Y', 'y', 'N', 'n' ];

if Ans in [ 'Y', 'y' ] then
    writeln ('Please vote on November 2.')
else
    writeln ('Please register to vote before October 15.')
```

▽

SECTION 1.3 EXERCISES

1. Using a compiler, check for syntax errors in the definitions and declarations from the program designed in the text in Section 1.1 and coded in Exercises 1 through 7 of Section 1.2.

2. Test on the computer the module *ReadStr* coded in Section 1.2.

3. Test and debug the program coded in Exercises 1 through 7 of Section 1.2. Enter and test the modules one at a time. For each module give appropriate write statements that would be used for debugging.

4. Add a stub procedure for sorting the names from your program from Exercise 3. Do not actually sort, but have a write statement indicating that the procedure will eventually sort.

5. Describe how the program from Exercise 3 can handle the error of a missing comma after a person's name.

6. Make appropriate changes to the program of Exercise 3 to read from and write to text files.

7. Describe data to test your program from Exercise 3.

8. Test and debug the procedures coded in Exercise 8 of Section 1.2 to find the maximum and minimum scores and who made them. For each module give appropriate write statements that would be used for debugging.

9. Describe data to test your program from Exercise 8.

In Exercises 10–12 test and debug the routines coded in Section 1.2.

10. Program coded in Exercise 9 to merge two sorted files of numbers into one output file.

11. Module coded in Exercise 10 to switch the values of two parameters, *X* and *Y*.

12. Error-handling procedure coded in Exercise 11.

▽

PROGRAMMING PROJECTS

For Programming Projects 1–4, enter, test, and debug the corresponding program you designed and coded in Sections 1.1 and 1.2, respectively.

1. Project 1, to maintain an interactive system to return a student's final letter grade in a course.

2. Project 2, to play craps.

3. Project 3, to play the higher-lower game.

4. Project 4, to produce a banker program.

▽

SECTION 1.4

Analysis of Algorithms

Throughout the book we discuss various algorithms and analyze their efficiency. The measure of the efficiency of an algorithm is called its **complexity** or **order of magnitude** and is a function of the number of data items.

For example, suppose an inventory list of n elements is stored in an array. One method of looking for a particular item in the array is the **sequential search**. With this algorithm, we start at the beginning of the array and examine each element in turn. If the item is discovered, we stop the search and return the index of that array element. If the item is not in the array, the search returns zero. In the **worst case** the item is not found or is the last (nth) element. For both situations we must examine all n elements of the array so the order of magnitude or complexity of the sequential search is n, written with **big oh** notation as $O(n)$. The execution time for this algorithm is proportional to n, that is, the algorithm executes in **linear time**. The actual run time depends on external factors such as the particular machine and compiler but is still related to n.

Definition
A function f is of **complexity** or **order at most $g(n)$**, written with **big oh** notation as $f = O(g)$, if there exist a positive constant c and a positive integer n_0 such that $$\|f(n)\| \le c \cdot \|g(n)\|$$ for all $n \ge n_0$.

By this definition we can see that an algorithm that takes $2n$ steps is of complexity n or $2n = O(n)$ since $(2n) \le 2 \cdot n$. We say that f and g are of **equal complexity**, written $O(f) = O(g)$, provided $f = O(g)$ and $g = O(f)$. Thus, with $n \le (2n)$ and $(2n) \le 2 \cdot n$, we have $O(n) = O(2n)$. In general, constant factors do not affect the complexity, so we usually drop them for simplicity.

An algorithm that takes time proportional to $5n^3 + 6n^2 + n + 7$ is actually $O(n^3)$ since the size of the n^3 greatly outweighs the size of the other terms. For instance, if n is 100, n^3 is 1,000,000, while n^2 is only 10,000 and $6n^2 + n + 7$ is 60,107. The running time, which is proportional to $5n^3 + 6n^2 + n + 7$, is dominated by the n^3 term. More formally,

$$5n^3 + 6n^2 + n + 7 \le 10n^3 \text{ for } n > 2$$

We say f is of **smaller complexity** than g, written $O(f) < O(g)$, if $f = O(g)$ but g is not $O(f)$. Certainly, for integers n greater than 1 we have $n^2 < n^3$, so that $n^2 = O(n^3)$. However, since there is no positive integer c, where $n^3 \le cn^2$, for all values of n greater than some number, we have $n^3 \ne O(n^2)$. Thus, $O(n^2) < O(n^3)$; an algorithm with order $O(n^2)$ is more efficient than one with order $O(n^3)$.

The expression $5n^3 + 6n^2 + n + 7$ is an example of a **polynomial**. Algorithms of order n to a power are called **polynomial-time algorithms**. A **polynomial** in n of **degree** m is an expression

$$a_m n^m + \ldots + a_2 n^2 + a_1 n + a_0$$

where the a's are real numbers and a_m is nonzero. Moreover, from the above discussion we observe that a polynomial of degree m has complexity $O(n^m)$; and $O(n^{m-1}) < O(n^m)$. Figure 1.3 summarizes with examples some of the rules of complexity.

Figure 1.3	
Some of the rules of complexity with examples	

Rule	*Example*
1. For constant k, $O(k) < O(n)$	1. $O(7) < O(n)$
2. For constant k, $O(kf) = O(f)$	2. $O(2n) = O(n)$
3. $O(|f| + |g|) = O(f) + O(g)$	3. $O(6n^2 + n) = O(6n^2) + O(n)$
4. For $O(f) \le O(g)$, $O(|f| + |g|) = O(g)$	4. $O(n^3 + n^2) = O(n^3)$
5. For polynomial f of degree m, $O(f) = O(n^m)$	5. $O(5n^3 + 6n^2 + n + 7) = O(n^3)$
6. $O(n^{m-1}) < O(n^m)$	6. $O(n^2) < O(n^3)$

A sequential search is a polynomial-time algorithm with order of magnitude $O(n)$. As we see later, a binary search is a more efficient method with **logarithmic-time** complexity of $O(\log_2 n)$. John Napier, a Scottish baron who considered mathematics a hobby, published his invention of logarithms in 1614. Unlike most other scientific achievements, his work was not built on that of others. His highly original invention was welcomed enthusiastically. It was found that by using logarithms, problems of multiplication and division could be reduced to much simpler problems of addition and subtraction.

By definition, m is the **logarithm to the base 2 of n**, $\log_2 n = m$, provided m is the exponent of 2 such that 2^m is n, or

$$\log_2 n = m \quad \text{if} \quad n = 2^m$$

Thus,

$$\log_2 8 \quad = 3 \quad \text{since } 8 \quad = 2^3$$
$$\log_2 32 \quad = 5 \quad \text{since } 32 \quad = 2^5$$
$$\log_2 1024 = 10 \quad \text{since } 1024 = 2^{10}$$

For an array of $n = 1023$ elements, a sequential search takes at most 1023 comparisons. A binary search, however, repeatedly cuts the problem in half and thus takes at most 10 comparisons, a dramatic improvement in efficiency.

A problem that takes a much longer time than one that is of complexity $O(n)$ or $O(\log_2 n)$ is listing all the subsets of a set of n elements. Recall that a **set**, S, is a collection of things. T is a **subset** of S if every element of T is in S. Since there are 2^n subsets, the problem of listing all the subsets of a set has order $O(2^n)$. For instance, a collection of $n = 3$ elements, such as $\{a, b, c\}$, has $2^3 = 8$ subsets: $\{a, b, c\}, \{a, b\}, \{a, c\}, \{b, c\}, \{a\}, \{b\}, \{c\}, \{\ \}$. For $n = 1024$ elements, 2^n is about 1.8×10^{308}—that's 18 followed by 307 zeros! If we could list a subset every nanosecond or billionth of a second, the process would take about 5.7×10^{291} years.

$$1.8 \times 10^{308} \times \frac{\text{sec}}{10^9 \text{ops}} \times \frac{\text{min}}{60 \text{ sec}} \times \frac{\text{hr}}{60 \text{ min}} \times \frac{\text{day}}{24 \text{ hr}} \times \frac{\text{yr}}{365.25 \text{ day}} = 5.7 \times 19^{291} \text{ yr}$$

By comparison, if we could make one comparison per nanosecond, a sequential search of 1024 elements would take about 0.000001 sec and a binary search would take only 0.00000001 sec. Thus, an algorithm that is of **exponential order**, such as 2^n, is totally impractical for large values of n.

Factorial order is even worse. Consider the **traveling salesperson problem** of finding the best route to take in visiting n cities away from home. Assume that there is a direct route between each pair of cities and that the salesperson does not want to visit any city twice. What are the number of possible routes? There are n cities that could be visited first. For the second city to visit, there are only $n - 1$ choices remaining. With each subsequent city, there is one less choice until there is only one choice for the last city. Thus, the total number of routes is n-factorial, n!

$$n! = n\,(n - 1) \cdots 3 \cdot 2 \cdot 1$$

To illustrate, suppose the salesperson has Atlanta, New Orleans, and Dallas in the territory. As diagrammed in the tree in Figure 1.4 there are $3! = 3 \cdot 2 \cdot 1 = 6$ possible routes.

For $n < 4$, 2^n is larger than $n!$. For instance, with $n = 3$, $2^3 = 8$, while $3! = 6$. It does not take long, however, for $n!$ to dramatically outpace 2^n. An n value of 10 yields 1024 for $2^n = 2^{10}$, but an $n!$ value in the millions,

$$n! = 10! = 3,628,800$$

With double the amount of data, only $n = 20$, we have

$$2^n = 2^{20} = 1,048,576 \approx 1.0 \times 10^6$$

Figure 1.4

Tree of possible routes through Atlanta, New Orleans, and Dallas

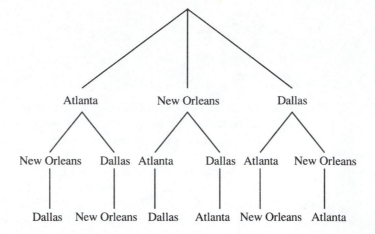

while 20! is over a trillion times as much,

$$n! = 20! \approx 2.4 \times 10^{18}$$

Similar problems are encountered in airline routing, telephone switching, and computer networking. As we have seen, with a complexity of $n!$ an exhaustive approach of finding the best of all possible routes is totally impractical. Consequently, a great deal of research has been done in developing other algorithms, perhaps not to find the best route but at least a good route. Generally, the aim in improving or creating better algorithms is to reduce the complexity. Thus, polynomial-time algorithms are usually more desirable than exponential ones. You should, however, know your data and your algorithm. For a small amount of data, a method that has a higher complexity might be better for a number of reasons such as program overhead, ease of implementation, or even fewer steps. For example, when $n < 16$, an algorithm with 2^n steps takes a shorter amount of time than one with n^4 steps. Of course, for larger n, the polynomial-time algorithm has a distinct advantage. Refer to Figure 1.5 for a comparison of the values of several functions of n.

Figure 1.5

Table comparing functional values for various values of n

$\log_2 n$	0	1	2	3	4	5
n	*1*	*2*	*4*	*8*	*16*	*32*
$n\log_2 n$	0	2	8	24	64	160
n^2	1	4	16	64	256	1,024
n^3	1	8	64	512	4,096	32,768
2^n	2	4	16	256	65,536	$4.29 \cdot 10^9$
10^n	10	100	10,000	10^8	10^{16}	10^{32}
$n!$	1	2	24	40,320	$2.09 \cdot 10^{13}$	$2.63 \cdot 10^{35}$
n^n	1	4	256	$1.68 \cdot 10^7$	$1.84 \cdot 10^{19}$	$1.46 \cdot 10^{48}$

◁

SECTION 1.4 EXERCISES

In Exercises 1–12, indicate which function, f or g, has the smaller complexity or that the functions have equal complexity.

	f	g		f	g
1.	$n^{5/4}$	n^5	**2.**	$\log_2(\log_2(n))$	$\log_2(n)$
3.	$n\log_2(n)$	2^n	**4.**	$\log_2(\log_2(n))$	$n\log_2(n)$
5.	n^n	$n!$	**6.**	n^2	$n\log_2(n)$
7.	2^n	3^n	**8.**	$50n^5 + n^2 + n$	n^5
9.	n	$\sqrt{n}$	**10.**	e^n	$n!$
11.	1	n	**12.**	$(631n - 255)/35$	n

Give the best big oh in Exercises 13–15.

13. $890n^{29}$ **14.** $8n^{3/2} + n^{2/5}$ **15.** $45\log_2(n) + 7n$

What is the run-time complexity based on n for each of the program segments in Exercises 16 and 17?

16. ```
for i := 1 to n do
    a[i] := y
```

**17.** ```
for i := 1 to do n do
    for j := 1 to n do
        for k := 1 to n do
            read (a[i, j, k])
```

If procedure Test has complexity O(X), what is the run-time complexity based on n for each of the program segments in Exercises 18 and 19?

18. ```
for i := 1 to n do
    Test(i,y)
```

**19.** ```
for i := 1 to n do
begin
    Test(i,y);
    write (y)
end {for}
```

For Exercises 20–26 graph each pair of functions for x ≥ 0 on the same coordinate system, and note which function has the smaller big oh value.

20. $f(x) = 1,$ $g(x) = x$ **21.** $f(x) = x,$ $g(x) = x^2$

22. $f(x) = x,$ $g(x) = \log_2(x), x > 0$ **23.** $f(x) = x^2,$ $g(x) = x^3$

24. $f(x) = x^2,$ $g(x) = 2^x$ **25.** $f(x) = 2^x,$ $g(x) = 3^x$

26. $f(x) = \sqrt{x},$ $g(x) = x$

In Exercises 27–32 find the complexity of the routine you designed in the indicated exercise from Section 1.1.

27. The Read-Data procedure in Exercise 2.

28. The Calculate-Total procedure in Exercise 4.

29. The Calculate-Average procedure in Exercise 5.

30. The Print-Those-above-Average procedure in Exercise 6.

31. The Maximum-Minimum procedure in Exercise 8.

32. The Merge procedure in Exercise 10.

33. Let $n = 64$. Suppose a step of an algorithm is executed every nanosecond (nsec), where $1 \text{ sec} = 10^9$ nsec.

   a. How long would it take to execute an algorithm that takes $\log_2(n)$ steps?
   b. How long for n^3 steps?
   c. How many years for 2^n steps?
   d. How many years for $n!$ steps?

34. A **prime** is an integer greater than 1 whose only positive factors are 1 and itself. Thus, 2, 3, 5, 7, 11, 13, and 17 are examples of primes, while $6 = 2 \times 3$ is not.

   a. Write a boolean function $primeP(n)$ that returns *true* if positive n is a prime and *false* otherwise. The function should first check if $n = 1$ (not a prime) or $n = 2$ (a prime). Then check to see if any whole number i from 2 through $n - 1$ divides n. If such a divisor is found, immediately return *false*. If none is found, return *true*.
   b. What is the complexity of the algorithm in Part a?
   c. Revise the function in Part a to test for i dividing n only while $i^2 \leq n$. For example, to discover that 59 is a prime we only need to check that no integer from 2 through 7 is a factor of 59. We note that $7^2 = 49 \leq 59$ and $8^2 = 64 > 59$. Suppose $59 = i \cdot j$, where i is greater than or equal to 8. For the product $i \cdot j$ to be 59, however, j must be less than 8 since $8 \cdot 8 = 64 > 59$.
   d. What is the complexity of the algorithm in Part c?

35. An array a of n numbers should already be in ascending order. Thus, for the sequence

   6, 2, 9, 5, 8, 7

which is supposed to be in ascending order, there are six pairs of integers that are out of order,

   (6, 2), (6, 5), (9, 5), (9, 8), (9, 7), and (8, 7)

A function to return the number of these out-of-order pairs in an array a takes each element $a[i]$ and finds all numbers $a[j]$ with $i < j$ but $a[i] > a[j]$. What is the complexity of this function?

36. a. Suppose $n = 100$ in Exercise 16 so that the assignment statement is executed 100 times. Thus, an amount of time to execute the segment is proportional to n, or the run-time complexity is $O(n)$. Suppose also that $k = 4$ processors can work in **parallel** to execute this loop; that is, all four computers are working simultaneously on different parts of the problem. One computer might be executing the loop for i from 1 to 25, while another does so for i from 26 to 50, etc. What is the run-time complexity?

b. What is the run-time complexity for k processors working in parallel to execute the loop in Exercise 16? Assume k divides n leaving a zero remainder.

c. Repeat Part a for $n = 103$.

d. Repeat Part b without the assumption that k divides n.

37. The segment below places the product of corresponding elements of two n-element arrays, a and b, into an array c and then computes the sum, dot, of those elements:

```
for i: = to n do
    c[i] := a[i] * b[i];

dot := 0;
for i: = 1 to n do
    dot := dot + c[i];
```

Thus, for arrays

a:	2	5	9	1	0	6	−1	6
b:	4	2	3	−5	4	1	8	2

we multiply corresponding elements to obtain

c:	8	10	27	−5	0	6	−8	12

and calculate the sum of these elements as

$$dot = 8 + 10 + 27 + -5 + 0 + 6 + -8 + 12 = 50$$

a. What is the complexity of the first loop?

b. Suppose n computers can work in parallel on this segment. (See Exercise 36.) What is the complexity of the first loop?

c. Suppose only one computer, working sequentially, performs the second loop. How many additions are executed?

d. What is the complexity of the second loop?

e. One way to compute the sum of the elements in c is to have $n/2$ computers work in parallel to compute the sum of adjacent values of c. Then $n/4$ computers calculate the sum of adjacent results. As Figure 1.6 indicates, the process continues until the answer is obtained. Using this technique, how many addition-time steps are needed for finding the sum of the elements of an 8-element array? (Two or more additions performed simultaneously take only one time step.)

f. Answer Part e for a 32-element array c.

Figure 1.6

Tree to compute a sum in parallel for Part e of Exercise 37

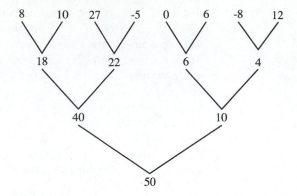

g. Using the technique of Part e, what is the complexity for finding the sum of the elements in an *n*-element array?

Fundamentals

Introduction

Various fundamental topics introduced in this chapter will be used throughout the text. In the first two sections we examine recursion or the process of a task calling itself. For a number of algorithms it is more natural to think of a recursive solution than an iterative one. We may find it necessary or desirable, however, to convert the recursive process to one that uses looping. In the second section we discuss how to make this conversion in a number of situations.

Another fundamental topic covered in this chapter is program verification or actually proving that the algorithms are correct. The goal of error-free programming, which is aided by the top-down design method discussed in Chapter 1, is advanced by this technique.

In the last section of this chapter we introduce the topic of abstract data type, the fundamental approach to data structures employed in this text. The word "abstract" is misleading, however. Instead of making work with data structures more remote, approaching each data structure as an abstract data type makes its study more understandable and its use easier and more organized.

Recursion

One important technique available in Pascal but not in Standard FORTRAN, COBOL, or BASIC is recursion. This powerful feature is used to develop a number of algorithms, procedures, functions, and even definitions in an elegant, top-down fashion. A **recursive** task is one that calls itself. With each invocation the problem is reduced until arriving at some terminal state.

Example 2.1

▼ Recursion can be used to define the syntax of a computer language formally. Languages defined in **Backus-Normal form (BNF)**, which employs recursion, can be recognized and translated more easily by a compiler. In BNF the symbol ::= is similar to the Pascal assignment symbol that means the term on the left is being defined by the expression on the right. A **nonterminal symbol** is in pointed brackets, < >, and can appear on the left in a definition. **Terminal symbols**, such as particular letters and digits, cannot be defined and, hence, can only be listed on the right-hand side of a definition. Adjacent symbols are concatenated or glued together, and a bar, |, represents "or."

The BNF description of a Pascal variable name shows that such a name must begin with a letter and then can be followed by any combination of letters and digits.

<variable> ::= <letter> | <variable><letter> | <variable><digit>
<letter>   ::= a | b | c | . . . | z
<digit>   ::= 0 | 1 | 2 | . . . | 9

Using this definition, Figure 2.1 demonstrates that the word *tx2a* can be recognized as a Pascal variable. **Parsing** is the process of recognizing that an item is part of a language, and the tree in Figure 2.1 is called a **parse tree**.

Figure 2.1

Parse tree for variable
name *tx2a*

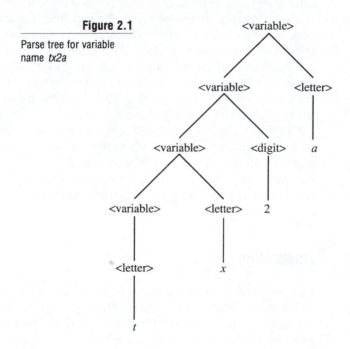

Notice that the definition of *variable* is recursive since we use <variable> to define <variable>. The recursive tasks cannot continue forever, however, and we have a **terminal case**, which is nonrecursive, of defining <variable> as a <letter>.

Example 2.2 **Factorial Function.**

Many definitions in computer science and mathematics are defined recursively. The definition of the factorial function was presented in the traveling salesperson problem of Section 1.4 as

$$n! = n \cdot (n - 1) \cdots 3 \cdot 2 \cdot 1 \quad \text{for } n > 0$$

Thus,

$$4! = 4 \cdot 3 \cdot 2 \cdot 1 = 4 \cdot (3 \cdot 2 \cdot 1) = 4 \cdot 3!$$

Moreover, by convention zero-factorial is defined as one:

$$0! = 1$$

These equalities motivate a recursive form of the definition:

$$n! = \begin{cases} 1 & \text{if } n = 0 \\ n(n - 1)! & \text{if } n > 0 \end{cases}$$

For a **terminal condition** of $n = 0$, the **terminal case** is $0! = 1$.

Using this definition, we can calculate $n!$ as n times $(n - 1)!$ if we know the value of $(n - 1)!$. The definition is recursive because n-factorial is itself defined in terms of a factorial. For example, 4! is $4 \cdot 3!$, where the factorial function of 3, 3!, is evaluated before the multiplication by 4. Notice the recursion— 4-factorial is defined in terms of 3-factorial. But wait . . . we must evaluate 3! before multiplying. At least we have a smaller problem with which to work. Using the definition once more we see that 3! is $3 \cdot 2!$. Not another factorial! We continue, however, because each time we are getting reduced problems. Eventually we must compute $n!$ for the smallest possible value of n, $n = 0$. When this condition is met, we can stop the recursive process of having the factorial function call itself and use the assignment in the first line of the definition, $n! = 0! = 1$. Because the recursive process terminates when the expression $(n = 0)$ becomes true, this equality is called the terminal condition; and the assignment for that condition, $0! = 1$, is called the terminal case. After achieving the terminal condition, we can then trace backwards, substituting, and eventually arrive at the value of 4!.

Figure 2.2 shows the steps to the terminal case in the evaluation of 4-factorial. Notice the similarity between that tree in this figure and the parse tree in Figure 2.1. In the factorial tree $n!$ is a nonterminal, while the numbers 4, 3, 2, and 1 are terminals. When the terminal condition of $n = 0$ is encountered, we can substitute the terminal case, $0! = 1$, and evaluate $1! = 1 \cdot 0!$ as $1 \cdot 1 = 1$. Knowing the value of 1!, we can compute 2! as $2 \cdot 1! = 2 \cdot 1 = 2$. Similarly, $3! = 3 \cdot 2! = 3 \cdot 2 = 6$, and so $4! = 4 \cdot 3! = 4 \cdot 6 = 24$. Figure 2.3 shows the steps involved in substituting values in reverse order.

This recursive definition has the ingredients of any recursive task:

Figure 2.2

Steps to arrive at the terminal case of evaluating 4! recursively

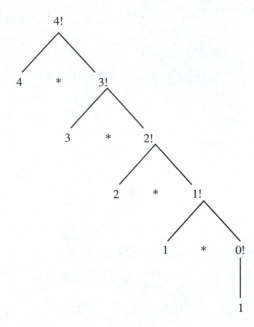

1. The task has a terminal case that is nonrecursive. (Here, 0! = 1.) As we will see in some exercises, the terminal case might be to do nothing.
2. The task is defined in terms of itself, working on a smaller version of the problem. (Here, $n! = n \, (n - 1)!$ for $n > 0$, but $(n - 1)!$ is a smaller problem than $n!$.)

This mathematical function can be translated into Pascal as below, where *NonNeg* has been defined as the type 0..*maxint*. The predefined constant *maxint* is the largest integer that our computer can use. As noted in Section 1.4, $n!$ can get very large quite rapidly. For example, 16! is 20,900,000,000,000. Because such a large integer is greater than *maxint* on most computers, in this implementation we declare that the function *factorial* returns a real number.

```
{ Function to evaluate n-factorial recursively.
  Assumption:    n is a nonnegative integer.

  Note: factorial is declared as real so that
        numbers larger than maxint can be returned. }

function factorial (n: NonNeg): real;
begin
   if n = 0 then
      factorial := 1
   else
      factorial := n * factorial(n - 1)
end;      { factorial }
```

Because a recursive invocation is not a loop, be careful to use an *if* statement as opposed to a *while* statement. The *if* tests to see whether the terminal

Figure 2.3

Steps in substituting values to evaluate 4!

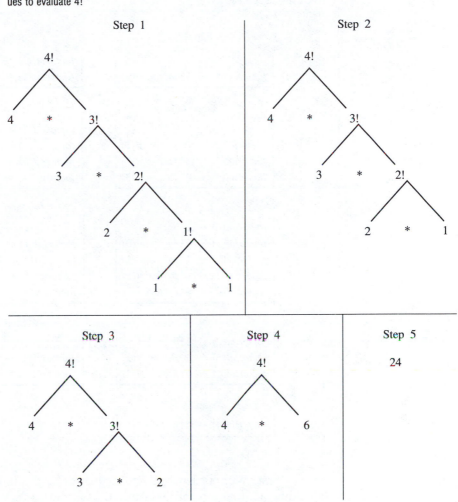

situation has been achieved. A recursive task must always have a terminal condition and should always work on a smaller problem with each recursive call.

When a function is invoked or a procedure is called, an **activation record** comes into existence. This record contains information about the routine, such as parameter values, local variables, and the return location after execution of the routine. With a statement such as

```
writeln( factorial(4) )
```

the function references in the form of activation records are stacked as illustrated in Figure 2.4. Once the terminal case, *factorial*(0) ← 1, is encountered in Step 5, each value of the function can be substituted in the expression from

Figure 2.4

Stack of function references and returns for *factorial(4)*

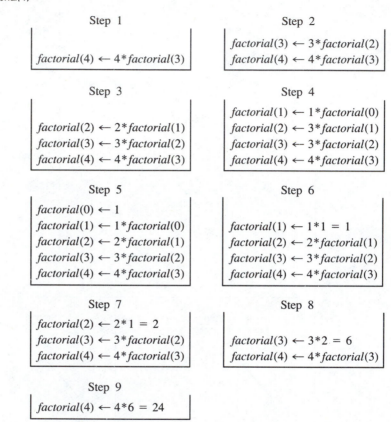

Step 1

factorial(4) ← 4*factorial(3)

Step 2

factorial(3) ← 3*factorial(2)
factorial(4) ← 4*factorial(3)

Step 3

factorial(2) ← 2*factorial(1)
factorial(3) ← 3*factorial(2)
factorial(4) ← 4*factorial(3)

Step 4

factorial(1) ← 1*factorial(0)
factorial(2) ← 3*factorial(1)
factorial(3) ← 3*factorial(2)
factorial(4) ← 4*factorial(3)

Step 5

factorial(0) ← 1
factorial(1) ← 1*factorial(0)
factorial(2) ← 2*factorial(1)
factorial(3) ← 3*factorial(2)
factorial(4) ← 4*factorial(3)

Step 6

factorial(1) ← 1*1 = 1
factorial(2) ← 2*factorial(1)
factorial(3) ← 3*factorial(2)
factorial(4) ← 4*factorial(3)

Step 7

factorial(2) ← 2*1 = 2
factorial(3) ← 3*factorial(2)
factorial(4) ← 4*factorial(3)

Step 8

factorial(3) ← 3*2 = 6
factorial(4) ← 4*factorial(3)

Step 9

factorial(4) ← 4*6 = 24

last to first. With each value returned through the function name, a corresponding activation record is removed from the stack. In the **stack** data structure, which we cover in detail in a later chapter, data can only be added to or removed from one end, the **top**, of the sequence. The last item placed on the stack must be the first item taken from the stack. This structure is well named, for it is analogous to a stack, say, of trays in a cafeteria. If you put back a tray, it goes on the top of the stack; the next person will pick up that tray. (For the sake of the analogy, we must assume that no one reaches into the middle of the stack.) The operation to place data on the top of the stack is called **push**; the **pop** operation removes data from the stack.

▲

| Example 2.3 | **Power Function.** |

▼   As another example of recursion, let us write a function to evaluate x^n where n is a nonnegative integer and x is a positive one. Since exponentiation is not implemented in Pascal, writing such a function could be useful in certain applications.

As a mathematical function, x^n with $x > 0$ could be defined as follows:

$$x^n = \begin{cases} 1 & \text{if } n = 0 \\ x \cdot x^{n-1} & \text{if } n > 0 \end{cases} \tag{1}$$

For instance, $5^0 = 1$, while

$$5^3 = 5 \cdot 5^2$$
$$5^2 = 5 \cdot 5^1$$
$$5^1 = 5 \cdot 5^0$$
$$5^0 = 1$$

Thus, substituting in reverse order, we have

$$5^1 = 5 \cdot 5^0 = 5 \cdot 1 = 5$$
$$5^2 = 5 \cdot 5^1 = 5 \cdot 5 = 25$$

and

$$5^3 = 5 \cdot 5^2 = 5 \cdot 25 = 125$$

We certainly could implement this definition in Pascal, but a better algorithm involves cutting the problem in half with each recursive reference. To write the mathematical definition we use the **floor function**, $\lfloor n \rfloor$, which is the largest integer less than or equal to n. Thus, $\lfloor 2.9 \rfloor = 2$, $\lfloor 5.1 \rfloor = 5$, and $\lfloor 7 \rfloor = 7$. Integer division using the *div* function divides and then takes the floor function. For instance, 7 *div* 2 is $\lfloor 7/2 \rfloor = \lfloor 3.5 \rfloor = 3$, and 14 *div* 2 is $\lfloor 14/2 \rfloor = \lfloor 7.0 \rfloor = 7$.

Suppose we want to evaluate x^{14}. By one of the properties of exponents,

$$x^{14} = (x^7)^2$$

Moreover, the square function, *sqr*, is built into Pascal. We have reduced the problem of evaluating x^{14} to a problem half its size, that of computing x^7. But what is x^7?

$$x^7 = x(x^3)^2$$

where the exponent 3 is $\lfloor 7/2 \rfloor$. We are now in a position to write a binary algorithm for evaluating x^n:

$$x^n = \begin{cases} 1 & \text{if } n = 0 \\ x \cdot (x^{\lfloor n/2 \rfloor})^2 & \text{if } n \text{ is odd} \\ (x^{\lfloor n/2 \rfloor})^2 & \text{otherwise} \end{cases} \tag{2}$$

In Pascal this function reads as follows:

```
{  A function to evaluate x^n in a binary fashion.
   Assumptions:    x is a positive integer.
                   n is a nonnegative integer.
```

```
     Note: Power is declared as real so that
           numbers larger than maxint can be returned. }
function Power (x: Pos; n: NonNeg): real;
begin
   if n = 0 then
      Power := 1
   else if odd(n) then
      Power := x * sqr( Power( x, n div 2) )
   else
      Power :=    sqr( Power( x, n div 2) )
end;        { Power }
```

Figure 2.5 shows the function references to $f(x) = x^n$ and the corresponding *Power* function pushed onto the stack. Figure 2.6 illustrates their values being popped in reverse order after the terminal condition has been achieved.

Figure 2.5

The stack of recursive function calls to the mathematical function $f(x) = x^n$ and the corresponding *Power* function.

Step 1

$5^{14} = (5^7)^2$	or	$Power(5,14) \leftarrow sqr(Power(5,7))$

Step 2

$5^7 = 5(5^3)^2$	or	$Power(5,7) \leftarrow 5 * sqr(Power(5,3))$
$5^{14} = (5^7)^2$		$Power(5,14) \leftarrow sqr(Power(5,7))$

Step 3

$5^3 = 5(5^1)^2$	or	$Power(5,3) \leftarrow 5 * sqr(Power(5,1))$
$5^7 = 5(5^3)^2$		$Power(5,7) \leftarrow 5 * sqr(Power(5,3))$
$5^{14} = (5^7)^2$		$Power(5,14) \leftarrow sqr(Power(5,7))$

Step 4

$5^1 = 5(5^0)^2$	or	$Power(5,1) \leftarrow 5 * sqr(Power(5,0))$
$5^3 = 5(5^1)^2$		$Power(5,3) \leftarrow 5 * sqr(Power(5,1))$
$5^7 = 5(5^3)^2$		$Power(5,7) \leftarrow 5 * sqr(Power(5,3))$
$5^{14} = (5^7)^2$		$Power(5,14) \leftarrow sqr(Power(5,7))$

Step 5

$5^0 = 1$		$Power(5,0) \leftarrow 1$
$5^1 = 5(5^0)^2$		$Power(5,1) \leftarrow 5 * sqr(Power(5,0))$
$5^3 = 5(5^1)^2$	or	$Power(5,3) \leftarrow 5 * sqr(Power(5,1))$
$5^7 = 5(5^3)^2$		$Power(5,7) \leftarrow 5 * sqr(Power(5,3))$
$5^{14} = (5^7)^2$		$Power(5,14) \leftarrow sqr(Power(5,7))$

Figure 2.6

The stack of recursive function values for the mathematical function $f(x) = x^n$ or the corresponding *Power* function after the terminal condition has been achieved (Note: The integer answer here would be returned as a real number by the function *Power*)

Step 6

$$5^1 = 5(1)^2 = 5$$
$$5^3 = 5(5^1)^2$$
$$5^7 = 5(5^3)^2$$
$$5^{14} = (5^7)^2$$

or

$$Power(5,1) \leftarrow 5 * sqr(1) = 5$$
$$Power(5,3) \leftarrow 5 * sqr(Power(5,1))$$
$$Power(5,7) \leftarrow 5 * sqr(Power(5,3))$$
$$Power(5,14) \leftarrow sqr(Power(5,7))$$

Step 7

$$5^3 = 5(5)^2 = 125$$
$$5^7 = 5(5^3)^2$$
$$5^{14} = (5^7)^2$$

or

$$Power(5,3) \leftarrow 5 * sqr(5) = 125$$
$$Power(5,7) \leftarrow 5 * sqr(Power(5,3))$$
$$Power(5,14) \leftarrow sqr(Power(5,7))$$

Step 8

$$5^7 = 5(125)^2 = 78125$$
$$5^{14} = (5^7)^2$$

or

$$Power(5,7) \leftarrow 5 * sqr(125) = 78125$$
$$Power(5,14) \leftarrow sqr(Power(5,7))$$

Step 9

$$5^{14} = (78125)^2 = 6103515625$$

or

$$Power(5,14) \leftarrow sqr(78125) = 6,103,515,625$$

Example 2.4

Towers of Hanoi.

The Towers of Hanoi game can be solved nicely with recursion. In the game there are three pegs (*A, B, C*) and *N* disks of varying sizes that can be stacked on a peg. The object is to move all the disks from one peg to another by moving one disk at a time, being careful never to place a larger disk on top of a smaller one.

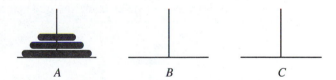

To simulate moving *Disk* 1 from *Peg A* to *Peg C*, we write

```
Move Disk 1 from Peg A to Peg C.
```

Suppose we are moving two disks, the top disk numbered 1 and the bottom numbered 2, from *Peg A* to *Peg C*.

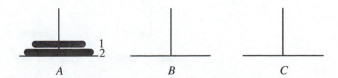

We first move *Disk* 1 to *B*.

Then we move *Disk* 2 to *C*.

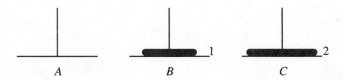

Finally, we move *Disk* 1 to *C*.

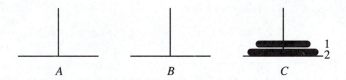

Similarly, suppose we want to move N disks from A to C and we know how to move $N - 1$ disks from any one peg to any other.

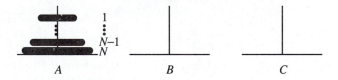

To move the N disks from A to C, we first move the top $N - 1$ disks by a series of legal moves from *Peg A* to *B*.

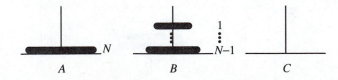

We then move *Disk N* from *A* to *C*.

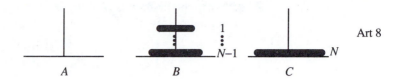

Art 8

Finally, we move the *N − 1* disks from *B* to *C*.

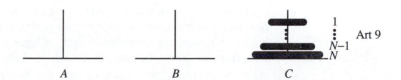

Art 9

We use the variables *FromPeg, AuxPeg,* and *ToPeg* to represent the peg from which we start, the auxiliary peg, and the peg to which we are moving the N disks, respectively. Following the above description, we design the procedure *Hanoi* to play the game as follows:

To call *Hanoi* to move N disks from *FromPeg* to *ToPeg* do the following:
    If N is 1 then
        Move Disk 1 from *FromPeg* to *ToPeg*
    else
        Call *Hanoi* to move N − 1 disks from *FromPeg* to *AuxPeg*.
        Move Disk N from *FromPeg* to *ToPeg*.
        Call *Hanoi* to move N − 1 disks from *AuxPeg* to *ToPeg*.

▽

SECTION 2.1 EXERCISES

In this and other exercise sets, you will write various functions and procedures. After you have written them, an excellent way to study the material is to implement and test these routines on the computer. In many cases you will need to write a main test program to handle input and output and to call the routine.

1. **a.** Using the fact that 4! = 24, evaluate 5!.
  b. Give the stacks for *factorial*(5) as in Figure 2.4.
  c. What kind of error could result from declaring *n* to be of type *integer* in the function *factorial*?
  d. What is the complexity of the *factorial* function of Example 2.1?
  e. Write a driver program and test the *factorial* function on the computer.
  f. Using the computer, add diagnostic statements to the *factorial* function

to print the values of appropriate variables when entering and leaving this function.

2. a. Write the first 5 terms of the sequence, $f(0)$ through $f(4)$, defined by the following function:

$$f(n) = \begin{cases} 3 & \text{if } n = 0 \\ 2f(n-1) + 1 & \text{if } n > 0 \end{cases}$$

b. Write this function in Pascal.

Note: The Advanced Placement (AP) Computer Science Examination tests "students' abilities to use computing in powerful, intelligent, and responsible ways." After taking a one-year AP computer science course in high school that is designed as a college freshman-year major's course in Pascal and introduction to data structures, a student may take the examination. If he or she scores high enough, many universities and colleges will give the student one or two semesters of credit in computer science. Several sample questions from the *AP Computer Science Examination* for various years are given throughout this book.*

3. The following appeared in the sample questions of the *1984 AP Computer Science Examination***:

```
program Main ;
    var z : integer ;
    function F(x : integer) : integer ;
    begin
        if (x = 1) or (x = 3) then
            F := x
        else
            F := x * F(x − 1)
    end ;
begin {Main}
    z := F( F(2) + F(5) )
end.
```

If *maxint* were large enough to allow the program above to be executed, then at the end of the program, the value of z would be

(A) 62
(B) 5! + 2!
(C) (5! + 2!)!
(D) (7!)!
(E) (62!) ÷ (2!)

---

*Permission to reprint the AP test questions does not constitute review or endorsement by the Educational Testing Service or the College Board of this publication as a whole or of any other testing information it may contain.

**AP question selected from *AP Computer Science Examination*, 1984. Reprinted by permission of Educational Testing Service, the copyright owner of the sample questions.

4. a. Write a recursive definition for <signed integer> using <digit>, <signed integer>, terminals "+", "−", and the digits.
   b. Using this definition, give a parse tree for +52.
   c. Give a parse tree for 42.
   d. Give a parse tree for −795.

5. A principal P of $3000 is deposited in a bank that compounds interest at a yearly rate of $R = 10\%$. The interest is also deposited in the account at the end of each year. If A_n is the amount present after n years, we have

$$A_0 = P = 3000$$
$$A_1 = A_0 + A_0R = A_0(1 + R) = A_0(1 + 0.10) = 3300$$
$$A_2 = A_1 + A_1R = A_1(1 + R) = A_1(1 + 0.10) = 3630$$

   a. Find A_3, A_4, and A_5.
   b. Write a recursive function *Amount* with parameters P, R, and n in Pascal to calculate the amount in the bank after n years.

6. a. Using the first definition of x^n as given in the text at (1) of Example 2.3, write a function *PowerLin* to calculate x^n.
   b. Using that definition, give the stack to evaluate 3^4 or *PowerLin*(3, 4).
   c. What is the largest number of elements that would be on the stack to evaluate 3^{42} or *PowerLin*(3, 42)?
   d. What is the complexity of *PowerLin*?
   e. Test this function on the computer with appropriate diagnostic statements.

7. a. Using the second definition of x^n as given in the text at (2) of Example 2.3, give the stack to evaluate 3^4 or *Power*(3, 4).
   b. What is the largest number of elements that would be on the stack to evaluate 3^{42} or *Power*(3, 42)?
   c. What is the complexity of *Power*?
   d. Which is the better algorithm, *PowerLin* of Exercise 6 or *Power*?

8. a. Alter the *Power* function of Example 2.3 to evaluate x^n for any real number x and any nonnegative integer n.
   b. One error that can result from the new definition occurs when $x = 0$ and $n = 0$. 0^0 is not 1 or 0; in fact, 0^0 is undefined, just as division by 0 is undefined. To avoid this error write a function that contains *Power* (or *PowerLin* of Exercise 6). The function first tests if $x = 0$ and $n = 0$. In that situation, the function calls an error-handling procedure, which prints an error message and halts execution. Otherwise, the procedure invokes *Power* (or *PowerLin*).
   c. A negative exponent results in the term being placed in the denominator with a positive exponent as in $2^{-3} = 1/2^3 = 1/8$. Alter the function from Part b to accommodate negative integer exponents.
   d. When n is real and x is positive, x^n can still be evaluated as $e^{n \ln(x)}$. Write this function nonrecursively, using the built-in exponential function, *exp*, and the built-in function for the natural logarithm, *ln*.

e. Write a function with real parameters x and n to evaluate x^n, $x \geq 0$. $0^n = 0$ for $n \neq 0$; but for $x \leq 0$, x^n cannot be evaluated using the function of Part d since $ln(x)$ is undefined for $x \leq 0$. If $x < 0$, call an error-handling procedure to print an error message and halt execution.

f. Design a function to evaluate x^n for any x and n. If n is an integer, invoke the function from Part a; otherwise invoke the function from Part e. One way to test that n is an integer is to see if n equals $trunc(n)$.

9. In about 1200 A.D. the mathematician Leonardo Fibonacci presented a sequence of numbers that has several applications to natural events. The terminal case defines the first two terms of the sequence, and any subsequent term is the sum of the two immediately preceding numbers. Thus, for $x_0 = x_1 = 1$, we have

$$x_2 = x_1 + x_0 = 1 + 1 = 2$$
$$x_3 = x_2 + x_1 = 2 + 1 = 3$$
$$x_4 = x_3 + x_2 = 3 + 2 = 5$$

a. Define this sequence with a recursive mathematical function.
b. Find x_{10}.
c. Write a Pascal function to find the nth Fibonacci number.

10. The following algorithm, developed by Euclid, finds the greatest common divisor, gcd, of two positive integers. For example, $gcd(18, 12) = 6$.

$gcd(x, y) \rightarrow d$
  Function to return the greatest common divisor of x and y
Input:
  x, y—positive integers
Output:
  d—positive integer
Algorithm:
  If $x > y$ then
    $gcd \leftarrow gcd(x - y, y)$
  else if $y > x$ then
    $gcd \leftarrow gcd(x, y - x)$
  else $gcd \leftarrow x$.

a. Verify that the algorithm works for $x = 18$ and $y = 12$ by showing the development of the stack.
b. Write gcd as a Pascal function.

11. Write a recursive function to find the sum of the first n elements of an array of real numbers. The recursive step is to add the nth element of the array to the sum of the first $n - 1$ elements. The terminal condition is true when $n = 1$.

12. Write a recursive boolean function to return *true* if x is a member of the first n elements of an array a.

13. Complete writing the recursive function to find the maximum of the first *n* elements of an array of real numbers with index of type *IndexType*.

```
function MaxInArray ( var a: ArrayType; n:   a   ):   b  ;
var
    Maxa: real;
begin
    if n = 1 then
        Maxa := a[n]
    else
        Maxa := MaxInArray (  c  ,   d  );

    if a[n] > Maxa then
        MaxInArray :=   e
    else
        MaxInArray := Maxa
end;
```

14. a. Write a recursive procedure to print the first *n* elements of an array in reverse order. Let *n* = 0 be the terminal condition.
   b. Write a recursive procedure to print the first *n* elements of an array in normal order.

15. Write a recursive boolean function to return *true* if the character string is a **palindrome,** that is, the string reads the same backwards as forwards. Examples of some palindromes are "dad" and "ABLE WAS I ERE I SAW ELBA." Parameters for the function are an array for the character string and *First* and *Last*, indices of the first and last elements of the part of the string being checked, respectively. If the *First* and *Last* elements are not equal, return *false*. If they are equal, however, repeat the process with the substring having indices *First* + 1 and *Last* − 1. Do not neglect the terminal condition.

16. Write a recursive function to evaluate *na,*

$$na = \underbrace{a + a + \cdots + a,}_{n \text{ summands}}$$

where *n* is a nonnegative integer and *a* is a real number. For example,

$$7 \cdot 3.1 = 3.1 + 3.1 + 3.1 + 3.1 + 3.1 + 3.1 + 3.1 = 21.7$$

n and *a* should be the parameters for the function.

17. a. Give the moves for moving three disks from *Peg A* to *Peg C* in the Towers of Hanoi game of Example 2.4.
   b. Code in Pascal the procedure *Hanoi* from Example 2.4 to simulate the Towers of Hanoi game.
   c. Write a recursive function to calculate the number of moves for *N* disks.

d. Suppose $N + 1$ pegs are available for the N disks in the game. How many moves are necessary?

18. a. What words written with zeros and ones are in the language defined by the following BNF description?

<S> ::= <S>0 | 1

b. By drawing a parse tree, show that 1000 is in the language.

Fill in the statements of this recursive Boolean function to return true if a particular string of n characters is in this language.

```
function InLang (var a: ArrayType; n: Positive):
                                           boolean;
begin
   if    c    then
         InLang := (a[1] = '1' )
   else if a[n] <> '0' then
         InLang :=    d
   else
         InLang :=    e
end;      { InLang }
```

19. a. What words written with zeros and ones are in the language defined by the following BNF description?

<S> ::= <S>0 | <S>1 | 00

b. By drawing a parse tree, show that 0001 is in the language.
c. Write a recursive boolean function to return *true* if a particular string of n characters is in this language.

20. A **syntax diagram** is a formal way of illustrating the syntax of a language. Figure 2.7 diagrams the BNF description of a Pascal variable from Example 2.1. To read the syntax diagram for a term, start at the left and follow the arrows. Branching indicates a choice and replaces the "or" symbol, |, in the BNF form. Nonterminal symbols appear in rectangles; terminals are in circles or ovals. Thus, *digit* is any one of 10 terminal symbols.

a. Draw a syntax diagram for the BNF description of S in Exercise 18.
b. Draw a syntax diagram for the BNF description of S in Exercise 19.

21. The number of **combinations** or subsets of r distinct objects chosen from n objects is

$$C(n, r) = \frac{n!}{r!(n - r)!}, 0 \le r \le n$$

For example, a 5-element set, such as $S = [0, 3, 5, 8, 9]$, has 10 2-element subsets or

$$C(5, 2) = \frac{5!}{2! \, 3!} = \frac{5 \cdot 4 \cdot 3 \cdot 2 \cdot 1}{2 \cdot 1 \cdot 3 \cdot 2 \cdot 1} = 10$$

Figure 2.7

Syntax diagram for *variable* for Exercise 20

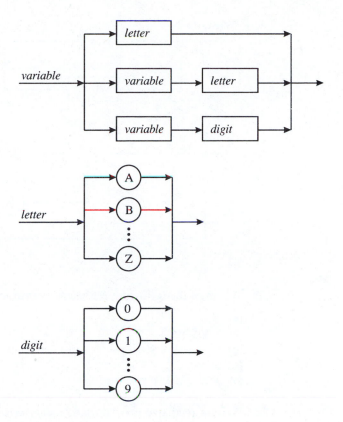

These 2-element subsets are [0, 3], [0, 5], [0, 8], [0, 9], [3, 5], [3, 8], [3, 9], [5, 8], [5, 9], and [8, 9]. Also, *S* has five 1-element subsets, [0], [3], [5], [8], [9]; so that,

$$C(5, 1) = \frac{5!}{1! \; 4!} = \frac{5 \cdot 4 \cdot 3 \cdot 2 \cdot 1}{1 \cdot 4 \cdot 3 \cdot 2 \cdot 1} = 5$$

Complete the following recursive mathematics formula for $C(n, r)$:

$$C(n, r) = \begin{cases} \dfrac{a}{b} & \text{if } n = r \\[2mm] \dfrac{a}{b} & \text{if } r = 0 \\[2mm] C(n - 1, r - 1) + C(n - 1, r) & \text{if } n > r > 0 \end{cases}$$

Write a Pascal function to implement this formula.

22. The following appeared in the sample questions of the *1984 AP Computer Science Examination**:

The following syntax diagram defines the syntax of a "whamo" in some fictitious programming language.

*AP question selected from *AP Computer Science Examination*, 1984. Reprinted by permission of Educational Testing Service, the copyright owner of the sample questions.

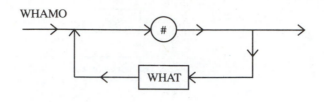

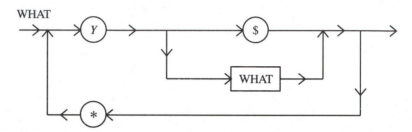

Which of the following represents a syntactically valid "whamo"?

(A) $Y \#$

(B) $* Y \$$

(C) $\# Y \# Y \$ \$ \#$

(D) $\# Y \$ * Y Y \$ \#$

(E) $\# Y \$ \# * Y \$ * Y \#$

23. Write a recursive procedure to merge two sorted arrays of the same type into a third array.

24. Write a recursive function to convert a character string of n digits to the corresponding integer number. For example, for the input string '5274', return the number 5274. Recall that $ord('5') - ord('0')$ is the number 5. The following calculations demonstrate the idea of the recursion:

$$5274 = (527)10 + 4$$

while

$$527 = (52)10 + 7$$

and

$$52 = (5)10 + 2$$

25. The decimal or base 10 number system, which we use every day, has 10 digits, while the binary or base 2 number system, which is used in the computer, has only the digits 0 and 1. The decimal number 5274 can be expanded in powers of 10 as

$$5 \cdot 10^3 + 2 \cdot 10^2 + 7 \cdot 10^1 + 4 \cdot 10^0 = 5 \cdot 1000 + 2 \cdot 100 + 7 \cdot 10 + 4 \cdot 1$$

The binary number 111001, expressed in powers of 2, yields the decimal equivalent:

$$111001 = 1 \cdot 2^5 + 1 \cdot 2^4 + 1 \cdot 2^3 + 0 \cdot 2^2 + 0 \cdot 2^1 + 1 \cdot 2^0$$
$$= 1 \cdot 32 + 1 \cdot 16 + 1 \cdot 8 + 0 \cdot 4 + 0 \cdot 2 + 1 \cdot 1$$
$$= 32 \quad + 16 \quad + 8 \quad + 0 \quad + 0 \quad + 1$$
$$= 57$$

Thus, 57 is the decimal equivalent of the binary number 111001. Modify the function from Exercise 24 to convert a nonnegative binary number to a decimal one.

26. To convert a nonnegative decimal integer *Num* to a binary number, repeatedly perform integer division (*div*) of successive quotients. The remainders, written in reverse order, are *Num* expressed in the base 2 number system. For example, consider conversion of 19:

$$
\begin{array}{ccccc}
9 & 4 & 2 & 1 & 0 \\
2\overline{)19} & 2\overline{)9} & 2\overline{)4} & 2\overline{)2} & 2\overline{)1} \\
\underline{18} & \underline{8} & \underline{4} & \underline{2} & \underline{0} \\
1 & 1 & 0 & 0 & 1
\end{array}
$$

Taking the remainders in reverse order, 19 is 10011 in the binary number system. Write a recursive procedure to print a nonnegative decimal integer in the binary number system.

27. a. Write a recursive procedure *Primes* to print all the prime factors of an integer, *Num*, which is greater than 1. In Exercise 34 of Section 1.4 we defined a prime as an integer greater than 1 whose only positive factors are 1 and itself. Thus, the prime factorizations of 40 and 126 are as follows:

$$40 \quad = 2 \cdot 2 \cdot 2 \cdot 5$$

$$126 = 2 \cdot 3 \cdot 3 \cdot 7$$

Use the procedure *PrimeFactor* below, whose only purpose is to call the recursive procedure *Primes*. This calling procedure passes *Primes* the arguments *Num* and 2, the first prime. With recursive calls to *Primes* we have arguments of a revised number and n or $n + 1$.

```
type
    Positive1 = 2..maxint;
procedure PrimeFactor (Num: Positive1);
    procedure Primes (Num, n: Positive1);
    ⋮
    end; {Primes}
begin    {PrimeFactor}
    Primes (Num, 2)
end;    {PrimeFactor}
```

b. Test *Primes* with *Num* = 40.

c. Test *Primes* with *Num* = 126.

▽

PROGRAMMING PROJECTS

1. One root of the polynomial function $f(x) = 2x^3 - 14x^2 + 31x - 22$ is $x = 2$ because $f(2) = 2 \cdot 2^3 - 14 \cdot 2^2 + 31 \cdot 2 - 22 = 0$. Thus, the graph of f crosses the x-axis at $x = 2$. We know another root is between $x = 3$ and $x = 4$ because $f(3) = 2 \cdot 3^3 - 14 \cdot 3^2 + 31 \cdot 3 - 22 = -1$ is negative, and $f(4) = 2 \cdot 4^3 - 14 \cdot 4^2 + 31 \cdot 4 - 22 = 6$ is positive. Thus, since f is continuous, having an unbroken graph, the graph crosses the x-axis, or f has a root, between $x = 3$ and $x = 4$. Cutting the interval in half, we find at $x = 3.5$, $f(3.5) = 2 \cdot 3.5^3 - 14 \cdot 3.5^2 + 31 \cdot 3.5 - 22 = 0.75$ is also positive. Therefore, a root must be between $x = 3$ and $x = 3.5$. We continue cutting the interval in half and testing the midpoint. We stop the procedure and return x as soon as the value of $f(x)$ is within some designated distance, say 0.001, of 0.

   Write a program to read the representation for a polynomial, a distance, *distance*, and two points, *First* and *Last*, and to print an approximation for a root x between those two points so that $f(x)$ is within *distance* of 0. Represent the polynomial by a list of its coefficients with their corresponding exponents. Print an error message if evaluations of the function at the two end points do not have opposite signs. Your program should define two recursive functions, one to calculate exponentiation and the other to return an approximation for a root of f between *First* and *Last*.

2. The number of combinations of r distinct objects chosen from n, $C(n, r)$, is also called a binary coefficient. (See Exercise 21.) These are the coefficients in the binomial expansion

$$(x + y)^n = C(n, 0)x^n + C(n, 1)x^{n-1}y + C(n, 2)x^{n-2}y^2 + \cdots$$
$$+ C(n, n - 2)x^2y^{n-2} + C(n, n - 1)xy^{n-1} + C(n, n)y^n$$

where n is a nonnegative integer. Using this formula we have

$$(x + y)^2 = x^2 + 2xy + y^2$$
$$(x + y)^3 = x^3 + 3x^2y + 3xy^2 + y^3$$

and

$$(x + y)^4 = x^4 + 4x^3y + 6x^2y^2 + 4xy^3 + y^4$$

   Write a program to read a nonnegative integer exponent n and to write out the binomial expansion of $(x + y)^n$. Use ^ to indicate exponentiation and display 5 terms per line. For example, write x^2 as $x ^ 2$. Use a recursive function to evaluate $C(n, r)$.

3. Exercise 25 of this section describes how to convert a nonnegative binary (base 2) number to its decimal (base 10) equivalent; Exercise 26 presents the

reverse process. Create a menu-driven program that will repeatedly give the user the options of converting a nonnegative number in a base less than 10 to a decimal number, or performing the opposite maneuver, or quitting. After selection, prompt the user for the other base and then for the number to be used in the conversion. Have error checking to verify that the user types an integer from 2 to 9 for the other base. Also, when a number is entered in another base, an error message should be issued if any digit not in the appropriate base is used. For example, with a base 2 number there are only 2 possible digits, 0 and 1; with a base 8 number the digits are 0, 1, 2, 3, 4, 5, 6, 7. Your conversion routines should be recursive as described in Exercises 25 and 26.

SECTION 2.2   Recursion vs. Iteration

In the text and exercises we have considered a number of problems that can be solved recursively. However, such a solution is not always the best because of efficiency considerations.

The stack in Figure 2.4 clarifies the behavior of the recursive function *factorial*, but in reality a more extensive **run-time stack** of **activation records** exists during execution. Each activation record contains the values of all local variables and parameters, such as n and *factorial*, and the return location for reentry to that instance of the routine. The run-time stack, however, is allotted only a certain amount of space in memory, which itself is finite. For instance, a reference to *factorial* with argument 100 to evaluate 100! results in a stack that has at least 300 items—100 values of n, 100 values for *factorial*(n), and 100 return locations. The run-time stack on a particular machine might not be able to handle the load, resulting in a run-time error message of STACK OVERFLOW.

Not only does a recursive solution usually gobble up more space than a nonrecursive one, but often the recursive routine consumes more time. Generally, a function reference or procedure call takes more time than a sequential execution of statements.

You might reasonably be asking at this point, "Then why use recursion at all?" Many times the most natural and understandable solution to a problem is a recursive one. As mentioned in Chapter 1, because computers have become faster with larger memories, the programmer's time is now a more important consideration than it was in the early days of the computer industry. Furthermore, there is experimental evidence that with some modern computers and compilers a recursive routine can actually execute faster than a nonrecursive counterpart. If we can readily develop a nonrecursive algorithm, however, we should do so. Moreover, sometimes we are forced to consider a nonrecursive solution after designing a recursive one because of stack overflow or speed considerations. In these cases we must convert the recursive idea to an iterative one.

Recursion takes a problem from its highest level, for instance the evaluation of *factorial*(4), to its lowest, as in the terminal case of *factorial*(0). In contrast, an iterative solution goes from the bottom up, here from *factorial*(0) to *factorial*(4). Iteration is implemented in structured Pascal with a *for*, *while*, or *repeat* loop.

Let us **solve** the recursive routine *factorial* or, in other words, find a nonrecursive definition for this function. The terminal case in the recursive definition will now become the initial case.

$$0! = 1 \text{ or } factorial(0) = 1$$

Using the recursive part, $n! = n(n - 1)!$, and proceeding from the lowest terms up to the nth case, we hope to discover how to program the function nonrecursively.

$$1! = 1 \cdot 0! = 1 \cdot 1 = 1$$
$$2! = 2 \cdot 1! = 2 \cdot 1 = 2$$
$$3! = 3 \cdot 2! = 3 \cdot 2 = 6$$
$$4! = 4 \cdot 3! = 4 \cdot 6 = 24$$

We start with $0! = 1$ as an initial value of the local variable *product*. The previous factorial, stored in *product*, is multiplied by the index at each iteration of the loop. Thus, the nonrecursive definition of *factorial* follows:

```
{ Nonrecursive version of the factorial function.
   Assumption: n is a nonnegative integer

   Note: NRfactorial is declared as real so that
   numbers larger than maxint can be returned. }

function NRfactorial (n: NonNeg): real;
   var
      product : real;          { ongoing value of the factorial }
      i       : integer;       { index }
   begin
      product: = 1;
      for i := 1 to n do
         product: = i * product;

   NRfactorial := product
   end;      { NRfactorial }
```

Since the nonrecursive *NRfactorial* is at least as easy to understand as the recursive *factorial*, the former is the more desirable implementation of the factorial function.

One type of routine that can be readily converted to an iterative solution is one that uses **tail recursion**, where the routine's last statement is only a recursive call. Some, though not all, compilers can even recognize tail recursion and automatically transform the routine to a nonrecursive form. Consider the solution to Exercise 14a of Section 2.1, which prints the first n elements of an array in reverse order:

```
{ Recursive procedure to print the first n elements
   of an array in reverse order }

procedure PrintReverse (var a: ArrayType;  n: NonNeg);
begin
   if n <> 0 then
   begin
      write (a[n]);
      PrintReverse(a, n - 1)
   end  { if }
end;     { PrintReverse }
```

Because the last action of this procedure is only to call itself, *PrintReverse* exhibits tail recursion. This would not be the case, however, if the call to the procedure were not the last statement or if that statement also included an operation such as addition. When tail recursion does exist, iteration can easily replace recursion by reassigning the parameter before looping to the first statement. The nonrecursive solution follows:

```
{ Nonrecursive version of procedure PrintReverse }

procedure NRPrintReverse (var a: ArrayType;  n: NonNeg);
begin
   while n <> 0 do
      begin
         write (a[n]);
         n := n - 1
      end  { while }
end;        { NRPrintReverse }
```

We could also use a *for* loop to decrement and test the terminal condition.

```
{ Alternative version of NRPrintReverse procedure }

procedure NRPrintReverse (var a: ArrayType;  n: NonNeg);
var
   i: integer;                      {index}
begin
   for i := n downto 1 do
      write (a[i])
end;   {NRPrintReverse}
```

Much research is being done on removing recursion in general. Another technique that converts the recursive solution to an iterative one simulates recursion by creating a stack. When we consider the stack data structure later, we show how to accomplish this conversion.

▽

SECTION 2.2 EXERCISES

In Exercises 1–18 find an iterative solution to the indicated problems from Section 2.1.

1. Example 2.3, Equation (1), for x^n.

2. Exercise 14b, a procedure to print the first n elements of an array in normal order.

3. Exercise 2, the function f, where

$$f(n) = \begin{cases} 3 & \text{if } n = 0 \\ 2f(n-1) + 1 & \text{if } n > 0 \end{cases}$$

4. Exercise 5b, a function *Amount* with parameters P, R, and n to calculate the amount compounded in the bank after n years.

5. Exercise 9, a function to find the nth Fibonacci number.

6. Exercise 10, the greatest common divisor function, *gcd*.

7. Exercise 11, a function to find the sum of the first n elements of an array of real numbers.

8. Exercise 12, a boolean function to return *true* if x is a member of the first n elements of an array a.

9. Exercise 13, a function to find the maximum of the first n elements of an array of real numbers.

10. Example 2.3, Equation (2), for x^n.

11. Exercise 15, a boolean function to return *true* if a character string is a palindrome.

12. Exercise 18, a boolean function to return *true* if a particular string of n characters is in the language defined by the BNF description

    $<S> ::= <S>0 \mid 1$

13. Exercise 19, a boolean function to return *true* if a particular string of n characters is in the language defined by the BNF description

    $<S> ::= <S>0 \mid <S>1 \mid 00$

14. a. Figure 2.7 presents one syntax diagram for the definition of a Pascal variable name. (See Exercise 20 of Section 2.1.) A nonrecursive version of *variable* is diagrammed in Figure 2.8. According to the diagram a single letter, such as x, is a legal variable name. Moreover, following the loop we see that a letter followed by any combination of letters and dig-

Figure 2.8

Syntax diagram for *variable* for Exercise 14

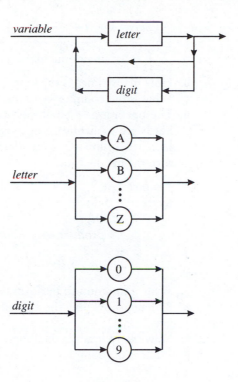

its, such as *TX2A*, is a variable. Draw a nonrecursive syntax diagram for *S* from Exercise 18 in Section 2.1, where

<S> ::= <S> 0 | 1

b. Exercise 19, where

<S> ::= <S> 0 | <S> 1 | 00

15. Exercise 23, a procedure to merge two sorted arrays into a third array.

16. Exercise 24, a function to convert a character string of *n* digits to the corresponding integer number.

17. Exercise 25, a function to convert a binary number to a decimal one.

18. Exercise 26, a procedure to print the binary equivalent of a nonnegative decimal number.

19. In Exercise 16 of Section 2.1 we considered a recursive operation to evaluate the product of *na*, where *n* is a nonnegative integer and *a* is a real number.

a. Design an algorithm to calculate the product *na* without using the operation * by adding *a* to itself *n* times:

$$na = \underbrace{a + a + \cdots + a}_{n \text{ summands}}$$

b. How many times is the loop in Part a executed?

c. What is the complexity of the algorithm in Part a?

d. The operations of multiplication and division by 2 are built into the hardware or firmware of most computers and, consequently, are very fast. The following is an algorithm that utilizes these operations to return the product *na*:

product ← 0
while *n* ≠ 0 do
    if *odd*(*n*) then
        product ← *product* + *a*
    a ← *a* * 2
    n ← *n* div 2

Write a function to perform this algorithm.

e. By hand show how the algorithm in Part d works in returning the product 7 · (3.1).

f. How many times is the loop in Part d executed?

g. What is the complexity of the algorithm in Part d?

▽

PROGRAMMING PROJECTS

For Projects 1–3 produce a nonrecursive version of corresponding project in Section 2.1.

1. Project 1, to find the root of a polynomial.

2. Project 2, to produce a binomial expansion. The number of combinations of *r* distinct objects chosen from *n* can be calculated nonrecursively as

$$C(n, r) = n! / (r!(n - r)!), \text{ where } 0 \le r \le n.$$

3. Project 3, for conversion from a base *b* ($2 \le b \le 9$) number to the base 10 equivalent and vice versa.

▽

SECTION 2.3

Induction and Program Verification

With the emphasis on structured programming has come the study of how to prove that programs are correct or that they do exactly what they are supposed to do. Such **program verification** can decrease debugging time and increase the efficiency of and confidence in a program. Moreover, with a complex program, testing every possible situation could take a prohibitive amount of time, so that program verification can be a valuable tool in showing that the program is correct.

Errors are prevalent, even in commercially produced software. One leader in the computer field, a superior programmer who reported on a major system he wrote, noted a rate of 40 errors per 1000 lines of code undetected by the compiler and 12 bugs not discovered by any testing before release. Such mistakes can produce erroneous results and cost time and money. Consequently, one major computer corporation uses methodologies based on verification to complete large software projects ahead of schedule and under budget. **Proof of the correctness** of a program seeks to prove that the program is right and, thus, to minimize errors.

Program verification is based in part on the proof technique of **mathematical induction**. As we will see, we can use induction to prove that iterative loops and recursive processes are correct.

In this section, we prove by mathematical induction that two formulas, useful in conversion of some routines from recursive to iterative definitions, are correct. Afterwards, we use induction as a program verification technique to show the correctness of a loop.

The first formula gives a fast way of computing the sum of the first n positive integers. The greatest mathematician of the 19th century, Carl Friedrich Gauss, discovered this formula while still a child. His teacher, undoubtedly, in an effort to gain some moments of peace, told the class to find the sum of the natural numbers from 1 to 100. To the amazement of teacher and class, almost immediately Gauss blurted out the correct answer of 5050. His technique consisted of writing the numbers in order and underneath this line in reverse order:

$$1 \quad 2 \quad 3 \quad 4 \ldots 97 \quad 98 \quad 99 \quad 100$$

$$100 \quad 99 \quad 98 \quad 97 \ldots 4 \quad 3 \quad 2 \quad 1$$

Each 2-element column has a sum of 101, and since there are 100 columns, the total is 100×101. Each number, however, appears twice, so the correct answer is half this amount:

$$1 + 2 + \cdots + 100 = \frac{100 \times 101}{2} = 5050$$

In general

$$1 + 2 + \cdots + n = \frac{n(n + 1)}{2} \quad \text{for all integers } n > 0$$

The ellipses indicate that we continue in the same fashion adding positive integers until we get to n. We call this formula $P(n)$. Proving that $P(n)$ is true for any positive integer n is a two-step process:

1. Prove $P(1)$. That is, prove that the statement $P(n)$ is true initially with $n = 1$.

2. Prove that if $P(k)$ is true, so is $P(k + 1)$. The statement $P(k)$, called the **induction hypothesis**, is formed by substituting k everywhere n occurs in the formula for $P(n)$. Similarly, by replacing n with $k + 1$ we convert

$P(n)$ to the statement $P(k + 1)$. Assuming the induction hypothesis, $P(k)$, we prove the next step, $P(k + 1)$.

To indicate how the method works, suppose we want to prove that we could climb to any rung of an infinitely long ladder. The rungs are numbered from the bottom up, 1, 2, 3, ... We are verifying we can climb to rung n for any positive integer n by the following two steps of induction:

1. Prove $P(1)$. We can get on the ladder at rung 1. After all, we must be able to begin somewhere, or there is no hope of climbing anywhere.

2. Prove $P(k)$ implies $P(k + 1)$. Assuming we can climb to an arbitrary rung, the kth, show that we can step to the next rung, the $k + 1$ rung.

Showing these two steps should prove to our friends that we can climb to any rung of the ladder.

Example 2.5.

▼ Now let us consider the more useful problem of verifying the formula $P(n)$:

$$1 + 2 + \cdots + n = \frac{n(n + 1)}{2}$$

is true for any positive integer n.

1. Prove $P(1)$.

Substituting 1 for n, we have only one term on the left:

$$P(1): \quad 1 = \frac{1(1 + 1)}{2}$$

2. Prove $P(k)$ implies $P(k + 1)$.

Substituting k for n, assume the sum of the first k positive integers is $k(k + 1)/2$:

$$P(k): \quad 1 + 2 + \cdots + k = \frac{k(k + 1)}{2}$$

Substituting $k + 1$ for n, prove the sum of the first $k + 1$ positive integers satisfies the formula

$$P(k + 1): 1 + 2 + \cdots + k + (k + 1) = \frac{(k + 1)((k + 1) + 1)}{2}$$

$$= \frac{(k + 1)(k + 2)}{2}$$

To prove $P(k + 1)$ we start with the induction hypothesis $P(k)$,

$$1 + 2 + \cdots + k = \frac{k(k + 1)}{2}$$

and add the next integer, $k + 1$, to both sides:

$$1 + 2 + \cdots + k + (k + 1) = \frac{k(k + 1)}{2} + (k + 1)$$

Now, the left-hand side is the sum of the first $k + 1$ positive integers and, thus, matches the left-hand side of $P(k + 1)$. We use some algebra to show that the right-hand sides are the same. First, we multiply and divide $k + 1$ by 2 to get a common denominator:

$$1 + 2 + \cdots + k + (k + 1) = \frac{k(k + 1)}{2} + \frac{2(k + 1)}{2}$$

Then, we add the two fractions:

$$1 + 2 + \cdots + k + (k + 1) = \frac{k(k + 1) + 2(k + 1)}{2}$$

Now, we factor out the common term $(k + 1)$ to obtain the right-hand side of $P(k + 1)$:

$$1 + 2 + \cdots + k + (k + 1) = \frac{(k + 1)(k + 2)}{2}$$

Having verified Steps 1 and 2 of the mathematical induction, we have shown that the formula

$$1 + 2 + \cdots + n = \frac{n(n + 1)}{2}$$

is true for all positive integers n.

Although we have expressed this sum mathematically, we can evaluate it using a recursive function in Pascal:

```
{ Recursive function to return the sum of the first
   n positive integers                               }

function SumNatural (n: Positive): Positive;
begin
   if n = 1 then
      SumNatural := 1
   else
      SumNatural := SumNatural (n - 1) + n
end;
```

We mirror the mathematical induction performed earlier to verify that the routine returns $n*(n + 1)/2$:

1. Prove $P(1)$ or that *SumNatural*(1) returns $1*(1 + 1)/2 = 1$.
      Clearly, the terminal condition, $n = 1$, yields *SumNatural* := 1.

2. Prove $P(k)$ implies $P(k + 1)$. That is, assuming *SumNatural*(k) *is* $k*(k + 1)/2$, prove *SumNatural* $(k + 1)$ returns $(k + 1)*(k + 2)/2$.
With $n = k + 1$,

$$SumNatural \leftarrow SumNatural((k + 1) - 1) + (k + 1)$$

or

$$SumNatural \leftarrow SumNatural(k) + (k + 1)$$

By the induction hypothesis *SumNatural*(k) is $k*(k + 1)/2$, so *SumNatural*(k) + $(k + 1)$ = $k*(k + 1)/2 + (k + 1)$, which is, as we saw earlier, $(k + 1)*(k + 2)/2$.

As a consequence of this formula, we should make one observation before continuing the discussion on program verification: If you need to add the first n positive integers, do not use the recursive function above or a loop, such as:

```
Sum := 0;
for i := 1 to n do
    Sum := Sum + i
```

Instead, use the formula

```
Sum := n * (n + 1) / 2
```

The function and the loop each have complexity $O(n)$ since there are n additions in each, while the latter assignment has complexity $O(1)$ since the number of operations does not depend on n.

| Example 2.6. |

The next formula will be useful in the chapter on binary trees. We wish to prove that the following equality, $P(n)$,

$$2^0 + 2^1 + 2^2 + \cdots + 2^n = 2^{n+1} - 1$$

is true for all nonnegative integers n. For example, with $n = 3$ we have

$$2^0 + 2^1 + 2^2 + 2^3 = 1 + 2 + 4 + 8 = 15$$

while

$$2^{n+1} - 1 = 2^{3+1} - 1 = 2^4 - 1 = 16 - 1 = 15$$

To prove the formula using mathematical induction we verify the two steps:

1. Prove the initial statement, $P(0)$.
With just one term on the left the statement $P(0)$,

$$2^0 = 2^{0+1} - 1,$$

is clearly true since $2^0 = 1$ and $2^1 - 1 = 1$.

2. Assuming $P(k)$,

$$2^0 + 2^1 + 2^2 + \cdots + 2^k = 2^{k+1} - 1$$

we wish to prove $P(k + 1)$:

$$2^0 + 2^1 + 2^2 + \cdots + 2^k + 2^{k+1} = 2^{k+2} - 1.$$

As we did in the first example, we add the $(k + 1)$ term to both sides of $P(k)$ and use algebra to simplify the right-hand side:

$$2^0 + 2^1 + 2^2 + \cdots + 2^k \quad\quad = 2^{k+1} - 1$$
$$\begin{aligned} 2^0 + 2^1 + 2^2 + \cdots + 2^k + 2^{k+1} &= (2^{k+1} - 1) + 2^{k+1} \\ &= 2^{k+1} + 2^{k+1} - 1 \\ &= 2(2^{k+1}) - 1 \\ &= 2^{k+2} - 1 \end{aligned}$$

Now we apply a similar technique in program verification. In Exercise 19, Part a, of Section 2.2 you were asked to find an iterative routine to calculate *na* for nonnegative integer *n* and real number *a* without using multiplication. One answer is the following segment:

```
i          : = n;
product    : = 0;
while i <> 0 do
    begin
        product : = product + a;
        i       : = i - 1
    end
```

We wish to show that this loop produces the correct answer for any non-negative integer *n*. An **invariant** is a statement that is true before and after each iteration of the loop. Figure 2.9 presents a diagram of the invariant

$0 \le i \le n$ and *product* is $n - i$ times *a*

for the above loop. This invariant corresponds to the formula $P(n)$ in each of the first two examples. There are four steps, each involving the invariant, to prove this loop is correct.

Steps to Prove a Loop Is Correct:

1. Show the invariant is true initially, before the loop is executed for the first time. This step corresponds to proving $P(n)$ for the initial value of

Figure 2.9

Diagram of the invariant, $0 \le i \le n$ and *product* is $n - i$ times *a*

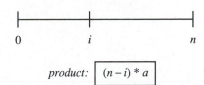

n. The initial case was $P(1)$ in the first example of this section and $P(0)$ in the second.

2. Show the invariant is true after each iteration of the loop. In terms of mathematical induction, this step involves showing $P(k)$ implies $P(k + 1)$.

3. Show that when the loop terminates, we have the desired result. That is, show $P(n)$ produces the correct answer.

4. Show that the loop will terminate. We must verify that we do not have an infinite loop. After all, Step 3 is meaningless if the loop never stops.

Example 2.7

▼ Following the four steps of program verification for a loop, we prove the correctness of the above loop:

1. Show the invariant,

   $0 \leq i \leq n$ and *product* is $n - i$ times *a*,

   is true initially.

   Before the loop is executed, *i* is initialized to be *n* and as such satisfies $0 \leq i \leq n$. Moreover, *product* is given an initial value of 0, which is certainly $n - i = n - n = 0$ times *a*.

2. Show the invariant is true after each iteration of the loop.

   Assume the invariant holds after the *k*th iteration of the loop where $k < n$ for $i = i_k$. In the $(k + 1)$ iteration of the loop, i_k is decremented by 1 so that the value of *i* after the $(k + 1)$ iteration is $i_{k+1} = i_k - 1 \leq n$. Moreover, since the loop terminates at $i = 0$, we must have $0 \leq i_{k+1}$.

   During the $(k + 1)$ iteration, *product* is also incremented by *a* so that after this iteration the value of *product*, called $product_{k+1}$, is *a* plus the value of *product* after the *k*th iteration, $product_k$. *That is,*

   $product_{k+1} = product_k + a$

   But $product_k$ is assumed to be $(n - i_k)*a$ so that

   $product_{k+1} = (n - i_k)*a + a$

   We can also use the fact that $i_{k+1} = i_k - 1$ or

   $i_{k+1} + 1 = i_k$

   or

   $-i_{k+1} - 1 = -i_k$

   Thus, substituting for i_k, we have

$$product_{k+1} = (n - i_{k+1} - 1)*a + a$$
$$= na - i_{k+1}a - a + a$$
$$= na - i_{k+1}a$$
$$= (n - i_{k+1})*a$$

Thus, the second part of the proof also holds.

3. Show that when the loop terminates, we have the desired result of *product* being *na*.

When the loop terminates, $i = 0$ and the invariant reads

$$0 \leq 0 \leq n \text{ and product is } (n - 0) \text{ times } a,$$

which is the desired result.

4. The loop will terminate when $i = 0$.

We are assured that this condition will be true eventually because i is initialized with the nonnegative value of n and is decremented by 1 each time through the loop.

This four-step process involving induction and using the invariant is an important technique in program verification of loop segments.

▽

SECTION 2.3 EXERCISES

1. Using mathematical induction prove *factorial*(n) from Example 2.2 of Section 2.1 returns $n! = n(n - 1) \cdots 3 \cdot 2 \cdot 1$.

2. **a.** Using the formula for the recursive function in Exercise 2 of Section 2.1,

$$f(n) = \begin{cases} 3 & \text{if } n = 0 \\ 2f(n - 1) + 1 & \text{if } n > 0 \end{cases}$$

find $f(4)$ and $f(5)$ without completely simplifying, in a manner similar to the evaluation of $f(0)$ to $f(3)$.

$$
\begin{array}{ll}
f(0) = & 3 \\
f(1) = & 2 \cdot 3 + 1 \\
f(2) = 2(2 \cdot 3 + 1) + 1 = & 2^2 \cdot 3 + 2 + 1 \\
f(3) = 2(2^2 \cdot 3 + 2 + 1) + 1 = & 2^3 \cdot 3 + 2^2 + 2 + 1
\end{array}
$$

b. Using the formula from Example 2.6 find the sum

$$2^0 + 2^1 + 2^2 + \cdots + 2^{n-1}$$

c. Using the formula from Example 2.6 show that $2^n \cdot 4 + 1$ is a simplified solution to $f(n)$, that is, a solution that does not involve the sum of $n + 1$ terms.

d. Using mathematical induction prove that the recursive function returns a value equal to this closed form solution.

3. Using the formula from Example 2.5 find the sum of the positive integers from 1 through $n - 1$:

$$1 + 2 + \cdots + (n - 1)$$

4. **a.** Find a simplified solution to the recursive function from Exercise 5, Section 2.1, for calculating the amount compounded in a savings account.
   b. Using mathematical induction prove that the recursive function returns a value equal to this simplified solution.

5. Prove that *PowerLin* from Exercise 6, Section 2.1, returns the value of x^n.

6. Using mathematical induction prove that the recursive function from Exercise 11, Section 2.1, returns the sum of the first n elements of an array of real numbers.

7. Using mathematical induction prove that the recursive function from Exercise 13, Section 2.1, returns the maximum of the first n elements of an array of real numbers.

8. Using mathematical induction prove that the recursive procedure from Exercise 14a, Section 2.1, prints the first n elements of an array in reverse order.

9. Using mathematical induction prove that the recursive procedure from Example 2.4 of Section 2.1 solves the Towers of Hanoi problem.

10. **a.** Find a simplified solution in mathematics to Exercise 17c, Section 2.1, for finding the number of moves for N disks in the Towers of Hanoi problem.
    b. Using mathematical induction prove that the recursive function returns a value equal to this simplified solution.

11. Prove by mathematical induction that if S is a set with n elements, then S has 2^n subsets. *Note:* For a set with $k + 1$ elements, separate out one of the elements, giving a set with k elements and a set with one element. Consider forming the subsets of the $(k + 1)$-element set from the subsets of the k-element set and the 1-element set.

12. The following appeared in the sample questions of the *1984 AP Computer Science Examination**:

    $i := 1;$
    while $(i < = Max)$ **and** $(String[i] <> Symbol)$ **do** $i: = i + 1$

    Which of the following is a loop invariant for the **while** loop above; i.e., which is true each time the while-condition is tested?

**AP question selected from *AP Computer Science Examination,* 1984. Reprinted by permission of Educational Testing Service, the copyright owner of the sample questions.*

(A) $i = Max$

(B) $i = i + 1$

(C) $String[j] = Symbol$ for all j such that $i < j$.

(D) $String[j] \neq Symbol$ for all j such that $i \leq j$.

(E) $String[j] \neq Symbol$ for all j such that $1 \leq j < i$.

13. a. State the invariant for the following program segment to find $n!$ for every nonnegative integer n.

```
i              := n;
factorial      := 1;
while ( i <> 0 )  do
    begin
        factorial    := factorial * i;
        i            := i - 1
    end        { while }
```

b. Using program verification, prove for any nonnegative integer n that this segment does find $n!$.

In Exercises 14–19:

a. State the invariant for the loop in the given exercise from Section 2.2.

b. Using the four-step process of program verification, prove this loop is correct.

14. Exercise 1, in which you used a loop to evaluate x^n by the formula in Equation (1), Example 2.3, of that section.

15. Exercise 4, in which you used a loop to calculate the amount compounded in a savings account.

16. Exercise 7, in which you used a loop to find the sum of the first n elements of an array of real numbers.

17. Exercise 8, in which you used a loop to write a boolean function to return *true* if x is a member of the first n elements of an array a.

18. Exercise 2, in which you used a loop to write a procedure to print the first n elements of an array in normal order.

19. Exercise 11, in which you used a loop to write a boolean function to return *true* if a character string is a palindrome.

SECTION 2.4

Abstract Data Types

A big deal was in the making, the biggest ever for the company, and the president was in no mood to hear the problems and questions of his subordinates. As vice presidents, lawyers, and secretaries listened intently, the boss spoke deliberately: "I don't care how you do it, just do it!" The object of his displeasure stuttered, "Well, I . . . I guess I . . ." A frown appeared on the president's face as he interrupted, "I really don't want to hear it! I told you I need you to shift our assets, and I've given you all the information you asked for. Now, please do your job and stop bothering me with how you plan to pull it off." He looked around the hushed room to make his point to everyone. "I've got enough on my mind putting this whole glorious mess together without getting bogged down in the minute details of how each of you do your part and without having to keep you informed of my every move." In a calmer and more encouraging tone, the president ended, "This deal is important. I sketched out the plan for it a year ago, and now I'm depending on each of you to somehow get your jobs done so I can do mine. I'm counting on you."

No, you haven't picked up the wrong book. Actually, this scene serves as an analogy of two important concepts in computer science, high-level design of programs and abstract data types. The president has designed an overall plan of attack for this deal that he is so touchy about, and now he is calling on subordinates to consider specific parts of the scheme in greater detail. Undoubtedly, some of those individuals will order others to carry out various specifics of their jobs. This hierarchy of command and work is reminiscent of the high-level design of a program, breaking the project down into smaller and smaller modules. As discussed in Chapter 1, programs designed from the top down in a modular fashion are far easier to develop and maintain.

The drama is also an analogy for the concept of an abstract data type. The president knows what tasks need to be done and he is depending on others to perform these duties correctly. Just as it was easier for the president to create the blueprint of the big deal in terms of objects such as assets and definite, larger operations on these objects, it will be easier for us to design major programs considering each data structure as a set of data objects and the basic operations performed on them. Moreover, while fitting all the pieces together, the president does not need or want to know the details of implementation; those details would only muddle his thinking about the larger goal. He does not care how his subordinates solve their tasks. Similarly, if we first consider data structures on a high level without concern for the implementation details, we will have a powerful tool that will simplify the process of handling data and extend naturally the concept of structured programming. Throughout the text we approach each data structure as an **abstract data type** (ADT), or a set of data objects and fundamental operations on this set, before implementing the structure and developing major applications. Not only is it more manageable to design algorithms with the high-level operations of an ADT, it is easier to study each data structure as an abstract data type before examining how to code the objects and operations in a computer language.

To illustrate another issue involved in data abstraction, the president wanted to remain isolated from the details of the individual tasks he had assigned. He gave each person the information needed, and he expected results. Moreover, he saw no need for subordinates to meddle in his affairs. This situation mirrors the concept of **encapsulation** for data structure operations. Within a program each such operation should be encapsulated or isolated with only its inputs, outputs, and action known to the user and with the behavior of the rest of the program unknown to the operation. As another analogy, a data structure operation is like a soft drink machine whose contents are not visible. You put the correct money in the slot, press the proper button, and get the drink you want. What goes on inside the machine is unknown and unimportant as long as you get your drink. If you do not put in enough money or if you press the wrong button, however, you will not get the soft drink you want. Similarly, each operation has particular inputs and assumptions that must be met to return the desired results.

After studying and using the data structure on the abstract data type level, we examine how the structure is represented and how the operations can be written in Pascal. Often, there are several ways to implement a particular ADT, just as for the hypothetical company there are probably many ways, some better than others depending on the situation, to do any one task. Advantages and disadvantages of these implementations and the circumstances which make one more desirable than another will be discussed. Throughout the book we examine ADTs and then consider their applications and implementations.

Several data types are built into Pascal, the most basic of which are *integer, real, char*, and *boolean*. These are all **scalar types** whose variables contain only one value. Enumeration and subrange types also fall in the category of scalar types. **Composite types,** such as *array, record, file,* and *set*, have more than one element. In this section we consider the scalar types, and in the next chapter we study the built-in composite types. In the following three chapters, we introduce strings, stacks, and queues along with an array implementation for each. After working with the type *pointer* and with linked lists, we discuss alternative implementations of the ADTs string, stack, and queue. In Section 8.5 we consider encapsulation with Pascal programs. In the remainder of the book we study sorting and the data structures of table, generalized set, binary tree, graph, and network that are not part of the definition of Pascal.

How might we define the data type *integer* on the abstract level? We need to give values that variables of that type can hold and the basic operations that can be performed with these variables. Other operations can be developed in terms of these basic ones. The basic operations are the axioms by which we define our structure. But just as in mathematics we can start out with a different set of axioms and basic definitions to define the same mathematical structure, so we can have different sets of basic operations to define the same data structure. We choose one set of basic operations for the ADT integer, realizing that we could have legitimately picked a different set or defined an operation in a slightly different way. Figure 2.10 gives one possible description of the ADT integer.

With this ADT we are not concerned with how the operations are represented in Pascal or how they are implemented in the computer. For instance, *IntegerAddition*(i, j) is represented as $i + j$ in Pascal. In LISP, however, $(+ \; i \; j)$ indicates this addition, while in FORTH $i \; j \; +$ accomplishes the same thing. At this high level of an abstract data type, we do not need to consider the syntax of a particular language.

In Pascal the same representation, $x + y$, is used for the addition two real numbers as well as two integers. The implementation is in fact very different. Because this operation is built in, we do not worry about these details. We use

Figure 2.10.

Formal definition of ADT integer

ADT Integer

Objects: Scalar elements with values in the set

$$\{\ldots, -3, -2, -1, 0, 1, 2, 3, \ldots\}$$

Operations:

Notation:

i, j, k — integers
nzi — nonzero integer
nni — nonnegative integer
e — integer data item
b — boolean value

StoreInteger(*i, e*)
Procedure to store *e*'s value in variable *i*

IntegerAddition(*i, j*) → *k*
Function to return the sum, *k*, of *i* and *j*

IntegerSubtraction(*i, j*) → *k*
Function to return the difference, *k*, of *i* and *j*

IntegerMultiplication(*i, j*) → *k*
Function to return the product, *k*, of *i* and *j*

IntegerDivision(*i, nzi*) → *k*
Function to return the quotient, *k*, of *i* divided by *nzi*

Remainder(*i, nzi*) → *nni*
Function to return the nonegative integer remainder,
nni, of *i* divided by *nzi*

EqualZero(*i*) → *b*
Function to return *true* if *i* equals zero, *false* otherwise

GreaterThanZero(*i*) → *b*
Function to return *true* if *i* is greater than zero, *false* otherwise

the operation with a clear understanding of what the symbol + does, if not how the computer performs the addition. Information on the details of how integer addition is accomplished is hidden from us.

To illustrate implementation on this low level, we need to review several terms. Everything in the computer is stored with strings of **bits** or zeros and ones. A **byte** is a string of contiguous bits that could encode a character, and on many computers there are eight bits in a byte. The term "byte" was coined in the late 1950s from "bite," but the spelling was changed to avoid an accidental drop of the e that would convert the word to "bit." Some had resisted use of the term "bit" ten years earlier, branding the acronym for "binary digit" as an "irresponsible vulgarity."

A **word** is a unit of information composed of a fixed number of bytes. For example, on an IBM 370 computer, there are 4 bytes or 32 bits in a word, while on a CRAY I supercomputer a word has 8 bytes or 64 bits. Though not true for all machines, in our discussion we assume that the smallest addressable unit in memory is a word. (Some machines are byte-addressable.) In the case of a **word-addressable** machine, words are numbered 0, 1, 2, and so forth with each number being the word's **address**.

In one computer an integer might be stored in two bytes and a real number in five, while on another machine an integer might be placed in a word and a real number in two words. Because of space limitations, any given computer cannot store every member of the set $\{\ldots, -3, -2, -1, 0, 1, 2, 3, \ldots\}$. Consequently, this mathematical set of integers is different from the set of integers in a computer. For instance, if a computer has a *maxint* of 32,767, its set of integers is the finite set $\{-32,768, -32,767, \ldots, -3, -2, -1, 0, 1, 2, 3, \ldots, 32,766, 32,767\}$; no integer sum could have a larger integer value than 32,767. Also, there are a variety of ways to encode integers as strings of bits, such as with one's complement, two's complement, and binary coded decimal notation. Integers and real numbers are even stored differently. Recall that a real number like 68.864 can be written as 0.68864×10^2. This real number is stored in two parts, the factional part 68864, called the mantissa, and the exponent. Actually, 68.864 also equals 0.269×2^8 and 0.269×16^2. Some computers store the exponent of 2, others of 16. Also, each part might be stored in a slightly different encoding scheme. These details, however, can be left for a computer organization course.

Because of the differences in storage of integers and real numbers, they must have different addition operations. We illustrate these differences by observing how we add numbers in the decimal number system. To perform the addition $573 + 14$ we start adding corresponding digits from the right to the left, taking care of a carry when necessary. Compare this procedure with finding the sum of 5.73 and 1.4. We do not start adding digits from right to left; we first line up the decimals. The computer must perform a similar process.

Certainly, the amount and form of storage and the method of encoding affect how integer addition is implemented, but we are not concerned with these details when writing a statement using addition at the high level of Pascal. The details of the operation of addition implementation are encapsulated so that the programmer is insulated from these considerations. The programmer only knows the syntax of using the operation, the needed input, and the expected results.

Certainly, there are a number of other operations involving integers than those listed in the ADT integer definition. Let us consider how we might define a few of these in terms of those basic operations. We are, in effect, considering applications of this structure.

Example 2.8

▼ How might we define the *succ* function that returns the successor to a given integer?

succ $(i) \rightarrow j$

Function to return the next larger integer

Input:
  i — integer
Output:
  j — integer
Algorithm:
  succ ← *IntegerAddition* (*i* , 1)

Notice we defined the behavior of the *succ* function in terms of one of the basic
▲ operations.

Most of the arithmetic operations appear in the list of basic operations. In
fact, as we have seen in Exercise 16 of Section 2.1 and Exercise 19 of Section
2.2, integer multiplication of *na* can be implemented recursively or iteratively
using integer addition, $a + a + \cdots + a$. Similarly, *IntegerDivision* can be
defined in terms of *IntegerSubtraction*. Thus, we could eliminate *Integer-
Multiplication* and *IntegerDivision* from the list of basic operations without
diminishing the potency of the ADT integer. For speed these operations are
often built into the hardware or firmware of a computer.

Example 2.9

▼ Another arithmetic operation, which is not listed, however, is unary minus,
written in Pascal with a minus in front of the number or variable as in $-i$. This
operation can be implemented quickly with *IntegerSubtraction* as follows:

UnaryMinus(*i*) → *k*
  Function to return the same magnitude as *i* but opposite sign
Input:
  i — integer
Output:
  k — integer
Algorithm:
▲ *UnaryMinus* ← *IntegerSubtraction*(0, *i*)

Example 2.10

▼ We define one form of the relational operators with the *EqualZero* and *GreaterThanZero* functions. Using these functions we can define functions to test the
equality and strict inequality of integers. The equality operation is defined as
follows:

Equal(*i*, *j*) → *b*
  Function to return *true* if *i* equals *j*
Input:
  i — integer
Output:
  b — boolean value

Algorithm:
  Equal ← *EqualZero*(*IntegerSubtraction* (*i, j*))

▲ Should the difference be zero, the integers are certainly equal.

Example 2.11

▼ The absolute value function is somewhat more involved, and the mathematical definition can be helpful:

$$|x| = \begin{cases} x & \text{if } x \geq 0 \\ -x & \text{if } x < 0 \end{cases}$$

Actually, since $-0 = 0$, $x = 0$ could be included in either line. Using this definition we can define the absolute value operation as follows:

abs(*i*) → **nni**
  Function to return the absolute value of *i*
Input:
  i — integer
Output:
  nni — nonnegative integer
Algorithm:
  if *GreaterThanZero*(*i*) then
      abs ← *i*
  else
▲   *abs* ← *UnaryMinus*(*i*)

We are certainly familiar with the implementation of the integer operations, such as *IntegerAddition*(*i, j*) as $i + j$ and *GreaterThanZero*(*i*) as $i > 0$. Thus, for clarity, we use this implementation form in defining other ADTs. Consequently, in checking to see if the ordinal values of two characters c_1 and c_2 are equal, we write the boolean expression

$$ord(c_1) = ord(c_2)$$

instead of using the ADT integer operations *EqualZero* and *IntegerSubtraction* to form the higher level expression

EqualZero (*IntegerSubtraction* ($ord(c_1)$, $ord(c_2)$))

(Appendix C contains the ordinal values or positions of many characters in the ASCII and EBCDIC encoding schemes.) Similarly, for other built-in types where there is little choice in implementation, such as for *array, file,* and *pointer,* we present the formal ADT definition to obtain a clear understanding of the data structure but thereafter use the Pascal code of the operations for clarity. Figure 2.11 summarizes the Pascal implementation of ADT integer.

Figure 2.11.

Summary of Pascal implementation of ADT integer operations

ADT Integer Implementation

Create an integer variable i

```
var
    i : integer;
```

StoreInteger(i, e)

```
i := e
```

IntegerAddition(i, j) → k

```
i + j
```

IntegerSubtraction(i, j) → k

```
i - j
```

IntegerMultiplication(i, j) → k

```
i * j
```

IntegerDivision(i, nzi) → k

```
i div nzi
```

Remainder(i, nzi) → nni

```
i mod nzi
```

EqualZero(i) → b

```
i = 0
```

GreaterThanZero(i) → b

```
i > 0
```

SECTION 2.4 EXERCISES

Define the operations in Exercises 1–10 in terms of ADT integer operations.

1. Procedure to increment i by 2.

2. Procedure to give i the value 0.

3. Boolean function to return *true* if i is greater than j.

4. Boolean function to return *true* if i is less than zero.

5. Boolean function to return *true* if i is less than j.

6. Function to return the units digit of an integer number. For example, if $i = 598$, the function should return 8.

7. Function to return the tens digit of an integer number. For example, if $i = 598$, the function should return 9.

8. *odd*

9. *ord*, where the ordinal value of an integer is the integer itself.

10. *sqr*

11. Implement *UnaryMinus* using *IntegerMultiplication*.

12. Write a formal definition of the ADT real with the operations of *StoreReal, RealAddition, RealSubtraction, RealMultiplication, RealDivision, Equal-Zero, GreaterThanZero*, and *trunc*.

Define the operations in Exercises 13–15 in terms of ADT real operations.

13. *UnaryMinus*

14. *round*

15. *sqr*

16. Write a formal definition of the ADT boolean with the operations of *StoreBoolean, And, Or,* and *Not*.

Define the operations in Exercises 17–20 in terms of ADT boolean operations.

17. *Nand*, which is "not and."

18. *Nor*, which is "not or."

19. *Xor*, which is "one or the other but not both."

20. *ord*, where *false < true*.

Using the appropriate ADT boolean and ADT integer operations, define the operations on integers in Exercises 21–24.

21. *GreaterOrEqualZero*, greater than or equal to zero.

22. *GreaterOrEqual*, greater than or equal.

23. *LessOrEqualZero*, less than or equal to zero.

24. *LessOrEqual*, less than or equal.

25. Write a formal definition of the ADT character with the operations of *StoreChar, ord,* and *chr*.

Define the operations in Exercises 26–28 in terms of ADT character operations.

26. *pred*

27. *succ*

28. *EqualChar*

29. Write a formal definition of ADT enumeration with the operations of *StoreEnumeration* and *ord*.

Define the operations in Exercises 30–31 in terms of ADT enumeration and ADT integer operations.

30. *EqualEnumeration*(i, j), a boolean function to return *true* if i equals j.

31. *GreaterThanEnumeration*(i, j), a boolean function to return *true* if i is greater than j.

32. How does the formal definition of the ADT integer subrange differ from that of the ADT integer?

▽

PROGRAMMING PROJECT

1. Write a program to read a text file and write to another text file the ordinal values (integer values from 0 to 255) of the characters with blanks separating them. Skip end-of-line marks. Then, read the second file, converting each ordinal number to a hexadecimal one and writing the results with no blanks to a third text file.

The ordinal value is in the base 10 decimal number system, while a hexadecimal value is in the base 16 number system. The base 16 number system has 16 digits, 0, 1, 2, 3, 4, 5, 6, 7, 8, 9, A, B, C, D, E, F, with the following equivalences:

Hexadecimal	*Decimal*
0 through 9	0 through 9
A	10
B	11
C	12
D	13
E	14
F	15

Often in mathematics we use a subscript to distinguish the number system. For example, with the ASCII encoding scheme, ord('H') = 72_{10} = 48_{16}; or the ordinal value of the character 'H' is the decimal number 72 and the hexadecimal number 48. Moreover, $4(16) + 8 = 72$.

To compute the hexadecimal equivalent of a decimal number in the range from 0 to 255, divide by 16. The quotient in base 16 is the most significant or leftmost digit while the remainder is the least significant. When we perform an integer division of 71 by 16, the quotient is 4 and the remainder is 8, so 72_{10} = 48_{16}. If we perform the same division by 16 on *ord*('m') = 109, the quotient is 6 and the remainder is 13_{10} = D_{16}. Thus, 109_{10} = $6D_{16}$.

Elementary Data Structures

Introduction

The introduction to abstract data types in Section 2.4 focused on predefined scalar types, such as *integer* and *char*. In this chapter we continue the study of abstract data types by examining various composite types that are built into Pascal—array, record, file, and set. After defining each as an ADT, we present its Standard Pascal implementation along with applications. Some of the details of how these types are implemented at the machine level are also included to enhance understanding of these composite types.

The discussion of arrays is augmented by a section on two methods of searching this structure for a particular item. We use these searching techniques in a variety of situations throughout the text.

ADT Array and Implementation

We have already employed one-dimensional arrays in applications in the text and exercises, and, in fact, this built-in type can be used to implement a number of data structures. Unless otherwise noted, we refer to a one-dimensional array simply as an "array." But what exactly is an array when considered as an abstract data type? A one-dimensional array is certainly a composite type, which is made up of at least one element. Moreover, there are a fixed number of elements of the same type arranged in a **linear order** or as a **sequence** such that there is a first element, a second, and so forth. An **index**, which is of a finite ordinal type, is used in accessing individual array elements. For each index there is an associated array element and vice versa, so that we can say there is a **one-to-one correspondence** between the set of index values and the set of array elements. Having discussed the data objects, what operations do we wish to perform on this structure? We need to be able to place a value into an element of the array and to get a value from it. The formal definition of ADT array is displayed in Figure 3.1.

Figure 3.1.

Formal definition of ADT array

ADT Array

Objects: Sequence of elements of the same type. An associated index has finite ordinal type. There is a one-to-one correspondence between the values of the index and the array elements.

Operations:
Notation:

    elType — type of each element of the array
    a   — one-dimensional array
    i   — index
    e   — item of type *elType*

StoreArray (*a, i, e*)
    Procedure to store *e*'s value in the *i*th element of array *a*
RetrieveArray (*a, i*) → *e*
    Function to return the value of the *i*th element in array *a*

Since you are already familiar with a number of applications of arrays, we consider implementation of these operations on both the software and the hardware levels. First, since the type *array* is built into Pascal, creation of an array is merely a matter of definition of types and declaration of variables. For instance, we can define *a* to be an array of 10 real numbers as follows:

```
const
    MaxNumEls   = 10;

type
    IndexType   = 1..MaxNumEls;
    ArrayType   = array [IndexType] of real;

var
    i           :  IndexType;
    a           :  ArrayType;
```

Just as execution of a program begins, in a process called **binding**, a starting address is established and enough memory is set aside for any array declared in the main Pascal program. This amount of allocated space is **static** and will not change during execution.

    There is **direct access** to an array; that is, we can access the element associated with a particular index *i* directly without examining each individual ele-

ment of the array. The ADT array operation *StoreArray* is realized in Pascal as
an assignment statement that specifies an individual element with an index.

```
a[i] := e
```

Later, we obtain the element's value for many reasons, such as printing to
a report, storing in a file, assigning to a variable, or comparing with another
value. Pascal implements this *RetrieveArray* operation as an array reference,

```
a[i]
```

Figure 3.2 gives a summary of the Pascal implementation of the ADT array. In
that figure and throughout the text, ellipses in a type definition indicate any
reasonable type.

Figure 3.2.

Summary of Pascal imple-
mentation of ADT array

ADT Array Implementation

Create an array *a* with elements of type *elType* and index of type *IndexType*

```
type
    IndexType  = ..........;    {type of index}
    elType     = ..........;    {type of array element}
    ArrayType  = array [IndexType] of elType;

var
    a          :  ArrayType;
    e          :  elType;
```

StoreArray(*a, i, e*)

```
a[i] := e
```

RetrieveArray(*a, i*) → *e*

```
a[i]
```

Some of the fastest computers use the array as a fundamental, built-in data
structure. The CRAY-2™ supercomputer, for example, has four processors
working in parallel along with another processor as an overseer. It usually operates fastest on data arranged in one-dimensional arrays that are multiples of
64 elements each.

This illustration suggests that besides considering one-dimensional arrays
on the abstract data type or the Pascal implementation level, we can examine
arrays on yet a lower level—the machine level. Arrays such as array *a* above are
usually stored contiguously in memory. As mentioned in Chapter 2, a word in
memory has an associated integer address. Suppose that in the computer under
consideration a word can store an integer and the next available location has
address 2854. This address of the first word of the array is called the **base address**. Figure 3.3 shows a pictorial representation of array *a* in memory.

Figure 3.3

Pictorial representation of a, an array of integers, in memory, assuming $base(a) = 2854$ with each integer occupying one word

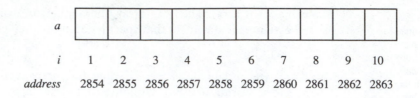

The computer does not store the address of every array element, just the base address ($base(a)$), upper bound (UB), and lower bound (LB) of the array. In this example,

$$base = 2854$$

$$LB = 1$$

$$UB = 10$$

Suppose the statement

```
a[4] := 138
```

is executed. To compute the memory address of $a[4]$, we add the base address, 2854, to the value of the index, 4, and then subtract 1. Thus, the address of $a[4]$ is

$$address(a[4]) = 2854 + 4 - 1 = 2857$$

and in general for this situation

$$address(a[i]) = base(a) + i - 1. \tag{1}$$

The number of elements in the array, called the **range**, is 10 as calculated by the following formula:

$$range = UB - LB + 1 \tag{2}$$

Many compilers will issue an out-of-range error message if we try to access an array element, such as $a[0]$ or $a[11]$, with an index whose value is not between the upper and lower bounds, inclusively.

There are some variations of formulas (1) and (2). For example, suppose a stores real numbers instead of integers with each real number occupying two words. As Figure 3.4 shows, in this case to calculate $address\ (a[i])$ the computer must multiply $i - 1$ by 2. Thus,

$$address(a[4]) = 2854 + 3 \cdot 2 = 2860$$

and

$$address(a[i]) = base(a) + (i - 1) \cdot 2$$

In general, if $elWidth$ is the number of words used to store an array element, the address of the ith element is computed as

$$address(a[i]) = base(a) + (i - 1) \cdot elWidth$$

Figure 3.4

Pictorial representation of *a*, an array of real numbers, in memory, assuming *base(a)* = 2854 with each real number occupying two words

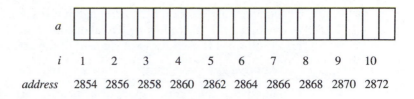

i	1	2	3	4	5	6	7	8	9	10
address	2854	2856	2858	2860	2862	2864	2866	2868	2870	2872

Additional work must be performed if *LB* is not 1. For example, suppose *IndexType* is defined as

    IndexType = 5..14;

The range is still $10 = 14 - 5 + 1$, but as shown in Figure 3.5,

$$address(a[8]) = 2854 + (8 - 5) \cdot 2 = 2860$$

As in (1), the lower bound, here 5 instead of 1, must be subtracted from the index *i* to obtain the relative position, so that

$$address(a[i]) = base(a) + (i - LB) \cdot elWidth$$

Figure 3.5

Pictorial representation of *a*, an array of real numbers, in memory, assuming *base(a)* = 2854, each real number occupies two words, and the index varies from 5 to 14.

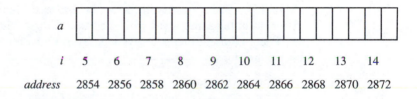

i	5	6	7	8	9	10	11	12	13	14
address	2854	2856	2858	2860	2862	2864	2866	2868	2870	2872

Enumeration types are also permissible for index types, such as

    Week   = (Mon, Tue, Wed, Thu, Fri, Sat, Sun);
    IndexType = Week;

Now, to evaluate the position we must take the ordinal of the index. The ordinal values, however, do start at zero so that $ord(Mon) = 0$ and $ord(Sun) = 6$. With the value of the lower bound of the index being 0, we have

$$address(a[Thu]) = 2854 + (ord(Thu)) \cdot 2$$

or in the most general case

$$address(a[i]) = base(a) + (ord(i) - ord(LB)) \cdot elWidth$$

and

$$range = ord(UB) - ord(LB) + 1$$

One very common application of arrays, already used in the program developed in Chapter 1, is to store character strings. (This application, the formal definition of ADT string, and another implementation will be discussed again in Chapter 4 and Section 8.2.) Although it is true that a character can be stored in one byte, with the following Pascal definition of *ArrayType* in some computers, a full word is used for each element of the array:

```
ArrayType = array [IndexType] of char;
```

Usually, when the array is packed as below, each character is stored in one byte:

```
ArrayType = packed array [IndexType] of char;
```

Thus, for

```
IndexType = 1..28;
```

and base = 2854 on a computer with 4 bytes per word, we have *elWidth* = 1/4 and

$$address(a[9]) = 2854 + (9 - 1) \cdot (1/4) = 2856$$

Using the same computation, we have

$$address(a[10]) = 2854 + (10 - 1) \cdot (1/4) = 2856.25$$

An address must be a whole number, so we take the floor function of this value, $\lfloor 2856.25 \rfloor = 2856$, to obtain the actual address. Elements $a[11]$ and $a[12]$ are also held in the same word with the same address but different byte positions.

Packing of character arrays has several advantages. Suppose we have the type definitions

```
IndexType = 1..10;
ArrayType = packed array [IndexType] of char;
```

and the variable declarations

```
a, b  : ArrayType;
```

We can make the assignment

```
a   := 'John Doe ';
```

as long as we are careful to pad the string constant 'John Doe ' to 10 characters, the number of elements in array *a*. Without *a* being packed, we would be forced to resort to the following awkward list of statements:

```
a[1]  := 'J';
a[2]  := 'o';
a[3]  := 'h';
a[4]  := 'n';
a[5]  := ' ';
a[6]  := 'D';
a[7]  := 'o';
a[8]  := 'e';
a[9]  := ' ';
a[10] := ' ';
```

Although it is not in Standard Pascal, many compilers allow us to read a string into a packed array using a statement such as

```
readln (a)
```

Values are read into *a* until the array is filled or until the end-of-line character is read. Standard Pascal *does* permit the statement

```
writeln (a)
```

which prints the entire string. For two packed arrays of character, *a* and *b*, having the same type, comparisons of *a* and *b* are also permissible, such as:

```
if a = b then
    writeln ('These strings are identical.')
else if a < b then
    writeln ('String ', a, ' occurs before string ',
             b, 'alphabetically.')
```

These comparisons are implemented character by character from left to right in the strings.

Two-Dimensional Arrays

Two-dimensional arrays have not one but two associated indices and, consequently, provide a good structure for the storage of tables in which each component has the same type. For example, suppose we wish to retain the number of car rentals for each Friday, Saturday, and Sunday over a two-week period. Figure 3.6 displays a picture of such a table.

Figure 3.6

The number of car rentals for each of Friday, Saturday, and Sunday over a two-week period

	Fri.	Sat.	Sun.
1	43	35	12
2	57	37	23

We might use the following Pascal type definitions and variable declaration:

```
type
    Week       = (Mon, Tue, Wed, Thu, Fri, Sat, Sun);
    RowIndex   = 1..2;
    ColIndex   = Fri..Sun;
    RentalType = array [RowIndex, ColIndex] of integer;
var
    rentals    : RentalType;
```

The possible array elements are as follows:

```
rentals[1, Fri] rentals[1, Sat] rentals[1, Sun]
rentals[2, Fri] rentals[2, Sat] rentals[2, Sun]
```

Notice that each first index is paired with every second index. The set of all these possible ordered pairs of indices,

$$\{ [1, \textit{Fri}], [1, \textit{Sat}], [1, \textit{Sun}], [2, \textit{Fri}], [2, \textit{Sat}], [2, \textit{Sun}] \},$$

is called the **cartesian product** of the set of row indices, {1, 2}, and the set of column indices, {*Fri, Sat, Sun*}. Notice that since *RowIndex* has 2 values and *ColIndex* has 3, their cartesian product has $2 \times 3 = 6$ ordered pairs. Similarly, the table of Figure 3.6 with its two rows labeled with the first index and its three columns labeled with the second has six elements. Had we considered four weeks instead of two, there would be four rows in the table with a resulting $4 \times 3 = 12$ number of entries. Thus, the range of the two-dimensional array is the product of the ranges of the individual indices.

Our ADT definition of a two-dimensional array must take into account that there are two indices, each of a finite ordinal type. Moreover, there is a one-to-one correspondence between the set of array elements and the cartesian product of the sets of first and second indices. Details of the definition of ADT two-dimensional array and of its Pascal implementation are covered in the exercises.

Though visualized as a table with rows and columns, a two-dimensional array cannot be implemented as such in the computer. Pascal compilers force storage to be contiguous and one row at a time in what is called **row-major order**. A FORTRAN compiler uses **column-major order,** storing the entire first column before storing the second, and so forth. Suppose the two-dimensional array begins at location 2854 with each element using one word of memory. A diagrammatic comparison of row-major and column-major orders is given in Figures 3.7 and 3.8.

Figure 3.7

Row-major order storage for array *rentals* of Figure 3.6

rentals	43	35	12	57	37	23
[*i, j*]	[1, *Fri*]	[1, *Sat*]	[1, *Sun*]	[2, *Fri*]	[2, *Sat*]	[2, *Sun*]
address	2854	2855	2856	2857	2858	2859

Figure 3.8

Column-major order storage for array *rentals* of Figure 3.6

rentals	43	57	35	37	12	23
[*i, j*]	[1, *Fri*]	[2, *Fri*]	[1, *Sat*]	[2, *Sat*]	[1, *Sun*]	[2, *Sun*]
address	2854	2855	2856	2857	2858	2859

To obtain the address of the array element *rental*[2, *Sat*] in row-major order storage, we start with the base address and add the total number of elements in the first row and the number of elements before column *Sat* in the second row, as follows:

$$address(rental[2, Sat]) = 2854 + 3 + 1 = 2857$$

Suppose we consider the array to cover a four-week period and wanted to find the location of *rental*[3, *Sat*]). We have

$$address(rental[3, Sat]) = 2854 + 2 \cdot 3 + 1 = 2861$$

Proceeding sequentially through the stored array, we must go through every element of rows 1 and 2 and then past the *Fri* element of row 3 to arrive at the desired *Sat* component. Where *LB1* is the lower bound for *RowIndex* and *UB2* and *LB2* are the upper and lower bounds, respectively, for *ColIndex*, we have for two-dimensional array *b*

$$address\ (b[i,j]) = base(b) +$$
$$[(ord(i) - ord(LB1)) \cdot (ord(UB2) - ord(LB2) + 1) +$$
$$(ord(j) - ord(LB2))] \cdot elWidth$$

In doing the exercises relative to memory addresses, try to reason out the answers as opposed to applying a formula. This formula is far easier to deduce numerically than to memorize symbolically.

▽

SECTION 3.1 EXERCISES

1. Write Pascal type definitions and variable declarations to create
  a. A boolean array with indices ranging from "A" to "Z".
  b. A real array *salary* with at most 500 elements.
  c. An unpacked character array, *Name*, with at most 20 elements.
  d. An integer array *a* with *IndexType* = 1..20

2. Code in Pascal a procedure *FileToArray* that reads values from a text file *Infile* into the array of Exercise 1b as long as there are elements in the file. Upon completion, *NumEls* should contain the number of elements actually in the array.

3. a. Code in Pascal a nonrecursive procedure *Blankout* that blanks out the array *Name* of Exercise 1c; that is, the procedure copies a blank character into each element.
  b. Write an invariant for the loop.
  c. Using program verification, prove this loop is correct.
  d. Write a recursive version of the procedure in Part a.

4. a. Code in Pascal a procedure that copies the first *n* elements of array *a* into array *b*, where both *a* and *b* have the same *elType*, *IndexType* =

1..*MaxNum*, and $1 \leq n \leq MaxNum$. Assume each of the first *n* elements of *a* has a value.

 b. Write an invariant for the loop.

 c. Using program verification, prove this loop is correct.

 d. Write a recursive version of the procedure in Part a.

5. a. Code in Pascal a procedure *StoreSqr* to store the square of the index in each corresponding element of the array *a* from Exercise 1d.

 b. Define a function to return the product of the values stored in *a*.

6. Code in Pascal a boolean function *ElInCommon* that returns *true* if two arrays of the same type have an element in common. Assume the data in each array is arranged in ascending order.

7. Code in Pascal a procedure *Compress(a, n)* that compresses the nonzero numbers of real array *a* from *a*[1] to *a*[*n*] by moving those elements to the first of the array. The procedure should maintain the order of the nonzero elements and change *n* to be the number of nonzero numbers.

In Exercises 8–11 the base address and the index type of integer array a *are given. If an integer occupies 1 word, compute the word address of* a[i] *for the indicated index value. Assume that this computer is word-addressable and there are 8 bits to a byte and 4 bytes to a word.*

	i	*base*	*IndexType*
8.	17	549	1..20
9.	54	1038	5..75
10.	*Sat*	3476	*Week*
11.	'E'	7720	'A'..'Z'

In Exercises 12–15 repeat Exercises 8–11, assuming a *is a real array and each real number occupies two words.*

In Exercises 16–19 repeat Exercises 8–11, assuming a *is a packed character array and each character occupies one byte.*

In Exercises 20–23 repeat Exercises 8–11, assuming a *is a packed boolean array and each boolean value occupies one bit.*

24. a. Main memory in a computer can be thought of as a one-dimensional array of bytes with each byte being a packed boolean array. Assume there are eight bits to a byte. Give type definitions and a variable declaration for *RAM*, random access memory of 512K, where 1K = 1024 bytes.

 b. Repeat Part a considering *RAM* to be a two-dimensional boolean array.

25. a. Create in Pascal a two-dimensional character array *Names* with at most 100 rows and 20 columns.

 b. Write a procedure to blank out this array using nested loops.

    c. Write an invariant for each loop.

    d. Using program verification, prove each loop is correct.

26. a. Create in Pascal a two-dimensional integer array *b*, which has rows labeled with the letters of the alphabet and columns labeled with the digits.

    b. Suppose the values for this array were previously stored in row-major order in text file *InFile*. Write a procedure to read values into *b*. *NumEls* should contain the number of elements actually in array *b* upon completion.

    c. In your nested loops, does the row or column index change most rapidly?

27. a. Suppose a two-dimensional real array *Profit* has rows labeled from 1 to 8 and a column type of *Week*. Write a procedure to compute and print each row total.

    b. Write an invariant for each loop.

    c. Using program verification, prove each loop is correct.

28. An alternate way to define a two-dimensional array is as an array of arrays. Complete the following type definitions to yield *RentalType* from this section.

```
RowType    = array [___a___] of integer;
RentalType = array [RowIndex] of ___b___;
```

29. Formally define ADT two-dimensional array.

In Exercises 30–34 the base address and RowIndex *and* ColIndex *types of integer array* b *are given. If an integer occupies one word, compute*

    a. The total number of elements in b.

    b. The space occupied by b,

    c. The word address of b[i,j] *for the indicated ordered pair of indices.*

Assume this computer is word-addressable; there are 8 bits in a byte and 4 bytes in a word; and the array is stored in row-major order.

	Ordered Pair of Indices	Base	RowIndex	ColIndex
30.	[0, 3]	1001	0..15	0..5
31.	[3, 0]	1001	0..15	0..5
32.	[2, 7]	2138	1..8	1..10
33.	[7, 2]	2138	1..8	1..10
34.	['Y', Fri]	345	'A'..'Z'	Week

In Exercises 35–39 repeat Parts b and c of Exercises 30–34, assuming b is a real array and each real number occupies two words.

In Exercises 40–44 repeat Parts b and c of Exercises 30–34, assuming b is a packed character array and each character occupies one byte.

In Exercises 45−49 repeat Parts b and c of Exercises 30−34, assuming b is a packed boolean array and each boolean value occupies one bit.

50. A three-dimensional array, *c*, can be pictured as a three-dimensional block of cells. Suppose *c* is declared as follows:

```
type
    Week      = (Tue, Wed, Thu, Fri, Sat, Sun);
    Month     = (Jan, Feb, Mar, Apr, May, Jun,
                 Jul, Aug, Sep, Oct, Nov, Dec);
    SliceType = Month;
    RowType   = 1..5;
    ColType   = Week;
    ArrayType = array [SliceType, RowType, ColType] of integer;
var
    c         : ArrayType;
```

A pictorial representation of *c* appears in Figure 3.9. This array is stored in row-major order, one row at a time and then one slice at a time. Suppose the computer has four bytes per word and a word can store an integer. For a base address of 7432 compute the address of the following elements:

a. *c*[*Jan*, 1, *Tue*]   **b.** *c*[*Mar*, 1, *Tue*]
c. *c*[*Jan*, 4, *Fri*]   **d.** *c*[*May*, 4, *Fri*]
e. *c*[*Dec*, 2, *Mon*]

51. The following appeared in the sample questions of the *1987 AP Computer Science Examination**:

An image can be represented as a grid of black and white cells. Two cells in an image are part of the same object if each is black and there is a sequence of moves from one cell to the other, where each move is either horizontal or vertical to an adjacent black cell. For example, the diagram below represents an image that contains two objects, one of them consisting of a single cell.

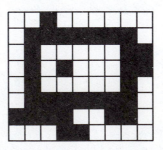

Figure 3.9

Pictorial representation of
three-dimensional array *c*
of Exercise 50

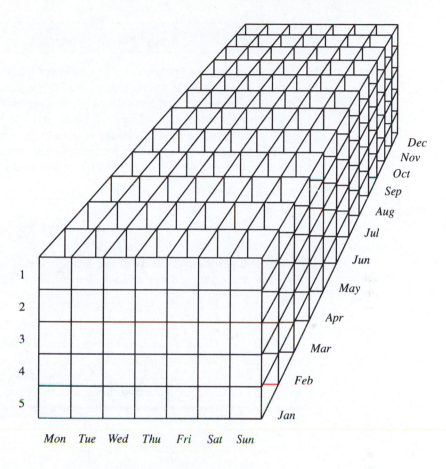

The following declarations are given.

const
> *Size* = 200;

type
> *CellType*   = (*Black, White*);
> *ImageType* = **array**[1..*Size*, 1..*Size*] **of** *CellType*;

Write a procedure with header

> **procedure** *EraseObject* (**var** *Image* : *ImageType*; *Row, Col* : *integer*);

such that

if 1 <= *Row* <= *Size* and 1 <= *Col* <= *Size* and *Image*[*Row, Col*] = *Black*,

then all cells in the same object as *Image*[*Row, Col*] are set to *White*;
otherwise, *Image* is unchanged. Your solution should have no more than
15 statements, and its execution time should be linear with respect to the
number of cells of the object.

▽

PROGRAMMING PROJECTS

1. Write a program to encode/decode a message from a file. This encryption scheme will swap characters. For example, every occurrence of the letter "A" might be encoded as a comma and vice versa. Thus, the same scheme that encodes a message can decode it. Some of the techniques we use in solving this problem are used in various computer games.

We must produce a random permutation of array elements. A **permutation** is an ordered arrangement. Thus, one permutation of the values

    0 1 2 3 4

is

    4 2 0 3 1

To create a permutation array of the integers 0 through 4, we first initialize an array p so that the value of each element is its index, such as:

      p: 0 1 2 3 4
    index: 0 1 2 3 4

Then for each i from 4 down to 1 we generate a random integer k from 0 to i and swap the values of $p[i]$ and $p[k]$. Thus, when $i = 3$, k will be a pseudo-random integer 0, 1, 2, or 3. If $k = 1$, we exchange the values in array elements $p[3]$ and $p[1]$. Figure 3.10 illustrates this process. For this project we need to write routines to accomplish each of the following tasks:

a. Initialize the permutation array p.
b. Swap the ith and kth array elements of p.
c. Generate a random integer from 0 to $n - 1$. Check to see if the computer system you are using has a built-in random number generator. If not, write your own using Appendix A.
d. Permute the elements of p as described above.

An array s is a **self-inverse permutation array** if s is a permutation array with the property that

    $s[i] = k$ if and only if $s[k] = i$

The following is one such array:

    s: 3 2 1 0 4
    index: 0 1 2 3 4

Notice that

    $s[0] = 3$ and $s[3] = 0$,
    $s[1] = 2$ and $s[2] = 1$,
    $s[4] = 4$.

Such an array can be used in the encryption scheme. The permutation can

Figure 3.10

Action to permute the elements of an array with changes in boldface

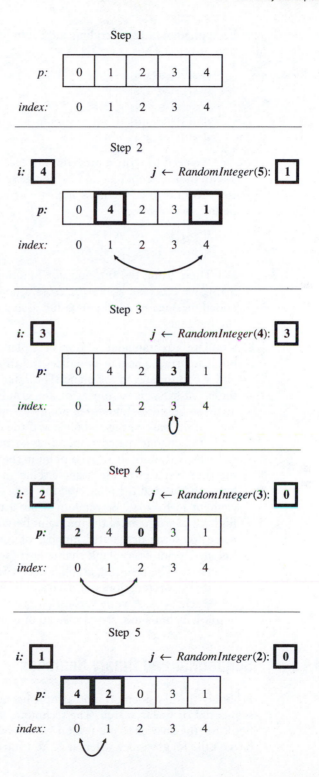

be applied once for encoding and again for decoding because the array is its own inverse. Thus, $s[s[i]] = i$:

$$s[s[0]] = s[3] = 0$$
$$s[s[1]] = s[2] = 1$$
$$s[s[2]] = s[1] = 2$$
$$s[s[3]] = s[0] = 3$$
$$s[s[4]] = s[4] = 4$$

We need to write a procedure to create a self-inverse permutation array s with indices from 0 to 255 by first generating a permutation array p. Then for i from 0 to 254 with a step size of 2, use adjacent elements from p to define s as follows:

$$s[p[i]] \quad\quad \leftarrow p[i + 1]$$
$$s[p[i + 1]] \leftarrow p[i]$$

Then, using the *ord* and *chr* functions and a self-inverse permutation array, we can read a message from a text file, encode it, and write the encoded message to another text file. Using the same program, we can decode the message.

2. Simulate a rectangular section of a plane with a packed two-dimensional boolean array. The pair of indices for an array element correspond to the x and y coordinates in the plane. The value of the array element is *true* when the point (x, y) is to appear on the graph, so initialize the elements of this array to be *false*. Take three points forming a triangle, two at the extreme ends of the base of the rectangle and the third in the middle of the opposite side, and change the corresponding elements in the two-dimensional array to be *true*. Randomly select a point in the plane. Then randomly pick one of the three vertices of the triangle. Find the integer coordinates of the point halfway between the point and the vertex. Change the corresponding array element to be *true*. At random select a triangle vertex again. Once more, find the coordinates of the midpoint between the point and the vertex. Continue for some designated number of times. Then, for every point on the "plane," print a nonblank character if the array element is *true* and a blank otherwise. The resulting graph is called Sierpinski's Triangle.

If your system does not have a built-in random number generator, refer to Appendix A. If your version of Pascal has graphics, you may choose to employ its built-in features instead of using the two-dimensional array.

| SECTION 3.2 | # Sequential and Binary Searches |

Probably the first method most people use to look for an item in an array is a **sequential** or **linear search**. The technique is akin to looking through a notebook for the answer to a question when you are sure the solution is there but haven't the foggiest idea where it is. You start at the beginning of the notebook, thumbing through every page looking for the answer. When you find it, you may jot down the answer or the page number on which it occurs. If you get to the end of the notebook without locating the answer you might throw your notes down in frustration—"It's not there!" If you had some recollection of where the answer was, you might have stopped searching well before the final page.

Let us consider this sequential search of an array a for a value x. If x is found, we wish to return the index where the value occurs; otherwise, we wish to return a value that is not a possible index to indicate that the search has failed. Often the index of an array starts with 1, and we can return 0 in case of search failure. With an unordered array, the entire array must be examined before we are positive x is not to be found. If the data in the array is ordered, however, we will halt as soon as we are past the point in the array where x should be. Figure 3.11 pictures a character array in ascending order. If we are searching for $x = $ 'G', we know we have failed when we compare $x = $ 'G' with $a[4] = $ 'H'. Since 'G' appears before 'H' in the alphabet, we are beyond the point where 'G' could occur. Figure 3.12 gives the algorithm for a sequential search of an array a, sorted into ascending order.

Figure 3.11

Character array a in ascending order

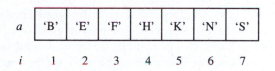

Figure 3.12.

Algorithm for sequential search

SeqSearch (**a, n, x**) → *i*
 Function to perform sequential search of array a for x
Input:
 a—array with elements of type *elType*
 n—number of elements in a
 x—item of type *elType* for which to search
Output:
 i—index of a where x is found, 0 if not found
Assumptions: The elements $a[1]$ through $a[n]$ are in ascending order.
Algorithm:

 $i \leftarrow 0$
 found ← *false*
 while $(i < n)$ and (not *found*) do
  $i \leftarrow i + 1$
  if $x \leq a[i]$ then
   found ← *true*
 if $x = a[i]$ then
  SeqSearch ← *i*
 else
  SeqSearch ← 0

What is the largest number of comparisons that can be made between x and an array element within the loop? That is, what is the maximum number of times the statement "if $x \leq a[i]$ . . ." is executed? Under what condition does this worst case scenario occur? In a sequential search of the array in Figure 3.11, if x = 'S', we must examine every element to deduce that *SeqSearch* should return 7. Also, if the value of x is beyond 'S', say 'T' or 'Z', then we must also make 7 comparisons and terminate with *SeqSearch* ← 0. As noted in Section 2.4, for an array of n elements, the worst case occurs when all n elements must be searched. Consequently, the sequential search algorithm has order $O(n)$ in these most unfavorable situations. Even on the average we must search about half of the n elements, so that in both the average and worst cases a sequential search is on the order of n.

$O(n)$ doesn't really seem so bad, but suppose there are a million elements (n = 1,000,000). Would you really want to look through a phone book sequentially to find the telephone number of J. Zwen? Of course, you will have to if the phone book or the array is not sorted, but is there a better way for an array arranged in ascending order? Indeed there is—a binary search.

A **binary search** comes close to how you would look for someone's name in the sorted phone book. You open the book and see if the name is there. If not, you decide which part of the opened book contains the name. Then you repeat the process with that part of the book. The search stops when you find the name or when you have subdivided the book so much that there is nothing left and you know the name must not be present. Notice how the idea of this search is recursive—each time you repeat the search on a smaller part of the book, and there is a way to stop. Although you may not open the phone directory exactly in the middle, in a binary search each recursive call cuts the problem in half. Division by 2 is built into the hardware or firmware of many computers and, consequently, is very fast. Moreover, division by a constant avoids repeated computation of a divisor.

Figure 3.13 shows a picture of the binary search of array a for x = 'K'. *First* and *Last* are the indices of the first and last elements, respectively, of the part of the array under consideration. *Mid* is the middle index of that subarray. Initially, *First* = 1 and *Last* = 7. To calculate the index of the middle element, we add the first and last indices and divide the result by 2. In this situation *Mid* = (1 + 7)/2 = 4. Suppose *Last* had been 8 so that (1 + 8)/2 = 4.5. To avoid noninteger values for *Mid*, we take the floor function or find the largest integer less than or equal to the result: $\lfloor (1 + 8)/2 \rfloor = \lfloor 4.5 \rfloor = 4$. Thus, the formula for the middle index is

$$Mid = \lfloor (First + Last)/2 \rfloor$$

Since x's value, 'K', is larger than that of this middle element, $a[4]$ = 'H', we no longer need to consider the left half of the array. Thus, we continue the search from just beyond the $a[4]$ element to the end of the array. In this subarray *First* = 5 and *Last* still is 7 with the resulting *Mid* = 6. Now, x = 'K' is less than $a[6]$ = 'N', so that we must take the left half of the subarray and change the

Figure 3.13

Picture of the binary
search of array *a* for
x = 'K' with changes
in boldface

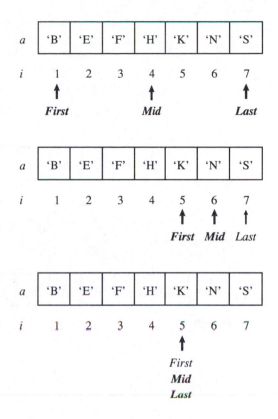

value of *Last* to 5. With *First* = *Last* = *Mid* = 5, *x* must be in that position if it is there at all. In this case *x* does equal *a*[5]. As shown in Figure 3.14, had *x* been 'L' instead of 'K', on the last step we would have assigned *First* a value of 6. Then *First* = 6 would have been larger than *Last* = 5 and the search would have terminated with the realization that *x*'s value was not in the array. Figure 3.15 gives the algorithm for a binary search.

In the search for *x* = 'K' or 'L' we initially examined an array of 7 elements. At the next recursive call we were searching a subarray of $\lfloor 7/2 \rfloor = 3$ elements, and lastly an array of $\lfloor 3/2 \rfloor = 1$ element. Thus, for $7 = 2^3 - 1$ elements, we need at most 3 comparisons. Even for $15 = 2^4 - 1$ elements, more than double the size, we only require 4 comparisons, because if the first comparison is *false*, we cut the problem in half and consider a subarray of $\lfloor 15/2 \rfloor = 7$ elements. What is the maximum number of comparisons in an array of $255 = 2^8 - 1$ elements? Figure 3.16 shows the number of elements in the subarray for each recursive invocation of the function. Each time the subarray under consideration is cut in half. In general, for $2^m - 1$ elements, at most *m* comparisons must take place because each time the problem is halved.

Figure 3.14

Picture of the binary
search of array *a* for
x = 'L' with changes in
boldface

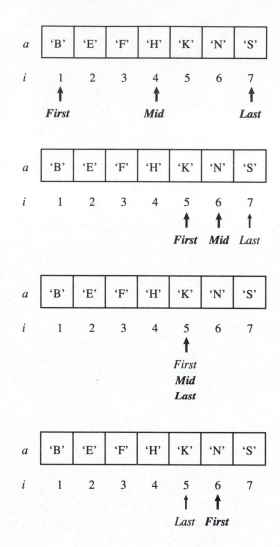

Suppose the number of elements *n* is not of the form $2^m - 1$. How many comparisons must be made? Figure 3.17 shows the search for *x* = 'S' or 'T' in an array of 20 elements, a search that requires 5 comparisons. Observe in Figure 3.18 that on each recursive call, we have a subarray half or less the size of the previous array. At the fourth invocation we are still considering a subarray with more than one element, so in the worst case we must divide the problem once more. Since 20 is between $2^4 - 1 = 15$ and $2^5 - 1 = 31$, we take the larger number and see that at most 5 comparisons are needed.

In general, for *n* elements, we find the smallest number of the form $2^m - 1$ such that

$$n \leq 2^m - 1$$

Figure 3.15.

Algorithm for binary search

$BiSearch(a, First, Last, x) \rightarrow i$

Function to perform binary search for x in array a from index *First* through index *Last*

Input:

    a — array with elements of type *elType*

    First — smallest index in subarray of a to be searched

    Last — largest index in subarray of a to be searched

    x — item of type *elType* for which to search

Output:

    i — index of a where x is found, 0 if not found

Assumptions: The elements of a are in ascending order, a's index type is $lb..ub$, and $0 < lb$. For a search of the entire array a, the first reference to this function should be $BiSearch(a, lb, ub, x)$.

Algorithm:

    if *First* > *Last* then
        $BiSearch \leftarrow 0$
    else
        $Mid \leftarrow \lfloor (First + Last)/2 \rfloor$
        if $x < a[Mid]$ then
            $BiSearch \leftarrow BiSearch(a, First, Mid - 1, x)$
        else if $x > a[Mid]$ then
            $BiSearch \leftarrow BiSearch(a, Mid + 1, Last, x)$
        else
            $BiSearch \leftarrow Mid$

Figure 3.16.

Number of elements in subarray of a, an array of 255 elements, used in successive calls of *BiSearch*

Call	*Size of Subarray*
1	$255 = 2^8 - 1$
2	$\lfloor 255/2 \rfloor = 127 = 2^7 - 1$
3	$\lfloor 127/2 \rfloor = 63 = 2^6 - 1$
4	$\lfloor 63/2 \rfloor = 31 = 2^5 - 1$
5	$\lfloor 31/2 \rfloor = 15 = 2^4 - 1$
6	$\lfloor 15/2 \rfloor = 7 = 2^3 - 1$
7	$\lfloor 7/2 \rfloor = 3 = 2^2 - 1$
8	$\lfloor 3/2 \rfloor = 1 = 2^1 - 1$

Then the number of comparisons is m, the exponent of 2. Following through the arithmetic, we have

$$n + 1 \le 2^m$$

Since $\log_2 (2^m) = m$, the exponent of 2 that yields 2^m, we have

$$\log_2 (n + 1) \le \log_2 (2^m)$$

or

$$\log_2 (n + 1) \le m$$

Figure 3.17

Binary search for x = 'S' or 'T' in an array of 20 elements with changes in boldface

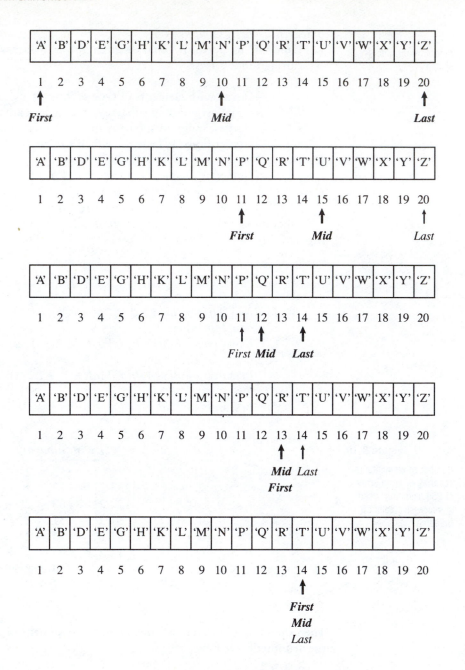

Figure 3.18.

Maximum size of subarray of an array a of 20 elements on each successive invocation of *BiSearch*

Call	Size of Subarray
1	20
2	10
3	5
4	2
5	1

Taking the **ceiling function** to obtain the next integer greater than or equal to $\log_2 (n + 1)$, we obtain

$$\lceil \log_2 (n + 1) \rceil = m$$

For example, with $n = 7$ elements, $\log_2 (7 + 1) = \log_2 (8) = \log_2 (2^3) = 3$. With $n = 20$ elements, we have $\lceil \log_2 (20 + 1) \rceil = \lceil \log_2 (21) \rceil = 5$ since $2^4 < 21 \le 2^5$.

Ignoring the added 1, which is insignificant for large values of n, we see that the binary search algorithm has complexity $O(\log_2 n)$. As we discussed in Section 1.4, $O(\log_2 n) < O(n)$, so the binary search is a more efficient technique than the sequential one. There is some overhead, however, such as the calculation of *Mid*. We consider an iterative version in the exercises; but in the case of the recursive implementation, the repeated invocation to the function requires time and space. Even with the recursive version, for about 20 or more sorted elements, the binary search is better than the sequential one. This technique can only be performed on a sorted array, however, so the overhead of sorting first might tip the scales in favor of a sequential method. If we must search frequently, sorting is worth the effort so that we will be able to use the binary search. In a later chapter we examine several sorting methods.

▽

SECTION 3.2 EXERCISES

1. Code in Pascal the sequential search function of Figure 3.12.

2. **a.** Generalize the algorithm in Figure 3.12 to work for an index of any finite ordinal type. The function should return the predecessor of the lower bound of the index if the item x is not found.
   b. Code Part a in Pascal.

3. Apply the binary search algorithm to find each of the following characters in array a of Figure 3.11. Give the index i for each comparison.

   a. 'E'   **b.** 'N'   **c.** 'D'
   d. 'S'   **e.** 'W'   **f.** 'F'

4. Apply the binary search algorithm to find each of the following characters in array a of Figure 3.17. Give the index i for each comparison.

   a. 'G'   **b.** 'C'
   c. 'R'   **d.** 'Z'

5. **a.** For the array in Figure 3.11 in the binary search for $x = $ 'K' or 'L' we compared x with $a[4]$, $a[6]$, and $a[5]$. List the other possible search orders of length 3.
   b. Are there any search sequences longer than 3?

6. **a.** In which situation(s) will at most one comparison ($x = a[i]$) need to be made in a sequential search?
   b. At most two comparisons?
   c. At most three comparisons?

7. Repeat Exercise 6 for a binary search.

8. Fill in the chart in Figure 3.19 for the worst case number of comparisons needed for a search of a sorted array with n elements using sequential and binary searches.

Figure 3.19

Chart for Exercise 8

n	1	$2^7-1=127$	$2^8-1=255$	$2^{10}-1=1,023$	$2^{20}-1=1,048,575$	$2^{24}-1=16,777,215$
SeqSearch						
BiSearch						

9. Repeat Exercise 8 for the chart in Figure 3.20.

Figure 3.20

Chart for Exercise 9

n	10	100	200	500	1000	5000	10,000	20,000	30,000	100,000	400,000	500,000
SeqSearch												
BiSearch												

10. a. In a sorted array of 127 elements we are searching for a value that is larger than any element stored in the array. Calculate the search time using a sequential search. Assume we are using a computer in which the time to execute various statements is given in the chart below:

Statement	Execution Time (in microsec)
Assignment statement:	
$i \leftarrow 0$	7
found $\leftarrow$ *false*	7
$i \leftarrow i + 1$	16
found $\leftarrow$ *true*	7
SeqSearch $\leftarrow i$	14
SeqSearch $\leftarrow 0$	7
Mid $\leftarrow \lfloor (First + Last)/2 \rfloor$	40
BiSearch $\leftarrow 0$	7
BiSearch $\leftarrow$ *Mid*	14
while $(i < n)$ and (not *found*) do	45
if $x \leq a[i]$ then	21
if $x = a[i]$ then	21

Statement	Execution Time (in microsec)
if *First* > *Last* then	21
if $x < a[Mid]$ then	21
if $x > a[Mid]$ then	21
Invocation of *SeqSearch*	70
Invocation of *BiSearch*	98

b. Repeat Part a for a binary search.

11. Repeat Exercise 10 for an array having a million elements.

12. Repeat Exercise 10 for an array having 19 elements.

13. a. Code in Pascal the *BiSearch* function of Figure 3.15.
 b. Test this function for a large array with various values for *First, Last,* and x. Print the index and array element values in each comparison.

14. a. Generalize the algorithm in Figure 3.15 to work for an index of any subrange type. The function should return an unused value of the index if the item x is not found.
 b. Code Part a in Pascal.

15. a. Design a nonrecursive binary search algorithm.
 b. Code Part a in Pascal.
 c. Give an invariant for the loop.
 d. Using program verification, prove that the algorithm is correct.

16. a. Suppose array *SAT* contains a sorted list of SAT scores for students. Write a procedure using a sequential search to return the high and low indices for the range of grades from *LowGrade* to *HighGrade*. For example, we may want the indices of the grades from 550 to 650. Assume there are no duplicates.
 b. What is the complexity of this **range search**?
 c. Repeat Part a using two binary searches.
 d. What is the complexity of the procedure in Part c?

17. Suppose numbers are fairly uniformly distributed throughout a sorted array a. An **interpolation search** is very similar to a binary search except the location of the desired element is estimated instead of calculated as the middle index. For example, suppose we are searching for $x = 2947$ in the subarray $a[51..100]$ with $a[51] = 2364$ and $a[100] = 6180$. For the linear interpolation formula we estimate the percentage of possible values occurring before $x = 2947$ in the range from 2364 to 6180:

$$\frac{x - a[51]}{a[100] - a[51]} = \frac{2947 - 2364}{6180 - 2364} = 0.15278$$

Thus, $x = 2947$ is about 15% of the distance from the first array value of 2364 to the last of 6180. We now compute this percentage of the distance between indices:

$$0.15278 \times (100 - 51) \approx 7.6$$

Truncating, we obtain 7. Thus, the estimated position of x is about 15% into the array a at index

$$51 + 7 = 58$$

For the interpolation search the first comparison is made between x and $a[58]$, not x and $a[Mid] = a[75]$. As with the binary search, however, if $a[58]$ is not the desired element, we recursively repeat the process on the subarray $a[51..57]$ or $a[59..100]$, depending on whether $x < a[58]$ or $x > a[58]$, respectively. With this technique of estimating the position of a key in an array of uniformly distributed keys, we have the potential of arriving at the target much faster.

a. Write the linear interpolation formula to calculate the estimated index in the general case using x, array a, and indices *First* and *Last*.

b. Design an interpolation search procedure.

c. What are the advantages and disadvantages of an interpolation search as compared with a binary search?

18. As in Exercise 17, the **interpolation-sequential search** for an item x in a sorted array a uses a linear interpolation formula to calculate the index i of the first array element to be compared with x. If x is not equal to $a[i]$, however, the search continues sequentially through elements in the subarray before $a[i]$ or after $a[i]$, depending on whether x is less than or greater than $a[i]$, respectively. Design a nonrecursive procedure to perform an interpolation-sequential search.

▽

PROGRAMMING PROJECT

1. A biologist is making a survey of the kind and number of vertebrates in a particular area. Write an interactive program to read the names and counts of various animals into an array of records as they are observed and then to print out the final totals. Do not sort the array by the names of the animals. The animals are observed at various times, so the counts for a particular vertebrate may have to be updated frequently. One method of storage is to order the records by decreasing value of their counts. When an animal is observed, the array is searched sequentially for the corresponding record. If found, the count field is incremented by the proper amount and the record is moved in front of all records with smaller counts. The record for a newly observed animal is added to the array in the proper location according to its count. Thus, records for the most frequently observed animals gravitate toward the first of the array where they can be accessed more rapidly in a sequential search.

The computer is not turned off while data is entered. When data entry is complete, display the final totals.

ADT Record and Implementation

For an array, all elements must be of the same type, and we reference items through an index. By contrast, components in a record can have a variety of types, and we specify an element using an identifier name. In the *ReadStr* procedure of Section 1.2 we used the record *StringType* with two major components or **fields**. One field, *length*, was of type a subrange of integers; and the other, *str*, had a composite type, that of an array of characters. As we saw in the same example, records can contain records in a hierarchical fashion; *elType* was a record with field *Name* of the record type *StringType* and with field *Grade*.

Records are useful in storing related data of different types and are the major data structure in the business-oriented language COBOL. Most versions of FORTRAN and BASIC do not contain this structure, but many more modern languages do, such as Pascal, Modula-2, C, and Ada.

With the added ability of having a variety of types for the individual elements, we lose the capability of referencing these components through an index. Using arrays, we could have a loop to process each element homogeneously, as in this segment to zero out the array:

```
for i := 1 to MaxNumEls do
    a[i] := 0
```

In a record structure, however, we must reference each individual field. Consider, for example, the following constant and type definitions and variable declarations:

```
const
    MaxNumStu       = 35;      {maximum number of students}
    MaxStr          = 20;      {maximum length of name}
    MaxNumGrades    = 6;       {maximum number of test grades}
    blank           = ' ';

type
    lengthType      = 0..MaxStr;
    GradeType       = 0..100;
    StrIndexType    = 1..MaxStr;
    GradeIndexType  = 1..MaxNumGrades;
    strType         = packed array [strIndexType] of char;
```

```
StringType        =   record
   length         :   lengthType;
   str            :   strType
end;

elType            =   record
   Name           :   StringType;
   Grade          :   array [GradeIndexType] of GradeType;
   Average        :   real;
   CourseGrade    :   char
end;

var
   student        :   elType;           {record of name, grades,}
                                        {average, and course grade}
   i              :   strIndexType;      {index for string}
   j              :   GradeIndexType;    {index for grades}
```

The pictorial diagram of this record is displayed in Figure 3.21.

Figure 3.21

Structure of record of
type *elType*

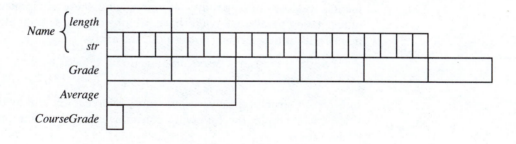

To reference the *Average* field of *student* we write the record identifier followed by a period and the field identifier, *student.Average*, while the third grade is *student.Grade*[3]. Since *Name* is itself of a record type, we must use the record, subrecord, and field identifiers. Thus, the length of this person's name is *student.Name.length*, while the name begins with a letter stored in *student.Name.str*[1]. The *with* statement can simplify the syntax when several fields are being referenced, as in the following:

```
with student do
     writeln (Name.str: 20, Grade[3]: 5,
          Average: 7:2, CourseGrade: 3);
```

To zero out number fields and blank out character fields of *student*, we must deal with each field individually as follows:

```
with student do
    begin
        with Name do
            begin
                length := 0;
                for i := 1 to MaxStr do
                    str[i] := blank
            end;   {with Name}
        for j := 1 to MaxNumGrades do
            Grade[j] := 0;
        Average := 0.0;
        CourseGrade := blank
    end   {with student}
```

Having reviewed Pascal records, let us define ADT records in Figure 3.22.

Figure 3.22.

Formal definition of ADT record

ADT Record

Objects: Finite collection of elements, called fields, of possibly different types. There is a one-to-one correspondence between a list of field identifiers and the collection of elements.

Operations:

Notation:

    R—record

    id—identifier that is a field's name

    e—item of the same type as that of the *id* field of record R

StoreRecord(R, id, e)

    Procedure to store e's value in the *id* field of R

RetrieveRecord(R, id) → e

    Function to return the value of the *id* field of R

As with the other structures covered so far, creation is a matter of employing the proper type definitions and variable declarations. To implement *StoreRecord(R, id, e)* we again use the assignment statement

```
R.id := e
```

RetrieveRecord(R, id) employs the field identifier as

```
R.id
```

As we will see, the record type is very useful in programming and is the basic component of a number of data structures. Figure 3.23 summarizes the Pascal implementation of the ADT record.

Figure 3.23.

Summary of Pascal implementation of ADT record

ADT Record Implementation

Create a record, R, with list of field identifiers, $(i_1, i_2, \ldots, i_n)$, and corresponding list of field types, $(t_1, t_2, \ldots, t_n)$

```
type
    t₁ = .............;   {type of a field}
    t₂ = .............;
        ⋮
    tₙ = .............;

    RecordType = record
              i₁ : t₁;
              i₂ : t₂;
                 ⋮
              iₙ : tₙ
    end;

var
    R : RecordType;
```

StoreRecord(R, id, e)

```
    R.id := e
```

RetrieveRecord(R, id) → e

```
    R.id
```

Another Pascal implementation of the ADT record is the variant record. Suppose we wish to store the grades of all students for a professor's courses in a file. Most of the records will have the fields of *elType* as presented earlier in this section. For students who withdraw, however, we only need to store their names and not use room for their no longer meaningful grades. Designations to indicate withdrawal and whether the student is a graduate or undergraduate will also be helpful to the professor. Besides grade records we need a header record for each class indicating the course title (as a character string), semester (as the character 'F', 'S', '1', or '2', representing fall, spring, summer session 1 or 2, respectively), and year (as an integer). Thus, in the same file we have three different kinds of records: class header record, withdrawal record, and grade record for both undergraduates and graduates. Therefore, we will use a **variant record** with a **fixed part** that is identical for all three and a **variant part** that is not. Each record begins with a fixed part, a character string to hold either the student or course name. The variant part begins with a *case* statement and is always at the end of the record definition. Figure 3.24 illustrates the structure of the following variant record, assuming each integer and unpacked character take up four bytes:

```
type
   ⋮
   RecCodeType        =    (header, withdraw, undergrad, grad);
   elType             =    record
      Name            :    StringType;
      case RecCode    :    RecCodeType of
         header       :    (semester    : char;
                            year         : integer);
         withdraw     :    ();
         undergrad,
         grad         :    (Grade        : array [GradeIndexType] of
                                           GradeType;
                            Average      : real;
                            CourseGrade  : char)
   end;   { elType }

var
   vStudent           :    elType;
   RecCodeChar        :    char;
   j                  :    GradeIndexType;
```

Figure 3.24

Structure of a variant
record with tag field
RecCode

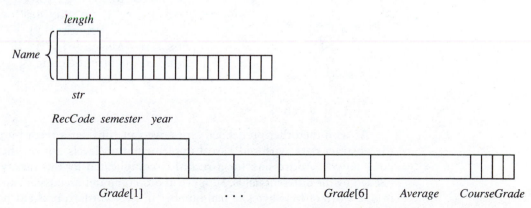

In this example, *RecCode* is the **tag field** whose value determines the structure of the rest of the record. For variable *vStudent*, if the value of *RecCode* is *header*, we can use the first variant field list and can reference the fields *vStudent.semester* and *vStudent.year*. A *RecCode* of *undergrad* or *grad* makes available fields *vStudent.Grade*, *vStudent.Average*, and *vStudent.CourseGrade*, and not the fields for semester and year. Parentheses surround each variant field list, and ( ) indicates an empty list.

Suppose that using interactive input we obtain a value for *vStudent*. First, we read the fixed part, *Name*, using the *ReadStr* procedure. Because we cannot read an enumeration type variable interactively, we read a character, 'H', 'W', 'U', or 'G', into the variable *RecCodeChar*. Then, with a *case* statement, we assign a value to the corresponding *RecCode* and read the appropriate remaining fields as below. For brevity we have omitted the interactive prompts for input from the user.

```
with vStudent do
    begin
        ReadStr (Name);
        readln (RecCodeChar);
        case RecCodeChar of

            'H'        :   begin
                               RecCode := header;
                               readln (semester, year)
                           end;  { 'H' }

            'W'        :   RecCode := withdraw;

            'U', 'G'   :   begin
                               if RecCodeChar = 'U' then
                                   RecCode := undergrad
                               else
                                   RecCode := grad;
                               for j := 1 to MaxNumGrades do
                                   readln (Grade[j]);
                               readln (Average);
                               readln (CourseGrade)
                           end { 'U', 'G' }
        end { case }
    end  { with }
```

As with the other predefined types, we can consider a record not only on the abstract data type and Pascal implementation levels but on the machine level as well. Addressing for a record is complicated by the variety of space needed by the different fields. Suppose in our computer an integer can be stored in one word of four bytes, a real number in two words, a packed character in one byte, and an unpacked character in one word. How much room is needed for a single record *student* as declared at the beginning of this section? The following enumerates the length for each field.

Field	Field Length		
student			
Name			
length	1 word	=	4 bytes
str	5 words	=	20 bytes
Grade	6 words	=	24 bytes
Average	2 words	=	8 bytes
CourseGrade	1 word	=	4 bytes
	15 words		60 bytes

If the base address is 6803 and if consecutive words have successive addresses, then the location of *Grade* is

$$6803 + (1 + 5) = 6809$$

Since *str* is a packed array, the word at location 6805 contains the fifth through the eighth characters of the name. A particular computer may have additional restrictions, such as requiring that each field begin at a new word address. In this case, even if *str* were declared to be a packed array of 18 characters (4.5 words), two bytes would be wasted and *Grade* would still be located at address 6809.

In the case of a variant record, storage must be provided for the longest possible record. For *vStudent* above, *RecCode* values of *undergrad* and *grad* indicate the longer form of the record. Thus, if an enumeration value uses one byte, the compiler will allot 61 bytes of storage for *vStudent*—24 bytes for the fixed part, 1 for *RecCode*, and 36 for the longest variant part.

▽

SECTION 3.3 EXERCISES

1. **a.** Create in Pascal a record *Stock* with a field identifier list of (*Code, Cost, Number*) and a corresponding type list of (*char, real, integer*).
   b. Write Pascal statements to store 'X' in *Code*, 346.59 in *Cost*, and 10 in *Number*.
   c. Write Pascal statements to print the values stored in this record.

2. **a.** Define in Pascal the type *NameType*, a packed array of 22 characters.
   b. Create in Pascal *Transcript*, a record with fields *Name* (of type *NameType*), *length*, and *GPA* (*real*).
   c. Create *Registrar*, an array of 500 records with the structure described in Part b.
   d. Design a procedure to read information interactively into this array of records.

     e. Design a hierarchy of routines to print the highest grade point average (*GPA*) and the names of everyone who achieved this average.

     f. Code Parts d and e in Pascal.

3. Give the identifier list and corresponding type list for *StringType* used in the program *AboveAverage* of Section 1.2.

4. Give the identifier list and corresponding type list for *elType* used in the program *AboveAverage* of Section 1.2.

5. Write a procedure in Pascal to print the values stored in the variant record *vStudent* in Section 3.3.

6. a. Create in Pascal a variant record *BankAccount*. The fixed part should have fields for *AccountNumber, date*, and *amount*. The tag field, *TransactionCode*, has possible enumeration values of *check, deposit, ATM-withdrawal, CardCharge*, and *CardPayment*. A check must have a field for the check number; a deposit or ATM withdrawal requires no extra fields; a credit card charge must hold the name of the business taking the charge; and a credit card payment needs a field for the interest payment.

     b. Write Pascal statements to read values into this record.

7. Suppose there are 8 bits to a byte and 4 bytes to a word. Assume a character is encoded in 1 byte but is stored in 1 word unless packed; an integer is stored in a word; a real number is stored in 2 words; the value for each new field must start at a new address; and the computer is word-addressable.

     a. Suppose *student* from this section needs storage and the next available location is at address 101. What is its base address?

     b. What is the address of *student.Grade*[3]?

     c. If a real variable, *x*, needs storage after *student*, what is its address?

     d. Suppose *str* was not packed. Repeat Parts a, b, and c.

8. Use the same assumptions presented in Exercise 7.

     a. Suppose *Registrar*[1] from Exercise 2c needs storage and the next available location is 722. What is its base address?

     b. How many words are needed to store *Registrar*[1]?

     c. What is the address of *Registrar*[2]?

     d. How many bytes are wasted from location 722 to the starting address of *Registrar*[2]?

     e. How much storage is needed for the array of records *Registrar*?

9. Use the same assumptions presented in Exercise 7 along with the assumption that an enumeration value uses 1 byte of storage. How many words are needed to store the record in Exercise 6a?

▽

PROGRAMMING PROJECT

1. Write a program to shuffle a fresh deck of cards, cut the deck, deal all the cards to four players, and write each player's hand. Each card's value should be written out, such as "3 of diamond" or "ace of spades."

To accomplish this project, create a record to contain the value of a playing card as a suit (*club, diamond, heart, spade*) and level, 1..13; and create an array *card* with indices from 0 to 51 to contain suits and levels of a deck of cards. Your program should contain the following routines at least:

a. An initialization procedure with nested loops to assign a value to each array element. For example, *card*[0] should be a record containing *club* and 1; *card*[1] should contain *club* and 2; *card*[13] should contain *diamond* and 1; and so on.

b. A procedure *swap(i, k)* to exchange the values for *card*[*i*] and *card*[*k*].

c. A function *RandomInteger(n)* to return a pseudorandom integer whose value is in the range 0..(*n* − 1). Check if the system you are using has a built-in random number generator. If not, write your own using Appendix A.

d. A procedure *shuffle* to shuffle the deck of cards. To accomplish this task for each *i* from 51 down to 1 generate a random integer *k* whose value is from 0 to *i*. Then swap the values for *card*[*i*] and *card*[*k*].

SECTION 3.4

ADT File and Implementation

A file structure provides a unique link between computer memory and a secondary storage medium such as a diskette, disk pack, or tape. Magnetic tape was introduced in the early 1950s as an external storage medium for the UNIVAC, the first commercially produced computer. At first some people would not believe that information was recorded on the tape since they could not see holes as they did on punch cards. At one plant, a fellow, not knowing about computer tape, received a delivery of tape he thought was no good since it had no adhesive back! Today, enormous amounts of information are stored for backup or additional processing. A bank's records, an airline's reservations, a pollster's voting surveys, a scientist's research—the list is endless—all are saved outside the computer.

The language COBOL provides various ways, from sequential to direct, of accessing this externally stored information. Unfortunately, Standard Pascal only provides for sequential access, one record after another, though some versions of the language do support various alternatives. In a sense the sequential file structure is similar to that of the array structure with each element having the same type, but with a file there is no associated index and there is no limit to the number of elements. Figure 3.25 presents the ADT file definition.

As with the other Pascal built-in data structures, creation can be handled with simple type definitions and variable declarations.

```
type
    elType    =  .............;
    FileType  =  file of elType;

var
    f             :   FileType;
```

Figure 3.25.

Formal definition of
ADT file

ADT File

Objects: Sequence of elements of the same type, *elType*. A **file pointer** indicates the next file element to be accessed.

Operations:

    Notation:

        elType — type of an element in the file; this type cannot be *file*
        f   — file
        e   — item of type *elType*
        b   — boolean value

    Rewrite(f)

        Procedure to move file pointer to beginning of file f and prepare f for output from computer

    StoreFile(*f, e*)

        While in output mode, procedure to copy *e*'s value into the next file element and advance file pointer

    Reset(f)

        Procedure to move file pointer to beginning of file f and prepare f for input to the computer

    EOF(f) → *b*

        Function to return *true* if the file pointer indicates the end-of-file marker

    RetrieveFile(*f, e*)

        While in input mode and with *EOF*(f) being *false*, procedure to copy the next file element into *e* and to advance the file pointer one position

If we declare f to be a *file* with elements of some type, then f is said to be a **user-defined** or a **binary file.**

Often a file exists on tape or disk secondary storage before and/or after execution of the program. Standard Pascal requires that such a file f be recorded in the *program* statement, as in

```
program FileEx (f);
```

Many versions of Pascal, such as Turbo Pascal, however, do not require the listing of each file in the program statement. Therefore, you should check the documentation for your version.

Upon declaration of the file f, the file pointer and buffer, called $f^\wedge$ or $f\uparrow$, are established as drawn in Figure 3.26. A **buffer,** which can contain a value of type *elType*, is an intermediate memory location between the file and main memory. On input the buffer contains a copy of the element indicated by the file pointer.

The *Rewrite* and *Reset* operations are implemented in Pascal as shown in the ADT file definition. As the descriptions of these operations reveal, in input mode you cannot find a record needing updating, make the changes, and then switch to output mode to write the updated record to the same position in the

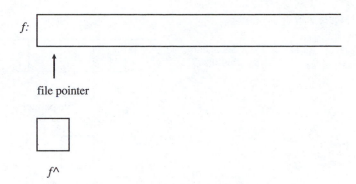

Figure 3.26

Diagram of file pointer
and buffer established by
declaration of file *f*

file. A switch to output mode with *rewrite(f)* would move the pointer from the particular record's position to the front of the file and destroy the entire file in the process. Thus, to update a record you must read the records one at a time, making changes as needed, and write the revised records to a temporary working file. To place the updated records in the original file, read the records one at a time from the working file and write them to the original file.

The operation *StoreFile(f, e)* can be written in Pascal as

```
write (f, e)
```

Actually, while in output mode, writing the value of *e* into the file is a two-stage process. First, the computer transfers *e*'s value to the buffer as shown in the transition from Step 1 to Step 2 of Figure 3.27. For emphasis in figures throughout the book, we have sketched in boldface memory locations and variables whose values change along with those new values. The boldface of Step 3 of Figure 3.27 illustrates the movement of the buffer's value to the file and the advancement of the file pointer. The transfer of the value in the buffer to the file is actually a move, not a copy, so that after execution *f^* is undefined, as indicated by the question mark in the box representing the buffer.

Though not available in many versions, including Turbo Pascal, Standard Pascal allows individual statements for the actions of Steps 2 and 3 of Figure 3.27. Standard Pascal implements Step 2, the copying of the value of *e* into the buffer *f^*, as the assignment statement

```
f^ := e
```

Step 3, to move the buffer's value to the file and to advance the file pointer, is implemented in Standard Pascal by the statement

```
put(f)
```

While in input mode, the buffer contains the current file entry needing processing. The Pascal statement

```
read(f, e)
```

implements the ADT file operation *RetrieveFile* by placing the buffer value into the variable *e*, advancing the pointer, and updating the buffer. The action of

Figure 3.27

Action of ADT file operation *StoreFile*(*f*, *e*), which can be implemented as *write* (*f*, *e*)

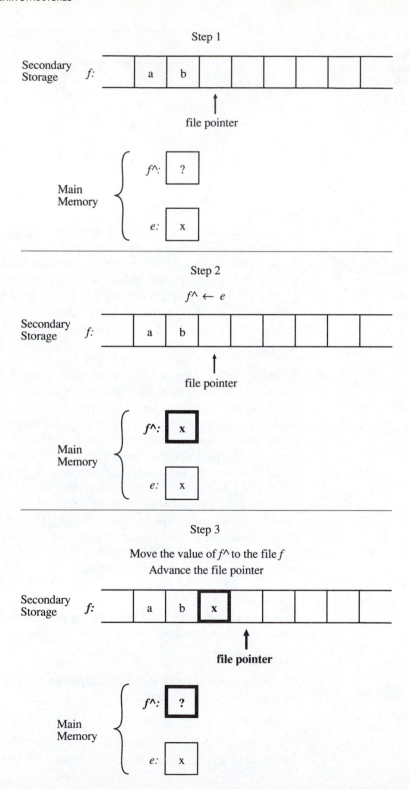

this operation is illustrated in Figure 3.28. As with *StoreFile, RetrieveFile* has two main steps, which have separate implementations in Standard Pascal. The assignment statement

```
e := f^
```

copies the buffer's value into *e* as indicated in Step 2 of Figure 3.28. The procedure call

```
get(f)
```

advances the file pointer and copies the file value indicated by the pointer into the buffer. (See Step 3 of Figure 3.28.) Turbo and several other versions of Pascal do not employ *f^*, *get*, and *put*, so check the documentation for your system before using these features.

On input we often must check to see if the file pointer indicates the end-of-file marker. This *eof(f)* check is accomplished in Pascal just as presented in the ADT file operations. For instance, we may read a nonempty file of scalar values and print its contents with the program segment below. A priming read is not used since the *eof* and *read* operations "look ahead" in the file.

```
reset(f);
while not eof(f) do
    begin
        read(f,e);
        writeln(e)
    end    {while}
```

Since input from and output to a user-defined file is accomplished one record at a time, data is not arranged in lines. Consequently, *eoln, readln, writeln,* and *page* are meaningless in this context.

A summary of a Pascal implementation of all the ADT file operations is presented in Figure 3.29.

Besides this user-defined or binary file, Pascal provides *text*, which is a predefined *file of char*. Moreover, the characters are arranged into lines so that the *eoln* operation should be included in the ADT text definition. The formal definition is considered in the exercises. Also, data is stored differently in user-defined and text files. In the latter, each character is translated separately into the encoding scheme, usually ASCII or EBCDIC, of that particular computer. (Appendix C contains these encoding schemes.) Since the ASCII system encodes the character "3" as 0011 0011, "7" as 0011 0111, and "2" as 0011 0010, a text file in ASCII stores the number 372 with the three bytes for the individual characters concatenated as

0011 0011 0011 0111 0011 0010

In reading a number from a text file, the computer must convert the number from its character string form to the number encoding of the computer. Similarly, on output the computer translates the binary number into a character

Figure 3.28

Action of ADT file operation *RetrieveFile*(*f*, *e*), which can be implemented as *read*(*f*, *e*)

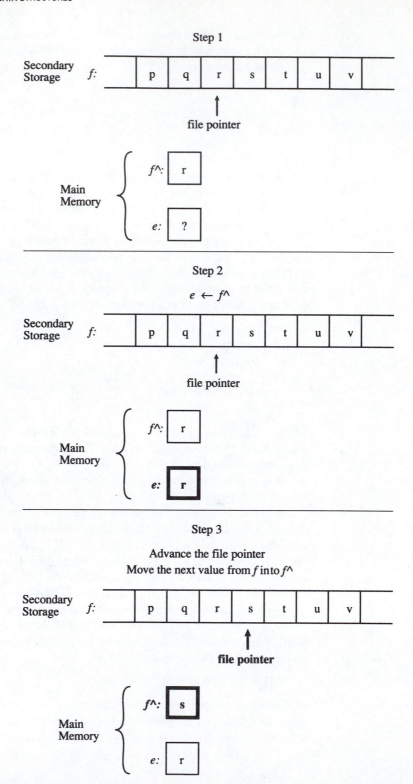

Figure 3.29.

Pascal implementation of
ADT file

ADT File Implementation

Create a file f with elements of type *elType*.

```
program FileEx (f);

type
    elType      =   .............;
    FileType    =   file of elType;

var
    f           :   FileType;
    e           :   elType;
```

Rewrite(f)

```
rewrite(f)
```

StoreFile(*f, e*)

```
write(f, e)
```

Reset(f)

```
reset(f)
```

EOF(f) → *b*

```
eof(f)
```

RetrieveFile(*f, e*)

```
read(f, e)
```

string. In a user-defined file, however, the number 372 is stored in a binary form, such as 0000 0001 0111 0100, exactly as it is in the computer. For input and output no conversion is necessary between the external file and main memory, so processing is faster. Also, information usually takes less space in a binary file than in a text file. Because of its method of storage, however, the programmer cannot use a text editor to create a binary file but must resort to programming. The program would read the data from the keyboard interactively or from an existing text file or compute the data in some way and then write that data to the binary file. Text files, however, can be generated and viewed with a text editor. In fact, the built-in *input* file with data from the keyboard and *output* file with information to the printer are actually of type *text*.

There are some differences between text and user-defined files in the implementation of the *read* and *write* procedures. Suppose we have the following record type definition and variable declaration:

```
type
    String20   =  packed array [1..20] of char;

    StuType  =  record
        Name  :  String20;
        Grade :  integer;
        GPA   :  real
    end;

var
    Student   : StuType;
```

If *StuFile* has type *file of StuType*, input is of the form

```
read (StuFile, Student)
```

Similarly, output to this binary file is accomplished an entire record at a time by the statement

```
write (StuFile, Student)
```

However, if *StuFile* is of type *text*, we must read and write values for the fields one at a time, as in

```
for i := 1 to 20 do
    read (StuFile, Student.Name[i]);
readln (StuFile, Student.Grade, Student.GPA)
```

and

```
writeln (StuFile, Student.Name, Student.Grade, Student.GPA)
```

The process of reading and writing values one at a time is called **stream I/O**. Standard Pascal can read a stream consisting of character, real, or integer numbers only, though many versions also permit reading string values. Real and integer values, such as for grade and grade-point average, are automatically transformed from text to binary on input by skipping leading blanks and end-of-line markers, reading, and converting the stream of characters that make up the number. This process is reversed when a number is written to a text file. In professional situations, most files are binary as opposed to text files.

▽

SECTION 3.4 EXERCISES

1. Consider the *text* file pictured in Figure 3.30. Give the output, contents of the file and buffer, and position of the file pointer after execution of each program segment starting with the same picture each time. Assume *blank* is an appropriately defined constant and *e* is a character variable.

a. `rewrite(f)`

b. Suppose in output mode

    `write(f, 'R')`

c. `rewrite(f);`
    `e := 'X';`
    `write(f, e)`

d. `rewrite(f);`
    `f^ := 'X';`
    `put(f);`
    `write(f, 24.5:4:1, blank);`
    `writeln(f, 37:2)`

e. `rewrite(f);`
    `for i := 2 to 6 do`
       `write(f, blank)`

f. `rewrite(f);`
    `write(f, 'FILE')`

g. `for i := 1 to 4 do`
      `begin`
         `rewrite(f);`
         `write(f, i:1)`
      `end      {for}`

Figure 3.30

Diagram of file and buffer for Exercises 1 and 2

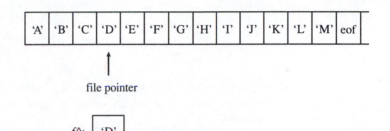

2. Repeat Exercise 1 using Figure 3.30 for the following program segments. Assume *x* is a character variable.

a. `reset(f)`

b. Suppose in input mode

    `get(f)`

c. Suppose in input mode

    `write(f^)`

d. `reset(f);`
    `while not eof(f) do`
      `begin`
         `read(f, x);`
         `write(x)`
      `end  {while}`

e. Suppose in input mode

    `write(f^);`
    `get(f);`

f. `for i := 3 to 6 do`
      `begin`
         `reset(f);`
         `read(f, x)`
      `end;  {for}`
    `writeln(x)`

g. `reset(f);`
    `for i := 1 to 6 do`
      `get(f);`
    `read(f, x);`
    `rewrite(f);`
    `for i := 1 to 6 do`
      `write(f, x)`

h. `reset(f);`
    `while not eof(f) do`
      `read(f, x);`
    `write (x)`

3. Repeat Exercise 1 using Figure 3.31. Assume *i* is an integer variable.

a. Suppose in output mode

```
i := 357;
writeln (f, i:3)
```

b. Suppose in output mode

```
writeln (f, 'KLM');
```

d. Suppose in output mode

```
for i := 1 to 4 do
    write(f, chr(ord
        ('A') + i) );
writeln (f)
```

c.
```
rewrite (f);
writeln (f);
writeln (f, 'X')
```

Figure 3.31

Diagram of file for Exercise 3; the end-of-line marker is indicated by ''eoln''

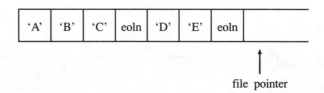

file pointer

4. Repeat Exercise 1 using Figure 3.32. Assume *ch*, *x*, and *y* are character variables, *word* is a packed array of three characters, and *i* is an integer variable.

a. Suppose in input mode

```
while not eoln (f) do
    begin
        read (f, ch);
        write (ch,
            blank)
    end  {while}
```

b. Suppose in input mode

```
while not eoln (f) do
    begin
        read (f, i);
        write (i, blank)
    end  {while}
```

c.
```
reset (f);
readln (f, ch);
writeln (ch);
readln (f, i);
writeln (i)
```

d.
```
reset (f);
while not eoln (f) do
    get (f);
get (f);
ch := f^
```

e. Suppose in input mode

```
for i := 1 to 3 do
    read (f, word[i]);
writeln(word)
```

5. Create in Pascal a file of real numbers

6. Create in Pascal a file of records where each record has fields for *Name*, *Date*, *Salary*, and *Tax*.

Figure 3.32

Diagram of file for Exercise 4; the end-of-line marker is indicated by "eoln," the end-of-file marker is shown as "eof"

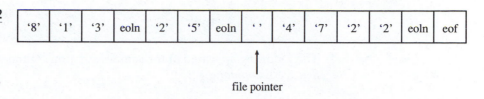

file pointer

Code in Pascal the routines in Exercises 7–10, and answer any other questions for each problem. All files are binary ones. Standard Pascal requires that any file that is a parameter for a procedure or a function, be a variable parameter.

7. a. A procedure to copy information from file *InFile* to file *OutFile*
   b. Write an invariant for the loop in Part a.
   c. Using program verification, prove this loop is correct.

8. a. A procedure to append information from file *AddFile* onto the end of file *OldFile*, placing all the records into *NewFile*
   b. Write an invariant for the second loop in Part a.
   c. Using program verification, prove this loop is correct.

9. a. A function to return the number of records in file *InFile*
   b. Write an invariant for the loop in Part a.
   c. Using program verification, prove this loop is correct.

10. Suppose the elements of *EmpFile* are of type *EmpType*, a record type with an *SSN* field and an *Info* field. Write a procedure to search the file for a record with *SSN* equal to *SearchSSN*. If found, print that record; otherwise, print a message that the record is not in the file.

11. Write a formal definition of ADT text.

12. Write a function to return the number of blanks in a text file. Be sure not to count the end-of-line marker as a blank.

13. a. Write a procedure to skip over blanks in the text file *OldFile* by reading to the next nonblank character or the end-of-line character, whichever comes first.
   b. Write a program to copy *OldFile* into *NewFile* with all strings of blanks replaced by a single blank.

14. Write a boolean function to return *true* if the present line of a text file contains two consecutive periods.

15. Suppose binary file *EmpFile* has records with a person's name as a packed array of characters, year of birth as an integer, and sex from the enumeration type (*female, male*). Write a procedure to generate two files, one with all the females and one with all the males. Omit the sex field in each of these new files.

▽

PROGRAMMING PROJECTS

1. The following appeared in the sample questions of the *1986 AP Computer Science Examination**:

Many Pascal programs take up more disk space than necessary because blanks used in indenting lines are saved. Write a complete program with the header

program *Compact(input, output, Infile, Outfile)*;

that can read any Pascal program from *Infile* and write to another file, *Outfile*, that would then contain the program compacted as follows: for each line of text, the leading blanks are replaced by an integer, followed by a blank, where the integer is the number of leading blanks in the original version. (Assume that there are no blank lines in the input file.)
For example, if *Infile* is

```
program xxx (input, output) ;
    var n : integer ;
    function F(n : integer) : integer ;
        begin
            F := n*n
        end ;
  .
  .
  .
```

then *Outfile* would be

```
0 program xxx(input, output) ;
2 var n : integer ;
2 function F(n : integer) : integer ;
4 begin
6 F := n*n
4 end ;
  .
  .
  .
```

2. Write a program to update a master file of inventory information with a transaction file of today's sales. An inventory record should contain fields for inventory number, description of the item, quantity present, and year-to-date sales and should be arranged in ascending order by inventory number. Another file of today's sales, also arranged in ascending order by inventory

---

*AP question selected from *AP Computer Science Examination*, 1986. Reprinted by permission of Educational Testing Service, the copyright owner of the sample questions.

number, has a record structure with inventory number, quantity sold, and price per item. Use the old inventory file as a backup and create a new, updated inventory file. Print a report of any updated inventory records. Also, produce an exception report to indicate errors such as records out of order and quantity sold being larger than quantity present. Other than the reports, all files should be user defined. Thus, you should write programs to initialize the inventory file and the file of today's sales from interactive input or from text files.

3. On January 1 your company must produce a year-end report and reinitialize the inventory file. Using an inventory file created in the last project, write a program to print a report of the entire file. Each new page of the report should have an appropriate title, column headings, date, and page number. Then write an interactive program to display the inventory number, description, and quantity present of each item. With a menu of choices, allow the user to add a new record whose inventory number precedes the present one, to change the description or quantity present, to delete the record, or to write the record without change. Whenever writing a record, initialize the year-to-date sales to be zero.

ADT Set and Implementation

In mathematics a **set** is a collection of things, perhaps even an infinite number of things. Some examples are the set of programs on your diskette and the set of natural numbers, 0, 1, 2, ... Of necessity, a set in the computer must be finite, so immediately we see some differences between the two. We first consider a set as a mathematical object, then an abstract data type, a structure in Pascal, and finally an object in memory.

In mathematics we write the set of weekdays or the set of weekend days as a list of the days surrounded by brackets:

weekdays = {*Mon, Tue, Wed, Thu, Fri*}
weekend = {*Sat, Sun*}

The order in which we write the elements is immaterial; {*Sat, Sun*} = {*Sun, Sat*}. Moreover, repetition of an element does not matter, so that {*Sat, Sun*} = {*Sat, Sun, Sat*}. The **universal set** is the set from which all the elements are taken in a particular context. Thus, for the above examples

alldays = {*Mon, Tue, Wed, Thu, Fri, Sat, Sun*}

is the universal set. The smallest set is the **empty set** or the set with no elements, { }. *Mon* is a member of or an element in the set *weekdays*, written

Mon ∈ *weekdays*

Since every element of *weekdays* belongs in *alldays*, we say that *weekdays* is a **subset** of *alldays* and write *weekdays* ⊆ *alldays*

Suppose we also have the set

SpecialDays = {*Mon, Thu, Sat*}

The set of elements that are in *SpecialDays* or *weekdays* or both is called the **union** of these two sets and is written

SpecialDays ∪ *weekdays* = {*Mon, Tue, Wed, Thu, Fri, Sat*}

The union of *weekdays* and *weekend* is the universal set or

weekdays ∪ *weekend* = *alldays*

If we picture two sets *A* and *B* as circles as in Figure 3.33, the shaded area of this **Venn diagram** indicates *A* ∪ *B*.

Figure 3.33

Venn diagram of *A* ∪ *B* shaded

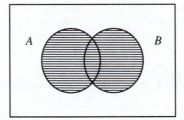

The set of elements that are simultaneously in *SpecialDays* and *weekdays* is called the **intersection** of these two sets, written

SpecialDays ∩ *weekdays* = {*Mon, Thu*}

Moreover, the intersection of *weekdays* and *weekend* is empty:

weekdays ∩ *weekend* = { }

The Venn diagram in Figure 3.34 pictures the intersection of sets *A* and *B*, *A* ∩ *B*, as the darker shaded portion where the circles overlap.

Set difference is a similar concept to the numeric difference or subtraction.

Figure 3.34

Venn diagram of *A* ∩ *B* shaded darkest

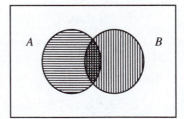

The **set difference** of *weekdays* and *SpecialDays* is the set of elements that are in *weekdays* but not in *SpecialDays*,

> *weekdays* − *SpecialDays* = {*Tue, Wed, Fri*}

For the set difference of *SpecialDays* and *weekdays*, we start with the elements in *SpecialDays* and take away the elements that are also in *weekdays*,

> *SpecialDays* − *weekdays* = {*Sat*}

Diagrams of the set differences $A - B$ and $B - A$ are shown in Figure 3.35.

Figure 3.35

(a) $A - B$; (b) $B - A$

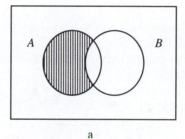
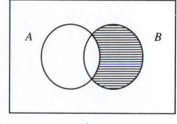

a   b

With these definitions in mind, we see that the operations in the ADT set definition in Figure 3.36 mirror their mathematical counterparts.

There are several implementations of the ADT set in Pascal. In this section we present the predefined type *set*, reserving other implementations until the exercises and later chapters. As with the creation of files and arrays, the creation of a set in Pascal involves definitions of the type of the elements and the structure itself and declaration of the variables of that set type. Paralleling the mathematical examples earlier in this section, we have

```
type
    Week          = (Mon, Tue, Wed, Thu, Fri, Sat, Sun);
    SetType       = set of Week;
var
    S,
    alldays,
    weekdays,
    weekend,
    SpecialDays  :  SetType;
```

We should emphasize that the structure is created at this point, but the sets themselves still do not have values. One limitation of Pascal is that we cannot read or write sets directly from standard input/output or any text file, though certainly we can perform input and output on the individual elements or assign a set constant to a set variable.

Figure 3.36.

Formal definition of
ADT set

ADT Set

Objects: Elements are of finite ordinal type and are members
of a mathematical set.

Operations:

Notation:

elType — finite ordinal type

S, T, V — sets with elements of type *elType*

e   — item of type *elType*

b   — boolean value

StoreSet(S, T)

Procedure to copy *T*'s value into *S*

EqualSet(S, T) → b

Function to return *true* if *S* is equal to *T*

IsInSet(S, e) → b

Function to return *true* if *e* is a member of *S*

Subset(S, T) → b

Function to return *true* if *S* is a subset of *T*

Union(S, T) → V

Function to return *V*, the union of sets *S* and *T*

Intersection(S, T) → V

Function to return *V*, the intersection of sets *S* and *T*

Difference(S, T) → V

Function to return *V*, the difference of sets *S* and *T*

MakeSetEmpty(S)

Procedure to make set *S* the empty set

MakeSet(e) → S

Function to return the set containing only *e*

Curly brackets, { }, indicate a comment in Pascal, while rectangular brackets, [ ], surrounding a list or subrange of elements denote a set. Thus, the function *MakeSet*(5) returns

    [5]

while *MakeSetEmpty*(S) is realized in Pascal as the assignment statement

    S := [ ]

As with arrays and records, *StoreSet*(S, T) is also produced by an assignment statement,

    S := T

Thus, for our example we can now give values to the previously declared variables:

```
alldays      := [Mon..Sun];
weekdays     := [Mon..Fri];
weekend      := [Sat, Sun];
SpecialDays  := [Mon, Thu, Sat];
```

The relational operation "=" can be used as in mathematics to implement *EqualSet*. Since the mathematical symbols ∈ and ⊆ are not in the ASCII or EBCDIC character set, *in* and <=, respectively, generate the operations of *IsInSet* and *Subset*. Examples of these boolean operations in Pascal follow:

```
if weekend = SpecialDays then ...
if Mon in weekdays then ...
if weekdays <= alldays then ...
```

The *IsInSet* operation is particularly useful when testing whether a variable is equal to any one of a number of values. For instance, suppose in the *ReadStr* procedure of Section 1.2 we wished to terminate reading the string upon finding a comma, period, semicolon, question mark, or exclamation point. Using a set constant and appropriately defined constants, we could write,

```
while not (ch in [comma, period, semicolon, question, exclaim])
   and (Length < MaxNumStu) do
```

This statement is certainly clearer and less cumbersome than the following:

```
while (ch <> comma) and (ch <> period) and
      (ch <> semicolon) and (ch <> question) and
      (ch <> exclaim) and (Length < MaxNumStu) do
```

The set difference operation, −, is available on any keyboard but ∪ and ∩ are not. Pascal substitutes + for the union symbol and * for intersection as in the expressions

```
weekdays + weekend
```

and

```
SpecialDays * weekdays
```

There is no confusion about the intent of a statement like $S + T$ or $S * T$, however, because of strong typing in Pascal. Since S and T would be declared as sets or numbers, the compiler recognizes the appropriate operation to be performed. Figure 3.37 summarizes the built-in Pascal implementation of all the ADT set operations.

An examination of implementation on the machine level shows the mathematical basis and reasons for the limitations of the predefined Pascal set. Once we declare a set, such as *weekdays*, to have the type

```
SetType = set of Week;
```

a string of 7 bits, one for each possible element of the set, is designated in memory. When the set variable is given a value, for each element in the set, its corre-

Figure 3.37.

Built-in Pascal implementation of ADT set operations

ADT Set Implementation

Create a set *S* with elements of type *elType*.

```
type
    elType   =   .............;
    SetType  =   set of elType;

var
    S, T     :   SetType;
    e        :   elType;
```

StoreSet(S, T)

```
S := T
```

EqualSet(S, T) → b

```
(S = T)
```

IsInSet(S, e) → b

```
(e in S)
```

Subset(S, T) → b

```
(S <= T)
```

Union(S, T) → V

```
(S + T)
```

Intersection(S, T) → V

```
(S * T)
```

Difference(S, T) → V

```
(S - T)
```

MakeSetEmpty(S)

```
S := [ ]
```

MakeSet(e) → S

```
[ e ]
```

sponding bit is set to 1; otherwise, that bit is cleared to 0. Thus, when the assignment statement

```
weekdays := [Mon..Fri]
```

is executed, the string 1111100 is stored in *weekday*'s location in memory. Figure 3.38 diagrams the situation in which bits 1 through 5, associated with *Mon* through *Fri*, are each 1 since those days are in *weekdays*.

Figure 3.38

Storage for
weekdays = [Mon..Fri]

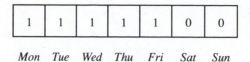

As shown in Figure 3.39, for

```
SpecialDays := [Mon, Thu, Sat]
```

we have the packed array of bits 1001010. Moreover,

```
alldays := [Mon..Sun]
```

is represented by a string of all ones, 1111111, while the empty set is stored as a string of zeros, 0000000.

Figure 3.39

Storage for *Special-Days = [Mon, Thu, Sat]*

The actions of the union and intersection operations are especially interesting on the hardware level. Execution of the statement

```
S := SpecialDays + weekdays
```

actually does cause addition of the two bit strings. Addition, however, is performed with a special arithmetic, called **boolean algebra**, that is at the basis of the design of computers, the manipulation of data and programs in the computer, and the logic of programs. When George Boole in 1847 wrote about the algebra that now bears his name, he was presenting an algebraic foundation for logic. But few appreciated Boole's genius. Born in England, the son of a poor shoemaker, George Boole was self-taught. Because of his work in logic he was given the position of professor of mathematics at Queens College, an honorable but not particularly respected position. Little did he or anyone else suspect that 100 years later his work would provide the theoretical basis for the design of electronic circuitry and, hence, of the computer.

In a boolean algebra the only digits are the bits 0 and 1. Moreover, $0 + 0 = 0$ and $1 + 0 = 0 + 1 = 1$, but surprisingly $1 + 1 = 1$. Actually, if we consider 1 to correspond to *true*, 0 to *false*, and + to be *or*, the result $1 + 1 = 1$ as "*true or true* is *true*" is not unexpected at all. Figure 3.40 presents the table for the + operation along with the corresponding one for *or*.

Therefore, as enumerated in Figure 3.41, the sum of the bit strings for *SpecialDays* and *weekdays* in this system is 1111110, which represents [*Mon..Sat*], the union of the two sets. Considering the representation again, we know zero indicates that the corresponding element, such as *Sun*, is not in the set. The

Figure 3.40

Tables for the boolean algebra operation + and corresponding *or* operation

x	y	x + y
0	0	0
0	1	1
1	0	1
1	1	1

x	y	x or y
false	false	false
false	true	true
true	false	true
true	true	true

Figure 3.41

Boolean algebra sum of corresponding elements that implements the union of *SpecialDays* and *weekdays*

	Mon	Tue	Wed	Thu	Fri	Sat	Sun
	1	0	0	1	0	1	0
+	1	1	1	1	1	0	0
	1	1	1	1	1	1	0

sum $0 + 0 = 0$ means that element is not in either set and so cannot be in the union. If an element, such as *Fri* or *Sat*, is in exactly one of the sets, the resulting sum is $0 + 1 = 1$ or $1 + 0 = 1$, indicating that the element will be in the union. And if the element appears in both sets, as with *Mon* through *Thu*, we have the sum $1 + 1$, which is 1. Being in both sets, the element clearly is in the union.

For intersection, the computer performs boolean algebra multiplication, one pair of corresponding elements at a time. Multiplication in boolean algebra is as we would expect, $1 * 1 = 1$, and any product involving 0 is 0. Boolean algebra multiplication corresponds to the Pascal *and*; and Figure 3.42 presents tables for both. Thus, multiplying the *Mon* bits for *SpecialDays* and *weekdays*, the *Tue* bits, then the *Wed* bits, and so on, we obtain the bit string 1001000, which represents the intersection [*Mon, Thu*]. Figure 3.43 details this operation. We see from this representation that the elements of a set must be of or-

Figure 3.42

Tables for the boolean algebra operation ∗ and corresponding *and* operation

x	y	x ∗ y
0	0	0
0	1	0
1	0	0
1	1	1

x	y	x and y
false	false	false
false	true	false
true	false	false
true	true	true

Figure 3.43

Boolean algebra product of corresponding elements that implements the intersection of *SpecialDays* and *weekdays*

	Mon	Tue	Wed	Thu	Fri	Sat	Sun
	1	0	0	1	0	1	0
∗	1	1	1	1	1	0	0
	1	0	0	1	0	0	0

dinal type, so that we can associate each possible element with a bit position in main memory. Compilers limit the number of possible elements in such a type, and in fact Standard Pascal does not allow a *set of integer*. Suppose, for instance, integers in a computer range from −32,768 to 32,767. If a *set of integer* were permissible, storage for just one set would consume $2 \cdot 32{,}768 = 65{,}536$ bits or 8192 bytes on a machine where there are 8 bits to a byte.

| **Example 3.1.** |

▼ Standard Pascal does not allow direct input and output of sets to text files. In this example, using pseudocode and ADT operations, we design a procedure to read the individual elements from a text file and place them in a set S. First, we initialize S to be the empty set; even if the file has no data, S will obtain the appropriate value. Then, as long as there are elements in the file, we read a datum, make a one-element set with that item, and assign to S the union of S and this one-element set. This process, inserting the elements from the file into S one element at a time, mimics the accumulation of the total of a list of numbers from a file.

GenerateSet(f, S)
    Procedure to generate a set containing values from file f
Input:
    f — file
Output:
    S — set containing values from f
Assumption:
    f and S have elements of the same type.
Algorithm:
    Reset(f)
    MakeSetEmpty(S)
    while not *EOF*(f) do
        RetrieveFile(f, e)
        $S \leftarrow S + \textit{MakeSet}(e)$

This operation *GenerateSet* could be written in abstract data type terms as a procedure, *GenerateSet*(f, S), or as a function returning a value for S, *GenerateSet*(f) → S. We must, however, code the operation in Pascal as a procedure since Standard Pascal only permits the return of scalar values through the function name. Again, we see the difference between higher level design and lower level implementation. It is easier to consider an operation initially on the ADT level without worry about coding details that may cloud our thinking about the more important overall design.
▲

▽

| **SECTION 3.5 EXERCISES** |

Evaluate the Pascal set expressions in Exercises 1−22.

    1. [1, 7, 3] + [3, 4, 5, 6, 7]   *2.* [1, 7, 3] * [3, 4, 5, 6, 7]

3. [1, 7, 3] − [3, 4, 5, 6, 7] **4.** [3, 4, 5, 6, 7] − [1, 7, 3]
5. [ ] + [2, 4, 6] **6.** [ ] * [2, 4, 6] **7.** [ ] − [2, 4, 6]
8. [2, 4, 6] − [ ] **9.** [1..7] + [2, 4, 6] **10.** [1..7] * [2, 4, 6]
11. [1..7] − [2, 4, 6] **12.** [2, 4, 6] − [1..7] **13.** 4 in [2, 4, 6]
14. 5 in [2, 4, 6] **15.** [1, 3] <= [1..5] **16.** [1, 3, 2] = [1..3]
17. [1..3] + [4..6] **18.** [1..3] * [4..6] **19.** [1..3] − [4..6]
20. [4..6] − [1..3] **21.** [1..3] + [4] **22.** [1..3] * [4]

23. a. Write the *GenerateSet* function of Example 3.1 in Pascal.
  b. Write an invariant for the loop in Part a.
  c. Using program verification, prove that this loop is correct.

24. Write definitions, declarations, and assignments to get *Vowels* and *Consonants* to be appropriate sets of capital letters.

In Exercises 25–30 code the routines in Pascal, and answer any questions for each problem.

25. Procedure to remove element *x* from *S*.

26. Function to return the size of set *S*, where *S* is a set of subrange type *start..finish*.

27. a. Procedure to make U the universal set whose elements are of subrange type *start..finish*.
  b. Write an invariant for the loop in Part a.
  c. Using program verification, prove that this loop is correct.

28. a. Procedure to make *C* the complement of a set *S*, the set of elements in the universal set but not in *S*. Assume *S* is a set of subrange type *start..finish*.
  b. Give the complement of *weekdays*.
  c. Give the complement of *SpecialDays*.
  d. Draw a Venn diagram of the complement of a set *A*.

29. a. Function to return *true* if sets *S* and *T* are disjoint, that is, not having any elements in common. Assume *S* and *T* are sets of subrange type *start..finish*.
  b. Are the sets *weekdays* and *weekend* disjoint?
  c. Are the sets *SpecialDays* and *weekend* disjoint?
  d. Draw a Venn diagram of disjoint sets *A* and *B*.
  e. Write a recursive version of the function in Part a that does not use the operation *.

30. a. Procedure to make *E* the exclusive-or of sets *S* and *T*, that is, the set of elements in *S* or *T* but not both. Assume *S* and *T* are sets of subrange type *start..finish*.
  b. Give the exclusive-or of *weekdays* and *weekend*.
  c. Give the exclusive-or of *weekdays* and *SpecialDays*.
  d. Give the exclusive-or of *SpecialDays* and *weekend*.

e. Give the exclusive-or of *SpecialDays* and *alldays*.

f. Draw a Venn diagram of the exclusive-or of *A* and *B*.

31. Let *S* and *T* be of type *packed array* [1..22] *of boolean*.

    a. Write a function to perform boolean addition of *S* and *T*.

    b. Write a procedure to print the corresponding bit string for a set of this type with 0 for *false* and 1 for *true*.

32. a. Write a recursive procedure *GenerateSubsets* to return an array of all subsets of set *S*, where *S* is a set of subrange type *start..finish*, and to return the number of such subsets. The terminal condition is that *S* is empty.

    b. What is the big oh for this algorithm?

PROGRAMMING PROJECT

1. Suppose you wish to work with sets of integers in the range from 1 to 500 but your version of Pascal only allows at most 256 different values. One alternative is to represent the set as a packed boolean array, *s*, of 500 elements. Thus, if *s*[359] = *true*, then 359 is in the set. Implement the ADT set operations for sets of integers from 1 to *n* using packed boolean arrays of *n* elements. Repeatedly read values from a text file for sets *S* and *T* and element *e* and print the results of the operations applied to these.

4

Strings

Introduction

For several applications, starting with the program in Section 1.2, it has been necessary to use an implementation of character strings, principally to hold names. In the first section of this chapter we cover the formal definition of the ADT string, and in the next section we consider the major implementation technique for this structure, namely arrays. After discussing linked lists in Chapter 8, we compare and contrast the array and linked list implementations of strings. Some versions of Pascal, such as UCSD and Turbo Pascal, provide built-in string operations, but Standard Pascal does not. (See Appendix B.) When such extensions are available, it is usually desirable to employ the predefined string operations as opposed to developing your own. Even when provided, however, we can consider the type *string* with an abstract data type approach, just as we studied arrays, records, files, and sets from that perspective.

ADT String

The language COBOL, the most common business-oriented language, was designed to handle input and output of strings easily because so many business applications involve manipulation of strings. One of the driving forces on the team that wrote COBOL in the late 1950s under the auspices of the Department of Defense was Grace Murray Hopper. She received her Ph.D. in mathematics from Yale in 1934 and taught at Vassar until World War II when she enlisted in the U.S. Naval Reserve. Her computing career was launched when she was assigned to work with the first electro-mechanical, large-scale digital computer, Mark I. In the early 1950s, she wrote the first compiler. An illustrious career in computing has also seen Rear Admiral Grace Hopper retire in 1986, the oldest officer in the U.S. military.

In the ADT string operations of Figure 4.1, notice a *StringIsFull* operation that is *true* when the string has no more room and *false* otherwise. This function is also employed in the *Concat* operation, which **concatenates** or glues together two strings. If the resulting structure is longer than the maximum allowable, the answer is **truncated** or cut off. Similarly, the operation *InsertString* uses *StringIsFull*. *InsertString(sub, s, pos)* inserts the substring *sub* into the string *s* starting at position *pos*. Again, if the result is too long, the final value of *s* is truncated to the maximum size. Similar truncation occurs when necessary with *AppendChar(s, c)* which appends a character, *c*, onto the end of the string, *s*. This operation is not the same as *InsertString(sub, s, LengthString(s) + 1)*, which appends a string *sub* onto the end of *s*. A variable holding a character is not a character string of length 1; the structures are different. *InsertString* has two strings and a position as input, while *AppendChar* has input of a string and a character. Figure 4.1 presents the formal definition of the ADT string; Figure 4.2 illustrates its actions. The following examples employ these basic operations.

Example 4.1

▼ In some applications we need to perform string operations involving a single character. For compatibility with most of the ADT string operations, we place the character into a one-character string.

The process, which follows, involves creating an empty string and then placing that character into the newly created string.

MakeString(s, c)
    Procedure to make *s* a string with the value of character *c* as its only
    character
Input:
    c — character
Output:
    s — string
Assumption:
    s can hold at least one character.
Algorithm:
    MakeStringEmpty(s)
▲   *AppendChar(s, c)*

Example 4.2

▼ In this example we design a procedure *DeleteSubstring* to delete the first occurrence of the substring *sub* from the string *s*. For future applications it will also be helpful to return the position, *pos*, at which the deletion occurs. If *sub* is not located, *s* is not changed.

This deletion operation varies from *DeleteString* in that the latter specifies a position and a length, not the substring itself. Of course, we use *DeleteString* to accomplish our task. The length of the substring can be obtained through

Figure 4.1

Formal definition of ADT string

ADT String

Objects: A finite sequence of characters

Operations:

Notation:

    s, sub, u — strings
    c   — item of type *char*
    b   — boolean value
    pos, lng — nonnegative integers

MakeStringEmpty(*s*)

Procedure to make *s* empty

StringIsEmpty(*s*) → *b*

Boolean function to return *true* if *s* is empty

StringIsFull(*s*) → *b*

Boolean function to return *true* if *s* is full

LengthString(*s*) → *lng*

Function to return the number of characters in *s*

Position(*sub, s*) → *pos*

Function to return the starting position of where the substring *sub* first appears in *s*. If *sub* is not found in *s*, 0 is returned. The character positions are numbered from left to right, starting with 1.

Concat(*u, s*)

Procedure to concatenate onto the end of *u* as many characters of *s* as possible until *StringIsFull*(*u*) is *true*

CopySubstring(*u, s, pos, lng*)

Procedure to make *u* a copy of the substring of *s* from the character at position *pos* for *lng* number of characters or to the end of the string, whichever occurs first. If *pos* is greater than *LengthString*(*s*) or less than 1 or if *lng* is less than 1, *u* becomes the empty string.

DeleteString(*s, pos, lng*)

Procedure to delete from *s* the substring starting at position *pos* for *lng* number of characters or to the end of the string, whichever occurs first. If *pos* is greater than *LengthString*(*s*) or less than 1, *s* is unchanged.

InsertString(*sub, s, pos*)

Procedure to insert *sub* as a substring into *s* starting at position *pos*. While *StringIsFull*(*s*) is *false*, the procedure concatenates the first *pos* − 1 characters of *s*, the characters of *sub*, and the remaining characters of *s*. If *pos* is greater than *LengthString*(*s*) + 1 or less than 1, *s* is unchanged.

RetrieveChar(*s, pos*) → *c*

Function to return the character at position *pos* in *s*. If *pos* is greater than *LengthString*(*s*) or less than 1, the function returns the *null* character, the character *chr*(0).

AppendChar(*s, c*)

Procedure to append character *c* onto the end of the string *s*. If *StringIsFull*(*s*) is *true* before execution of the operation, *s* remains unchanged.

Figure 4.2

Examples of the actions of ADT string operations

Examples of the Actions of ADT String Operations

MakeStringEmpty(s): $s \leftarrow$ ' ' , the empty string

StringIsEmpty('') $\rightarrow$ *true*
StringIsEmpty(' ') $\rightarrow$ *false*

For s = 'RING'
StringIsFull(s) $\rightarrow$ *true* if s can hold a maximum of 4 characters
StringIsFull(s) $\rightarrow$ *false* if s can hold a maximum of 6 characters
LengthString('STRING') $\rightarrow$ 6

Position('ISS', 'MISSISSIPPI') $\rightarrow$ 2
Position('RA', 'STRING') $\rightarrow$ 0

For u = 'CON'
Concat(u, 'CAT'): $u \leftarrow$ 'CONCAT'

CopySubstring(u, 'STRING', 3, 2): $u \leftarrow$ 'RI'
CopySubstring(u, 'STRING', 3, 4): $u \leftarrow$ 'RING'
CopySubstring(u, 'STRING', 3, 97): $u \leftarrow$ 'RING'
CopySubstring(u, 'STRING', 9, 2): $u \leftarrow$ ' '
CopySubstring(u, 'STRING', 0, 2): $u \leftarrow$ ' '

For s = 'STRING'
DeleteString(s, 3, 2): $s \leftarrow$ 'STNG'
DeleteString(s, 3, 4): $s \leftarrow$ 'ST'
DeleteString(s, 3, 18): $s \leftarrow$ 'ST'
DeleteString(s, 9, 2): $s \leftarrow$ 'STRING'
DeleteString(s, 0, 2): $s \leftarrow$ 'STRING'

For s = 'STRING'
InsertString('OLL', s, 4): $s \leftarrow$ 'STROLLING' if *StringIsFull(s)*
                                         remains *false*
InsertString('ENT', s, 7): $s \leftarrow$ 'STRINGENT' if *StringIsFull(s)*
                                         remains *false*
InsertString('OLL', s, 4): $s \leftarrow$ 'STROLL' if *StringIsFull(s)* is *true*
InsertString('OLL', s, 9): $s \leftarrow$ 'STRING'
InsertString('OLL', s, 0): $s \leftarrow$ 'STRING'

RetrieveChar('STRING', 3) $\rightarrow$ 'R', as a character, not a string
RetrieveChar('STRING', 7) $\rightarrow$ *null*

For s = 'STRING'
AppendChar(s, 'Y'): $s \leftarrow$ 'STRINGY' if *StringIsFull(s)* is *false*
AppendChar(s, 'Y'): $s \leftarrow$ 'STRING' if *StringIsFull(s)* is *true*

LengthString(*sub*) and the position through *Position*(*sub*, *s*). With these arguments, *DeleteString* can accomplish the mission of *DeleteSubstring*, as illustrated in Figure 4.3. In this and many other designs of operations in the text, we indicate corresponding steps from example figures next to statements in the algorithms. Following the action in the drawing along with the algorithm should help in understanding the process.

Figure 4.3

Action of *DeleteSubstring*(*sub*, *s*, *pos*) from Example 4.2

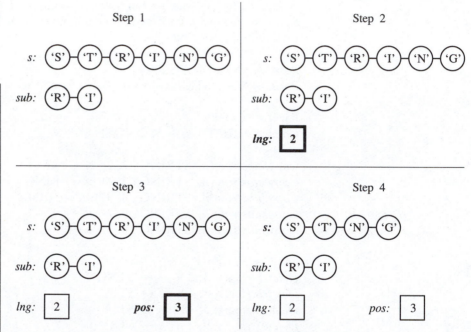

DeleteSubstring(*sub*, *s*, *pos*)
   Procedure to delete the first occurrence of the substring *sub* in the string *s* and to return the position of the deletion in *pos*. If *sub* cannot be found, *s* is unchanged and a value of 0 is returned for *pos*.
Input:
   sub, *s* — strings
Output:
   s   — revised string
   pos — position where the deletion occurs or 0
Assumptions:
   s and *sub* exist.

Figure	Algorithm
{4.3}	
{Step 2}	*lng* ← *LengthString*(*sub*)
{Step 3}	*pos* ← *Position*(*sub*, *s*)
{Step 4}	*DeleteString*(*s*, *pos*, *lng*)

But will we have an error if *sub* cannot be located in *s*? If *sub* cannot be found, *Position(sub, s)* returns 0. Moreover, the procedure call *DeleteString(s, pos, lng)* leaves *s* unchanged when *pos* is out of the range from 1 to *LengthString(s)*. Thus, without an error and with *pos* being assigned a zero value, the ADT string operation definitions allow us to deal with the case of *sub* not being found.

▲

| Example 4.3 |

▼ *DeleteSubstring* only eliminates the first occurrence of a substring, *sub*, in string *s*. To cause *s* to contain no copies of *sub*, we repeatedly call *DeleteSubstring* until the position of *sub* in *s* is zero, indicating *sub* cannot be found. The definition of the operation to delete all occurrences of a substring follows:

*DeleteAllSub(**sub, s**)*
    Procedure to delete all occurrences of the substring *sub* in the string *s*
Input:
    sub, s — strings
Output:
    s — revised string
Assumptions:
    s and *sub* exist.
Algorithm:
    repeat
        DeleteSubstring(sub, s, pos)
▲   until *pos* = 0

▽

SECTION 4.1 EXERCISES

For Exercises 1–11, starting with the following assumptions, give the result of the operation(s):
    s = 'GEORGIA' and has a maximum size of 10
    a = 'A' and has a maximum size of 5
    u = 'ATLANTA' and has a maximum size of 10
    v has a maximum size of 30
    n and *i* are integer variables
    b is a boolean variable
The following are character constants:
    blank   = ' '
    comma = ','
    e   = 'E'

1. *MakeStringEmpty(s)*

2. *n ← LengthString(s)*

3. *b ← StringIsFull(s)*

4. *n ← Position('G', s)*

5. *CopySubstring(v, u, 4, 3)*

6. *DeleteString(s, 6, 2)*
      AppendChar(s, e)

7. *DeleteSubstring*(*a*, *u*, *pos*)

8. *DeleteAllSub*(*a*, *u*)

10. *MakeString*(*asterisk*, '*')
$n \leftarrow LengthString(u) + 1$
for *i* from *n* downto 1 do
    InsertString(*asterisk*, *u*, *i*)

9. *AppendChar*(*u*, *comma*)
AppendChar(*u*, *blank*)
CopySubstring(*v*, *u*, 1, 9)
Concat(*v*, *s*)

11. *CopySubstring*(*v*, *u*, 1, 5)
CopySubstring(*u*, *u*, 6, 2)
Concat(*u*, *v*)

Use pseudocode and ADT string operations to define the routines in Exercises 12–21.

12. Procedure *AppendAsterisks*(*s*) to pad string *s* (a maximum of 20 characters) with asterisks.

13. Procedure *LineToString* to read a line from a text file into a string.

14. Procedure *StringToFile* to write a string to a text file; use *RetrieveChar*.

15. Procedure *Copy*(*s*, *oldpos*, *lng*, *newpos*) to make a copy at *newpos* of the substring starting at *oldpos* of length *lng*.

16. Procedure *DeleteToEnd*(*s*, *pos*) to delete from *s* the substring starting at position *pos* to the end of *s*. If *pos* is greater than *LengthString*(*s*) or less than 1, *s* is unchanged.

17. Procedure *DeleteToFirst*(*s*, *pos*) to delete from *s* the substring starting at the beginning of *s* through position *pos*. If *pos* is greater than *LengthString*(*s*) or less than 1, *s* is unchanged.

18. Procedure *Caps* to change every lowercase letter in a string to uppercase.

19. Procedure *Move*(*s*, *oldpos*, *lng*, *newpos*) in string *s* to move the substring starting at *oldpos* of length *lng* to *newpos*. Note that the *newpos* value is the position in the original *s*. If *newpos* is beyond *oldpos* (*newpos* > *oldpos*), deletion of the substring affects the position of the insertion.

20. Function *SentencePosition*(*s*, *pos*) to return the starting location of a sentence that contains position *pos*. Assume two blanks separate sentences and consecutive blanks appear nowhere else.

21. Procedure *DeleteSentence*(*sub*, *s*) to delete from *s* the first sentence containing *sub*. Delete from the start of that sentence to the beginning of the next. If *sub* is not found, *s* is not changed. Assume two blanks separate sentences and consecutive blanks appear nowhere else. Use *SentencePosition* from Exercise 20.

SECTION 4.2

Array Implementation of Strings

With the ADT string we have two major implementation techniques, arrays and linked lists. We consider the former in this section and postpone the linked list implementation until a later chapter. For the *ReadStr* procedure in Section 1.2 we used the array implementation. In fact, several versions of Pascal that support string operations employ arrays to form this structure.

We can generate the structure of a string with a record containing a length field and a packed or unpacked array of characters. Figure 4.4 draws a diagram of the following creation of a string:

```
const
    MaxLength   =  . . . . . . . . . . ;
type
    lengthType  =  0..MaxLength;
    IndexType   =  1..MaxLength;
    StringType  =  record
        length   :   lengthType;
        el       :   packed array [IndexType] of char
    end;
var
    s  :  StringType;
```

Figure 4.4

Diagram of a string implemented with an array

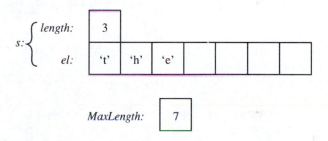

The value of *s.length* is initialized to zero by the *MakeStringEmpty* procedure. *AppendChar*, *Concat*, and *InsertString* usually increase the length, while *DeleteString* has the opposite effect. Also, the procedure *CopySubstring* generates a string with an appropriate length value. The functions *StringIsEmpty*, *StringIsFull*, *LengthString*, and *RetrieveChar* also must have an accurate value of *s.length* to execute properly.

For this array implementation, the length is particularly significant. The ADT operations *CopySubstring*, *DeleteString*, *InsertString*, and *RetrieveChar* all use the *LengthString* operation to check that a position indicator, *pos*, is in the proper range. The function *StringIsFull* returns *true* if the length is *MaxLength*:

$$StringIsFull \leftarrow (LengthString(s) = MaxLength)$$

Moreover, the *StringIsFull* operation is used in *Concat*, *InsertString*, and *AppendChar* to determine if truncation is needed or not.

Several of the array implemented string operations execute with a complexity of $O(1)$; regardless of the number of characters, *sLng*, in the string, the operation requires a constant amount of time. These rapid routines are *MakeStringEmpty, StringIsEmpty, StringIsFull, LengthString, RetrieveChar,* and *AppendChar.*

CopySubstring, Concat, DeleteString, and *InsertString* execute in linear time based on some or all of the following: the length of a string (*sLng*), the starting position of a substring (*pos*), and the length of a substring (*lng*). For example, the procedure call *CopySubstring(u, s, pos, lng)* returns in *u* the substring of *lng* number of characters starting at position *pos*. Retrieval of these elements from s is immediate through array references, *s.el[pos]*, *s.el[pos + 1]*, ..., *s.el[pos + lng − 1]*. Thus, the main work of the procedure, which is illustrated in Figure 4.5, is involved with the element-by-element copy to a new string.

```
{ Procedure to return in u the substring of s from
  position pos for lng characters                        }


procedure CopySubstring (var u, s: StringType; pos, lng: lengthType);
var
    oldIndex,                        {index for s}
    copyIndex  :  lengthType;        {index for u}

begin
    if (pos < 1) or (pos > s.length) or (lng < 0) then
        u.length := 0
    else
        begin                               {Fig. 4.5}
            oldIndex  := pos − 1;           {Step 1}
            copyIndex := 0;

            while (oldIndex < s.length) and (copyIndex < lng) do
                begin                                    {Steps 2,3}
                    oldIndex          := oldIndex + 1;
                    copyIndex         := copyIndex + 1;
                    u.el[copyIndex]   := s.el[oldIndex]
                end;   { while }

            u.length := copyIndex
        end    { else }
end;   { CopySubstring }
```

Notice that there are three assignment statements within the *while* loop that are executed a maximum of *lng* times for a total of $3 \cdot lng$ number of statements. With the two statements before and the one after the loop, a maximum of $3 \cdot lng + 3$ assignment statements are executed when a string of *lng* characters is returned. For the example in Figure 4.5, we executed $3 \cdot 2 + 3 = 9$ assignment statements. Had *lng* been 4, the number would have been $3 \cdot 4 + 3 = 15$ statements. Clearly, the complexity of this problem is linear with respect to

Figure 4.5

Action of *CopySub-string*(*u*, 'STRING', 3, 2)

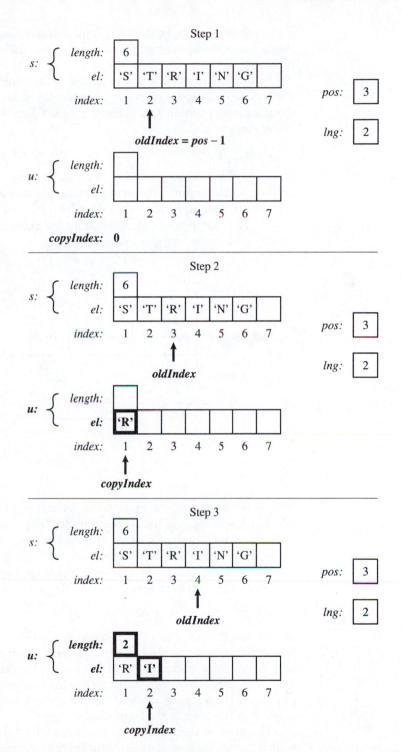

the length *lng*. Similarly, the array implemented *Concat* operation copies *sLng* characters of the second string onto the end of the first and so has complexity $O(sLng)$.

Figure 4.6 shows the action of the procedure call *DeleteString(s, 2, 3)*. With *sLng* = *LengthString(s)* = 9, this call results in the movement of array elements from position *pos* + *lng* = 2 + 3 = 5 to the end of the string, a total of five elements,

$$sLng - (pos + lng) + 1 = sLng - pos - lng + 1 = 9 - 5 + 1 = 5$$

Thus, the *DeleteString* procedure is of linear order, $O(sLng - pos - lng)$, depending on the length of the string and the position and length of the substring. For a short string *s*, little work is done by the computer for a deletion, while a considerable number of statements must be executed to delete a one-element substring from the first of a long string.

Figure 4.6

Action of *DeleteString(s, 2, 3)*

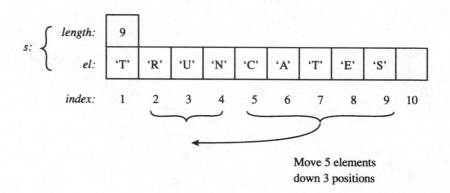

Move 5 elements
down 3 positions

For an array implementation the procedure call *InsertString(sub, s, pos)* also has linear complexity. Ignoring truncation, however, the complexity only depends on the length of *s*, *sLng*, and the position of the insertion, *pos*, not the length of the substring, *lng*. As with deletion, the first phase of the insertion is to move *sLng* − *pos* − *lng* + 1 array elements, but then we must copy into *s* the *lng* number of characters of *sub*. With

$$(sLng - pos - lng + 1) + lng = sLng - pos + 1$$

we see that the complexity of *InsertString* is $O(sLng - pos)$. For a long substring, *sub*, we do not need to move as many array elements to make room for *sub*, but we must install that large number of characters into *s*. (See Figure 4.7.) Thus, the complexity of *InsertString* depends entirely on the length of *s* and the position of the insertion. Insertion at the end of a long string requires much less work than insertion at the beginning.

The most straightforward implementation of the *Position* function is not of linear order. Instead, the complexity of the function reference *Position(sub, s)* is $O(lng \cdot sLng)$, where *lng* is the length of the pattern whose position is to be

Figure 4.7

Action of *Insert-String*(*sub*, *s*, 2)

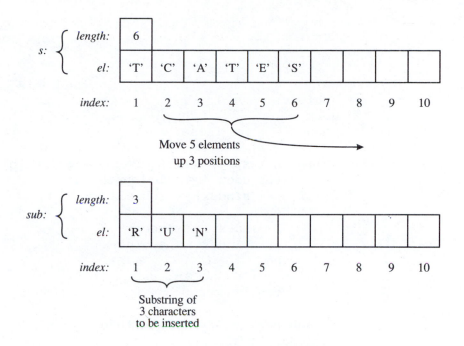

located in *s*, a string of length *sLng*. Figures 4.8 and 4.9 show the search for a pattern *sub* of 3 characters in a string *s* of 10 characters. We begin with each character of *s* (Figure 4.8), marking the starting location and looking for the pattern *sub*. Figure 4.9 illustrates the search for the pattern starting at location 6 with *mark* = 6. As soon as we realize we do not have a match at a position, we back up and start again at the next location after *mark*. Thus, the algorithm requires a maximum of about *lng* · *sLng* = 3 · 10 = 30 comparisons. We do add a condition to stop the *repeat* loop as soon as it is impossible for there to be enough characters left in *s* to match *sub*,

$$(sIndex + sub.length - 1 > s.length)$$

```
{ Function to return the position of sub in s }

function Position (var sub, s: StringType): lengthType;
var
    mark,                           {index of s to mark the
                                     starting}
                                    {position of a
                                     comparison          }
    subIndex,                       {index of sub}
    sIndex      :   IndexType;      {index of s}
    pos         :   LengthType;     {position of sub in s}
    stop        :   boolean;        {boolean variable; becomes true}
                                    {when corresponding elements of}
                                    {s and sub are not equal        }
```

```
begin
    sIndex    := 1;
    pos       := 0;

    repeat                                      {Fig. 4.8}
        subIndex    := 1;
        mark        := sIndex;
        stop        := false;
                                                {Fig. 4.9}
        while (not stop) and (sIndex <= s.length) and
                (subIndex <= sub.length) do
            if s.el[sIndex] = sub.el[subIndex] then
                begin
                    sIndex := sIndex + 1;
                    subIndex := subIndex + 1
                end
            else
                stop := true;

        if subIndex > sub.length then
            pos := mark
        else
            sIndex := mark + 1

    until (pos > 0) or (sIndex + sub.length - 1 > s.length);
    Position := pos
end;        { Position }
```

Some other pattern-matching algorithms have a smaller complexity than the big oh value of $O(lng \cdot sLng)$ for this brute-force approach. One of the advantages of structured programming with data abstraction is that if we find a better algorithm for an operation, we can easily replace one implementation by another without disturbing the rest of the program.

The speed of the pattern match is particularly important for long strings. For example, if we are using a word processor to type a 30-page term paper and need to change every occurrence of "Fig." to "Figure," a slow searching operation can make this simple modification very frustrating indeed.

The **Boyer-Moore string search** is usually a much faster algorithm for the *Position* operation than the one presented above. In an initialization procedure, we establish an array *dist* to associate each character, *ch*, in the character set with its distance from the end of the pattern *sub*. First, for all characters, we assign the length of *sub* to *dist*[*ch*]. Thus, for *sub* = 'POSITION' *dist*['A'] = 8, *dist*['B'] = 8, etc. Then we assign *dist*['P'] = 7, *dist*['S'] = 5, and *dist*['T'] = 3, since they are 7, 5, and 3 places from the end of the substring, respectively. For the repeated letters 'O' and 'I' we take the rightmost occurrence, so that

Figure 4.8

Action of *repeat* loop
in *Position* ('XXY',
'XXXXXXXXXY')

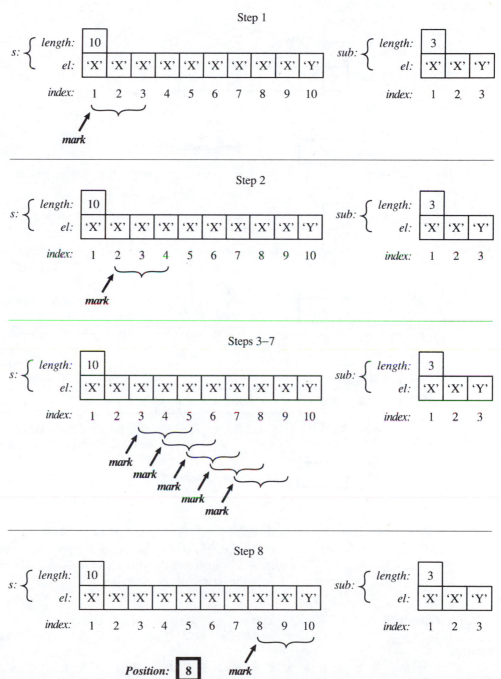

Step 1

Step 2

Steps 3–7

Step 8

Figure 4.9

Action of *while* loop for *mark* = 6 in *Position*('XXY', 'XXXXXXXXXY')

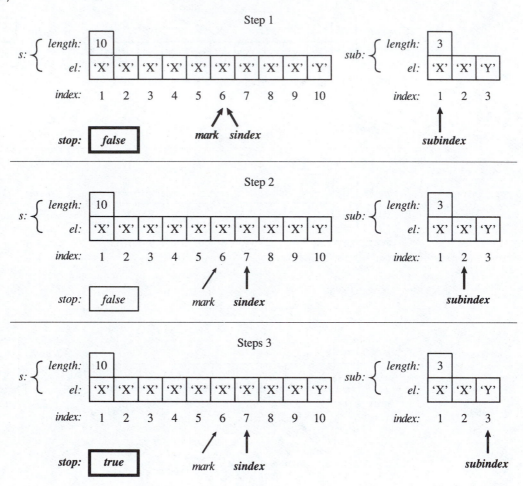

dist['O'] = 1 and *dist*['I'] = 2. We leave *dist*('N') as 8 for this last character in *sub*. For *sub* = 'FUNCTION', where the last character is repeated, we assign 5 to *dist*('N'). Figure 4.10 illustrates the *dist* array for *sub* = 'POSITION' and a character set of only the letters of the alphabet.

Figure 4.10

The array *dist* for *sub* = 'POSITION'

sub.el:	P	O	S	I	T	I	O	N
index:	1	2	3	4	5	6	7	8

dist:	8	8	8	8	8	8	8	8	2	8	8	8	8	8	1	7	8	8	5	3	8	8	8	8	8	8
index:	A	B	C	D	E	F	G	H	I	J	K	L	M	N	O	P	Q	R	S	T	U	V	W	X	Y	Z

In searching for the position of a substring we initialize *mark* to be the length of the substring and start checking at the end of the pattern instead of at the beginning as we did with the brute-force method. If a mismatch is located, we make the assignment

$$mark \leftarrow mark + dist[s.el[mark]]$$

For example, consider *s* = 'UXWVBYQXYZRS' and *sub* = 'XYZ' as in Figure 4.11. The distance values are as noted in *dist* of Step 1 with $dist['X'] = 2$, $dist['Y'] = 1$, and all other distances being 3. Initially, we assign $mark \leftarrow 3$ (Step 2). Since the value of $s.el[3] = 'W'$ does not equal $sub.el[3] = 'Z'$ and $dist['W'] = 3$, we know 'W' does not occur in the pattern *sub*. Moreover, a pattern match will not involve any of the first three characters. Thus, there is no need to make comparisons involving letters appearing before 'W' in *s*. Consequently, in Step 3 we add $dist['W'] = 3$ to *mark* to obtain $mark = 6$, and check the sixth character in *s*. We have $s.el[mark] = 'Y' \neq 'Z'$; but as indicated by $dist['Y'] = 1 < 3$, 'Y' does occur one from the right in *sub*. Therefore, it is possible that the fifth, sixth, and seventh elements of *s.el* could contain 'X', 'Y', and 'Z', respectively. We adjust *mark* by $dist['Y'] = 1$ so that *mark* now is 7 (Step 4). Once more, $s.el[mark]$ is not $sub.el[3]$. Also, this inequality along with $dist['Q'] = 3$ indicates that 'Q' is not in *sub*. Skipping three places, we adjust *mark* to be $mark + dist['Q']$ or $7 + 3 = 10$ (Step 5). At this point we discover a match and return the appropriate starting position for the match. The algorithm for the Boyer-Moore string search follows:

Position(*sub*, *s*) → *pos*
   Position function implemented with the Boyer-Moore string search
   algorithm
Algorithm:
   Initialize the array *dist*
   $mark \leftarrow LengthString(sub)$
   $found \leftarrow false$

   while (not *found*) and ($mark \leq LengthString(s)$) do
      $subIndex \leftarrow LengthString(sub)$
      $sIndex \quad \leftarrow mark$
      while ($s.el[sIndex] = sub.el[subIndex]$) and ($subIndex > 0$) do
         $subIndex \leftarrow subIndex - 1$
         $sIndex \quad \leftarrow sIndex - 1$
      if $subIndex > 0$ then
         $mark \quad \leftarrow mark + dist[s.el[mark]]$
      else
         $found \quad \leftarrow true$

   if *found* then
      $position \leftarrow mark - LengthString(sub) + 1$
   else
      $position \leftarrow 0$

Figure 4.11

Action of the Boyer-Moore string search for substring 'XYZ' in string 'UXWVBYQXYZRS'

Step 1

sub. el:	X	Y	Z
index:	1	2	3

dist:	3	3	3	3	3	3	3	3	3	3	3	3	3	3	3	3	3	3	3	3	3	3	3	<u>2</u>	<u>1</u>	<u>3</u>
index:	A	B	C	D	E	F	G	H	I	J	K	L	M	N	O	P	Q	R	S	T	U	V	W	X	Y	Z

Step 2

dist:	3	2	3	3	3	1	3	2	1	3	3	3
s.el:	U	X	W	V	B	Y	Q	X	Y	Z	R	S
index:	1	2	3	4	5	6	7	8	9	10	11	12

sub.el:	X	Y	Z
index:	1	2	3

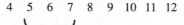

mark

Step 3

dist:	3	2	3	3	3	1	3	2	1	3	3	3
s.el:	U	X	W	V	B	Y	Q	X	Y	Z	R	S
index:	1	2	3	4	5	6	7	8	9	10	11	12

sub.el:	X	Y	Z
index:	1	2	3

mark

Step 4

dist:	3	2	3	3	3	1	3	2	1	3	3	3
s.el:	U	X	W	V	B	Y	Q	X	Y	Z	R	S
index:	1	2	3	4	5	6	7	8	9	10	11	12

sub.el:	X	Y	Z
index:	1	2	3

mark

Step 5

dist:	3	2	3	3	3	1	3	2	1	3	3	3
s.el:	U	X	W	V	B	Y	Q	X	Y	Z	R	S
index:	1	2	3	4	5	6	7	8	9	10	11	12

sub.el:	X	Y	Z
index:	1	2	3

position   *mark*

With the example in Figure 4.11 we compare letters from *sub* with six letters from *s*: 'W', 'Y', 'Q', 'Z', 'Y', 'X'. Using the first algorithm for *Position*, however, there would be 11 comparisons with letters from *s*: 'U', 'X', 'W', 'W', 'V', 'B', 'Y', 'Q', 'X', 'Y', 'Z'. We consider again the speed of those two algorithms and the implementation of the Boyer-Moore search in the exercises.

▽

SECTION 4.2 EXERCISES

Code in Pascal the operations of ADT string listed in Exercises 1–10 using the array implementation (record with length and array) discussed in the text.

1. *MakeStringEmpty*

2. *StringIsEmpty*

3. *StringIsFull*

4. *LengthString*

5. *Concat*

6. *CopySubstring*

7. *DeleteString*

8. *InsertString*

9. *RetrieveChar*

10. *AppendChar*

11. **a.** Write an initialization procedure as part of the implementation of the Boyer-Moore algorithm to assign the substring length to every element of *dist*. Then, for each character *ch* in *sub* except the last, assign the distance of *ch* from the end to *dist*[*ch*].

   b. Implement *Position* using the Boyer-Moore algorithm.

   c. How many comparisons are made of string elements of *s* in Figure 4.11 using the Boyer-Moore search for the substring 'YQ'?

   d. How many comparisons are made of string elements of *s* in Figure 4.11 using the first version of the function *Position* in the text and the substring 'YQ'?

   e. Suppose that for a string *s* of 300 elements and a pattern *sub* of 3 elements, *dist*[*s.el*[mark]] is always 3, and *sub* is not found in *s*. How many string element comparisons will be made by the Boyer-Moore method?

   f. In the situation where *dist*[*s.el*[*mark*]] is always the length of the substring and *sub* is not in *s*, give the complexity of the algorithm in terms of the length of *s* (*sLng*) and the length of *sub* (*lng*).

For Exercises 12−24, code each routine from the referenced exercise or example in Section 4.1 using an implementation with arrays.

12. Procedure *MakeString*(*s*, *c*) of Example 4.1 to make *s* a string with the value of character *c* as its only character.

13. Procedure *DeleteSubstring*(*sub*, *s*, *pos*) of Example 4.2 to delete the first occurrence of the substring *sub* in the string *s* and to return the position of the deletion in *pos*.

14. Procedure *DeleteAllSub*(*sub*, *s*) of Example 4.3 to delete all occurrences of the substring *sub* in the string *s*.

15. Procedure *AppendAsterisks*(*s*) of Exercise 12 to pad string *s* with a maximum of 20 asterisks.

16. Procedure *LineToString* of Exercise 13 to read a line from a text file into a string.

17. Procedure *StringToFile* of Exercise 14 to write a string to a text file.

18. Procedure *Copy*(*s*, *oldpos*, *lng*, *newpos*) of Exercise 15 to make a copy at *newpos* of the substring starting at *oldpos* of length *lng*.

19. Procedure *DeleteToEnd*(*s*, *pos*) of Exercise 16 to delete from *s* the substring starting at position *pos* to the end of *s*. If *pos* is greater than *LengthString*(*s*) or less than 1, *s* is unchanged.

20. Procedure *DeleteToFirst*(*s*, *pos*) of Exercise 17 to delete from *s* the substring starting at the beginning of *s* through position *pos*. If *pos* is greater than *LengthString*(*s*) or less than 1, *s* is unchanged.

21. Procedure *Caps* of Exercise 18 to change every lowercase letter in a string to uppercase.

22. Procedure *Move*(*s*, *oldpos*, *lng*, *newpos*) of Exercise 19 to move in string *s* the substring starting at *oldpos* of length *lng* to *newpos*.

23. Function *SentencePosition*(*s*, *pos*) of Exercise 20 to return the starting location of a sentence that contains position *pos*. Assume two blanks separate sentences and consecutive blanks appear nowhere else.

24. Procedure *DeleteSentence*(*sub*, *s*) of Exercise 21 to delete from *s* the first sentence containing *sub*. Delete from the start of that sentence to the beginning of the next. If *sub* is not found, *s* is not changed. Assume two blanks separate sentences and consecutive blanks appear nowhere else.

25. A common implementation of strings involves packed arrays of characters whose index type is 0..255. The zero-element contains the length of the string encoded as a character. For example, suppose the identifier for the array is *s* and the length of the string is 70. Then *s*[0] contains *chr*(70), which is the letter "F" in ASCII. To obtain the length of the string we find the ordinal value of *s*[0], *ord*(*s*[0]). Since in many computers a character is encoded in 8 bits and since 8 bits can in turn encode integers from 0 to 255, in such a computer a string can have a maximum length of 255. Implement the ADT string using this structure.

SECTION 4.3

String Applications

Countless computer programs employ character strings—a name is read or a title to a report is written, and strings are brought into play. The source code for a program itself is actually a string of characters that can be manipulated with edit commands that echo the ADT string operations. In this section we consider some of these applications of strings.

Example 4.4.

Comparing Strings.

Reports, such as a list of students with grades or products with prices, are often presented so that the elements of a string field, perhaps *name* or *product*, are listed in alphabetical order. In a later chapter we discuss various sorting techniques, but at the heart of any of these methods is the ability to compare two strings lexically. In this example we design a boolean function *LessOrEqual-String(s, u)* that returns *true* if s is the same as u or occurs before u in lexical order.

A computer encoding scheme translates a character, c, to a string of bits. This association dictates an ordering of the characters. In fact, the string of zeros and ones could be interpreted as a decimal number, $ord(c)$, as well. For instance, in the ASCII system, the lowercase letter "a" is encoded as 1100001 with a corresponding decimal, ordinal value of 'a' = 97. The letter "b," next alphabetically, has the next largest ordinal value of ord('b') = 98. Every character has a corresponding ordinal value decreed by the encoding scheme. In the most commonly used systems, ASCII and EBCDIC, lexically larger letters have greater ordinal values. In the ASCII system, character digits such as "3" appear before the capital letters, which are before the lowercase letters, while the reverse is true with EBCDIC. Appendix C contains these encoding schemes.

With the computer we compare two strings, s and u, as we would by hand. We start at the left, comparing strings character by character. As soon as we encounter a difference, the character with the lower ordinal value indicates the string that is lexically smaller. If one string is exhausted before any difference can be found between the two, that string is declared to be less than the other; for example, the word "table" occurs before "tables" in the dictionary. This comparison of characters c and d can be made using the function ord with the boolean expression $(ord(c) \leq ord(d))$. Exercise 25 of Section 2.4 covered the ADT character with basic operations of *StoreChar*, *ord*, and *chr*. In fact, with the Pascal implementation of *char*, we can make a direct comparison without resorting to the function *ord*. Thus, the condition ('a' <= 'b') is *true*, and we can test the relative order of characters with the boolean expression $(c <= d)$.

To isolate elements for the character-by-character comparison, we use the ADT string operation *RetrieveChar*. If we exhaust one string with the loop index, *i*, being greater than *LengthString(s)* or *LengthString(u)*, then we terminate the *while* loop that drives the tests. As illustrated in the comparison of 'IS' and 'I' in Figure 4.12, when $i = 2$ in Step 2, we have $i > 1 = LengthString('I')$. Thus, in Step 3 we assign *LessOrEqualString* the value of the boolean expression (*LengthString*('IS') <= *LengthString*('I')), which is *false*. In this case, the shorter string is the lexically smaller one. Had *s* and *u* been the same string,

Figure 4.12

Action of *LessOrEqualString*('IS', 'I')

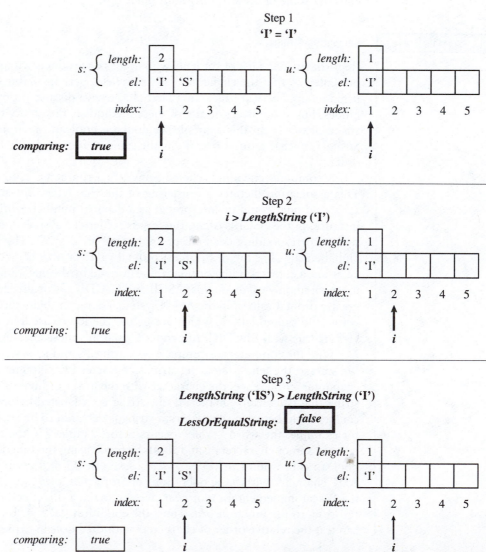

LessOrEqualString would have received a value of *true* because, in fact, the first string would have been lexically less than or equal to the second.

In the character-by-character comparison we also halt the loop, in this case with a boolean variable *comparing* being *false*, if two corresponding characters from *s* and *u* disagree. Then *LessOrEqualString* is *true* or *false* based on whether or not the character from *s* is less than the character from *u*. Figure 4.13 shows the action of *LessOrEqualString*('EAT', 'EBB'). Iteration stops when *i* = 2 with *comparing* ← *false* since the second characters, 'A' and 'B',

Figure 4.13

Action of *LessOrEqual-String*('EAT', 'EBB')

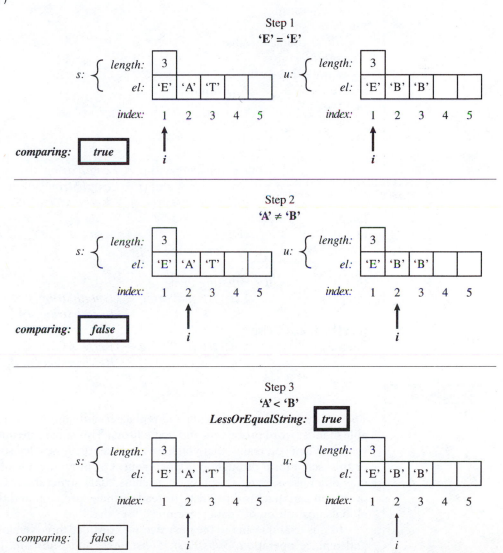

disagree. In this situation *LessOrEqualString* is assigned the value of a boolean expression,

$$LessOrEqualString \leftarrow (RetrieveChar(\text{'EAT'}, 2) \leq RetrieveChar(\text{'EBB'}, 2))$$
$$= (\text{'A'} <= \text{'B'})$$
$$= true$$

Following is the algorithm for this boolean function that systematically compares two strings:

LessOrEqualString(s, u) → b

   Boolean function to return *true* if string *s* appears before string *u* in the ordering of the encoding scheme of the computer being used

Input:

   s, *u* — strings

Output:

   b   — boolean value

Assumptions:

   s and *u* have values.

Figure	**Algorithm**
{4.12–4.13}	
{Step 1}	*comparing* ← *true*
	i ← 1
	while *comparing* and $(i \leq LengthString(s))$
	and $(i \leq LengthString(u))$ do
	if $(RetrieveChar(s, i) = RetrieveChar(u, i))$ then
{Step 2}	*i* ← *i* + 1
{4.13}	else
{Step 2}	*comparing* ← *false*
{4.12}	if *comparing* then
{Step 3}	$LessOrEqualString \leftarrow (LengthString(s) \leq$
	$LengthString(u))$
{4.13}	else
{Step 3}	$LessOrEqualString \leftarrow (RetrieveChar(s, i) \leq$
	$RetrieveChar(u, i))$

Example 4.5.

The ability to find one substring and replace it with another in a string is available in most word processors and text editors. This substitute operation is convenient when you realize that you have consistently misspelled someone's name or misused a term throughout a document. Or, in typing a lengthy paper you may often use a term or expression, such as "data structures." On the original draft you can quickly type "dst" instead of the expression and then perform a global substitution of "data structures" for "dst."

   In this example and in the next two we consider three versions of this find-and-replace operation, *SubstFirst*, *SubstNext*, and *SubstAll*. The procedure

Figure 4.14.

Action of *Update*(*s*, 7, 3, ' the ')

Step 1

new: ' the '   *lng:*   3

s: 'Of all t choices, t first one was t best.'
↑
pos

. . . .

Step 2

new: ' the '   *lng:*   3

s: 'Of all**choices, t first one was t best.'
↑
pos

. . . .

Step 3

new: ' the '   *lng:*   3

s: 'Of all **the choices, t first one was t best.'
↑
pos

call *SubstFirst*(*new, old, s*) changes the value of string *s* with the string *new* substituted for the first occurrence of the substring *old* in *s*. We use the function *Position* to obtain the first position of *old* in *s* and then update *s*.

It is useful to define this update position as a separate operation. The *UpdateString*(*s, pos, lng, new*) procedure is passed the string, *s*; a position, *pos*, at which the update is to occur; the number of characters, *lng*, to remove at location *pos*; and the string *new* to insert at *pos*. Figure 4.14 shows the execution of the procedure call

UpdateString(*s*, 7, 3, ' the '),

for

s = 'Of all t choices, t first one was t best.'

This invocation removes the three characters at position 7, the letter "t" surrounded by blanks, and at that same position places the word "the" with accompanying blanks to give *s* the value

'Of all **the** choices, t first one was t best.'

The design of this procedure follows:

UpdateString(*s, pos, lng, new*)
Procedure to update string *s* at position *pos* by replacing *lng* number of characters with the string *new*. If *pos* is greater than *LengthString*(*s*) or less than 1, *s* is unchanged. If necessary, *s* is truncated to the maximum number of characters it can contain.

Input:

    s, new   — strings

    pos, lng — nonnegative integers

Output:

    s   — revised string

Assumption:

    s is defined.

Figure	**Algorithm**
{4.14}	
{Step 2}	*DeleteString*(*s, pos, lng*)
{Step 3}	*InsertString*(*new, s, pos*)

Figure 4.15

Action of *SubstFirst*
(' the ', ' t ', *s*)

Step 1

old: ' t '   *LengthString*(*old*): 3
new: ' the '

s: 'Of all t choices, t first one was t best.'

. . . .

Step 2

old: ' t '   *LengthString*(*old*): 3
new: ' the '

s: 'Of all t choices, t first one was t best.'
                ↑
               pos

. . . .

Step 3

old: ' t '   *LengthString*(*old*): 3
new: ' the '

s: 'Of all **the choices, t first one was t best.**'
             ↑
           pos

Armed with this update procedure we complete the definition of *Subst-First*. Figure 4.15 illustrates the action of the following design:

SubstFirst(*new, old, s*)

    Procedure to substitute string *new* for the first occurrence of the substring *old* in string *s*. If *old* cannot be found, *s* is not changed. If necessary, the string is truncated to the maximum allowable for *s*.

Input:

    new, old, s — strings

Output:
    s   — revised string
Assumptions:
    new, old, and *s* have values; *old* is not an empty string.

Figure	Algorithm
{4.15}	
{Step 2}	*pos* ← *Position*(*old, s*)
{Step 3}	*UpdateString*(*s, pos, LengthString*(*old*)*, new*)

Example 4.6

Suppose the string *s* is

    'Table t contains t information.'

The first occurrence of the substring ' t ' is not an abbreviation for ' the ' but is the name of the table, *t*. We want the ability to find the next position of the string ' t ' at or beyond location *fromPos* and then update. Thus, a procedure call *SubstNext*(*new, old, s, fromPos*) invokes the *NextPosition* function as well as calling *UpdateString*. Afterwards, *fromPos* advances just beyond where the update occurred. The procedures *SubstNext* and *SubstFirst* are similar, as seen by comparisons of their definitions and actions. (Compare Figures 4.16 and 4.15.)

SubstNext(*new, old, s, fromPos*)
    Procedure to substitute string *new* for the first occurrence of the substring *old* in string *s* at or beyond the location *fromPos* and to update *fromPos*. If *old* cannot be found, *s* is not changed. If necessary, the string is truncated to the maximum allowable for *s*.
Input:
    new, old, s — strings
    fromPos   — nonnegative integer
Output:
    s   — revised string
    fromPos   — revised nonnegative integer
Assumptions:
    new, old, and *s* have values; *old* is not an empty string.

Figure	Algorithm
{4.16}	
{Step 2}	*pos* ← *NextPosition*(*old, s, fromPos*)
	if *pos* > 0 then
{Step 3}	*UpdateString*(*s, pos, LengthString*(*old*)*, new*)
{Step 4}	*fromPos* ← *pos* + *LengthString*(*new*)
	else
	fromPos ← 0

The *NextPosition* function, which is crucial to the *SubstNext* procedure, certainly invokes the *Position* function. *NextPosition*(*sub, s, fromPos*), how-

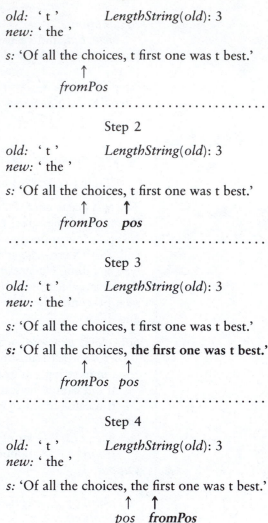

Figure 4.16.

Action of *SubstNext* ('the', 't', *s*, *fromPos*), where *fromPos* = 12

Step 1

old: 't'   LengthString(old): 3
new: 'the'

s: 'Of all the choices, t first one was t best.'
           ↑
        fromPos

Step 2

old: 't'   LengthString(old): 3
new: 'the'

s: 'Of all the choices, t first one was t best.'
           ↑   ↑
        fromPos **pos**

Step 3

old: 't'   LengthString(old): 3
new: 'the'

s: 'Of all the choices, t first one was t best.'

s: 'Of all the choices, **the first one was t best.'**
           ↑   ↑
        fromPos pos

Step 4

old: 't'   LengthString(old): 3
new: 'the'

s: 'Of all the choices, the first one was t best.'
              ↑   ↑
             pos **fromPos**

ever, is to return the position of *sub*, not necessarily from the first of the string, but from position *fromPos*. Thus, we split *s* into two substrings, *first*, storing the substring of *s* up to but not including position *fromPos*, and *last*, storing the substring of *s* from position *fromPos* to the end of *s*. References to the *CopySubstring* procedure with appropriate arguments generate both substrings. The procedure call *CopySubstring(last, s, fromPos, LengthString(s))*, gives *last* the substring of *s* starting at position *fromPos* and containing a maximum of *LengthString(s)* characters. We could use a more precise count of characters as *LengthString(s) − fromPos + 1*, but such accuracy is unwarranted. By the definition of *CopySubstring*, if the end of the string is encountered, the

Figure 4.17.

Action of *NextPosition*
(' t ', *s, fromPos*) with
fromPos = 12

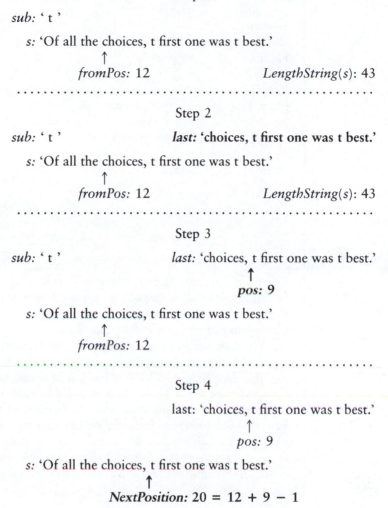

Step 1

sub: ' t '

s: 'Of all the choices, t first one was t best.'

↑

fromPos: 12   *LengthString*(*s*): 43

. . . .

Step 2

sub: ' t '   **last: 'choices, t first one was t best.'**

s: 'Of all the choices, t first one was t best.'

↑

fromPos: 12   *LengthString*(*s*): 43

. . . .

Step 3

sub: ' t '   *last:* 'choices, t first one was t best.'

↑

***pos:* 9**

s: 'Of all the choices, t first one was t best.'

↑

fromPos: 12

. . . .

Step 4

last: 'choices, t first one was t best.'

↑

pos: 9

s: 'Of all the choices, t first one was t best.'

↑

NextPosition: 20 = 12 + 9 − 1

substring to that point is returned. After generating *first* and *last*, with *Position*(*sub, last*) we search the substring *last* for *old*. The resulting position, *pos*, is the location of *sub* in *last*, not in *s*. Thus, we calculate the location in *s* as *pos* + *fromPos* − 1. Of course, if *sub* is not found in *last*, we want to return a value of zero for *NextPosition*. The following definition of *NextPosition* is reflected in the example in Figure 4.17.

NextPosition(*sub, s, fromPos*) → *pos*
Function to return the starting position of the substring *sub* in *s* at or beyond the location *fromPos*. If *sub* cannot be found or if *fromPos* is beyond *LengthString*(*s*), then 0 is returned.

Input:
  sub, s — strings
Output:
  fromPos — positive integer
Figure   **Algorithm**
{4.17}
{Step 2}   *CopySubstring(last, s, fromPos, LengthString(s))*
{Step 3}   *pos ← Position(sub, last)*
             if *pos = 0* then
                  NextPosition ← 0
             else
▲ {Step 4}   *NextPosition ← pos + fromPos − 1*

Example 4.7.

▼ The procedure call *SubstAll(new, old, s)* should substitute *new* for every appearance of the substring *old* in string *s*. If necessary, the string is truncated to the maximum allowable for *s*. We develop a recursive version of this operation, leaving an iterative one for the exercises.

First, we assign to *pos* the position of the pattern *old* in the string *s*. If *old* is located, the string is split into the section before and after the pattern. The variable *last* is assigned the substring of *s* immediately after *old*, while *s* is changed to be the substring before *old*. The value of *new* is then concatenated onto the end of *s*. Using a recursive invocation to *SubstAll*, we revise *last* with *new* replacing every occurrence of the pattern *old*. Once *last* has been completely edited, that string is concatenated onto the end of *s*. Figure 4.18 illustrates the action of this *SubstAll* procedure. We describe the design of this procedure in pseudocode and leave the higher-level design and implementation for the exercises.

SubstAll(*new, old, s*):
Figure   **Pseudocode for Algorithm**
{4.18}
{Step 2}   *pos ←* the position of *old* in *s*
             If *pos > 0* then
{Step 3}   Let *last* get a copy of the substring in *s* after *old*
{Step 4}   Let the value of *s* be changed to be a copy of the substring in
                     s before *old*
{Step 5}   Concatenate *new* onto the end of *s*
{Step 6}   Recursively call *SubstAll* to substitute *new* for every
                     occurrence of *old* in *last*
{Step 7}   Concatenate *last* onto the end of *s*

Figure 4.18.

Action of *SubstAll*(' the ',
' t ', s)

Step 1

new: ' the '   *old:* ' t '   *LengthString*(old): 3
    s: 'Of all t choices, t first one was t best.'   *LengthString*(s):   41

....

Step 2
pos ← *Position*(old, s)

new: ' the '   *old:* ' t '   *LengthString*(old): 3
    s: 'Of all t choices, t first one was t best.'   *LengthString*(s):   41
        ↑
       pos

....

Step 3
CopySubstring(last, s, 10, 41)

s: 'Of all t choices, t first one was t best.'   *LengthString*(s): 41
    ↑
   pos   **last:** 'choices, t first one was t best.'

....

Step 4
CopySubstring(s, s, 1, 6)

s: 'Of all'   **LengthString(s): 6**
last: 'choices, t first one was t best.'

....

Step 5
Concat(s, new)

new: ' the '
    s: 'Of all the '   **LengthString(s): 11**
last: 'choices, t first one was t best.'

....

Step 6
SubstAll(new, old, last)

new: ' the '   *old:* ' t '   *LengthString*(old): 3
    s: 'Of all the '   *LengthString*(s):   11
last: 'choices, the first one was the best.'

....

Step 7
Concat(s, last)

s: 'Of all the choices, the first one was the best.'   **LengthString(s): 47**
▲ *last:* 'choices, the first one was the best.'

▽

SECTION 4.3 EXERCISES

For Exercises 1–7 code the routines in Pascal using an implementation with arrays.

1. *LessOrEqualString* of Example 4.4.

2. Boolean function *InAlphaOrder* to return *true* if an array of names with last name first is in alphabetical order.

3. Procedure *LexLess(s, t, Small)* to return the lexically smaller string *Small*.

4. *UpdateString* of Example 4.5.

5. *SubstFirst* of Example 4.5.

6. *NextPosition* of Example 4.6.

7. *SubstNext* of Example 4.6.

8. a. Write pseudocode with ADT string operations to design *SubstAll* of Example 4.7.
   b. Implement the function in Part a.

9. a. Design a nonrecursive version of *SubstAll* from Example 4.7.
   b. Implement the function in Part a.

10. a. Design a recursive version of *LessOrEqualString* from Example 4.4.
   b. Implement the function in Part a.

11. a. Design a function *CompareStrings(s, t)* to return 1 if $s > u$; 0 if $s = u$; and -1 if $s < u$.
   b. Implement the function in Part a.

▽

PROGRAMMING PROJECTS

1. The AAB company has dealings with a number of other organizations, the names of which are stored in a permanent text file. The president would like a list of those organizations, printed formally without abbreviations such as "Co." for "Company," "Inc." for "Incorporated," "U." for "University," "Inst." for "Institute," and "Lab." for "Laboratory." Write a program that will produce the desired report for the president. Have another text file of abbreviations with corresponding words that can be read into two arrays of strings before processing the file of organizations.

2. A video store has the following information about movies stored in a binary file, sorted by title:

title	— movie title
available	— boolean value that is *true* if at least one copy of the movie is available in the store
rating	— G, PG, R, or X
category	— *comedy, drama, action,* or *SelfHelp*
ShelfNumber	— integer value from 1 to 300 indicating the shelf number where the movie can be found

Write a program to create this binary file from interactive input or from a text file.

Write another program that will provide a lookup function for customers. Read the binary file into an array of records and interactively ask for the manager's password. Repeatedly give the customer a menu of choices:

a. Find a title . . .
b. Find the title(s) that contains . . .
c. Quit (for management use only)

Based on the choice, prompt the customer for all or part of a title. Display the corresponding information indicated by the records, one record at a time. After a record is displayed, give the user the option of seeing the next record if there is one or returning to the main menu. The management wants this program to run all day. Therefore, if someone selects 3, ask for the password to quit. An incorrect password should result in a return to the menu. Be sure to give appropriate prompts and error messages for incorrect choices.

3. Design a line editor for a text file that responds to the following commands:

a. EDIT '*filename*'
Enters edit mode. Causes the file *filename* to be read into an array of strings and initializes *CurrentLine* to be 1. Assume that each line in the file is 80 characters or less. While in edit mode, a prompt of * appears on the screen.

b. *n*
(*n* is a positive integer.) Displays line *n* and changes *CurrentLine* to be *n*.

c. d
Delete the current line.

d. s
Indicates that a substitution is desired on *CurrentLine*. Prompt the user for the string to find, *FindString*, and the replacement string, *ReplaceString*. Then, on the current line change the first occurrence of *FindString* to *ReplaceString*. Display the edited line.

e. i
Indicates that an insertion is desired on *CurrentLine*. Prompt the user for a cursor position. The user should type a number that indicates the char-

acter position for the insertion. A value larger than 80 indicates that the string will be appended onto the end of the line. Next, prompt the user for the string to be inserted.

f. b

Indicates that a line is to be inserted before *CurrentLine*. Prompt the user for this line.

g. r

Indicates that *CurrentLine* should be replaced. Prompt the user for the replacement.

h. t

Type the file on the screen.

i. q

Quit edit mode and save the file.

Be sure to give an error message if a command cannot be interpreted.

4. Some word processors allow the user to employ embedded commands to give instructions on how the document should be printed. Suppose an embedded command must start with a period, appear at the beginning of a line, and be followed by a blank before the actual text. Suppose also that at most one embedded command can appear on a line. Read a text file that includes embedded commands and follow the commands to print the document in the desired format.

Use each of the commands listed below in your text file and produce a document that is at least two pages long.

Commands that must appear at the beginning of the text file:

.Pn	Sets the page length as n printed lines long; $3 \le n \le 50$.
.Sn	Sets the number of spaces between lines; $0 \le n \le 3$.
.Nc	Print the page number in column c, $1 \le c \le 75$.
.T*heading*	Print *heading* as a header centered at the top of each page. The page number should appear on one line and the heading on the next.
.Fn	Have n blank lines after the *heading*, $1 \le n \le 10$.

The following commands can appear in the body of the text:

.C	Center this line.
.Ln	Print n blank lines, $1 \le n \le$ page length.
.In	Indent the following text n spaces, $1 \le n \le 50$.
.Un	Unindent the following text n spaces. There is no change in indentation if not preceded by the embedded indent command.

5

Stacks

Introduction

In Section 2.1 we discussed how recursion is implemented in the computer by use of a run-time stack. An activation record for each invocation of a recursive function to itself is placed or pushed onto the stack until the terminal condition is met. Then, one by one and in reverse order, the references are taken or popped from the stack and appropriate values substituted. Besides employing stacks when executing functions and procedures, many computers and some calculators use stacks to perform arithmetic.

In this chapter we expand our understanding of the stack structure, first defining stack as an abstract data type. If your version of Pascal has a built-in string type, this will be the first data structure we have covered that is not formally implemented on your system. We discuss an implementation with arrays of the ADT operations, postponing one with linked lists until Chapter 8. Finally, we use the ADT operations to develop various applications of stacks.

ADT Stack

A **stack** is an appropriate data structure in situations when the last data placed into the structure is the first processed. The acronym **LIFO** symbolizes the situation—*Last In, First Out;* and the name "stack" itself is descriptive. For example, at a salad bar we typically take the top plate from a stack of salad plates. If the plates are recessed into a spring-loaded receptacle, we only have access to the top plate. For example, we cannot get to the third plate from the top without removing the two above it, one at a time. If we put a plate back, it goes on top of the stack. The pop and push operations are illustrated with a stack of plates in Figure 5.1. The ADT stack definition in Figure 5.2 projects the basic characteristic illustrated with the plates—all activity occurs at the **top** of the stack. The following examples define additional stack operations.

Figure 5.1

Pushing onto and popping from a stack of plates

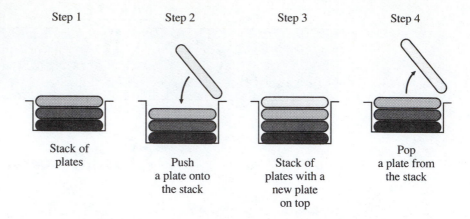

Step 1   Step 2   Step 3   Step 4

Stack of
plates

Push
a plate onto
the stack

Stack of
plates with a
new plate
on top

Pop
a plate from
the stack

Figure 5.2.

Formal definition of ADT stack

ADT Stack

Objects: A finite sequence of elements of the same type, *elType*.

Operations:
    Notation:
      elType — type of an element in the stack
      s   — stack
      e   — item of type *elType*
      b   — boolean value

MakeStackEmpty(*s*)
    Procedure to make *s* empty
StackIsEmpty(*s*) → *b*
    Boolean function to return *true* if *s* is empty
StackIsFull(*s*) → *b*
    Boolean function to return *true* if *s* is full
Push(*s, e*)
    Procedure to place an item with *e*'s value into *s*; assume there is room
    in *s* for this new item
Pop(*s, e*)
    Procedure to take the top item or the last item placed into nonempty *s*
    out of *s* and give its value to *e*; assume *s* is not empty initially

Example 5.1.

▼ In some applications we wish to use the value of the top item on the stack, perhaps for comparison or assignment, but do not want to remove this item from the stack. This *RetrieveStack* procedure involves popping the top item from the stack, assigning that value to a variable, and then pushing the same item once more onto the stack.

Even though *RetrieveStack* can be defined in terms of *Pop* and *Push*, if the operation is to be used frequently in an application, it would be better to consider *RetrieveStack* as one of the basic ADT stack operations. The list of abstract data type operations is not absolute for any data structure and can be logically expanded or contracted to meet the needs of a particular application. Figure 5.3 shows the action of this operation, which is designed below using *Pop* and *Push*.

Figure 5.3

The action of *Retrieve-Stack(s)*

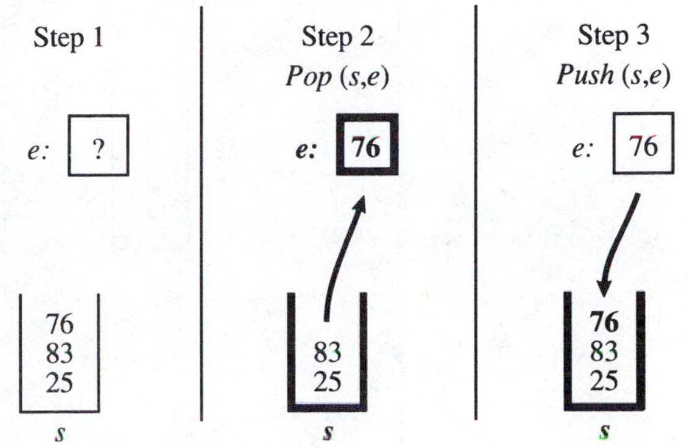

Step 1

Step 2
Pop (s,e)

Step 3
Push (s,e)

$e:$?

$e:$ 76

$e:$ 76

76
83
25

s

83
25

s

76
83
25

s

RetrieveStack(s, e)
   Procedure to assign to *e* the value at the top of the stack, leaving the stack unchanged; assume *s* is not empty
Input:
   s — stack
Output:
   e — value of item at the top of *s*
Assumption:
   s is nonempty.

Figure	Algorithm
{5.3}	
{Step 2}	*Pop(s, e)*
{Step 3}	*Push(s, e)*

Example 5.2.

Suppose the data in a stack *s* are numbers. Design a procedure that replaces the top two elements with their sum. Figure 5.4 illustrates the action of this *Add-Top* procedure. We pop the top element, 7, to be the second operand, and then pop the new top element, 5, to be the first. Afterwards, we push the sum *operand1* + *operand2* = 12 onto the stack.

We assume that *s* is nonempty before calling *AddTop*, but we can only be sure that the stack contains one element. With the basic ADT stack operations, reference is only made to the top of the stack. *StackIsEmpty(s)* being *false* does not give us a clue as to whether *s* has one or a thousand elements. Thus, the

Figure 5.4

Action of *AddTop* proce-
dure on a stack of at least
two numbers

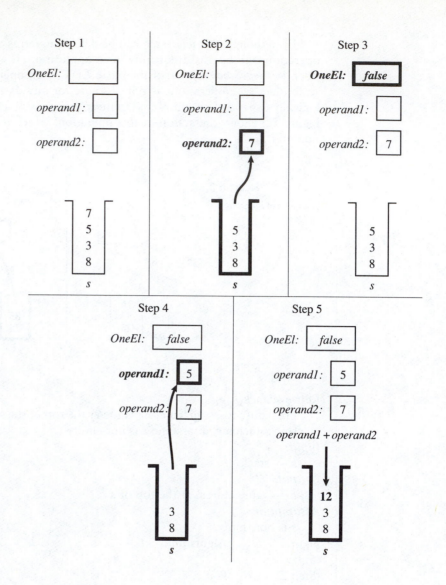

routine *AddTop* must handle the situation where the stack contains exactly
one number. In this case, shown in Figure 5.5, we pop the top and only element; discover that now the stack is empty; and, consequently, replace the element and change a flag, *OneEl*, to be *true*. In Figure 5.4 we have more than
one element, so that *OneEl* is assigned the value *false*.

The pseudocode and ADT stack operations for *AddTop* follow:

AddTop(s, OneEl)
Procedure to replace the top two elements of a nonempty stack, *s*, of
numbers with their sum. If *s* contains only one number, we leave the
stack unchanged.

Figure 5.5

Action of *AddTop* from Example 5.2, where the stack has one element

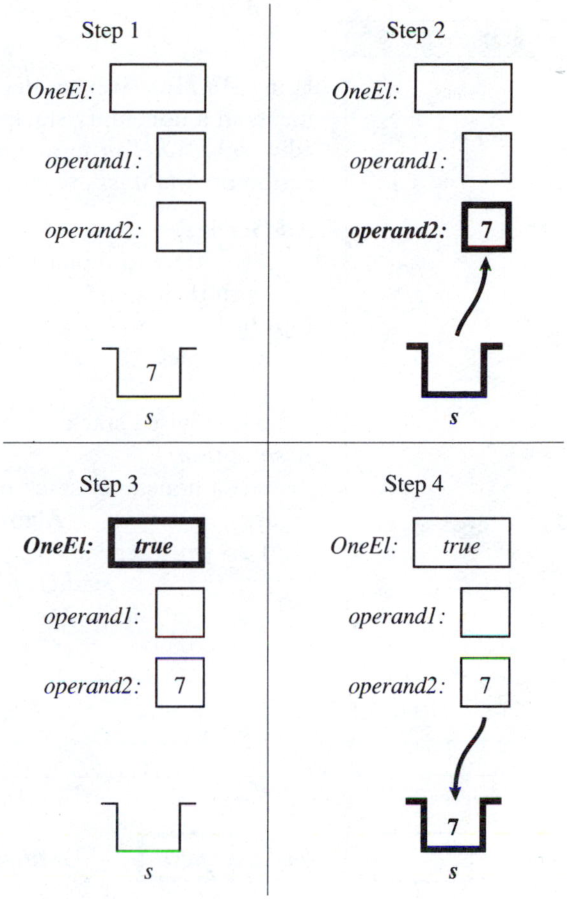

Step 1

OneEl: [ ]

operand1: [ ]

operand2: [ ]

[7]
s

Step 2

OneEl: [ ]

operand1: [ ]

operand2: [**7**]

[ ]
s

Step 3

OneEl: [**true**]

operand1: [ ]

operand2: [7]

[ ]
s

Step 4

OneEl: [true]

operand1: [ ]

operand2: [7]

[7]
s

Input:

    s — stack

Output:

    s — revised stack

    OneEl — boolean variable that becomes *true* when the input stack only has one element

Assumption:

    s is a nonempty stack of numbers.

Figure	Algorithm
{5.4, 5.5}	
{Step 2}	*Pop(s, operand2)*
{5.5}	if *StackIsEmpty(s)* then
{Step 3}	*OneEl ← true*
{Step 4}	*Push(s, operand2)*
{5.4}	else
{Step 3}	*OneEl ← false*
{Step 4}	*Pop(s, operand1)*
{Step 5}	*Push(s, operand1 + operand2)*

Example 5.3.

▼ Using *AddTop*, we can design an operation, *AddStack*, to replace all the elements in a nonempty stack of numbers with their sum. This procedure repeatedly calls *AddTop* until *OneEl* is *true*. Figure 5.6 shows an example of the action of *AddStack*, whose design follows:

AddStack(s)
　　Procedure to replace the elements of a nonempty stack, s, of numbers
　　with their sum
Input:
　　s — stack
Output:
　　s — revised stack
Assumption:
　　s is a nonempty stack of numbers.

Figure	**Algorithm**
{5.6}	repeat
	AddTop(s, *OneEl*)
	until *OneEl*

Figure 5.6

Action of *AddStack*

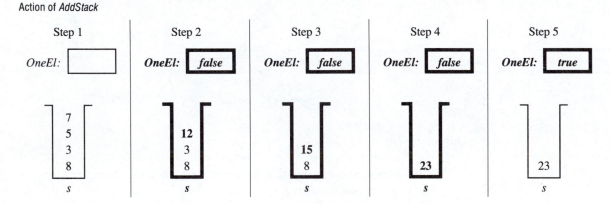

▲

Example 5.4.

▼ In this example we design a recursive procedure *PrintStackUp* to print the elements of a stack from bottom to top, leaving the stack unchanged when execution is complete. *StackIsEmpty*(s) is the terminal condition because there is nothing to print in an empty stack. When the stack has at least one element, we pop the top element, *e*. Before proceeding we recursively call *PrintStackUp* to print the remainder of the stack from bottom to top. With those elements writ-

Figure 5.7

Action of *PrintStackUp(s)*
from Example 5.4

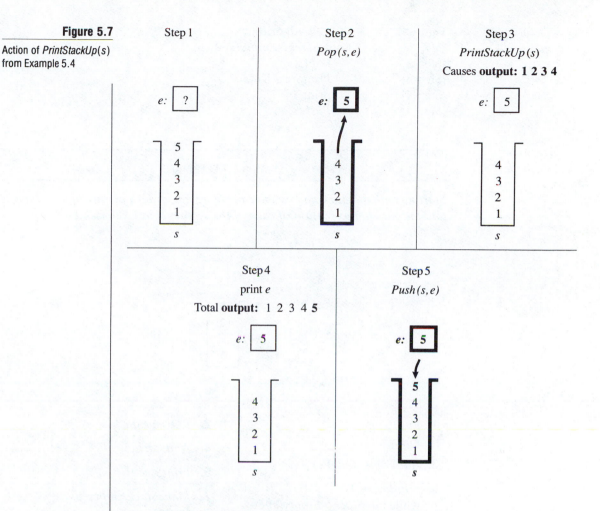

Step 1

Step 2
Pop(s, e)

Step 3
PrintStackUp(s)
Causes **output: 1 2 3 4**

Step 4
print *e*
Total **output:** 1 2 3 4 **5**

Step 5
Push(s, e)

ten in the desired order, we can print the value of *e* and push *e* back onto the stack. The value of this top element is recorded only after all the elements beneath it have been printed. Thus, the output lists the elements of the stack from bottom to top. Figure 5.7 demonstrates the action of this *PrintStackUp* procedure, the design of which follows:

PrintStackUp(s)
   Procedure to print the elements of a stack from bottom to top, leaving
   the stack unchanged
Input:
   s — stack
Output:
   Elements of *s* printed from bottom to top
Assumption:
   s exists.

Figure	Algorithm
{5.7}	if not *StackIsEmpty*(*s*) then
{Step 2}	*Pop*(*s*, *e*)
{Step 3}	*PrintStackUp*(*s*)
{Step 4}	print *e*
{Step 5}	*Push*(*s*, *e*)

SECTION 5.1 EXERCISES

Starting with the stack and variable in Figure 5.8, draw a picture of any changes and output after execution of each of the segments in Exercises 1–7.

Figure 5.8

Stack *s* and variable *e* for Exercises 1–7

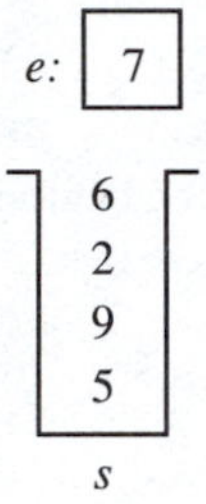

e: 7

6
2
9
5

s

1. *Push*(*s*, *e*)
  Push(*s*, *e*)

3. *AddTop*(*s*, *OneEl*)

6. *product* ← 1
  while not *StackIsEmpty*(*s*) do
      Pop(*s*, *e*)
      product ← *product* ∗ *e*
  Push(*s*, *product*)

2. *RetrieveStack*(*s*, *e*)

4. *AddStack*(*s*)

5. *PrintStackUp*(*s*)

7. *MakeStackEmpty*(*u*)
  Push(*u*, *e*)
  Pop(*s*, *e*)
  Push(*u*, *e* ∗ *e*)

8. The following appeared in the sample questions of the *1984 AP Computer Science Examination**:

Suppose an input list consists of the numbers 1, 2, 3, 4, 5, 6 and there are three operations that can be performed, using only one stack *S*:

  i. Copy next input to output list.
  ii. Push next input onto *S*.
  iii. Pop *S* and output the popped integer.

*AP question selected from *AP Computer Science Examination*, 1984. Reprinted by permission of Educational Testing Service, the copyright owner of the sample questions.

Which of the following is NOT a possible output list that could be achieved using these operations?

(A) 1 2 3 4 5 6
(B) 6 5 4 3 2 1
(C) 2 4 6 5 3 1
(D) 3 4 5 6 1 2
(E) 1 2 5 6 4 3

9. Suppose input, consisting of the integers 1, 2, and 3 in that order, is pushed onto a stack *s*. Only when a number is popped from the stack is it written. If possible, with appropriate pushes and pops show how to print each of the following permutations of the input stream.

a. 1 2 3   ***b.*** 1 3 2   **c.** 2 1 3
d. 2 3 1   **e.** 3 1 2   **f.** 3 2 1

Using pseudocode and ADT stack operations and notation, define the operations in Exercises 10–28. Also, answer any other questions about the operations.

10. Procedure *SwapStack* to exchange the top two elements on a stack.

11. a. Procedure *Dup* to duplicate the top element on a stack.
b. What is the complexity of *Dup*?

12. Procedure *SaveVariables* to save the values of variables x, y, and z by placing them onto an existing stack, *s*. The process of storing the local variables is handled by the operating system before a call to another routine. When writing in an assembly language, the programmer is responsible for saving these values.

13. Procedure *RestoreVariables* to recover the values saved by *SaveVariables* of Exercise 12.

14. a. Procedure *ClearStack* to remove all the elements from a stack.
b. Write an invariant for the loop.
c. Using program verification, prove this loop is correct.

15. a. Procedure *FileToStack* to read from a line of a file of integers and place each datum in a stack. Assume the file pointer initially indicates the first element of a line of the file.
b. What is the complexity of *FileToStack*?
c. Write an invariant for the loop.
d. Using program verification, prove this loop is correct.

16. Procedure *PrintStack* to print the elements in a stack from top to bottom, leaving the stack empty.

17. Procedure to print data from a file of integers in reverse order. Use *FileToStack* and *PrintStack* from Exercises 15 and 16, respectively.

18. Recursive procedure *Append*(*s, u*) to append a stack *u* on top of stack *s* so that *u*'s top element is on the top. The procedure should cause *u* to be empty.

19. Nonrecursive version of procedure *PrintStackUp* from Example 5.4 to print the elements of a stack from bottom to top.

20. a. Nonrecursive procedure *NRCopyStack* to make a copy of a stack.
b. Design a recursive version of *NRCopyStack* from Part a.

21. a. Procedure *Bottom* to place the bottom element of the stack *s* into *e*, making *s* empty.
b. Write an invariant for the loop.
c. Using program verification, prove this loop is correct.

22. Recursive version of *AddStack* from Example 5.3.

23. a. Procedure *AddStack2* that is a revision of *AddStack* of Example 5.3. *AddStack2* initializes *sum* to be 0; pops the elements from the stack, accumulating their sum in *sum*; and then pushes the value of *sum* onto the stack. For *AddStack2* the stack can be empty initially.
b. What is the total number of statements executed (incuding those of *AddTop*) with *AddStack* for a stack of *n* elements?
c. What is the complexity of *AddStack*?
d. What is the total number of statements executed with *AddStack2* for a stack of *n* elements?
e. What is the complexity of *AddStack2*?

24. Procedure *AddStack3* that first checks that the stack is not empty before calling *AddStack2* of Exercise 23. An error-handling procedure should be called for an empty initial stack, and a sum of 0 returned by *AddStack3*.

25. Procedure *AddStack4*, a recursive version of *AddStack2* from Exercise 23.

26. a. Procedure *DeleteStack* to delete an item *e* from a stack *s*, leaving the stack otherwise unchanged; assume *e* is in the stack
b. Revise the procedure in Part a to handle the situation of *e* not being in *s*.

27. Procedure *RemoveBlanks* to remove all blanks from a stack of characters, leaving the stack otherwise unchanged.

28. a. Nonrecursive boolean function *EqualStack* to return *true* if two stacks are identical, ordered in the same way. The function should leave the stacks unchanged.
b. Recursive version of *EqualStack* from Part a.

29. In Exercise 26 of Section 2.1 we discussed how to convert a positive decimal integer to a binary number by repeatedly dividing by 2 and printing the remainders in reverse order. Using a stack to store the remainders, design a nonrecursive version of this procedure.

Array Implementation of Stacks

As with many data structures, a stack can be implemented with an array or with a linked list. For the former we will use a record with two main fields; one is the index of the top element in the stack and the other is the array itself. The creation of such a structure follows:

```
const
    MaxNumEls  = . . . . . . . . . . ;

type
    IndexType  = 1..MaxNumEls;
    elType     = . . . . . . . . . . ;
    stack      = record
        top    : 0..MaxNumEls;
        el     : array [IndexType] of elType
    end;

var
    s : stack;
    e : elType;
```

The bottom element of a stack will be the first element of the array, *s.el*[1]; the top item is at the other end of the array, the array item whose index is *s.top*, *s.el*[*s.top*]. Figure 5.9 pictures a stack along with its storage in such a record.

Figure 5.9

Stack along with its implementation with an array

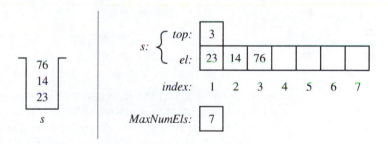

Notice that *s.top* is of type 0..*MaxNumEls*, and the array indices begin at 1. The zero value for *top* is used to indicate an empty stack as demonstrated in Figure 5.10. Thus, the *MakeStackEmpty* procedure consists of a simple assignment.

```
{ Procedure to make the stack s empty }

procedure MakeStackEmpty (var s: stack);
begin                                          { Figure 5.10 }
    s.top := 0
end;
```

Figure 5.10

Empty stack along with its implementation with an array

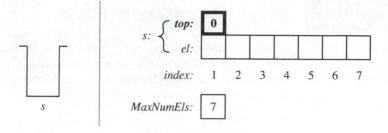

Moreover, the boolean function *StackIsEmpty(s)* tests whether *top* is equal to zero.

```
{ Boolean function to return true if the stack s is empty }

function StackIsEmpty (var s : stack): boolean;
begin
    StackIsEmpty := (s.top = 0)
end;
```

This array implementation pushes to and pops from the end of the array because insertions and deletions are easier there. As shown in Figure 5.11, insertion of *e* at the end consists of incrementing *s.top* to point to the next element and then assigning *e* to that element.

```
{ Procedure to push an element, e, onto a stack, s }

procedure Push (var s: stack; e: elType);
begin                                   { Figure 5.11 }
    s.top          := s.top + 1;        { Step 2 }
    s.el [s.top] := e                   { Step 3 }
end;
```

Had we placed the top at the first array element, pushing an element onto the stack would require that we move all other elements in the array to make room for the addition. This time-consuming process has complexity $O(n)$ for *n* stack items. Insertion at the end, however, is of the order $O(1)$, taking a constant amount of time regardless of the number of elements.

As with all array insertions, we must be careful not to add an element to an already full array. An array reference beyond the maximum allowable index results in an OUT-OF-RANGE error. Thus, in most applications before we push, we check with *StackIsFull* that there is room in the array. If the array is full, typically we call an error-handling procedure, as the following segment does:

```
if StackIsFull (s) then
    StackFullError
else
    Push (s, e)
```

Figure 5.11

Action of *Push*(*s, e*) on a stack along with its implementation with an array

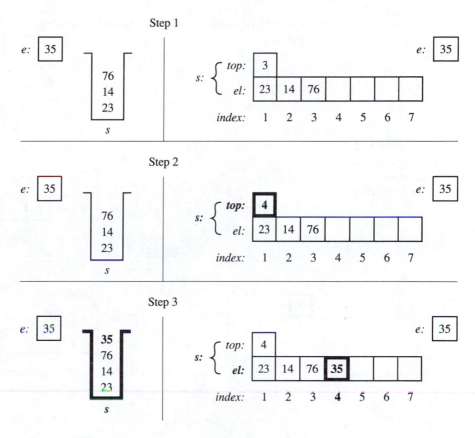

This error-handling procedure, *StackFullError*, might print an error message and then cause termination of the program. The *StackIsFull* function, with its check for a full stack, tests if the index *s.top* is equal to the maximum possible index, *MaxNumEls*, of the array.

```
{ Boolean function to return true if the stack is full }
```

```
function StackIsFull (var s: stack): boolean;
begin
    StackIsFull := (s.top = MaxNumEls)
end;
```

Pop performs the reverse process of the operation *Push*, placing the value at the top of the stack into *e* and then decrementing the *top* by 1. Figure 5.12 illustrates this process, coded below:

```
{ Procedure to pop an element from a stack, s,
    and place the value in e }
```

```
procedure Pop (var s: stack; var e: elType);
begin                                    { Figure 5.12 }
    e      := s.el [s.top];              { Step 2 }
    s.top := s.top - 1                   { Step 3 }
end;
```

Figure 5.12

Action of *Pop* operation on a stack along with its implementation with an array

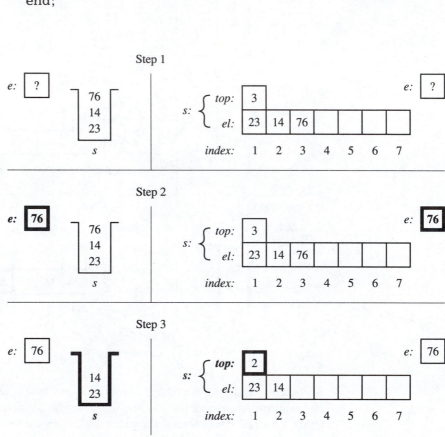

Now, instead of worrying about being full, before calling push, we must be sure the stack *s* is not already empty. If *StackIsEmpty(s)* is *true* with an *s.top* value of zero, we usually call another error-handling routine using a segment such as:

```
if StackIsEmpty(s) then
    StackEmptyError
else
    Pop(s, e)
```

Figure 5.13 shows a summary of the array implementation of ADT stack.

Figure 5.13.

Array implementation of ADT stack

An Array Implementation of ADT Stack

Create a stack, *s*, with each element of type *elType* and with a maximum of *MaxNumEls* number of elements.

```
const
   MaxNumEls = ...........;
type
   IndexType = 1..MaxNumEls;
   elType    = ...........;
   stack     = record
      top    : 0..MaxNumEls;
      el     : array [IndexType] of elType
   end;
var
   s : stack;
   e : elType;
```

***MakeStackEmpty*(*s*)**

```
procedure MakeStackEmpty (var s: stack);
begin
   s.top := 0
end;
```

StackIsEmpty*(*s*) → *b

```
function StackIsEmpty (var s : stack): boolean;
begin
   StackIsEmpty := (s.top = 0)
end;
```

StackIsFull*(*s*) → *b

```
function StackIsFull (var s: stack): boolean;
begin
   StackIsFull := (s.top = MaxNumEls)
end;
```

***Push*(*s, e*)**

```
procedure Push (var s: stack; e: elType);
begin
   s.top        := s.top + 1;
   s.el [s.top] := e
end;
```

***Pop*(*s, e*)**

```
procedure Pop (var s: stack; var e: elType);
begin
   e     := s.el [s.top];
   s.top := s.top - 1
end;
```

For Exercises 1–22, code each routine from the referenced exercise or example in Section 5.1 using an implementation with arrays.

1. a. Procedure *RetrieveStack* of Example 5.1 to obtain the top value on the stack.
  b. Implement *RetrieveStack* without a push and a pop but with an array reference.

2. Procedure *AddTop* of Example 5.2 to pop the top two elements and push their sum onto the stack.

3. Procedure *SwapStack* from Exercise 10 to exchange the top two elements on a stack.

4. Procedure *Dup* from Exercise 11 to duplicate the top element on a stack.

5. Procedure *SaveVariables* from Exercise 12 to save the values of variables x, y, and z by placing them onto a stack.

6. Procedure *RestoreVariables* from Exercise 13 to recover the values saved by *SaveVariables*.

7. Procedure *ClearStack* from Exercise 14 to remove all the elements from a stack.

8. Procedure *FileToStack* from Exercise 15 to read from a line of a text file and place each character in a stack.

9. Procedure *PrintStack* from Exercise 16 to print the elements in a stack from top to bottom.

10. Procedure from Exercise 17 to print data from a file in reverse order.

11. Recursive procedure *Append(s, u)* from Exercise 18 to append a stack u on top of stack s so that u's top element is on the top. The procedure should cause u to be empty.

12. Recursive procedure *PrintStackUp* from Example 5.4 to print the elements of a stack from bottom to top.

13. Nonrecursive version of *PrintStackUp* from Exercise 19.

14. a. Nonrecursive procedure *NRCopyStack* from Exercise 20a to make a copy of a stack.
  b. Recursive version of *NRCopyStack* from Exercise 20b.

15. Procedure *Bottom* from Exercise 21 to place the bottom element of the stack s into e, making s empty.

16. Recursive version of *AddStack* from Exercise 22.

17. Procedure *AddStack2* from Exercise 23 that initializes *sum* to be 0; pops the elements from the stack, accumulating their sum in *sum*; and then pushes the value of *sum* onto the stack.

18. Procedure *AddStack3* from Exercise 24 that first checks that the stack is not empty before calling *AddStack2*.

19. Procedure *AddStack4* from Exercise 25 that is a recursive version of *AddStack2*.

20. Procedure *DeleteStack* from Exercise 26 to delete an item *e* from a stack *s*, leaving the stack otherwise unchanged; assume *e* is in the stack.

21. Procedure *RemoveBlanks* from Exercise 27 to remove all blanks from a stack of characters.

22. Boolean function *EqualStack* from Exercise 28a to return *true* if two stacks are identical, ordered in the same way. The procedure should leave the stacks unchanged.

SECTION 5.3 Applications of Stacks

Stacks are used extensively, from storage of values and return location upon a procedure call, to evaluation of arithmetic expressions, to a technique for computer game theory. We consider some of these applications in this section.

Example 5.5 **Removal of Recursion.**

Recall from Section 2.1 that we demonstrated how recursion is implemented with stacks. In Section 2.2 we pointed out that many routines can be developed naturally with recursion, but that a recursive task usually takes more time and space than a nonrecursive counterpart. In fact, in a recursive call for a large value of an argument we may obtain a STACK-OVERFLOW error message, indicating that the run-time stack is full. We can, however, simulate recursion iteratively by implementing our own stack. Usually an iterative routine executes faster than the recursive one and, presumably, a user-defined stack can grow larger than the fixed-size run-time stack.

Consider the *factorial* function of Section 2.1:

```
{ Function to evaluate n-factorial recursively.
  Assumption: n is a nonnegative integer          }

function factorial (n: NonNeg): real;
begin
   if n = 0 then
      factorial := 1
   else
      factorial := n * factorial (n - 1)
end;
```

In Figure 2.4 we showed the stack of function references and returns for *factorial*(4). At Step 4 the stack is as in Figure 5.14. Actually, we are stacking the values for *n*—4, 3, 2, 1—until we get to the terminal case *factorial*(0) ← 1. Then we start substituting into the statement

$$factorial(n) = n * factorial(n - 1)$$

The values of *n*, popped from the stack, are multiplied times the last evaluation of the *factorial* function, *factorial*(*n* − 1). The action of building the stack of values of *n* and then substituting back is illustrated in Figure 5.15 with the variable *Afactorial* containing the accumulated value of the factorial.

Figure 5.14

Stack of function references for *factorial*(4) from Figure 2.4

Step 4

factorial(1) ← 1 * *factorial*(0)
factorial(2) ← 3 * *factorial*(1)
factorial(3) ← 3 * *factorial*(2)
factorial(4) ← 4 * *factorial*(3)

We keep pushing and decrementing *n* until *n* is 0, the terminal condition. Then we assign *Afactorial* the terminal value 1. Afterwards, we continue assigning to *Afactorial* the product of the popped value of *n* and previous value of *Afactorial* until the stack is empty.

We do, however, need to be careful that we are not attempting to push a value onto a full stack. If *StackIsFull*(*s*) becomes *true* before *n* becomes 0, we terminate the stack-building process, call an error-handling procedure to print an error message and to empty the stack or to halt, and return some erroneous value for *factorial*, such as −1. The factorial function with simulated recursion follows:

```
{Function to evaluate n-factorial with simulated recursion.
    Assumption: n is a nonnegative integer                    }

function factorial (n: NonNeg): real;
var
    s         : stack;
    Afactorial : real;

begin                                              {Figure 5.15}
    {*** Build stack of values of n ***}
    MakeStackEmpty (s);                            {Step 1}

    while (n > 0) and (not StackIsFull(s)) do      {Steps 2-9}
        begin
            Push (s, n);                           {Steps 2, 4, 6, 8}
            n := n - 1                             {Steps 3, 5, 7, 9}
        end; {while}
```

Figure 5.15

Values of *n* stacked and
then popped for the
evaluation of 4-factorial

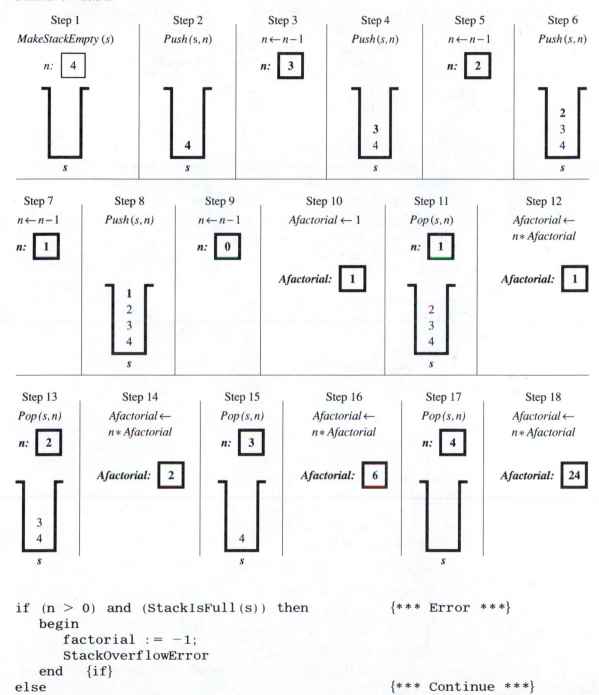

```
if (n > 0) and (StackIsFull(s)) then          {*** Error ***}
   begin
      factorial := -1;
      StackOverflowError
   end   {if}
else                                          {*** Continue ***}
```

```
      begin
         {*** Terminal case ***}                    {Step 10}
         Afactorial := 1;

         {*** Build factorial from stack ***}       {Steps 11-18}
         while not StackIsEmpty (s) do
            begin
               Pop (s, n);                           {Steps 11, 13, 15, 17}
               Afactorial := n * Afactorial          {Steps 12, 14, 16, 18}
            end; {while}
         factorial := Afactorial
      end {else}
end;
```

This technique is useful for simulating a recursive function or procedure in which there is only one reference or call of the routine to itself, such as illustrated in the following recursive function form:

```
{ Form of a recursive function that can be readily converted
  to a nonrecursive function using a stack }

function RecFnc ( n: integer ): ...........;
begin
   if TerminalCondition(n) then
      RecFnc := TerminalValue(n)
   else
      begin
         PreStatements(n);
         RecFnc := RecFnc( f(n) );
         PostStatements(n)
      end {else}
end;
```

TerminalCondition(n) is the terminal condition, such as ($n = 0$). *TerminalValue*(n) is the value of the function when the terminal condition is *true*, e.g., *factorial* := 1. *PreStatements*(n) are the statements, if any, executed before the recursive reference of the function to itself. In the case of the recursive *factorial* function, there are no prestatements. For simplicity, we separate the recursive reference of *factorial* from the expression. Thus,

```
factorial := n * factorial(n - 1)
```

can be written as two statements:

```
Afactorial := factorial(n - 1);
Afactorial := n * Afactorial
```

In the recursive reference, $f(n)$ means a function of n, often ($n - 1$). *PostStatements*(n) are the statements, if any, executed after the recursive call, e.g., *Afac-*

torial := *n* * *Afactorial*. Again, in building we must be careful to handle a situation in which the stack is full.

As in the nonrecursive version of *factorial* above, to simulate the recursion we define a nonrecursive alternative to *RecFnc* as follows:

```
{ Simulation of recursion in function RecFnc with a stack }

function SimRecFnc ( n: integer ): ...........;
var
    s          : stack;
    LocalRecFnc : ..........;

begin
    {*** Build stack ***}
    MakeStackEmpty(s);
    while (not TerminalCondition(n)) and (not StackIsFull(s)) do
        begin
            PreStatements(n);
            Push(s, n);
            n := f(n)
        end;    {while}

    if (not TerminalCondition(n)) and StackIsFull(s) then
        begin                                      {*** Error ***}
            SimRecFnc := ErrorValue;
            StackOverflowError
        end    {if}
    else                                         {*** Continue ***}
        begin
            {*** Terminal case ***}
            LocalRecFnc := TerminalValue(n);
            {*** Build value of function from stack ***}
            while not StackIsEmpty(s) do
                begin
                    Pop(s, n);
                    PostStatements(n)
                end;    {while}
            SimRecFnc := LocalRecFnc
        end {else}
end;
```

▲

| Example 5.6. | **Postfix Notation.** |

▼ The familiar way of writing an arithmetic expression, such as *A* + *B*, is called **infix notation**. The binary operation + is placed between the two operands, *A* and *B*. The same expression can be written in **postfix notation** as *A B* +. Some calculators require that the expression be entered in postfix form, and some computers accept infix form but convert the expression to postfix notation before execution.

The stack-oriented language FORTH uses postfix notation, such as 4 3 5 + *, for expressions. The story goes that Charles Moore, its creator, wanted to call the new language FOURTH to indicate that it was a fourth-generation language. The computer system he was using, however, allowed only five-character names, hence the shortened, but meaningful, name FORTH.

When the expression is in postfix notation, such as $A \ B +$, during execution the operands are pushed onto the stack as the expression is read from left to right. When an operator such as + is encountered, the top two items are popped from the stack; the binary operation is evaluated; and the result is pushed onto the stack. For example, suppose $A = 5$ and $B = 3$. Figure 5.16 demonstrates the execution of $A \ B +$. Notice that when the two numbers are popped, the top number, 3, is stored in the second operand, *operand2*, while the number beneath it, 5, is eventually placed into *operand1*. With the proper order established, the answer *operand1* + *operand2* = 5 + 3 = 8 is pushed onto the stack.

Figure 5.17 shows the stack during evaluation of the postfix expression $A \ B \ C + D * -$ with $A = 5$, $B = 3$, $C = 1$, and $D = 2$. We first evaluate $3 + 1 = 4$ or $B + C$; then we compute $4 * 2 = 8$ or $(B + C) * D$; finally, we have $5 - 8 =$

Figure 5.16

Stack used in evaluation of postfix expression $A \ B +$ with $A = 5$ and $B = 3$

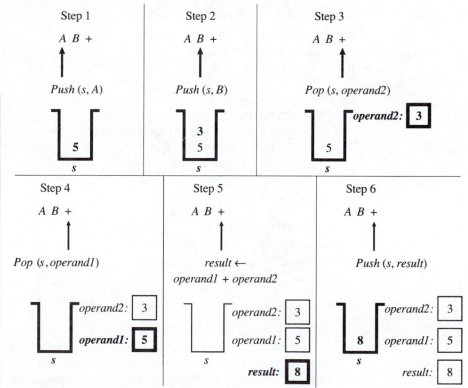

Figure 5.17

Stack used in evaluation of
postfix expression
$A\ B\ C + D * -$ with
$A = 5$, $B = 3$, $C = 1$,
and $D = 2$

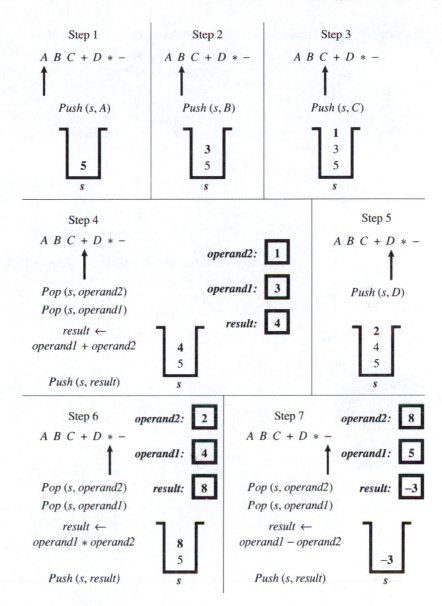

−3 or the expression $A - (B + C) * D$ in infix notation. Thus, the postfix expression $A\ B\ C + D * -$ is equivalent to the infix expression $A - (B + C) * D$. One tremendous advantage of postfix notation is that parentheses are unnecessary. For this infix expression, however, parentheses are essential. Since the operator $*$ has a higher priority than $+$, without parentheses, as in $A - B + C * D$, the product $C * D$ would be performed before addition of B. A routine to use a stack to convert expressions from postfix to infix notation is covered in the exercises.

Example 5.7.

Converting Infix Notation to Postfix.

▼

We can also use stacks to take an expression from its infix form to postfix notation. Before considering this conversion, recall that operator precedence means that ∗ and / have higher priority than + and −; that is, for $7 + 3 * 2$, $3 * 2$ is evaluated as 6 and then the result is added to 7. When two operations with the same priority are present, as in $12 / 3 * 2$, the operations are evaluated from left to right. First we calculate $12 / 3$ as 4, then $4 * 2$ as 8. Of course, parentheses overcome the natural operator priority.

In postfix and infix notation the operands appear in the same order. Moreover, in postfix notation the operator always appears after its operands. Thus, in converting the infix expression $A − (B + C) * D$ we move from left to right, recording the operands in order. When the minus operator, left parenthesis, and plus operator are encountered, we push them onto an operator stack as shown in Figure 5.18.

Upon finding the right parenthesis,), we pop and record all operators to the left parenthesis, (, because parentheses surrounding an expression override the usual operator priority. The left parenthesis is then popped and thrown away because parentheses are not used in postfix notation. (See Figure 5.19.)

Figure 5.18

First part of the conversion of the infix expression $A − (B + C)*D$ to postfix using an operator stack

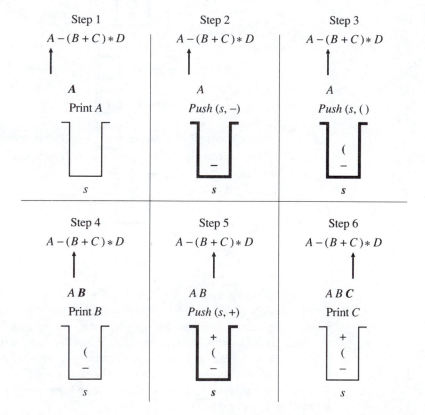

Figure 5.19

Continuation from Figure 5.18 of the conversion of the infix expression $A - (B + C)*D$ to postfix; upon finding the right parenthesis, pop and record all operators to the left parenthesis, then pop(

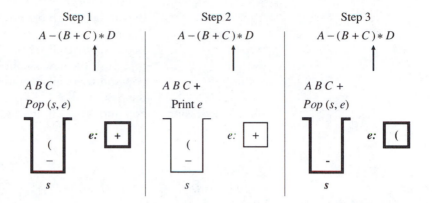

The next operator, $*$, has greater priority than the operator on the stack, $-$, so we also push $*$ onto the stack. We want to evaluate the product before the difference, and the last in, first out characteristic of stacks guarantees that multiplication will be performed first.

Had any operators with equal or higher precedence been on top, we would have popped, written them, and pushed the new operator onto the stack. For example, suppose the expression were $A / (B + C) * D$, with division in place of the subtraction of the example. In this case, the division operator / would be on the stack when the multiplication operator $*$ was encountered. Because division shares equal priority with multiplication and because the symbol / appears to the left of $*$ in the expression, we want to pop and write / and then push $*$, indicating that division is to occur before multiplication. This order corresponds to the way equal priority of operators is resolved for most cases (except two exponentiations) in mathematics and in the majority of programming languages: When two operators have the same precedence, the one on the left is evaluated first. (It is interesting that the computer language APL has an order of priority that deviates significantly from that of mathematics and Pascal, namely, all operations have the same precedence and expressions are evaluated from right to left, except when overridden by parentheses.)

In the present example, $A - (B + C) * D$, after recording D, we come to the end of the expression. Finally, the operators on the stack are popped and recorded as in Figure 5.20.

The algorithm for conversion from infix to postfix notation for an expression with operators chosen from $+$, $-$, $*$, and / follows:

Initialize an operator stack, s.
While not at the end of the infix expression do the following:
    Read the next symbol.
    In case the symbol is

        An operand   : Write the operand
        '('   : Push '(' onto s

')'	: Pop and write all operators until encountering '(', then pop '('
'*' or '/'	: Pop and write all '*' and '/' operators from the top; push the new symbol ('*' or '/')
'+' or '−'	: Pop and write all operators from the top; push the new symbol ('+' or '−')
end-of-expression	: Pop and write all operators

Figure 5.20

Continuation from Figure 5.19 of the conversion of the infix expression $A - (B + C) * D$ to postfix; push *, print D, pop and print *, pop and print −

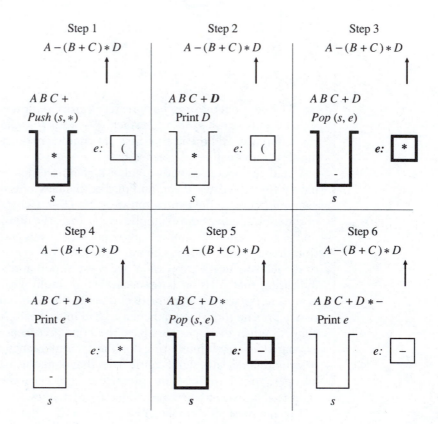

SECTION 5.3 EXERCISES

1. Consider the following recursive procedure form, *RecProc*, in which there is only one statement where the procedure calls itself. As was done in Example 5.5 with *SimRecFnc* for a recursive function, write the general form of a nonrecursive *SimRecProc* procedure to simulate recursion by use of a stack.

```
{ Form of a recursive procedure that can be readily
  converted to a nonrecursive procedure using a stack }

procedure RecProc ( n: integer );
begin
    if TerminalCondition(n) then
        TerminalCase(n)
    else
        begin
            PreStatements(n);
            RecProc( f(n) );
            PostStatements(n)
        end    {else}
end;
```

In Exercises 2–7, simulating the recursion by means of a stack, write a non-recursive version of the routine from the referenced exercise in Section 2.1.

2. The following function from Exercise 2:

$$f(n)= \begin{cases} 3 & \text{if } n = 0 \\ 2f(n-1) + 1 & \text{if } n > 0 \end{cases}$$

3. Function *Amount* with parameters *P*, *R*, and *n* from Exercise 5 to calculate the amount compounded in the bank after *n* years.

4. Function *PowerLin* to evaluate x^n for nonnegative integer *n* and positive integer *x* from Exercise 6.

5. Function from Exercise 11 to find the sum of the first *n* elements of an array of real numbers.

6. Procedure from Exercise 14a to print the first *n* elements of an array in reverse order.

7. Function from Exercise 16 to evaluate *na* for nonnegative integer *n* and real number *a*.

8. a. Evaluate the following postfix expression $A\,B - C\,/$, where $A = 17$, $B = 3$, and $C = 2$.
   b. Display the changing stack as demonstrated in Example 5.6.

9. Repeat Exercise 8 for $A\,B\,C\,D - * +$, where $A = 25$, $B = 2$, $C = 18$, and $D = 13$.

10. Without substituting values for the variables, we can convert an expression from postfix to infix notation. Employing the same process covered in Example 5.6, we push operands onto the stack. Upon encountering an operator, we pop the top two operands and push the resulting expression back onto the stack, being careful to surround this expression with parentheses.

Figure 5.21

Stack used to convert the postfix expression $A B C + D * -$ to the infix expression $(A - ((B + C) * D))$

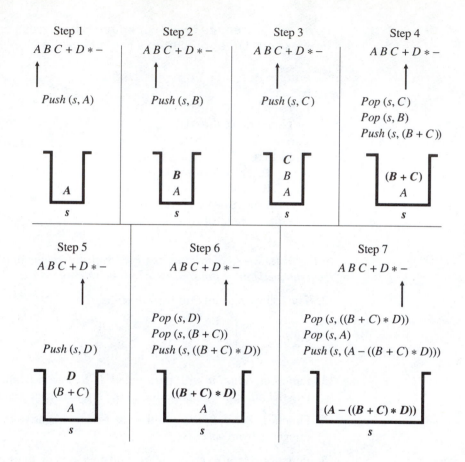

Step 1
$A B C + D * -$
Push (s, A)

Step 2
$A B C + D * -$
Push (s, B)

Step 3
$A B C + D * -$
Push (s, C)

Step 4
$A B C + D * -$
Pop (s, C)
Pop (s, B)
Push $(s, (B + C))$

Step 5
$A B C + D * -$
Push (s, D)

Step 6
$A B C + D * -$
Pop (s, D)
Pop $(s, (B + C))$
Push $(s, ((B + C) * D))$

Step 7
$A B C + D * -$
Pop $(s, ((B + C) * D))$
Pop (s, A)
Push $(s, (A - ((B + C) * D)))$

Figure 5.21 shows the conversion of the postfix expression $A B C + D * -$ to the infix expression $(A - ((B + C) * D))$. Show the stack, converting the expression of Exercise 8, $A B - C /$, to infix notation.

11. Repeat Exercise 10 for expression $A B + C D - /$.

In Exercises 12–15, using the algorithm in Example 5.7, convert the infix expression to postfix notation.

12. $A + B * C$

13. $A + B - C$

14. $(A + B) * C$

15. $(A * B / C) / (A - D)$

16. The Towers of Hanoi game presented in Example 2.4 can be solved iteratively. We establish three stacks to simulate the three pegs. The algorithm follows:

While the game is not complete do the following:
Move Disk 1 (the smallest) clockwise to the next peg.
Move any top disk except Disk 1.

There is always only one legal move for that second step in the loop.

a. Play the game by hand for four disks.
b. Write a nonrecursive procedure to play the game.

▽

PROGRAMMING PROJECTS

1. Write a program to read a text file and print whether or not a line is a palindrome, that is, the line reads the same backward as forward. Use stacks to implement the program as follows: As a line is read, push each character onto stack s and stack u. Then transfer the information from stack u to stack r so that r is in reverse order. Then, repeatedly popping elements from s and r, test for equality.

2. **a.** Write a program to find the ways of making 51¢ in change using 10 coins. You may use from 1 to 7 pennies, 1 to 7 nickels, and 1 to 4 dimes. Use a stack to backtrack to the last place where you had a choice of coins.
   b. Repeat Part a where you read the amount of change, the number of coins, and the constraints.

3. Write a program to read an expression in postfix notation and evaluate the answer, as was done by hand in Example 5.6 and Exercises 8 and 9. Assume an expression is only composed of operators, $+$, $-$, $*$, $/$, and variables A, B, C, D, E, F, with no blanks. Before reading the expression, read or assign values for the variables.

4. Write a program to read expressions in postfix notation and to convert them to infix notation. Assume the only operators are $+$, $-$, $*$, $/$, along with left and right parentheses, and the only variables are single characters with no blanks in the expression. Use a blank, another special symbol, or the end-of-line character to terminate the expression.

5. Write a program to read expressions in infix notation and convert them to postfix notation. One method of handling operator precedence is to assign a priority to each operator and the left parenthesis as follows:

Operator	Priority
(	0
+ or −	1
* or /	2

Use the same assumptions as in Project 4, except design the program to ignore blanks so that any number of blanks can separate parts of an expression.

Figure 5.22

Play of the Four Queens
Problem

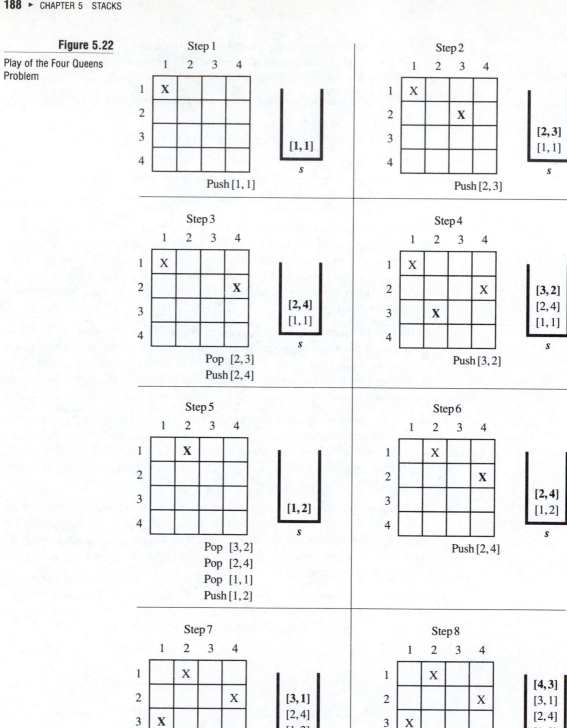

6. The **Eight Queens Problem** asks you to place 8 queen chess pieces on an 8 x 8 board so that no two queens lie in the same row, same column, or same 45° diagonal. Let us illustrate the solution with 4 queens on a 4 x 4 board. In what is called a **depth-first search**, we place queens one row at a time until we arrive at a solution or an impossible situation. If we reach such a dead-end, we **backtrack** to the last place where we had a choice of placing a queen and choose a different position. The stack data structure is ideal for keeping track of the choices so that the most recent queen position is readily available. We stack a position as an ordered pair of row and column numbers.

Figure 5.22 demonstrates one solution. In Step 1 we place a queen in position [1, 1]. Step 2 handles the second row. Since position [2, 1] is in the same column as [1, 1] and since [2, 1] is on a diagonal with [1, 1], we chose position [2, 3]. With these choices, however, there is no position for a queen on the third row; positions [3, 1] and [1, 1] share a column as do [3, 3] and [2, 3]; [3, 2] and [2, 3] are on a diagonal as are [3, 4] and [2, 3]. Thus, backtracking, we pop [2, 3] and instead pick position [2, 4] of the second row. Then [3, 2] is a legal possibility. With this position, however, there is no place for a queen in row 4. We pop [3, 2], but find no other possibility in row 3. Position [2, 4] is popped, but we have exhausted the choices in row 2. Consequently, we must pop [1, 1], and move the first queen to [1, 2]. After this choice, the game moves quickly to its goal by pushing positions [2, 4], [3, 1], and [4, 3] onto the stack. Depth-first search and backtracking are reconsidered in Chapter 12.

a. Play the game with four queens and an initial board position of [1,4].
b. Write a program to play the game for n queens where n is read. Print changes to the stack as they occur and print the final board positions of the queens.

6

Queues

Introduction

In the last chapter we described a stack as analogous to a stack of salad plates in a spring-loaded receptacle, where the addition or removal of a plate only occurs at the top. By contrast, we can use the queue structure to model a line of people waiting at the salad bar. A person gets in line at the back and, after filling a plate with salad, leaves from the front.

In the first section of this chapter we see striking similarities between the abstract data type definitions of stack and queue. As with our studies of strings and stacks, after presenting the formal definitions, we consider an array implementation of the ADT queue. A linked list implementation is presented in Chapter 8. In the last section of this chapter, we use this queue structure in a simulation of a waiting line.

SECTION 6.1 ## ADT Queue

The order of arrival of an element is as important in a queue (pronounced like the letter q) as it is in a stack. The basic operations of both are similar as well—make the structure empty, test if it is empty or full, place an element in or take an element out of the structure. The crucial difference is in that last operation. With stacks we have LIFO (Last In, First Out) behavior, where the element pushed onto the stack most recently is the first element we pop. Queues, however, obey the **FIFO** rule, *First In, First Out*, where the element that has been in the structure the longest is the one that is available for deletion. With stacks all activity is at the top, while with queues, we take elements from the front and add elements to the rear.

A queue is just a line, like a line of people waiting to get tickets to a concert. The person waiting the longest gets his or her ticket first; someone just arriving goes to the end of the line. We **dequeue** or delete a person from the front of the line and **enqueue** or insert someone at the rear. As another example, when entering an ice cream shop you may need to get a number that establishes an order of arrival into the shop. The person with the lowest number gets ice cream first; the latest person to enter pulls off the highest number thus far. Enqueuing and dequeuing are illustrated in Figure 6.1, and the ADT queue is presented in Figure 6.2.

In some situations a *RetrieveQueue* operation is also desirable. The procedure call *RetrieveQueue*(*q*, *e*) assigns the front item of a queue *q* to *e* without changing *q*. We discussed a corresponding operation for stacks in Example 5.1

Figure 6.1

Example of enqueuing and dequeuing with a queue

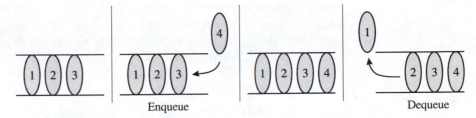

Enqueue   Dequeue

Figure 6.2.

Formal definition of ADT queue

ADT Queue

Objects: A finite sequence of elements of the same type. The **front** item has been in the queue the longest, and the **rear** item entered the queue most recently.

Operations:

Notation:

elType	—	type of an element in the queue
q	—	queue
e	—	item of type *elType*
b	—	boolean value

MakeQueueEmpty(*q*)
  Procedure to make *q* empty
QueueIsEmpty(*q*) → *b*
  Boolean function to return *true* if *q* is empty
QueueIsFull(*q*) → *b*
  Boolean function to return *true* if *q* is full
EnQueue(*q*, *e*)
  Procedure to place an item with *e*'s value into *q* at the rear; assume there is room in *q* for this new item
DeQueue(*q*, *e*)
  Procedure to take the front item out of *q* and give its value to *e*; assume *q* is not empty initially

of Section 5.1. The *RetrieveStack*(*s*, *e*) designed in that example popped the top item for *e* and then immediately pushed that value back onto *s*. Since the push operation reinstalls the item at the top, *RetrieveStack* does not alter the stack.

The sequence of operations

DeQueue(*q*, *e*)
EnQueue(*q*, *e*)

does not, however, accomplish a comparable task for queues. Certainly, by the action of the first operation *e* obtains the value of the front item. But enqueuing does not restore *q* to its original form since that operation installs an item at the rear, not the front. The situation is analogous to a line of people where if the front person gets out of line, he or she must go to the end to get back in line. To restore the queue to its original form using only the operations of Figure 6.2, we must in turn dequeue and enqueue every element of *q*. Though possible, this design, which manipulates every element of the queue, is highly undesirable. Thus, when needed for an application, it is better to add *Retrieve-Queue* to the ADT queue package of operations. The description of this auxiliary operation follows:

RetrieveQueue(*q*, *e*)
　　Procedure to assign the value of the front element of the queue *q* to *e*,
　　leaving *q* unchanged; assume *q* is not empty

Example 6.1

▼ We define an operation *AppendQueue*(*q*, *p*) to append queue *p* onto the end of queue *q*, leaving *p* empty. If we run out of room in *q*, the excess elements will remain in *p* and we will call an error-handling procedure.

Leaving the iterative version for the exercises, we design a recursive algorithm for *AppendQueue*. If *p* is empty, there is nothing to append. Consequently, the terminal condition is *QueueIsEmpty*(*p*), while the terminal case is void. If queue *p* is not empty, we must check that *q* is not full and so can accept an element. Being full is an error situation for this operation.

Elements leave *p* in the same order that they should enter *q*. Thus, we dequeue the front element from *p* and immediately enqueue that element at the rear of *q*. At this point, *p* has one less element while *q* has one more. By a recursive call to *AppendQueue* with these revised queues as parameters, we complete the operation. Had we called *AppendQueue* before *EnQueue*, the elements of *p* would have been appended in reverse order. Figure 6.3 shows the action of the following design for the *AppendQueue* operation:

AppendQueue(*q*, *p*)
　　Procedure to append queue *p* onto the end of queue *q*, leaving *p* empty;
　　if excess elements remain in *p*, the procedure calls an error-handling
　　procedure
Input:
　　q, *p* — queue
Output:
　　q　　— revised queue

Assumptions:
    q and p have been initialized.

Figure	**Algorithm**
{6.3}	if not *QueueIsEmpty*(p) then
	if *QueueIsFull*(q) then
	QueueIsFullError
	else
{Step 2}	*DeQueue*(p, e)
{Step 3}	*EnQueue*(q, e)
{Step 4}	*AppendQueue*(q, p)

Figure 6.3

Action of *AppendQueue*(q, p) of Example 6.1

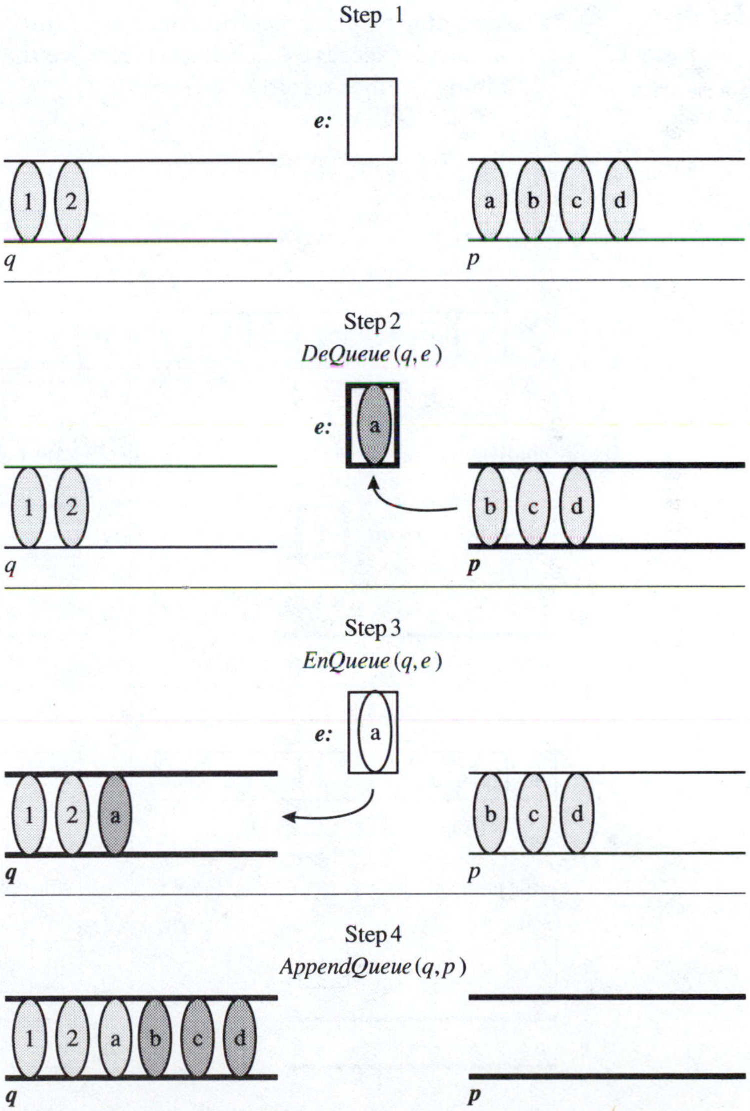

Step 1

Step 2
DeQueue(q,e)

Step 3
EnQueue(q,e)

Step 4
AppendQueue(q,p)

▼ In this example we write a procedure *ScrollDown* to place records from a file *f* into a queue *q* until the number of entries exceeds 24. We then remove the front queue item before adding another record to *q* from *f*. This situation is comparable to displaying up to 24 lines on a terminal screen; then as more lines are added to the bottom, the top lines scroll off the screen.

After initializing the file to read from the beginning and the queue to be empty, we enqueue up to 24 records. If more records are in *f*, we dequeue an item before enqueuing each new item. Figures 6.4–6.7 illustrate the algorithm that follows:

ScrollDown(q, f)

Procedure to place records from a file *f* into a queue *q* until the number of entries exceeds 24. Thereafter, remove the front queue item before adding another record to *q* from *f*.

Figure 6.4

First part of the action of *ScrollDown* from Example 6.2; the initialization and the situation during one execution of the first *while* loop

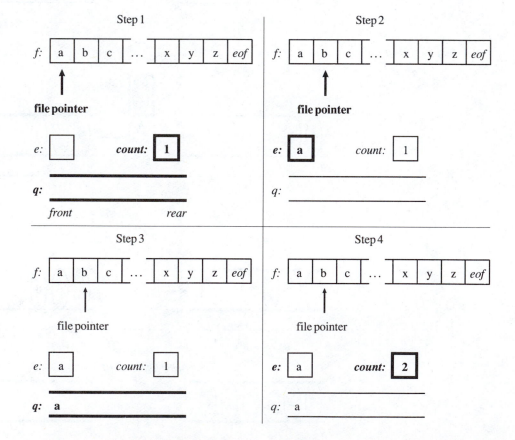

Figure 6.5

Continuation from Figure 6.4 of the action of *ScrollDown* from Example 6.2; the situation at the end of the execution of the first *while* loop

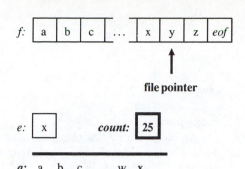

Figure 6.6

Continuation from Figure 6.5 of the action of *ScrollDown* from Example 6.2; the situation during one execution of the second *while* loop

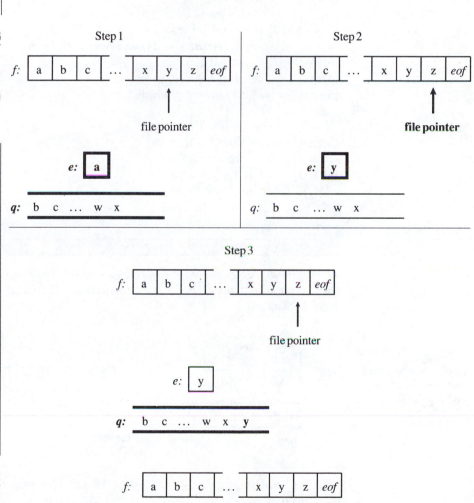

Figure 6.7

Continuation from Figure 6.6 of action of *ScrollDown* from Example 6.2; the situation at the end of execution

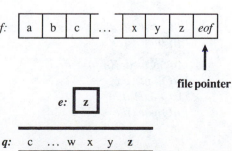

Input:
  f — file
Output:
  q — queue
Assumption:
  An element of *f* has the same type as an element of *q*.

Figure	Algorithm
{6.4}	
{Step 1}	*Reset (f)*
	MakeQueueEmpty(q)
	count ← 1
	while (*count <= 24*) and not *EOF(f)* do
{Step 2}	read(*f, e*)
{Step 3}	*EnQueue(q, e)*
{Step 4}	*count ← count + 1*
{6.5}	
{6.6}	while not *EOF(f)* do
{Step 1}	*DeQueue(q, e)*
{Step 2}	read (*f, e*)
{Step 3}	*EnQueue(q, e)*
{6.7}	

SECTION 6.1 EXERCISES

Starting with the queue q, *the variables* e *and* x, *and the file* f *in Figure 6.8, draw a picture of any changes after execution of each of the segments in Exercises 1–7.*

Figure 6.8

Queue *q*, variables *e* and *x*, and file *f* for Exercises 1–7

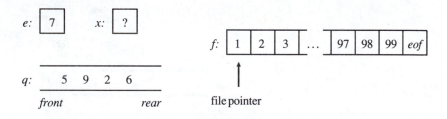

1. *EnQueue(q, e)*
   EnQueue(q, e)

4. *MakeQueueEmpty(u)*
   EnQueue(u,e)
   DeQueue(q,e)
   *EnQueue(u,e * e)*

2. *DeQueue(q,e)*

3. *RetrieveQueue(q, e)*

5. *product ← 1*
   while not *QueueIsEmpty(q)* do
      DeQueue(q, e)
      *product ←product * e*
   EnQueue(u, product)

6. while not *QueueIsEmpty*(*q*) do
  DeQueue (*q*, *e*)
  if not *QueueIsEmpty*(*q*)
    DeQueue(*q*, *x*)
    EnQueue(*q*, *e* + *x*)

7. *ScrollDown*(*u*,*f*)

Using pseudocode and ADT queue operations and notation, design the routines in Exercises 8–20. Also, answer any other questions about the operations.

8. Function *AddQueue* to return the sum of all the elements in a queue of numbers.

9. Procedure *ClearQueue* to remove all the elements from a queue.

10. a. Procedure *PrintQueue* to print the elements in a queue from front to rear, leaving the queue empty.
  b. Recursive procedure *PrintRevQueue* to print the elements from a queue in reverse order and leave the queue empty.

11. Function *LengthQueue* to return the number of elements in the queue, leaving the queue unchanged.

12. Procedure *RetrieveRear* to return the last element from a queue *q*, leaving *q* unchanged.

13. Boolean function *EqualQueue* to return *true* if two queues are identical, ordered in the same way. The function should leave the queues unchanged.

14. Procedure *Replace*(*q*, *e*, *x*) to replace every occurrence of element *e* in queue *q* with the value of *x*.

15. a. Recursive procedure *Reverse* to reverse the order of the elements in a queue.
  b. Design a nonrecursive version of *Reverse* using a stack.

16. Nonrecursive version of *AppendQueue* from Example 6.1 to append one queue to the end of another.

17. a. Procedure *SelectFile*(*q*, *f*, *probability*) to create a queue *q* and to place into *q* any item from a file *f* that is less than the constant *probability*.
  b. Write an invariant for the loop.
  c. Using program verification, prove this loop is correct.

18. a. Procedure *SwapQueue* to exchange the front two elements on the queue.
  b. Find the complexity of this operation.
  c. Find the complexity of the procedure *SwapStack* from Exercise 10, Section 5.1.

19. Procedure *PositionsToQueue*(*q*, *sub*, *s*) to place into a new queue *q* the starting positions in order of every occurrence of the substring *sub* in the string *s*.

20. Boolean function *Palindrome* that returns *true* if the elements from a queue, listed in order, form a palindrome, which reads the same front to back as back to front. To perform this operation, copy items from the queue into a stack and then compare.

21. a. What is the complexity of the *RetrieveQueue* operation designed with only the operations of Figure 6.2?
   b. What is the complexity of the *RetrieveStack* operation of Example 5.1, Section 5.1?

SECTION 6.2 | # Array Implementation of Queues

As with stacks, arrays and dynamic linked lists are the primary implementation tools of queues. The latter method will be discussed in Chapter 8.

We consider one approach to the array implementation of queues in the text and explore several alternatives in the exercises. For the present, we have the indices range from 0 to *MaxNum*, 0..*MaxNum*, so that the size of the array, *QueueSize*, is one more than *MaxNum*. For example, if the index is of type 0..4, the queue has room for 5 elements or *QueueSize* = 5. (See Figure 6.9.)

Figure 6.9

Array with index of type 0..4 implementing a queue

Since activity occurs at both ends of a queue, we need a variable to point to the tail or rear as well as one to indicate the head or front. By holding the index of the oldest element, *front* points to the front of the queue. Similarly, *rear* maintains the index of the youngest queue element.

As Figure 6.10 displays, we initialize the empty queue so that *front* is 1 and *rear* is 0. The first element is inserted into the array element *el*[1] with the queue growing toward the end, as suggested in the array implementation of stacks from Section 5.2. For *EnQueue*, *rear* is incremented by one to point to the next available cell and then the item is inserted as in Figure 6.11. Dequeu-

Figure 6.10

Array implementation of an empty queue

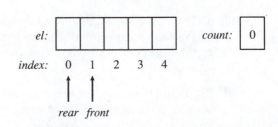

Figure 6.11

Enqueuing the first time with an array implementation of a queue

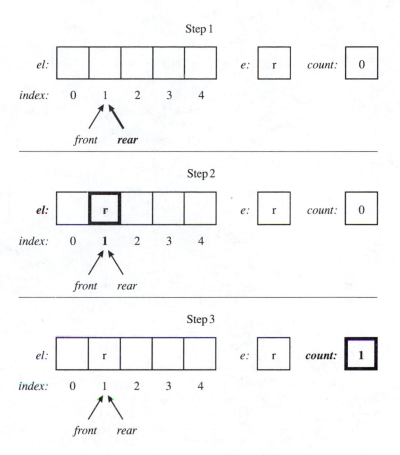

ing, however, removes elements from the opposite end from stack popping. The first time $DeQueue(q, e)$ is executed, e is assigned the value of $el[1]$ and *front* is incremented by one so that the queue starts with $el[2]$. (See Figure 6.12.) Figure 6.13 illustrates a queue after several enqueuing and dequeuing operations.

With these operations the queue drifts toward the end of the array. To avoid having this end as a barrier, we make the structure circular, using modulo arithmetic to wrap around. Thus, for *EnQueue* we increment *rear*, taking the result modulo *QueueSize*,

```
rear := (rear + 1) mod QueueSize
```

As the transition from Figure 6.13 to Figure 6.14 shows, for an index type of 0..4 and *QueueSize* of 5, if *rear* points to $el[4]$, $EnQueue(q, e)$ wraps *rear* to the beginning of the array,

$$rear \leftarrow (4 + 1) \bmod 5 = 5 \bmod 5 = 0$$

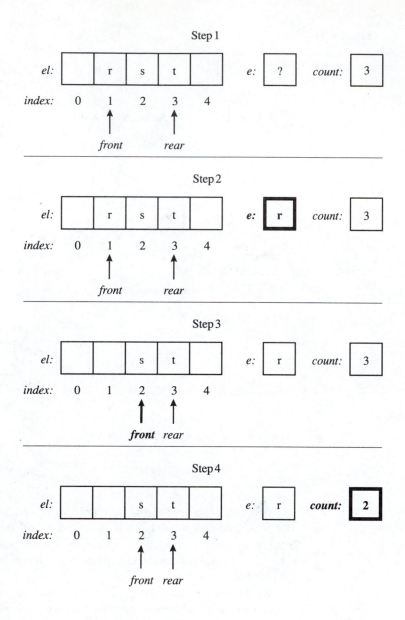

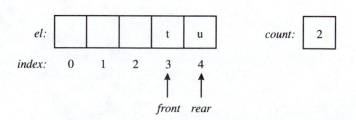

before inserting the new element

$el[rear] \leftarrow e$

DeQueue(q, e) makes the assignment of the front queue element to *e* before incrementing *front* modulo *QueueSize*.

```
e      := el[front];
front  := (front + 1) mod QueueSize
```

Figure 6.14

Starting with Figure 6.13, a wraparound for enqueuing in a circular array implementation of a queue, drawn two ways

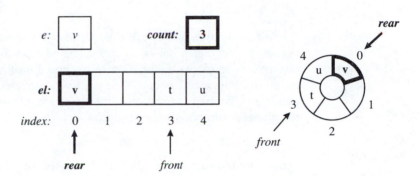

Figures 6.15 and 6.16 picture situations in which there is no more room in the array. We must be careful to check for a full structure before enqueuing, or else the tail element might destroy the front of the queue. Observe that in the full queue, *rear* points to the element immediately before the first queue element. Again employing modulo arithmetic, we see that the following condition is *true* in a full queue:

```
( front = ( (rear + 1) mod QueueSize ) )
```

Figure 6.15

Example of a full queue with *front* = 3 = *rear* + 1 = 2 + 1, implemented with an array and drawn two ways

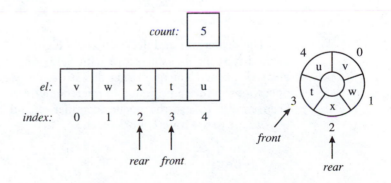

Figure 6.16

Example of a full queue
with *front* = 0 =
((*rear* + 1) mod 5) =
((4 + 1) mod 5), imple-
mented with an array and
drawn two ways

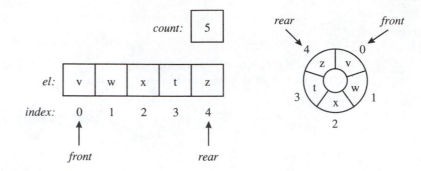

We must also make sure the queue is not empty before attempting the operation *DeQueue*. But as Figures 6.10 and 6.17 show, the above condition is also true in an empty queue. Obviously, we cannot have the same test for both an empty and a full queue. One method of overcoming this difficulty is to maintain a count of the number of elements in the queue. When *count* is zero, the queue is empty, but the condition

```
( count = QueueSize )
```

being *true* indicates a full queue. Of course, we must remember to increment *count* by 1 when enqueuing and to decrement *count* by the same amount when dequeuing.

Figure 6.17

Example of an empty
queue, implemented with
an array and drawn two
ways

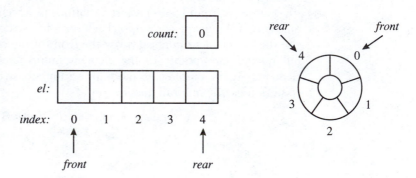

The definitions and declarations in Figure 6.18 create the queue. We have defined type *queue* as a record with fields for *front, rear, count,* and *el,* the array of queue elements. Using this structure, we implement the ADT queue operations in the same figure. In referencing *front, rear, count,* and *e,* we have been careful to use the queue identifier *q* and the field identifier, such as *q.front,* or to use a *with* block, such as

```
with q do
   begin

      .........

   end    { with }
```

Figure 6.18.

Array implementation of
ADT queue

An Array Implementation of ADT Queue

Create a queue q with each element of type *elType* and with a maximum of *MaxNum* number of elements.

```
const
    MaxNum    = . . . . . . . . . . ;
    QueueSize = . . . . . . . . . . ;        {1 more than MaxNum}

type
    elType    = . . . . . . . . . . ;
    indexType = 0..MaxNum;
    countType = 0..QueueSize;
    arrayType = array [indexType] of elType;

    queue     = record
        front,
        rear    : indexType;
        count   : countType;
        el      : arrayType
    end;

var
    q : queue;
    e : elType;
```

MakeQueueEmpty(*q*)

```
procedure MakeQueueEmpty (var q: queue);
begin
    q.front := 1;
    q.rear  := 0;
    q.count := 0
end;
```

QueueIsEmpty(*q*) → *b*

```
function QueueIsEmpty (var q : queue): boolean;
begin
    QueueIsEmpty := (q.count = 0)
end;
```

QueueIsFull(*q*) → *b*

```
function QueueIsFull (var q: queue): boolean;
begin
    QueueIsFull := (q.count = QueueSize)
end;
```

Figure 6.18.
continued

EnQueue(*q, e*)

```
procedure EnQueue (var q: queue; e: elType );
begin
    with q do
        begin
            rear        : = (rear + 1) mod QueueSize;
            el [rear]  : = e;
            count       : = count + 1
        end   { with }
end;
```

DeQueue(*q, e*)

```
procedure DeQueue (var q: queue; var e: elType );
begin
    with q do
        begin
            e      : = el [front];
            front : = (front + 1) mod QueueSize;
            count : = count −1
        end   { with }
end;
```

Auxiliary Operation:

RetrieveQueue(*q, e*)

```
procedure RetrieveQueue (var q: queue; var e: elType );
begin
    e : = q.el [q.front]
end;
```

For completeness we also include the *RetrieveQueue* operation described in the last section. As discussed, we can implement *RetrieveQueue* in a tedious fashion using *EnQueue* and *DeQueue*. The implementation here only involves an array reference.

▽

SECTION 6.2 EXERCISES

In Exercises 1–15 code in Pascal the operations from Section 6.1 using the array of records implementation discussed in this section.

1. *AppendQueue* from Example 6.1 to append one queue to the end of another.

2. *ScrollDown* from Example 6.2 to place records from a file *f* into a queue *q* until the number of entries exceeds 24. Thereafter, remove the front queue item before adding another record to *q* from *f*.

3. Function *AddQueue* from Exercise 8 to return the sum of all the elements in a queue of numbers.

4. Procedure *ClearQueue* from Exercise 9 to remove all the elements from a queue.

5. a. Procedure *PrintQueue* from Exercise 10a to print the elements in a queue from front to rear, leaving the queue empty.
  b. Recursive procedure *PrintRevQueue* from Exercise 10b to print the elements from a queue in reverse order and leave the queue empty.

6. Function *LengthQueue* from Exercise 11 to return the number of elements in the queue *q* without destroying *q*.

7. Procedure *RetrieveRear* from Exercise 12 to return the last element from a queue *q* leaving *q* unchanged.

8. Boolean function *EqualQueue* from Exercise 13 to return *true* if two queues are identical, ordered in the same way. The function should leave the queues unchanged.

9. Procedure *Replace*(*q, e, x*) from Exercise 14 to replace every occurrence of element *e* in queue *q* with the value of *x*.

10. a. Recursive procedure *Reverse* from Exercise 15a to reverse the order of the elements in a queue.
  b. Nonrecursive version of the procedure in Part a.

11. Nonrecursive version of *AppendQueue* from Exercise 16 to append one queue to the end of another.

12. Procedure *SelectFile*(*q, f, probability*) from Exercise 17a to create a queue *q* and to place into *q* any item from a file *f* that is less than the constant *probability*.

13. Procedure *SwapQueue* from Exercise 18a to exchange the front two elements on the queue.

14. Procedure *PositionToQueue* from Exercise 19 to place into a new queue the starting positions in order of every occurrence of substring *sub* in string *s*.

15. Boolean function *Palindrome* from Exercise 20 that returns *true* if the elements from a queue, listed in order, form a palindrome, which reads the same front to back as back to front.

16. In the array implementation of ADT queue discussed in this section, the field *rear* is unnecessary. Write a function, *ComputeRear*, to return the index *rear*, given *front* and *count*.

17. Another implementation of ADT queue using an array of records is as follows: We have *front* point to the array element (modulo *QueueSize*) before the first in the queue. Thus, as Figure 6.19 shows, initially *front* and *rear* are both zero. We do not use a counter to determine an empty and full queue, but sacrifice one array element, the one pointed to by *front*. The sacrificed element is never filled. Figure 6.20 illustrates another situation in such an implementation, a queue containing two elements.

Figure 6.19

An empty queue implemented as in Exercise 17 with an array and a sacrificed element

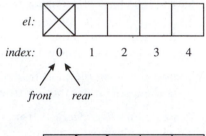

Figure 6.20

A queue of two elements after several enqueuing and dequeuing operations implemented as in Exercise 17 with an array and a sacrificed element

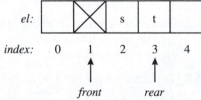

a. What is the relationship of *front* and *rear* in an empty queue?
b. What is the relationship of *front* and *rear* in a full queue?
c. Code in Pascal each of the ADT queue operations using this implementation.

18. Another implementation of ADT queue using an array of records involves having an extra boolean field *empty* in every record. When *empty* is *true* (*false*), that array element is empty (filled). With this configuration *count* is unnecessary. Using this implementation, code in Pascal the following ADT queue operations:

a. *MakeQueueEmpty(q)*
b. *QueueIsEmpty(q)*
c. *QueueIsFull(q)*
d. *EnQueue*; be sure to assign the appropriate value to the *empty* field of the added element.
e. *DeQueue*; be sure to assign the appropriate value to the *empty* field of the deleted element.

19. A **deque** is a double-ended queue where insertions and deletions can occur at either end.

a. Define ADT deque
b. Implement the ADT deque as an array.

▽

PROGRAMMING PROJECT

---

1. Design a program to read and display records from a file based on interactive commands. The command $+n$, where n is a positive integer, causes n records to be read, displayed on the screen, and stored in a data structure. At most 15 lines should be displayed at one time. The structure should hold the 50 most recently read records. The command $-n$ causes the bottom n lines not to be printed as the display scrolls down n lines. For example, $+5$ reads and displays and stores 5 lines. Then $+25$ reads and displays 25 more records, scrolling the oldest records off the screen so that records 16 through 30 are shown. Then command -10 causes lines 5 through 20 to be shown. If the command $+12$ follows, the screen displays records 18 through 30 along with two additional records read from the file. If $+n$ causes the *EOF* condition to be *true*, then ignore the excess value.

▽

SECTION 6.3

Queue Applications

Many applications of queues fall in the area of **simulation**, where the computer is used to imitate and study such occurrences as serving customers in a post office. With a computer model of a "real-life" situation, many "what if" questions can be examined to determine the best course of action; and investigations that are too costly, dangerous, or lengthy can be studied in depth.

Queues are used in the simulation of waiting-line events. For instance, with the post office customers, we might be interested in the average waiting time, in the maximum or minimum wait, or in the longest line.

Example 6.3

Simulation of Waiting Line.

▼

For the simulation of customer service in a post office, we consider a simplified situation in which there is one line, one postal worker, a fixed customer time at the service window or transaction time (*TransactionTime*), and a fixed probability (*ProbabilityArrive*) that a customer will arrive in any one minute. We also must know how long the simulation will run (*SimulationTime*). Thus, the model will have a simulated clock (*clock*) that will count off the minutes from the start of the simulation, when $clock = 0$.

To determine if at a certain time a new customer will arrive, we obtain a random number (*Random*) between 0 and 1. If *Random* is less than *ProbabilityArrive*, we process an arrival. For example, a *ProbabilityArrive* of 0.25 means there is a 25% chance that in any one minute a customer will arrive or that on the average a customer arrives every 4 minutes. We need *Random* to return random numbers uniformly distributed from 0 to 1. That is, 25% of the time *Random* will return a number between 0 and 0.25. This random number is obtained from a function reference to a random number generator. Such a function may be built into the version of Pascal that you are using, but if not, the design in Appendix A displays such a function.

John von Neumann introduced the first algorithm for generating random numbers with the computer. He also is attributed with originating the idea of storing programs as well as data in the memory of the computer. The brilliant von Neumann, born in Budapest, Hungary, in 1903, received his Ph.D. in mathematics at age 22. He contributed significantly to a variety of areas including the mathematical foundation of quantum theory, logic, theory of games, economics, nuclear physics, meteorology, as well as theory and applications in early computer science. Many stories tell of his phenomenal memory, reasoning ability, and computational speed. It is said that he could memorize a column of the telephone book at a glance, and that he had mastered calculus by age 8. Dr. von Neumann headed a team that built one of the earliest computers. The first test of the machine was to execute a program to find the smallest power of 2 with its fourth decimal digit from the right being 7. The computer and von Neumann began calculating at the same time . . . von Neumann won!

Returning to our simulation, when a computer-generated, pseudo random number is less than the probability that a customer will arrive in any one minute, i. e., the condition

$$(Random < ProbabilityArrive)$$

is *true*, we enqueue a customer. But what does it mean to "enqueue a customer"? For this example we are only concerned with the waiting time. Thus, we let the arrival time (*ArrivalTime*), determined by the value of *clock*, represent the customer in the queue. Therefore, this simulation is **time driven** with events being regulated by the value of the clock.

We need another clock, comparable to a timer counting down, that displays the amount of time remaining to serve the customer at the window (*WindowTimeLeft*). As a customer moves to the window to have a transaction processed, *WindowTimeLeft* is set to *TransactionTime*. As *clock* is incremented by 1 to simulate the passing of 1 minute of time,

$$clock \leftarrow clock + 1$$

WindowTimeLeft is decremented by 1 until it is zero,

$$WindowTimeLeft \leftarrow WindowTimeLeft - 1.$$

When *WindowTimeLeft* becomes zero, the transaction is complete, the customer at the window leaves the post office, and the postal worker is available to assist another customer.

The customer stepping to the window to be served is symbolized by a dequeue of an arrival time (*ArrivalTime*). Since the clock has remained ticking, we can calculate the length of time the customer had to wait (*wait*) as

$$wait \leftarrow clock - ArrivalTime$$

This value of *wait* can be used in the computation of the average or maximum waiting time. A hierarchy chart of the program is diagrammed in Figure 6.21. Pseudocode for the various routines follows.

Figure 6.21

Hierarchy chart for the
program of Example 6.3

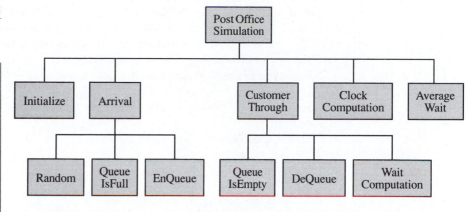

PostOfficeSimulation
> Program to simulate a waiting line at a post office and print the average
> wait

Read Input:
> *TransactionTime*
> *ProbabilityArrive*
> *SimulationTime*

Printed Output:
> *AverageWait* — average time a customer waits

Algorithm:
> *Initialize* (*CustomerQueue, clock, WindowTimeLeft, WaitSum,*
>   *CustomerCount, TransactionTime, ProbabilityArrive,*
>   *SimulationTime*)
> while *clock < SimulationTime* do
>   *Arrival* (*ProbabilityArrive, CustomerQueue, clock*)
>   *CustomerThrough* (*CustomerQueue, WindowTimeLeft,*
>   *WaitSum, CustomerCount, Transaction Time, clock*)
>   *ClockComputation* (*clock, WindowTimeLeft*)
> *AverageWait* (*WaitSum, CustomerCount*)

Initialize (***CustomerQueue, clock, WindowTimeLeft, WaitSum,***
CustomerCount, TransactionTime, ProbabilityArrive, SimulationTime)
> Procedure to initialize

Output:

CustomerQueue	—	queue of customer arrival times
clock	—	clock counting minutes
WindowTimeLeft	—	time left for customer at a window
WaitSum	—	accumulated sum of waits for customers that have been served
CustomerCount	—	accumulated number of customers that have been served

seed — global variable; seed for random number generator; the variable is unnecessary if a built-in random number generator is used

TransactionTime — time of a transaction

ProbabilityArrive — probability that a customer will arrive at any one minute

SimulationTime — length of time for simulation

Algorithm:

    MakeQueueEmpty(CustomerQueue)

    Initialize the following to 0:
        clock
        WindowTimeLeft
        WaitSum
        CustomerCount

    seed ← ....
        { Assign global variable *seed* an appropriate value for the random number generator, as suggested in Appendix A. The statement is unnecessary if we use a built-in random number generator. }

    Read the following:
        TransactionTime
        ProbabilityArrive
        SimulationTime

Arrival (*ProbabilityArrive, CustomerQueue, clock*)

    Procedure to test if there is an arrival and if so to process the arrival

Input:

    ProbabilityArrive
    CustomerQueue
    clock

Output:

    CustomerQueue

Algorithm:

    if *Random* < *ProbabilityArrive* then
        if *QueueIsFull (CustomerQueue)* then
            FullQueueError
        else
            EnQueue (CustomerQueue, clock)

CustomerThrough (*CustomerQueue, WindowTimeLeft, WaitSum, CustomerCount, TransactionTime, clock*)

    Procedure to take the front customer from the line to serve

Input:

    CustomerQueue
    WindowTimeLeft

    WaitSum
    CustomerCount
    TransactionTime
    clock
Output:
    CustomerQueue
    WindowTimeLeft
    WaitSum
    CustomerCount
Algorithm:
    if *WindowTimeLeft* = 0 then
        if not *QueueIsEmpty* (*CustomerQueue*) then
            DeQueue (*CustomerQueue, ArrivalTime*)
            WaitComputation (*WaitSum, ArrivalTime, CustomerCount,*
                clock)
            WindowTimeLeft ← *TransactionTime*

WaitComputation (***WaitSum, ArrivalTime, CustomerCount, clock***)
    Procedure to compute the total waiting time and number of customers
    that have been served thus far
Input:
    WaitSum
    ArrivalTime
    CustomerCount
    clock
Output:
    WaitSum
    CustomerCount
Algorithm:
    wait   ← *clock* − *ArrivalTime*
    WaitSum   ← *WaitSum* + *wait*
    CustomerCount ← *CustomerCount* + 1

ClockComputation (***clock, WindowTimeLeft***)
    Procedure to change the clocks by one minute
Input:
    clock
    WindowTimeLeft
Output:
    clock
    WindowTimeLeft
Algorithm:
    clock ← *clock* + 1
    if *WindowTimeLeft* > 0 then
        WindowTimeLeft ← *WindowTimeLeft* − 1

AverageWait (*WaitSum, CustomerCount*)
    Procedure to calculate the average wait
Input:
    WaitSum
    CustomerCount
Printed Output:
    AvgWait
Algorithm:
    if *CustomerCount* = 0 then
        AvgWait ← 0
    else
        AvgWait ← *WaitSum* / *CustomerCount*
    Print *AvgWait*

▽

SECTION 6.3 EXERCISES

1. Code in Pascal the program from Example 6.3 using an array implementation of the queue.
2. Alter the appropriate routine(s) of Example 6.3 to calculate and print the longest wait, too.
3. Alter the appropriate routine(s) of Example 6.3 to calculate and print the longest line, too.
4. Write a driver program to execute *PostOfficeSimulation* in Example 6.3 as often as the user desires. The *ProbabilityArrive, TransactionTime*, and *SimulationTime* should remain constant. Observe the variation in the results.
5. Write a driver program to execute the program in Example 6.3 a given number of times. The *ProbabilityArrive* and *TransactionTime* should vary with each execution of the program. Observe the variation in the results.
6. Alter the program of Example 6.3 to accommodate a transaction time of less than or equal to 5 minutes that varies for each customer. This time can be calculated by using *RandomInteger*.
7. In a **priority queue** the order established is based on a priority value associated with each element. The element with the highest priority is removed first. For instance, a priority queue of jobs exists in a mainframe computer. Typically, jobs that request less time and space have a higher priority.

    a. Define ADT priority queue.
    b. Implement the ADT priority queue using arrays.

▽

PROGRAMMING PROJECTS

1. Alter the appropriate routines of Example 6.3 to have two service windows but only one waiting line. The person at the front of the line goes to the next

available window. Also, have the transaction time be different for each window, where one postal employee is faster than the other.

2. Alter the appropriate routines in Example 6.3 to have two service windows, each with its own waiting line. Suppose a person entering the post office always picks the shorter line and never switches lines.

3. As described in Exercise 7, suppose that as a user submits a job to be executed on a mainframe computer, that job is assigned an integer priority from 1 to 8. In case two jobs have the same priority, the first job submitted will execute first. As in Example 6.3, simulate the action of this job queue, calculating the average wait time. Randomly assign a priority (*priority*) and execution time (*ExecutionTime*) for each job. Suppose the execution time is never more than the exponential of the priority, *exp*(*priority*).

4. When a large program will not completely fit in the main memory of the computer, the operating system may use a technique called **paging** to give the programmer the impression that virtually unlimited storage is available. The program is split into fixed-size segments called **pages**; pages are fetched or brought into main memory as needed from secondary storage. Suppose primary storage has room for three pages at one time. One technique is to maintain this area of storage as a queue, always replacing the page that has been in memory the longest. Of course, if a page is already in memory, we make no change in the queue. Reference to external storage does consume extra time. Thus, the hope with a queue is that after execution within a set of pages, execution will continue in another set of pages. Write a program to simulate paging. Read an input stream of positive integers indicating the new program pages needed in order for execution. With each datum print the contents of memory. Upon completion, print the total number of page faults. Such a fault occurs when a new page is fetched into main memory, copying over another page. For example, suppose a program is broken into five pages numbered 1, 2, 3, 4, 5 and the input stream is 1 2 3 4 3 4 5 2 5. Output might be as follows:

Input	Memory	Fault?
1	1	no
2	1 2	no
3	1 2 3	no
4	2 3 4	yes
3	2 3 4	no
4	2 3 4	no
5	3 4 5	yes
2	4 5 2	yes
5	4 5 2	no

Number of faults: 3

5. Simulate counseling of students in a computer science department. Students can be advised by any faculty member. When a student arrives at the department, he or she checks with the secretary to obtain an advisement folder and to learn which faculty member to see. The secretary assigns a student to the faculty member with the shortest waiting line. After being advised, the student returns the advisement folder to the secretary and indicates the advisor's name. Faculty members, too, check in and out with the secretary. If a faculty member must leave, the secretary reassigns the students waiting to see him or her to other advisors. The chairperson of the department never leaves, so there is always a line available.

The simulation is **event driven**—the simulation is driven by the events of a student or faculty member arriving or leaving. Have the program be interactive. Ask the person's status (faculty member or student), name, and whether he or she is checking in or out. For a student who is checking in, assign the student to a faculty member. For a student who is leaving, ask the name of the advisor. When a faculty member leaves before consulting with all his or her students, reassign those students.

Lists

Introduction

The only built-in data type that we have not covered is that of *pointer*. The predefined structures discussed so far are static; their amount of storage is established at compile time. Pointers, however, allow us to allocate memory dynamically, as needed.

After studying pointers, we devote the rest of the chapter to the abstract data type linked list. Manipulations of linked lists pictorially precede the formal ADT definition. In the last two sections of the chapter we will see that pointers provide the linking mechanism for most implementations of linked lists. An array implementation of linked lists is developed in the exercises.

ADT Pointer and Implementation

A pointer variable is a special kind of variable, one that does not hold the data item itself but the memory address of where the value is located. Only when a special statement is executed is memory set aside for this data value and the pointer assigned the datum's address. Until this time, the pointer does not hold a meaningful address, and the memory eventually designated for the data value is free to be used for other purposes.

There does not seem to be a big advantage to dynamic memory allocation with a pointer referencing only one data cell. Typically, however, the cell has an information portion and at least one pointer area itself. Thus, we can link one cell to another, much as a train is composed of a number of cars linked together. Each rail car is a box that holds cargo and that has a link to the next car. If a train needs to transport more, another car can be added. If a rail car is no longer needed, it can be removed from the train. The **linked list** with analogy to the train is very important to the study of data structures. Not only is it valuable in itself, but along with arrays, the linked list is a major implementation tool for other structures.

The dynamic memory allocation of linked lists has some important advantages over the static memory allocation of arrays. With arrays the programmer must decide the maximum number of elements needed, and the compiler must allocate the appropriate amount of memory before execution even begins. If the programmer has underestimated, the program will eventually end abnormally. If there is an overestimate, not only is space monopolized from the beginning, but too much is set aside. Also, as we will see, insertion and deletion is easier in a sorted linked list than in a sorted array. Figure 7.1 displays an ADT pointer definition.

Figure 7.1.

Formal definition of ADT pointer

ADT Pointer

Objects: *nil and memory addresses of data values of type Node*

Operations:
  Notation:
    P, Q — pointers to memory addresses of data values of type *Node*
    e — item of type *Node*
    b — boolean value
  New(P)
    Procedure to allocate memory for datum of type *Node* and to place its address into P
  Dispose(P)
    Procedure to free memory for datum of type *Node* whose address is in P and to make P undefined
  StorePointer(P, Q)
    Procedure to copy Q's value into P
  StoreNode(P, e)
    Procedure to copy e's value into the node whose address is stored in P
  RetrieveNode(P) → *e*
    Function to return the value of the node whose address is stored in P
  EqualPointer(P, Q) → *b*
    Function to return *true* if P and Q store the same memory address

For creation in Pascal of a pointer variable that holds the address of a data value of type *Node*, we use the caret ^ or the up arrow symbol ↑ to write the type definition:

```
type
    pointer = ^Node;
    Node    = ..........;
```

and the variable declaration:

```
var
    P, Q   :   pointer;
```

As a result of this declaration, room enough for an address is allocated to *P*, but no address is placed in *P*, so its value is undefined, and no space is established for a data item of type *Node*. Perhaps, as shown in Figure 7.2, the compiler allocates the location 1486 for *P* while *P*'s value is undefined.

Figure 7.2

Memory allocated for pointer *P* at location 1486, where *P*'s value is undefined

P | ? |

address   1486

With this variable being undefined, a comparison involving *P* would result in an error. We can, however, assign the pointer a special built-in constant, *nil*, to indicate that *P* does not point to a memory location. With the value of *nil* or of a memory address, *P* would no longer be undefined. Typically, in a linked list the last pointer in the chain is assigned the value *nil*, thus flagging that node as the last, much like the caboose in a train. As with most other store operations, the ADT pointer operation *StorePointer(P, nil)*, which places *nil* in *P*, is implemented with an assignment statement,

```
P := nil
```

As Figure 7.3 shows, we use a slash in the rectangle for *P* to indicate that the pointer has the value *nil*.

Figure 7.3

Symbolism for memory allocated to pointer *P* at location 1486, where *P* has the value *nil*

P

address   1486

One implementation of the ADT operation *New* is the Pascal procedure of the same name. As shown in Figure 7.4,

```
new (P)
```

allocates space for a node and places its address in *P*. Although the node has a position in memory, its value is undefined at this point. In the example in Figure 7.4, location 1486 contains *P*'s value, 5497, which is the address of the

Figure 7.4

Example of memory after *new(P)* has been executed for pointer variable *P*; in this example, *P* points to memory location 5497

Cell that can hold
data of type *Node*

P | 5497

address 1486

?

5497

node pointed to by *P*. The address *in P*, as well as the address *of P*, is immaterial and varies with each run of the program. Thus, we cannot reference this address, just as we cannot discover the address for any variable. Throughout this book, instead of inventing contrived addresses, we picture the situation as in Figure 7.5.

Figure 7.5

An alternate diagram for Figure 7.4, which gives an example of memory after *new(P)* has been executed for pointer variable *P*

Cell that can hold
data of type *Node*

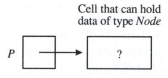

If Q has the same type as P and if Q already has a value of *nil* or the address of a node, we can copy that address into P with the ADT pointer operation of *StorePointer(P, Q)* or in Pascal with the assignment statement

    P := Q

Figures 7.6 and 7.7 illustrate the effects on memory of such assignments.

To test equality of pointers, the ADT pointer operation *EqualPointer(P, Q)* is matched by the boolean expression

    (P = Q)

Figure 7.6

Action of $P := Q$, where Q has the value *nil*

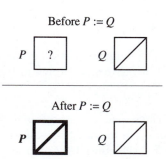

Figure 7.7

Action of *P* : = *Q*, where *Q* has the value of the address of a cell that can hold a data value of type *Node*

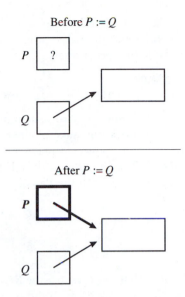

Before *P* := *Q*

P ?

Q

After *P* := *Q*

P

Q

It should be emphasized that we are testing if *P* and *Q* contain the same address. The values to which they point could be the same without the addresses being identical. Certainly, if *P* = *Q* so that they hold the same address, the corresponding values are the same. Figure 7.8 gives several examples of values for the boolean expression (*P* = *Q*). When there is no confusion, we sometimes omit the rectangular representation for a pointer variable, as shown in Figure 7.9.

Figure 7.8

Several examples of values for the boolean expression (*P* = *Q*)

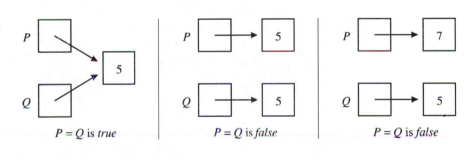

P   *P*   5   *P*   7

Q   5   *Q*   5   *Q*   5

P = Q is *true*   *P = Q* is *false*   *P = Q* is *false*

Figure 7.9

An alternate diagram for Figure 7.8

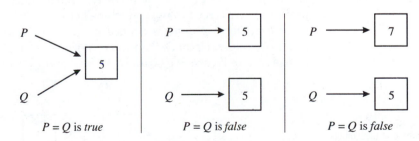

P   *P* ⟶ 5   *P* ⟶ 7

Q   5   *Q* ⟶ 5   *Q* ⟶ 5

P = Q is *true*   *P = Q* is *false*   *P = Q* is *false*

We have seen how to assign and compare pointers, but how do we assign and reference the value pointed to by *P*? For example, suppose we have *P*, a variable of type *pointer*,

```
type
    pointer = ^integer;
```

so that *P* will point to a memory location that can contain an integer. This location does not have a separate name but is only referenced through the pointer as *P*^. Thus, to place the integer 5 in that location as shown in Figures 7.8 or 7.9, we would use the ADT pointer operation *StoreNode(P, 5)*, which is put into effect with the Pascal assignment

```
P^  := 5
```

or

```
P↑  := 5
```

To print that value, we use the *RetrieveNode(P)* operation, implemented as P^ or P↑, in conjunction with the *write* or *writeln* procedure:

```
writeln (P^)
```

As a note of caution, until the operation *New(P)* is executed, we cannot use *StoreNode(P, e)*. Moreover, a call to *StoreNode* must precede an invocation to *RetrieveNode*.

Often *Node* is of type record. For instance, suppose we have the type definitions

```
type
    pointer  = ^Node;
    Node     = record
        info : integer;
        next : pointer
    end;

var
    P, Q     : pointer;
```

Here we have the only situation in Pascal in which a type (*Node*) can be referenced (*pointer* = ^*Node*) before it is defined. Since *Node* has a pointer field itself, we were forced to use something before its definition. Notice the indirect recursion, where *pointer* is defined in terms of *Node* and *Node* is defined in terms of *pointer*. Upon declaration of variables *P* and *Q*, we have the situation as pictured in Figure 7.10 with room in *P* and *Q* for addresses.

Figure 7.10

Memory after declaration of variables *P* and *Q*

Figure 7.11

Memory after execution of
new(P)

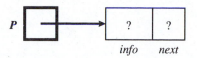

If the statement

new (P)

is executed, we have the situation as shown in Figure 7.11. Notice that the node has two fields, an information field and a pointer field. As with all records, we reference the individual fields using a period and the field identifier. We do not have a record identifier, however, and must use the pointer variable *P* with the caret ^ or up arrow ↑. Thus,

P^. info

refers to the information field, while

P^. next

is the pointer field. Figure 7.12 shows the result of the following assignments:

P^. info : = 5;
P^. next : = nil

As mentioned above, a slash through the rectangle for the *next* field represents the value *nil*.

Figure 7.12

Memory after execution
of *P^.info* : = 5 and
P^.next : = nil

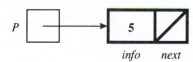

To emphasize the difference between the address stored in a pointer variable and the value to which *P* points, observe the difference in the assignments

P : = Q

and

P^. info : = Q^. info

as shown in Figure 7.13. On a higher level these statements are also quite different. The first assignment is a Pascal realization of the ADT pointer operation *StorePointer(P, Q)*. The second assignment involves the ADT record function *RetrieveRecord(Q^, info)* to return the value in the information field *Q^.info* and the ADT record procedure *StoreRecord* to place this value in the information field *P^.info* of the node pointed to by *P*:

StoreRecord(P^, info, RetrieveRecord (Q^, info))

Figure 7.13

Comparison of the effects of $P := Q$ and $P^\wedge .info :=$ $Q^\wedge .info$

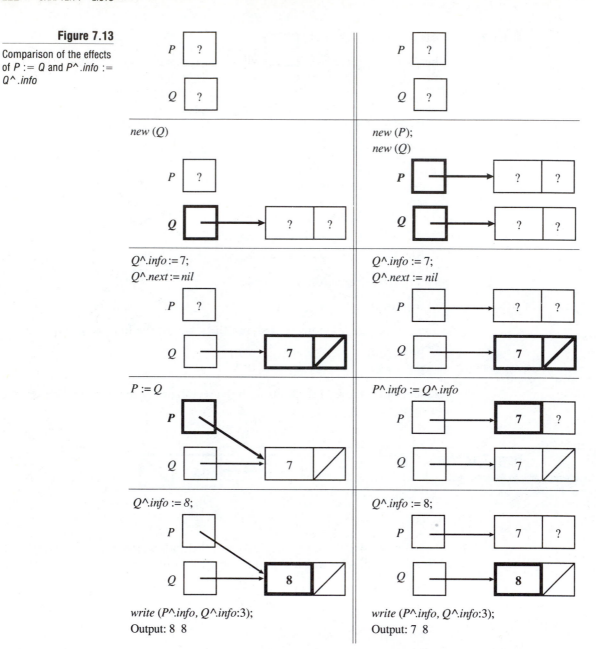

As with variables of the other predefined types, such as *integer, record*, and *array*, when using pointer variables in the design of algorithms, for clarity we use pseudocode that is very close to Pascal syntax. For structures that are not predefined, such as stacks, queues, and linked lists, we adhere to the ADT operation terminology.

Example 7.1	**Create a Node with Information.**

▼

When we consider linked lists, it will be important for us to be able to place a data item *e* into the information portion of a new node. For the time being we will ignore the *next* field, leaving it undefined. Figure 7.14 diagrams the steps of this procedure, which the following pseudocode and ADT pointer operations define:

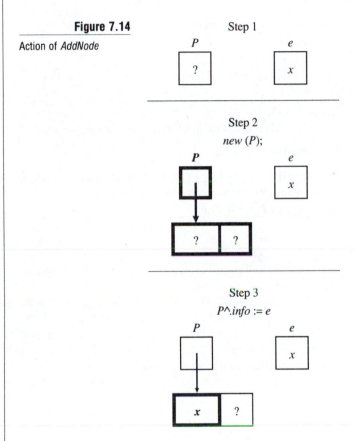

Figure 7.14

Action of *AddNode*

AddNode (*P, e*)

    Procedure to place a data item *e* into the information portion of a new
    node pointed to by *P* ; such a node has fields for information and a link

Input:

    e — item having the type of the information portion of a node to which
         P can point

Output:

    P — pointer

Figure	Algorithm
{7.14}	
{Step 2}	*New* (P)
{Step 3}	P^.*info* ← *e*

We perform a statement-by-statement conversion to Pascal:

```
{ Procedure to place information into a new node
pointed to by P }


procedure AddNode (var P: pointer; e: InfoType);
begin
   new(P);
   P^.info := e
end;
```

The ADT *Dispose* operation, which can be written in Pascal as

```
dispose(P)
```

reverses the effect of *new*(P) by deallocating memory space. Suppose P points to a memory cell that can hold an item of type *Node*. If the link is broken by reassigning P, such as by

```
P := nil    or    P := Q    or    new(P)
```

the memory cell is still allocated, as pictured in Figures 7.15–7.17, but cannot be reached.

To avoid abandoning the cell, we should free the unneeded cell before performing any of the other operations. (See Figures 7.18–7.20.) Alternative implementations of the ADT pointer operations *New* and *Dispose* are discussed in Section 8.1. Figure 7.21 summarizes the implementations of the ADT pointer operations discussed in this section.

Figure 7.15

Action of P := *nil*

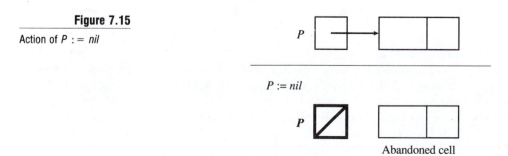

Figure 7.16

Action of $P := Q$

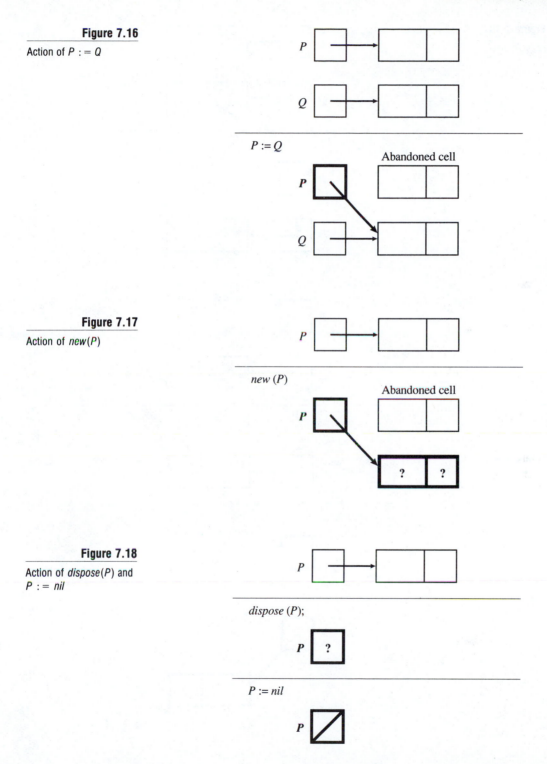

Figure 7.17

Action of *new*(P)

Figure 7.18

Action of *dispose*(P) and
$P := nil$

Figure 7.19

Action of *dispose(P)* and
P := *Q*

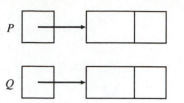

dispose (P);

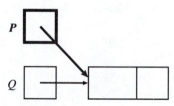

P := *Q*

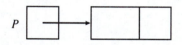

Figure 7.20

Action of *dispose(P)* and
new(P)

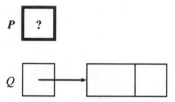

dispose (P);

new (P)

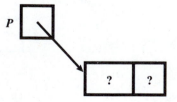

Figure 7.21.

Summary of one Pascal
implementation of ADT
pointer

An ADT Pointer Implementation

Create a pointer, *P*, which points to an element of type *Node*:

```
type
    pointer = ^Node;
    Node    = . . . . . . . . . . ;

var
    P : pointer;
```

New(P)

```
new (P)
```

Dispose(P)

```
dispose (P)
```

StorePointer(P, Q)

```
P := Q
```

StoreNode(P, e)

```
P^ := e
```

RetrieveNode(P) → e

```
P^
```

EqualPointer(P, Q) → b

```
(P = Q)
```

▽

SECTION 7.1 EXERCISES

*Assume the following type definition and variable declaration for Exercises
1−5:*

```
type
    pointer = ^real;

var
    P, Q     : pointer;
```

For Exercises 1–5 show a diagram of memory after execution of each statement, and give the output.

1. new (P) ;
   P^ : = 14.5;
   new (Q) ;
   Q^ : = 23.8;
   writeln (P^:5:1, Q^:5:1) ;
   P : = Q;
   P^ : = 36.1;
   writeln (P^:5:1, Q^:5:1) ;
   Q : = nil

2. new (P) ;
   P^ : = 14.5;
   new (Q) ;
   Q^ : = 23.8;
   writeln (P^:5:1,
      Q^:5:1) ;
   P^ : = Q^;
   writeln (P^:5:1,
      Q^:5:1) ;
   Q : = nil;
   writeln (P^:5:1)

3. new (P) ;
   P^ : = 14.5;
   Q : = P;
   writeln (P^:5:1, Q^:5:1)

4. new (P) ;
   P^ : = 14.5;
   Q : = P;
   if P = Q then
      writeln ('1. yes') ;
   new (Q) ;
   if P = Q then
      writeln ('2. yes') ;
   Q^ : = 14.5;
   if P = Q then
      writeln ('3. yes')

5. new (P) ;
   P^ : = 14.5;
   Q : = P;
   if P^ = Q^ then
      writeln ('1. yes') ;
   new (Q) ;
   Q^ : = 14.5;
   if P^ = Q^ then
      writeln ('2. yes')

Assume the following type definitions and variable declarations for Exercises 6–10:

```
type
   pointer  = ^Node;
   Node     = record
      info  : integer;
      ptr   : pointer
   end;

var
   P, Q, R  : pointer;
```

For Exercises 6–10 show a diagram of memory after execution of each statement.

6. new (P) ;
   P^.info : = 3;
   Q   : = P;
   Q^.ptr   : = nil

7. new (P) ;
   P^.info : = 4;
   new (Q) ;
   Q^.info : = 7;
   Q^.ptr   : = nil;
   P^.ptr   : = Q

8. new (P) ;
    P^.info := 5;
    new(P^.ptr)

10. new (P) ;
    P^.info := 8;
    new (Q) ;
    Q^.info := 9;
    P^.ptr := Q;
    Q^.ptr := P

9. new (P) ;
    Q   := P;
    P^.info := 6;
    new (R) ;
    R^.info := 7;
    P^.ptr := R;
    Q   := Q^.ptr

Assume the definitions and declarations used for Exercises 6–10, and consider the situation pictured in Figure 7.22. For Exercises 11–18 show a diagram of memory after execution of the segment and give any output.

Figure 7.22

Diagram of memory for Exercises 11–18

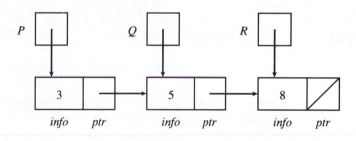

11. writeln(P^.info) ;
    P := P^.ptr;
    writeln(P^.info) ;
    P := P^.ptr;
    writeln(P^.info)

15. new (R) ;
    R^.info := 4;
    R^.ptr := Q;
    P^.ptr := R

17. new (Q) ;
    Q^.info := 2;
    Q^.ptr := P

12. dispose (P)

13. P := nil

14. P^.ptr := Q^.ptr;
    dispose (Q)

16. Q^.ptr := nil;
    dispose (R)

18. new (Q) ;
    Q^.info := 9;
    Q^.ptr := R^.ptr;
    R^.ptr := Q

19. Implement in Pascal the creation of a pointer variable *R* that can point to a character.

20. Implement in Pascal the creation of a variable *Emp* of type *pointer* that can point to a node that has record type *Node*. *Node* has two fields, *info* and *next*. The *info* field has two subfields, *name* and *salary*; while *next* is of type *pointer*.

For Exercises 21–24 do the following:
 a. Using pseudocode and ADT pointer operations and notation, define the operations.
 b. Code Part a in Pascal.

21. A procedure *MakeEmpty(P)* to give *P* the value *nil*.

22. Allocate memory for a character and place the letter "A" in that location. Use Exercise 19.

23. Allocate memory for a data cell pointed to by *Emp* of Exercise 20 and place "Evans, Joe" in the name field, 23005.75 in the salary field, and *nil* in *next*.

24. A procedure to advance a pointer *P* to point to the next node in a linked list. Use the definitions and declarations before Exercise 6 and refer to Figure 7.22.

SECTION 7.2

Linked List

Besides the advantages of dynamic memory allocation afforded by some implementations of linked lists, insertions and deletions can be easier and much faster in such a list than in an array. Consider, for instance, an array of names maintained in alphabetical order. The following are relevant constant and type definitions and variable declarations:

```
const
    MaxNum      = 100;              {maximum number of names}
                                   {in array Name             }


type
    StringType = packed array [1..20] of char;
    ArrayType  = array [1..MaxNum] of StringType;
    IndexType  = 0..MaxNum;


var
    Name        : ArrayType;       {array of names}
    TargetName  : StringType;      {particular name}
    i,                             {index}
    NumNames,                      {number of names in array Name}
    TargetLoc   : IndexType;       {index of TargetName}
```

Suppose *NumNames* number of names are arranged in the array *Name* and the name in *TargetName* needs to be inserted in the *TargetLoc* position. Perhaps this array holds a class roll; someone has added the course, and we wish to maintain our alphabetization. Figure 7.23 illustrates such a situation with *NumNames* = 7, *TargetName* = "Evans, Beth," and *TargetLoc* = 3.

Figure 7.23

Array of names with name "Evans, Beth" to be inserted

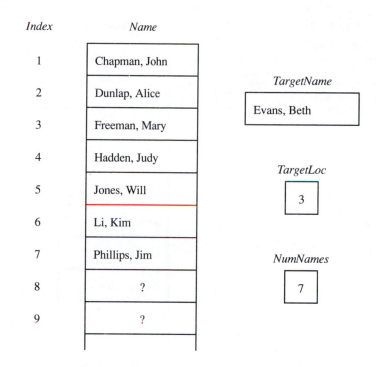

To accomplish the insertion we must first move by one position all the names from the third member to the end of the roll. We start at the end of the list, copying the name "Phillips, Jim" into the eighth array element. Then we copy *Name*[6] into *Name*[7], and so forth. A *for* loop can be used to perform this process:

```
for i := NumNames downto TargetLoc do
   Name[i + 1] := Name[i]
```

We start from the end and work down to the *TargetLoc* because copying from the other direction (*NumNames* to *TargetLoc*) would erroneously place the third name, "Freeman, Mary," in each of the third through the eighth array elements. With the additional statement to increment the number of names in the array,

```
NumNames := NumNames + 1
```

we have prepared the array for insertion of the target name. (See Figure 7.24.) As shown in Figure 7.25 we complete the process with the assignment

```
Name[TargetLoc] := TargetName
```

As Figure 7.24 indicates, for this situation we had to move five of the seven array values to make room for the target. In the worst case, where the new name belongs at the first of the roll, all array elements must be moved. Thus,

Figure 7.24

Array of Figure 7.23 after moving down one position all the names from the third position to the end of the roll and incrementing *NumNames*

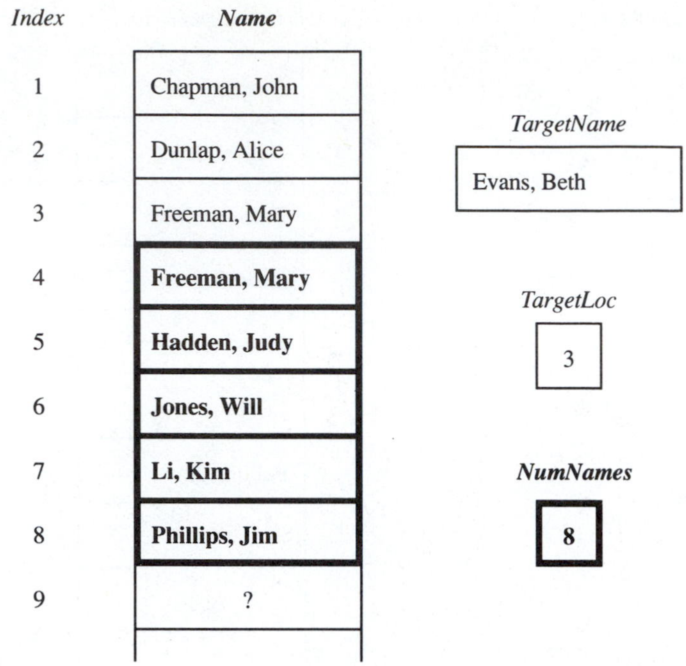

Index	Name
1	Chapman, John
2	Dunlap, Alice
3	Freeman, Mary
4	**Freeman, Mary**
5	**Hadden, Judy**
6	**Jones, Will**
7	**Li, Kim**
8	**Phillips, Jim**
9	?

TargetName

Evans, Beth

TargetLoc

3

NumNames

8

Figure 7.25

Array of Figure 7.24 after insertion of the target name

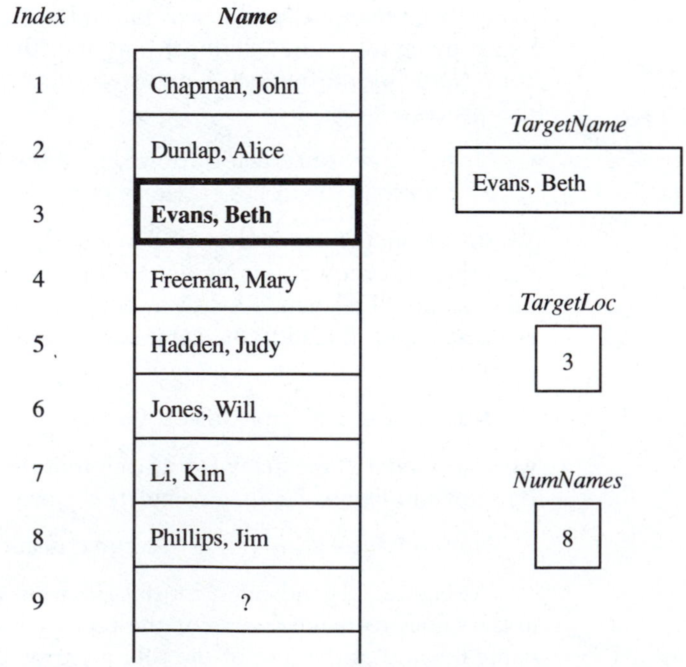

Index	Name
1	Chapman, John
2	Dunlap, Alice
3	**Evans, Beth**
4	Freeman, Mary
5	Hadden, Judy
6	Jones, Will
7	Li, Kim
8	Phillips, Jim
9	?

TargetName

Evans, Beth

TargetLoc

3

NumNames

8

for *n* names this insertion has a worst case complexity of $O(n)$. Deletion of a name poses a similar situation. In our example, if "Chapman, John" drops the course, all other array elements must be moved up to fill in the vacant position.

A linked list data structure for the roll, however, will accomplish insertion and deletion at an indicated location in the list with a complexity of $O(1)$, an order in which the number of array elements is irrelevant. Figure 7.26 shows the linked list with *cur* pointing to the current insertion location and *prev* indicating the previous node such that the new node will connect in between the two. The pointer *head* holds the address of the first element in the roll and *Target* points to the node to be inserted.

Figure 7.26

Linked list of names with "Evans, Beth" to be inserted

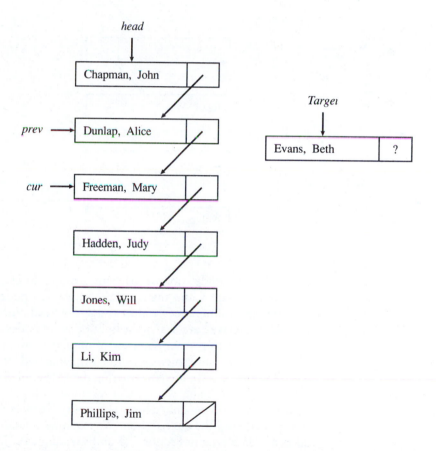

As shown in Figure 7.27, without moving anything in memory we can change one link, add another, and have the node properly inserted. Even if the target name is "Allen, Jill," change a couple of links, and we are through. (See Figures 7.28 and 7.29.) Regardless of the insertion point, the amount of work is the same.

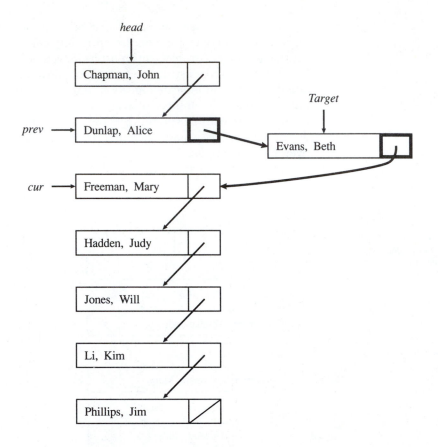

Figure 7.27

Linked list from Figure 7.26 after insertion of a node containing "Evans, Beth"

Similarly, for deletion we just route around the element to be removed without moving names and then free the unwanted node. Figures 7.30 and 7.31 picture removal of names within and at the head of the roll, respectively.

Although we have drawn the links between nodes as arrows, such diagrams are not meant to restrict our view of implementation. In fact, as we see later, the linked list data structure can be implemented not only with pointers but also with arrays. We are constructing data structures using data structures.

For the time being, we consider several drawings to aid our understanding of operations involving linked lists. The formal definition of the ADT linked list is postponed until the next section. We examine various implementations of this abstract data type in Section 7.4 and variations of linked lists in Section 7.5.

The first and last elements in the linked list must be marked in some way. In Figure 7.32, as in Figures 7.26–7.31, *head* is a pointer to the first element, while a slash in the link portion signals the terminal node.

Insertion and deletion can take place anywhere—the first, last, or interior of the list. To find the appropriate location, we must **traverse** or travel through the list from the beginning. *Cur* and *prev* indicate the current and previous

Figure 7.28

Linked list from Figure 7.26 with ''Allen, Jill'' to be inserted

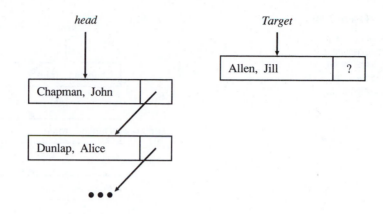

Figure 7.29

Linked list from Figure 7.28 after insertion of a node containing ''Allen, Jill''

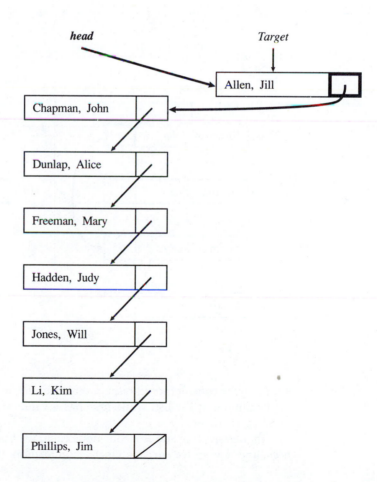

Figure 7.30

Deletion within a linked
list by routing around the
element to be removed
(Step 2) and then free-
ing the unwanted node
(Step 3)

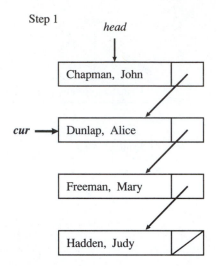

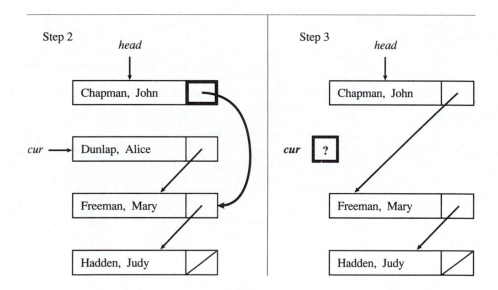

nodes under consideration, respectively. Initially, as in Figure 7.33 *cur* starts at
the beginning of the list, while *prev* has a value of *nil*, drawn with a slash instead of an arrow.

To advance *cur* and *prev* one node each, we first advance the back pointer,
prev, and then move *cur*, in an inchworm fashion. (See Figure 7.34.) If we trav-

erse the entire list, we arrive at a situation where *cur* falls off the end of the list. Figure 7.35 shows the *cur* box with a slash indicating a value of *nil* and the end of the list.

In traversing a list we might be looking for the location at which to insert a new node. Suppose the node to be added, which is pointed to by *Target*, must go between nodes indicated by *prev* and *cur*. Let us see how to accomplish this in the three situations of insertion at the head, middle, or tail of the linked list.

When *cur* = *head*, we have the situation detailed in Figure 7.36. Notice we link in the target node and then change the value of *head*.

Figure 7.31

Deletion at the head of a linked list by routing *head* around the element to be removed (Step 2) and then freeing the unwanted node (Step 3)

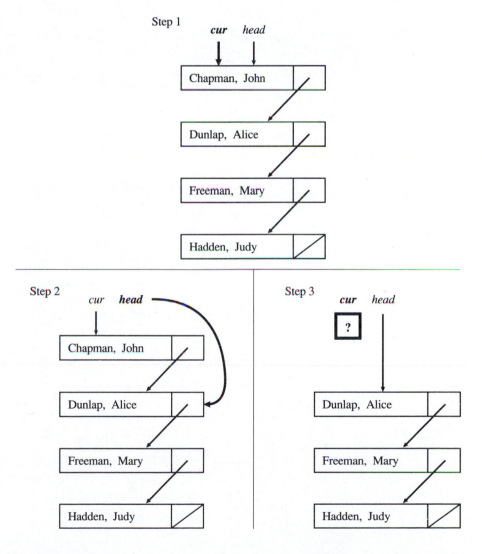

Figure 7.32

Linked list with *head* pointing to the first node and a slash, indicating *nil*, in the link portion of the last node

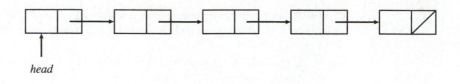

Figure 7.33

Start of a traversal of a linked list with *cur* pointing to the first node of the list

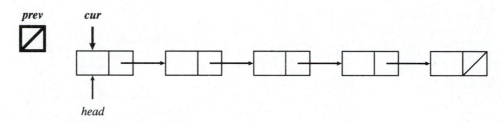

Figure 7.34

Steps to advance *prev* and *cur* one node each

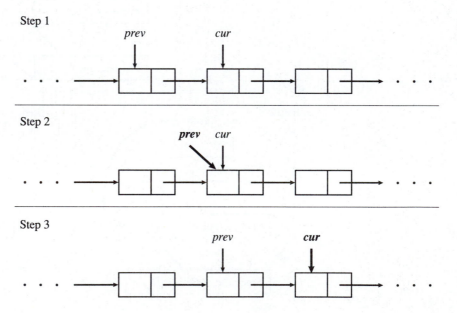

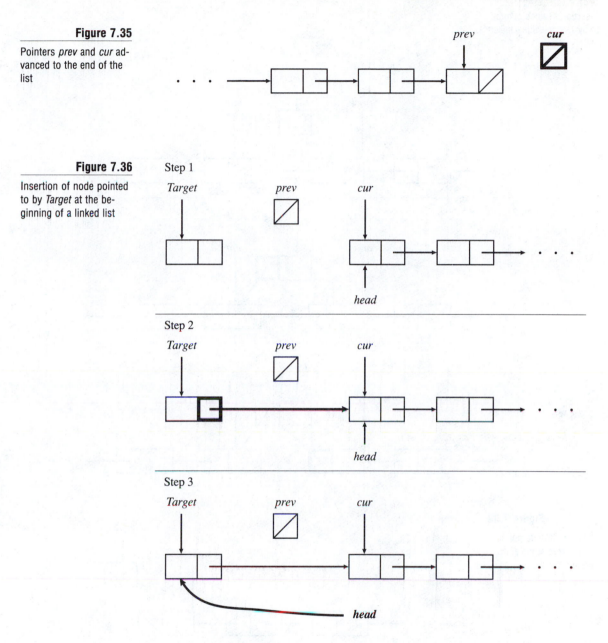

Figure 7.35

Pointers *prev* and *cur* advanced to the end of the list

Figure 7.36

Insertion of node pointed to by *Target* at the beginning of a linked list

Figures 7.37 and 7.38 illustrate insertion within and at the end of the linked list, respectively. Notice in both of these situations that we first make the target's link identical to the value of *cur*. Then we change the link of the previous node to connect the target's node.

Figure 7.37

Insertion of node pointed to by *Target* inside a linked list

Step 1

Step 2

Step 3

Figure 7.38

Insertion of node pointed to by *Target* at the end of a linked list

Step 1

Step 2

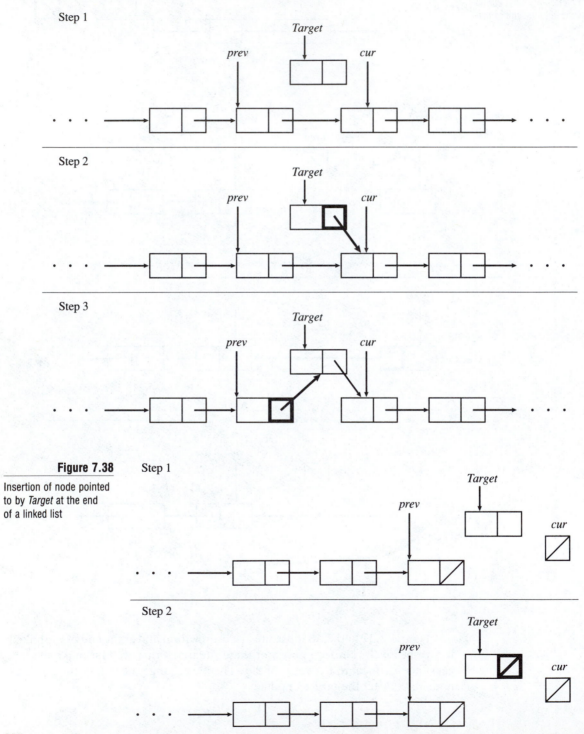

Figure 7.38   Step 3

continued

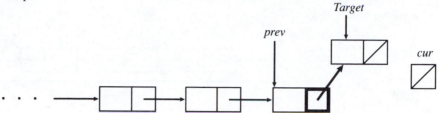

We next consider deletion at either end and the middle of the linked list. *Cur* points to the node to be deleted while *prev* indicates the previous node. As with insertion, deletion at the beginning of the list poses a unique situation in that we must adjust the *head*. Figure 7.39 shows deletion of the head node.

Removal of a later cell is detailed in Figures 7.40 and 7.41. In all three situations the last step involves freeing the deleted node. In both cases where the node is not at the head, we first change the link of the previous node to be the link of the current node before freeing the node pointed to by *cur*.

Figure 7.39

Deletion at the head of a linked list

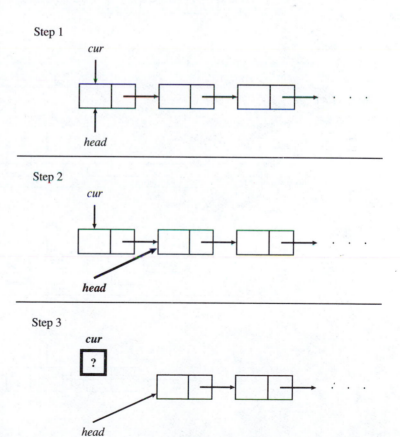

Figure 7.40

Deletion within a linked list

Step 1

Step 2

Step 3

Figure 7.41

Deletion at the end of a linked list

Step 1

Step 2

Step 3

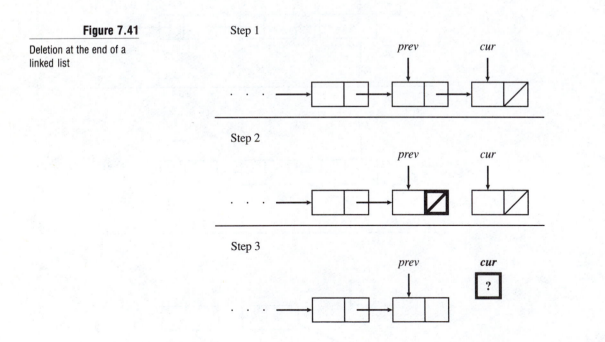

In the following sections we consider other operations involving linked lists.

SECTION 7.2 EXERCISES

1. **a.** Give an invariant for the loop at the beginning of this section to move array elements one position.
   b. Using program verification, prove the loop is correct.
   c. Are there any error situations that might arise?
   d. Write an insertion procedure with proper error handling to insert *TargetName* into an array *Name* of *NumNames* number of elements at location *TargetLoc*.

2. **a.** Write a procedure to delete an array element at *TargetLoc*.
   b. Give an invariant for the loop in Part a.
   c. Using program verification, prove the loop is correct.
   d. What is the worst case complexity of this procedure?

3. **a.** Draw sketches to show the steps of deletion of a target node that contains "Chapman, John" in the linked list of Figure 7.26.
   b. Repeat Part a for "Freeman, Mary."
   c. Repeat Part a for "Phillips, Jim."

4. Consider a linked list whose information portion is arranged in ascending order. In searching for the target information, under what circumstances would we stop traversing the list? That is, how do the current node's information and the target node's information compare?

5. **a.** What is the worst case complexity for a search of a linked list?
   b. Is a binary search possible on a linked list? Why or why not?

6. **a.** Draw a picture involving *head* to indicate an empty list.
   b. What indicates that the array *Name* of this section is empty?

7. Suppose a linked list contains integers in ascending order as shown in Figure 7.42.

Figure 7.42

Linked list for Exercises 7 and 8

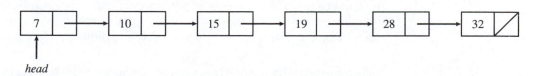

head

a. Draw each step with *cur, prev,* and *Target* for searching from the head of the list for a node containing 17 and, if not present, inserting a node pointed to by *Target* and containing 17.

b. Repeat Part a for the number 3.

c. Repeat Part a for the number 10.

d. Repeat Part a for the number 37.

8. Use the linked list in Figure 7.42.

a. Draw each step with *cur* and *prev* for searching from the head of the list for a node containing 28 and, if present, deleting it.

b. Repeat Part a for the number 7.

c. Repeat Part a for the number 12.

d. Repeat Part a for the number 32.

9. a. With *cur* and *prev* starting at appropriate locations at the beginning of a linked list, draw a series of figures to traverse the list until *cur* points to the third node and *prev* points to the second. Then draw figures to delete the third node.

b. What error situation might arise?

10. Suppose we have two nonempty lists, *L1* and *L2,* pointed to by *head1* and *head2,* respectively. Draw figures to remove the first node from *L1* and install it as the first node in *L2.*

11. The following appeared in the sample questions of the *1984 AP Computer Science Examination**:

In a certain card game, cards are distributed into seven separate piles. The rules of the game permit selecting a card in one pile and moving it, together with all cards on top of it, to the top of another pile. The cards that are moved are not to be reordered. Of the following data structures, which would be most appropriate to use in simulating this aspect of such a game?

(A) Seven singly linked lists

(B) Seven one-dimensional arrays

(C) Seven stacks

(D) Seven queues

(E) Seven sets

SECTION 7.3

ADT Linked List

With the drawings from the last section in mind, we are now ready to define ADT linked list. The formal definition appears in Figure 7.43. Remember that though we refer to variables pointing to nodes, those variables are not necessarily of type *pointer.* As we will see, such a variable may point to a node in

---

* AP question selected from *AP Computer Science Examination,* 1984. Reprinted by permission of Educational Testing Service, the copyright owner of the sample questions.

Figure 7.43.

Formal definition of ADT
linked list

ADT Linked List

Objects: Finite sequence of nodes. All the nodes have the same type; each node has two parts, an information portion, *info*, and a field, *next*, that points to the following node in the list. A special variable, in this definition called *head*, points to the first node of the list.

Operations:

Notation:

InfoType	— type of information portion of a node
L	— linked list
head	— points to the first node of *L*
cur, prev	— point to nodes in *L*
P	— points to a node, not necessarily in *L*
e	— item of type *InfoType*
b	— *boolean value*
null	— special constant value for a pointing variable; indicates the variable is not pointing to a node

MakeListEmpty(*cur*)
Procedure to give *cur* the *null* value

ListIsEmpty(*head*) → *b*
Boolean function to return *true* if *L* is empty

ToFirst(*head, cur*)
Procedure to make *cur* point to the first node in *L*

AtFirst(*head, cur*) → *b*
Function to return *true* if *cur* points to the first node in the list

AtEnd(*cur*) → *b*
Function to return *true* if *cur* points to the last node in the list; if *cur* is *null* or does not point to the last node, return *false*.

InsertFirst(*head, Target*)
Procedure to insert the node pointed to by *Target* as the first element in *L*

InsertLater(*prev, Target*)
Procedure to insert a node pointed to by *Target* into *L* after the node indicated by *prev*; assume *prev* points to a node in *L*

DeleteFirst(*head*)
Procedure to delete the first node in *L*; assume *head* points to a node

DeleteLater(*prev*)
Procedure to remove the node after the one pointed to by *prev*; assume *prev* points to a node which is not the last node in the list

Advance(*cur*)
Procedure to advance *cur* to point to the next node in *L*. If *cur* presently points to the last node, *MakeListEmpty(cur)* is executed. Assume *cur* points to a node

StoreInfo(*cur, e*)
Procedure to give *e*'s value to the information portion of the node indicated by *cur*; assume *cur* points to a node.

Figure 7.43.

continued

StoreNext(*cur*, *P*)
>   Procedure to give *P*'s value to the *next* field of the node indicated by *cur*; assume *cur* points to a node

RetrieveInfo(*cur*) → *e*
>   Function to return the information in the node indicated by *cur*; assume *cur* points to a node

RetrieveNext(*cur*) → *P*
>   Function to return the value of the *next* field from the node indicated by *cur*; assume *cur* points to a node

another way, say, by holding its index in an array. Before we consider implementation, we develop some further operations defined using pseudocode and the ADT linked list operations.

Example 7.2

▼ We will write pseudocode with ADT operations to read records from a file *f* into a linked list, with the first node indicated by *head*. The first record will go in the head node and the last record will appear at the tail. To facilitate repeated insertion at the end of the linked list, we will employ an additional pointer, *tail,* to indicate the last node on the list.

Step 1 of Figure 7.44 pictures the initialization of the empty list and the file for reading. As Step 2 shows, we read the first datum from the file into a variable *e*; and then in Step 3 we transfer that information into a node whose location is indicated by *Target*. In Section 7.1 we detailed node creation and information insertion with the pointer operation *AddNode*. As we will see, this procedure could have been implemented in the context of arrays as well. Regardless of the encoding in Pascal, we picture the formation of this node as in Step 3 of Figure 7.44. In Step 4 this newly created node is inserted at the beginning of the list. We use a slash in the *next* field to indicate that the field has a null value and that this is the last node in the linked list. Now we initialize *tail* to point to the last and only node in the list. (See Step 5 of Figure 7.44.)

After establishing what happens at the beginning of the linked list, we are ready to repeat the sequence of steps drawn in Figure 7.45 as long as the file pointer does not indicate the end-of-file marker. Note that we are always inserting at the end of the list.

Because insertion at the beginning of a linked list changes the value of *head* but a later insertion does not, we must treat installation of the first datum from the file independently from that of the other data. Thus, at the head of the list we use the operation *InsertFirst*, but afterwards we employ *InsertLater*. Moreover, initially we point *tail* to the head node with the *ToFirst* operation. Once *tail* points to a list node, we can use the operation *Advance* to proceed to the next node in the linked list. Being careful to handle the empty file situation even for the initial case, we write the steps for this *ReadList* procedure in pseudocode and ADT operations as shown below.

Figure 7.44

Initial action of *Read-List*(*head, f*) from Example 7.2

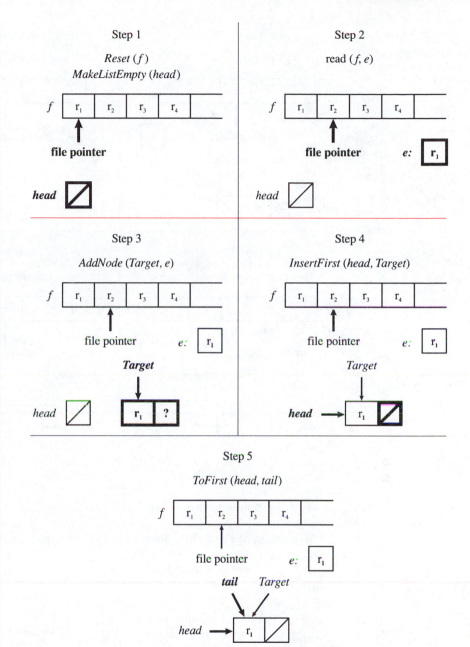

Step 1

Reset (*f*)
MakeListEmpty (*head*)

Step 2

read (*f, e*)

Step 3

AddNode (*Target, e*)

Step 4

InsertFirst (*head, Target*)

Step 5

ToFirst (*head, tail*)

ReadList(*head, f*)
Procedure to read records from a binary file *f* into a linked list, with the first node of the list indicated by *head* and containing the first element of *f*
Input:
    f   — file

Figure 7.45

One iteration of the *while* loop for *ReadList*(*head*, *f*) of Example 7.2

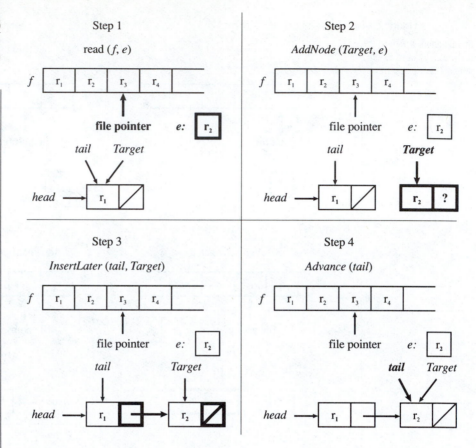

Output:
    head — points to linked list
Assumption:
    An element of *f* and the information field of a node of the linked list have the same type.

Figure	Algorithm
{7.44}	
{Step 1}	*Reset* (*f*)
	MakeListEmpty (*head*)
	if not *EOF* (*f*) then
{Step 2}	read (*f*, *e*)
{Step 3}	*AddNode* (*Target*, *e*)
{Step 4}	*InsertFirst* (*head*, *Target*)
{Step 5}	*ToFirst* (*head*, *tail*)
{7.45}	
	while not *EOF* (*f*) do
{Step 1}	read (*f*, *e*)
{Step 2}	*AddNode* (*Target*, *e*)

	{Step 3}	*InsertLater (tail, Target)*
▲	{Step 4}	*Advance (tail)*

Example 7.3	**Search and Delete**.

▼ Suppose a linked list pointed to by *head* already exists with the information portions of the nodes of type *InfoType*, arranged in ascending order with no two nodes containing the same information. From a file *f* we read values of type *InfoType*. Each node with one of these values is to be deleted from the list.

As long as the linked list is not empty, for every record in the file, we read a value into a variable, *e*. Then we search the list for the node containing *e*'s value. If found, we delete that node. Pseudocode for the *DeleteValues(head, f)* task is as follows:

Start at the beginning of the file *f*.
While there is data in *f* and the list is not empty do
    Read a datum from the file into *e*.
    Search for a node containing *e*'s value.
    If found then
        Delete that node
  else
        Say the node was not found.

Two procedures are evident from this pseudocode, a search and a delete procedure.

The search of the linked list in ascending order is sequential and stops on one of three conditions:

1. *e* is equal to the information portion of the node pointed to by *cur*, in which case we have found the node to be deleted.

2. *e* is less than the information portion of the node pointed to by *cur*. Thus, we have already passed the place in the list where *e* should be found without locating the value.

3. *cur* points to the last node in the list. There are no more nodes in the list to be searched. The value of *e* must be there, if in the list at all.

When the search halts, we also want *prev* pointing to the node immediately before *cur*'s node. Should *cur* be at the head of the list, *prev* will have the null value. Thus, parameters for the search routine include *head* and *e* as well as *cur* and *prev*.

In the search we first initialize as *true* a boolean variable, *continue*, that will indicate whether we should continue searching or not. Also, we place *cur* and *prev* in their proper locations at the beginning of the list as shown in an example in Figure 7.46.

While *cur* does not point to the last node and *continue* is *true*, we check whether we have found the place in the list where the value of *e* should be located. If *e* remains larger than the information part of the list node, we advance *prev* and then *cur*. If a match is found or if we are already past where *e* should

Figure 7.46

Initialization in
Search(*head, prev, cur,
e*) from Example 7.3

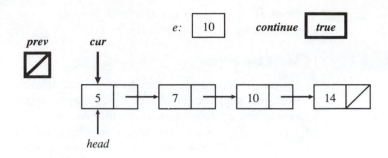

Figure 7.47

Example of search from
Example 7.3 to advance
cur to point to the node
containing *e* = 10

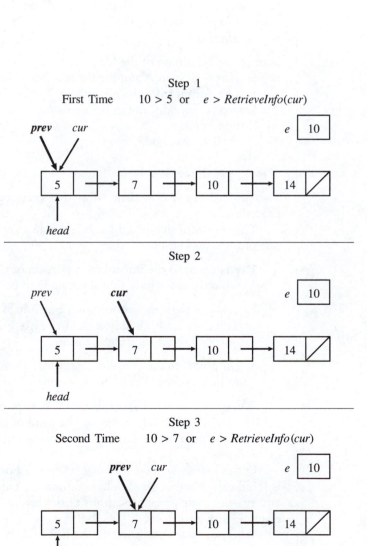

Step 1

First Time   10 > 5 or   *e > RetrieveInfo*(*cur*)

Step 2

Step 3

Second Time   10 > 7 or   *e > RetrieveInfo*(*cur*)

Figure 7.47

continued

Step 4

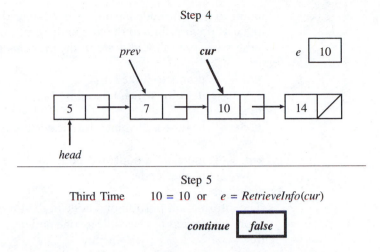

Step 5

Third Time   10 = 10 or   *e* = *RetrieveInfo*(*cur*)

continue | *false*

be found, we change *continue* to be *false* so that the search will halt. Supposing the value sought is in the third node, the search would proceed as in Figure 7.47 with each iteration of the loop indicated. Had *e*'s value been in the first node, traversal would stop immediately, leaving the situation as pictured in Figure 7.48.

Figure 7.48

Example of search from Example 7.3 to advance *cur* to point to the node containing *e* = 5

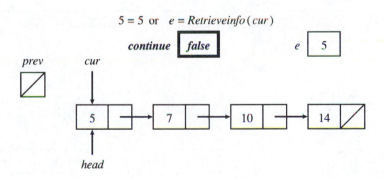

Had *e*'s value been 8 or 9, the search of this list would have terminated in the same place as shown in Figure 7.47 with 9 < 10 or *e* < *RetrieveInfo*(*cur*). If the search had been for a value larger than any in the list, for example 17, the process would have culminated with *AtEnd*(*cur*) being *true* as pictured in Figure 7.49. The search procedure illustrated in Figures 7.46–7.49 is designed as follows:

Search (*head, prev, cur, e*)
   Procedure to search for *e*'s value in an ordered linked list pointed to by *head*. If found, *cur* should point to that node; otherwise, *cur* should

point to the first node having a value larger than *e* or to the last node in the list. If *cur* points to the first node, *prev* should have the null value; otherwise, *prev* should point to the previous node.

Input:
    head — points to linked list
    e   — item for which to search

Output:
    prev — has the null value or indicates the node before that pointed to by *cur*
    cur   — indicates a node; if a node has the same value as *e*, *cur* points to that node.

Assumptions:
    The information portion of a node of the linked list and *e* have the same type. The linked list has at least one node.

Figure	Algorithm	
{7.46}	*ToFirst*(*head, cur*)	{ Initialize }
	MakeListEmpty(*prev*)	
	continue ← *true*	
{7.47}	while not *AtEnd*(*cur*) and	
	continue do	{ Search loop }
	if *e* > *RetrieveInfo*(*cur*) then	{ Keep searching }
{Steps 1, 3}	*prev* ← *cur*	
{Steps 2, 4}	*Advance*(*cur*)	
	else	{ At or beyond location }
{Step 5} or {7.48}	*continue* ← *false*	
{7.49}		

Figure 7.49

Result of search from Example 7.3 to advance *cur* to point to the node containing *e* = 17; *AtEnd*(*cur*) is *true*; node not found, *e* > *RetrieveInfo*(*cur*)

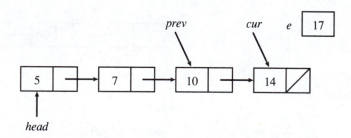

Since in the examples of Figures 7.48 and 7.47 *e* is found, we delete the node as in Figures 7.50 and 7.51, respectively. If as in Figure 7.49 the information portion of the node indicated by *cur* does not match *e*'s value, we should print a message stating that the value is not found. As suggested in these figures, the delete procedure that follows must handle deletion of the first node differently from deletion of a later one.

Figure 7.50

Node containing 5 deleted from the beginning of the list

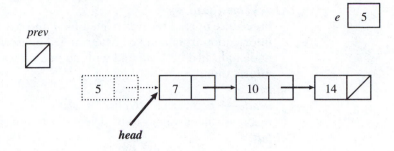

Figure 7.51

Node containing 10 deleted from inside the list

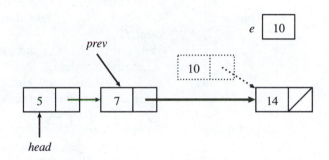

*Delete(**head, prev**)*

Procedure to delete the node after the one pointed to by *prev* from the linked list pointed to by *head*. If *prev* has the null value, the procedure deletes the first node.

Input:

head — points to linked list

prev — indicates node before the one to be deleted

Output:

head — points to modified linked list

Assumption:

prev has the null value or indicates a node in the nonempty linked list pointed to by *head*.

Figure	Algorithm	
{7.48}	if *ListIsEmpty(prev)* then	{ Found at head }
{7.50}	*DeleteFirst(head)*	
{7.47, Step 4}	else	{ Found inside }
{7.51}	*DeleteLater(prev)*	

The entire process of reading values from a file and deleting the nodes containing that information is repeated as long as there is data in the file. Pseudocode using ADT operations for the procedure follows:

DeleteValues(*head*, *f*)

> Procedure to read records from a file *f* and delete nodes with that information from a linked list arranged in ascending order with the first node indicated by *head* and with no two nodes containing the same information.

Input:
> *head* — points to linked list
> *f* — file of values to be deleted from linked list

Output:
> *head* — points to linked list

Assumptions:
> An element of *f* and an information portion of a node are of the same type.

Figure	**Algorithm**	
	Reset(*f*)	
	while (not *EOF* (*f*)) and (not *ListIsEmpty*(*head*)) do	
	read *e* from file *f*	
{7.46−7.49}	*Search*(*head*, *prev*, *cur*, *e*)	
{7.47−7.48}	if *e* = *RetrieveInfo*(*cur*) then	{ Found }
{7.50−7.51}	*Delete*(*head*, *prev*)	
{7.49}	else	{ Not found }
	print message that *e* was not found	

SECTION 7.3 EXERCISES

Using pseudocode and ADT linked list operations and notation, define the operations in Exercises 1−19. Also, answer any other questions for each problem.

1. Procedure to exchange values in two nodes pointed to by *cur* and *prev*. Assume *cur* and *prev* point to nodes that contain information.

2. Procedure from Exercise 10, Section 7.2 to remove the first node from a linked list pointed to by *head1* and install it as the first node in a linked list pointed to by *head2*.

3. Procedure to form a list with two nodes, the first with the value of *x* and the second with the value of *y*.

4. Procedure *InsertTailList*(*head*, *tail*, *Target*) to insert the target node at the end of the linked list with head and tail pointers *head* and *tail*, respectively. Be sure to handle the situation where the list is initially empty and to continue to have *tail* point to the last node.

5. a. Nonrecursive function *Size* to return the number of nodes in a linked list pointed to by *head*.
   b. Find a recursive version of the function in Part a.

6. Boolean function *EqualList*(*P*, *Q*) to return *true* if the two lists are identical, ordered in the same way.

7. **a.** Nonrecursive procedure to print the values in the information fields of the nodes of a linked list pointed to by *head*.
   b. Find a recursive version of the procedure in Part a.

8. Procedure to read records from a file and insert each datum in turn at the beginning of a linked list.

9. Procedure *Split*(*prev*, *head2*) to split a linked list into two lists. The second list, starting at the node after the one indicated by *prev*, gets a head pointer, *head2*. Assume *prev* points to a node.

10. **a.** Procedure to make a copy of a linked list.
    b. Draw a series of figures for a linked list with three elements to illustrate Part a.

11. **a.** Nonrecursive function to return the sum of the values stored in a linked list of numbers.
    b. Find a recursive version of the function in Part a.

12. Boolean function to return *true* if the key values in a list are in order.

13. Procedure to delete the third node in a linked list; be sure to handle the situations where the list has fewer than three nodes.

14. **a.** Procedure to append a linked list with pointer *headExtra* onto the end of a linked list with pointer *head*.
    b. Draw a series of figures to illustrate Part a.

15. Suppose a linked list, pointed to by *head*, already exists with elements arranged in ascending order. From a file *f* read values of type *InfoType*. Add nodes with this information to the list, maintaining the order. If the value already is in the list, do not duplicate the node.

16. **a.** Procedure to merge two sorted linked lists, destroying the original lists.
    b. Draw a series of figures for linked lists with three elements to illustrate Part a.

17. **a.** Nonrecursive procedure to free all the nodes in a linked list.
    b. Find a recursive version of the function in Part a.

18. Function to point to the predecessor of the node indicated by *cur*.

19. Procedure to delete from a linked list the node with the largest value; if more than one node contain this largest value, delete the first such node.

20. **a.** Write an invariant for the loop in *ReadList* of Example 7.2.
    b. Using program verification, prove this loop is correct.

21. **a.** Write an invariant for the loop in the procedure *Search* of Example 7.3.
    b. Using program verification, prove this loop is correct.

Linked List Implementations

We have previously referred to two major implementations of linked lists, one using arrays and the other pointers. After presenting pointers and a dynamic memory allocation approach, we consider development with arrays and static memory allocation.

For the linked list we need the structure established in Section 7.1 of using pointers to nodes. The information portion of the node can be as small as a bit or as large as a record with numerous fields. The pointer portion holds the location of yet another node. The following type definitions and variable declarations generate the creation of a list pointed to by *head* with information fields of type *InfoType*. In various operations in this section we need additional pointers of *cur*, *prev*, and *P*, as well as variable *e* of type *InfoType* and boolean variable *b*.

```
type
    InfoType  = ..........;
    pointer   = ^Node;
    Node      = record
         info :  InfoType;
         next :  pointer
    end;

var
    head,          { Pointer to the first node in the list }
    cur,
    prev,
    P          : pointer;
    e          : InfoType;
    b          : boolean;
```

The special constant, *nil*, is used to indicate a null pointer in this dynamic allocation of linked lists. Thus, *MakeListEmpty(cur)* is generated with an assignment statement as follows:

```
{ Procedure to give cur a null value }

procedure MakeListEmpty (var cur : pointer);
begin
    cur := nil
end;
```

ListIsEmpty(head), to test if the list pointed to by *head* does not hold any nodes, returns the value of a boolean expression that uses the relational operator =.

```
{ Boolean function to return true if head points to an empty list }
```

```
function ListIsEmpty (head: pointer): boolean;
begin
   ListIsEmpty := (head = nil)
end;
```

The effect of this assignment is the same as that of an *if* statement:

```
if head = nil then
   ListIsEmpty := true
else
   ListIsEmpty := false
```

In reality, we are using the ADT pointer operation for testing equality of pointers, *EqualPointer*(*head, nil*). A note of caution—until we execute *MakeListEmpty*(*head*) or *head* := *nil*, *head*'s value is undefined. Comparison of *nil* with an undefined variable with most compilers results in an error.

After initialization and as the list develops, *head* continues to indicate the first node. Thus, *ToFirst*(*head, cur*) is generated by the ADT pointer operation *StorePointer*(*cur, head*) and is implemented by a procedure with a Pascal assignment statement:

```
{ Procedure to point cur toward the list pointed to by head     }

procedure ToFirst(head: pointer; var cur : pointer);
begin
   cur := head
end;
```

AtFirst(*head, cur*) tests with a boolean expression to see if *cur* points to the first node in the list:

```
{  Boolean function to return true if cur points to the first
   node in the linked list to which head points                }

function AtFirst (head, cur : pointer): boolean;
begin
   AtFirst := (cur = head)
end;
```

This function is an implementation of the ADT pointer operation *EqualPointer*(*head, cur*).

AtEnd(*cur*) also employs the relational operator = to test. We use the fact that the *next* field of the last node in the list will be *nil* to complete the function.

```
{ Boolean function to return true if cur points to the last
   node in a linked list                                     }
```

```
function AtEnd (cur: pointer): boolean;
begin
   if (cur = nil) then
      AtEnd := false
   else
      AtEnd := (cur^.next = nil)
end;
```

Notice how careful we are to make sure that *cur* really points to a node before we attempt to access the *next* field of that node. Without such a precaution, if *cur* had the value *nil*, the program would end abnormally.

Figures 7.36 through 7.38 of Section 7.2 show the cases of insertion anywhere in the list. Considering the two main situations of insertion at the head and beyond the head node, we should construct a procedure *Insert*, as shown in the structured diagram of Figure 7.52.

Figure 7.52

Structured diagram for
Insert

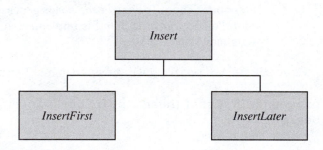

Insertion at the beginning of the list requires adjustment of *head* to point to a new first node. We must be careful, however, to link this node to the list before changing the value of *head* or else all reference to the rest of the list will be lost. Figures 7.53 and 7.54 illustrate a wrong and right sequence of events, respectively, of attaching a node pointed to by *Target* to the beginning of the list.

As Figure 7.53 shows, when we change the value of *head* before we attach *Target*'s node, we lose the reference to the list; no pointer contains the address of the list. Thus, *InsertFirst(head, Target)* must be implemented in the following order:

```
{ Procedure to insert a node pointed to by Target at the
   beginning of the linked list pointed to by head      }

procedure InsertFirst ( var head: pointer; Target: pointer );
begin
   Target^.next := head;
   head         := Target
end;
```

Figure 7.53

Wrong way to insert node at beginning of list

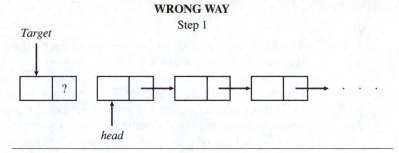

WRONG WAY

Step 1

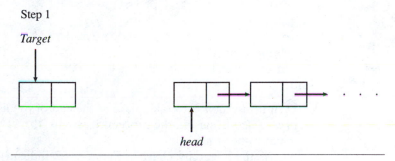

Step 2

LOST!

Figure 7.54

Correct way to insert node at beginning of list

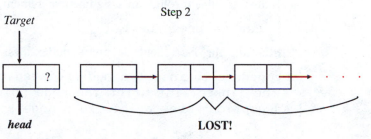

Step 1

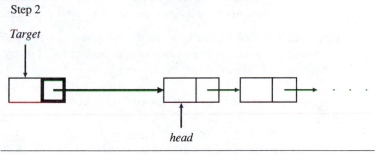

Step 2

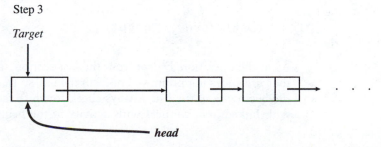

Step 3

The *StoreRecord* ADT record operation can be used to place values in the information field of this node before or after insertion into the list.

The *InsertLater(prev, Target)* operation will not alter the value of *head*. Figures 7.37 and 7.38 of Section 7.2 detail how we first change the pointer field of *Target*'s node and then the pointer field of the *prev* node to link in the new node. In those figures we employ an extra pointer, *cur*, to indicate the node ahead of *prev*'s node. For the Pascal implementation, *cur* is a local variable that obtains its value through an assignment statement,

        cur := prev^.next

After all, the *next* field of *prev*'s node does point to the next node.

```
{ Procedure to insert a node pointed to by Target inside
   the linked list after the node pointed to by prev   }
{ Assumption: prev points to a node }

procedure InsertLater ( prev, Target: pointer );
var
    cur             : pointer;
begin
    cur             := prev^.next;
    Target^.next := cur;
    prev^.next    := Target
end;
```

Even if insertion is to take place at the end of the list with the value of *cur = prev^.next* being *nil*, the procedure assigns *Target^.next* the appropriate terminal value of *nil*.

As the hierarchy chart in Figure 7.52 indicates, to accomplish insertion anywhere in the list, we define the *Insert* procedure with two parts:

```
{ Procedure to insert a node pointed to by Target in the
   linked list after the node pointed to by prev or at
   the head should prev be nil                          }

procedure Insert ( var head: pointer; prev, Target: pointer );
begin
    if ListIsEmpty(prev) then
        InsertFirst(head, Target)
    else
        InsertLater(prev, Target)
end;
```

As in the operation *Delete* from the last section, *ListIsEmpty(prev)* indicates that *prev* does not point to a node in the list, so that activity is to take place at the beginning of the list. Always check for the exceptional case. In particular, with linked lists, we deal with activity at the beginning of the list differently from later in the list. Otherwise, *head* could hold an incorrect value and the list could be lost forever.

Figure 7.39 of Section 7.2 illustrates this special case for deletion. When we delete the first node, we not only want to advance *head* to point to the second node, but we also want to release the memory occupied by the abandoned node. To accomplish this removal, we use another pointer, *cur*, to hold the position of the first node. Then after advancing the *head*, we dispose of the extra node. Using the *Advance* procedure to be presented shortly, the *Delete-First* procedure reads as follows:

```
{ Procedure to delete the first node in a linked list }
{ Assumption: head points to a node                   }

procedure DeleteFirst ( var head: pointer );
var
    cur : pointer;
begin
    ToFirst (head, cur);
    Advance (head);
    dispose (cur)
end;
```

It is important to hold the position of the first node in *cur* before advancing *head* or else the reference to the former head node will be lost. The error of forgetting to dispose will not immediately, or perhaps ever, affect the performance of the linked list. If, however, there are a number of deletions without nodes being released for further use, we may eventually obtain an OUT OF MEMORY error message.

Elsewhere, the *DeleteLater* operation generates a deletion of a node, where *prev* references the previous node. As with several other routines, we use a local pointer variable, *cur*, to point to the node after *prev*'s node. Figures 7.40 and 7.41 of Section 7.2 illustrate this procedure, implemented with pointers as follows:

```
{ Procedure to delete a node not at the
  beginning of a linked list           }
{ Assumption: prev points to a node    }

procedure DeleteLater ( prev : pointer );
var
    cur : pointer;
begin
    cur := prev^.next;
    Advance (prev^.next);
    dispose (cur)
end;
```

We break the existing link of the *prev* node by advancing its *next* pointer to reference the node after the one indicated by *cur*. As with the *Insert* procedure, the *Delete* procedure, discussed in Example 7.3 of Section 7.3, takes into consideration activity at the beginning of the list.

Advancing a pointer changes its value to the address of the following node. As shown in Figure 7.55, *cur*'s *next* field, *cur*^.*next*, already points to this node. Even when *cur* references the last node in a list, as in Figure 7.56, the *next* field has the proper value, *nil*, for *cur* to fall off the end of the list. Thus, the procedure for advancing involves only an assignment statement.

Figure 7.55

cur^.*next* points to the node following the one pointed to by *cur*

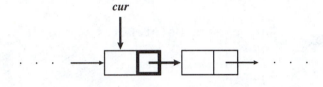

Figure 7.56

cur^.*next* is *nil*

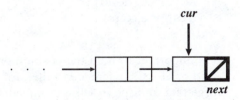

```
{ Procedure to advance cur to point
    to the next node in a linked list }
{ Assumption: cur points to a node  }

procedure Advance (var cur: pointer);
begin
    cur := cur^.next
end;
```

The *StoreInfo* operation assigns a value to the information portion of the current node.

```
{ Procedure to store a value in the information
    field in a linked list                      }
{ Assumption: cur points to a node              }

procedure StoreInfo (cur: pointer; e: InfoType);
begin
    cur^.info := e
end;
```

Similarly, *StoreNext* alters the value of *next*:

```
{ Procedure to store a value in the
  next field in a linked list       }
{ Assumption: cur points to a node }

procedure StoreNext (cur, P: pointer);
begin
   cur^.next := P
end;
```

The function *RetrieveInfo* returns the information portion of a node. For the given implementation, the value returned through *RetrieveInfo* is assumed to be of a scalar type, *InfoType*. Because of Pascal restrictions, if we need to return a value of a composite type, such as record or array, we must implement the *RetrieveInfo* operation as a procedure and return the value through a variable parameter.

```
{ Function to return the information portion
  of a node in a linked list                 }
{ Assumptions: cur points to a node and InfoType
  is a scalar type                              }

function RetrieveInfo (cur: pointer): InfoType;
begin
   RetrieveInfo := cur^.info
end;
```

Returning the *next* field of the node pointed to by *cur*, the definition of the function in a linked list *RetrieveNext* follows:

```
{ Function to return the pointer field of a
  node in a linked list          }
{ Assumption: cur points to a node }

function RetrieveNext (cur: pointer): pointer;
begin
   RetrieveNext := cur^.next
end;
```

As with all pointers, however, the value of *RetrieveNext* cannot be printed.

Figure 7.57 summarizes this dynamic memory allocation implementation of ADT linked list.

Figure 7.57

Summary of one Pascal
dynamic memory alloca-
tion implementation of
ADT linked list

A Dynamic Memory Allocation Implementation
of ADT Linked List

Create a linked list pointed to by *head* where each node has two parts, an information portion, *info*, and a field, *next*, that points to the following node in the list.

```
type
    InfoType = . . . . . . . . . . . ;
    pointer   = ^Node;
    Node      = record
        info  :  InfoType;
        next  :  pointer
    end;
var
    head      :  pointer;
```

MakeListEmpty(*cur*)

```
procedure MakeListEmpty (var cur : pointer);
begin
    cur := nil
end;
```

ListIsEmpty(*head*) → *b*

```
function ListIsEmpty (head: pointer): boolean;
begin
    ListIsEmpty := (head = nil)
end;
```

ToFirst (*head, cur*)

```
procedure ToFirst (head: pointer; var cur : pointer);
begin
    cur := head
end;
```

AtFirst(*head, cur*) → *b*

```
function AtFirst (head, cur : pointer): boolean;
begin
    AtFirst := (cur = head)
end;
```

AtEnd(*cur*) → *b*

```
function AtEnd (cur: pointer): boolean;
begin
    if (cur = nil) then
        AtEnd := false
    else
        AtEnd := (cur^.next = nil)
end;
```

Figure 7.57

continued

InsertFirst(head, Target)

```
procedure InsertFirst ( var head : pointer; Target: pointer );
begin
    Target^.next :=    head;
    head          := Target
end;
```

InsertLater(prev, Target)

```
{ Assumption: prev points to a node }
procedure InsertLater ( prev, Target : pointer );
var
    cur   : pointer;
begin
    cur := prev^.next;
    Target^.next := cur;
    prev^.next   := Target
end;
```

DeleteFirst(head)

```
{ Assumption: head points to a node }
procedure DeleteFirst ( var head: pointer );
var
    cur : pointer;
begin
    ToFirst(head, cur);
    Advance(head);
    dispose(cur)
end;
```

DeleteLater(prev)

```
{ Assumption: prev points to a node }
procedure DeleteLater ( prev : pointer );
var
    cur   : pointer;
begin
    cur := prev^.next;
    Advance(prev^.next);
    dispose(cur)
end;
```

Advance(cur)

```
{ Assumption: cur points to a node }
procedure Advance (var cur: pointer);
begin
    cur := cur^.next
end
```

Figure 7.57

continued

StoreInfo(cur, e)

```
{ Assumption: cur points to a node }
procedure StoreInfo (cur: pointer; e: InfoType);
begin
   cur^.info := e
end;
```

StoreNext(cur, P)

```
{ Assumption: cur points to a node }
procedure StoreNext (cur, P: pointer);
begin
   cur^.next := P
end;
```

RetrieveInfo(cur) → e

```
{ Assumptions: cur points to a node; InfoType is
  scalar }
function RetrieveInfo (cur: pointer): InfoType;
begin
   RetrieveInfo := cur^.info
end;
```

RetrieveNext(cur) → P

```
{ Assumption: cur points to a node }
function RetrieveNext (cur: pointer): pointer;
begin
   RetrieveNext := cur^.next
end;
```

Array Implementation of Linked Lists

An alternative implementation involves arrays of records. Here, the *next* field points to the next node by holding its index instead of its actual memory address. The special *null* value is an unused index, usually zero, instead of the pointer value *nil*; and the variables *head, cur, prev*, and *P* are now of the index type as opposed to being of the pointer type.

To create this version of the linked list, we can use the following definitions and declarations, where *MaxNumEls* is an appropriately defined constant for the maximum value of the index:

```
const
   MaxNumEls  = ............;
type
   InfoType   = ............;
   PointRange = 0..MaxNumEls;
   IndexType  = 1..MaxNumEls;
```

```
Node          = record
   info       : InfoType;
   next       : PointRange
end;
ArrayType     = array[IndexType] of Node;
var
   head,
   cur,
   prev,
   P          : PointRange;
   a          : ArrayType;
```

To illustrate an array implementation of a linked list, suppose a list of names needs to be maintained in alphabetical order. Over a period of time, due to additions and deletions, the array might appear as shown in Figure 7.58. In this figure *head* holds the index, 3, of the first node in the linked list. The *next* field of that node contains 1, which is the index of the next node in the linked list. The last node, the one with the name "Phillips, Jim," has a *next* field with the null value of zero. This array is redrawn as a linked list in Figure 7.59 with each *next* field containing the index of the node that is to follow.

When a node is to be added, we must find a free node, copy the name into the *info* field, and insert the node into the linked list. There are several ways to indicate a free node in this example. We could place a special value, such as blanks or an asterisk, in the *info* field; we could expand *PointRange* to include −1 and place this in the *next* field; or we could keep a list of available nodes as pictured in Figures 7.58 and 7.59.

One convenient way to implement the ADT linked list with arrays is to use a global array containing all the linked lists and the list of available nodes. In a sense, the dynamic implementation with pointers treats the structure globally as well. We may declare *head* to be the only variable parameter for a procedure, and within the procedure we may change several nodes in the linked list. Moreover, making the array global allows implementation routines to have the same parameters as the corresponding ADT operations. Thus, we can have a package containing all the ADT linked list operations implemented dynamically with pointers and another containing the operations implemented statically with arrays. Although Standard Pascal does not, some versions of Pascal allow such packages to be compiled separately. After the design of a program we can decide on which implementation package is best. Even after coding a program in Pascal it is a simple matter to switch ADT implementation packages without changing the body of the program. The topic of such an encapsulation of a structure is covered in greater detail in Section 8.5.

Regardless of the method of implementing with arrays the ADT linked list, we are still limited by the maximum number of elements. Eventually, if there are enough insertions, we will run out of room in the array. Thus, this implementation does not hold the advantage of dynamic memory allocation with the capability of having an enormous number of additions to the list. As with a dynamic one, however, this static memory allocation implementation does

Figure 7.58

Static memory allocation of a linked list

index	info	next
1	Dunlap, Alice	8
2	?	10
3	Chapman, John	1
4	Hadden, Judy	5
5	Jones, Will	6
6	Li, Kim	7
7	Phillips, Jim	0
8	Freeman, Mary	4
9	?	0
10	?	9

head

3

avail

2

Figure 7.59

Linked list represented by array in Figure 7.58

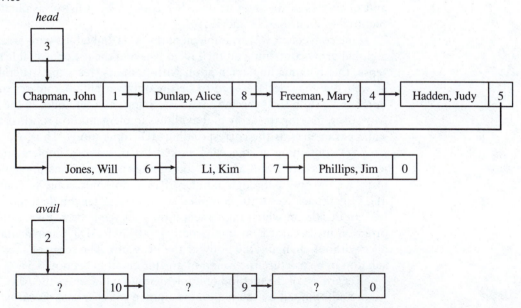

have the advantage of worst case insertions and deletions being of complexity $O(1)$. These operations along with a Pascal array implementation of the other ADT linked list operations are covered in the exercises.

SECTION 7.4 EXERCISES

1. Give the value of each expression by referring to Figure 7.60.

 a. P^. info

 b. P^. next^. info

 c. R^. next

Figure 7.60

Linked list for
Exercises 1–5

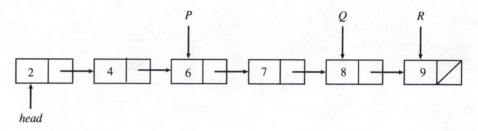

For Exercises 2–5, starting with Figure 7.60, draw the list after execution of the segment.

2. R^. next   := Q;
   head^. info := 1;
   P   := P^. next

3. P^. info := head^. info;
   Q   := nil;
   P   := P^. next^. next;
   head   := R

4. Q^. next := nil;
   R^. next := head;
   head   := R

5. new (Q) ;
   Q^. info := 10;
   R^. next := Q

6. Use the array implementation of a linked list pictured in Figure 7.61 and declared as follows:

```
const
    MaxNumEls  = 9;
type
    PointRange = 0..MaxNumEls;
    IndexType  = 1..MaxNumEls;
    Node       = record
        info   : char;
        next   : PointRange
    end;
    ArrayType  = array[IndexType] of Node;
```

```
var
    P,
    Q,
    head,
    avail          : PointRange;
    A              : ArrayType;
```

a. List in order the indices of the linked list pointed to by *head*.
b. List in order the indices of the linked list pointed to by *avail*.
c. Draw with boxes and arrows the linked list pointed to by *head* with *P* and *Q* properly placed.
d. Draw with boxes and arrows the linked list pointed to by *avail*.

Figure 7.61

Array implementation of a linked list for Exercises 6–11

index	info	next
1	a	3
2	d	6
3	e	0
4	c	2
5	b	4
6	g	7
7	h	0
8	k	9
9	m	1

head

5

avail

8

P

2

Q

7

7. Give the value of each expression using the linked list in Figure 7.61.
   a. A[head].info
   b. A[Q].next
   c. A[A[P].next].info

For Exercises 8–11, starting with Figure 7.61, draw the list after execution of the segment.

8.
```
P := A[P].next;
A[head].info := 'i';
A[P].next := 0;
Dispose(Q)
```

9.
```
New(P);
A[P].info := 'n';
A[P].next := 0;
A[Q].next := P
```

10. `A[Q].next := avail;` **11.** `Dispose(Q);`
   `avail      := head;`   `P   := A[P].next;`
   `head       := 0`   `A[P].next := 0`

In Exercises 12 and 13, the subfields of the info *portion of a node are given. Define the types and declare the variable* head *to create a dynamic memory allocation implementation of a linked list structure.*

12. *Count* of type *integer*

13. *SSN, name, salary*

14. Repeat Exercise 12 using a static memory allocation implementation.

15. Repeat Exercise 13 using a static memory allocation implementation.

In Exercises 16–38 code in Pascal each routine from Section 7.3:
   i. Using a dynamic memory allocation implementation.
   ii. Using a static memory allocation implementation.

16. *Readlist* from Example 7.2 to read records from a file *f* into a linked list with the first node of the list containing the first element of *f*.

17. *Search* from Example 7.3 to search for *e*'s value in an ordered linked list pointed to by *head*.

18. *Delete* from Example 7.3 to delete the node after the one pointed to by *prev* from the linked list pointed to by *head*; if *prev* has the null value, delete the first node.

19. *DeleteValues* from Example 7.3 to read records from a file and delete nodes with that information from a linked list arranged in ascending order with no two nodes containing the same information.

20. Procedure from Exercise 1 to exchange values in two nodes pointed to by *cur* and *prev*, assuming neither *cur* nor *prev* has a null value.

21. Procedure from Exercise 2 to remove the first node from a linked list pointed to by *head1* and install it as the first node in a linked list pointed to by *head2*.

22. Procedure from Exercise 3 to form a list with two nodes, the first with the value of *x* and the second with the value of *y*.

23. Procedure *InsertTailList(head, tail, Target)* from Exercise 4 to insert the target node at the end of the linked list.

24. Nonrecursive function *Size* from Exercise 5 to return the number of nodes in a linked list pointed to by *head*.

25. Boolean function *EqualList(P, Q)* from Exercise 6 to return *true* if the two lists are identical, ordered in the same way.

26. a. Nonrecursive procedure from Exercise 7a to print the values in the information fields of the nodes of a linked list pointed to by *head*.
   b. Recursive version of the procedure from Exercise 7b.

27. Procedure from Exercise 8 to read records from a file and insert each datum in turn at the beginning of a linked list.

28. Procedure *Split(prev, head2)* from Exercise 9 to split a linked list into two lists. The second list, starting at the node after the one indicated by *prev*, gets a head pointer, *head2*. Assume *prev* points to a node.

29. Procedure from Exercise 10 to make a copy of a linked list.

30. **a.** Nonrecursive function from Exercise 11a to return the sum of the values stored in a linked list of numbers.
    b. Recursive version of the procedure from Exercise 11b.

31. Boolean function from Exercise 12 to return *true* if the key values in a linked list are in order.

32. Procedure from Exercise 13 to delete the third node in a linked list.

33. Procedure from Exercise 14 to append a linked list with pointer *headExtra* onto the end of a linked list with pointer *head*.

34. Procedure from Exercise 15 to add nodes with information from a file to an ordered list.

35. Procedure from Exercise 16 to merge two sorted linked lists.

36. **a.** Nonrecursive procedure from Exercise 17a to free all the nodes in a linked list.
    b. Recursive version of the procedure from Exercise 17b.

37. Function from Exercise 18 to point to the predecessor of the node indicated by *cur*.

38. Procedure from Exercise 19 to delete from a linked list the node with the largest value; if more than one node contain this largest value, delete the first such node.

39. Write a recursive procedure to reverse the links in a dynamic memory allocation implementation of a linked list.

40. Write a recursive procedure for Exercise 38 above to point to the first occurrence of the largest value from a linked list. Use this pointer to delete that node.

41. Write a recursive boolean function for Exercise 31 above to return *true* if the key values in a linked list are in order.

▽

PROGRAMMING PROJECTS

1. An alphabetical listing of members of a school's chorus is stored in a file. Membership in the chorus changes frequently, however. Write a program

for the choral director that will read this file into a linked list and provide the following menu of choices:

p — Print a listing of members.
a — Add a member.
d — Delete a member.
s — Save the changes.
q — Quit.

Upon quitting, if any changes have been made in the membership since the last save, warn the director that not all changes have been saved. Have the director press "s" and return to save or "q" and return to exit without saving.

2. A company selling athletic equipment has bought mailing lists, each sorted by name, from three different sports magazines. The files exist on disk as text files. The company wants to send its catalog to anyone appearing on one of these lists. In many cases a person subscribes to two or even three of the magazines, however, and the company wishes to cut down on the expense of duplicate mailings. Write a program to produce mailing labels for the catalogs. Use a linked list of names of those to receive a catalog to help eliminate duplicates.

3. A grocer wishes to have a computerized shopping guide for customers. This guide will display a list of frequently purchased items, such as milk, bread, soft drinks, etc., along with the isle on which each is located. On the screen the customer sees each item, one after another, and is able to say "y" (yes) or "n" (no) to each. Print a list for the customer to use of all desired items with associated isles.

   In the morning the grocer starts the program, which reads products and isles from a file into a linked list. For customer convenience the file and linked list should be maintained as sorted by isle number. The program initially allows the grocer to add or delete items or to change isle numbers and then to save the revised list in the file. Once this initialization is complete, the computer displays a friendly message awaiting the first customer.

SECTION 7.5

Variations of Linked Lists

In Section 7.4 we discussed two implementations of the ADT linked list, one with dynamic and the other with static memory allocation. Both methods had a variable, often called *head*, to indicate the first node in the list; and both had a null value for the link portion of the final node. Greater variation is possible, however, and different approaches are often useful in applications. In this section we discuss additional implementations of the ADT linked list as well as two other linked structures, doubly and multiply linked lists.

Because linked lists are most often realized with dynamic memory allocation, we use that approach throughout this section. As covered in the exercises, however, these ideas can be mirrored with arrays.

In Section 7.4 *head* was declared of type *pointer*. We could, however, designate that this variable contain additional information about the list, such as the number of nodes. A picture of the structure created below appears in Figure 7.62.

```
type
    InfoType      = . . . . . . . . . . ;
    pointer       = ^Node;
    Node          = record
        info      :  InfoType;
        next      :  pointer
    end;
    headType      = record
        NumNodes  :  0..maxint;
        headPtr   :  pointer
    end;

var
    head          :  headType;
```

Figure 7.62

Linked list with *head* also
containing the length of
the list

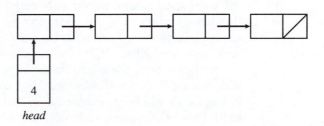

head

This count of nodes, or other information such as a maximum or minimum value, could be useful in certain applications. In Example 7.2 of Section 7.3, when insertion always occurred at the end of a linked list, we found it useful to have a tail pointer as well. Such an enhancement of the structure reappears in Chapter 8 in a discussion of a linked list implementation of queues.

Some programmers prefer a linked list implementation that uses a **dummy first node** such as in Figure 7.63. This node is not the logical first node of the list but either holds no meaningful information or holds a particular value from the list, such as a maximum. Because the dummy node is always present, even an empty list contains this extra item. (See Figure 7.64.) The main advantage of such a dummy node, however, is that with it we can avoid the special cases involved with insertion and deletion of the logical first node. For instance, deletion of the logical first node or insertion of a new such node does not change

Figure 7.63

Linked list implemented with a dummy first node

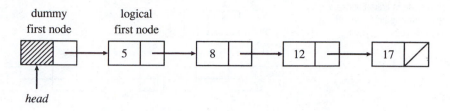

Figure 7.64

MakeListEmpty(*head*) for linked list implementation with dummy first node

the value of *head* as shown in Figures 7.65 and 7.66, respectively. This implementation makes the ADT linked list operations of *InsertFirst* and *DeleteFirst* unnecessary. A dummy node does, however, consume extra space and require additional processing to advance past it.

All the implementations of linked lists so far have been **linear** with *head* somehow indicating the first node and with the last node having a null link field. In a **circular linked list,** the last node is linked to the first as in Figure 7.67. In fact, there is no first or last node since the structure is circular. We still, however, must have a variable (*list* in Figure 7.67) that points to some node in the list.

Figure 7.65

Deletion of logical first node in linked list with dummy first node of Figure 7.63

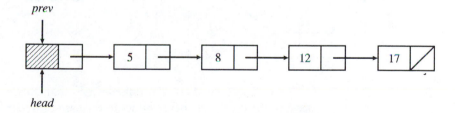

DeleteLater (*prev*)

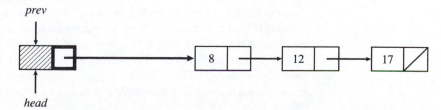

Figure 7.66

Insertion of a new logical
first node in linked list
with dummy first node of
Figure 7.63

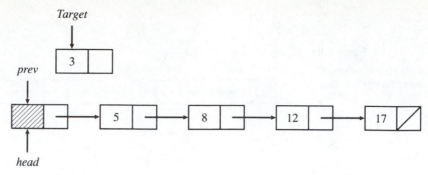

InsertLater (prev, Target)

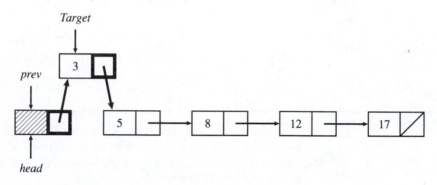

Figure 7.67

Example of a circular
linked list drawn two ways

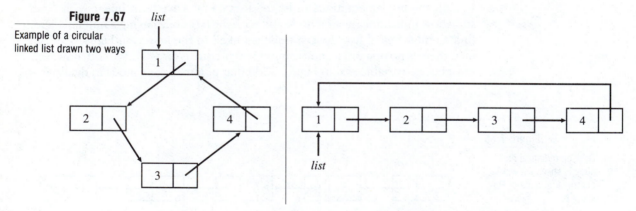

One advantage of circular linked lists is that starting from any node we can traverse the list to any other node. In the case of linear linked lists, a pointer P to a node inside the list does not help us get to earlier nodes. As shown in Figure 7.68, we cannot traverse the first part of the list without knowledge of the value of *head*. In this linked list, the last node does not have a successor; in a circular linked list, every node has a successor. Moreover, *list*, a pointer to the circular linked list, does not need to remain fixed as a pointer to a linear linked list does. Often, however, it is convenient to maintain the elements in some order, say ascending, with a list pointer indicating the first, or perhaps even the last, logical node. In fact, *tail* is a good choice for a circular list pointer, because through it we can also have a pointer, *tail^.next*, to the first node. (See Figure 7.69.)

Figure 7.68

A pointer *P* to reference the inside of a linked list does not help us get to earlier nodes

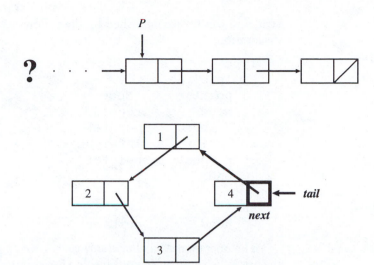

Figure 7.69

Circular linked list with pointer to the tail node and reference to the first node through *tail^ .next*

The linear and circular linked lists presented thus far both have the characteristic of having one pointer per node. Sometimes applications demand a slightly different structure with resulting changes in the operations. One major disadvantage of a **singly linked list**, with a single link per node, is that even though it is adjacent, there is no easy way to find the predecessor of a node. Suppose *cur* points to a node. To cause *prev* to point to the previous node, we must have *prev* traverse the list from the head to the appropriate node. This situation is analogous to a fictional train in which you can only walk from the engine toward the caboose. As soon as you walk through a door, it slams shut and locks. If you wish to go back one car, you must get off the train, climb back on at the engine, and start the walk back once more.

A **doubly linked list** can solve the problems of traversing the list in either direction and of finding the immediate predecessor of a node. Figure 7.70 gives an example of such a doubly linked list.

Figure 7.70

Example of a doubly linked list

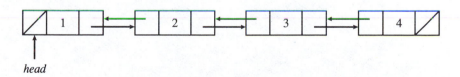

We actually have a slightly different abstract data type from that of ADT linked list. The objects are a sequence of nodes having three parts, an information portion, a field that points to the successor node, and a field that points to the predecessor node in the list. A special variable to point to the first node in the list is still used. We add and substitute several operations to the ADT linked list operations shown in Figure 7.43 of Section 7.3. The creation of this structure can be accomplished by the following type definitions and variable declaration:

```
type
    InfoType = ..........;
    pointer  = ^Node;
    Node     = record
        prior : pointer;
        info  : InfoType;
        next  : pointer
    end;

var
    head        : pointer;
```

The operation *MoveBack(cur)* causes *cur* to point to the previous node in the list. When inserting a node inside a list, four links must be attached as shown in Figure 7.71. Insertion at the tail, as in Figure 7.72, however, only involves alteration of three pointers. Thus, we keep the *InsertFirst* operation, change *InsertLater* to *InsertInside*, and add the operation *InsertLast*. Similarly, we need to include an extra delete operation, *DeleteLast*, to handle the excep-

Figure 7.71

Action of *Insert-Inside(prev, Target)* in a doubly linked list with a local variable *cur*

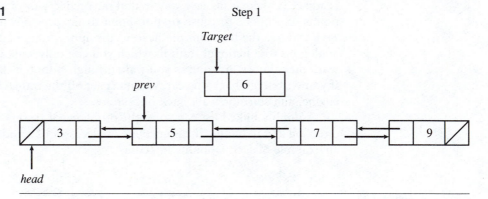

Step 1

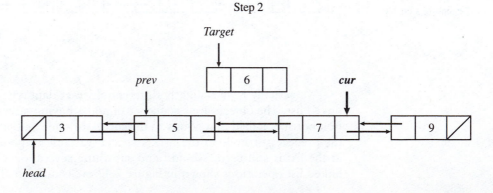

Step 2

Figure 7.71

continued

Step 3

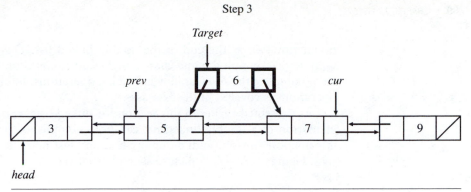

Step 4

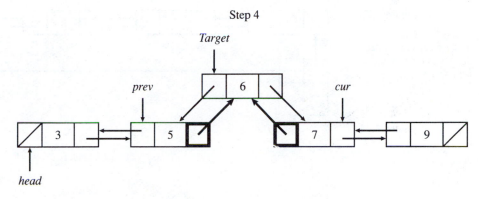

Figure 7.72

Action of *InsertLast*(*tail*, *Target*) in a doubly linked list

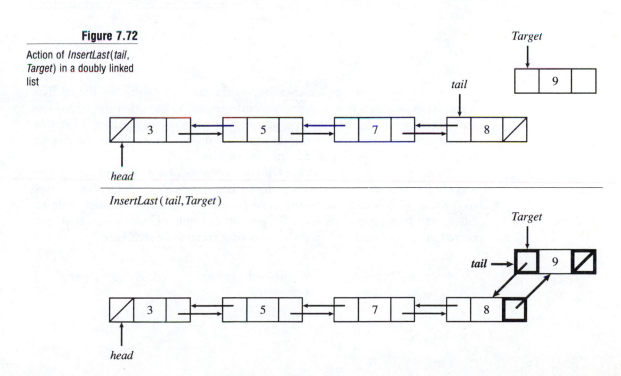

InsertLast (*tail*, *Target*)

279

tional situation at the end of the doubly linked list. *DeleteLater* is adjusted with a corresponding name change to *DeleteInside*. *StorePrior* and *RetrievePrior* complete the ADT doubly linked list operations. Implementation of these operations is covered in the exercises.

As presented earlier in this section for linked lists, variations of the implementation of a doubly linked list can be accomplished with *head* having an information portion, with a dummy first and last node, or with a circular design. Figures 7.73–7.75 picture such alternatives.

Figure 7.73

Doubly linked list with head having an information portion and head and tail pointers

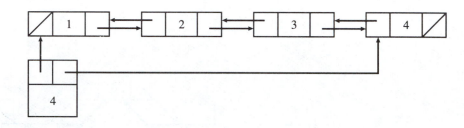

Figure 7.74

Doubly linked list with dummy first and last nodes

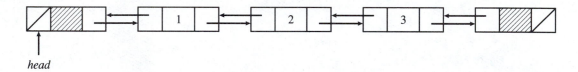

head

Regardless of the implementation, in the context of doubly linked lists, traversal in one direction is the inverse of traversal in the other direction—we cover the same nodes in the opposite order. We can, however, have a list with two or more link portions per node where we do not have this inverse characteristic. Such is the realm of **multiply linked lists**.

Perhaps information held in each node consists of a name and salary. One set of links could alphabetize while another could indicate the salary from lowest to highest. In this case we would need pointers to indicate the first node for each sorting. Figures 7.76 and 7.77 give an example of such a situation, presented in the two orders, while the following creates the structure:

```
type
    NameType     = packed array [1..20] of char;
    InfoType     = record
        name     : NameType;
        salary   : real
    end;
```

Figure 7.75

Two diagrams of a circular doubly linked list

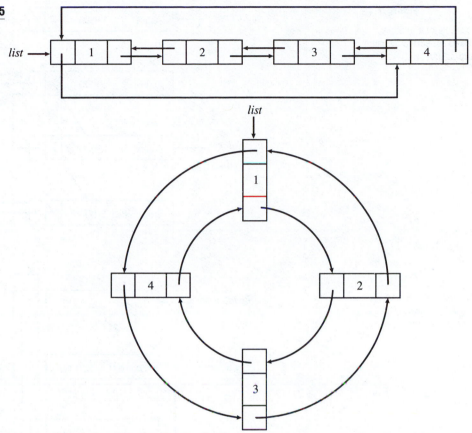

```
pointer      = ^Node;
Node         = record
   info      : InfoType;
   nextName,
   nextSalary : pointer
end;

var
   headName,
   headSalary   : pointer;
```

Various linked list structures will be used to implement a number of other data structures in the remainder of the book. We present an application of a multiply linked list in the following example.

Figure 7.76

Example of a multiply linked list sorted by name and salary

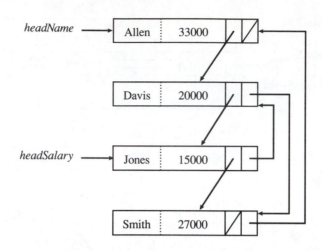

Figure 7.77

Multiply linked list of Figure 7.76 drawn by increasing salary

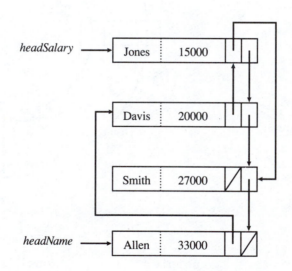

Example 7.4

Sparse Matrix.

▼ A **matrix** is a rectangular array of numbers. An obvious implementation of a matrix is a two-dimensional array such as that discussed in Section 3.1 and created below:

```
type
    IntegerArray = array[1..MaxRow, 1..MaxCol] of
                        integer;
var
    A : IntegerArray;
```

This straightforward approach has serious drawbacks for a very large, **sparse matrix**, a matrix with almost all entries being zero. For example, suppose a team of people will be doing a vegetational analysis of California. Starting on the coast and going straight inland, they report how many plants in each of 1000 species is present in each of 300 sample areas. With 1000 species and 300 samples, the resulting matrix would contain $1000 \times 300 = 300,000$ counts, most of which would be zero. Storage of such a large matrix would be prohibitive on many computers. Thus, using multiply linked lists, we will design a structure for holding only the nonzero elements.

Suppose we consider a smaller example with a 4×5 matrix A, having 4 rows and 5 columns:

$$A = \begin{bmatrix} 0 & 0 & 0 & 55 & 0 \\ 34 & 0 & 0 & 28 & 0 \\ 0 & 0 & 0 & 0 & 0 \\ 0 & 0 & 83 & 0 & 0 \end{bmatrix}$$

In our structure we certainly want to store each nonzero number as well as the row and column in which the number occurs. Moreover, we will have a *right* link that points to the next element in that row and a *down* pointer to the next value in that column. At the beginning of each row that contains at least one nonzero number, there will be a dummy header node with the row number, zero for the column number, and appropriate links. Similarly, each nonzero column will be topped by a dummy header node giving the column number, zero as the row number, and links. For convenience, we will also store the dimension, 4×5, in the dummy header node for the matrix, while pointer A holds the location of the matrix. This structure can be created by the following:

```
const
    MaxRow      = 4;
    MaxCol      = 5;

type
    pointer     = ^Node;
    Node        = record
        row     : 0..MaxRow;
        column  : 0..MaxCol;
        info    : integer;
        right,
        down    : pointer
    end;

var
    A           : pointer;
```

The matrix above placed in this configuration would appear as shown in Figure 7.78.

Figure 7.78

Multiply linked list implementation of sparse matrix of Example 7.4

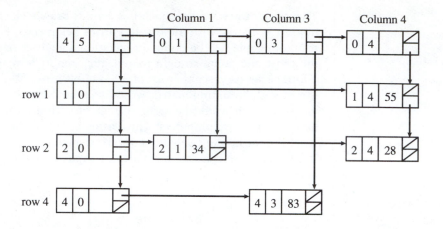

One variation of this structure is to make the linked list in every row and every column circular, looping back to the dummy header node. Moreover, the dummy header node for the row (column) could hold the number of elements in that row (column). As we will see in the exercises, this multiply linked list structure is important in situations where we must perform operations, such as multiplication, on matrices.

▽

SECTION 7.5 EXERCISES

1. Using a dummy first node, implement dynamically all the ADT linked list operations.

2. Using a dummy first node, implement statically all the ADT linked list operations.

3. Using a circular linked list with a tail pointer instead of *head*, implement dynamically all the ADT linked list operations.

4. Using a circular linked list with a tail pointer instead of *head*, implement statically all the ADT linked list operations.

5. Give a formal definition of ADT doubly linked list.

6. **a.** Give a diagram of the action of the ADT doubly linked list operation *InsertFirst*.
   b. Repeat Part a for *DeleteLast*.
   c. Repeat Part a for *DeleteInside*.
   d. Repeat Part a for *DeleteFirst*.

7. Implement ADT doubly linked list dynamically.

8. Draw a diagram like Figure 7.77 to store the following sparse matrix:

$$A = \begin{bmatrix} 0 & 0 & 5 & 0 & 0 & 0 & 0 & 0 \\ 0 & 0 & 0 & 1 & 0 & 8 & 3 & 0 \\ 0 & 0 & 0 & 0 & 0 & 0 & 0 & 0 \\ 0 & 0 & 9 & 0 & 0 & 0 & 0 & 0 \\ 0 & 0 & 0 & 0 & 0 & 0 & 0 & 0 \\ 0 & 0 & 0 & 0 & 0 & 0 & 0 & 2 \\ 6 & 0 & 0 & 0 & 0 & 0 & 0 & 0 \end{bmatrix}$$

9. Alter the diagram from Exercise 8 to have the head node for the matrix store the number of nonzero elements in the matrix as well as the dimension of the matrix. A header for a row (column) should also store the number of matrix nodes in that row (column).

In Exercises 10–33, using the structure of Example 7.4, write in Pascal the requested routines to implement an ADT sparse matrix structure.

10. Procedure *MakeMatEmpty*

11. Function *MatIsEmpty*

12. Procedure *ToFirstMat*

13. Function *AtFirstMat*

14. Function *AtEndRow*

15. Function *AtEndCol*

16. Procedure *InsertRowHead*

17. Procedure *InsertColHead*

18. Procedure *Insert*

19. Procedure *DeleteRowHead*

20. Procedure *DeleteColHead*

21. Procedure *Delete*

22. Procedure *AdvanceDown*

23. Procedure *AdvanceRight*

24. Procedure *StoreInfo*

25. Procedure *StoreRow*

26. Procedure *StoreCol*

27. Procedure *StoreRight*

28. Procedure *StoreDown*

29. Function *RetrieveInfo*

30. Function *RetrieveRow*

31. Function *RetrieveCol*

32. Function *RetrieveRight*

33. Function *RetrieveDown*

Using pseudocode and the ADT sparse matrix operations in Exercises 10–33, design the operations in Exercises 34–41.

34. Procedure *ToRow*(A, i, cur) that points *cur* to the dummy header node of row *i*; if there is no such row in the representation (i.e., the row in the matrix contains all zeros), *cur* gets the null value.

35. Procedure *ToCol*(A, j, cur) that points *cur* to the dummy header node of column *j*; if there is no such column in the representation (i.e., the column in the matrix contains all zeros), *cur* gets the null value.

36. Procedure *ConstRowProd*(A, i, c) that will multiply the *i*th row of matrix A by the integer *c*.

37. Procedure *ConstColProd*(*A, j, c*) that will multiply the *j*th column of matrix *A* by the integer *c*.

38. Procedure *ConstProd*(*A, c*) that will multiply the matrix *A* by the integer *c*.

39. Function *RowSum*(*A, i*) to return the sum of the elements in the *i*th row of the matrix pointed to by *A*.

40. Function *ColSum*(*A, j*) to return the sum of the elements in the *j*th column of the matrix pointed to by *A*.

41. Function *MatSum*(*A*) to return the sum of the elements in the matrix pointed to by *A*.

42. Write a procedure to erase all the elements in a circular linked list.

43. The following appeared in the sample questions of the *1984 AP Computer Science Examination**:

Each record in a mailing list contains a name, address, social security number, and possibly some pointer or integer fields for linking records. The list is very seldom changed. There are two operations to be performed frequently: printing mailing labels ordered by zip code, and finding a particular record given its social security number. Assume that efficiency in both space and time is important.

Of the following, which is the best way to store the mailing list records in order to solve the problem above?

(A) Using two arrays, one ordered by social security number and one by zip code.
(B) Using one array, ordered by social security number, with records linked in zip code order.
(C) Using two linked lists, one ordered by social security number and one by zip code.
(D) Using one array, ordered only by social security number.
(E) Using one array, ordered by zip code and by social security number within each zip code.

▽

PROGRAMMING PROJECTS

1. A finite fixed-length sequence of bits, called a **deBruijn sequence**, can be used to produce a binary encoding scheme. When such a sequence of 2^n bits is arranged in a circle, each consecutive n bits is different, and thus, the sequence can encode 2^n different characters. As Figure 7.79 illustrates, the se-

---

* AP question selected from AP Computer Science Examination, 1984. Reprinted by permission of Educational Testing Service, the copyright owner of the sample questions.

Figure 7.79

Diagram of deBruijn
sequence for encoding
8 characters

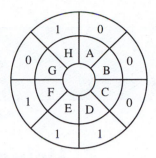

quence of $2^3 = 8$ bits, 00011101, can encode 8 characters, where 3 consecutive bits encode a character:

000 A	001 B	011 C	111 D
110 E	101 F	010 G	100 H

Design a program to read the characters and deBruijn sequence for a wheel from a text file. From another file read and print a message and then encode and print the encoded form of the message. From still another file, read and print an encoded message and decode and print the decoded message.

Use the the deBruijn sequence

10100010011000001110111110010101

to encode the following sequence of 32 characters: blank, period, comma, question mark, colon, dash, letters A−Z. Use a circular linked list modeling the figure to store this sequence of bits and characters.

2. Create a program to read from a file into a sparse matrix a hypothetical vegetational analysis of California. Besides the sparse matrix entries, read the names of the species and the identification codes for the sample areas from the file into two one-dimensional arrays, respectively. For ease of searching, have both lists sorted. In the sparse matrix, information about the ith species should be contained in row i, and column j should contain information about the jth sample area.

   After reading the information, give the user a menu of choices:

   a. Find the count for a particular species in a sample area.
   b. List all sample areas in which a particular species was observed.
   c. List all observed species in a particular sample area.
   q. Quit.

3. As described in the first paragraph of Project 2, read from a file into a sparse matrix a hypothetical vegetational analysis of California. From this information produce two reports, a listing of how many different species occur in each sample area and a listing for each species of its total observed count in the study.

8

Using Linked Lists

Introduction

In the last chapter we developed the abstract data type linked list along with several implementation techniques. With this background we are now in a position to use this structure in various applications. Moreover, we will see that the abstract data types of string, stack, and queue, previously implemented statically with arrays, can be implemented dynamically with linked lists. For each ADT we discuss the advantages and disadvantages of these two implementation techniques. Faced with a choice in the coding of the abstract data types, in the last section we reconsider how we should develop Pascal programs with ADT objects and operations hidden so they can be used like built-in types.

Applications of Linked Lists

Throughout the text we use linked lists as an implementation tool for other data structures. In this section we consider several additional applications of this important structure.

Example 8.1. ### Memory Management.

One useful application is the dynamic memory allocation implementation of linked lists themselves. In Section 7.1 we presented the ADT pointer operation *Dispose(P)*, which made the node pointed to by *P* available and made *P* undefined. We also discussed one Pascal implementation,

```
dispose (P)
```

Unfortunately, some versions of Pascal do not handle the *dispose* procedure in the way the corresponding ADT operation is defined. These flawed versions change the value of *P* to undefined but do not free the node for further use. Thus, many insertions and deletions in a linked list could eventually result in an OUT-OF-MEMORY error. In situations where we anticipate much activity in a linked list and where we are using such a version of Pascal, we should handle **memory management** ourselves.

To manage these nodes we establish and maintain a linked list of available nodes. We use procedures *Allocate* and *Free* to implement the ADT operations *New* and *Dispose*, respectively. Initially, we create an empty list. When *Allocate(P)* is called the first time or any time the list of available nodes is empty, the built-in Pascal procedure *new(P)* is executed. *Free(P)* does not employ the Pascal procedure *dispose(P)* but restores the node to the linked list of available nodes. Such a node is then free to be used in a later call of *Allocate*.

Making this linked list of available nodes global, our main program would have the same definitions and declarations for the creation of the list of available nodes as for the main linked list:

```
type
    InfoType  =  ............;
    pointer   =  ^Node;
    Node      =  record
        info  :  InfoType;
        next  :  pointer
    end;
var
    P,
    avail,
    head      :  pointer;
```

In this example, *avail* points to the linked list of available nodes, while *head* points to the linked list being developed for another application with nodes of the same type. Before using the *Allocate* operation to obtain a node for our main list, we must establish the list of available nodes with *MakeListEmpty(avail)*. Recall from Section 7.4 that this operation assigned *nil* to *avail*.

Figures 8.1 and 8.2 illustrate the two situations that can arise when calling

Figure 8.1

Action of *Allocate(P)* when the list of available nodes is empty

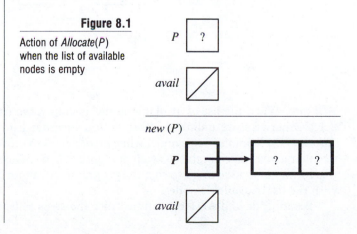

Figure 8.2

Action of *Allocate(P)*
when the list of available
nodes is not empty

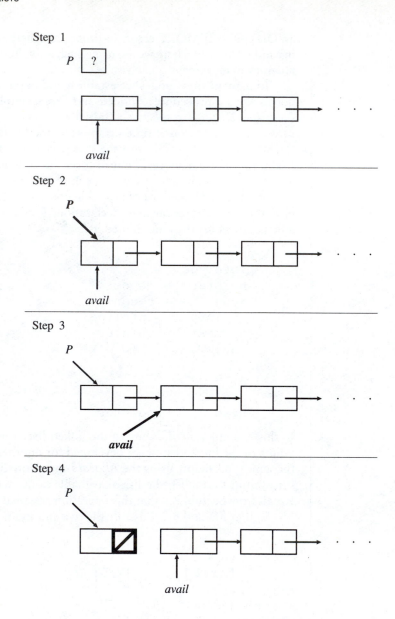

Allocate. When the list of available nodes is empty, we use *new*. (See Figure 8.1.) Otherwise, we unlink the first node from that list. After execution of *Allocate(P)*, *P* points to this node, while *avail* points to the new head node. Notice that care is taken in the last step of Figure 8.2 to change the link portion of this former first node to *nil* so that the programmer cannot accidentally tamper with the list of available nodes.

Pseudocode and ADT operations trace the steps reflected in these figures.

***Allocate**(P)*
Procedure to allocate memory for datum and to place its address into *P*
Input:
P — pointer
Output:
P — pointer to a node
Assumptions:
Pointer *avail* has been declared globally of the same type as *P*. The list of available nodes pointed to by *avail* has been established.

Figure	**Algorithm**
{8.1}	if *ListIsEmpty*(*avail*) then
	new(*P*)
{8.2}	else
{Step 2}	*ToFirst*(*avail*, *P*)
{Step 3}	*Advance*(*avail*)
{Step 4}	*MakeListEmpty*(*P*^.*next*)

Figure 8.3

Action of *Free*(P)

Step 1

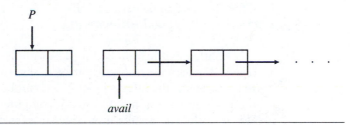

Step 2

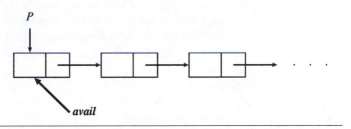

Step 3

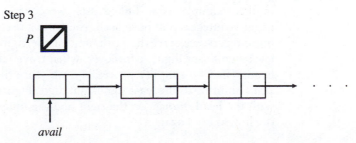

Free(*P*) restores the node pointed to by *P* to the head of the available list with *InsertFirst*(*avail*, *P*). One extra precaution is taken by breaking *P*'s link to this node. Without such an action, the programmer would have access to the entire list of available nodes through *P*.

Figure 8.3 illustrates the action of the operation *Free*, which is designed as follows:

Free(P)
    Procedure to free memory for datum whose address is in *P* and to make *P* empty; assume *P* initially points to a node
Input:
    P — pointer
Output:
    P — pointer with value *nil*
Assumptions:
    Pointer *avail* has been declared globally as the same type as *P*. The list of available nodes pointed to by *avail* has been established. *P* points to a node.

Figure	Algorithm
{8.3}	
{Step 2}	*InsertFirst*(*avail*, *P*)
▲ {Step 3}	*MakeListEmpty*(*P*)

Another application of linked lists allows virtually infinite precision for integers. Integers are stored in a fixed amount of space. The built-in constant *maxint* retains the largest integer that can be stored in the computer on which the program is running. On many computers the value of *maxint* is 32,767. When arithmetic results in a larger integer number, some computers indicate an error, others convert the number to a real number with a limited number of significant digits, and still others simply drop the most significant digits. We can use a linked list to overcome these problems and to store all the digits of virtually any integer. Moreover, we can perform arithmetic on these very large numbers. As in Example 8.1, we are using linked lists to manage memory ourselves.

Example 8.2.

Addition of Large Integers.

▼

In this example using linked lists, we cover arithmetic on very large, nonnegative integers that have been read from a text file. When adding or multiplying integers, we start the arithmetic at the right side of the numbers with the least significant digits. Moreover, when traversing a linked list, we start at the head. Thus, to simplify processing, we store the digits of the linked list with *head* pointing to the least significant digit. Figure 8.4 displays such an example with the head, *num1*, on the right and the links pointing to the left, to clarify the linked list storage.

Figure 8.4

Linked list to store the integer 63872 for Example 8.2

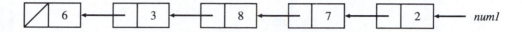

When reading the character string "63872" we start with the most significant digit. Thus, each digit character in turn is converted to a digit number and inserted at the head of the list. Notice that this building of the linked list from a file varies from that presented in Example 7.2 of Section 7.3 in which insertion of each new node occurred at the tail. Figure 8.5 illustrates each step of the placement of the most significant digit of 63872 into the linked list, and Figure 8.6 continues the building of the linked list for the next two digits. Following is the algorithm for the process of reading the character string representation of the integer and placing each corresponding numeric digit into a linked list:

ReadNumIntoList(num, f)
  Procedure to read a nonnegative integer as a character string from a text file *f* and place each digit as a number into a linked list pointed to by *num* so that the least significant digit is in the first node

Input:
  f   — text file containing a nonnegative integer on a line
Output:
  num — pointer to linked list of the digits of a number
Assumptions:
  f stores one nonnegative integer per line with no leading blanks. *Reset(f)* has been previously executed.

Figure	Algorithm
{8.5}	
{Step 1}	*MakeListEmpty(num)*
	while not *eoln(f)* do
{Step 2}	read (*f, ch*)
{Step 3}	*AddNode(P, ord(ch) − ord('0'))*
{Step 4}	*InsertFirst(num, P)*
	readln (*f*) {advance past *eoln* marker}

Suppose that, as in Step 1 of Figure 8.7, *num1* and *num2* point to two such linked lists. Figures 8.7–8.9 detail how we perform addition on these numbers, placing the answer in a linked list pointed to by *result*. Step 2 of Figure 8.7 shows that when adding the least significant digits, 2 and 1, the sum is placed in the linked list, while the carry is given a value of 0. In Step 1 of Figure 8.8 the sum of the next digits, 7 and 5, however, is 12. Thus, 2 is inserted and *carry* is changed to 1. Then 8, 9, and the carry of 1 are added to give 18. Once more,

Figure 8.5

Initial action of *ReadNum-IntoList*(num, f) in Example 8.2

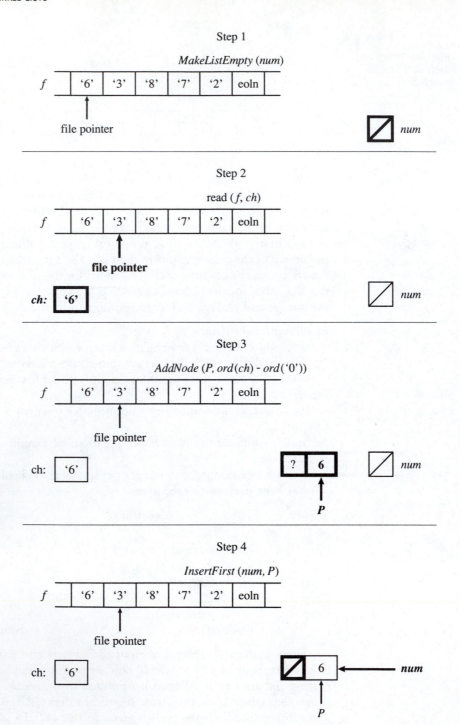

Figure 8.6

Action of *ReadNumInto-List*(*num*, *f*) in Example 8.2 for the second and third executions of the *while* loop

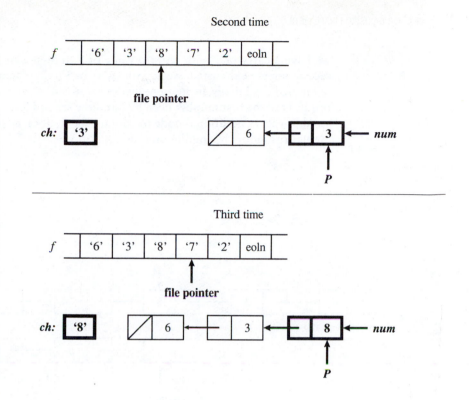

Figure 8.7

Initial action before execution of the first *while* loop of *InfIntegerAdd*(*num1*, *num2*) from Example 8.2

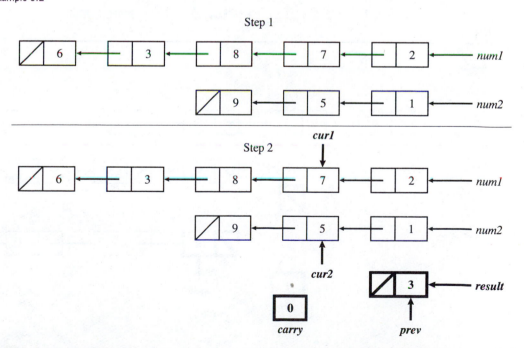

295

we have a carry of 1 with an *info* value of 8 in Step 2 of Figure 8.8. With the second integer exhausted, we add the carry of 1 to 3, placing 4 in the list (Step 1 of Figure 8.9). Finally, in Step 2 of Figure 8.9, 6 plus a carry of 0 is copied into the result. Had the first number been 872 and the second 951, as in Figure 8.10, we would need an additional node to contain the final carry of 1. The following is an algorithm for the infinite precision addition:

Figure 8.8

Action of *InfInteger-Add*(*num1*, *num2*) for the first *while* loop; continued from Figure 8.7

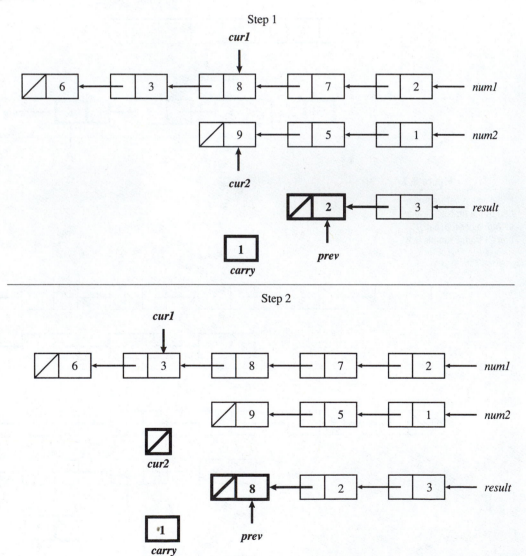

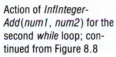

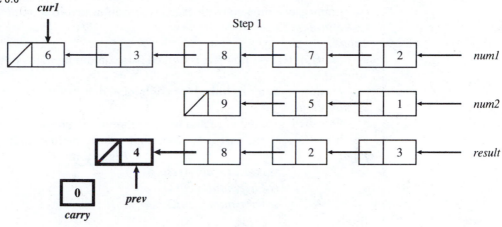

Step 1

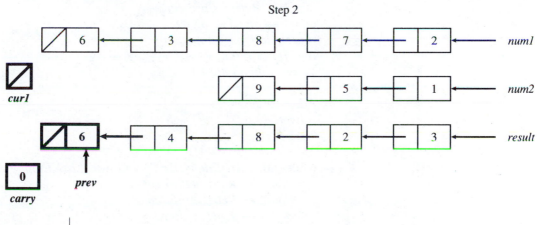

Step 2

Figure 8.10

Linked lists after addition of 872 and 951

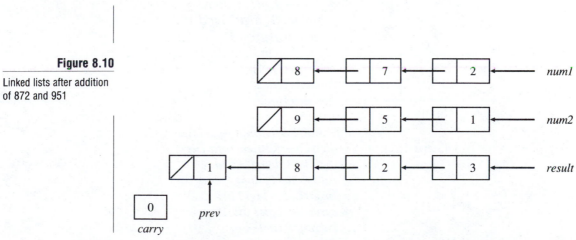

297

InfIntegerAdd(*num1, num2*) → *result*

> Function to return a pointer to a linked list storing digits of the sum of nonnegative integers with digits stored in linked lists pointed to by *num1* and *num2*

Input:

> *num1, num2* — pointers to linked lists containing digits of the summands

Output:

> *result* — pointer to linked list containing digits of the sum

Assumptions:

> One digit is stored in each node; summands are nonnegative; neither input list is empty; the least significant digits are in the first nodes.

Figure	Algorithm
	MakeListEmpty(*result*)
	ToFirst(*num1, cur1*)
	ToFirst(*num2, cur2*)
{8.7}	
{Step 2}	*digit1* ← *RetrieveInfo*(*cur1*)
	digit2 ← *RetrieveInfo*(*cur2*)
	digit3 ← *digit1* + *digit2*
	AddNode(*P, digit3 mod* 10)
	InsertFirst(*result, P*)
	carry ← *digit3 div* 10
	Advance(*cur1*)
	Advance(*cur2*)
	ToFirst(*result, prev*)
{8.8}	
	while (not *ListIsEmpty*(*cur1*)) and (not *ListIsEmpty*(*cur2*)) do
{Steps 1, 2}	*digit1* ← *RetrieveInfo*(*cur1*)
	digit2 ← *RetrieveInfo*(*cur2*)
	digit3 ← *digit1* + *digit2* + *carry*
	AddNode(*P, digit3 mod* 10)
	InsertLater(*prev, P*)
	carry ← *digit3 div* 10
	Advance(*cur1*)
	Advance(*cur2*)
	Advance(*prev*)
{8.9}	
	while (not *ListIsEmpty*(*cur1*)) do
{Steps 1, 2}	*digit1* ← *RetrieveInfo*(*cur1*)
	digit3 ← *digit1* + *carry*
	AddNode(*P, digit3 mod* 10)
	InsertLater(*prev, P*)
	carry ← *digit3 div* 10
	Advance(*cur1*)
	Advance(*prev*)

{8.10}

while (not *ListIsEmpty*(*cur2*)) do
    digit2 ← *RetrieveInfo*(*cur2*)
    digit3 ← *digit2* + *carry*
    AddNode(*P*, *digit3 mod* 10)
    InsertLater(*prev*, *P*)
    carry ← *digit3 div* 10
    Advance(*cur2*)
    Advance(*prev*)

if *carry* <> 0 then
    AddNode(*P*, *carry*)
    InsertLater(*prev*, *P*)

InfIntegerAdd ← *result*

Example 8.3.

LISP-Like Functions.

The only complex data structure built into the computer language LISP is list. LISP, which is particularly good at manipulating symbols, is used extensively in artificial intelligence, the study of having the computer exhibit humanlike intelligence. An **atom**, which is a string of letters and/or digits, is the fundamental unit in LISP. A **list** is a set of parentheses enclosing any number of atoms and lists, such as $B = (b)$ or $L = (a\,b\,(c\,d\,e)\,f)$. These atoms and lists can be stored as a linked list of atoms and linked lists as in Figures 8.11 and 8.12.

Figure 8.11

Linked list of atoms and linked lists storing the LISP list $L = (a\,b\,(c\,d\,e)\,f)$

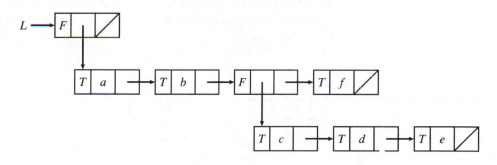

Figure 8.12

Storage for atom $A = a$ and list $B = (b)$

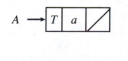
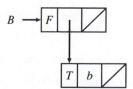

The nodes have three fields:

1. A boolean field, *atom*.

2. Depending on the value of *atom*, either an information field (*info*) holding data, such as "a," or a pointer field (*list*).

3. A pointer, *next*.

If *atom*'s value is *true*, the node holds an atom; if false, the node contains a pointer to a list. In Figure 8.12, *a* is an atom, so that *A* points to a node that stores *a* in an *info* field; (*b*) is a list, so that *B* indicates a node with a field *list*, which is a pointer to another node. Variant records, covered in Section 3.3, can be employed in the implementation of this **generalized list structure**.

```
type
    GeneralizedList  = ^Node;
    Node             = record
        next             : GeneralizedList;
        case atom        : boolean of
            true         : (info : char);
            false        : (list : GeneralizedList)
    end;

var
    A,
    B,
    L : GeneralizedList;
```

Because of the requirement of Pascal for the variant part of the record to be last, we declare the *next* field first in the definition of *Node*. For ease in reading the diagram from left to right, however, we have drawn the *next* field last in each block. Figure 8.13 associates the field identifiers with the segments of blocks.

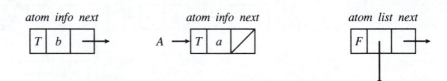

In LISP for $L = (a\ b\ (\ c\ d\ e\ )\ f)$, the function reference $car(L)$ returns the first item in the list,

$$car(L) = a$$

while function invocation $cdr(L)$ returns the rest of the list:

$$cdr(L) = (b\ (c\ d\ e)\ f)$$

Figure 8.14 illustrates the actions of these two functions.

Figure 8.14

Action of *car(L)* and
cdr(L) for the list *L* in
Figure 8.11

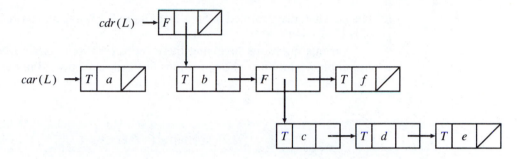

Figure 8.15

Diagram of *cons(M, N)*
using the lists *M* = (*g h*)
and *N* = (*i j k*)

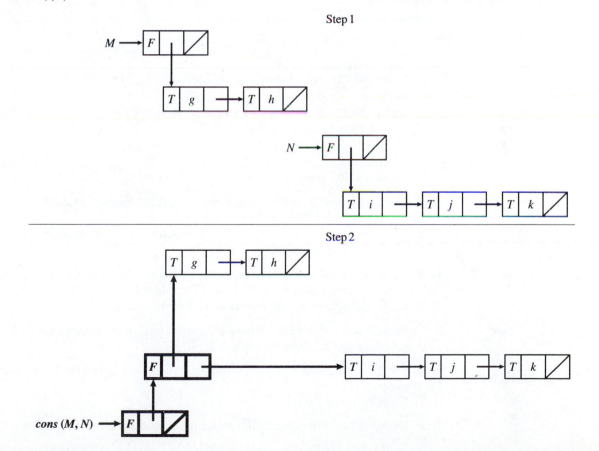

For lists $M = (g\ h)$ and $N = (i\ j\ k)$, pictured in Step 1 of Figure 8.15, the function reference $cons(M, N)$ returns a list with the list M as the first element and with the elements of N following:

$$cons(M, N) = ((g\ h)\ i\ j\ k)$$

The new list, diagrammed in Step 2 of Figure 8.15, has one more element than N has.

Various questions involving these representations, other LISP functions, and implementation of the operations in Pascal are covered in the exercises.

▽

SECTION 8.1 EXERCISES

1. For the procedures *Allocate* and *Free*, as designed in Example 8.1, show drawings of the linked lists pointed to by *head* and *avail* after execution of each line in the following sequence:

   Allocate(*head*); *StoreInfo*(*head*, 1)
   Free(*head*)
   Allocate(*head*); *StoreInfo*(*head*, 2)

2. Repeat Exercise 1 for the following sequence:

   MakeListEmpty(*head*)
   Allocate(*Q*); *StoreInfo*(*Q*, 1); *InsertFirst*(*head*, *Q*)
   Allocate(*P*); *StoreInfo*(*P*, 2); *InsertFirst*(*head*, *P*)
   Allocate(*T*); *StoreInfo*(*T*, 3); *InsertLater*(*Q*, *T*)
   DeleteFirst(*head*)
   DeleteLater(*Q*)
   Free(*head*)
   Allocate(*P*); *StoreInfo*(*P*, 4)

3. **a.** Code in Pascal a dynamic memory allocation implementation of the procedure *Allocate* from Example 8.1.
   b. Code in Pascal a dynamic memory allocation implementation of the procedure *Free* from Example 8.1.

4. **a.** Code in Pascal a dynamic memory allocation implementation of the procedure *ReadNumIntoList* from Example 8.2.
   b. Code in Pascal a recursive version of this procedure.

5. Code in Pascal a dynamic memory allocation implementation of the function *InfIntegerAdd* from Example 8.2.

6. **a.** Design a recursive procedure *PrintBack* to print a linked list in reverse order.
   b. Code Part a in Pascal.

7. **a.** Design a function *ConstMulti* to return a pointer to the product of an

integer stored in a linked list, as in Example 8.2, by a positive integer constant.

    b. Code Part a in Pascal.

8. Larger real numbers than integers can be held in the computer. Write a function to return the real number equivalent of the integer held in a linked list.

9. **a.** Using *div* and *mod*, design a procedure to take a nonnegative integer stored in a variable and place each digit in a linked list.

    b. Code Part a in Pascal.

    c. Revise your procedure in Part b to store 4 digits of the number in each node.

    d. Revise *InfIntegerAdd* of Exercise 5 to add nonnegative integers stored as in Part c.

    e. Revise *ConstMulti* of Exercise 7 similarly.

10. The built-in Pascal set covered in Section 3.5 requires that the elements be of a finite ordinal type because the set is stored as a bit string. We can expand the ADT set definition by implementing sets with linked lists. In this situation, elements can be of any type except *file*. Use pseudocode and ADT linked list operations to design the following:

    a. Procedure, *SetToList*, to read data from a file and store them in a linked list representing a set, placing each new element at the head.

    b. Procedure, *PrintSet*, to print the set stored in a linked list.

    c. Procedure, *ElimDuplicates(P)*, to eliminate all duplicates beyond *P* of the node pointed to by *P*.

    d. Procedure, *ElimAllDuplicates(S)*, to eliminate all duplicates in set *S*.

    e. All ADT set operations as given in Section 3.5, assuming no duplicates.

    f. Function, *SizeSet*, to return the number of elements in a set, assuming it has no duplicates.

    g. Boolean function, *IsDisjoint*, to return *true* if two sets are disjoint.

    h. Function, *XORSet*, to return the exclusive-or of two sets.

11. Give a dynamic memory allocation implementation of the package in Exercise 10.

12. Give a static memory allocation implementation of the package in Exercise 10.

13. Suppose set *S* has *m* elements and set *T* has *n* elements. Find the complexity of the following routines designed in Exercise 10e.

    a. *Union*   **b.** *Intersection*   **c.** *IsIn*

    d. *Subset*   **e.** *EqualSets*

14. Repeat Exercise 10 using ordered linked lists.

15. Repeat Exercise 13 for ordered linked lists.

Similar to the figures for Example 8.3, draw block diagrams for the generalized lists in Exercises 16–23.

16. $A = c$ **17.** $B = (c)$ **18.** $C = ((c))$

19. $D = (((c)))$ **20.** $E = (a\ (b\ (c)))$ **21.** $F = (\ )$

22. $G = ((a\ b)\ (c)\ (e\ (f\ g))\ (\ )\ h)$

23. $H = (setq\ a\ (plus\ b\ c))$, the LISP statement that corresponds to the Pascal assignment statement $a := b + c$.

24. Find $car(G)$ and $cdr(G)$ for the list in Exercise 22.

25. Find $car(H)$ and $cdr(H)$ for the list in Exercise 23.

26. Find $cons(B, H)$ for the lists in Exercises 17 and 23. Draw a block diagram for this new list.

In Exercises 27–35 implement the LISP-like functions in Pascal. Refer to Example 8.3.

27. Boolean function $atomP(L)$, which returns *true* if L is an atom.

28. Boolean function $listP(L)$, which returns *true* if L is a list.

29. $car(L)$

30. $cdr(L)$

31. $cons(M, N)$

32. Function $Length(L)$, which returns the number of items at the highest level of list L. For example, for the list L of Figure 8.11, $Length(L) = 4$.

33. Function $append(M, N)$, which returns the concatenation of lists M and N. For example, for $M = (g\ h)$ and $N = (i\ j\ k)$, $append(M, N)$ is $(g\ h\ i\ j\ k)$.

34. Recursive procedure $PrintGenList(L)$ that prints a generalized list as a LISP atom or list.

35. Recursive procedure $FileToGenList(f, L)$ to read LISP atoms and/or lists, one per line of text file f, into a generalized list structure L.

▽

PROGRAMMING PROJECTS

1. Design a program to read a positive integer value n, to calculate $n!$ (n-factorial), and to print the answer as an integer. Use linked list storage as in Example 8.2. Test your program for a value of n where $n!$ is larger than *maxint* on your computer.

2. In Section 1.4 a polynomial of degree m was defined. One example of a polynomial of degree 6, with 6 being the largest exponent from a term with a nonzero coefficient, is

$$4 + 5x + x^3 + 2x^6$$

We can rewrite this polynomial with every term from the constant to x^6 displayed as

$$4x^0 + 5x^1 + 0x^2 + 1x^3 + 0x^4 + 0x^5 + 2x^6$$

One way to represent this polynomial in a linked list is to store the coefficients as in Figure 8.16. The constant polynomial $4 = 4x^0$, having degree 0, would be stored as in Figure 8.17; the zero polynomial with no nonzero coefficients and, consequently, with no degree would be represented by Figure 8.18.

Figure 8.16

Linked list storing the polynomial for Project 2

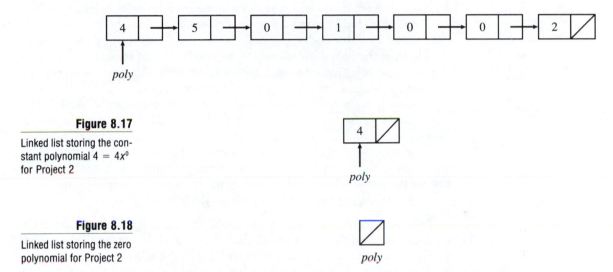

Figure 8.17

Linked list storing the constant polynomial $4 = 4x^0$ for Project 2

Figure 8.18

Linked list storing the zero polynomial for Project 2

Create a polynomial package to help beginning algebra students check their homework. The algebra students want to have the computer be able to find the following:

a. The degree of a polynomial.
b. The sum of two polynomials. For example, the polynomial sum $(12x + 15x^2 + 27x^3) + (8 + 10x + 18x^2)$ is calculated as $8 + 22x + 33x^2 + 27x^3$ by adding corresponding coefficients.
c. The product of a polynomial P by a constant, b. For example, $4 + 5x + 9x^2$ times 2 is the polynomial $8 + 10x + 18x^2$.
d. The product of a polynomial P by ax, where a is a constant. For example, $4 + 5x + 9x^2$ times $3x$ is the polynomial $12x + 15x^2 + 27x^3$.
e. The product of a polynomial P by $ax + b$, where a and b are constants. For example, $4 + 5x + 9x^2$ times $3x + 2$ is the polynomial $8 + 22x + 33x^2 + 27x^3$, which is the sum of the results of the examples in Parts c and d.

The polynomial program should be menu-driven, giving the students the choice of the above alternatives. The coefficients of a polynomial are read interactively and placed into a dynamic linked list. In displaying the polynomial on the screen we can use the notation x^n to indicate x^n. Be sure to trim unnecessary zeros off the end of the polynomial. For example, the polynomial $4 + 5x + 9x^2 + 0x^3 + 0x^4$ is equal to $4 + 5x + 9x^2$.

3. During execution of programs written in list processing languages, such as LISP, there is periodic **garbage collection** or reclamation of no longer used storage space for memory management. Usually, there are two passes over memory, one pass to mark used cells and the other to reclaim unused (and unmarked) cells.

In this project we simulate computer memory as *mem*, an array of records, each record having *info* and *next* fields and a boolean field, *mark*. Variables *head* and *avail* hold the indices of the first nodes in linked lists of information and of available nodes, respectively. Suppose, however, that deletion of a node from the linked list pointed to by *head* does not restore that node to the available list. Consequently, upon execution of *Allocate* an empty list pointed to by *avail* should trigger a garbage collection.

Use a file of data, each record starting with the character 'A' or 'D'. The character 'A' indicates the record is to be inserted at the head of the linked list pointed to by *head*, while 'D' means the record is to be deleted. Perform garbage collection when necessary and print the information in the linked lists pointed to by *head* and *avail* after each garbage collection. Be sure to handle the situation where the memory array, *mem*, is completely filled.

Your program should at least contain the following procedures:

a. *InitializeMemory* to initialize the entire array as a linked list of available nodes pointed to by *avail* with the value in each *mark* field being *false*.
b. *GarbageColln* to call routines *MarkUsed* and *Reclaim*.
c. *MarkUsed* to follow the linked list pointed to by *head*, changing each *mark* field to be *true*.
d. *Reclaim* to place unused cells in a list of available nodes and to assign *false* to each *mark* field.
e. *Allocate* procedure to call *GarbageColln* when appropriate.

4. Suppose that in the memory simulation of Project 3 the list of available cells starts at a location *avail* and is contiguous. Thus, the *Reclaim* procedure also performs compaction, where the linked list pointed to by *head* is placed at the end of the array *mem* and the linked list of available nodes is established at the other end. Revise the *Reclaim* procedure to perform this compaction.

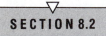

Linked List Implementation of Strings

In Chapters 4, 5, and 6 we considered the abstract data types of string, stack, and queue, respectively, along with implementations with arrays and applications.

After discussing linked lists in the last chapter, we are now ready to consider a dynamic memory allocation implementation with linked lists for each ADT.

Figure 8.19 presents diagrams of possible packed array and linked list implementations of the length 3 string 'the'. Several positions are wasted in the array, while the exact number of nodes is allocated in the linked list. Moreover, with the dynamic linked list implementation of strings, worry over truncation in a full string is all but eliminated. Therefore, we define *StringIsFull* as always *false*. But different problems arise with this implementation. Several operations, *CopySubstring, DeleteString, InsertString, RetrieveChar*, have a position argument that is an integer. In each, the linked list must first be searched sequentially to arrive at the appropriate numeric position. With arrays, however, the position merely becomes the index. Of course, the actual installation and removal of substrings is far easier with a linked list.

Figure 8.19

Diagram of array and linked list storage of the string 'the'

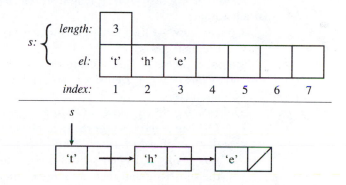

Another disadvantage of a linked list of characters is the space overhead. In a packed array of characters, each character occupies one byte in memory. When dynamically allocated, the character probably consumes a word, which may be longer than one byte. Moreover, the value of a pointer, which is a memory address, also consumes several bytes of storage. Of course, we do allocate and free nodes for the characters only as needed instead of maintaining a statically allocated array.

Figures 8.20 and 8.21 summarize the advantages and disadvantages of each of these implementations. The actual coding of the operations and variations of the basic implementations are covered in the exercises.

As indicated in these figures, the major disadvantage of the array implementation is the fixed number of permissible characters in any string, sometimes leading to truncation. Dynamic implementation of strings with linked lists overcomes this disadvantage but has a tedious search for a numeric position. As indicated in the conclusions of Figure 8.21, this dynamic implementation is most useful in situations where we do not know the maximum string size but it is very important to avoid truncation. Considering truncation the lesser of the evils in a majority of the applications, most versions of Pascal that have built-in string operations choose to implement strings with arrays.

Figure 8.20

Discussion of array implementation of ADT string

Array Implementation of ADT String

Notation

> $sLng$ — length of string s
>
> lng — length of substring sub
>
> pos — position of substring sub in s

Advantages

> Search for an integer position immediate—$O(1)$; advantageous for the search phase of *CopySubstring, DeleteString, InsertString, Retrieve-Char*
>
> *CopySubstring* fast—$O(lng)$: $O(1)$ search phase, $O(lng)$ copy phase
>
> *RetrieveChar* fast—$O(1)$: $O(1)$ search phase, $O(1)$ retrieval phase
>
> *AppendChar* fast—$O(1)$: $O(1)$ search phase, $O(1)$ installation phase; append to end
>
> *LengthString* fast—$O(1)$; length stored in record with the array

Disadvantages

> *Concat* slow—$O(lng)$; copy elements of the second string onto the end of the first
>
> Removal phase of *DeleteString* slow—$O(sLng - pos - lng)$; move $sLng - pos - lng + 1$ entries from deletion point on to close up the deleted characters
>
> *DeleteString* fairly slow—$O(sLng - pos - lng)$: $O(1)$ search phase, $O(sLng - pos - lng)$ removal phase
>
> Installation phase of *InsertString* slow—$O(sLng - pos)$; move $sLng - pos - lng + 1$ entries from the insertion point on to make room for the substring and then copy lng elements into s
>
> *InsertString* fairly slow—$O(sLng - pos)$: $O(1)$ search phase, $O(sLng - pos)$ installation phase
>
> *Position* slow—$O(lng \cdot sLng)$ for the brute-force algorithm, Boyer-Moore algorithm faster in most cases
>
> Must know the maximum number of entries in string initially—Check *StringIsFull* before executing *Concat, InsertString*, and *AppendChar*; possible truncation

Conclusions

> Truncation, because of insertion into a full string, is the major disadvantage of this implementation. Insertion into and deletion from an array involves movement of elements and is time consuming in a lengthy string. In applications where the strings are shorter, insertion and deletion are not a big consideration.

Figure 8.21 Discussion of dynamic linked list implementation of ADT string	**Dynamic Linked List Implementation of ADT String**

Notation

> $sLng$ — length of string s
>
> lng — length of substring sub
>
> pos — position of substring sub in s

Advantages

> Insertion phase of *InsertString* fast—$O(1)$
>
> Removal phase of *DeleteString* fast—$O(1)$
>
> Do not need to know the maximum number of entries in the string initially—*StringIsFull* is always *false*

Disadvantages

> Must search sequentially for a numeric position—$O(n)$; not advantageous for the search phase of *CopyString, DeleteString, RetrieveChar,* and *InsertString*
>
> *Concat* slow—$O(sLng + lng)$: $O(sLng)$ search phase to find the end of the first string, $O(lng)$ copying the second string; if linked list has a tail pointer, *Concat*—$O(lng)$
>
> *CopyString* slow—$O(pos + lng)$: $O(pos)$ search phase, $O(lng)$ copy phase
>
> *DeleteString* slow—$O(pos)$: $O(pos)$ search phase, $O(1)$ removal phase
>
> *InsertString* slow—$O(pos + lng)$: $O(pos)$ search phase, $O(lng)$ installation phase
>
> *AppendChar* slow—$O(sLng)$: $O(sLng)$ search phase to find the end of the string, $O(1)$ installation phase; if linked list has a tail pointer, *AppendChar* fast—$O(1)$
>
> *RetrieveChar* slow—$O(pos)$: $O(pos)$ search phase, $O(1)$ retrieval phase
>
> *Position* slow—$O(lng \cdot sLng)$ for the brute-force algorithm
>
> Overhead of storage room for pointers

Conclusions

> The sequential search for a numeric position is a big disadvantage. Moreover, though nodes for characters are only added as needed, the pointers do consume memory space. The performance of the *Concat* and *AppendChar* operations, however, can be significantly improved by the use of a tail pointer. This implementation should be used in situations where it is important not to truncate and when we do not initially know the maximum string size.

▽

SECTION 8.2 EXERCISES

1. Implement the ADT string with dynamic linked lists. First design the operations on the higher level of pseudocode and ADT linked list, then code each operation in Pascal.

2. ADT string can be implemented with a combination of arrays and linked lists. In this situation the information in a node consists of a packed array of characters. The head node should maintain front and tail pointers as well as the length of the string. If all the characters from a node are deleted, that node can be removed. If some but not all characters of a node are deleted or there are positions unused, those elements should be marked with a special unused character, perhaps '#'. Elements so marked are not considered part of the string and are not counted in the length.

   a. Implement the ADT string with this structure where the array size is 16.
   b. Implement a garbage collection routine to delete the unused characters and the nodes consisting entirely of the unused character.

3. Suppose that for the combined linked list/array implementation of strings presented in Exercise 2 we also store in each node a count of the actual number of characters of the string in that node. Implement ADT string using this arrangement where each node contains an array of 32 characters.

4. Explain the complexity of the linked list implementation of the string operations as presented in the summary of Figure 8.21.

For Exercises 5–10 use a linked list implementation of ADT string.
   a. Employ pseudocode and ADT linked list operations to design the routines.
   b. Code the routines in Pascal.

5. Procedure *PointFreeString*(s) that frees all the characters of the string pointed to by *s*. Assume *s* exists.

6. Procedure *PointDeleteWord*(s, p) to delete from the string pointed to by *s* the substring starting after the position indicated by *p* to the end of the word. If *p* has the null value and a word appears at the beginning of the string, delete that word. Assume a word is a contiguous string of letters. If the character after the one indicated by *p* points to a nonletter, do not delete anything.

7. Function *PointPosition*(sub, s) to return a pointer to the node where the substring indicated by the pointer *sub* can first be found in the string indicated by the pointer *s*. If *sub* does not appear in *s*, return *nil*.

8. Procedure *PointInsert*(sub, s, p) to insert the pattern pointed to by *sub* as a substring into the string pointed to by *s* after the position indicated by *p*; if *p* has the value *nil*, insert *sub* at the beginning of *s*.

9. Function *PointCopy*(s, fromPtr, toPtr) to return a pointer to a copy of the substring of the string pointed to by *s* from the position pointed to by *fromPtr*, up to but not including the position indicated by *toPtr*. If *fromPtr* is *nil* or if *toPtr* indicates an earlier or the same node as *fromPtr* does, return *nil*. If *toPtr* is *nil* but *fromPtr* is not, return a pointer to a copy of the sub-

string from the position pointed to by *fromPtr* through the end of the string.

10. Procedure *PointDelete(s, fromPtr, toPtr)* to delete from the string pointed to by *s* the substring from the position pointed to by *fromPtr*, up to but not including the node indicated by *toPtr*. If *fromPtr* is *nil* or if *toPtr* indicates an earlier node than *fromPtr*, *s* is unchanged. If *toPtr* is *nil* but *fromPtr* is not, delete the substring from the position pointed to by *fromPtr* through the end of the string.

▽

PROGRAMMING PROJECT

1. Read a form letter from a text file into a string, implemented with a linked list. Use the character '#' to indicate that a return is needed in the resulting letter. For example, suppose the text file reads as follows:

April 22##*FirstName* *LastName*#*Street*#*CityState*##
Dear *FirstName*:##Congratulations! You have won one of the following gifts: a car, a boat, a house, a ten-month vacation to Hawaii, a million dollars in spending money, or a toaster. *FirstName*, all you have to do to claim your prize is to call us at 555-1111 and make plans to visit us at Mt. RipOff Retreat. Call today! See you soon.##Sincerely, ###Mr. U. R. RippedOff

The resulting form letter, with appropriate wrapping of text for the body of the letter, reads as follows:

April 22

FirstName *LastName*
Street
CityState

Dear *FirstName*:

Congratulations! You have won one of the following gifts: a car, a boat, a house, a ten-month vacation to Hawaii, a million dollars in spending money, or a toaster. *FirstName*, all you have to do to claim your prize is to call us at 555-1111 and make plans to visit us at Mt. RipOff Retreat. Call today! See you soon.

Sincerely,

Mr. U. R. RippedOff

From another user-defined file read records containing information about the first and last names, street address, and city-state. For each record print a "personalized" letter with the appropriate information inserted.

Linked List Implementation of Stacks

With a dynamic linked list implementation of stacks we still need to be concerned about not popping from an empty stack; but as long as there is enough memory, the stack never becomes filled. Moreover, space for stack elements is allocated only as needed. Most computers implement the run-time stack, which holds activation records for each function invocation and procedure call, as an array. Consequently, we may obtain a STACK OVERFLOW error message while using recursion. For applications involving stacks, we have the flexibility of choosing a static or dynamic implementation. As we will see, unlike some of the string operations, all of the stack operations can be implemented easily and efficiently with dynamic linked lists.

The creation of the stack follows the typical linked list structure:

```
type
    elType  = ...........;
    stack   = ^Node;
    Node    = record
        el    : elType;
        next  : stack
    end;

var
    s : stack;
```

Here, *stack* is the identifier for the pointer type; the pointer variable, *s*, is the variable we have often called *head*. Since we already maintain a pointer at the beginning of the list, we consider the top of the stack to be there. Figure 8.22 shows a stack along with its storage in a linked list.

Figure 8.22

Stack with linked list
representation

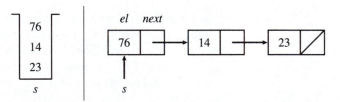

The *MakeStackEmpty* operation now reduces to the ADT linked list operation *MakeListEmpty*. This operation, the result of which is pictured in Figure 8.23, is implemented dynamically as follows:

```
{ Procedure to make the stack s empty }

procedure MakeStackEmpty (var s: stack);
begin                                    { Figure 8.23 }
    s := nil                             { MakeListEmpty }
end;
```

Figure 8.23

Empty stack with linked list implementation

Similarly, *StackIsEmpty* tests if *s* is *nil*, just as the dynamic memory allocation of *ListIsEmpty* does:

```
{ Boolean function to return true if the stack s is empty }

function StackIsEmpty (s : stack): boolean;
begin
    StackIsEmpty := (s = nil)                { ListIsEmpty }
end;
```

As mentioned earlier, one major advantage of a dynamic linked list implementation of the ADT stack is that the stack can grow virtually indefinitely. Since we need not check if the stack is full, the operation *StackIsFull* degenerates to always being *false*:

```
{ Boolean function always returns false; stack never full }

function StackIsFull (s: stack): boolean;
begin
    StackIsFull := false
end;
```

Because we maintain the top at the beginning of the list, *Push*(*s, e*) first places *e*'s value in a newly created node and then inserts that node at the beginning of the linked list. The pointer operation *AddNode* from Example 7.1 of Section 7.1 accomplishes the first task, and the ADT linked list operation *InsertFirst* produces the second. Figure 8.24 demonstrates the process outlined below:

Push(*s, e*):   { Figure 8.24 }
    AddNode(*p, e*)   { Step 2 }
    InsertFirst(*s, p*)   { Step 3 }

Figure 8.24

Action of *Push* along
with a linked list imple-
mentation

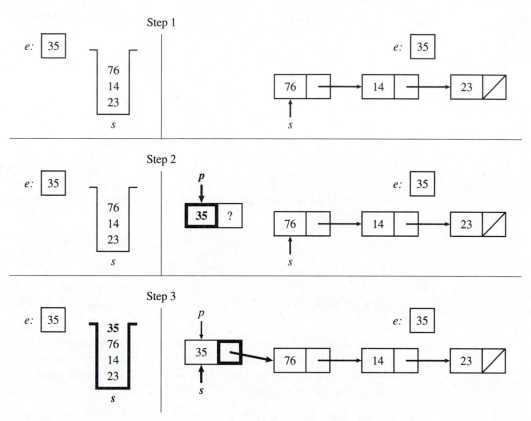

These operations translate into the following procedure:

```
{ Procedure to push an element, e, onto a stack, s }

procedure Push (var s: stack; e: elType);
var
    p : stack;
begin                              { Figure 8.24 }
    new(p);                        { Step 2—AddNode }
    p^.el    := e;
    p^.next := s;                  { Step 3—InsertFirst }
    s        := p
end;
```

As we discussed in Example 8.1 of Section 8.1, *new(p)* is but one implementation of the ADT linked list operation *New(p)*. Depending on the version of Pascal used, you may choose to maintain your own list of available nodes.

Thus, for the *Pop* procedure, after unlinking the node at the top of the stack, we could use *dispose* or our own version of the ADT linked list operation *Dispose(p)*, such as the procedure *Free(p)* from Example 8.1 of Section 8.1. Before execution of the operation *DeleteFirst*, however, we must store the value for that first node into *e*. Pseudocode and ADT linked list operations for the *Pop* operation follow:

Pop(s, e):   { Figure 8.25}
    e ← RetrieveInfo(s)   { Step 2 }
    DeleteFirst(s)   { Step 3 }

Figure 8.25

Action of *Pop* along with a linked list implementation

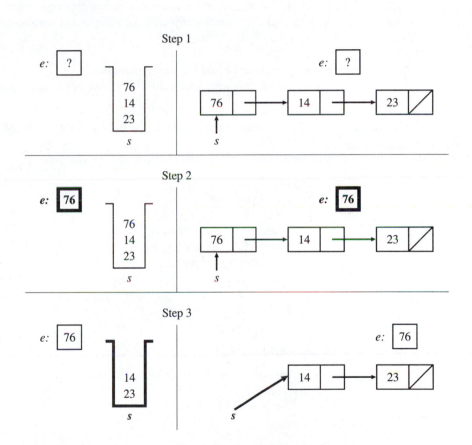

Figure 8.25 illustrates this process, coded as follows:

```
{ Procedure to pop an element from a stack, s,
   and place the value in e                      }
{ Assumption: The stack is not empty.            }
```

```
procedure Pop (var s: stack; var e: elType);
var
   p: stack;
begin                            { Figure 8.25 }
   e := s^.el;                   { Step 2—RetrieveInfo }
   p := s;                       { Step 3—DeleteFirst }
   s := s^.next;
   dispose(p)
end;
```

Depending on the application, we may choose to add *RetrieveStack* to our list of ADT stack operations. Leaving the stack unchanged, *RetrieveStack(s, e)* returns the value of the top element through the parameter *e*. As pointed out in Example 5.1 of Section 5.1, we can define this operation with successive calls to *Pop* and *Push* or directly with an assignment statement, such as

```
e := s^.el
```

for the dynamic linked list implementation.

Figure 8.26 summarizes this linked list implementation of ADT stack.

Figure 8.26

Linked list implementation of ADT stack

A Dynamic Linked List Implementation of ADT Stack

Create a stack *s* with each element of type *elType*.

```
type
   elType  = ...........;
   stack   = ^Node;
   Node    = record
      el    : elType;
      next  : stack
   end;

var
   s : stack;
```

MakeStackEmpty(s)

```
procedure MakeStackEmpty(var s: stack);
begin
   s := nil
end;
```

StackIsEmpty(s) → b

```
function StackIsEmpty(s : stack): boolean;
begin
   StackIsEmpty := (s = nil)
end;
```

Figure 8.26

continued

StackIsFull(*s*) → *b*

```
function StackIsFull(s: stack): boolean;
begin
   StackIsFull := false
end;
```

Push(*s*, *e*)

```
procedure Push (var s: stack; e: elType);
var
   p : stack;
begin
   new(p);
   p^.el   := e;
   p^.next := s;
   s       := p
end;
```

Pop(*s*, *e*)

```
{ Assumption: The stack is not empty. }
procedure Pop (var s: stack; var e: elType);
var
   p: stack;
begin
   e := s^.el;
   p := s;
   s := s^.next;
   dispose(p)
end;
```

▽

SECTION 8.3 EXERCISES

For Exercises 1–23, code each routine from the referenced exercise in Section 5.1 using an implementation with linked lists. (These operations are implemented with arrays in Section 5.2 Exercises.)

1. a. Procedure *RetrieveStack* of Example 5.1 to obtain the top value on the stack.

  b. Implement *RetrieveStack* without a push and a pop but with an assignment statement.

2. Procedure *AddTop* of Example 5.2 to pop the top two elements and push their sum onto the stack.

3. Procedure *SwapStack* from Exercise 10 to exchange the top two elements on a stack.

4. Procedure *Dup* from Exercise 11 to duplicate the top element on a stack.

5. Procedure *SaveVariables* from Exercise 12 to save the values of variables x, y, and z by placing them onto a stack.

6. Procedure *RestoreVariables* from Exercise 13 to recover the values saved by *SaveVariables*.

7. Procedure *ClearStack* from Exercise 14 to remove all the elements from a stack.

8. Procedure *FileToStack* from Exercise 15 to read from a line of a text file and place each character in a stack.

9. Procedure *PrintStack* from Exercise 16 to print the elements in a stack from top to bottom.

10. Procedure from Exercise 17 to use *FileToStack* and *PrintStack* from the previous two exercises to print data from a file with each line printed in reverse order.

11. Recursive procedure *Append(s, u)* from Exercise 18 to append a stack u on the top of stack s so that u's top element is on the top. The procedure should cause u to be empty.

12. Recursive procedure *PrintStackUp* from Example 5.4 to print the elements of a stack from bottom to top.

13. Nonrecursive version *PrintStackUp* from Exercise 19.

14. **a.** Nonrecursive procedure *NRCopyStack* from Exercise 20a to make a copy of a stack.
    b. Recursive version of *NRCopyStack* from Exercise 20b.

15. Procedure *Bottom* from Exercise 21 to place the bottom element of the stack s into e, making s empty.

16. Recursive version of *AddStack* from Exercise 22.

17. Procedure *AddStack2* from Exercise 23 that initializes *sum* to be 0; pops the elements from the stack, accumulating their sum in *sum*; and then pushes the value of *sum* onto the stack.

18. Procedure *AddStack3* from Exercise 24 that first checks that the stack is nonempty before calling *AddStack2*.

19. Procedure *AddStack4* from Exercise 25 that is a recursive version of *AddStack2*.

20. Procedure *DeleteStack* from Exercise 26 to delete an item e from a stack s leaving the stack otherwise unchanged; assume e is in the stack.

21. Procedure *RemoveBlanks* from Exercise 27 to remove all blanks from a stack of characters.

22. **a.** Boolean function *EqualStack* from Exercise 28a to return *true* if two stacks are identical, ordered in the same way. The procedure should leave the stacks unchanged.

    b. Nonrecursive version of *EqualStack* from Exercise 28b.

23. Nonrecursive function from Exercise 29 to convert a positive decimal integer to a binary number.

24. Summarize the advantages and disadvantages of the array and dynamic linked list implementations of the ADT stack.

▽

PROGRAMMING PROJECT

1. Write a program to read pairs of very long integers from a file and to print out their sums as integers. To accomplish this task revise Example 8.2 of Section 8.1 using a stack to read a nonnegative integer from a text file into a stack. After insertion, the top element of the stack should be the least significant digit. Revise *InfIntegerAdd* of that example to place the sum in a stack with the least significant digit being on the bottom. *PrintStackUp* of Exercise 12 or 13 and *PrintStack* of Exercise 9 could be used to print the input numbers and the result, respectively.

▽

SECTION 8.4

Linked List Implementation of Queues

With a dynamic linked list implementation of queues we do not have the same worries over wrapping around or filling the structure as we do with an array implementation. We do have the overhead of space consumed by each pointer, but we allocate and deallocate space for each queue element only as needed. Moreover, as with stacks, both static and dynamic implementations yield the same complexity for each ADT operation.

In Section 7.5 we mentioned several alternatives to the conventional linked list implementation. One involved having a tail as well as a head pointer. Here, we use that variation with the queue *q*, declared to be the type of a record containing head and tail pointers, called *front* and *rear*, respectively. Again, we must be careful to use a *with* block or the record and field identifiers as in *q.front* and *q.rear*. The following type definitions and variable declarations create the queue:

```
type
    elType   = ...........;
    pointer  = ^Node;
    Node     = record
        el   : elType;
        next : pointer
    end;
```

```
queue   = record
   front,
   rear : pointer
end;

var
   q : queue;
   e : elType;
```

As with the dynamic implementation of stacks, memory size is our only limitation on the size of the queue. Thus, we define *QueueIsFull*(*q*) always to be *false*.

Like the linked list operation *MakeListEmpty*, to define *MakeQueue-Empty* we assign the value *nil* to the head pointer, *q.front*. It is unnecessary to tamper with the rear pointer as well.

Information is always taken from the front of a queue and from the top of a stack. This information comes from the node indicated by the front queue pointer, such as *q.front*, or the stack pointer, such as *s*. Thus, implementations of the ADT queue operations *DeQueue*(*q,e*) and *RetrieveQueue*(*q,e*) mimic the implementations in Section 8.3 of the ADT stack operations *Pop*(*s, e*) and *RetrieveStack*(*s, e*), respectively. Figure 8.27 details the dequeuing process.

Figure 8.27

Dequeuing with a linked list implementation of a queue

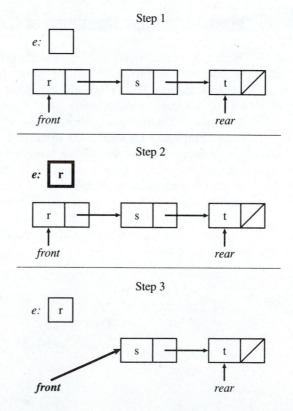

The *EnQueue* operation should also look familiar. In Example 7.2 of Section 7.3, we read items from a file and inserted them at the tail of a linked list. In the definition of *EnQueue*, after placing the new information in a target node, we consider two situations. If the queue is empty, we insert that node at the beginning, being careful to point both *front* and *rear* to this element. If the queue is not empty, we use the ADT linked list operation *InsertLater* to install the target node at the end of the queue. Then we point *rear* toward the addition. Figures 8.28 and 8.29 illustrate these two cases. *EnQueue* is defined below using pseudocode and ADT linked list operations. We consider implementation of this and other ADT queue operations in the exercises. Because we

Figure 8.28

Enqueuing with a linked list implementation of an initially empty queue

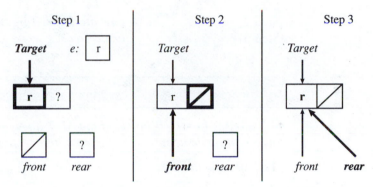

Figure 8.29

Enqueuing with a linked list implementation in a queue that is not empty

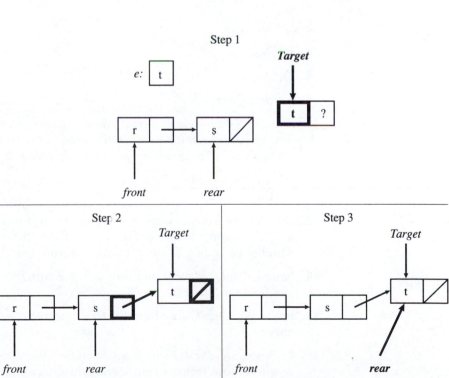

implement *q* as a record with two pointer fields, for the Pascal code in those exercises you should use a *with* block or *q.front* and *q.rear*, instead of just *front* and *rear*, respectively.

EnQueue(q, e):

Figure	Algorithm
{8.28 and 8.29}	
{Step 1}	*AddNode(Target, e)*
{8.28}	if *ListIsEmpty(front)* then
{Step 2}	*InsertFirst(front, Target)*
{Step 3}	*ToFirst(front, rear)*
{8.29}	else
{Step 2}	*InsertLater(rear, Target)*
{Step 3}	*Advance(rear)*

▽

SECTION 8.4 EXERCISES

In Exercises 1–6 code in Pascal the ADT queue operations using the dynamic linked list implementation discussed in this section.

1. *MakeQueueEmpty*

2. *QueueIsEmpty*

3. *QueueIsFull*

4. *EnQueue*

5. *DeQueue*

6. *RetrieveQueue*

In Exercises 7–21 code in Pascal the operations from Section 6.1 using the dynamic linked list implementation discussed in this section. (These operations are implemented with arrays in Section 6.2 Exercises.)

7. *AppendQueue* from Example 6.1 to append one queue to the end of another.

8. *ScrollDown* from Example 6.2 to place records from a file *f* into a queue *q* until the number of entries exceeds 24. Thereafter, remove the front queue item before adding another record to *q* from *f*.

9. Function *AddQueue* from Exercise 8 to return the sum of all the elements in a queue of numbers.

10. Procedure *ClearQueue* from Exercise 9 to remove all the elements from a queue.

11. **a.** Procedure *PrintQueue* from Exercise 10a to print the elements in a queue from front to rear, leaving the queue empty.

     b. Recursive procedure *PrintRevQueue* from Exercise 10b to print the elements from a queue in reverse order and leave the queue empty.

12. Procedure *LengthQueue* from Exercise 11 to return the number of elements in the queue *q* without destroying *q*.

13. Procedure *RetrieveRear* from Exercise 12 to return the last element from a queue *q*, leaving *q* unchanged.

14. Boolean function *EqualQueue* from Exercise 13 to return *true* if two queues are identical, ordered in the same way.

15. Procedure *Replace(q, e, x)* from Exercise 14 to replace every occurrence of element *e* in queue *q* with the value of *x*.

16. a. Recursive procedure *Reverse* from Exercise 15a to reverse the order of the elements in a queue.
     b. Nonrecursive version of the procedure in Part a.

17. Nonrecursive version of *AppendQueue* from Exercise 16.

18. Procedure *SelectFile(q, f, probability)* from Exercise 17a to create a queue *q* and to place into *q* any item from a file *f* that is less than the constant *probability*.

19. Procedure *SwapQueue* from Exercise 18a to exchange the front two elements on the queue.

20. Procedure *PositionToQueue* from Exercise 19 to place into a new queue the starting positions in order of every occurrence of substring *sub* in string *s*.

21. Boolean function *Palindrome* from Exercise 20 that returns *true* if the elements from a queue, listed in order, form a palindrome, which reads the same front to back as back to front.

22. Code in Pascal the post office simulation program from Example 6.3 of Section 6.3 using a dynamic linked list implementation of the queue.

23. Implement the ADT deque of Exercise 19 in Section 6.2 with dynamic linked lists.

24. Implement the ADT priority queue of Exercise 7 in Section 6.3 with dynamic linked lists.

▽

PROGRAMMING PROJECTS

1. Repeat Project 1 of Section 6.3 using a dynamic linked list implementation.

2. Repeat Project 2 of Section 6.3 using a dynamic linked list implementation.

SECTION 8.5   Encapsulation and Pascal

One of the major goals of data abstraction is to encapsulate the structure so that details of implementation are hidden from the user. With such information hidden the programmer can consider major operations as opposed to becoming lost in a sea of details.

Unfortunately, Standard Pascal forces us to handle these details when writing a program. For example, in a simulation of a waiting line in a post office, in the main program we must define the global type *queue*. Upon looking at such a program we are struck immediately with implementation details—from the type definitions it is obvious whether we are using an array or linked list implementation. Moreover, the operations, defined as procedures or functions, directly follow. To program with abstract data types we should know the kinds of objects and operations, and for the operations we should know the required input to obtain the desired output. In Standard Pascal, the forced appearance of such things as type, function, and procedure definitions compromises the ideals of data abstraction. Thus, with Standard Pascal we have an added responsibility to isolate as much as possible the implementation of the ADT operations and the implementation of the application program. One helpful technique is to place all the creation and implementation details of the ADT together, boldly demarcated by skipped lines and several comment lines of all asterisks.

Additionally, though Standard Pascal does not, some versions allow us to store source code in another file. For example, this other file, perhaps called *QueueFile*, could contain all relevant type definitions for a queue as well as definitions of the ADT queue operations. We omit these definitions in the application program and use an *include* compiler directive, perhaps written as

```
{$include QueueFile}
```

where these definitions should occur. Upon compilation, this statement directs the compiler to read *QueueFile* and include its statements at this location in the program. *QueueFile* is not separately compiled, however, but the included statements are compiled along with the main program. Thus, information still is not hidden from the main program—we could manipulate the queue without using one of the ADT queue operations. Moreover, because code is directly inserted, inadvertently we could have the same identifier declared twice, once for a variable in *QueueFile* and once for a different variable in the main program.

Partially in response to this deficiency in Standard Pascal, its creator, Niklaus Wirth, introduced the language Modula-2 in 1980. With Modula-2 one can define a pair of independently compiled **modules** for each ADT. A **definition module** contains the definitions of constants, types, procedures, and functions and the declarations of variables that are to be known to the "outside world." An **implementation module** encapsulates the implementation details of the objects in the definition module as well as definitions of identifiers that are completely local to the unit. If at one time we must use a queue of integers and another time a queue of characters, however, we must have two copies of the queue available, one with the type of a queue element, *elType*, defined as *integer*, the other with *elType* = *char*.

Some versions of Pascal, such as the newest ones of Turbo Pascal for both the IBM PC and the Macintosh, provide a similar facility with **units**. A unit has two sections, an **interface section**, corresponding to the definition module of Modula-2, and an **implementation section** similar to Modula-2's implementation module. If such units are available in your version of Pascal, their use is highly recommended. The unit can be independently debugged and used repeatedly, leading to more error-free programs. Also, units can help us to employ the abstract data type in designing programs on a high level. For example, suppose we are writing a waiting-line simulation program involving the abstract data type queue. Presumably, we will already have compiled units implementing the ADT queue with arrays and linked lists. After the design and coding are complete, we can determine which implementation is best and use that unit. Our program's coding should not be affected by the choice of units. Unfortunately, we may need to recompile the unit to define a particular *elType* in our application. Appendix B provides additional details about the development and application of units with Turbo Pascal.

Developed under the direction of the Department of Defense to be used in real-time and large-scale systems, the computer language Ada provides even better features for abstract data types. The language derives its name from Lady Ada Augusta Lovelace, considered to be the first programmer. Born in the early 1800s, she was the daughter of the poet Lord Byron. She became fascinated with the work of Charles Babbage, who conceived the idea of the analytical engine, a machine to solve general arithmetic problems. Babbage even thought of using punched cards to enter data and operations. His engine contained most of the major features of modern digital computers. Ada Lovelace's writings on Babbage's work reveal that she envisioned the concepts of loop and subroutine. Ada died at an early age, and Babbage's analytical engine, called "Babbage's folly" by his critics, was never completed. Unfortunately, his ideas were far beyond the technology of the times.

In the language Ada the **package** corresponds to the Modula-2 definition and implementation modules and the Turbo Pascal unit. As with the others, the package can be separately compiled; can group definitions of constants, types, procedures, and functions and declarations of variables; and can hide information, such as implementation details. Similar to the Turbo Pascal unit, the Ada package has two major parts, a declaration section and the package body.

A more advanced feature of Ada, however, is the **generic package**, which allows the same package to be used for elements of different types. For example, we could have a generic package to implement ADT queue regardless of whether the type of a queue element is *integer* or *char*. Once a generic package for the ADT queue is available, we can create "instances" of the generic package for a particular element type. If the generic package is *GenericQueue*, we obtain an integer instance of the structure by using the type *integer* as an argument in the following statement:

```
package IntegerQueue is new GenericQueue (integer);
```

Similarly, with the argument *char*, the statement

```
package CharQueue is new GenericQueue (char);
```

makes available all the queue operations where the type of a queue element is *char*.

The generic package is a powerful feature of Ada that promotes the ideals of data abstraction in program development. The language is, however, larger and more complicated than Pascal or Modula-2.

With Pascal we should use whatever encapsulation features are available on our system to contain the implementation details of an abstract data type: careful separation from the rest of the program, included files, or separately compiled units. Such encapsulation can help us produce better quality programs faster.

CHAPTER

▽
9

Tables

Introduction

The abstract data type definition of table in the first section of this chapter reveals a structure that can be organized based on the value in a particular field or fields. Using this organization, information can be retrieved, inserted, deleted, or processed in a variety of ways.

In Section 9.2 we compare and contrast four implementations of ADT table involving a static memory allocation with ordered and unordered arrays and a dynamic memory allocation with ordered and unordered linked lists. The hash table of Section 9.3 provides an additional, powerful method of implementation for ADT table. In studying binary trees in the next chapter we will discover yet another such implementation. As will be discussed, the best method of implementation to use depends largely on the particular application.

▽
SECTION 9.1

ADT Table

Undoubtedly, you have consulted tables many times. Let us examine the characteristics of tables to discern how we should define that abstract data type. For example, consider the table in Figure 9.1 of students in a course along with their year in college and grade point average (GPA).

This table, like most, is composed of records, although there is no requirement that this be the case. For instance, the first column by itself is a table of students in the course.

The records in this table are arranged alphabetically in the first column so that it is easy to look up a student's name and corresponding record. The name identifies the record; thus, the name field is a key to the table. A **key** is a field or composite of fields that uniquely identifies an entry in a table.

Figure 9.1

Table of students in a
course sorted by name

Name	Year	GPA
Adams, Keith	3	3.21
Blackwell, Henry	1	2.00
Davis, Susan	1	3.50
Hinkel, Chris	2	1.94
Jordan, Ann	4	3.05
Patterson, Lynn	1	2.00
Suarez, Rosa	3	2.82
Williams, George	2	3.64

The table need not be sorted by key, however, but in any manner convenient for searching. Perhaps we wish to ask questions by year. For instance, who in the course is a freshman? Or what is the average GPA for sophomores in the course? In this case, arrangement of the table by class as in Figure 9.2 would be most appropriate.

Figure 9.2

Table of students from
Figure 9.1 sorted by year

Name	Year	GPA
Blackwell, Henry	1	2.00
Davis, Susan	1	3.50
Patterson, Lynn	1	2.00
Hinkel, Chris	2	1.94
Williams, George	2	3.64
Adams, Keith	3	3.21
Suarez, Rosa	3	2.82
Jordan, Ann	4	3.05

Certainly, we need to be able to search a table, retrieving records that answer a question. The operations of insertion and deletion are also essential for manipulation of a table. Often it is necessary to process the entire table in some manner. Performing some action on or with every entry in a table is called **traversing** the table. When we process an entry in the table we say we are **visiting** that element. A visit to an element is a routine that could perform innumerable duties from printing the record to comparing a field with a constant. In the ADT table definition of Figure 9.3, we define a traversal operation. In the definition, *Traverse* has as a parameter a user-defined procedure, *Visit*, which gives instructions about what action to perform upon a visit to an entry. For the actual implementation in Pascal, we will call *Visit* but not use this procedure as a parameter. Though permissible in Standard Pascal, some versions do not allow functions and procedures as parameters. We develop the following examples on the higher abstract data type level and postpone a comparison of various implementations until the next section.

Figure 9.3

Formal definition of ADT table

ADT Table

Objects: A finite sequence of elements such that each element has a key that uniquely identifies the entry and that is the element or is a subfield of the element.

Operations:
    Notation:

elType	— type of an element in the table
keyType	— type of the key
t	— table
e	— item of type *elType*
k	— item of type *keyType*
b	— boolean value

***MakeTableEmpty*(*t*)**
    Procedure to make *t* empty
TableIsEmpty*(*t*) → *b
    Boolean function to return *true* if *t* is empty
TableIsFull*(*t*) → *b
    Boolean function to return *true* if *t* is full
KeyTableEl*(*e*) → *k
    Function to return *e*'s key
KeyFound*(*t, k*) → *b
    Boolean function to return *true* if an entry with key *k* is found in *t*
***InsertTable*(*t, e*)**
    Procedure to insert *e* into *t*; assume *e* is not already in *t*
***DeleteTable*(*t, k*)**
    Procedure to delete entry with key *k* from *t*; assume such an entry is in *t*
RetrieveTable*(*t, k*) → *e
    Function to return the entry with key *k* in *t*; assume *k* is a key in *t*
***Traverse*(*t, Visit*(*ArgumentList*))**
    Procedure to execute *Visit*(*ArgumentList*) for every element in *t*, where *Visit* is a user-specified procedure and *ArgumentList* is a list of arguments

Example 9.1.

▼ With pseudocode and the ADT table operations, we define the function *SizeTable*, which returns the number of entries in the table.

Because we must count every element in the table, we employ the traversal procedure to travel through the table. Visiting an element consists of incrementing a counter that was previously initialized to be zero. Thus, we define the visit procedure as the following successor routine:

Successor(*count*)
 Procedure to increment *count* by 1
Input/Output:
 count — counter
Assumption:
 Upon entry to the procedure *count* has a nonnegative integer value.
Algorithm:
 count ← *count* + 1

With this visit procedure defined, we can establish the function *SizeTable* as follows:

SizeTable(*t*) → *count*
 Function to return the number of entries in table *t*
Input:
 t　　 — table
Output:
 count — number of entries in table *t*
Assumption:
 Table *t* exists.
Algorithm:
 count ← 0
 Traverse(*t*, *Successor*(*count*))
 SizeTable ← *count*

▲

| Example 9.2. |

▼ In many applications we must frequently update information in a table. To change the value of an item, we first delete the old entry and then insert the new, revised one as the following procedure reflects:

Update(*t*, *e*):
 Procedure to update the item that has *e*'s key in table *t* to contain *e*'s information; assume *e*'s key is a key in *t*
Input:
 t — table
 e — item of the same type as an element of *t*
Output:
 t — updated table
Assumption:
 There exists an entry in table *t* with the same key as *e*'s.
Algorithm:
 DeleteTable(*t*, *KeyTableEl*(*e*))
 InsertTable(*t*, *e*)

Even though *Update* can be implemented with *DeleteTable* and *InsertTable*, in applications where updating is frequently used, it is wise to include this procedure as an ADT table operation. In that case, we could implement the operation
▲ by finding the appropriate record and changing its value.

| Example 9.3. | **Relational Data Base.** |

▼ The table structure is the main component of a relational data base. A **data base** is a collection of integrated data for a variety of applications, stored to minimize repetitions. A relational data base is composed of many tables, called **relations**. Various set operations can be performed on these tables. For instance, taking the table in Figure 9.1 and a similar table for the students in another course, the union of these two is another table of records for students who are in one, the other, or both classes. Let us define a function to form the union, *t3*, of tables *t1* and *t2*.

First, we copy all of *t1*'s elements into *t3*. Then for each element *e* of *t2*, if *e* is not already in *t3*, we insert that item into *t3*. The pseudocode for this routine is as follows:

t3 ← *t1*
For each element *e* in *t2* do
    If *e* is not in *t3* then
        Insert *e* into *t3*

We have broken the problem into two major parts: a procedure call *CopyTable(t3, t1)* that makes a copy *t3* of table *t1*; and a procedure call *CompleteTable(t3, t2)* that places additional elements from *t2* into *t3*. Thus, we define *UnionTable* as follows:

UnionTable(t1, t2)* → *t3
    Function to return the union of tables *t1* and *t2*
Input:
    t1, t2 — tables
Output:
    t3   — table
Assumptions:
    Tables *t1* and *t2* exist and are of the same type.
Algorithm:
    CopyTable(t3, t1)
    CompleteTable(t3, t2)

The *CopyTable* routine initializes *t3* to be empty before traversing *t1*. In the traversal, a visit to an element of *t1* is defined as its insertion into *t3*,

    InsertTable(t3, e)

Thus, this *CopyTable* procedure is defined as follows:

CopyTable(t3, t1)
    Procedure to make a copy, *t3*, of table *t1*
Input:
    t1 — table
Output:
    t3 — table

Assumption:
 Table *t1* exists.
Algorithm:
 MakeTableEmpty(t3)
 Traverse(t1, InsertTable(t3, e))

Once the table *t1* is copied, we traverse *t2*. In this case, a visit to an item of *t2* consists of checking whether the element's key is found in *t3*. If found, we do nothing; but if not found, we insert that element. Thus, we visit each entry *e* of *t2* as follows:

InsertNew(*t3, e*)
 Procedure to insert an element *e* into table *t3* if *e* is not already in that
 table; if *e* is already present, nothing is done
Input:
 t3 — table
 e — item of the same type as an element of *t3*
Output:
 t3 — revised table
Assumption:
 Table *t3* exists.
Algorithm:
 if not *KeyFound(t3, KeyTableEl(e))* then
  InsertTable(t3, e)

The entire traversal of *t2* with this *InsertNew* visit procedure is written in ADT operations as below:

CompleteTable(*t3, t2*)
 Procedure to place additional elements from *t2* into *t3*
Input:
 t3, t2 — tables
Output:
 t3 — revised table
Assumptions:
 Tables *t3* and *t2* exist and are of the same type.
Algorithm:
 Traverse(t2, InsertNew(t3, e))

SECTION 9.1 EXERCISES

In Exercises 1–6, starting with Figure 9.4 each time, give a picture of any output or changes in the variable x *of type* elType, *the variable* k *of type* keyType, *or the tables* tbl *and* s, *ordered by key, after execution of each sequence of pseudocode and ADT table operations.*

Figure 9.4

Picture of table *tbl*, item *x*, and key *k* for Exercises 1–6

tbl			*x:*			*k: ?*
key	info		key	info		
372	'a'		493	'd'		
481	'b'					
592	'a'					
863	'c'					

1. $k \leftarrow KeyTableEl(x)$

2. $Traverse(tbl, write(e \wedge .info))$

3. $InsertTable(tbl, x)$
$DeleteTable(tbl, 592)$
$x \leftarrow RetrieveTable(tbl, 372)$

3. $MakeEmptyTable(s)$
$x \leftarrow RetrieveTable(tbl, 863)$
$InsertTable(s, x)$

5. $x.key \leftarrow 481$
$x.info \leftarrow 'd'$
$Update(tbl, x)$

6. $MakeEmptyTable(s)$
$InsertTable(s, x)$
$x.key \leftarrow 201$
$InsertTable(s, x)$
$tbl \leftarrow UnionTable(tbl, s)$

7. For the table of Figure 9.1, write an operation to remove the record with key name 'Jordan, Ann.'

8. Write pseudocode and ADT table operations to produce a report of the freshmen from the table in Figure 9.1. First write the visit procedure and then the traversal.

9. Write pseudocode and ADT table operations to print the average GPA of the sophomores from the table in Figure 9.1.

Using pseudocode and ADT table operations and notation, define the operations in Exercises 10–15.

10. Boolean function *EqualKey(e, k)*, which returns *true* if *e*'s key is equal to *k*.

11. Function *IntersectTable(s, t)*, which returns the intersection of tables *s* and *t*.

12. Boolean function *DisjointTable(s, t)*, which returns *true* if tables *s* and *t* have no elements in common. Use the functions *IntersectTable* from Exercise 11 and *TableIsEmpty*.

13. Boolean function *Subtable(s, t)*, which returns *true* if every key of table *s* is in table *t*. The visit procedure *TestInTable*, given below, makes the boolean variable *IsInTable true* if key *k* of table *s* is in table *t*.

TestInTable(e, t, IsInTable)
Procedure called by a traversal of a table to make the boolean variable *IsInTable true* if item *e* is an element of table *t*; if not, it makes *IsInTable false*

Input:
>   *e* — item of same type as an element of *t*
>   *t* — table

Output:
>   *IsInTable* — boolean variable that returns *true* if item *e* is an
>   element of table *t*

Assumption:
>   Table *t* exists.

Algorithm:
>   *k ← KeyTableEl(e)*
>   *IsInTable ← KeyFound(t, k)*

14. Boolean function *EqualTable(s, t)* that returns *true* if tables *s* and *t* are equal; use the *Subtable* function from Exercise 13.

15. Boolean function *TableInOrder(t)* that returns *true* if the elements are traversed so that the keys of the elements are in ascending order. Assume the keys are positive integers.

▽

SECTION 9.2

Table Implementations

There are a number of implementations of ADT table. In this section we cover some involving arrays and linked lists. Hashing tables are discussed in the next section, and tables created using binary trees are developed in a later chapter.

A linked list implemented dynamically or an array of records, in both cases with data ordered or unordered, can provide the structure for a table. We discuss the advantages and disadvantages of each of these four methods and leave the details of coding the operations in Pascal for the exercises. For brevity, in this section we use "linked list" to mean "linked list implemented with dynamic memory allocation."

The characteristics of a particular application determine the best implementation of ADT table. Of the ADT table operations, *InsertTable*, *DeleteTable*, *RetrieveTable*, *Traverse*, and *KeyFound* usually require the most time. In fact, the other operations are all of complexity $O(1)$, requiring a fixed amount of time, regardless of the size of the table. *InsertTable*, *DeleteTable*, and *RetrieveTable* are different than the *Insert*, *Delete*, and *RetrieveInfo* operations of linked lists, respectively. For example, a typical call to the linked list *Delete* procedure is of the form *Delete(head, prev)*, where *prev* points to the node before the one designated for deletion. When *DeleteTable(t, k)* is executed, however, the table must first be searched for the element with key *k* before the entry can be deleted. Thus, deletion in a table requires two steps, one to search for a key and the other to remove the corresponding element.

Recall that a binary search has complexity $O(\log_2 n)$, while a sequential search generally requires more time to execute, on the order of $O(n)$. Thus, those structures, such as an ordered array, on which it is possible to perform a binary search are better suited for the search phase of *InsertTable, Delete-Table, RetrieveTable*, and *KeyFound*. A sorted array is such a structure.

The actual removal of an item is easier in a linked list, however, than in an ordered array. As we have seen, removal of an entry has complexity $O(1)$ in a linked list but $O(n)$ in an array where we must move elements to fill in the void. With an unordered array, however, we can move the last element into the position of the deletion for a removal complexity of only $O(1)$.

Once the search for a key is complete, the actual return of the value of the entry can be accomplished easily through an array reference, such as $a[i]$, or through a pointer reference, such as *cur^.info*. The work of *KeyFound* also depends primarily on the search, after which the function returns a value of *true* or *false*.

We can readily traverse in any of these implementations. If, however, we wish to traverse in an ordered fashion, say to print names in alphabetical order, then an ordered arrangement is desirable. As we will see in a later chapter, $O(n \log_2 n)$ is the best complexity we can achieve in sorting a table.

In an ordered table we must also search for the location where we install the new entry. For this search, ordered arrays have the advantage over ordered linked lists. The actual installation of the item, however, is easier in a linked list with a complexity of $O(1)$. In an ordered array, all entries from the insertion point to the end of the array must be moved before introducing the new item; thus, the worst case complexity of the installation phase of the array implementation of *InsertTable* is $O(n)$.

One technique of building an ordered table from an unordered file is to read each element and to insert it into a relative position. With an ordered array this building process for the n elements requires $O(\log_2 n)$ search time and $O(n)$ installation time for each element, with a resultant insertion time of $O(\log_2 n + n) = O(n)$ per element. Thus, using this building technique, the total amount of time to build the table is of order $O(n^2)$, where we take the product of n (the number of elements) and n (the insertion time of order $O(n)$ for one element). With a similar technique on an ordered linked list, the building process also has complexity $O(n^2)$: each of the n elements requires a maximum search time on the order of $O(n)$ with a fast installation time of $O(1)$.

Another alternative for building an ordered table from an unordered file is to insert items one after another as read, delaying sorting until we have read all the elements. The unordered insertion of n elements in the table requires time on the order of $O(n)$. As indicated earlier, the best sorting techniques have a complexity of $O(n \log_2 n)$. Thus, the total process uses time on the order of $O(n + n \log_2 n) = O(n \log_2 n)$, which is certainly better than the $O(n^2)$ method described above.

In unordered situations, there is no lengthy search for an insertion point. The end of an array and the head of a linked list are both convenient locations. In both these cases, *InsertTable* can be performed with a complexity of $O(1)$. Thus, the initial building of a table from a file of n elements can be performed in time on the order of $O(n \cdot 1) = O(n)$.

We must, however, be careful that the array structure is not filled, testing with the ADT table operation *TableIsFull* before insertion. Linked lists do not have this limitation; so that in this context, *TableIsFull*(*t*) is always defined as *false*.

Figures 9.5–9.8 summarize the advantages and disadvantages of the ADT table implementations of ordered array, unordered array, ordered linked list, and unordered linked list. In each figure, conclusions give the situations in which that implementation is best suited. Notice that none of these provides fast procedures for all the operations *InsertTable*, *DeleteTable*, *RetrieveTable*, and *KeyFound*. The hash table, covered in the next section, can do this, but in a hashing context, ordered traversal is difficult.

We can see from this analysis that none of these four linear methods can satisfactorily support frequent retrievals, insertions, and deletions in an environment where we have a large table whose maximum size is unknown. In the next section we discuss another implementation, hashing, that will meet

---

Figure 9.5

Discussion of ordered array implementation of ADT table

Ordered Array Implementation of ADT Table

Advantages

Binary search possible—$O(\log_2 n)$; advantageous for the search phase of *InsertTable*, *DeleteTable*, *RetrieveTable*, and *KeyFound*

RetrieveTable fairly fast—$O(\log_2 n)$: $O(\log_2 n)$ search phase, $O(1)$ return phase, and $O(\log_2 n + 1) = O(\log_2 n)$

KeyFound fairly fast—$O(\log_2 n)$: $O(\log_2 n)$ search phase, $O(1)$ return phase

Traverse in sorted order fast—$O(n)$: from 1 to n each of the n elements is visited

Disadvantages

Installation phase of *InsertTable* slow—$O(n)$; move all entries from the insertion point on to make room

InsertTable slow—$O(n)$: $O(\log_2 n)$ search phase, $O(n)$ installation phase, and $O(n + \log_2 n) = O(n)$

Removal phase of *DeleteTable* slow—$O(n)$; move all entries from deletion point on to close up the vacated position

DeleteTable slow—$O(n)$: $O(\log_2 n)$ search phase, $O(n)$ removal phase

Building a table from unsorted data slow—$O(n \log_2 n)$: n elements, $O(1)$ *InsertTable* phase for each of the n elements, at least $O(n \log_2 n)$ sorting phase; and $O(n + n \log_2 n) = O(n \log_2 n)$

Must know the maximum number of entries in table initially—check *TableIsFull* before executing *InsertTable* or building a table

Conclusions

This structure is advantageous when there will be a number of enquiries or ordered reports from the table but few insertions and deletions when the table is large. You must also have a good concept of the size of the table before beginning.

Figure 9.6

Discussion of unordered array implementation of ADT table

Unordered Array Implementation of ADT Table

Advantages

InsertTable fast—$O(1)$; insertion at the end of array; no search necessary; installation immediate

Removal phase of *DeleteTable* fast—$O(1)$: move last entry to deletion point

Building table from unsorted data fast—$O(n)$: starting at the beginning of the array, insert the n elements one after another

Disadvantages

Sequential search—$O(n)$; binary search not possible; not advantageous for the search phase of *DeleteTable, RetrieveTable*, and *KeyFound*

DeleteTable slow—$O(n)$: $O(n)$ search phase, $O(1)$ removal phase, and $O(n + 1) = O(n)$

RetrieveTable slow—$O(n)$: $O(n)$ search phase, $O(1)$ return phase, and $O(n + 1) = O(n)$

KeyFound slow—$O(n)$: $O(n)$ search phase, $O(1)$ return phase

Traverse in sorted order slow—sorting at least of order $O(n \log_2 n)$

Must know the maximum number of entries in table initially—check *TableIsFull* before executing *InsertTable* or building a table

Conclusions

An unordered array is advantageous when we must perform frequent unordered traversals of the table, such as performing some computation on or comparison with each table entry. Insertions are easy, so building the table is too; but we must know the maximum number of elements before commencing. This structure is not desirable in situations where there are frequent deletions from, enquiries into, or ordered traversals of a large table.

Figure 9.7

Discussion of ordered linked list implementation of ADT table

Ordered Linked List Implementation of ADT Table

Advantages

Installation phase of *InsertTable* fast—$O(1)$

Removal phase of *DeleteTable* fast—$O(1)$

Traverse in sorted order fast—$O(n)$: from first to last each of the n elements is visited

Do not need to know the maximum number of entries in table initially—*TableIsFull* is always *false*

Disadvantages

Sequential search—$O(n)$; binary search not possible; not advantageous for the search phase of *InsertTable, DeleteTable, RetrieveTable*, and *KeyFound*

InsertTable slow—$O(n)$: $O(n)$ search phase, $O(1)$ installation phase

DeleteTable slow—$O(n)$: $O(n)$ search phase, $O(1)$ removal phase

RetrieveTable slow—$O(n)$: $O(n)$ search phase, $O(1)$ return phase

KeyFound slow—$O(n)$: $O(n)$ search phase, $O(1)$ return phase; when the

Figure 9.7

continued

key is not in the table, the search can halt just beyond where the item
should be

Building a table from unsorted data slow—$O(n \log_2 n)$: n elements, $O(1)$
InsertTable phase for each of the n elements, at least $O(n \log_2 n)$ sorting phase; and $O(n + n \log_2 n) = O(n \log_2 n)$

Overhead of links

Conclusions

An ordered linked list structure is advantageous for situations when there
are frequent ordered traversals and when we may not know the maximum
size of the table. This structure is not desirable for enquiries into the table,
such as for airline reservations. Insertions and deletions are time consuming in large tables.

Figure 9.8.

Discussion of unordered
linked list implementation
of ADT table

Unordered Linked List Implementation of ADT Table

Advantages

InsertTable fast—$O(1)$; at head of the linked list; no search necessary; installation immediate

Removal phase of *DeleteTable* fast—$O(1)$

Building table from unsorted data fast—$O(n)$: insert each of the n elements at the head of the list

Do not need to know the maximum number of entries in table initially—
TableIsFull is always *false*

Disadvantages

Sequential search—$O(n)$; binary search not possible; not advantageous
for search phase of *DeleteTable*, *RetrieveTable*, and *KeyFound*

DeleteTable slow—$O(n)$: $O(n)$ search phase, $O(1)$ removal phase

RetrieveTable slow—$O(n)$: $O(n)$ search phase, $O(1)$ return phase

KeyFound slow—$O(n)$: $O(n)$ search phase, $O(1)$ return phase

Traverse in sorted order slow—sorting at least of order $O(n \log_2 n)$

Overhead of links

Conclusions

An unordered linked list is fast for building a table and for performing additional insertions, particularly when we do not know the ultimate size of
the table. Frequent enquiries into, deletions from, or sorted traversals of a
large table are time consuming.

---

this challenge. If we also wish to perform ordered traversals, binary trees, covered in a later chapter, have distinct advantages.

▽

SECTION 9.2 EXERCISES

1. Using an array of records, ordered by name, create a table to store the information in Figure 9.1 of Section 9.1.

2. a. Why must the ADT table operation *RetrieveTable* be implemented in Pascal as a procedure instead of a function when a record is returned?

   b. Why must the operation *UnionTable* of Example 9.3 in Section 9.1 be coded in Pascal as a procedure instead of a function when the tables are implemented as arrays?

3. Using ordered arrays, implement the ADT table.

4. Use the table created in Exercise 1 to implement Exercise 8 from Section 9.1 to produce a report of the freshmen from the table in Figure 9.1. First write the visit procedure and then the traversal.

5. Use the table created in Exercise 1 to implement Exercise 9 from Section 9.1 to print the average GPA of the sophomores.

6. Using unordered arrays, give implementations of the ADT table operations that differ from those of Exercise 3.

7. Using a linked list of records ordered by name, create a table to store the information in Figure 9.1 of Section 9.1.

8. Using ordered linked lists, implement the ADT table.

9. Using the table created in Exercise 7, repeat Exercise 4.

10. Using the table created in Exercise 7, repeat Exercise 5.

11. Using unordered linked lists, give implementations of the ADT table operations that differ from those of Exercise 8.

12. a. Give an array implementation of the function *SizeTable* from Example 9.1 of Section 9.1.

   b. Repeat Part a for a linked list implementation.

For Exercises 13–16, code the requested routine using an implementation with
   a. ordered arrays   *b. unordered arrays*
   c. ordered linked lists   *d. unordered linked lists*

13. Suppose a particular application requires a large number of updates. Revise the implementation of *Update* from Example 9.2, Section 9.1, so that the table entry is not deleted and the revised item inserted, but so that the entry is updated in place.

14. Operation *UnionTable* from Example 9.3, Section 9.1. Since only scalar values can be returned through a function name in Standard Pascal, implement this operation as a procedure.

15. Operation *IntersectTable* from Exercise 11, Section 9.1. Since only scalar values can be returned through a function name in Standard Pascal, implement this operation as a procedure.

16. Boolean function *Subtable(s, t)* of Exercise 13, Section 9.1, which returns *true* if every entry in table *s* is in table *t*.

17. Code a procedure *BuildTable*(*t*, *f*) that builds a table *t* from an unsorted file *f* using an unordered array implementation.

18. Repeat Exercise 17 for an unordered linked list implementation.

19. Suppose a table is implemented as an unordered linked list. With the **move-to-front technique**, every time a table element is accessed the node is moved to the front of the list. Thus, frequently referenced elements tend to appear toward the front of the table, minimizing the number of probes in a sequential search. Such a technique is useful when the number of records is small or the execution time for the usual sequential search is almost good enough.

    a. Implement the *RetrieveTable* operation using this strategy.
    b. Suppose a record that is accessed infrequently is retrieved. How is the future performance of the algorithm affected?

20. Suppose a table is implemented as an unordered array. With the **transpose technique**, after a table element is referenced, the entry is swapped with the element just in front of it. Thus, frequently accessed records gradually move to the front of the array to be located more rapidly in a sequential search. This technique is useful on small data sets and where storage space is limited or pointers are not available in the computer language being used.

    a. Implement the *RetrieveTable* operation using this strategy.
    b. Suppose a particular table element is accessed frequently for a short period of time, after which it is seldom referenced. Which technique responds best to this situation, the transpose technique of this exercise or the move-to-front technique of Exercise 19?

21. Suppose a table *t* is implemented as an ordered linked list, and a number of records need to be updated. One technique is to sort and place all the updates into a file *f*. Starting at the beginning of the file and the beginning of the table, keys are compared. Where a match occurs, we update the table entry. When a file record does not appear in the table, the entry is inserted. Implement the merge search procedure.

▽

PROGRAMMING PROJECTS

1. Suppose a table has a search key composed of several fields. A query asks for all records with each field within a certain range, between specific upper and lower bounds. **Range searching** is the process of retrieving records with the appropriate key field values. Consider an array of student records with search fields for name, age, and grade point average (GPA).

    Write a program to build an unordered table from a file, to interactively ask for the desired ranges, and using a sequential search to find and print the names of all students between a range of ages and a range of GPAs. For example, the user may interactively request the names of students between the ages of 18 and 21 whose GPA is in the range from 3.4 to 4.0.

The following are auxiliary questions for Project 1:

a. For an unordered arrangement of n elements, find the cost (complexity) of building the table.

b. The amount of storage required is on the order of what big oh value?

c. What is the complexity of the sequential range search of n elements on m search fields?

d. Give the advantages and disadvantages of the sequential range search.

2. For the range searching of Project 1 the **projection technique** stores the data two times, once sorted by age and once by GPA. Two binary searches are performed on the array of records sorted by age to find the range of students between 18 and 21 years old. This range is called a **projection**. Similarly, two binary searches are performed on the array of records sorted by GPA to find lower and upper bounds of indices of students with averages between 3.4 and 4.0. Then a sequential search is performed on the projection with the smaller number of records. For example, if the first projection revealed 5000 students between the ages of 18 and 21 and the second projection contained 1000 students with averages between 3.4 and 4.0, we would search sequentially through the smaller number of records for the students in the other category. Thus, we would search through those records in the second projection for students between the ages of 18 and 21. This technique is particularly useful when one of the ranges contains few records.

Write a program to build a table from a file where the data is stored two times, sorted by age and GPA. Then the program should interactively ask for the desired ranges and using a projection search should find and print the names of the students in the desired ranges.

The following are auxiliary questions for Project 2:

a. Usually, we must sort the records by each field, instead of reading the table from a file sorted two different ways. Suppose a set of n records can be sorted on one field with a complexity of $O(n \log_2 n)$. What is the complexity to sort the records on all of the m search fields?

b. The amount of storage required for this technique is on the order of what big oh value?

c. Suppose for $n = 8192$, 5000 students are between the ages of 18 and 21, and 1000 students have GPAs between 3.4 and 4.0. What is the maximum number of comparisons with the projection technique to find all students in both ranges?

d. Repeat Part c for the sequential technique of Project 1.

e. It has been shown that the average case complexity of the projection range search of n records on m search fields is $O(n^{1-1/m})$. Is this complexity better or worse than that for a sequential range check? (See Project 1.)

f. Give the advantages and disadvantages of this projection range check.

3. Consider the table described in Project 1. Suppose queries are often made about students in a specified range of ages and range of GPAs. One method of implementing the table is with a two-dimensional array d of pointers to linked lists of records. The array serves as a directory. Suppose this array has four rows representing GPA categories 0.00−0.99, 1.00−1.99, 2.00−2.99, and 3.00−4.00 and five columns representing age categories of "19 or younger," 20, 21, 22, and "23 or older." Thus, $d[4, 2]$ is a pointer to a linked list of records for students with a GPA between 3.0 and 4.0 who are 20 years old.

   Write a program to build the table as described above from a file, to interactively ask for the desired range of ages and range of GPAs, and to print a report of all names of students simultaneously in both ranges. For example, the query might be to find all students between the ages of 22 and 24 with a GPA between 1.75 and 3.25.

   The following are auxiliary questions for Project 3:

   a. What is the complexity for building this table?
   b. What is the amount of storage for the table in terms of the number of table elements, n?

4. A nursery keeps in a master text file the date and an alphabetical listing of names and counts of the plants currently in stock. Each evening an unsorted transaction file is created. Each record in the transaction file begins with 'A' or 'S' indicating an arrival of a shipment or a sale of a plant, respectively. After that character is the quantity and the name of the plant. Write a program to update the master file with the transaction file and print a report of the plants currently in stock. When a plant sells out, remove its record from the revised master file. New plants, of course, should be added.

   The management wishes to keep a one-day backup of the master file. Therefore, interactively ask the user for the name of the old master file and its date. A mismatch of date stored in the file and the typed date should result in an error message giving the file date and a prompt for a new file and date. Also, ask for the name of today's date and the name of the master file to be created.

SECTION 9.3   Hash Table

In the last section we discussed four linear implementations of ADT table—ordered and unordered array, ordered and unordered linked list. As we saw, none of these methods efficiently supports a lot of activity from all the operations of insertion, deletion, and retrieval.

Each of these operations usually begins with a search for a key, k, comparing k with other keys until the proper location is found. A **hash table** implementation uses a different approach, one that computes the location with a **hash function**. Jumping immediately to the desired record is a direct access approach, much like direct access of data on a disk. In fact, hashing can be used for external disk storage of files. This method contrasts with the comparative searches encountered so far. The sequential search technique compares the key with every record until the desired entry is discovered, like sequential access of a tape file. A binary search is a significant improvement over a sequential one, but requires that records be sorted and still does not allow for a direct computation of the record location.

Suppose we want to store the records from Figure 9.9 into a table. Only the keys are listed here since the information portion is irrelevant in computing the location of the record. Perhaps the key is a product's stock number and the information portion has subfields containing the product's description, quantity on hand, warehouse number, year-to-date sales, and so on.

Figure 9.9

Data to be stored in a table

key	information
3542	....
9179	....
7406	....
5081	....
6598	....
5370	....

One implementation of a hash table involves placing this data into an array of records, declared in a similar fashion to the following:

```
const
    MaxNum    = ............;
    TableSize = ............;   { One more than MaxNum }
    MaxKey    = 9999;

type
    IndexType = 0..MaxNum;
    keyType   = 0..MaxKey;
    infoType  = ............;

    elType    = record
        key   : keyType;
        info  : infoType
    end;
    table     = array [IndexType] of elType;
```

```
var
    t  :  table;
    k  :  keyType;
    h  :  IndexType;
    e  :  elType;
```

One method of storage, called **relative storage,** is to have the array large enough so that a key is actually the index of a record. For the data in Figure 9.9, the resulting table would require a range of 10,000 elements with indices from 0 to 9999. Certainly, such a configuration produces extremely fast retrieval, insertion, and deletion operations with the search phase having complexity $O(1)$. For instance, $RetrieveTable(t, k)$ dissolves merely to an array reference, $t[k]$. But we only have six items listed, meaning space for 9994 records is wasted. We have a trade-off of time for space. Had the key been as large as a Social Security number, a prohibitively large number of records, one billion, would be needed for this relative organization.

Suppose we are confident that the number of records will never exceed 10. In this case we want to find a hash function that will map each possible key to an array index in the range 0 to 9. With a maximum of 10 elements, we might select one of the digits of the key as the index, using the built-in *div* and *mod* functions. For example, the hash function selecting the least significant digit is

$$hash(k) = k \ mod \ 10$$

the remainder when k is divided by 10. Thus, the record with key 3542 will have index 2,

$$hash(3542) = 3542 \ mod \ 10 = 2$$

The entire placement of the data from Figure 9.9 into a table using this **digit selection** hash function is shown in Figure 9.10.

Figure 9.10

Data from Figure 9.9 placed into a hash table implemented with an array of records; the hash function selects the least significant digit of the key, *hash(k) = k mod 10*

Table *t*

index	key	information
0	5370	....
1	5081	....
2	3542	....
3		
4		
5		
6	7406	....
7		
8	6598	....
9	9179	....

The same hash function used for insertion is used in the search to retrieve or delete items from the table. For instance, *RetrieveTable*(6598), to retrieve the entry with key 6598, involves finding the least significant digit,

$$hash(6598) = 6598 \bmod 10 = 8$$

Then if $t[8].key$ is the desired key, 6598, the retrieval function just returns the table entry $t[8]$.

But suppose the least significant digit of the stock number is not random but indicates something like a perishable or nonperishable stock item, with 0 or 2, respectively. In this case, all keys would map to 0 or 2, clearly an undesirable situation. Thus, it is better for a hash function to involve the whole key. Expanding our table to contain 11 entries, we can use the entire key in the computation of the remainder when the key is divided by 11 for the hash function:

$$hash(k) = k \bmod 11$$

For example, when the key 5370 is divided by 11, the remainder is 2. Thus, the record with key 5370 is mapped to table location with index 2, $t[2]$. The result of this storage technique is shown in Figure 9.11. One of the earliest hash functions, this **remainder method** has the advantage of fast computation, especially when the *mod* function is built into the computer hardware.

Figure 9.11

Data from Figure 9.9 placed into a hash table implemented with an array of records; remainder hash function, $hash(k) = k \bmod 11$. The following are the keys with the hash values (their remainders modulo 11) in parenthesis: 3542 (0), 9179 (5), 7406 (3), 5081 (10), 6598 (9), 5370 (2)

Table t

index	key	information
0	3542	....
1		
2	5370	....
3	7406	....
4		
5	9179	....
6		
7		
8		
9	6598	....
10	5081	....

The integer 11, being a prime number, was a good choice for the table size, *TableSize*. Recall that a **prime** is an integer larger than 1 whose only positive divisors are 1 and itself. The only positive integers that divide into 11, leaving a zero remainder, are 1 and 11. Suppose we pick as our divisor the nonprime number 14, which has factors of 2 and 7 as well as 1 and 14. It can be shown mathematically that any key k that has a factor of 2 (or 7) will have a **hash** value, $hash(k)$, that has a factor of 2 (or 7). Thus, since any even number has a factor of 2, any even key maps to an even index. Similarly, odd numbers, having no factor of 2, map to odd indices. It is desirable for keys to be dispersed in what appears to be a random fashion throughout the table. The mapping of even and odd keys to even and odd locations, respectively, certainly does not appear random. To illustrate the problem, suppose again that all keys had a least significant digit of 0 or 2. Instead of the 10,000 possible keys distributing randomly through the 14 elements, they would all map to one of seven positions, 0, 2, 4, 6, 8, 10, or 12. In conclusion, when employing the remainder method for calculating the hash function, use a prime number for the divisor, *TableSize*.

We consider other hash functions in the exercises, but let us now turn our attention to the situation where two keys are mapped to the same location. Suppose we wish to insert another record into the table of Figure 9.11, this item with a key of 6855. Since

$$hash(6855) = 6855 \bmod 11 = 2$$

we first consider inserting the item into $t[2]$. But $t[2]$ is already occupied by a record with key 5370. We have a **collision** with two keys having the same hash value. There are two categories of techniques for deciding what to do in case of a collision, **open** and **chained addressing**.

In open addressing we employ some technique to search through the table for an empty location at which to insert the record. The simplest open addressing method is **linear probing**, where we continue from the hash location on, looking for the next available position. In our example $t[2]$ and $t[3]$ are occupied, so we must insert the new item at index 4. (See Figure 9.12.)

We must have some way of telling whether an array entry does or does not contain meaningful data. One method is for *MakeTableEmpty(t)* to place an *empty* value, perhaps zero or blanks, into the key field of every record in the

Figure 9.12

Table from Figure 9.11 with record having key 6855 inserted into $t[4]$ after collision at index 2 and linear probing

Table *t*

index	key	information
0	3542	....
1		
2	5370	....
3	7406	....
4	**6855**	....
5	9179	....
6		
7		
8		
9	6598	....
10	5081	....

table. Another value, *deleted*, could be used in the key field to indicate that the record has been deleted. Of course, these special values of *empty* and *deleted* cannot be legitimate key values. We must mark a removed record as deleted instead of empty for otherwise we could break a chain of **probes** or inquiries into the table. For example, suppose we now delete the record in table location 3 from the table in Figure 9.12. When trying to find the record with key 6855, we first probe the table at location 2. Not finding the desired element, we proceed to entry $t[3]$. If that element had a key of *empty* instead of *deleted*, we would wrongly assume that our search for key 6855 should terminate with *KeyFound*(6855) being *false*. As Figure 9.13 shows, the value of *deleted*, however, tells us that record $t[3]$ is available for insertion but is part of a chain, in this case to the table entry $t[4]$. If in our chain of probes we encounter the *empty* value, the search terminates. In the case of insertion we have located an available cell, while *KeyFound* returns a value of *false*.

Figure 9.13

Hash table from Figure 9.12 with the record in $t[3]$ marked as *deleted* so that the chain of probes to the record with key 6855 is not broken

0	3542	....
1	*empty*	
2	5370	....
3	***deleted***	
4	6855	....
5	9179	....
6	*empty*	
7	*empty*	
8	*empty*	
9	6598	....
10	5081	....

Another approach is to add a field, *status*, to the table record, such as:

```
type
    . . .
    elType      =   record
        key     :   keyType;
        info    :   infoType;
        status  :   (empty, full, deleted)
    end;
    table       =   array [IndexType] of elType;
var
    t           :   table;
```

The status field is initialized to the value *empty*. Moreover, deletion of a record from location h only involves assigning a value of *deleted* to $t[h]$.*status*, leaving the remainder of the record as unaltered garbage. Upon insertion, we must be careful to change $t[h]$.*status* to *full*. Regardless of the method of indicating an empty or occupied table entry, execution of the ADT table operation *Make-TableEmpty*(*t*) must initialize every table entry to be empty.

Assuming we have marked the status of a record in some way, suppose we need to insert a record with a key of 8644 in a table that is not filled, such as that of Figure 9.12. Since

$$hash(8644) = 8644 \bmod 11 = 9$$

we would like to place the record into *t*[9]. But we are thwarted in our efforts and must keep probing the table for an available location. With *t*[10] filled as well, we wrap around the table examining *t*[0] before discovering that location 1 is available. The wraparound can be achieved by using modulo *TableSize*. We calculate

    h : = hash(k)

If a collision occurs, we repeatedly add 1, computing the result modulo *Table-Size*, until encountering a free entry:

if not *TableIsFull*(*t*) then
    repeat
        $h \leftarrow (h + 1) \bmod TableSize$
    until (*t*[*h*] is *empty*) or (*t*[*h*] is *deleted*)

Thus, for $h = 10$,

    $h + 1 = 11$

but

    $(h + 1) \bmod TableSize = 11 \bmod 11 = 0$

Figure 9.14 shows insertion of the record with key 8644 at index 1.

Figure 9.14

Hash table from Figure 9.12 with record having key 8644 inserted into *t*[1] after collision at index 9 and linear probing that wraps around the table, illustrating primary clustering

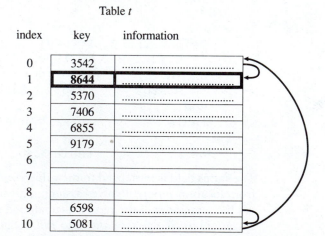

Table *t*

index	key	information
0	3542	....
1	**8644**	....
2	5370	....
3	7406	....
4	6855	....
5	9179	....
6		
7		
8		
9	6598	....
10	5081	....

One disadvantage of linear open addressing is that any key that maps to a location h will follow the same path, searching for an available cell. For example, the key 2297 also hashes to 9,

$$hash(2297) = 2297 \bmod 11 = 9$$

With a linear approach to resolve this collision, we follow the same path as that of 8644, first examining index 9, then 10, then 0. This clustering of records that follow the same path from the hash location is called **primary clustering.** Since now $t[1]$ is also occupied, as are $t[2]$ through $t[5]$, we must go to index 6 before finding a suitable entry position. (See Figure 9.15.) The probing path for the key 2297 started merging with other hash values and paths in a situation called **secondary clustering.** The longer the sequence of keys, the greater the probability for a new key to collide with an element of that chain and for the sequence itself to coalesce with others. Much study has been performed on how to avoid such clustering.

Figure 9.15

Table from Figure 9.14 with record having key 2297 inserted into $t[6]$ after collision at index 9 and linear probing, illustrating secondary clustering

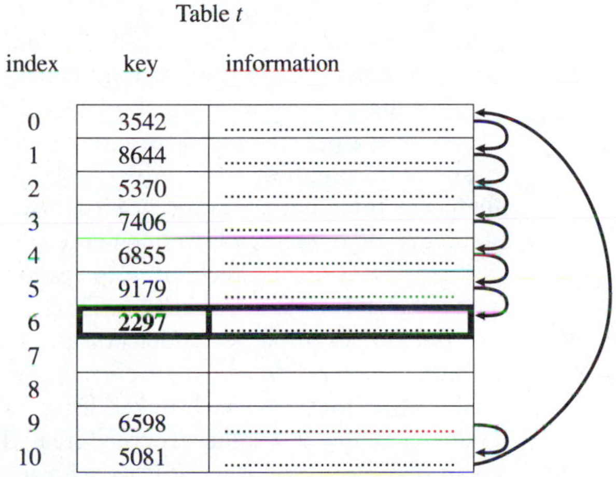

Table t

This clustering certainly slows the hashing process because we must examine element after element before finding an empty cell for the record with key 2297. Moreover, the table is getting full; with only two more insertions, there will be no more room. We are again encountering a major disadvantage of a strictly array implementation of a data structure—we must know the maximum number of entries before execution of the program and should test *TableIsFull(t)* before attempting an insertion.

Moreover, even if not completely filled, with few vacant slots in the table performance can be severely degraded. The **load factor,** a measure of the saturation of a table, is the ratio of the number of items in the table, n, and the number of table locations, *TableSize*:

load factor = n / *TableSize*

Thus, for the table in Figure 9.15 we have

load factor = 9/11 = 0.82 = 82%

Load factors of 60% or 70% are common, but a table that is 82% full is undesirable.

It is interesting that if the load factors for a large and a small table are equal, then the average search times for both tables are the same. Thus, for hash tables that are 60% filled, on the average the number of probes will be the same for a table size of 100,000 as for a table size of 100.

Before execution of a hashing procedure, we can use the desired load factor to determine an appropriate table size. Suppose we estimate that the maximum number of entries in a table will be $n = 95$ and because of performance considerations, we want a maximum load factor of 70%. Thus,

0.70 = 95 / *TableSize*

or cross multiplying,

TableSize = 95 / 0.70

Since *TableSize* should be a prime, we make the size of the table 137, the first prime number greater than n/(load factor) = 135.7.

During execution, if we start encountering much degradation in the efficiency of the operations because of a high load factor, one possibility is to re-hash the information into a larger table. Another approach is initially to implement the table with a different structure, one involving our expandable data structure of dynamically implemented linked lists. With linked lists we use a chained addressing technique to resolve collisions and to expand the table as needed.

For our example, consider not an array of 11 records but an array of 11 pointers, each pointer being the head of a linked list of records with keys that hash to that location. Each linked list is called by the descriptive name **bucket**. Figure 9.16 illustrates the structure created below. With 12 nodes and 11 buckets in that figure, we were able to achieve a load factor greater than 1.

load factor = 12 / 11 = 1.09 = 109%

By contrast, with an array implementation the maximum load factor is 1, which occurs with a completely filled table.

```
const
    MaxNum     =  10;
    TableSize  =  11;     { One more than MaxNum }
    MaxKey     =  9999;

type
    IndexType  =  0..MaxNum;
    keyType    =  0..MaxKey;
    infoType   =  ...............;
```

Figure 9.16

Implementation of a hash
table using an array of
pointers to linked lists

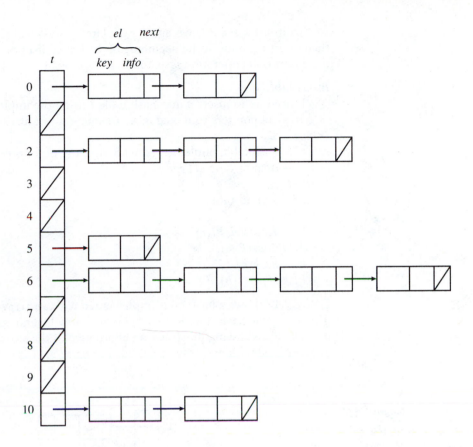

```
elType      =   record
    key     :   keyType;
    info    :   infoType
end;

pointer     =   ^Node;
Node        =   record
    el      :   elType;
    next    :   pointer
end;
table       =   array [IndexType] of pointer;

var
    t   :   table;
    k   :   keyType;
    h   :   IndexType;
    e   :   elType;
```

To insert a record, we again calculate its hash value $hash(key) = h$ and then insert the node at the beginning of the linked list pointed to by $t[h]$. Thus, the *InsertTable* operation is as follows:

InsertTable(t, e)
>   Procedure to insert *e* into hash table *t* using the implementation of an array of pointers to linked lists; assume *e* is not already in *t*
Input:
>   *t* — hash table implemented with an array of pointers to linked lists
>   *e* — item of type *elType*
Output:
>   *t* — revised table
Algorithm:
> $k \leftarrow KeyTableEl(e)$
> $AddNode(P, e)$
> $h \leftarrow hash(k)$
> $InsertFirst(t[h], P)$

Figure 9.17 shows a hash table implemented with an array of pointers to linked lists, using the hash function $hash(k) = k \bmod 11$ and storing data from Figure 9.9. This drawing illustrates an alternative to the corresponding hash table implemented with an array of records in Figure 9.11.

Figure 9.17

Data from Figure 9.9 placed into table implemented with an array of pointers to linked lists; remainder hash function, $hash(k) = k \bmod 11$. The following are the keys with the hash values in parenthesis: 3542 (0), 9179 (5), 7406 (3), 5081 (10), 6598 (9), 5370 (2)

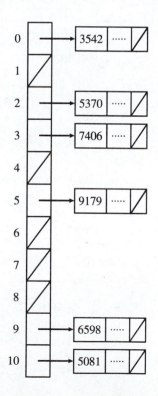

Suppose, as in Figure 9.12, we wish to insert a new record with key 6855. Since 6855 hashes to 2 with

$$hash(6855) = 6855 \bmod 11 = 2$$

we insert a node containing the record with key 6855 at the beginning of the linked list pointed to by $t[2]$. Similarly, with

$$hash(8644) = 8644 \bmod 11 = 9$$

a node with key 8644 is placed at the head of $t[9]$'s linked list. For the table in Figure 9.17, Figure 9.18 demonstrates the results of *InsertTable(t, e)* for *KeyTableEl(e)* = 6855 and *KeyTableEl(e)* = 8644. Figures 9.12 and 9.14 show the same insertions in the table implemented with an array of records.

Figure 9.18

Hash table of Figure 9.17 after insertion of records with keys 6855 and 8644 and hash values of 2 and 9, respectively

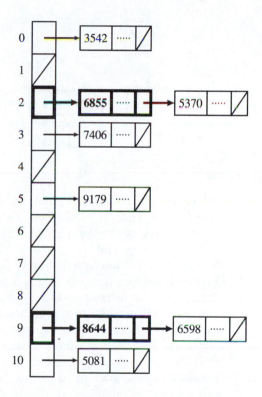

As Figure 9.15 did in the earlier implementation, Figure 9.19 illustrates the insertion of a record with key 2297 and hash value 9,

$$hash(2297) = 2297 \bmod 11 = 9$$

into an array of pointers to linked lists. Notice that with an array of pointers we have avoided the time-consuming ordeal of finding an empty table location in case of a collision. Primary and secondary clustering and concern about the table being full are no longer problems during insertion.

Figure 9.19

Hash table of Figure 9.18 after insertion of a record with key 2297 and hash value of 9

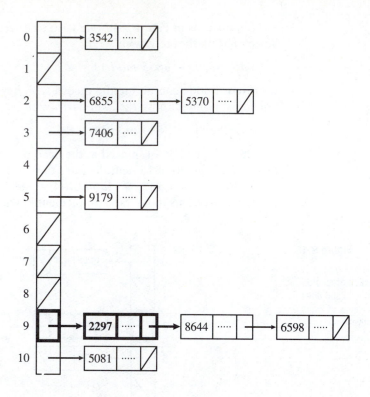

KeyFound, DeleteTable, and *RetrieveTable* also involve computation of $hash(k) = h$. Then, the linked list with a head pointer of $t[h]$ is searched sequentially. The dynamic implementation is very efficient in terms of the number of probes into the table for a search. Moreover, within the limits of computer memory size, this implementation of the hash table never fills. As linked lists lengthen, however, the searching process slows. This method also has the advantage that we delete a record by changing links so that the removed node does not interfere with future searches. In contrast, with the array implementation a deleted element must be marked as such and still appears in a probe sequence. The linked list implementation does not require a field or fields to mark the element as empty, full, or deleted and does not need to initialize each element of a new table to be empty. Of course, each element of the array of pointers must be initialized as *nil*, but this array is typically much smaller than the one used in the array implementation. This dynamic allocation does, however, require extra room for each pointer.

Should each linked list be ordered, *KeyFound* would be faster than in unordered linked lists, ceasing at the proper node or just beyond where it should be. But insertion, not always occurring at the head, would be slower.

Many alternatives for implementation of ADT table have been developed. Hashing certainly provides a relatively fast approach for insertion, deletion, and retrieval. Imagine, however, the difficulty in printing a report ordered by the key. In a later chapter we discuss a binary tree implementation of ADT table that allows for searches with a complexity of $O(\log_2 n)$ and a fast ordered traversal.

▽

1. Write a hash function in Pascal to return the specified digit(s) of a four-digit key.

   a. The 10s digit; e.g., for a key of 9183, return 8. Accomplish this task by first dividing by 10 and then taking the quotient modulo 10.
   b. The 100s digit; e.g., for a key of 9183, return 1.
   c. The two least significant digits; e.g., for a key of 9183, return 83.
   d. The middle two digits; e.g., for a key of 9183, return 18.

2. For the hash function $hash(key) = key \bmod 11$, calculate the hash value for a key of

   a. 2769   b. 73692   c. 9164563   d. 55528

   Note: If the remainder function, *mod*, is not built into your calculator, compute its value as follows:

   To compute $9179 \bmod 11$, type

   $$9179 \;\boxdot\; 11 \;\boxminus$$

   With the result of 834.45455 on a display of 10 characters, subtract the integer part, 834:

   $$\boxminus\; 834 \;\boxminus$$

   Multiply the resulting fractional part, 0.45455, by the divisor 11:

   $$\boxtimes\; 11 \;\boxminus$$

   The result is 5, the value of $hash(9179)$. If you obtain a number such as 4.9999999, round this value to the nearest integer (here, 5) to obtain $hash(key)$. Should your calculator have a memory, you will find it convenient to store the divisor, here 11.

3. Repeat Exercise 2 for the hash function $hash(key) = key \bmod 101$.

4. Suppose the key is a four-digit integer $d_3 d_2 d_1 d_0$ and the hashing function is defined as the sum of the digits,

   $$hash(d_3 d_2 d_1 d_0) = d_3 + d_2 + d_1 + d_0,$$

   in a process called **folding**.

   a. Evaluate $hash(2769)$.
   b. What is *TableSize*?
   c. Write this function in Pascal.

5. Repeat Exercise 4 for the hash function that computes the sum of pairs of digits,

$$hash(d_3d_2d_1d_0) = d_3d_2 + d_1d_0.$$

6. A character string, such as a name, can be used as a key. We must, however, convert the string or part of the string to a numeric value.

   a. Write a hash function in Pascal to take the first character of a string, find its decimal encoding using the *ord* function, and return the answer modulo 13.

   b. Using the fact that in the ASCII encoding scheme *ord*('C') = 67, evaluate this hash value for the name "CAMPBELL JAMES."

   c. The ASCII scheme encodes 128 characters, so that using that system *ord*(*ch*) ranges from 0 to 127. We can calculate the ordinal value of each of the first two characters of the name, multiplying the first number by 128 and adding the result, such as

$$128 \, ord(\text{`C'}) + ord(\text{`A'})$$

Calculate this value modulo 107.

   d. Write a hash function in Pascal for Part c.

   e. Similarly to Part c, how would you convert the first three characters to a number?

7. A mailing list is stored in a hash table based on a five-digit zip code. Suppose about 80% of the zip codes begin with 303. For those, the hash function returns the last two digits. For the other zip codes, the hash function takes the entire number modulo the prime 19 and then adds 100.

   a. Evaluate *hash*(30342).

   b. Evaluate *hash*(94550).

   c. Write this hash function.

   d. What is *TableSize* for this table?

8. A Social Security number (SSN) can be used as a key, but the nine-digit number is often too large an integer to be stored conventionally in the computer. Suppose SSN has been read into a nine-element character array, *key*. Write a hash function to convert the key into three three-digit numbers, to add these numbers, and to return the result modulo the prime 997. Recall that a three-digit number is

$$d_2d_1d_0 = 100 \, d_2 + 10 \, d_1 + d_0$$

In Exercises 9–19, code in Pascal the requested operations to implement the ADT table. Assume the table is created as the array of records at the beginning of this section. Also, assume that 0 and 1 are never keys so that a 0 in t[h].key indicates the entry is empty, while 1 indicates the entry is deleted. The TableSize *is the number of array elements,* MaxNum + 1.

  9. *MakeTableEmpty*(*t*), which zeros out all key fields of the table.

10. *TableIsEmpty*(*t*); the table is empty when every key is 0, indicating that no item was ever inserted there, or the key is 1, indicating that the item that was there has been deleted.

11. *TableIsFull*(*t*)

12. *KeyTableEl*(*e*)

13. Remainder hash function, *hash*, that returns the key modulo *TableSize*.

14. Linear probing function, *LinearProbe*, which when given a key *k* and a hash position *h* returns the next index modulo *TableSize* of an array element that is available (with a key value of 0 or 1) or has a key value of *k*. This function is called by the routines *InsertTable*, *DeleteTable*, *RetrieveTable*, and *KeyFound* if an initial probe using the function *hash* is unsuccessful.

15. *KeyFound*(*t*, *k*)

16. *InsertTable*(*t*, *e*)

17. *DeleteTable*(*t*, *k*); be sure to change the key field value of the deleted item to 1.

18. *RetrieveTable*(*t*, *k*); since only scalar values can be returned through a function name in Standard Pascal, implement this operation as a procedure.

19. *Traverse*(*t*, *Visit*(*ArgumentList*)); leave the *Visit* procedure undefined.

20. **a.** Suppose 89 items are in a table of size 250. What is the load factor?
    b. Suppose a table is implemented as an array of linked lists. Find the load factor for a table with 389 nodes and 250 buckets.

21. Suppose we want to have a table implemented as an array with a maximum load factor of 65%, and we anticipate a maximum of 50 entries. What is the best estimate of the table size?

22. Repeat Exercise 21 for a maximum load factor of 70% and a maximum of 200 entries.

23. **a.** Declare a global variable *NumElsFilled* of type 0..*TableSize* to keep a tally of the number of elements that are filled in the array implementation of the ADT table. For an empty table *NumElsFilled* is zero, while for a full table this variable's value is *TableSize*.
    b. Which table operations from Exercises 9–19 should be altered by inclusion of *NumElsFilled*, and how should they be changed?

24. **a.** Suppose an extra boolean field, *empty*, is included in the array representation of a table. When this field contains *true*, the array element is considered available. If *empty* is *true* and the key is nonzero, the record was previously deleted. If *empty* is *false*, the table element is filled. Redefine the type *Table* to include this *empty* field.

b. Which table operations from Exercises 9–19 should be altered by this definition and how should they be changed?

25. Code a rehash function, *QuadraticRehash*, to replace the function of Exercise 14. For this function the probe sequence should examine the locations that are the squares of the integers beyond the original hash position h,

$$h + 1^2, h + 2^2, h + 3^2, h + 4^2, \ldots$$

26. Suppose a hash table is implemented as an array of n records with linear probing. If all but one entry is filled, find the following:

a. The least number of comparisons for *InsertTable*.
b. The most.
c. The average.

27. In an **ordered hashing**, when a collision occurs if k, the key of the element to be inserted, is less than tk, the key of the table entry, their values are exchanged and the search continues using tk. Thus, during insertion, a smaller key will displace a larger key in its path.

a. Redesign *InsertTable* of Exercise 16 to accomplish ordered hashing.
b. Redesign *KeyFound* of Exercise 15 to accomplish ordered hashing.
c. What are the advantages and disadvantages of ordered hashing?

28. The presence of many deleted items in an array-implemented hash table can make some probe sequences quite long. An *in situ* rehash reinserts table items in the existing table, removing deleted entries and improving efficiency. The status field of each entry should be of enumeration type (*empty, full, deleted, rehashed*). Write an *in situ* rehash that uses the following algorithm:

For each full table entry x do the following:
　　Change the entry's status to *empty*
　　Calculate the hash index h
　　If $t[h].status$ is *empty* or *deleted*, insert the item and change the
　　　　status to *rehashed*.
　　else if $t[h].status$ is *rehashed*, handle the collision with an
　　　　appropriate hash sequence.
　　else if $t[h].status$ is *full*, change the entry's status to *rehashed*, swap
　　　　x and $t[h].el$, and continue the process with $t[h].el$.

In Exercises 29–38 code the requested operations to implement the ADT table. Assume the table is created as the array of pointers to linked lists created at the end of this section.

29. *MakeTableEmpty*(t)

30. *TableIsEmpty*(t)

31. *TableFull*(t), which should be constantly *false* because of the dynamic nature of this implementation.

32. *KeyTableEl(e)*

33. Probing procedure, *Probe*. When given a key, *k*, this procedure calculates a hash position and causes the pointer *prev* to point to the node before the one with a key value of *k*. If *k* is in the head node, *prev* is *nil*. If *k* is not found, *prev* points to the last node in the list. This procedure is called by the routines *DeleteTable*, *RetrieveTable*, and *KeyFound*.

34. *KeyFound(t, k)*

35. *InsertTable(t, e)*

36. *DeleteTable(t, k)*

37. *RetrieveTable(t, k)*; since only scalar values can be returned through a function name in Standard Pascal, implement this operation as a procedure.

38. *Traverse(t, Visit(ArgumentList))*; leave the *Visit* procedure undefined.

39. Suppose a hash table is implemented as an array of 64 pointers to unordered linked lists with a total of *n* entries.

   a. Find the least number of comparisons for *RetrieveTable*.
   b. Find the most.
   c. Find the average.
   d. How many pointers are stored in the table?

40. In the linked list implementation of a table as presented in the text, the array of pointers contains only pointer information.

   a. Adjust the type definitions so that the array also contains table information. Be sure you have a field within the array for marking the element as empty.
   b. Implementation of which ADT table operations will be affected by this change? Describe in English how to adjust the implementations.

41. Suppose a table record contains 300 bytes, four of which hold an integer key that ranges from 0 to 999.

   a. Using relative storage, how many bytes are needed for the table?
   b. Suppose at most 200 of the table positions are needed. How many bytes will be used?
   c. How many bytes will be wasted?
   d. One alternative is to have a 1000-element index array, *index*, and a 200-element table array, *t*. Relative storage is used for the index array, so that for key *k*, *index[k]* contains the location in *t* of the record associated with *k*. For example, suppose *k* = 734 and *index[734]* = 59. Then *t[59]* contains the record for key 734. Moreover, if *index[734]* = 0, there is no record with key 734 in table *t*. Assuming the key is stored in both *index* and *t*, how many bytes are needed for the storage of these two tables?
   e. Implement the ADT table using this structure.

▽

PROGRAMMING PROJECTS

1. A lookup table for the 36 standard Pascal reserved words is static. A **minimal perfect hash function** places these words into an array in 36 contiguous positions with no collisions. One such function is

    $hash(key) \leftarrow length(key) +$
    the value of the key's first character +
    the value of the key's last character

    where the value of a character is determined by the following list:

A—11	B—15	C—1	D—0	E—0
F—15	G—3	H—15	I—13	J—0
K—0	L—15	M—15	N—13	O—0
P—15	Q—0	R—14	S—6	T—6
U—14	V—10	W—6	X—0	Y—13
Z—0				

    Thus,

    $hash(\text{'ARRAY'}) = 5 + 11 + 13 = 29$

    The character values range from 0 to 15 and the hash values range from 2 to 37.

       Write a program to read an alphabetical listing of the Pascal reserved words, place these words in the hash table, and print the resulting table.

2. From a file read in records that have a four-digit key and a product name. Using the hash function

    $hash(k) = k \bmod 11$

    implement a hash table as an array of 11 records. Have the program detect a load factor of 80%, print the table with associated hash values, store the table information in another file, and print a message alerting the user that the data needs to be placed into a larger table.

3. The **random method** of hashing uses the key as the seed for the random number generator. The random number that is returned, $0 < Random < 1$, is then multiplied by the number of entries in the hash table to locate the address of the record. Should collision occur, the next pseudorandom number in the sequence is computed to be used in evaluation of the new address. Appendix A presents a random number generator.

       Write a program to build from a file such a hash table implemented as an array of records and to print the table with associated hash values. Then, interactively perform retrievals, insertions, and deletions on the table as requested. Print the table again upon termination of execution.

4. A **symbol table** for a program stores a list of all identifiers with their associated addresses. Design a program to read another program from a text file. Generate the symbol table as an array of linked lists with each node storing an identifier, a pointer to the next node in the bucket, and a pointer to a linked list of line numbers on which the identifier occurs. Use the hash function described in the next paragraph. After processing the input, print hash values with associated identifiers and line numbers.

   An identifier name starts with a letter and contains only letters and digits. For this project assume identifiers are no longer than 20 characters. Encode the letters as 10 through 35 and the digits as themselves. Suppose the function *hash* first computes the sum s of the encoded form of the first two characters. Then the function multiplies the encoded first character by 10 and adds this product to s. Thus, to evaluate *hash*('X2MOS'), we have $s = 33 + 2 = 35$, where 33 is the encoded letter 'X', and a hash value of $330 + 35 = 365$.

CHAPTER 10

Binary Trees

Introduction

The tree is one of the most important structures in computer science. A diagram of a tree, such as in Figure 10.1, can look much like an upside-down version of a live tree. We have already used this structure to display hierarchy charts (Figure 1.1), parse trees for a variable name (Figure 2.1), and steps in the evaluation of 4! (Figures 2.2 and 2.3). Trees are used extensively in a variety of areas including artificial intelligence, computer graphics, and compiler design.

The first section of this chapter introduces tree terminology and the next defines the abstract data type binary tree. Two binary tree implementations involving pointers are presented in Sections 10.3 and 10.4. With the first of these implementations, the natural way to develop many of the algorithms is recursively. The second method, using threaded trees, illustrates a nonrecursive alternative. Binary search trees and AVL trees of Sections 10.5 and 10.6, respectively, provide ways of organizing data that are usually very efficient. As we observe in the last section of this chapter, applications of binary trees are abundant.

SECTION 10.1 | Tree Terminology

A tree is a special case of a **graph,** which is a set of **nodes** (**vertices** or **points**) and a set of **edges** (**arcs**) joining pairs of nodes. As with all trees, the graph in Figure 10.1a is **connected**; that is, the drawing is in one piece; it is possible to move along edges from any node to any other one. Moreover, this graph has no **cycles,** so that we cannot travel in a circular fashion through any part of the graph. We present more formal definitions of these terms in Chapter 12. Accepting these concepts intuitively for now, we define a **tree** as a connected graph with no cycles.

Figure 10.1

Example of a rooted tree
drawn two ways

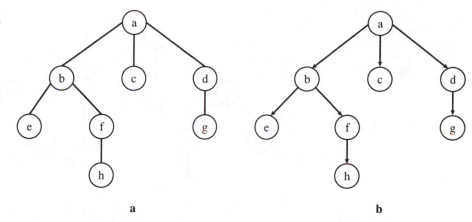

a   b

Often in computer science we consider the edges of a tree pointing downward as in Figure 10.1b. In this case, the vertex at the top (here, *a*) is specially
designated as the **root**; thus the structure is called a **rooted tree**. Throughout
this chapter we discuss rooted trees, which for brevity we call "trees." Moreover, a downward pointing direction of the edges is implied in the figures.

In the tree of Figure 10.1 we say that *b* is the **parent** of nodes *e* and *f* because there is an edge going from *b* down to each. Moreover, **siblings** *e* and *f*
are **children** of *b*. There is a **path** from node *b* to node *h* because there is a
sequence of edges from *b* to *f* to *h*. Continuing with the same family-tree terminology, the **descendants** of *b* are *e*, *f*, and *h*, the nodes that can be reached by
paths from *b*. Moreover, the **ancestors** of *f* are *b* and *a*, the nodes found on the
path from the root *a* to *f*. Nodes *c*, *e*, *g*, and *h* are **leaf nodes** because they have
no edges coming downward from them. The other nodes, *a*, *b*, *d*, and *f*, each
have at least one child and are **internal nodes**.

The level of the root is 1; nodes *b*, *c*, and *d* are at level 2; *e*, *f*, and *g* share
level 3; while *h* is the only node at level 4. The **level** of a node *n* is the number of
vertices in the path from the root to *n*. The maximum level in this tree is 4, so
we say the tree has **height** 4.

Figure 10.2 shows a **subtree**, *s*, of the tree *t* in boldface. We can say that *s* is
a subtree because *s* is itself a tree and every node and edge of *s* is in *t*. As the
figure illustrates, the root of *s* is *b*.

We now come to the primary object of this chapter—binary trees. A rooted
tree is a **binary tree** if every node has at most two children, one drawn to the
left, called the **left child**, and one to the right, the **right child**. Thus, we draw
edges from a node downward to the left or right, never straight down or to the
side. Figures 10.3–10.6 give examples of several binary trees, but Figure 10.1
is not a binary tree since *a* has three children.

Figure 10.3 shows a tree with root *a*, a left subtree with root *b*, and a right
subtree with root *c*. Being a leaf node, *c* has no children and empty left and
right subtrees. Figure 10.4 illustrates an empty tree with the root containing no
information.

Figure 10.2

Tree *t* with subtree *s* in boldface along with *s* diagrammed separately

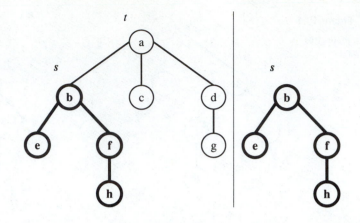

Figure 10.3

Example of binary tree

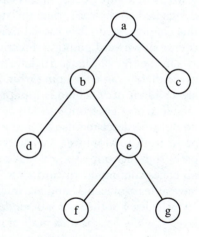

Figure 10.4

Example of binary tree

Figure 10.5

Example of binary tree

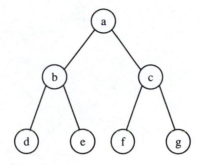

Figure 10.6

Example of binary tree

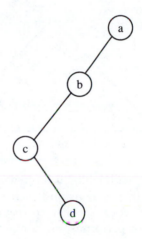

In Chapter 11 we discuss heaps, which are complete binary trees with a special characteristic. A **complete binary tree** (sometimes called almost complete binary tree) is defined as a binary tree where

1. All of its leaves are on level $n - 1$ or level n.

2. On levels 1 through $n - 2$ every node has exactly two children.

3. On level n the leaves are as far to the left as possible.

Figure 10.5 presents a complete binary tree with all leaves on level 3, while leaves are on levels 3 and 4 of the complete binary tree in Figure 10.7. With leaves on three levels, the tree in Figure 10.3 is not complete; nor is the binary tree of Figure 10.6 complete, because it violates the second condition of the definition. Observe in Figure 10.8 the outlines of the two possible shapes of complete binary trees.

Figure 10.7

Example of a complete
binary tree with leaves on
two levels

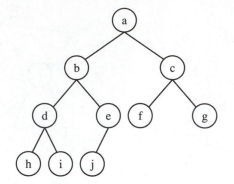

Figure 10.8

Outlines of the two pos-
sible shapes of complete
binary trees

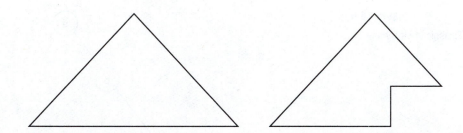

As with tables, it is often essential in applications that we **traverse** or travel through a tree visiting each node. Recall that visiting a node means calling some sort of user-defined **visit** procedure. For example, a visit procedure might print or perform some computation with the information in that node. There are three major orders used for traversals: preorder, inorder, and postorder.

Figure 10.9 displays a general picture of a binary tree. The root and left and right subtrees each may or may not be empty. In any of these traversals we always visit the left subtree before the right. The names of the three traversals indicate the order in which we visit the root. With a **preorder traversal**, we visit the root before the subtrees. For an **inorder traversal**, the root is visited in order, between the processing of the left and right subtrees. The root is visited last in a **postorder traversal**. Whichever the order, traversing a subtree repeats recursively the given ordered traversal. Suppose for now that a visit to a node

Figure 10.9

General picture of a binary
tree

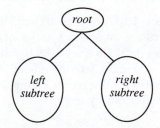

Figure 10.10

A small binary tree

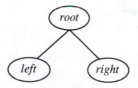

means printing its information. For the small tree of Figure 10.10, the traversal orders are as follows:

Preorder traversal: **root**   *left*   *right*
Inorder traversal: *left*   **root**   *right*
Postorder traversal: *left*   *right*   **root**

In a comparison of the preorder, inorder, and postorder traversals we see that the visit to the root gravitates from first to middle to last, respectively.

A dotted curve with arrows encasing this binary tree may help you to picture the order of the traversals. (See Figure 10.11.) We can think of traveling past each node indicated by the dotted curve, visiting only as dictated by one of the three traversal techniques.

Figure 10.11

Curve with arrows encasing the binary tree of Figure 10.10

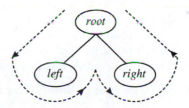

Below is a recursive algorithm for each type of traversal:

Preorder Traversal:
     if the root is not empty then
         visit the root
         traverse the left subtree
         traverse the right subtree
Inorder Traversal:
     if the root is not empty then
         traverse the left subtree
         visit the root
         traverse the right subtree

Postorder Traversal:

  if the root is not empty then
    traverse the left subtree
    traverse the right subtree
    visit the root

The binary tree of Figure 10.12 presents a more detailed example than a three-element tree. For inorder traversal we place the visit of the root between the traversals of the left and right subtrees, respectively. Thus, as shown below, for the inorder traversal of the binary tree in Figure 10.12 we have

Inorder traversal: *d   b   e   a   c   g   f*

Figure 10.12

A binary tree drawn with a dotted curve to aid traversal

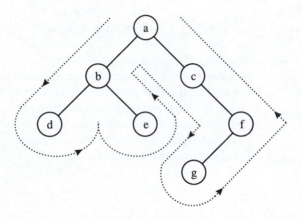

In the following we use indentation to indicate statements that are part of the traversal of one subtree and boldface to emphasize a visit.

Inorder Traversal of Binary Tree in Figure 10.12:

  Traverse the left subtree of *a*
    Traverse the left subtree of *b*
      Traverse the left subtree of *d* — empty, do nothing
      Visit the root *d*
      Traverse the right subtree of *d* — empty, do nothing
    Visit the root *b*
    Traverse the right subtree of *b*
      Traverse the left subtree of *e* — empty, do nothing
      Visit the root *e*
      Traverse the right subtree of *e* — empty, do nothing
  Visit the root *a*
  Traverse the right subtree of *a*
    Traverse the left subtree of *c* — empty, do nothing

Visit the root *c*
Traverse the right subtree of *c*
    Traverse the left subtree of *f*
        Traverse the left subtree of *g* — empty, do nothing
        Visit the root *g*
        Traverse the right subtree of *g* — empty, do nothing
    Visit the root *f*
    Traverse the right subtree of *f* — empty, do nothing

The root is visited last in a postorder traversal and first in a preorder traversal. For these traversals we visit the nodes of Figure 10.12 as follows:

Postorder traversal: *d* *e* *b* *g* *f* *c* *a*
Preorder traversal: *a* *b* *d* *e* *c* *f* *g*

Detailed descriptions of these traversals are requested in the exercises.

Certain binary trees and traversals allow us to alphabetize and search quickly. Others enable us to display expressions with infix notation and convert easily to postfix notation. In the following sections we examine a number of binary tree operations and applications.

SECTION 10.1 EXERCISES

1. Consider the binary tree in Figure 10.13.

Figure 10.13

Binary tree for Exercise 1

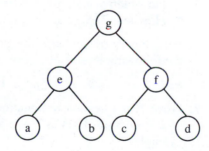

a. What is the root?
b. What is the parent of *d*?
c. List the children of *g*, if any.
d. List the siblings of *d*, if any.
e. Give the descendants of *f*, if any.
f. Give the ancestors of *c*, if any.
g. What is the level of *c*?
h. What is the height of the tree?
i. List all the leaf nodes.
j. List all the internal nodes.
k. Draw the left subtree of *g*.
l. Draw the right subtree of *f*.
m. Draw all the complete subtrees.
n. Give the preorder traversal.
o. Give the inorder traversal.
p. Give the postorder traversal.

Figure 10.14

Binary tree for Exercise 2

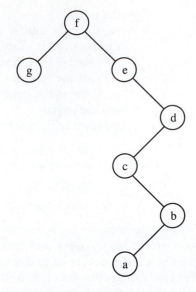

Figure 10.14

Binary tree for Exercise 2

2. Repeat Exercise 1 for the binary tree in Figure 10.14.

3. Similar to the inorder traversal in the text, give a detailed description for a postorder traversal of the binary tree in Figure 10.12.

4. Similar to the inorder traversal in the text, give a detailed description for a preorder traversal of the binary tree in Figure 10.12.

5. **a.** How many edges are in a tree with 5 nodes?
   b. How many edges are in a tree with n nodes?

6. For a binary tree, what is the greatest number of nodes that can appear at the following levels?

   a. 1   **b.** 2   **c.** 3   **d.** 4   **e.** n

7. Prove by mathematical induction that in a binary tree there is a maximum of 2^{n-1} nodes at level n. *Note:* See your answers in Exercise 6 for specific examples.

8. What is the maximum number of nodes that can appear in a binary tree of each of the following heights:

   a. 1   **b.** 2   **c.** 3   **d.** 4   **e.** n
   f. Write your answer to Part e without using a long sum by applying the formula from Example 2.6 of Section 2.3.

9. We can consider the tree of height n with the maximum number of nodes to be composed of a root and two subtrees of height $n - 1$. Complete the recursive definition to find the maximum number of nodes in a binary tree of height n.

$$f(1) = \underline{\quad a \quad}$$
$$f(n) = \underline{\quad b \quad} \text{ for } n \geq 2$$

10. A **full binary tree** is a binary tree where every node has 0 or 2 children but never just 1.

   a. Draw two full binary trees having 2 internal nodes.
   b. Draw five full binary trees having 3 internal nodes.
   c. Give an example of a full binary tree that is not complete.
   d. Give an example of a complete binary tree that is not full.

11. Fill in the details of the proof of the following theorem: A full binary tree t with i internal nodes has $2i + 1$ nodes and $i + 1$ leaves. (See Exercise 10.) **Proof:** Each of the i internal nodes has 2 children. (**a.** Why?) Thus, there are a total of __b__ children in the tree. Only one node, __c__, is not a child. Therefore, there are $2i + 1$ nodes in t. Consequently, there are $i + 1$ leaves. (**d.** Why?)

12. Play in a tennis tournament can be represented by a full binary tree. The players' names are listed at the leaf nodes; the internal nodes indicate matches. The winner of a match continues to the next match indicated by the tree, while the loser is eliminated. How many matches will be played in a tournament with 53 contestants? (See Exercise 11.)

▽

SECTION 10.2

ADT Binary Tree

With a foundation in the terminology, we are now ready to define the ADT binary tree. You will notice a number of similarities between this definition and those of the ADT linked list and the ADT table. Like doubly linked lists, each node of the binary tree has an information portion as well as left and right links. As with tables the element field is a key or has a key subfield. We can consider each node indicated by t to be the root of its own subtree so that the node's left (right) link points to its left (right) subtree. Principally because of the three portions of the node, most operations are tripled. For example, instead of just a *Retrieve* operation, we have operations to retrieve each of the three portions of the node, *RetrieveRoot*, *RetrieveLeft*, *RetrieveRight*. The action of many of the binary tree operations are illustrated in Figures 10.15–10.25. The formal definition of ADT binary tree appears in Figure 10.26.

Figure 10.15

Action of *MakeTree-Empty(t)*

$t:$

Figure 10.16

Action of *ToRoot*(*t, cur*)

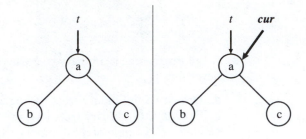

Figure 10.17

Action of *ToLeft*(*t*)

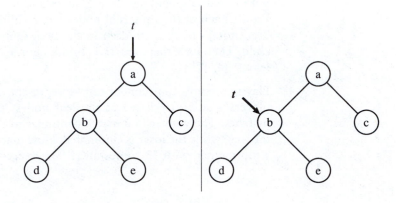

Figure 10.18

Action of *InsertRoot*(*t, e*)

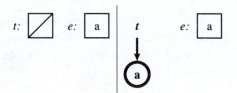

Figure 10.19

Action of *InsertLeft*(*t, e*)

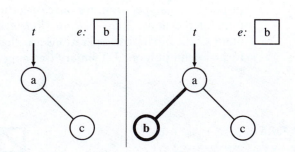

Figure 10.20

Action of *DeletePtLeft(t)*

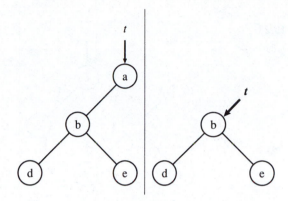

Figure 10.21

Action of *DeletePtRight(t)*

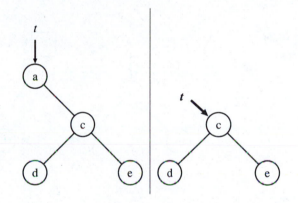

Figure 10.22

Action of *StoreRoot(t, e)*

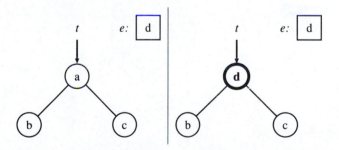

Figure 10.23

Action of *StoreLeft(t, cur)*

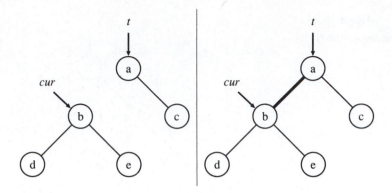

Figure 10.24

Action of *e ← Retrieve-Root(t)*

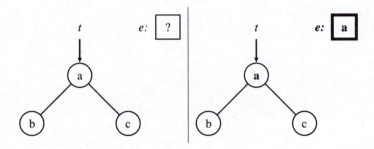

Figure 10.25

Action of *cur ← Retrieve-Left(t)*

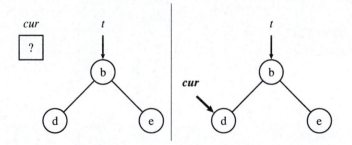

Figure 10.26

Formal definition of ADT
binary tree

ADT Binary Tree

Objects: A binary tree structure of nodes. All the nodes have the same type; each node is the root of a subtree and has three parts, an element portion, *el*, and fields, *left* and *right*, that point to the left and right subtrees of the root, respectively. Moreover, each node has a key that identifies the entry and that is the *el* field or is a subfield of *el*.

Operations:

    Notation:

        elType   — type of the element portion of a node

        keyType — type of the key

        t, cur   — binary trees; that is, *t* and *cur* point to nodes, where each node is the root of a binary tree structure

        e   — item of type *elType*

        k   — item of type *keyType*

        b   — boolean value

        n   — nonnegative integer

MakeTreeEmpty(*t*)

    Procedure to make *t* empty

TreeIsEmpty(*t*) → *b*

    Function to return *true* if *t* is empty

ToRoot(*t, cur*)

    Procedure to make *cur* point to the node to which *t* points

ToLeft(*t*)

    Procedure to make *t* point to the left subtree of *t*; assume *t* points to a node

ToRight(*t*)

    Procedure to make *t* point to the right subtree of *t*; assume *t* points to a node

InsertRoot(*t, e*)

    Procedure to point *t* to a new node containing *e* in the *el* field; assume before execution that *t* does not point to a node

InsertLeft(*t, e*)

    Procedure to create a left child for *t*'s node, placing *e* in the *el* field of the new node; assume before execution that *t* points to a node that has no left child

InsertRight(*t, e*)

    Procedure to create a right child for *t*'s node, placing *e* in the *el* field of the new node; assume before execution that *t* points to a node that has no right child

DeleteRoot(*t*)

    Procedure to delete *t*'s node; assume before execution that *t* points to a node that has no children

DeletePtLeft(*t*)

    Procedure to delete the node pointed to by *t* and point *t* to the node's left child; assume before execution that *t* points to a node that has no right child

Figure 10.26

continued

DeletePtRight(*t*)

Procedure to delete the node pointed to by *t* and point *t* to the node's right child; assume before execution that *t* points to a node that has no left child

StoreRoot(*t, e*)

Procedure to place *e*'s value in the *el* field of the node indicated by *t*; assume *t* points to a node

StoreLeft(*t, cur*)

Procedure to place *cur*'s value in the *left* field of the node indicated by *t*; assume *t* points to a node

StoreRight(*t, cur*)

Procedure to place *cur*'s value in the *right* field of the node indicated by *t*; assume *t* points to a node

RetrieveRoot(*t*) → *e*

Function to return the value in the *el* field indicated by *t*; assume *t* points to a node

RetrieveLeft(*t*) → *cur*

Function to return the value of the *left* field of the node indicated by *t*; assume *t* points to a node

RetrieveRight(*t*) → *cur*

Function to return the value of the *right* field of the node indicated by *t*; assume *t* points to a node

KeyTreeEl(*e*) → *k*

Function to return key of *e*

Height(*t*) → *n*

Function to return the height of the tree pointed to by *t*

PreorderTraverse(*t, Visit*(*ArgumentList*))

Procedure to perform a preorder traversal on the tree pointed to by *t*, executing *Visit*(*ArgumentList*) for every element in *t*, where *Visit* is a user-specified procedure and *ArgumentList* is a list of arguments

InorderTraverse(*t, Visit*(*ArgumentList*))

Procedure to perform an inorder traversal on the tree pointed to by *t*, executing *Visit*(*ArgumentList*) for every element in *t*, where *Visit* is a user-specified procedure and *ArgumentList* is a list of arguments

PostorderTraverse(*t, Visit*(*ArgumentList*))

Procedure to perform a postorder traversal on the tree pointed to by *t*, executing *Visit*(*ArgumentList*) for every element in *t*, where *Visit* is a user-specified procedure and *ArgumentList* is a list of arguments

Example 10.1.

▼ In this example we design a procedure *DeleteAll* to delete every node of a binary tree pointed to by *t*. We cannot correctly apply *DeleteRoot*(*t*) and throw away the entire tree at once because the operation has the assumption that the node indicated by *t* has no children. Thus, we must eliminate the root's left and right subtrees before deleting the root. The postorder traversal performs exactly in that order, visiting the root only after traversing the left and right subtrees. With this traversal, our visit procedure can be *DeleteRoot*. When we visit a root, we have already traversed its left and right subtrees, eliminating a node with each visit. Consequently, no children remain for that root, and we can correctly apply the *DeleteRoot* operation.

The outline below details this postorder traversal for the small tree in Figure 10.27. In that figure dotted areas indicate a deletion.

{10.27}   traverse the left subtree of *a*
                        traverse the left subtree of *b* — empty, do nothing
                        traverse the right subtree of *b* — empty, do nothing
{Step 2}   **visit the root *b* — delete *b***
                traverse the right subtree of *a*
                        traverse the left subtree of *c* — empty, do nothing
                        traverse the right subtree of *c* — empty, do nothing
{Step 3}   **visit the root *c* — delete *c***
{Step 4}   **visit the root *a* — delete *a***

Figure 10.27

Action of *DeleteAll*(*t*)

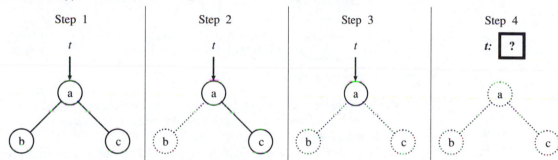

The algorithm for the *DeleteAll* procedure follows:

***DeleteAll*(*t*)**
     Procedure to delete every node in the binary tree *t*
Input:
     t — points to a binary tree
Output:
     t — points to a revised binary tree
Assumption:
     t exists.

Figure	Algorithm
▲ {10.27}	*PostorderTraverse*(*DeleteRoot*(*t*))

Example 10.2.

▼ The **predecessor** of a vertex in a traversal is the node visited immediately before that vertex. For this example we are interested in developing a procedure *InorderPredOfRoot* to point *cur* to the inorder predecessor of the root of the tree indicated by *t*. Since the left subtree of *t* is traversed immediately before visiting the root, the predecessor must be to the left. For example, in Figure 10.28 the inorder predecessor of node *a* is *k*, a node in the left subtree.

Figure 10.28

Initial step of finding the inorder predecessor of the root *a*

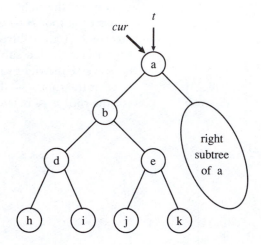

If the left subtree is empty, there is no inorder predecessor of the root; for an inorder traversal of such a tree, we visit the root first. In this case the procedure call *InorderPredOfRoot(t, cur)* makes *cur* empty.

If the left subtree is not empty, as in Figure 10.28, then the inorder predecessor of the root is in that subtree. Moreover, in that tree the predecessor of *a* is the very last node visited in the traversal of the subtree with root *b*. Consideration of the inorder traversal until the visit of the root *a* helps us in developing an algorithm:

Traverse the left subtree of *a*
    Traverse the left subtree of *b*
    . . .
    Visit *b*
    Traverse the right subtree of *b*
        Traverse the left subtree of *e*
        . . .
        Visit *e*
        Traverse the right subtree of *e*
            Traverse the left subtree of *k* — empty, do nothing
            Visit *k*
            Traverse the right subtree of *k* — empty, do nothing
Visit *a*

Figure 10.29

Find the inorder predecessor (*k*) of the root (*a*) by
taking an initial left and
then continuing to the
right as far as possible

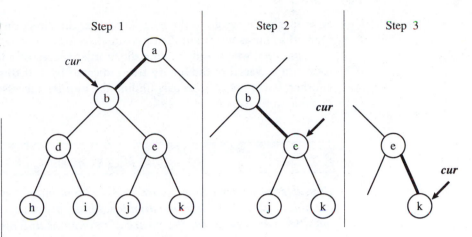

Notice that once we are to the left of the root *a*, the work involved in traversing the left subtrees and visiting their roots is unnecessary. As Figure 10.29
illustrates and the following algorithm states, we can find the inorder predecessor of the root by first moving to the left subtree and then by traveling to the
right until we arrive at a node that has no right child.

InorderPredOfRoot(**t, cur**)
  Procedure to cause *cur* to point to the inorder predecessor of the root
  of the binary tree pointed to by *t*; if the root does not have an inorder
  predecessor, *cur* becomes empty
Input:
  t   — points to the root of a binary tree
Output:
  cur — points to the inorder predecessor of the root in the binary tree
        pointed to by *t*
Assumption:
  t exists.

Figure	Algorithm
{10.28}	*ToRoot*(*t, cur*)
{10.29}	
{Step 1}	*ToLeft*(*cur*)
	if not *TreeIsEmpty*(*cur*) then
	while not *TreeIsEmpty*(*RetrieveRight*(*cur*)) do
{Steps 2−3}	*ToRight*(*cur*)

The **successor** of a node is the next node visited in a given traversal method.
In the exercises we cover the procedure *InorderSuccOfRoot*(*t, cur*) to cause
cur to point to the inorder successor of the root of the binary tree indicated by
t. The only difference between *InorderPredOfRoot* and *InorderSuccOfRoot*
algorithms is a switch of *Left* for *Right* and *Right* for *Left*. For the successor,
we need a later node, so we first go to the right. For the predecessor, which is

an earlier node, we go to the left. Whichever the direction we take initially, we then go as far as we can in the opposite direction.

Note that we are only finding the inorder successor and predecessor of the root in a traversal of the binary tree indicated by *t*. If this tree is a subtree of another, we are not necessarily finding the inorder successor or predecessor of *t*'s node in the supertree.

▽

SECTION 10.2 EXERCISES

Consider the binary tree in Figure 10.30 with pointers t, p, *and* cur, *character variables* e *and* x, *and integer variable* i. *Show any changes in memory or output after execution of each sequence of operations in Exercises 1–15.*

Figure 10.30

Binary tree for Exercises 1–15

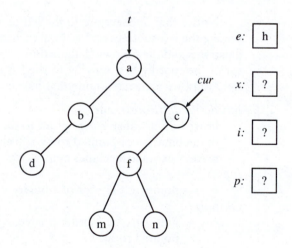

1. *InsertRight(cur, e)*

2. *ToRoot(t, cur)*
   ToLeft(cur)
   DeletePtLeft(cur)
   StoreLeft(t, cur)

3. *MakeTreeEmpty(cur)*
   InsertRoot(cur, e)
   x ← RetrieveRoot(t)
   InsertRight(cur, x)

4. *StoreRoot(t, RetrieveRoot(cur))*

5. $i \leftarrow Height(t) + Height(cur)$

6. $ToLeft(cur)$
$e \leftarrow RetrieveRoot(RetrieveRight(cur))$
$StoreRoot(t, e)$

7. $InorderSuccOfRoot(t, cur)$

8. $InorderSuccOfRoot(cur, p)$

9. $InorderPredOfRoot(t, cur)$

10. $InorderPredOfRoot(cur, p)$

11. $ToRoot(t, cur)$
while not $TreeIsEmpty(RetrieveLeft(cur))$
    $ToLeft(cur)$
$x \leftarrow RetrieveRoot(cur)$
$InsertLeft(cur, e)$

12. $PreorderTraverse(t, Write(RetrieveRoot(t)))$

13. $InorderTraverse(t, Write(RetrieveRoot(t)))$

14. $PostorderTraverse(t, Write(RetrieveRoot(t)))$

15. $StoreRight(t, RetrieveLeft(cur))$
$DeletePtLeft(cur)$

16. Using pseudocode and ADT binary tree operations and notation, complete the definition below of a routine to read a binary file and to place each datum into a binary tree. The first element from the file is inserted in the root. For the other items, use an integer random number generator that returns 0 or 1 to determine whether to send the item to the left or right, respectively. If there is a child in that direction, generate another random 0 or 1 to pick the direction from the child. Continue the process until the item can be inserted.

GenerateTree(t, f)
Input: f - file   *Output:* t - tree
Algorithm:
    $Reset(f)$
    $MakeTreeEmpty(t)$
    if not $EOF(f)$ then   {place first item in root}
        $read(f, e)$
        _____**a**_____

    while not $EOF(f)$ do   {process next item}
        $read(f, e)$
        $ToRoot(t, cur)$
        $continue \leftarrow true$

```
            while continue do                        {find location}
                if RandomInteger(2) = 0 then         {go left}
                                                     {left subtree empty}
                    if TreeIsEmpty(RetrieveLeft(cur)) then
                        InsertLeft(cur, e)
                        continue ← false
                else                                 {left subtree not empty}
                        ToLeft(cur)
                else                                 {go right}
                    if ____b____ then                {right subtree empty}
                          ____c____
                          ____d____
                else                                 {right subtree not empty}
                          ____e____
```

Using pseudocode and ADT binary tree operations and notation, define the routines in Exercises 17–28.

17. Boolean function *LeftIsEmpty*(*t*) to return *true* if the root pointed to by *t* does not have a left child.

18. Boolean function *RightIsEmpty*(*t*) to return *true* if the root pointed to by *t* does not have a right child.

19. Boolean function *IsLeaf*(*t*) to return *true* if the root pointed to by *t* is a leaf.

20. Function *SizeTree* to return the number of nodes in a tree; see Example 9.1 of Section 9.1.

21. Function *LeafCount* to return the number of leaves in a binary tree; use a traversal and *IsLeaf* of Exercise 19.

22. Function *InternalNodeCount* to return the number of internal nodes in a binary tree.

23. Boolean function *EqualKey*(*t*, *k*) to return *true* if the node pointed to by *t* has key *k*.

24. Function *MaxInTree* to return the maximum value held in a binary tree; assume *t* is not empty.

25. Procedure *InorderSuccOfRoot* that causes *cur* to point to the inorder successor of the root in the binary tree indicated by *t*; assume *t* is not empty.

26. Boolean function *IsInTree*(*t*, *item*) to return *true* if the value of an element, *item*, is in any node of the tree pointed to by *t*. Use a traversal with a visit procedure *Compare*(*t*, *item*, *elFound*). This visit procedure should make the parameter *elFound true* or *false* depending on whether the value in the node equals *item* or not. If found, abort the traversal.

27. Function *Parent*(*t*, *cur*) to return a pointer to the parent of the node pointed to by *cur* in the tree indicated by *t*. If *cur*'s node is the root, return the null value. Assume *t* is not empty and that *cur* points to a node of the tree. Use a preorder traversal.

28. Procedure *CopyTree(s, t)* that makes a copy, *s*, of a tree, *t*. Use a preorder traversal because we want to install the root of a subtree first.

Binary Tree Implementation

ADT binary tree can be implemented with the static memory allocation of arrays or the dynamic memory allocation of pointers. We choose the latter for presentation in the text and leave the development with arrays for the exercises.

The type definitions and variable declarations that create the binary tree are very similar to those for the creation of linked lists except for the addition of another pointer field and the inclusion of a key field.

```
type
    NonNeg      =   0..maxint;
    keyType     =   ...........;
    infoType    =   ...........;
    elType      =   record
        key     :   keyType;
        info    :   infoType
    end;

    BinaryTree  =   ^Node;
    Node        =   record
        left    :   BinaryTree;
        el      :   elType;
        right   :   BinaryTree
    end;

var
    t,
    cur    :   BinaryTree;
    e      :   elType;
    k      :   keyType;
    b      :   boolean;
    n      :   NonNeg;
```

The exact definitions, of course, depend on the application. Often the key field contains all the data stored in the node, so that the *keyType* and *elType* are identical. In this situation, we do not have *infoType* and vary type definitions accordingly.

```
    keyType  =  ...........;
    elType   =  keyType;
```

Figure 10.31

A binary tree viewed as a graph and as a linked structure

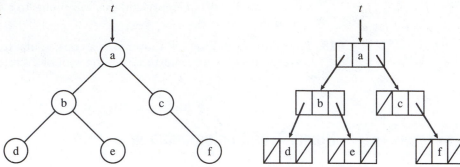

Figure 10.31 presents the binary tree viewed two ways, as a graph and as a linked structure. The *left* and *right* pointers associated with each node indicate the left and right subtrees of that node, respectively. Notice the slashes through some pointer fields of the schematic indicating a value of *nil* and no corresponding subtrees.

Several of the ADT binary tree operations manipulate or test a pointer: *MakeTreeEmpty, TreeIsEmpty, ToLeft, ToRight*. Others assign or return a value: *RetrieveRoot, RetrieveLeft, RetrieveRight, StoreRoot, StoreLeft, StoreRight, KeyTreeEl*. The insert and delete operations are reminiscent of insertions and deletions in linked lists where the location of the action is an argument for the procedure. These operations contrast with those of *InsertTable* and *DeleteTable* where the locations must first be found before installation or removal of a node.

As an example, consider the procedure *InsertLeft*(*t, e*) that inserts a node containing the value of *e* as the left child of the node pointed to by *t*. The ADT definition of this operation assumes that before execution of the operation, *t* is not empty, that is, not *nil*; but *t*'s node has no left child, or ($t^\wedge.left = nil$). Such a situation is depicted in Figure 10.32.

The ADT pointer operation *New* can be used to point $t^\wedge.left$ toward a new node; the ADT binary tree operations of *StoreRoot* and *MakeTreeEmpty* can be employed to fill the node. An intermediate pointer (*cur*) to the new node, though unnecessary, does make the action of the operation more understandable. Figure 10.33 demonstrates the ADT-level design of *InsertLeft*.

Figure 10.32

Binary tree on which *InsertLeft*(*t, e*) can be performed because ($t^\wedge.left = nil$)

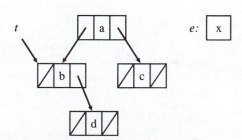

Figure 10.33

Action of *InsertLeft*(t, e) on the binary tree of Figure 10.32

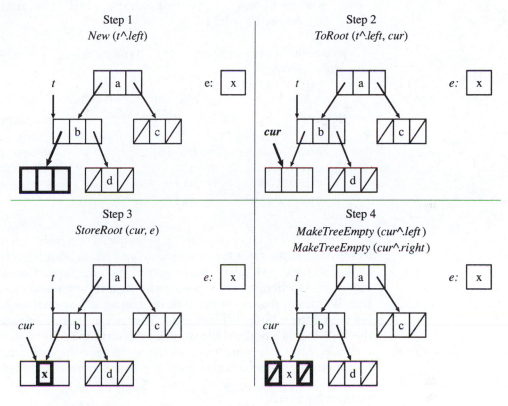

Step 1
New (t^.left)

Step 2
ToRoot (t^.left, cur)

Step 3
StoreRoot (cur, e)

Step 4
MakeTreeEmpty (cur^.left)
MakeTreeEmpty (cur^.right)

InsertLeft(**t, e**)
Procedure to create a left child for *t*'s node, placing *e* in the *el* field of the new node

Input:
t — points to a binary tree
e — value of type *elType*

Output:
none

Assumptions:
t is not empty, but its node has no left child.

Figure	Algorithm
{10.33}	
{Step 1}	*New(t^ .left)*
{Step 2}	*ToRoot(t^ .left, cur)*
{Step 3}	*StoreRoot(cur, e)*
{Step 4}	*MakeTreeEmpty(cur^ .left)*
	MakeTreeEmpty(cur^ .right)

The following is a Pascal implementation of this design:

```
{  Procedure to create a left child for t's node,
      placing e in the el field of the new node.
   Assumptions: t is not empty, but its node has
      no left child.}

procedure InsertLeft (t: BinaryTree; e: elType};
var
     cur : BinaryTree;

begin                                 {Figure 10.33}
   new (t^.left);                     {Step 1}
   cur          := t^.left;           {Step 2}
   cur^.el      := e;                 {Step 3}
   cur^.left    := nil;               {Step 4}
   cur^.right   := nil
end;
```

The *DeletePtRight* procedure employs the ADT pointer operation *Dispose* to free the deleted node for further use. But first, as with linked lists, we must change a crucial link or risk losing part of the binary tree. Consider the tree in Figure 10.34 where we wish to eliminate *t*'s node and point *t* to the right subtree. We cannot dispose of the node containing *a*, however, without abandoning the subtree whose root contains *c*. Thus, we have another pointer, *cur*, hold the address of *a*'s node, while we point *t* toward the root of the right subtree, *c*'s node. After this maneuver, we can safely free the unwanted node. ADT operations define this deletion process, which is mirrored in Figure 10.35.

DeletePtRight(*t*)

Procedure to delete the node pointed to by *t* and point *t* to the node's right child

Figure 10.34

Binary tree on which *DeletePtRight*(*t*) can be performed because (*t^.left = nil*)

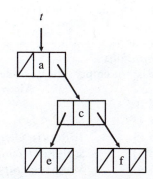

Figure 10.35

Action of *DeletePtRight(t)* on the binary tree of Figure 10.34

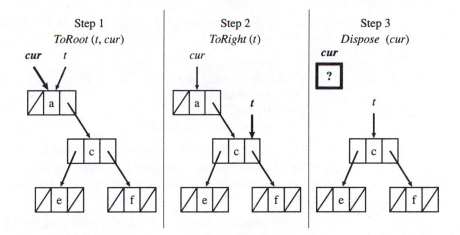

Step 1
ToRoot (t, cur)

Step 2
ToRight (t)

Step 3
Dispose (cur)

Input:
     t — pointer to the root of a binary tree
Output:
     t — revised pointer to the root of a binary tree
Assumption:
     The node to be deleted has no left child.

Figure	Algorithm
{10.35}	
{Step 1}	*ToRoot(t, cur)*
{Step 2}	*ToRight(t)*
{Step 3}	*Dispose(cur)*

A Pascal implementation of the operation *DeletePtRight* follows the above design:

```
{ Procedure to delete the node pointed to by t and point t
     to the node's right child.
  Assumption: The node to be deleted has no left child. }

procedure DeletePtRight (var t: BinaryTree);
var
   cur: BinaryTree;
begin                                    {Figure 10.35}
   cur    := t;                          {Step 1}
   t      := t^.right;                   {Step 2}
   dispose(cur)                          {Step 3}
end;
```

Four ADT binary tree operations—the three traversals and *Height*—involve the entire tree. As with many binary tree operations, these operations can be easily designed with recursion. In fact, in the first two sections of this chapter we elaborated upon a recursive definition of the traversals. For example, we defined the inorder traversal of a binary tree as follows, calling the traversal from within the traversal:

Inorder Traversal:
    If the root is not empty then
        Traverse the left subtree
        Visit the root
        Traverse the right subtree

We assume that *Visit* is a previously defined procedure. Perhaps the data portion of each node contains only an integer key and a real number or a character as information. The visit routine prints the element using the following definition:

```
{ Procedure to print information held in the node
      pointed to by t }
{ Assumption: key and info are of a scalar type }

procedure Visit (t: BinaryTree);
begin
    writeln(t^.el.key, ' ', t^.el.info)
end;
```

With this definition, execution of the recursive procedure below causes the data stored in the nodes to be printed "in order." The preorder and postorder traversals are defined similarly with only a change in the location of the call to the visit procedure.

```
{ Procedure to traverse inorder the binary tree
      pointed to by t.
  Assumption: Visit is a previously defined
      procedure with a parameter of type
      BinaryTree. }

procedure InorderTraverse (t: BinaryTree);
begin
    if t <> nil then
        begin
            InorderTraverse(t^.left);
            Visit(t);
            InorderTraverse(t^.right)
        end    { if }
end;           { InorderTraverse }
```

We can also employ recursion to define the operation *Height*. Recall that the height of a tree is the greatest level of the tree. Since we are calculating a maximum level, we need a function to return the larger of two integers. Many languages have such a function built in, but Standard Pascal does not, so for completeness we include its definition.

```
{ Function to return the maximum of two integers }

function max (i, j: integer): integer;
begin
    if i > j then
        max := i
    else
        max := j
end;
```

Returning to the design of the function *Height*, consider the empty binary tree in Figure 10.36. Since that tree has no nodes, its height is 0. Thus, we have

if *TreeIsEmpty*(*t*) then
    Height ← 0

In a recursive definition, this *if* statement becomes the terminal condition.

Figure 10.36

An empty binary tree

t:

A binary tree with a root and left and right subtrees, as illustrated in Figure 10.9, has a height of at least 1. In fact, if we know the height of its left subtree is 5 and of its right subtree is 3, we can say the height of the entire binary tree is:

$1 + max(3, 5) = 1 + 5 = 6$

Since one of the subtrees has 5 levels of nodes, when we include the root, there are a total of 6 levels of nodes. Thus, the height is one more than the maximum height of the left and right subtrees. The recursive step reads:

Height ← 1 + *max* (height of left subtree, height of right subtree)

The Pascal definition of *Height* is as follows:

```
{ Function to return the height of the binary tree
      pointed to by t }

function Height (t: BinaryTree): NonNeg;
begin
    if t = nil then
        Height := 0
    else
        Height := 1 + max(Height(t^.left), Height(t^.right))
end;
```

A summary of all the ADT binary tree operations appears in Figure 10.37.

Figure 10.37

A dynamic linked list implementation of ADT binary tree

Dynamic Linked List Implementation of ADT Binary Tree

Create a binary tree pointed to by *t*.

```
type
   NonNeg      = 0..maxint;
   keyType     = ...........;
   infoType    = ...........;
   elType      = record
      key    : keyType;
      info   : infoType
   end;
   BinaryTree = ^Node;
   Node       = record
      left   : BinaryTree;
      el     : elType;
      right  : BinaryTree
   end;

var
   t,
   cur  :  BinaryTree;
   e    :  elType;
   k    :  keyType;
   b    :  boolean;
   n    :  NonNeg;
```

MakeTreeEmpty(*t*)

```
procedure MakeTreeEmpty (var t: BinaryTree);
begin
   t := nil
end;
```

TreeIsEmpty(*t*) → *b*

```
function TreeIsEmpty (t: BinaryTree): boolean;
begin
   TreeIsEmpty := (t = nil)
end;
```

Figure 10.37

continued

ToRoot(*t, cur*)

```
procedure ToRoot (t: BinaryTree; var cur : BinaryTree);
begin
    cur := t
end;
```

ToLeft(*t*)

```
{ Assumption: t points to a node. }
procedure ToLeft (var t: BinaryTree);
begin
    t := t^.left
end;
```

ToRight(*t*)

```
{ Assumption: t points to a node. }
procedure ToRight (var t: BinaryTree);
begin
    t := t^.right
end;
```

InsertRoot(*t, e*)

```
{ Assumption: t does not point to a node. }
procedure InsertRoot (var t: BinaryTree; e: elType);
begin
    new(t);
    t^.el       := e;
    t^.left     := nil;
    t^.right    := nil
end;
```

InsertLeft(*t, e*)

```
{ Assumptions: t points to a node, but its node has
      no left child.}
procedure InsertLeft (t: BinaryTree; e: elType);
var
    cur : BinaryTree;
begin
    new (t^.left);
    cur          := t^.left;
    cur^.el      := e;
    cur^.left    := nil;
    cur^.right   := nil
end;
```

Figure 10.37

continued

InsertRight(t, e)

```
{ Assumptions: t points to a node, but its node has
    no right child.}
procedure InsertRight (t: BinaryTree; e: elType);
var
   cur : BinaryTree;
begin
   new (t^.right);
   cur         := t^.right;
   cur^.el     := e;
   cur^.left   := nil;
   cur^.right  := nil
end;
```

DeleteRoot(t)

```
{ Assumption: t points to a node, but its node has
    no children. }
procedure DeleteRoot (var t: BinaryTree);
begin
   dispose(t)
end;
```

DeletePtLeft(t)

```
{ Assumptions: t points to a node, but its node has
    no right child.}
procedure DeletePtLeft (var t: BinaryTree);
var
   cur:  BinaryTree;
begin
   cur   := t;
   t     := t^.left;
   dispose(cur)
end;
```

DeletePtRight(t)

```
{ Assumptions: t points to a node, but its node has
    no left child.}
procedure DeletePtRight (var t: BinaryTree);
var
   cur:  BinaryTree;
begin
   cur   := t;
   t     := t^.right;
   dispose(cur)
end;
```

Figure 10.37

continued

StoreRoot(*t, e*)

```
{ Assumption: t points to a node.}
procedure StoreRoot (t: BinaryTree; e: elType);
begin
   t^.el := e
end;
```

StoreLeft (*t, cur*)

```
{ Assumption: t points to a node.}
procedure StoreLeft (t, cur: BinaryTree);
begin
   t^.left := cur
end;
```

StoreRight(*t, cur*)

```
{ Assumption: t points to a node.}
procedure StoreRight (t, cur: BinaryTree);
begin
   t^.right := cur
end;
```

RetrieveRoot(*t*) → *e*

```
{ Assumption: t points to a node. }
{ Note: If elType is a scalar type, we can implement
        RetrieveRoot as a function. }
procedure RetrieveRoot (t: BinaryTree, var e: elType);
begin
   e := t^.el
end;
```

RetrieveLeft(*t*) → *cur*

```
{ Assumption: t points to a node.}
function RetrieveLeft (t: BinaryTree): BinaryTree;
begin
   RetrieveLeft := t^.left
end;
```

RetrieveRight(*t*) → *cur*

```
{ Assumption: t points to a node.}
function RetrieveRight (t: BinaryTree): BinaryTree;
begin
   RetrieveRight := t^.right
end;
```

Figure 10.37

continued

KeyTreeEl(*e*) → *k*

```
function KeyTreeEl (e: elType): keyType;
begin
   KeyTreeEl := e.key
end;
```

Height(*t*) → *n*

```
{ Assumption: Function max has been previously defined. }
function Height (t: BinaryTree): NonNeg;
begin
   if t = nil then
      Height := 0;
   else
      Height := 1 + max(Height(t^.left), Height(t^.right))
   end;
```

PreorderTraverse(*t, Visit*(*ArgumentList*))

```
{ Assumption: Function Visit previously defined. }
procedure PreorderTraverse (t: BinaryTree);
begin
   if t <> nil then
      begin
         Visit(t);
         PreorderTraverse (t^.left);
         PreorderTraverse (t^.right)
      end { if }
end;
```

InorderTraverse(*t, Visit*(*ArgumentList*))

```
{ Assumption: Function Visit previously defined. }
procedure InorderTraverse (t: BinaryTree);
begin
   if t <> nil then
      begin
         InorderTraverse(t^.left);
         Visit(t);
         InorderTraverse(t^.right)
      end   { if }
end;
```

Figure 10.37

continued

PostorderTraverse(t, Visit(ArgumentList))

```
{ Assumption: Function Visit previously defined. }
procedure PostorderTraverse (t: BinaryTree);
begin
    if t <> nil then
        begin
            PostorderTraverse(t^.left);
            PostorderTraverse(t^.right);
            Visit(t)
        end    { if }
end;
```

▽

SECTION 10.3 EXERCISES

In Exercises 1–15 code in Pascal the routines from Section 10.2.

1. Procedure *GenerateTree* from Exercise 16 to read a binary file and to place each datum into a binary tree, where the position of insertion is determined by a sequence of random 0s and 1s. The resulting tree can be used in testing routines in the exercises.

2. Procedure *DeleteAll* from Example 10.1 to delete all the nodes from a binary tree.

3. Procedure *InorderPredOfRoot(t, cur)* from Example 10.2 to point *cur* toward the inorder predecessor of the root in the binary tree indicated by *t*.

4. Boolean function *LeftIsEmpty(t)* from Exercise 17 to return *true* if the root pointed to by *t* does not have a left child.

5. Boolean function *RightIsEmpty(t)* from Exercise 18 to return *true* if the root pointed to by *t* does not have a right child.

6. Boolean function *IsLeaf(t)* from Exercise 19 to return *true* if the root pointed to by *t* is a leaf.

7. Function *SizeTree* from Exercise 20 to return the number of nodes in a tree.

8. Function *LeafCount* from Exercise 21 to return the number of leaves in a binary tree.

9. Function *InternalNodeCount* from Exercise 22 to return the number of internal nodes in a binary tree.

10. Boolean function *EqualKey*(*t, k*) from Exercise 23 to return *true* if the node pointed to by *t* has key *k*.

11. Function *MaxInTree* from Exercise 24 to return the maximum value held in a binary tree.

12. Procedure *InorderSuccOfRoot*(*t, cur*) from Exercise 25 to point *cur* toward the inorder successor of the root in the binary tree indicated by *t*.

13. Boolean function *IsInTree*(*t, item*) from Exercise 26 to return *true* if the value of an element *item* is in any node of the tree pointed to by *t*.

14. Function *Parent*(*t, cur*) from Exercise 27 to return a pointer to the parent of the node pointed to by *cur* in the tree indicated by *t*. If *cur*'s node is the root, return *nil*. Assume *t* is not empty and that *cur* points to a node of the tree.

15. Procedure *CopyTree*(*s, t*) from Exercise 28 that makes a copy *s* of a tree, *t*.

16. Using the binary tree of Figure 10.31, trace the steps of execution of the function *Height*.

17. Design and code a recursive version of the function *SizeTree* of Exercise 7 so that its definition is similar to that of the *Height* function.

18. Design and code a recursive version of the function *IsInTree* of Exercise 13 so that its definition is similar to that of the *Height* function.

19. Design and code a recursive boolean function *EqualTrees* that returns *true* if two binary trees are identical.

20. The function *SumofLevels* below is used to return the sum of all the levels of nodes in the binary tree pointed to by *t*. For example, the sum of all the levels of nodes for the binary tree in Figure 10.32 is $1 + 2 + 2 + 3 = 8$. The only action of *SumofLevels* is to return the value of the recursive function reference *RecSumofLevels*(*t*, 1), where 1 is the level of a nonempty root.

    a. Complete the following function definitions:

```
{ Function to call RecSumofLevels for the entire tree }
{ Assumption: t is not empty                          }

function SumofLevels (t: BinaryTree): NonNeg;

{  Recursive function to return the sum of all the levels
   of nodes in the two subtrees of the root pointed to by
   t plus the level of the root }
```

```
function RecSumofLevels (t: BinaryTree; level: NonNeg): NonNeg;
   begin   { RecSumofLevels }
      if TreeIsEmpty (t) then
         RecSumofLevels := __i__
      else
         RecSumofLevels := __ii__ +
            RecSumofLevels(RetrieveLeft(t), level + 1) + __iii__
   end       { RecSumofLevels }

begin   { SumofLevels }
   SumofLevels := __iv__
end;      { SumofLevels }
```

b. Show the action of *SumofLevels* on the binary tree in Figure 10.32.

21. Define the function *AvgLevel* to return the average level of a node in a binary tree. Use *SizeTree* and *SumofLevels* from Exercises 7 and 20, respectively.

22. As in Exercise 20, define a function *FindLevel* that will return the level of the node to which *cur* points in the binary tree indicated by *t*. Have *FindLevel* reference a recursive function *RecLevel* with parameters *t*, *cur*, and *level*.

23. Using a stack, write a nonrecursive procedure to perform an inorder traversal of a binary tree.

24. Implement the ADT binary tree with arrays of records much as we did for linked lists in Section 7.4. One field, *el*, holds the element portion. Fields *left* and *right* hold the indices of the left and right children, respectively. The null value for an index is zero.

25. Give the advantages and disadvantages of the array and linked implementations of ADT binary tree. Refer to Exercise 24.

SECTION 10.4

Threaded Tree

Suppose in a particular application we must frequently perform an inorder traversal of a binary tree. One method to avoid recursion and the resulting space requirements for a stack is to implement the binary tree as a **threaded tree**. This technique does not remove recursion as we did in Section 2.2 by creating our own stack. Instead, we alter the structure of the implemented binary tree.

As discussed in the last three sections, for an inorder traversal we recursively traverse the left subtree, visit the root, and then traverse the right subtree. Thus, if the right subtree of a node is not empty, the **inorder successor** of that node, the next node to be visited with an inorder traversal, will be found in that right subtree. If, however, a node has an empty right subtree, then its right link is *nil*. A *nil* right link tells us a limited amount of information about the inorder successor—the successor is not on the right, but where exactly is it? In Section 10.3, when necessary, we used recursion and a stack to backtrack to the inorder successor. For a binary tree with a long chain of nodes to the left, however, the stack can be quite large. Also, the recursive procedure calls are time consuming.

By holding valuable information in the right links, a threaded tree implementation of the ADT binary tree does not need to use recursion or a stack. In a threaded tree any right link that was formerly *nil* now is a **thread** or link that points to the inorder successor of that node in the tree. Figure 10.38 illustrates a tree with dotted lines for the threads and with the vertex numbers indicating the order of traversal. Notice that the last node visited, 10, which is as far to the right as possible, is the only node with no inorder successor. Thus, in a threaded tree this node is the only one with a *nil* right link.

To determine if the right link is a thread or not, each node will have an additional boolean field, *thread*, as given in the following definitions:

Figure 10.38

Tree with and without threads

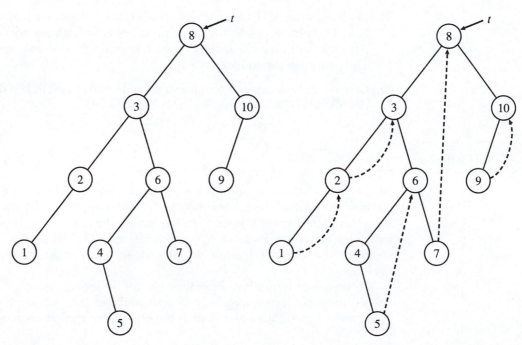

```
type
   BinaryTree  =   ^Node;
   Node        =   record
      left      :   BinaryTree;
      el        :   elType;
      right     :   BinaryTree;
      thread    :   boolean
   end;
var
   p   :   BinaryTree;
```

When $p^\wedge.thread$ is *true*, $p^\wedge.right$ is a thread that points to the inorder successor of p's node. If $p^\wedge.thread$ is *false*, then $p^\wedge.right$ is a link that points to p's nonempty right subtree.

Let us observe how to use the threads to traverse the tree in Figure 10.38. Initially, we visit the last node on the left; then we must find that node's inorder successor. For the tree of Figure 10.38 we follow the thread from node 1 to node 2, visiting the latter. Then we follow another thread to node 3. After visiting, we note that node 3 has a nonempty right subtree, which must contain node 3's inorder successor. We move to that right subtree and repeat the entire process, now starting with node 6. To reiterate, we do the following:

While there are more nodes to visit do the following:
   Travel to the left as far as possible and then visit that node.
   Follow threads back up the tree as far as possible, visiting as we go.
   Go to the right.

The formal definition in pseudocode and ADT operations of the inorder traversal of a threaded tree follows. The coding in Pascal is left for the exercises.

ThreadedInorderTraverse(t, Visit(ArgumentList))
   Procedure to perform an inorder traversal on the threaded binary tree pointed to by *t*, executing *Visit(ArgumentList)* for every element in the tree, where *Visit* is a user-specified procedure and *ArgumentList* is a list of arguments
Input:
   t — pointer to the root of a threaded binary tree
Output:
   Depends on the *Visit* procedure
Assumption:
   t exists.
Algorithm:
   ToRoot(t, cur)
   while not *TreeIsEmpty(cur)* do

      while not *TreeIsEmpty(cur^.left)* do
         ToLeft(cur)

> *Visit*(*ArgumentList*)
>
> **while** *cur^.thread* **and not** *TreeIsEmpty*(*cur^.right*) **do**
>   *ToRight*(*cur*)
>   *Visit*(*ArgumentList*)
>
> *ToRight*(*cur*)

Another advantage of threaded trees is that from any node we can travel through the rest of the tree. With the recursive version of the inorder traversal we must start from the root and build up the stack to find some inorder successors of nodes.

The designs for the threaded tree implementation of most of the remaining ADT binary tree operations are covered in the exercises. To aid in their development, we will make a few comments here about the operations *InsertLeft*, *InsertRight*, *DeletePtLeft*, and *DeletePtRight*. The operations *PreorderTraverse* and *PostorderTraverse* are not covered for the present implementation in the exercises since the threading of this section is for an inorder traversal. Quite often, however, only one kind of traversal method is needed anyway.

Figure 10.39 shows the action of *InsertLeft*(*t, e*), which inserts a vertex containing information from *e* to the left of the node pointed to by *t*. It is assumed that *t*'s node initially has no left child. The newly inserted node has a thread to its parent, the node indicated by *t*.

Figure 10.39

Action of *InsertLeft*

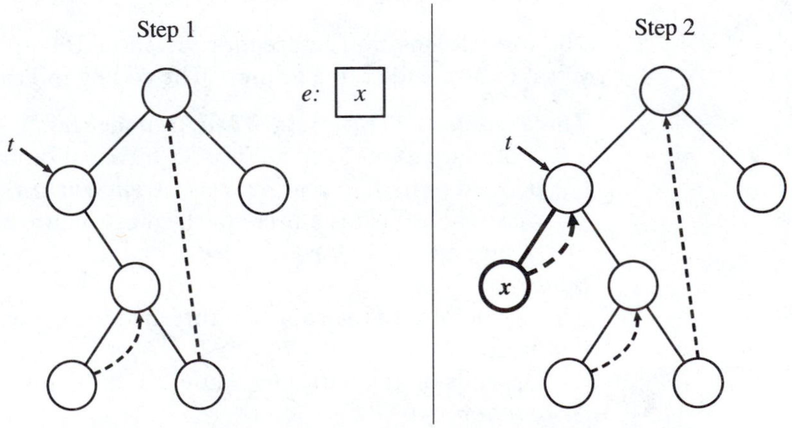

For *InsertRight*(*t, e*) in Figure 10.40, before insertion, *t*'s right link is a thread pointing to the inorder successor. After insertion, the right link of the new node becomes a thread to that same element.

Assuming no left child, *DeletePtRight*(*t*) removes *t*'s node and points *t* toward its right child. As indicated in Figure 10.41, no other links or pointers need to be changed.

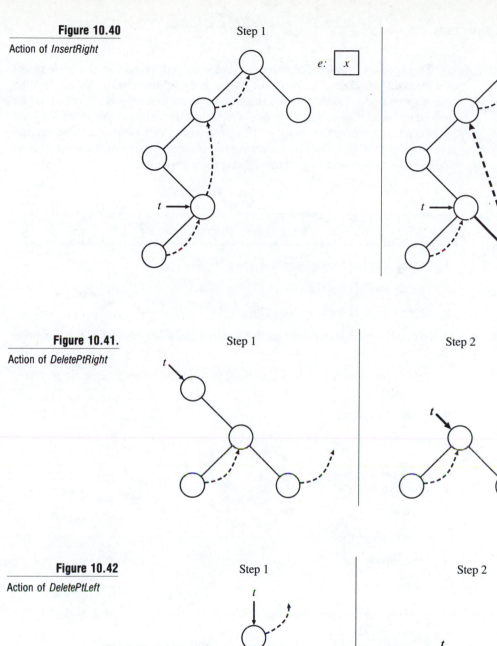

Figure 10.40

Action of *InsertRight*

Step 1

e: [*x*]

Step 2

Figure 10.41.

Action of *DeletePtRight*

Step 1

Step 2

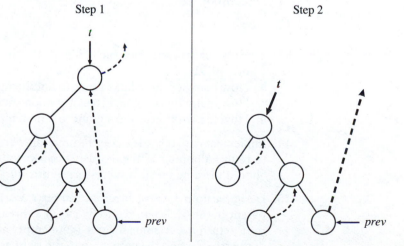

Figure 10.42

Action of *DeletePtLeft*

Step 1

Step 2

The action of *DeletePtLeft*(*t*) is more involved, requiring the adjustment of a thread. For clarity Figure 10.42 shows *prev* pointing to the inorder predecessor of *t*'s node. Consequently, there is a thread from the node indicated by *prev* to its inorder successor, *t*'s node. As part of the deletion this thread should be altered to contain the value of *t*^.*right*, which is a pointer to the inorder successor of *t*'s node. Thus, in removing the node indicated by *t* we connect its predecessor to its successor (if one exists) via a thread.

SECTION 10.4 EXERCISES

1. Sketch threads for the tree in Figure 10.30.

2. Sketch threads for the tree in Figure 10.6.

3. Sketch threads for the tree in Figure 10.7.

In Exercises 4–12 implement with threaded trees the given ADT binary tree operations.

4. *InorderTraverse* as described in the *ThreadedInorderTraverse* algorithm of this section.

5. *MakeTreeEmpty*

6. *InsertRoot*. Be sure to initialize *thread* to be *true*.

7. *InsertLeft*

8. *InsertRight*

9. *DeletePtLeft*

10. *DeletePtRight*

11. *DeleteRoot*

12. *Height*

13. **a.** How many links (not including *t*) are in the tree of 6 nodes in Figure 10.31?
  b. How many of these links point to a nonempty subtree?
  c. How many links are in a tree of *n* nodes that is not threaded?
  d. How many of these links point to a nonempty subtree?

14. Implement with threaded trees the function *ThreadedInorderSuccessor*(*cur*) to return a pointer to the inorder successor of the node pointed to by *cur*. Should there be no such successor, return *nil*.

15. Design a nonrecursive function *Parent*(*t, cur*) to return a pointer to the parent of the node pointed to by *cur* in a threaded tree. If *cur*'s node is the root, return *nil*. Assume the tree is not empty and that *cur* points to a node of the tree. To find the parent, go to the right as far as possible, then follow

Figure 10.43

Five situations involving
cur for *Parent(t, cur)* in
Exercise 15

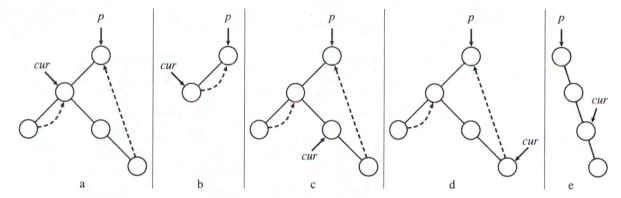

the thread (if one exists) to a node. Figure 10.43 illustrates several possibilities with pointer *p* indicating this node. As shown, the parent of *cur*'s
node is *p*'s node as in Parts a or b of Figure 10.43; or the parent is on the
right of *p*'s left subtree as in Parts c and d. If after going to the right from
cur as far as possible no thread exists, then the parent of *cur*'s node is the
root or a descendant of the root to the right as in Part e.

*In Exercises 16–19 using threaded trees code in Pascal the routines from Sec-
tion 10.2.*

16. Procedure *GenerateTree* from Exercise 16 to read in a binary file and to
place each datum into a threaded binary tree, where the position of insertion is determined by a sequence of 0s and 1s.

17. Boolean function *RightIsEmpty(t)* from Exercise 18 to return *true* if the
root pointed to by *t* does not have a right child.

18. Boolean function *IsLeaf(t)* from Exercise 19 to return *true* if the root
pointed to by *t* is a leaf.

19. Function *SizeTree* from Exercise 20 to return the number of nodes in
a tree.

20. Another method of tree traversal without using a stack is to reverse a
pointer as you pass through a node the first time and restore the pointer
when you return to the node. A boolean field *reversal* of the node is assigned *true* when there is a reversal of the left link. A limited amount of the
implemention of a traversal using this technique is described here.

    a. Starting with the situation in Step 1 of Figure 10.44 and using pseudo-
code and ADT binary tree operations, design a procedure *DownLeft(P,
Q, R)* to produce Step 2.

Figure 10.44

Action of *DownLeft(P, Q, R)* for Exercise 20a

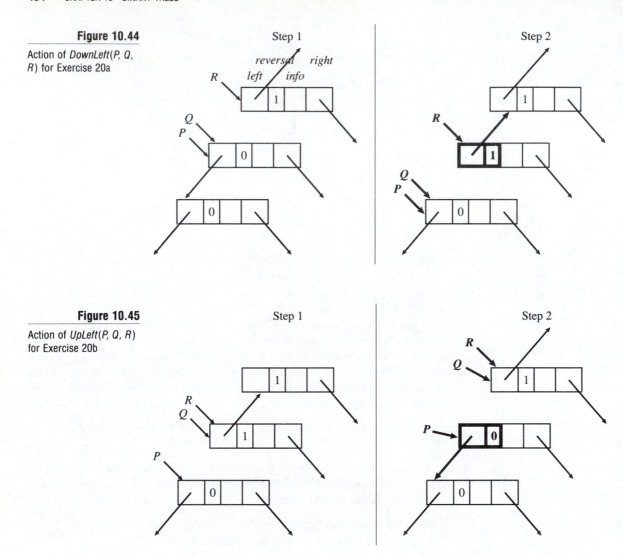

Figure 10.45

Action of *UpLeft(P, Q, R)* for Exercise 20b

b. Using pseudocode and ADT binary tree operations, design a procedure *UpLeft(P, Q, R)* to restore a left pointer as shown in Figure 10.45.

SECTION 10.5 ▽

Binary Search Tree

There are an abundance of applications of binary trees. One of the most prominent leads to an alternative implementation of the ADT table. Recall from Chapter 9 that array implementations have the disadvantage of requiring a knowledge of the maximum number of elements in advance. With an ordered array, although ordered traversals and searches are fast, table insertions and deletions are not. Unordered arrays permit rapid insertions, but deletions, ordered traversals, and searches are tedious. The linked list implementations have the advantage of dynamic memory allocation. Although an ordered traversal is straightforward in an ordered linked list, searches and the search phases of deletions and insertions are slow. Unordered linked lists provide fast insertions but slow ordered traversals, searches, and deletions. The hash table implementation gives us fast searches, insertions, and deletions but ordered traversals are difficult. With a particular type of binary tree, called a **binary search tree**, however, we have the advantage of an expandable linked structure along with fast ordered traversals, searches, insertions, and deletions. We do not need to know the maximum number of elements, but it is possible for the search of the tree for a key to have the same complexity as that of a binary search in an ordered array, $O(\log_2 n)$.

In fact, a binary search tree is ordered, as the building of such a tree shows. The first element to be inserted in the binary tree is placed at the root. If the value of the next element (or of the key) is less than that of the root, that element is installed as the left child. If greater, the element becomes the right child. For the third datum the same comparison is made with the root. As each datum is passed to the left or right, if another node r is encountered, the process of comparison to determine direction is recursively repeated with r being the root.

For example, consider the words

INTEGER, CHAR, REAL, ARRAY, FILE, SET, RECORD

INTEGER is placed in the root as shown in Step 1 of Figure 10.46. Because CHAR is lexically less than INTEGER, we insert CHAR as a left child of the root (Step 2). Starting again at the root, REAL > INTEGER, so that now the root in the developing tree has a right child (Step 3). The fourth word, ARRAY, is also less than the root word, INTEGER, so ARRAY is sent to the left. But another word, CHAR, has already been inserted. Consequently, we repeat the left/right decision process, this time comparing ARRAY and CHAR. With ARRAY < CHAR and with CHAR having no left child, ARRAY is inserted in a node to the left (Step 4). The word FILE initially follows the same path as ARRAY. Alphabetically, FILE is less than INTEGER so we go to the left. But FILE > CHAR, so FILE becomes the right child of CHAR (Step 5). The word SET, being greater than INTEGER and greater than REAL, is moved as far as possible to the right (Step 6). RECORD too goes to the right until comparison with SET sends it to the left (Step 7).

The ordering established for the binary search tree is clearly recursive as the algorithm reveals. In this algorithm and throughout this section, instead of writing the retrieve pointer function references, such as $RetrieveLeft(t)$ or $RetrieveRight(t)$, we employ the Pascal implementations, such as $t\char94.left$ or $t\char94.right$, respectively. Sometimes, $t\char94.left$ or $t\char94.right$ is an argument to a procedure, where the corresponding parameter is variable. Since execution of the procedure may change the value of such a link, the retrieve function reference for the argument does not accurately express the possible change in value of the link. Without ambiguity, however, we will be able to continue to use the ADT

Figure 10.46

Binary search tree with
words INTEGER, CHAR,
REAL, ARRAY, FILE, SET,
RECORD inserted

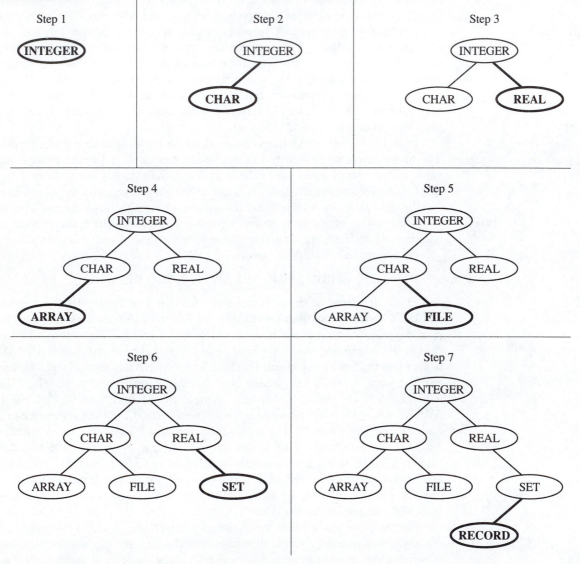

binary tree operation *RetrieveRoot(t)* instead of a Pascal implementation of
$t^\wedge.el$. If this element is a record, we must use a procedure implementation of
the operation because a Pascal function cannot return a composite type.

InsertBST(t, e)

Procedure to insert an element *e* into the binary search tree pointed to by *t*
Input:

　　t — points to a binary search tree
　　e — value of the same type as a node element
Output:

　　t — points to a revised binary search tree
Assumption:

　　The item *e* has the type of an element of the tree to which *t* points.

Figure	Algorithm
{10.46}	
{Step 1}	if *TreeIsEmpty(t)* then
	InsertRoot(t, e)
	else
{Step 2}	if *e < RetrieveRoot(t)* then
	InsertBST(t^.left, e)
{Step 3}	else if *e > RetrieveRoot(t)* then
	InsertBST(t^.right, e)

Notice that because no action is taken when $e = RetrieveRoot(t)$, duplicates are eliminated from the tree. We can, of course, amend the algorithm if
duplicates are desirable for a particular application.

One tremendous advantage of a binary search tree is that ordered traversals are possible. In fact, with a visit printing the value of the node, an inorder traversal of the tree just built yields an alphabetical listing of the words:

ARRAY, CHAR, FILE, INTEGER, REAL, RECORD, SET

Not only can we perform a sorted traversal easily, searches can be performed with the same speed as insertions. For example, suppose we are searching for the word FILE in the binary search tree in Step 7 of Figure 10.46. For
the search, proceed in the same fashion as for an insertion. FILE < INTEGER,
so check the left subtree for the word FILE. Immediately, we have cut the number of words to check in half; FILE is not at the root or in the right subtree of
three words. Then we have FILE > CHAR, and we have again halved the problem. Instead of three words to consider, we are left with one possibility; and, in
fact, we find the word FILE. Suppose, however, we are searching for the word
BOOLEAN. BOOLEAN is less than INTEGER alphabetically; BOOLEAN <
CHAR and BOOLEAN > ARRAY; but ARRAY has no right child, so the search
terminates in BOOLEAN not being found. Notice for the words BOOLEAN
and FILE, the number of words to be searched was cut in half with each comparison, so that a maximum of three comparisons was needed. The right side of
the tree, however, is not as balanced as the left, and we need four comparisons

to search for the words RECORD and RECURSION. The binary search tree search algorithm follows:

SearchBST(t, cur, k)
>   Procedure to point *cur* to the node that contains key *k* in the binary search tree indicated by *t*. If the key is not found, *cur* becomes *nil*.

Input:
>   *t*   — points to a binary search tree
>   *k*   — value of the same type as the key field in a node

Output:
>   *cur* — points to a node with key *k* in the binary search tree pointed to by *t*

Assumption:
>   *k* has the type of a key in binary search tree pointed to by *t*.

Algorithm:
```
    if TreeIsEmpty(t) then            { Key not in tree }
        cur ← nil
    else
        TreeEl   ← RetrieveRoot(t)
        TreeKey ← KeyTreeEl(TreeEl)

        if     k < TreeKey then
            SearchBST(t^.left, cur, k)
        else if k > TreeKey then
            SearchBST(t^.right, cur, k)
        else     { Key found }
            cur ← t
```

In the algorithm if *TreeIsEmpty(t)* is *true*, the operation stops with *cur* becoming *nil*. The procedure also terminates when *t* points to the node containing key *k*, *k = TreeKey*. In this case, we assign *cur* the value of *t*.

This search can be used to define other tablelike operations of *KeyFoundBST* and *RetrieveBST*. The boolean function reference *KeyFoundBST(t, k)* returns *true* if the entry with key *k* is found in the binary search tree indicated by *t*. With the assumption that *KeyFoundBST(t, k)* is *true*, the function reference *RetrieveBST(t, k)* returns the entry with key *k*.

The procedure call *DeleteBST(t, e)* to delete the node containing *e* from the binary search tree pointed to by *t* works under the same assumption and a similar search. But how is the removal of the node achieved? Let us consider various situations in the binary search tree of Figure 10.47, which is used to sort the letters G, S, A, Z, T, D, B, R, E. Suppose we wish to delete the node with letter A. With no left child, A can be removed by use of the procedure call *DeletePtRight(t^.left)*. This call also correctly shifts the subtree whose root contains D into position as the left subtree. (See Figure 10.48.)

Similarly, for the appropriate value of *cur* in Figure 10.49 and with Z's node having no right child, *DeletePtLeft(cur^.right)* can be used to eliminate Z and move T up one level. To summarize, if the node to be deleted has an empty right subtree, we use *DeletePtLeft*; with no left subtree, we employ

Figure 10.47

Binary search tree used to sort the letters G, S, A, Z, T, D, B, R, E

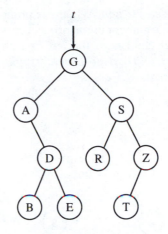

Figure 10.48

Deletion of A from Figure 10.47 through *Delete-PtRight(t^.left)*

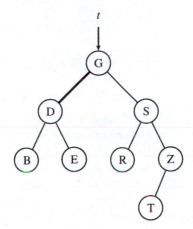

Figure 10.49

Deletion of Z from binary search tree with *Delete-PtLeft(cur^.right)*

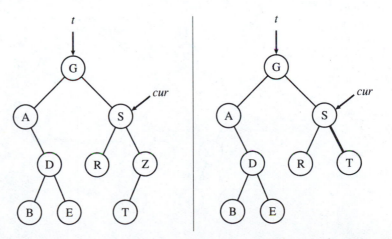

DeletePtRight. When *cur* points to the parent of the soon-to-be-deleted node, the argument of the procedure is *cur^.left* or *cur^.right*, depending on whether that child is to the left or right, respectively. As Figure 10.50 shows, either *DeletePtLeft* or *DeletePtRight* can eliminate a leaf where *cur* points to the parent.

Figure 10.50

Deletion of leaf T from binary search tree with *DeletePtRight(cur^.left)* or *DeletePtLeft(cur^.left)*

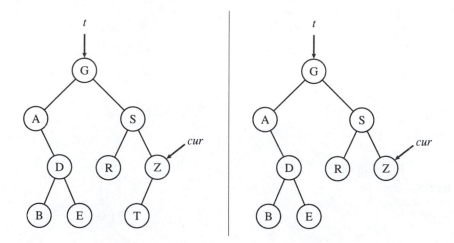

The letter G is a different matter. If we try to shift A up to be the root, the ordering of the table will be destroyed. Since D > A, D should be in the right subtree; but as Figure 10.51 shows, D is erroneously still on the left. We have a similar problem if we move S to the root. (See Figure 10.52.) First, S has two children, R and Z. What happens to them as we try to maintain the binary quality of the tree? Second, R should be in the left subtree since R < S. Clearly, we need to find an alternative.

Figure 10.51

Trying to delete the root of the binary search tree of Figure 10.47 by erroneously moving A into that position

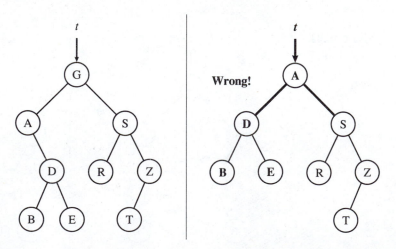

Figure 10.52

Trying to delete the root of the binary search tree of Figure 10.47 by erroneously moving S into that position

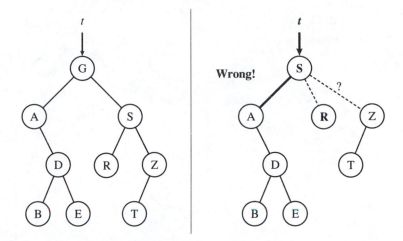

We can turn to a procedure from Section 10.2 for help. *InorderPredOf-Root* of Example 10.2 causes a pointer to indicate the node visited immediately before root G in an inorder traversal of the tree. As we discovered, to find this node, we go to the left subtree and then travel as far as possible to the right. Thus, in Figure 10.47, the inorder predecessor of G is E. Recall that the inorder traversal can alphabetize these letters as

A, B, D, E, G, R, S, T, Z

Every other letter in the left subtree is less than E, and every one in the right subtree is greater because no letter of the tree appears between E and G. Thus, to delete G, we point *cur* to the inorder predecessor E of G as in Step 1 of Figure 10.53. Then we copy E into the root (Step 2). E now appears twice in the table, at the root and in the left subtree. The original E, as with any inorder predecessor, has no right child, however. Therefore, we just repeat the *DeleteBST* process, which calls *DeletePtLeft*, this time to delete the original E from the left subtree. (See Figure 10.53, Step 3.)

Using a search technique similar to that found in *InsertBST* or *SearchBST*, the following algorithm handles the three main situations of deletion of a node: the node has no left child, has no right child, or has both.

DeleteBST(t, k)

Procedure to delete the node with key *k* from the binary search tree pointed to by *t*.

Input:

    t — points to a binary search tree

    k — value of the same type as a key

Output:

    t — points to a revised binary search tree

Assumption:

    An element with key *k* exists in the binary search tree pointed to by *t*.

Figure 10.53

Steps of deleting G from
the binary search tree in
Figure 10.47

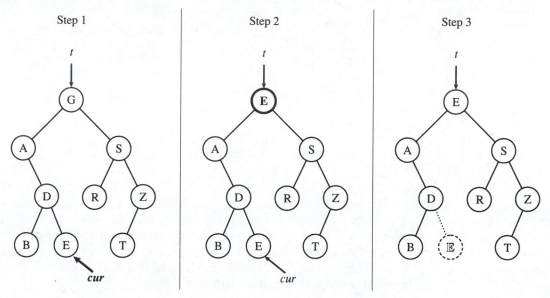

Figure	Algorithm	
	if $k < KeyTreeEl(RetrieveRoot(t))$ then	{ Search }
	DeleteBST(t^.$left$, k)	
	else if $k > KeyTreeEl(RetrieveRoot(t))$ then	
	DeleteBST(t^.$right$, k)	
	else { Element found }	
{10.48, 10.50}	if $TreeIsEmpty(t$^.$left)$ then	
	DeletePtRight(t)	
{10.49}	else if $TreeIsEmpty(t$^.$right)$ then	
	DeletePtLeft(t)	
{10.53}	else	
{Step 1}	InorderPredOfRoot(t, cur)	
{Step 2}	StoreRoot(t, RetrieveRoot(cur))	
{Step 3}	DeleteBST(t^.$left$, KeyTreeEl(RetrieveRoot(cur)))	

▽

SECTION 10.5 EXERCISES

1. Insert the words TREE, TABLE, BINARY, and NETWORK into the binary
   search tree of Figure 10.46.

2. a. Build a binary search tree with the following numbers: 29, 18, 25, 33, 20, 35, 30.
   b. Write the results of an inorder traversal of this tree, where the visit procedure prints the value in the node.
   c. How many comparisons are needed in a search for 29?
   d. For 35?   **e.** For 20?   **f.** For 17?   **g.** For 19?
   h. Show the tree after deletion of 20.
   i. Of 25.   **j.** Of 18.
   k. What is the inorder predecessor of 29?
   l. Show the tree after deletion of 29.
   m. What is the inorder predecessor of 33?
   n. Show the tree after deletion of 33.

3. a. Build a binary search tree with the following numbers: 15, 50, 36, 28, 53, 40, 44, 60, 22.
   b. Write the results of an inorder traversal of this tree where the visit procedure prints the value in the node.
   c. How many comparisons are needed in a search for 50?
   d. For 51?   **e.** For 45?   **f.** For 12?
   g. Show the tree after deletion of 15.
   h. Of 50.   **i.** Of 36.   **j.** Of 53.

Code in Pascal the binary search tree operations of Exercises 4–11. Use a procedure implementation of RetrieveBST.

4. *InsertBST*

5. Procedure *InsertDupBST*, a revision of *InsertBST* that also inserts duplicates.

6. Procedure *BuildBST* that builds a binary search tree from a file of data.

7. *SearchBST*

8. *KeyFoundBST*

9. *RetrieveBST*

10. *DeleteBST*

11. Boolean function *IsBST* that returns *true* if a binary tree is a binary search tree.

12. Implement the ADT table using the ADT binary tree and binary search tree operations.

13. Discuss advantages and disadvantages of the binary search tree implementation of the ADT table.

14. a. Draw the shape of a binary search tree with three nodes that requires a maximum of three comparisons. Do not fill in values at the nodes.

    b. Draw the shape of a binary search tree with three nodes that requires a maximum of two comparisons.

    c. Draw the shape of a binary search tree of seven nodes that requires a maximum of seven comparisons.

    d. Draw the shape of a binary search tree of seven nodes that requires a maximum of three comparisons.

    e. Draw the shape of a binary search tree of 15 nodes that requires the greatest possible number of comparisons.

    f. Draw the shape of a binary search tree of 15 nodes that requires the least possible number of comparisons.

    g. For a binary search tree of $2^m - 1$ nodes, what is the greatest number of possible comparisons?

    h. Describe the shape of the tree that requires that number of comparisons for some items.

    i. For a binary search tree of $2^m - 1$ nodes, what is the shape of the tree that requires the least number of possible comparisons?

    j. In the tree from Part i, what are the least and greatest number of comparisons?

    k. What is the range of the worst-case complexity for a search in a binary search tree of $n = 2^m - 1$ nodes?

15. Let h be the height of a binary search tree of n nodes. Express the worst-case complexity of each of the following operations in terms of h and/or n.

    a. *InsertBST*

    b. *DeleteBST*

    c. *RetrieveBST*

    d. *InorderTraverse*

16. a. Define a function to return the minimum key in a binary search tree.

    b. Define a function to return the maximum key in a binary search tree.

    c. Let h be the height of a binary search tree of n nodes. Express the complexity of the function in Part a in terms of h and/or n.

17. a. What is the cost (in big oh notation) of storage of a binary search tree?

    b. What is the best-case complexity for the process of building a binary search tree?

    c. What is the worst-case complexity?

    d. What is the best-case complexity for the search of a binary search tree?

    e. What is the worst-case complexity?

18. One variation on building a binary search tree is to always pick the median of a set as the value placed at the root. Thus, for building a tree with the words INTEGER, CHAR, REAL, ARRAY, FILE, SET, RECORD, we would first insert the middle word alphabetically, INTEGER. In this situation the tree remains balanced.

    a. Repeat Exercise 2, Part a, using medians.

    b. Repeat Exercise 3, Part a, using medians.

c. Suppose you are using a procedure to find a median of a range of array elements, and the algorithm has complexity $O(3n)$. Find the complexity of the procedure to build the binary search tree using medians.

d. Find the complexity of the procedure to search such a binary search tree.

▽

PROGRAMMING PROJECTS

1. Design a program to read a text file and perform word analysis. The program should isolate each word, placing the word into a binary search tree. Each node should contain a word and the number of times it has occurred in the text. Print the number of distinct words in alphabetical order along with their frequency. For simplicity assume each word is a contiguous sequence of letters.

2. A linguist wishes to analyze all two-letter sequences that occur in a particular text. For example, in the phrase "insert in linked list" the frequency of each two-letter sequence is as follows:

Two-Letter Sequence	Frequency
ed	1
er	1
in	3
is	1
ke	1
li	2
hk	1
ns	1
rt	1
se	1
st	1

One data structure to hold the sequences and their frequencies involves an array *first* of pointers indexed by the letters of the alphabet. Each of these array elements points to a binary search tree consisting of the second characters along with the frequency of that sequence. For the phrase above, *first*['i'] is a pointer to a binary search tree containing the letters "n" and "s" with associated frequencies 3 and 1, respectively. Figure 10.54 displays this structure.

Write a program to read a text file and print out all two-letter sequences in alphabetical order along with their frequencies.

Figure 10.54

Array *first* for Project 1

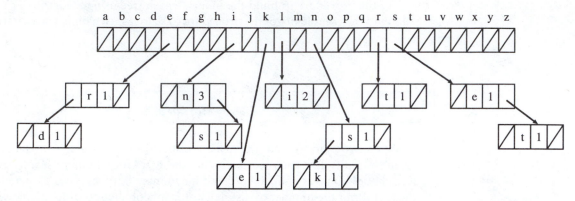

The following is an auxiliary question for Project 2:

As in Figure 10.54, sketch the appearance of this structure after analysis of the following saying by Benjamin Franklin: "If you would be loved, love and be lovable."

SECTION 10.6 **AVL Tree**

In a binary search tree that has the most desirable shape, the complexity of the search operation is at most $O(\log_2 n)$. This best-case scenario occurs when the tree is very bushy, as in Figure 10.55. And we only need to make at most $\lceil \log_2 7 \rceil = 3$ comparisons to search for any item in this tree of $n = 7$ nodes.

Figure 10.55

Binary search tree with 7 nodes and at most 3 comparisons for any search

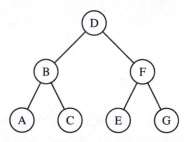

But suppose we insert letters into the tree in the following order: A B C D E F G. Unfortunately, the resulting binary search tree in Figure 10.56 is linear, called a **skewed tree**; and to perform a search for G or any lexically greater letter requires $n = 7$ comparisons. The search has degenerated to a sequential one with the resulting poor run-time performance of $O(n)$. Imagine the impact of this change in the shape of the tree for $n = 2^{10} - 1 = 1023$ items. The best

Figure 10.56

Skewed binary search tree with 7 nodes and at most 7 comparisons for any search

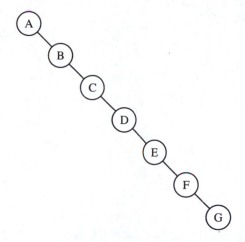

possible situation will result in a full binary tree of height 10 and a search length of at most $\lceil \log_2(2^{10} - 1) \rceil = 10$. If, however, the structure has 1023 nodes strung out in a line, the height and maximum number of comparisons in a search will be $n = 1023$, more than 100 times the value obtained with the better tree.

Both trees hold the same data but their structure is radically different, due solely to a variation in the order of insertion; and that difference has a big impact on the performance of the search operations. The operation of searching is particularly important since we must search not only for the retrieval of values, but as a prerequisite to the building of the tree and to most insertions and deletions. Much research has been done in methods of reorganizing binary search trees to minimize the height and, thus, to maximize the searching efficiency. One alternative is to store data in an AVL tree. An **AVL tree** (named after its creators G. M. *Adel'son-Vel'skii* and E. M. *Landis*) is a type of binary search tree where the heights of left and right subtrees of any node are equal or differ by 1. Because the tree remains **height balanced**, the worst-case complexity of a search is $O(\log_2 n)$.

For any node in a binary tree we define its **balance factor** to be the height of the left subtree minus the height of the right subtree. Using pseudocode and the ADT binary tree operation *Height*, for a pointer t to the node, the balance factor can be defined as

BalanceFactor(t) ← *Height*(t^.*left*) − *Height*(t^.*right*).

For an AVL tree, the balance factor for each node is 0, 1, or -1, depending on whether the left and right subtrees have the same height, the height of the left is one more than the right, or the height of the right is one more than the left, respectively. Figure 10.57 displays an AVL tree with balance factors beside the nodes. By contrast, the tree in Figure 10.58 is not an AVL tree since nodes C and G have balance factors of -2 and 2, respectively.

Figure 10.57

AVL tree with balance factors indicated by the nodes

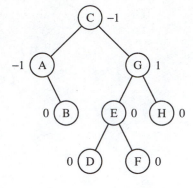

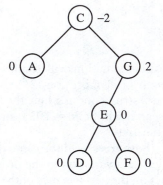

In studying the AVL tree we are actually considering an alternative implementation of the binary search tree. The type definitions and variable declarations are very similar to those found in Sections 10.3 and 10.5. As with threaded binary trees in Section 10.4, however, we have an extra field, called *balance*, with each node's record. This field stores the balance factor for that vertex. The type definition of *Node* follows:

```
type
  . . .
  AVL          =    ^Node;
  Node         =    record
    left       :    AVL;
    el         :    elType;
    right      :    AVL;
    balance    :    -2..2
  end;
```

In the text we consider various situations for the insertion, leaving the details of the coding in Pascal for the exercises. Moreover, we do not attempt to be comprehensive in covering this topic. Instead, we try to impart the concept underlying AVL trees and one method of rebalancing a binary search tree.

Rebalancing is not always necessary. For example, if we insert a letter greater than H into the AVL tree of Figure 10.57, we still have an AVL tree. Figure 10.59 displays this tree with the letter J inserted, with the balance factors updated, but with no further adjustments. In fact, it has been shown that rebalancing after an insertion is only necessary about half of the time.

Figure 10.59

AVL tree of Figure 10.57 after insertion of H

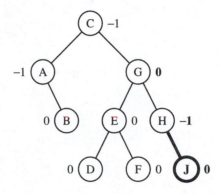

We encounter a situation where we must rebalance, however, when we attempt to insert the letter A into the AVL tree of Step 1 in Figure 10.60. Inserting as we would in a binary search tree yields the unbalanced tree of Step 2. To reorganize this tree into an AVL tree again, we must eliminate the balance factor of 2 for the root. This reorganization is accomplished by shifting some nodes to the right to adjust the subtrees' heights, while at the same time maintaining the ordering of a binary search tree. We achieve this goal in Step 3 through a **right rotation** around a pivot of G. Not only have we reduced the height of the tree and the resulting maximum search length from 4 to 3, we have maintained the binary search tree. Figure 10.61 generalizes this situation for the insertion, where each oval before insertion stands for a subtree of height *h*.

The action of the right rotation, presented in detail in Figure 10.62, is mirrored in the pseudocode for the right-rotation operation below. We have ignored the balance factors in this and other procedures because their consideration is rather involved for some of the operations. We have covered this topic as an introduction to the concept of rebalancing and to the advantages of height-balanced trees. Interested students may wish to refer to an upper-level data structures textbook for a more detailed discussion of AVL trees.

***RightRotation*(*t*)**
        Procedure to perform a right rotation on the tree *t*
Input:
        t — points to a binary tree
Output:
        t — points to a revised binary tree
Assumption:
        t exists.

Figure 10.60

Insertion of A into an AVL tree

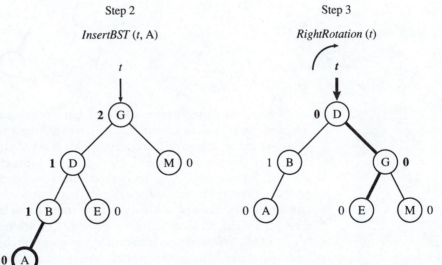

Figure 10.61

Generalization of the situation in Figure 10.60, where each oval stands for a subtree of height h or $h + 1$ as indicated

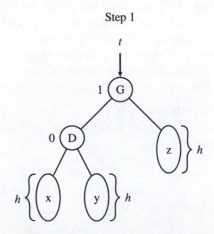

Figure 10.61

continued

Step 2

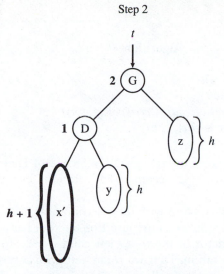

Step 3

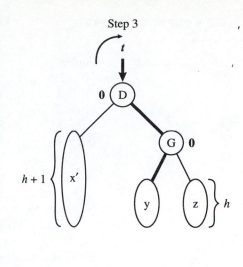

Figure 10.62

Action of *RightRotation*(*t*) on tree in Step 2 of Figure 10.61

Step 1

Step 2

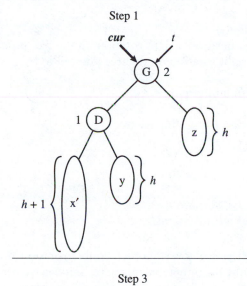

Step 3

Step 4

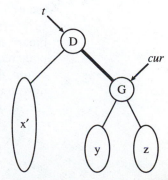

Figure	Algorithm
{10.62}	
{Step 1}	*ToRoot(t, cur)*
{Step 2}	*ToLeft(t)*
{Step 3}	*StoreLeft(cur, RetrieveRight(t))*
{Step 4}	*StoreRight(t, cur)*

The mirror image of the tree shape in Step 2 of Figure 10.61 has a root with a balance factor of −2 needing a left rotation. Such a rotation is considered in the exercises.

Another possibility arises with the insertion of D in the tree of Step 1, Figure 10.63. As Step 2 indicates, after insertion the root has a balance factor of 2, while the balance factor of the root's left child is −2. To rebalance this tree requires a double rotation. First we rotate left with a pivot of the left child, node C; then we rotate right with a pivot of the root, node K. This double rotation, pictured in Figure 10.63, can be achieved by calling the procedure *LeftRotation* followed by *RightRotation*.

LeftRightRotation(t)
Procedure to perform a right rotation on the tree pointed to by $t^\wedge.left$
and then a right rotation on the tree pointed to by t
Input:
t — points to a binary tree
Output:
t — points to a revised binary tree
Assumption:
t exists.

Figure	Algorithm
{10.63}	
{Step 3}	*LeftRotation(t^.left)*
{Step 4}	*RightRotation(t)*

In the exercises we cover another double rotation procedure, *RightLeftRotation*. Actually, the only rebalancing techniques we need to restore an AVL tree after insertion or deletion are the two single rotations, left and right, and the two double rotations, left-right and right-left.

Certainly, algorithms for AVL trees are more involved than those for the binary search trees. When needed, rebalancing takes computer time, and each node requires an additional field for the balance factor. If in a particular application there are significantly more retrievals than insertions and deletions, however, a rebalancing technique is probably worth the effort, time, and space.

Figure 10.63

Action of the double left-right rotation after insertion of D in an AVL tree

Step 1

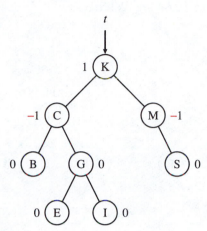

Step 2

InsertBST (t, D)

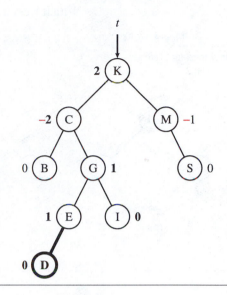

Step 3

LeftRotation (t^.left)

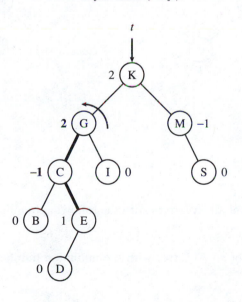

Step 4

RightRotation (t)

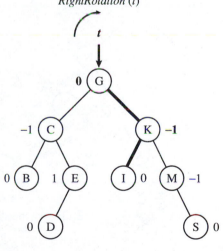

1. Which trees in Figure 10.64 are AVL trees?

Figure 10.64

Binay trees for Exercises
1, 6, and 7

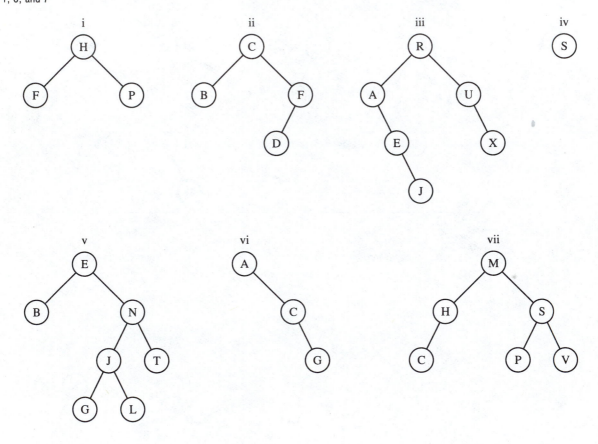

2. Draw the shapes of all AVL trees with the following number of nodes:

    a. 2   **b.** 3   **c.** 4   **d.** 6   **e.** 7

3. Draw the shape of an AVL tree with the minimum number of nodes and with a height of

    a. 1   **b.** 2   **c.** 3   **d.** 4   **e.** 5

For Exercises 4–6 insert the letter in the indicated AVL tree, if necessary, rebalancing and indicating the type of rotation. Draw the resulting AVL tree with balance factors.

4. H in Figure 10.60, Step 3

5. F in Figure 10.60, Step 1

6. E in Figure 10.64, Part ii

7. Perform a rotation on Part v of Figure 10.64 to convert the tree to an AVL tree.

8. Deletion of node B in Figure 10.57 causes the tree to become unbalanced. Perform a rotation to restore the tree to an AVL tree.

9. Code the procedure *RightRotation* in Pascal.

10. a. Draw a situation similar to that of Figure 10.60 where a left rotation is needed.
    b. Design a procedure *LeftRotation* to accomplish this left rotation.
    c. Code this procedure in Pascal.

11. Code the procedure *LeftRightRotation(t)* in Pascal as designed in the text.

12. a. Design the procedure *LeftRightRotation(t)* in Pascal by relinking and without calling *LeftRotation* and *RightRotation*.
    b. Code this design in Pascal.

13. a. Draw a situation similar to that of Figure 10.63 where a right-left rotation is needed.
    b. Design a procedure *RightLeftRotation* to accomplish this double right-left rotation by calling procedures for single rotations.
    c. Code this procedure in Pascal.
    d. Design *RightLeftRotation(t)* by relinking and without calling *LeftRotation* and *RightRotation*.
    e. Code this procedure in Pascal.

14. Let $f(h)$ be the minimum number of vertices in an AVL tree of height h. Consider such a tree to be composed of a root, a left AVL subtree of height $h - 1$, and a right AVL subtree of height $h - 2$, where each subtree has a minimum number of nodes. Complete the recursive definition of f.

$$f(1) = \underline{\quad a \quad}$$
$$f(2) = \underline{\quad b \quad}$$
$$f(h) = \underline{\quad c \quad} + \underline{\quad d \quad} + \underline{\quad e \quad}, \text{ for } h \geq 3$$

15. It can be shown that the average path length in a random binary tree of n nodes is $2\ln(n) - 1.845$, where $\ln(n) = \log_e(n)$. For the worst case, where the tree is linear, the average path length is $n/2$. In a balanced tree, however, the average path length is proportional to $\log_2(n)$.
    a. Calculate $\log_2(n)$, $2\ln(n) - 1.845$, and $n/2$ for $n = 2^{10} = 1024$.
    b. Repeat Part a for $n = 2^{20} = 1,048,576$.
    c. Use the fact that $\log_2(n) = \ln(n)/\ln(2)$ to show that there is only about a 38% increase in the average path length from the optimum binary tree to the random one constructed without concern for balancing.

    d. Based on Part c, is the random situation close to the optimum or to the worst case?

    e. For large *n* and random data, is it best to balance the binary search tree?

SECTION 10.7 More Applications of Binary Trees

In Section 10.5 we covered binary search trees, which provide a binary tree structure with an associated ordering. Such trees allow us to search with a worst-case complexity of $O(\log_2 n)$ for height-balanced trees, the same order as a search for an item in an ordered array. (See Exercises 14–17 of Section 10.5.) In this section we cover some additional applications of binary trees.

Example 10.3.

Expression Tree.

▼

An expression, such as A ∗ B / (C + D ∗ E), can be stored in a binary tree with each binary operator at a node, the root of a tree, with its first operand in the left subtree and its second operand in the right. To see this placement, we first write the expression with full parentheses, taking into account operator precedence:

$$((A * B) / (C + (D * E)))$$

Figure 10.65

Steps to store the expression A ∗ B / (C + D ∗ E) in an expression tree

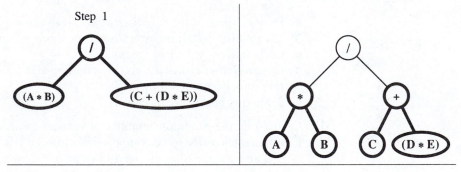

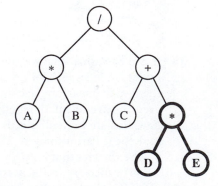

The outside parentheses group operands (A * B) and (C + (D * E)), and the operator is division , /. Thus, as Step 1 of Figure 10.65 demonstrates, / is at the root, the expression (A * B) is in the left subtree, and (C + (D * E)) is in the right. Repeating the process with each operand, we have the tree of Step 2 with * and + now in internal nodes and A, B, and C in leaf nodes. Step 3 of Figure 10.65 completes the process.

Performing a postorder traversal of this **expression tree** produces the expression in postfix notation: A B * C D E * + /. Similarly, a preorder traversal yields **prefix form** of the expression: / * A B + C * D E. Moreover, an inorder traversal returns the infix expression as long as we are careful to surround each subexpression with parentheses. Printing a left parenthesis before and a right parenthesis after traversal of each subtree of the expression yields this infix expression with full parentheses, ((A * B) / (C + (D * E))).

Applications of trees are prevalent in computer science. In the next three examples and in the exercises we consider some uses of binary trees in artificial intelligence, game theory, and character encoding.

The brilliant mathematician Alan Turing made an impact on computer science in each of these areas. In 1936 he developed the Turing machine, which is a simple mathematical model of a computer. In work, done before the invention of the first computer in the 1940s, Turing developed the concept of computability theory. He showed that some functions cannot be computed; there are problems for which no algorithmic solution exists.

Alan Turing's concepts were published when he was only 25 years old. A little more than five years later he was heading the British team that broke the code of the German high command in World War II. Before the decade of the 1940s was over, he was working on the idea of a computer displaying intelligence, what we know now as artificial intelligence (AI). He wrote the first program for playing chess, a problem in AI that still poses challenges. In fact, each year computer chess championships are held in which the best chess programs compete.

Example 10.4.

Decision Tree.

A **decision tree** can be employed in some artificial intelligence and software engineering applications. In this binary tree a series of yes/no questions are stored in internal nodes. A "yes" answer indicates a branch in one direction, while a "no" points in the other direction. The leaf nodes store the decision. Figure 10.66 presents a decision tree to determine whether to accept or reject a customer for a store credit card, and if accepted, to determine the credit limit. For example, a customer who has a major credit card, good credit, does not own a house, but has a salary over $15,000 is eligible for a card with a limit of $500.

Figure 10.66

Decision tree for Example 10.4

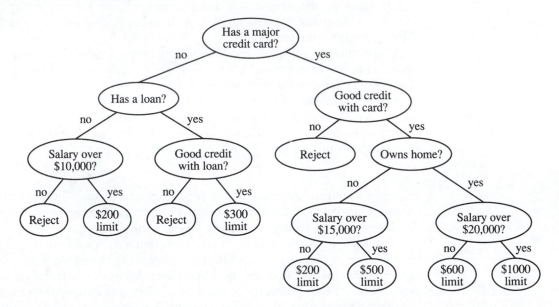

Example 10.5.

Game Tree.

▼

Sometimes the possible moves in a game are represented in a binary **game tree**. Suppose a value indicating the desirability of a game situation to you is assigned to each node at a certain level of the tree. Perhaps the value is a count of board pieces, the amount of center control of the board, or a number located in a table. Figure 10.67 illustrates a situation where one of two choices must be made for each board situation. If it is your move at the root, you have two possible choices. Presuming that higher values are more advantageous, you would undoubtedly choose the move with the maximum value, the move represented on the left. Had it been your opponent's move, however, that person should have picked the move indicated on the right to obtain a minimum value of 2.

Step 1 of Figure 10.68 pictures a larger tree with your possible moves at the top and at level 3. Finding yourself at any of the four game situations of level 3, you are forced to make a left or a right choice. You should take the

Figure 10.67

Part of a tree for Example 10.5

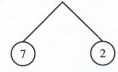

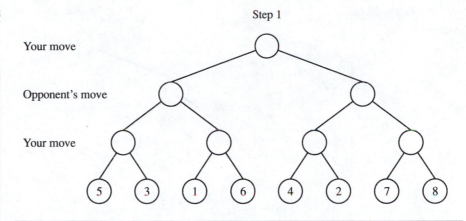

Figure 10.68

Development of minimax
tree for Example 10.5

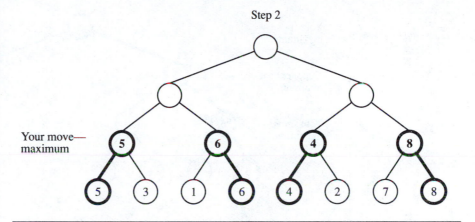

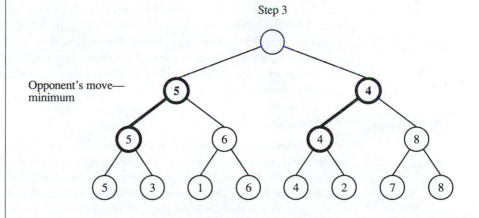

Figure 10.68

continued

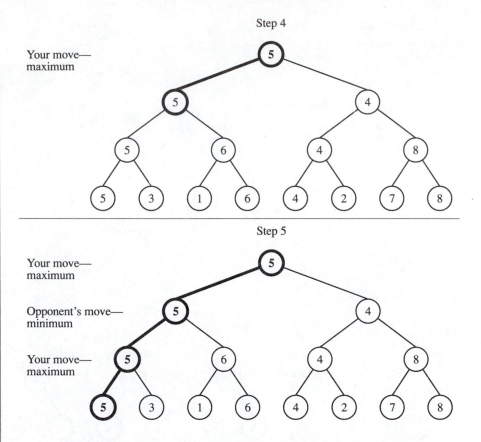

direction that will yield the highest score. Step 2 indicates these maximum values. But at level 2 your opponent wishes to make a move that is detrimental to you. Thus, your opponent should always take the direction with a minimum value as shown in Step 3. Your move, however, will be a maximum. Step 4 displays the completed **minimax tree.** Presuming that your opponent will choose the minimum value, Step 5 marks the series of moves to secure the best possible situation for you.

| **Example 10.6.** | **Huffman Code.**

▼ A **Huffman code** encodes so that the bits of one character's code do not appear at the first of another character's representation. Thus, the codes for the characters can be of different lengths, with characters such as "e" that appear frequently having a shorter encoding structure. This contrasts with the ASCII encoding system where every character is represented by a seven-bit structure. For a lengthy text, encoding with a Huffman code can use significantly fewer bits than encoding with the ASCII system.

The binary tree in Figure 10.69 represents a Huffman code for the lowercase letters, blank, and period. A left branch indicates a zero bit and a right

Figure 10.69

Binary tree containing a
Huffman code for Ex-
ample 10.6

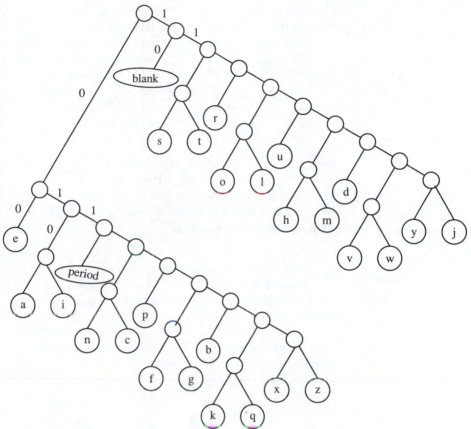

edge, the bit one. The information portions of the leaves store the characters;
internal nodes contain no data. Referring to the tree in Figure 10.69, we see
that the short string 00 encodes the most frequently encountered letter, "e,"
and no other letter starts with 00. To find the code for "m," we follow the path
from the root to "m." As we travel through the tree we write down the bits, a 0
bit for each left branch and 1 for each right one. Thus, "m" is encoded as
11111101.

   To decode a string we follow the path from the root indicated by the bit
string (0 → left, 1 → right) until we arrive at a leaf. We write down the letter
and start the process over with the next bit in the string. Thus, the bit string

   11111111110100110011100011100101111101111110111011111111
   00011100011111110011010101100000111001111111010111111110000
   1111010111100110

encodes "jason murdered. send help." The following grouping of bits helps to
show the encoding for each letter:

1111111111	→ j	0100	→ a	1100	→ s
111100	→ o	011100	→ n	10	→ blank
11111101	→ m	111110	→ u	1110	→ r
11111110	→ d	00	→ e	1110	→ r
00	→ e	11111110	→ d	0110	→ period
10	→ blank	10	→ blank	1100	→ s
00	→ e	011100	→ n	11111110	→ d
10	→ blank	11111100	→ h	00	→ e
111101	→ l	011110·	→ p	0110	→ period

Notice that the message is encoded with 130 bits, whereas ASCII would demand 189 bits for the same characters.

The following algorithm decodes and prints a message from a line of a text file using a tree similar to the tree of Figure 10.69, which is already stored in memory and pointed to by t.

Decode(f, t)

    Procedure to decode a message on a line of a text file. The message is encoded with a Huffman code, and the tree for decoding is already stored in memory and is pointed to by t.

Input:

    f — text file with each line containing an encoded message

    t — points to a tree containing a Huffman code

Printed output:

    Decoded message

Algorithm:

```
ToRoot(t, cur)                                      {Start at top}

while not eoln(f) do
    read(f, ch)
    if ch = '0' then
        ToLeft(cur)                                 { Move to left }
        if TreeIsEmpty(RetrieveLeft(cur)) then      { Character found }
            print the information in cur's node
            ToRoot(t, cur)                          {Start over}
    else if ch = '1' then
        ToRight(cur)                                { Move to right }
        if TreeIsEmpty(RetrieveRight(cur)) then     { Character found }
            print the information in cur's node
            ToRoot(t, cur)                          {Start over}
    else
        NotABitError

if cur ≠ t then                                     { Bits left over }
    IncorrectCodeError
readln(f)                                           { Skip eoln marker }
```

Only bits '0' and '1' are to appear in the message, which is terminated with an end-of-line marker. The procedure *NotABitError* will be called if any other characters appear. If there are bits left over at the end of the message, we call the *IncorrectCodeError* procedure. For example, suppose after writing a decoded letter we have the final bit string 1111. Since these four bits do not encode any character, we must have an error. Perhaps a bit was omitted from the encoded message.

▽
SECTION 10.7 EXERCISES

1. Draw an expression tree to contain the expression (A + B) * C − D / E.

2. Repeat Exercise 1 for A − B * C / D + E.

3. Design a function to evaluate an expression held in a tree. Assume the information portion of each node holds a character that is a binary operator, '+', '−', '*', '/', or a letter from 'A' to 'F'. The values of the variables should be previously read or assigned.

4. Draw a decision tree to determine someone's eligibility to register to vote in a county. A person can register in that county if he or she is 18 or older; a resident of the county; appears in person at the county courthouse with a valid driver's license or picture identification; or mails in the proper form.

5. Design a procedure to store the information from a decision tree in a file in preorder form.

6. **a.** Complete the values in the minimax tree of Figure 10.70.

Figure 10.70

Minimax tree for Exercise 6, Part a

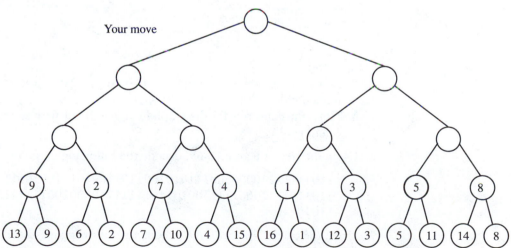

b. Design functions *YourMove* and *OpponentsMove* to return the values in a minimax tree, presuming positive values are stored in the leaves. Suppose that before a value is computed for a node, a zero is stored in the information field.

7. In game theory graphs are often used to discover how to play a game to win. Suppose the graph in Figure 10.71 maps the possible moves in a game. Starting with *s*, the object is to arrive at the goal *g*. One path is from *s* to *a* to *g*, but there are other possibilities. A game tree can be used to list all the paths where we exclude cycles. After all, we do not want to go in circles by following cycles such as *s, a, d, b, s, a, d, b*. Figure 10.71 gives the tree of all possible paths from *s* to *g*, where no node is repeated in the path from the root. Notice that there are four noncyclic paths that arrive at the goal.

Figure 10.71

Graph and associated game tree for Exercise 7

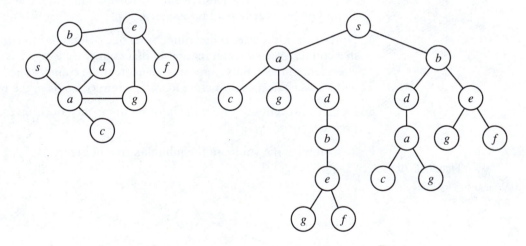

a. Draw the game tree for the graph in Figure 10.71 with starting position *a* and goal *d*.

b. Draw the game tree for the graph in Figure 10.71 with starting position *b* and goal *c*.

8. Using the tree of Figure 10.69, decode the following message:

110111111000010011101010011011001011100101111001111110
110110111100011111001011011111110000100111111001000111
11010110

9. Using the tree of Figure 10.69, encode the following message:

the butler did it.

10. a. Does the following decode a legal message using the tree of Figure 10.69?

　　　　0111110001110101111001

b. Why or why not?

11. Write in Pascal the procedure *Decode* from Example 10.6.

▽

PROGRAMMING PROJECTS

1. Design a program to read an expression in prefix notation and place the operators and operands in an expression tree. Then write the expression in infix notation with full parentheses and in postfix notation. Assume the only operators are binary, the variables are single letters, the constants are single digits, and there are no blanks.

2. Design a program to read the information of Figure 10.66 from a text file and store that information in a decision tree. Then interactively question a customer using the tree and return the applicant's eligibility for a credit card and credit limit.

In the file have the data stored in prefix order with the string for a node stored on one line. Information for an internal node ends with a question mark. An answer ends with a period.

3. Design a program to read a Huffman code from a file and place it in an encoding tree. The text file containing the code has a string of bits followed by a blank and the character that the string encodes on each line. Then read a message, print the encoded message, and send that message in Huffman code to a binary file containing boolean values with *true* representing 1 and *false* 0. Reading from the same or another binary file of boolean values until encountering the end-of-file marker, decode and print the message.

4. Write a program for the computer to play the game Nim with a user. The game starts with a certain number of sticks. Players take turns, each removing 1, 2, or 3 sticks. The last player to pick up a stick loses. Have the computer pick at random the number of sticks and who goes first. If one exists on your system, use a built-in random number generator. If not, create your own, such as the one described in Appendix A.

Have the computer play intelligently using a minimax technique. Use -1 and $+1$ for losing and winning moves, respectively. One method of computing the number of sticks to pick up involves two indirectly recursive procedures, one to determine the present player's move and the other to evaluate the move of an intelligent opponent.

CHAPTER 11

Sorting

Introduction

One major application in computer science is the sorting of information in a table. Files and reports may require that data be arranged with names in alphabetical order, stock numbers in ascending order, or dollar amounts in descending order. In this chapter we present several algorithms for sorting and examine their complexities. There is no one best method. As we will discover, different collections of data, implementations, and circumstances demand different sorting techniques.

Insertion Sort

Often data is stored in an array or linked list of records where sorting applies to a key field or fields. For presentation of the basic techniques, however, we concentrate on sorting an array or linked list of characters. These ideas can easily be extended to a much larger record with key field. Later in the chapter we consider alternative implementations of these techniques for records that are large in comparison to the key.

The first technique to be studied, the **insertion sort**, is a straightforward method that is useful for small collections of data, about 100 records or less. As we will see later, the method can also be used in conjunction with more efficient sorting techniques.

To illustrate the process, suppose you have a loose-leaf folder of notes for a course. Luckily, you have numbered the pages because just as you walk into the cafeteria you trip, and notes fly everywhere. Now you are faced with the arduous task of putting the notes back in order.

You grab one page, then another. You place this second page in order, either before or after the first page. Then you pick up a third page and insert that page into its proper, relative position. Your folder of sorted papers is growing. Suppose that with each new paper you start at the back of the folder, comparing page numbers with the new item. As long as the page numbers in the folder are greater than the number on the new page, you keep searching. Eventually, you can stop searching and slip the paper into its proper location.

We will now illustrate the insertion sort with an array a of n characters. For simplicity we omit the quotations around each character in the examples of this chapter.

For implementation of this technique it will be easier to place a sentinel value in array element $a[0]$. This value should be smaller than any possible data item. Thus, for a character array the character with ordinal number 0, *null*, is an appropriate choice. For an array of integers, we would use $-maxint$.

Figure 11.1 illustrates the concept of an insertion sort. Initially, the boldfaced subarray with $a[0]$ and $a[1]$, abbreviated $a[0..1]$, in Step 1 is certainly sorted. Thus, we start by inserting the second character, D, into the appropriate location to maintain the alphabetical order (Step 2). Now, the boldfaced subarray of the first three elements, $a[0..2]$, is in alphabetical order, and we turn our attention to the third character, Z (Step 3). We take each element, $a[i]$, one at a time from i equals 2 to i equals n. Before insertion of the value of $a[i]$, the subarray from $a[0]$ to $a[i-1]$ is sorted; after insertion, $a[0..i]$ is correctly ordered.

Figure 11.1

Action of insertion sort on an array

continued on next page

Figure 11.1

continued

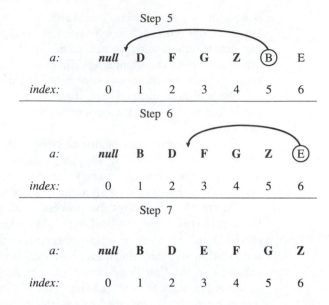

Using the ADT table operation *InsertTable* we present the general outline of the insertion sort below. Before invoking *InsertTable*($a[0..(i-1)]$, *temp*), the subarray $a[0]$, $a[1]$, . . . , $a[i-1]$ is sorted. Thus, when $i = 2$, only the subarray $a[0..1]$ is sorted. We insert $a[2]$ so that on the next iteration, $a[0..2]$ is ordered.

InsertionSort(a, n):
    $a[0]$ ← a low sentinel value
    for i from 2 to n do
        temp ← $a[i]$
        InsertTable($a[0..(i-1)]$, *temp*)

On each iteration of the *for* loop, the value of $a[i]$, which is to be inserted, is stored in a temporary variable, *temp*. But how do we implement *InsertTable* ($a[0..(i-1)]$, *temp*) on an array? Recall from our discussion of an ordered array implementation of tables in Section 9.2 that we find the appropriate location for *temp* and move the elements from that location to the end of the subarray up one element. Because this upward movement destroys the old value of $a[i]$, we need *temp* to hold the value for further processing. The search phase to find the location *loc* in the sorted subarray starts by comparing *temp* with the largest element, $a[i-1]$. If *temp* is greater than or equal to that element, *temp* belongs at the end. If not, we continue searching down the subarray as long as the entries are larger than *temp*. We are guaranteed to find a stopping point, because $a[0]$ contains the sentinel value, which is smaller than any of the other array elements. The installation phase moves all the subarray elements in $a[loc..(i-1)]$ up one position. Then we assign *temp* to the array element $a[loc]$.

    $a[loc]$ ← *temp*

Instead of separate iterations for the search and installation phases of *InsertTable*, we can combine the two. Figure 11.2 illustrates the insertion of *temp* = F, the value of *a*[4], into the subarray *a*[0..3]. We start at the top of the subarray, moving elements up one at a time until we find the location for *temp*. After execution of this loop, we have found the proper location, *loc*, for *temp* and also have made room for the value. All that remains is to copy *temp* into *a*[*loc*]. The following gives a more detailed design of the insertion sort.

InsertionSort(a, n)

Procedure to perform an insertion sort on the first *n* elements of an array *a*

Input:

    a — array

    n — number of elements

Output:

    a — revised array

Assumption:

    Array *a* is declared to have a subrange index type 0..*m* with *n* ≤ *m*.

Figure	Algorithm
	$a[0] \leftarrow$ a low sentinel value
	for *i* from 2 to *n* do
{11.2}	
{Step 1}	*temp* $\leftarrow a[i]$
	loc $\leftarrow i$
{Steps 2–4}	while $a[loc - 1] > temp$ do
	$a[loc] \leftarrow a[loc - 1]$
	loc $\leftarrow loc - 1$
{Step 5}	$a[loc] \leftarrow temp$

Figure 11.2

Combined search and installation phase of *InsertTable*(*a*[0..3], F)

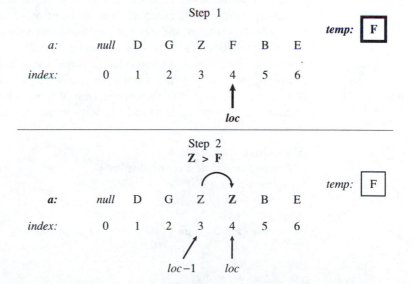

Step 1

temp: F

a: null D G Z F B E

index: 0 1 2 3 4 5 6

↑
loc

Step 2
Z > F

temp: F

a: null D G Z Z B E

index: 0 1 2 3 4 5 6

loc −1 *loc*

continued on next page

Figure 11.2

continued

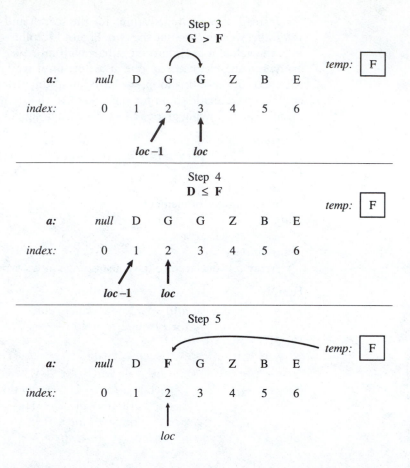

In some instances sentinel values are hard to find. For example, suppose our array contains real numbers that can be positive or negative. Unlike *maxint* for the largest integer, there is no predefined constant in Standard Pascal for the largest or smallest real number that can be stored in the particular computer we are using; and we want to make our procedure machine independent. To terminate looping when *temp* is smaller than $a[1]$, one technique employs an extra test, $(loc > 1)$, instead of the comparison of *temp* with a sentinel value in $a[0]$. Such an algorithm reads as follows with variations from the above algorithm marked in boldface:

Alternative Algorithm
{ No assignment of a sentinel value }
for i from 2 to n do
    $temp \leftarrow a[i]$
    $loc \leftarrow i$
    while $(\textbf{loc} > \textbf{1})$ **and** $(a[loc - 1] > temp)$ do
        $a[loc] \leftarrow a[loc - 1]$
        $loc \leftarrow loc - 1$
    $a[loc] \leftarrow temp$

If *temp* is smaller than every element in the subarray $a[1..(i-1)]$, execution of the loop stops with $loc = 1$, the proper location for the insertion. We have avoided the extra space of storing a sentinel value, which may be difficult to find, at the expense of an additional test for every iteration of the loop.

For comparison with other techniques we need to calculate the complexity of this operation, which in part depends on the data. Perhaps the data were read from a file into the array and were already sorted or were substantially sorted. But perhaps the data were stored in the file in descending or reverse order, the opposite of alphabetical order. Quite often with raw data, the order is **random** with each possible arrangement equally likely to occur.

In *InsertionSort* the outer *for* loop is executed $n-1$ times, for i from 2 to n. On the ith iteration to find and prepare the location for *temp*, the value of the ith array element, we execute the *while* loop. If $a[i]$ is already in its proper location as in Step 3 of Figure 11.1, the *while* loop is skipped. Thus, our best situation is where the data is already sorted. The inner loop is never executed, while the outer loop is processed $n-1$ times for a total complexity of $O(n)$.

In contrast, data in reverse order, such as

null Z G F E D B

present the worst possible situation. As demonstrated in Step 5 of Figure 11.1, to place B, the value of $a[5] = temp$, into the sorted subarray, we must compare *temp* with each subarray element from $a[4]$ down to $a[0]$. Thus, the *while* loop is executed four times, for $loc = 5, 4, 3,$ and 2. For each i from 2 to n this inner loop performs $i-1$ iterations.

Number of times *while* loop executed:	1 2 3 . . . $(n-1)$
Index i of *for* loop:	2 3 4 . . . n

Consequently, starting with an array in descending order, the insertion sort to place the array in ascending order requires a total number of $\frac{1}{2}n^2 - \frac{1}{2}n$ iterations of the *while* loop:

$$
\begin{aligned}
1 + 2 + 3 + \ldots + (n-1) &= (n-1)n/2 \\
&= (n^2 - n)/2 \\
&= \tfrac{1}{2}n^2 - \tfrac{1}{2}n
\end{aligned}
$$

Thus, the complexity of the insertion sort in this worst possible case is **quadratic** or $O(n^2)$.

The complexity of the average case is no better. For a randomly sorted table, on the average we will need to search through one-half of the subarray to find the proper location for *temp*. For each i from 2 to n, the inner loop will be executed on the average $(i-1)/2$ times.

Average number of times *while* loop executed:	$\frac{1}{2} \cdot 1 \quad \frac{1}{2} \cdot 2 \quad \frac{1}{2} \cdot 3 \ldots \frac{1}{2} \cdot (n-1)$
Index i of *for* loop:	2 $\quad$ 3 $\quad$ 4 . . . $\quad n$

On the average the total number of executions of the inner loop is

$$\tfrac{1}{2} \cdot 1 + \tfrac{1}{2} \cdot 2 + \tfrac{1}{2} \cdot 3 + \ldots + \tfrac{1}{2} \cdot (n-1) \quad \begin{aligned} &= \tfrac{1}{2} \cdot ((n-1)n/2) \\ &= \tfrac{1}{2} \cdot (\tfrac{1}{2}n^2 - \tfrac{1}{2}n) \\ &= \tfrac{1}{4}n^2 - \tfrac{1}{4}n \end{aligned}$$

Therefore, the complexity of the insertion sort for randomly and reverse sorted data is $O(n^2)$ and for already sorted data, $O(n)$.

The number of moves also has an effect on the efficiency of an algorithm. Except when $a[loc - 1]$ is less than or equal to *temp*, each comparison made in the inner loop results in the upward movement of an array element. Thus, when data are already ordered, there is no movement of data in the one pass through the array. Moreover, in the average and worst cases, the number of assignments of data has the same complexity as the number of comparisons, namely $O(n^2)$.

Besides efficiency considerations, the stability of a sort of a particular collection of data may be important. The insertion sort has the desirable quality of being **stable**; that is, if two table elements *e1* and *e2* have the same key and *e1* appears earlier than *e2* before sorting, *e1* is located before *e2* after sorting. For instance, let us assume we have a table of names and addresses that is already sorted by name. Suppose we need to have a listing of these people by city. In resorting the table, this time with the key being the city, we would like to maintain the names in alphabetical order for each city. With the *while* loop of the algorithm, we keep moving down the subarray, searching for the insertion location as long as $a[loc - 1] > temp$. As soon as $a[loc - 1]$ is less than or equal to *temp*, we stop the search. The element $a[loc - 1]$ is unchanged while *temp* is placed in the next element, $a[loc]$.

SECTION 11.1 EXERCISES

1. a. As in Figure 11.1, show the steps of an insertion sort on the following data: M S C R T F P.
  b. How many comparisons of elements did you make for this sort?
  c. How many moves of elements did you make for this sort?

2. Repeat Exercise 1 for this data: C D F M R S T.

3. Repeat Exercise 1 for this data: T S R M F D C.

4. a. Code the procedure *InsertionSort* in Pascal for an array of characters.
  b. Revise the procedure in Part a for an array of strings. Refer to Example 4.4 of Section 4.3 for a string comparison function.

5. a. Design the insertion sort for a doubly linked list implementation where the sorted part is built toward the tail.
  b. Code Part a in Pascal.

6. a. In the worst case how many moves of information are made in the insertion sort of the doubly linked list from Exercise 5?

b. In the worst case how many moves are made in an insertion sort of an array?

7. Suppose 10,000 student records, each record with a Social Security number key and a total size of 300 characters, are stored in a file. In the worst case, what is the total number of characters that would be moved in an insertion sort?

8. **a.** Design a recursive version of the *InsertTable* procedure for the insertion sort of an array.
   b. Code Part a in Pascal.

9. **a.** Give an invariant for the inner loop of *InsertionSort*.
   b. Using program verification, prove this loop is correct.
   c. Give an invariant for the outer loop of *InsertionSort*.
   d. Using program verification, prove this loop is correct.

10. Revise the program of Sections 1.1 and 1.2 to sort the records by name after reading.

11. Repeat Exercise 1 for this data: M_1 M_2 S C_1 R C_2, where $M_1 = M_2$ and $C_1 = C_2$.

12. Consider data in record format where each item has a unique part number in the range from 0 to 9999 and a classification code, A, B, C, or D.

   a. For a randomly sorted file, read, sort by part number, print a report of the information, and store this sorted information in a file.
   b. Read the output file of Part a and print a report sorted by classification code, with a blank line before each code change.
   c. On the printed report of Part b, are the part numbers sorted within a code?
   d. Is this sort stable?

13. A **bubble sort** has the following algorithm:

   repeat until the array is sorted:
       sorted ← true
      pass through the unsorted subarray
          if a pair of adjacent elements are out of order
            swap their values
            sorted ← false

   For an array of n elements, after the first pass through the array, we are guaranteed that $a[n]$ contains the proper value; the largest value has "bubbled" to the top, which in this case is the end of the array.

   a. Illustrate the action of this algorithm on the data in Exercise 1.
   b. Code the procedure *Bubblesort*.
   c. What is the average complexity of this method?
   d. Illustrate the action of this algorithm on the data in Exercise 2.
   e. What is the complexity when the data is already sorted?

   f. Illustrate the action of this algorithm on the data in Exercise 3.
   g. What is the complexity when the data is in reverse order?
   h. Illustrate the action of this algorithm on the data in Exercise 11.
   i. Is this technique stable?

SECTION 11.2

Selection Sort

One disadvantage of the insertion sort of an array is the amount of movement of data. In the random and worst cases, the number of moves is on the order of $O(n^2)$. In an array of lengthy records those reassignments can be quite time-consuming. One alternative is to use the **selection sort**. The number of moves with this technique is always on the order of $O(n)$.

To illustrate the selection sort, suppose you are working for the school library to organize the volumes of an old encyclopedia. Unfortunately, some volumes are missing; there are duplicates of others; shelf space is limited; and each book is heavy to move. You look through all the books, selecting the one with the smallest volume number. Once found, you swap that book with the first one. Then, starting with the next book, you look for the smallest volume number in the remaining books and exchange that book with the one in the second position. The process is repeated until only one book remains in the unsorted section of books. Of course, that book must have the largest volume number and, consequently, must already be in place.

Figure 11.3 illustrates the selection sort for a small array a of n characters. On each step the sorted subarray appears in boldface. As the last step shows, once the first $n - 1$ least items are in place, the last element must contain the maximum value. Thus, we repeat the process $n - 1$ times as follows:

SelectionSort(a, n)
   Procedure to perform a selection sort on the first n elements of an array a
Input:
   a — array
   n — number of elements
Output:
   a — revised array
Assumption:
   Array a is declared to have a subrange index type $1..m$ with $n \leq m$.

Figure	Algorithm
{10.3}	

        for i from 1 to $n - 1$ do
           $MinIndex \leftarrow IndexOfMin(a, i, n)$
           $swap(a[i], a[MinIndex])$

In this design a function invocation returns the index of the smallest element in the subarray of a from the ith index to the end of the array, while a procedure swaps that element and the ith one. As shown below, the *Index-*

Figure 11.3

Action of selection sort on
an array

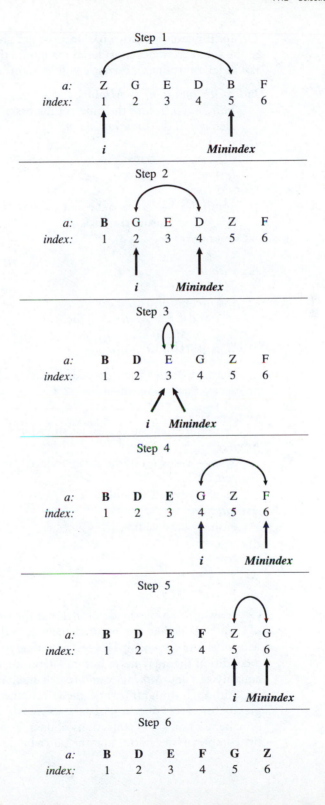

OfMin function has three parameters, the array and the low and high indices of the subarray under consideration. Should the minimum element be repeated, the index of its first occurrence will be returned.

IndexOfMin(a, i, n) → *MinIndex*
  Function to return the index of the first occurrence of the minimum
  element in the subarray $a[i..n]$
Input:
  a   — array
  i, n   — indices
Output:
  MinIndex — index of the first occurrence of the minimum element in the
                  subarray $a[i..n]$
Assumption:
  $i \leq n$.
Algorithm:
  MinIndex ← *i*
  for *j* from $i + 1$ to *n* do
      if $a[j] < a[MinIndex]$ then
          MinIndex ← *j*
  IndexOfMin ← *MinIndex*

Recall that the swap procedure uses a temporary variable to handle the proper exchange of elements.

swap(x, y)
  Procedure to swap the values stored in variables *x* and *y*
Input:
  x, y — variables of the same declared type
Output:
  x, y — revised variables
Assumption:
  x and *y* have values.
Algorithm:
  temp ← *x*
  x   ← *y*
  y   ← *temp*

A swap is always made of $a[i]$ and the minimum element in the subarray $a[i..n]$, even if that minimum element is $a[i]$. We could switch only if *i* and *MinIndex* are not equal. This test would be performed every time, however, for a condition that may never occur. Therefore, it is more efficient not to test for equality of *i* and *MinIndex* and to call *swap* on each iteration.

Although straightforward, the selection sort algorithm has quadratic complexity for every collection of data, as we will show. Therefore, this sort should only be used on small collections of data, about 100 items or less. To discover the complexity we notice that the outer loop is a *for* loop that always executes

$n - 1$ times. The inner *for* loop, found in the *IndexOfMin* function, is performed $n - (i + 1) + 1 = n - i$ times. Thus, the total number of executions of the *if* statement in the inner loop is:

$$(n - 1) + \ldots + 3 + 2 + 1 = (n - 1)n / 2 = \tfrac{1}{2}n^2 - \tfrac{1}{2}n.$$

Regardless of the data—ordered, random, or reverse ordered—the number of comparisons in a selection sort is on the order of $O(n^2)$. For an already sorted array, this performance is not nearly as good as $O(n)$ attainable with the insertion sort.

For random and reverse ordered data, however, fewer assignment statements are executed in a selection sort than in an insertion sort. Since the call to *swap* is in the outer loop of the selection sort, not the inner, an exchange of elements occurs exactly $n - 1$ times. Thus, regardless of the data the number of moves is constant and is on the order of $O(n)$. When each element is a lengthy record with a small key so that comparisons are fast and when the data are probably not in order already, the selection sort can display a considerable savings over the insertion sort. In this case, both techniques have a complexity of $O(n^2)$ for the number of comparisons; but the number of moves in a selection sort is proportional to n, instead of n^2 as with the insertion sort. If the data is already sorted, however, the insertion sort is preferable with about $O(n)$ comparisons and number moves. By contrast, in this situation the selection sort has about $O(n^2)$ comparisons and $O(n)$ moves.

Moreover, the selection sort is not stable; records with duplicate keys do not necessarily remain in the same order. The problem comes when the first occurrence of a key may be swapped to a position after the second occurrence of the same key. Figure 11.4 illustrates such a situation where $M_1 = M_2$.

Figure 11.4

Example to show that the selection sort is not stable

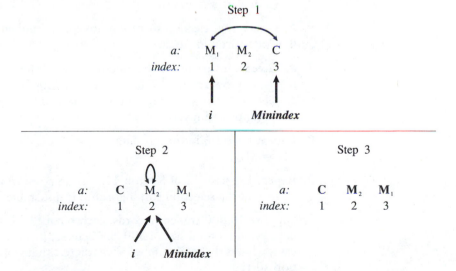

The algorithm for *SelectionSort* is probably easier to understand than that of *InsertionSort*, but in most cases the former holds no real advantage over the latter. For unsorted arrays with large records, the selection sort does result in less movement of array values. As Exercise 6 of Section 11.1 shows, even that advantage is lost for a linked list implementation of the table.

▽

SECTION 11.2 EXERCISES

1. a. As in Figure 11.3, show the steps of a selection sort on the following data: M S C R T F P.
   b. How many comparisons of elements did you make for this sort?
   c. How many moves of elements did you make for this sort?

2. Repeat Exercise 1 for this data: C D F M R S T.

3. Repeat Exercise 1 for this data: T S R M F D C.

4. a. Code the procedure *SelectionSort* in Pascal for an array of characters.
   b. Code the procedure *IndexOfMin* in Pascal for an array of characters.
   c. Code the procedure *swap* in Pascal for an array of characters.
   d. Revise the procedure in Part a to have embedded code instead of separate routines for finding the index of the minimum element and for swapping.
   e. Revise the procedure in Part d for an array of strings. Refer to Example 4.4 of Section 4.3 for a string comparison function.

5. a. Design a recursive selection sort procedure.
   b. Code Part a in Pascal.

6. a. Design the selection sort for a linked list implementation.
   b. Code Part a in Pascal.

7. a. Give an invariant for the loop of *IndexofMin*.
   b. Using program verification, prove this loop is correct.
   c. Give an invariant for the loop of *SelectionSort*.
   d. Using program verification, prove this loop is correct.

8. Repeat Exercise 1a for this data: G_1 M_1 G_2 C B M_2 A where $G_1 = G_2$ and $M_1 = M_2$.

9. Repeat Exercise 12 of Section 11.1 using a selection sort. Design data to show that the selection sort algorithm is not stable.

10. Suppose 10,000 student records, each record with a Social Security number key and a total size of 300 characters, are stored in a file. In the worst case, what is the total number of characters that would be moved in a selection sort?

Quicksort

The **quicksort** technique has far better performance, on average, than the insertion and selection sorts. For random ordering, quicksort has complexity $O(n \log_2 n)$, while an insertion or a selection sort is on the order of $O(n^2)$. In Figure 1.5 of Chapter 1 we note for $n = 32$, $n^2 = 1024$, but $n \log_2 n$ is only 160. Considering a much larger n, for $n = 2^{12} = 4096$, we have

$$n \log_2 n = 2^{12} \log_2 2^{12} = (2^{12})12 = 49{,}152$$

but

$$n^2 = 2^{12} \cdot 2^{12} = 2^{24} = 16{,}777{,}216.$$

For $n = 2^{12}$, n^2 is over 300 times larger than $n \log_2 n$:

$$\frac{n^2}{n \log_2 n} = \frac{n}{\log_2 n} = \frac{2^{12}}{\log_2(2^{12})} = \frac{2^{12}}{12} = \frac{1024}{3} = 341\tfrac{1}{3}$$

Suppose we have an array of letters to arrange alphabetically. Initially, to explain the technique we will not draw the letters in an array structure but as the collection in Figure 11.5. The exact position of the letters in the array during processing will be covered shortly.

Figure 11.5

Quicksort of elements in an array without the details of the partition

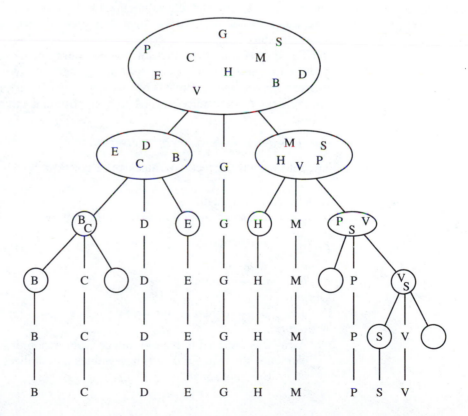

First, an array element called the **pivot** is picked; suppose the letter G is chosen as the pivot. As shown in level 2 of the tree in Figure 11.5, the array is then partitioned into a subarray of letters less than G alphabetically, G itself, and a subarray of items greater than G. This pivot, G, is now in its proper and final location for the sorted array. We then recursively repeat the process on each subarray. Quicksort is a **divide and conquer** algorithm—we conquer the sort by dividing the problem into smaller problems upon which we perform the same process.

Executing a quicksort on the reduced collection of those letters greater than G, level 3 of Figure 11.5 shows the letter M being picked as the pivot. Only H is less than M in that set, while P, S, and V are greater. When we perform a quicksort on a one-element subarray, such as with H, we have a terminal condition for the recursive algorithm. Note that in partitioning, one part or the other may be empty. For example, partitioning with P as pivot at level 4, both S and V are greater than P. Thus, the collection of elements from S and V that are less than P is empty. Certainly, discovery of an empty subarray should also be a terminal condition.

The procedure call *Partition(a, first, last, loc)* picks a pivot element from the subarray of elements $a[first. .last]$. The procedure returns the proper location, *loc*, for this pivot and the array *a* with the subarray $a[first . . (loc - 1)]$ containing elements less than or equal to the pivot, $a[loc]$ equaling the pivot, and $a[(loc + 1)..last]$ having values greater than or equal to the pivot. We consider the details of this partition algorithm after a description of the main quicksort procedure.

For the recursion of quicksort we need arguments of the array identifier and the first and last indices of the subarray being sorted. We stop performing this sorting when the array has one element, *first* = *last*, or none, *first* > *last*. For an array *a* with indices from 1 to *n*, the original call to this sorting procedure is:

Quicksort(a, 1, n)

The following is the recursive quicksort algorithm.

Quicksort(a, first, last)
   Procedure to perform quicksort on the subarray of *a* from index *first* to
   last.
Input:
   a   — array
   first, last — indices
Output:
   a   — revised array
Assumptions:
   Array *a* is declared to have an integer subrange index type; array
   elements a[first], . . ., a[last] have values; and indices *first* and *last*
   are within that range.

Figure	Algorithm
{11.5}	if *first* < *last* then
	Partition(*a, first, last, loc*)
	Quicksort(*a, first, loc* − 1)
	Quicksort(*a, loc* + 1, *last*)

How do we perform the partition at the heart of the quicksort algorithm? As with insertion sort, we use a sentinel value. Before execution begins a value greater than or equal to any data value should be placed at the end of the array in $a[n + 1]$. Figure 11.6 pictures this initialization with a sentinel of Z in $a[11]$ for the example given earlier.

Figure 11.6

Initialization with a sentinel of Z in $a[11]$ for quicksort

n: 10

a:	G	B	S	E	V	M	P	H	D	C	**Z**
index:	1	2	3	4	5	6	7	8	9	10	11

The pivot can be any of the array elements, say the leftmost one:

$pivot \leftarrow a[first]$

As Figure 11.7 shows, we also initialize two indices, *i* and *loc*, to indicate the outside bounds of the elements to be divided into two collections.

Figure 11.7

Initialization of indices, *i* and *loc*, to indicate the outside bounds of the elements to be divided into two collections for quicksort

In the partition we wish to have the elements less than or equal to *pivot* toward the left and those greater than or equal toward the right. Thus, we start incrementing the left index pointer, *i*, until *i* indicates an element that should be toward the right; that is, an element greater than or equal to the pivot. (See Figure 11.8.)

Figure 11.8

Increment *i* until *i* indicates an element that
should be toward the right

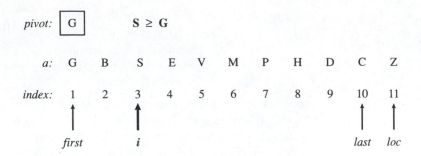

repeat
$\quad i \leftarrow i + 1$
until $a[i] \geq pivot$

Similarly, we decrement *loc*, the right index, to point to a value that should be toward the left of the array, an element less than or equal to the pivot. (See Figure 11.9.)

Figure 11.9

Decrement *loc* until *loc*
indicates an element that
should be toward the left

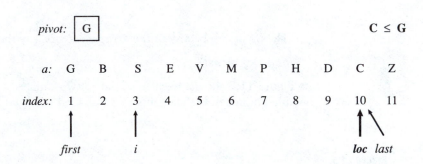

repeat
$\quad loc \leftarrow loc - 1$
until $a[loc] \leq pivot$

At this point $a[i]$ contains a value that should be on the right, while the item in $a[loc]$ should be on the left. Thus, as Figure 11.10 pictures, we swap the two values.

$swap(a[i], a[loc])$

The process continues with *i* moving to the right again, searching for an element larger than *pivot*, and with *loc* moving to the left, seeking a smaller one. Figure 11.11, Step 1, shows *i* stopping at 5 ($a[5] = V \geq G$) and *loc* at 9 ($a[9] = D \leq G$). As before, we switch the values in $a[5]$ and $a[9]$. (See Step 2.)

After this exchange, the movement of *i* and *loc* begins again. This time, *i* halts at 6 with $a[6] = M \geq G$. The index *loc*, however, does not halt until index 5 with $a[5] = D \leq G$. Notice in Figure 11.12 that indices *i* and *loc* have

Figure 11.10

Swap elements to place them on the proper sides of the array

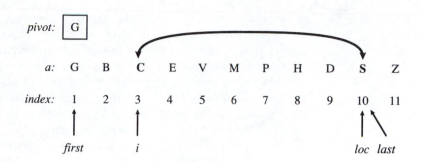

Figure 11.11

Starting with Figure 11.10, repetition of process in Figures 11.8–11.10

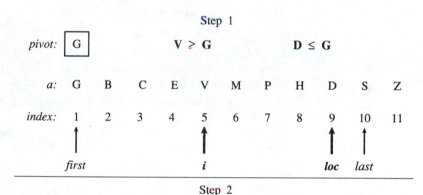

Figure 11.12

Starting with Figure 11.11, movement of *i* up and *loc* down, but no swap because *i* ≥ *loc*

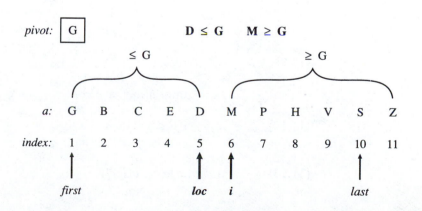

passed each other. Notice also that the array elements from *first* = 1 to *loc* = 5 are all less than or equal to the pivot, while those from *i* = 6 to *last* = 10 are all greater than or equal to G. We certainly do not want to swap *a*[5] and *a*[6]; such an exchange would destroy the partition.

The only remaining step of the partition is to place the pivot, G, between the two collections of elements. The index *loc* marks the position where the pivot should be. Presently, in array element *a*[*loc*] we have a value, D, that belongs on the left. Since G is also on the left in *a*[*first*], as in Figure 11.13 we move G to its proper location as a separator by switching *a*[*first*] and *a*[*loc*],

$$swap(a[first], a[loc])$$

The entire partition algorithm is as follows:

Partition(a, first, last, loc)
> Procedure to partition array *a* from index *first* to index *last* so that for some array element, *pivot*, the subarray *a*[*first*..(*loc* − 1)] contains elements less than or equal to *pivot*; *a*[*loc*] = *pivot*; and the subarray *a*[(*loc* + 1)..*last*] contains elements greater than or equal to *pivot*.

Input:
> *a* — array
> *first, last* — indices

Output:
> *a* — partitioned array
> *loc* — location of *pivot*

Assumptions:
> *first* and *last* + 1 are in the index range for *a*; *first* < *last*; array elements *a*[*first*], ... , *a*[*last*] have values; *a*[*last* + 1] has a sentinel value greater than any array element from *a*[*first*] to *a*[*last*].

Figure	Algorithm
{11.7}	$i \leftarrow first$
	$loc \leftarrow last + 1$
	$pivot \leftarrow a[first]$
	while $i < loc$ do
{11.8}	repeat
	$\quad i \leftarrow i + 1$
	until $a[i] \geq pivot$
{11.9}	repeat
	$\quad loc \leftarrow loc - 1$
	until $a[loc] \leq pivot$
{11.10}	if $i < loc$ then
	$\quad swap(a[i], a[loc])$
{11.12}	
{11.13}	$swap(a[first], a[loc])$

Figure 11.13

Movement of the pivot, G, into its proper location

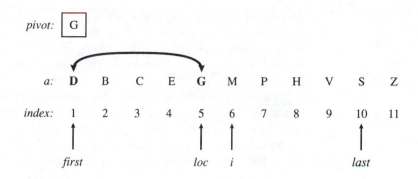

For speed in the quicksort procedure, the partition and the swap are usually coded directly instead of as procedure calls. Indeed, in the best situation the quicksort is a very fast sorting method with a complexity of $O(n \log_2 n)$. For random data and for each recursive call the array is split approximately in half. Figure 11.14 diagrams recursive calls in this ideal situation for an array of 15 elements. In all, there are a total of 15 calls to *Quicksort*,

$$1 + 2 + 4 + 8 = 15$$

Notice that the resulting tree has four levels. As with the number of comparisons in a binary search, which cuts the problem in half each time (see Section 3.2), the number of levels is:

$$\lceil \log_2(n + 1) \rceil = \lceil \log_2 16 \rceil = \lceil \log_2 2^4 \rceil = 4$$

Figure 11.14

Recursive calls to *Quicksort* in the ideal situation for an array of 15 elements

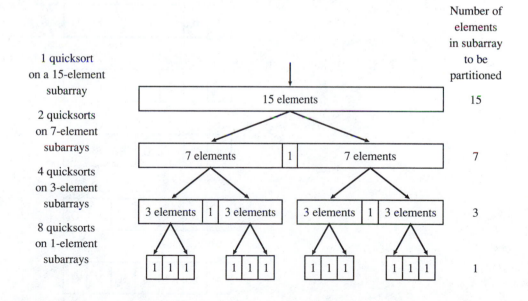

At each of the four levels approximately $n = 15$ comparisons are made of an array element and the pivot. Thus, the total number of comparisons is about $n \log_2 n$. Moreover, most of the activity is in the two inner *repeat* loops that move i and *loc*. These loops are very simple and, consequently, extremely rapid.

The worst possible situation occurs when the original data is already sorted in alphabetical or reverse alphabetical order. In these cases, choosing the pivot as the first element always creates an empty subarray. Figure 11.15 demonstrates such a disastrous situation. Notice that for $n = 7$ array elements, we have 7 levels of the tree, each level requiring about 7 comparisons. Thus, the complexity for

Figure 11.15

Recursive calls to *Quicksort* in the worst situation for an array of seven elements

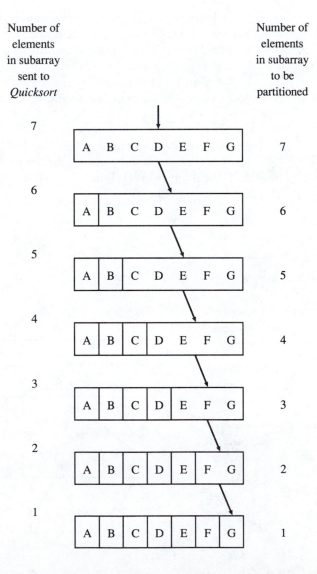

Number of elements in subarray sent to *Quicksort*

Number of elements in subarray to be partitioned

this situation is $O(n^2)$, a very poor performance indeed. Alternative choices for the pivot to avoid such degradation are covered in the exercises.

<hr>

SECTION 11.3 EXERCISES

1. a. Suppose $n = 2^{10}$. Evaluate n, n^2, $n \log_2 n$.
   b. Suppose $n = 2 \cdot 2^{10} = 2^{11}$. Evaluate n, n^2, $n \log_2 n$.
   c. Comparing the answers for Parts a and b when n was doubled, how did n^2 change?
   d. When n was doubled, how did $n \log_2 n$ change?

2. Evaluate n^2 and $n \log_2 n$ for n equal to

   a. $2^8 = 256$ **b.** $2^{13} = 8192$ **c.** 25,000

3. a. With the first element as the pivot illustrate the partition of the following array similar to that shown in Figures 11.7–11.13:

     h: M A D N R E C P H

   b. How many swaps were made?
   c. Complete the quicksort on this array, drawing a tree of calls to *Quicksort* as in Figure 11.5 and sketching the action of each partition.
   d. How many calls to *Quicksort* were there?

4. Repeat Exercise 3 for the array

   h: S T B A E D V C U H F I G

5. Repeat Exercise 3 for the array

   h: B D E F H K

6. Repeat Exercise 3 for the array

   h: K H F E D B

7. a. Show the steps of the partition of the array

     h: A_1 A_2 A_3

     where $A_1 = A_2 = A_3$.
   b. How many swaps were made?
   c. Is the algorithm stable?

8. Code in Pascal the *Quicksort* algorithm. Place the code for the partition directly in the routine, not as a separate procedure.

9. The **median-of-three** method avoids the very poor performance of quicksort when the data is sorted or reverse sorted. Instead of choosing $a[first]$ as the pivot, the median of the *first*, *last*, and middle element in the subarray is computed and swapped into $a[first]$ before the partition. For example, the median of the values A, P, and C is C since $A \leq C \leq P$. To compute the index of the middle element, add *first* and *last* and perform an integer division by 2 on the sum. Of course, we do not want to perform this maneuver unless the subarray has at least three elements.

    a. Perform the median-of-three method to find the pivot for the array in Exercise 3.

    b. Repeat Part a for the array in Exercise 4.

    c. Revise the coding of the procedure *Quicksort* to employ the median-of-three method.

10. Repeat Exercise 5c using the median-of-three method. (See Exercise 9.)

11. Repeat Exercise 6c using the median-of-three method. (See Exercise 9.)

12. Use a technique similar to quicksort to design a procedure to find the *k*th smallest element in an array. Choose a pivot and partition the array into subarrays of elements less than, equal to, or greater than the pivot. If the first subarray has *k* or more elements, continue the process on that subarray. If not and if the first two arrays together have greater than or equal to *k* elements, then the *k*th smallest element is the pivot. Otherwise, the *k*th smallest element is in the subarray of elements greater than the pivot, so search in that area of the array.

13. Suppose a table is implemented as a linked list with *head* being a pointer. We can perform a quicksort by partitioning the list into three lists: a list of nodes with information less than the value in the head node, a list of nodes with information equal to, and a list of nodes with information greater than that of the node pointed to by *head*. After recursively performing a quicksort on the first and third of these lists, we link the three lists together to create the final sorted version.

    a. Write procedure *QuicksortList* that implements the following algorithm:

        QuicksortList(*head*, *tail*)
            Procedure to perform a quicksort on a linked list
        Input:
            head — pointer to the linked list
        Output:
            head — pointer to the sorted linked list
            tail   — pointer to the last node of the sorted linked list
        Algorithm:
        If not *ListIsEmpty*(*head*) then
            PartitionList(*head*, *LessHead*, *LessTail*, *EqualHead*, *EqualTail*,
                        MoreHead, *MoreTail*).

        {* * * Sort *Less* list; point *head*; attach *Less* list to *Equal* list * * *}
        If not *ListIsEmpty*(*LessHead*) then
            QuicksortList(*LessHead*, *LessTail*)
            ToFirst(*LessHead*, *head*)
            StoreNext(*LessTail*, *EqualHead*)

{* * * Sort *More* list; attach *Equal* list to *More* list; point *tail* * * *}
If not *ListIsEmpty*(*MoreHead*) then
    QuicksortList(*MoreHead, MoreTail*)
    StoreNext(*EqualTail, MoreHead*)
    tail ← *MoreTail*
else
    tail ← *EqualTail*

b. The partitioning into three sublists is accomplished by traversing the list, inserting each node at the tail of the appropriate *Less, Equal,* or *More* list. The *InsertTailList* procedure of Exercise 4 of Section 7.3 (implementation in Exercise 23 of Section 7.4) accomplishes the insertion. Write the partition procedure whose algorithm is below:

PartitionList(head, LessHead, LessTail, EqualHead, EqualTail, MoreHead, MoreTail)
Procedure to perform a partition of a linked list pointed to by *head* into three disjoint lists: nodes with information less than that of the first node (*Less* list), those with information equal to that of the first node (*Equal* list), those with information greater than that of the first node (*More* list)
Input:
  head   — pointer to the linked list
Output:
  head   — pointer to the partitioned linked list
  LessHead — pointer to the first node of the list of nodes with values less than the head node
  LessTail — pointer to the last node of the list of nodes with values less than the head node
  EqualHead — pointer to the first node of the list of nodes with values equal to the head node
  EqualTail — pointer to the last node of the list of nodes with values equal to the head node
  MoreHead — pointer to the first node of the list of nodes with values greater than the head node
  MoreTail — pointer to the last node of the list of nodes with values greater than the head node
Algorithm:
{* * * Initialize the first node of list as the first node of *Equal* list * * *}
ToFirst(*head, EqualHead*)
ToFirst(*head, EqualTail*)

{* * * Initialize *Less* and *More* lists * * *}
MakeListEmpty(*LessHead*)
MakeListEmpty(*MoreHead*)

While not *AtEnd*(*EqualTail*) do the following:
    {* * * if next node has information less than that in   * * *}
    {* * * *EqualHead*'s node, move that node to *Less* list * * *}
    if *RetrieveInfo*(*RetrieveNext*(*EqualTail*)) < *RetrieveInfo*(*EqualHead*)
        ToFirst(*EqualTail*, *Target*)
        Advance(*Target*)
        StoreNext(*EqualTail*, *RetrieveNext*(*Target*))
        InsertTailList(*LessHead*, *LessTail*, *Target*)
    {* * * if next node has information greater than that in * * *}
    {* * * *EqualHead*'s node, move that node to *More* list * * *}
    else if *RetrieveInfo*(*RetrieveNext*(*EqualTail*)) > *RetrieveInfo*(*EqualHead*)
        ToFirst(*EqualTail*, *Target*)
        Advance(*Target*)
        StoreNext(*EqualTail*, *RetrieveNext*(*Target*))
        InsertTailList(*MoreHead*, *MoreTail*, *Target*)
    {* * * if next node has information equal to that in   * * *}
    {* * * *EqualHead*'s node, expand *Equal* list to include that node * * *}
    else
        Advance(*EqualTail*)

c. Does this algorithm handle duplicate records?
d. Is this algorithm stable?
e. What is the best case complexity of this algorithm?
f. What is the average case complexity of this algorithm?
g. What is the worst case complexity of this algorithm?

▽

PROGRAMMING PROJECT

1. Write a program to read in data from a file, sort, and rewrite the sorted data to the same file. Have the program combine quicksort and insertion sort. Quicksort should work on the larger arrays, partitioning them into smaller ones. As soon as a subarray is size 10 or less, terminate the sort. Then with the total array partitioned into smaller chunks that are ordered relative to each other, perform an insertion sort on that array.

SECTION 11.4

Heapsort

The advantage of the heapsort technique is that its worst and average case performances are both of complexity $O(n \log_2 n)$. Though generally not as fast as quicksort, the heapsort algorithm presented here is nonrecursive, thus eliminating worry about STACK-OVERFLOW errors.

As defined in Section 10.1, a complete binary tree has all of its leaves on level $n - 1$ or level n; on levels 1 through $n - 2$ every node has exactly two children; and on level n the leaves are as far to the left as possible. A **heap** is a complete binary tree, where the value stored in a node is greater than or equal

Figure 11.16

A heap

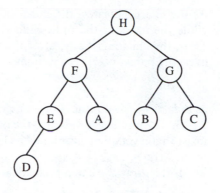

to the values of its children. There is, however, no ordering between the left and right children. Figure 11.16 presents such a heap with a characteristic shape of a complete tree. (See Figure 10.8.)

One reason for studying complete binary trees is that trees with this structure can be stored in an array without the large overhead of link storage. The array h,

$$h: \ \text{H F G E A B C D}$$
$$\textit{index:} \ \ 1 \ 2 \ 3 \ 4 \ 5 \ 6 \ 7 \ 8$$

contains the complete binary tree of Figure 11.16, and Figure 11.17 shows the tree with the corresponding array indices. Notice that $h[1] = $ H contains the root; $h[2] = $ F and $h[3] = $ G are the root's children. We picture the elements of the array entirely filling a level of the tree before advancing to the next level down. The indices of each array element and its children are as follows:

Index of the Element	Indices of the Children	
	Left	Right
1	2	3
2	4	5
3	6	7
4	8	none

Figure 11.17

The heap in Figure 11.16 with corresponding array indices

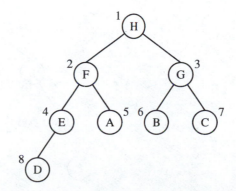

As the chart indicates, the index of a left child is double that of the parent, while the index of the right child is one more than twice the parent's index. Thus, the children, if any, of $h[p]$ are located in $h[2p]$ and $h[2p + 1]$. Moreover, the parent of $h[c]$ is at index

$c\ div\ 2$

as long as $h[c]$ is not the root. For example, the parent of $h[6]$ is $h[3]$ with 6 *div* 2 = 3. The element $h[3]$ is also the parent of $h[7]$ since 7 *div* 2 = 3. Because we insist that a complete graph fills its leaf nodes to the left first, there are no gaps in the array.

If the array were in alphabetical order as

$h:$ A B C D E F G H

then the corresponding binary tree would be as shown in Figure 11.18. This diagram has the shape of a heap but does not satisfy the condition that the value at a node is greater than or equal to the values of its children. For the heapsort we will take an unordered array, such as found in Figure 11.19, and rearrange the elements to form a heap, such as in Figure 11.16. Then we will transform the structure to be sorted, as in Figure 11.18.

As with the insertion sort, we start with a one-element subarray, expanding and rearranging the subarrays until the whole array stores a heap. Figures

Figure 11.18

Binary tree for the sorted array $h:$ A B C D E F G H

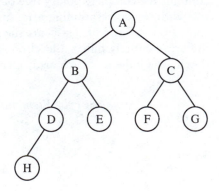

Figure 11.19

Binary tree for the unordered array $h:$ D B G E A H C F

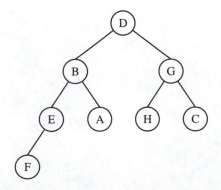

11.20–11.22 detail the conversion to a heap of the complete binary tree stored in array h,

> $h:$ D B G E A H C F

Starting with a subarray of two elements, as in Step 1 of Figure 11.20, the root is $h[1] =$ D and the left child is $h[2] =$ B. Because D > B, this subarray cer-

Figure 11.20

Start of conversion of array $h:$ D B G E A H C F to a heap

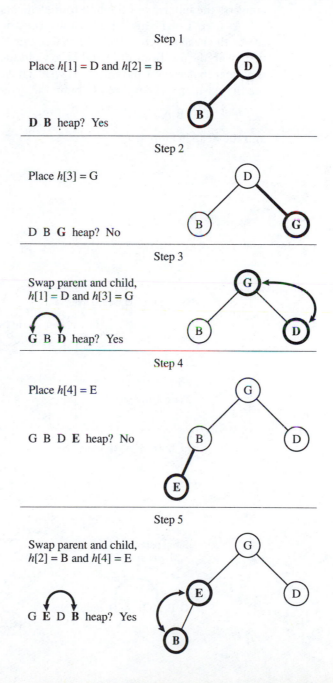

Step 1

Place $h[1] =$ D and $h[2] =$ B

D B heap? Yes

Step 2

Place $h[3] =$ G

D B **G** heap? No

Step 3

Swap parent and child, $h[1] =$ D and $h[3] =$ G

G B **D** heap? Yes

Step 4

Place $h[4] =$ E

G B D **E** heap? No

Step 5

Swap parent and child, $h[2] =$ B and $h[4] =$ E

G **E** D **B** heap? Yes

tainly is a heap. But placement of $h[3]$ = G as the right child presents problems because the parent, D, is less than the child, G. This difficulty can be overcome by switching parent and child as in Step 3.

Having filled levels 1 and 2, we consider the next value, E, to be the left-most element of level 3, the left child of B. (See Figure 11.20, Step 4.) Again, there is a problem with the heap, but exchanging parent for child in Step 5 converts the subarray of the first four elements into a heap.

As Step 1 of Figure 11.21 shows, the addition of the small value A preserves the heap structure, but the placement of H in Step 2 does not. We must first swap the positions of D and H to yield the array and tree in Step 3. But H is greater than its new parent, G, as well. Thus, we repeat the process, exchanging the position of G and H to obtain the array

   h: H E G B A D C F

and the heap in Step 4.

Figure 11.21

Continuation from Figure 11.20 of conversion of array h to a heap

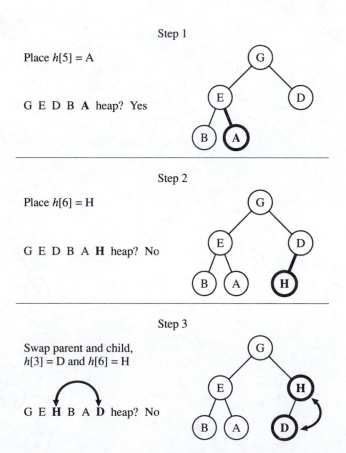

Step 1

Place $h[5]$ = A

G E D B **A** heap? Yes

Step 2

Place $h[6]$ = H

G E D B A **H** heap? No

Step 3

Swap parent and child,
$h[3]$ = D and $h[6]$ = H

G E **H** B A **D** heap? No

Figure 11.21

continued

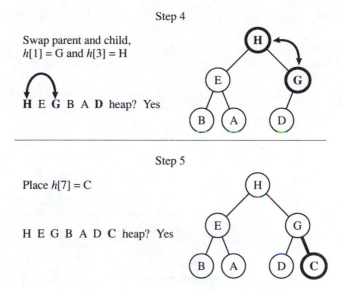

Step 4

Swap parent and child,
$h[1] = G$ and $h[3] = H$

H E **G** B A **D** heap? Yes

Step 5

Place $h[7] = C$

H E G B A D C heap? Yes

The small value C is readily added to the heap in Step 5 of Figure 11.21. With the addition of F, however, we must perform two exchanges to move the value into an acceptable location for the heap. (See Figure 11.22, Steps 1–3.)

The algorithm *PlaceInHeap* below places the value of $h[childNX]$ in a heap. Before execution, we assume the subarray from index 1 to index $childNX - 1$ forms a heap. After execution, the larger subarray $h[1..childNX]$ is a heap. The general description of the algorithm follows:

while (not a heap) and (child is not at the root) do
    find the parent
    if parent and child are out of order then
        swap parent and child
        move child up the tree one level
    else
        we have a heap

A more detailed description of the method is given below:

PlaceInHeap(h, childNX)
    Procedure to add the value of $h[childNX]$ to the heap $h[1..(childNX - 1)]$ so that the subarray $h[1..childNX]$ is a heap
Input:
    h — array
    $childNX$ — index of h
Output:
    h — revised array

Figure 11.22

Continuation from Figure 11.21 of conversion of array *h* to a heap

Step 1

Place $h[8] = F$

H E G B A D C **F** heap? No

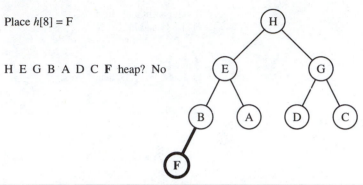

Step 2

Swap parent and child,
$h[4] = B$ and $h[8] = F$

H E G **F** A D C **B** heap? No

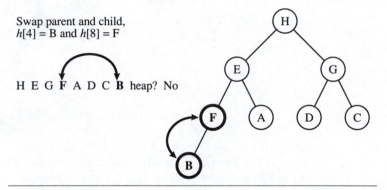

Step 3

Swap parent and child,
$h[2] = E$ and $h[4] = F$

H **F** G **E** A D C B heap? Yes

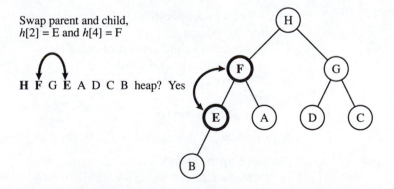

Assumptions:

The index type of *h* is a subrange starting with 1; *childNX* is a positive integer greater than 1; the subarray $h[1..(childNX - 1)]$ is a heap; *h* is defined for indices from 1 to *childNX*.

Figure	Algorithm
	parentNX ← *childNX* div 2
	heap ← *false*
{11.20}	while (not *heap*) and (*childNX* > 1) do
{Step 2}	if $h[parentNX] < h[childNX]$ then
{Step 3}	*swap*($h[parentNX]$, $h[childNX]$)
	childNX ← *parentNX*
	parentNX ← *childNX* div 2
	else
	heap ← *true*

To build the entire heap from the complete binary tree in *h*, as Figures 11.20−22 indicate, we process the array from $i = 2$ to *n*, the number of elements in *h*.

BuildHeap(*h*, *n*)

Procedure to convert a complete binary tree of *n* elements stored in array *h* to a heap

Input:

h — array storing a complete binary tree

n — number of elements in *h*

Output:

h — revised array

Assumptions:

The index type of *h* is a subrange starting with 1; *n* is within that subrange; *h* is defined for indices from 1 to *n*.

Figure	Algorithm
{11.20−22}	for *childNX* from 2 to *n* do
	PlaceInHeap(*h*, *childNX*)

Once we have a heap, we must sort it. Again we generate progressively larger sorted subarrays. As pictured in Figure 11.23, the array *h* is split in two. The first part of the array is a diminishing heap and the end is a growing sorted array.

Figure 11.23

Array *h* split into a diminishing heap and a growing sorted array

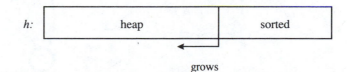

Figure 11.24

Heap stored in array *h*

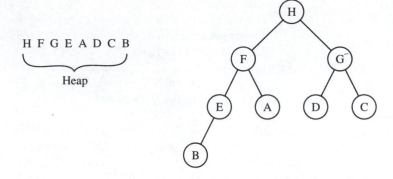

H F G E A D C B

Heap

Figures 11.24–11.30 present a detailed description of the sort of *h*. Because *h* of Figure 11.24 stores a heap, the root or $h[1] = $ H contains the largest element in the array. In the sorted array, however, that value should be in the last element, so we switch the value in the root with the last value in the heap,

$$swap(h[1], h[8]).$$

Now, as Step 1 of Figure 11.25 shows, the subarray consisting of only $h[8] = $ H is sorted, but the subarray $h[1..7]$ is not a heap.

To get the maximum element on top again, we find the largest child of B, in this case G, and exchange their positions. (See Figure 11.25, Step 2.) Now the largest value of the heap is in the root. We still violate the definition of "heap," however, for the subtree with root B. B is smaller than both its children, D and C. Again we locate the larger child and swap the parent with that child (Step 3). Array *h* now contains a heap in elements $h[1]$ through $h[7]$ and a sorted sub-

Figure 11.25

Swap of value at root, H, with last element in heap; conversion of subarray $h[1..7]$ to form a heap

Step 1

Swap root and last node of heap, $h[1] = $ H and $h[8] = $ B

B F G E A D C   H

Heap? No   Sorted

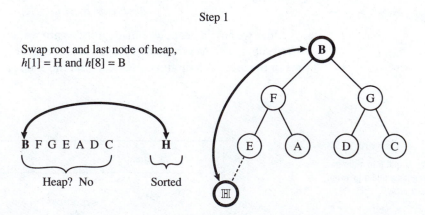

Figure 11.25

continued

Step 2

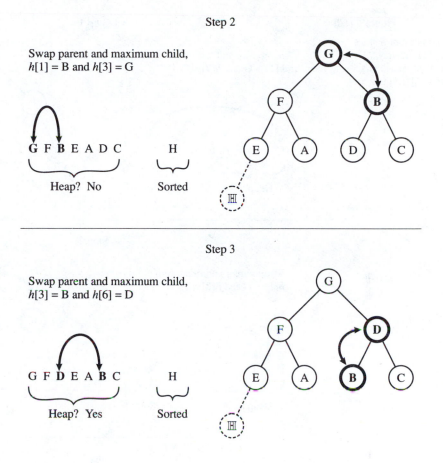

Swap parent and maximum child,
$h[1] = B$ and $h[3] = G$

G F B E A D C   H

Heap? No   Sorted

Step 3

Swap parent and maximum child,
$h[3] = B$ and $h[6] = D$

G F D E A B C   H

Heap? Yes   Sorted

array in $h[8]$. Dotted arcs and nodes in the figures indicate elements that are no longer part of the heap but are part of the sorted subarray.

This process is repeated over and over in Figures 11.26–11.30 until the entire array is sorted as in Figure 11.30, Step 3. With each major step, the value in the root, $h[1]$, is swapped with the last element in the heap, $h[sortNX]$. Then the subarray from $h[1]$ to $h[sortNX - 1]$ is converted again to a heap. If the new value at the root is smaller than a child, the reheap swaps that value with the larger of the two children. Following that value down the tree, the process is repeated until the value is larger than its children or until the value is in a leaf. The following presents the general detailed outline of the *Reheap* procedure which, if necessary, moves the root $h[1]$ down the array so that the corresponding complete tree is a heap.

Figure 11.26

Placement of G in the
sorted subarray, $h[7..8]$,
and conversion of sub-
array $h[1..6]$ to a heap

Step 1

Swap root and last node of heap,
$h[1] = G$ and $h[7] = C$

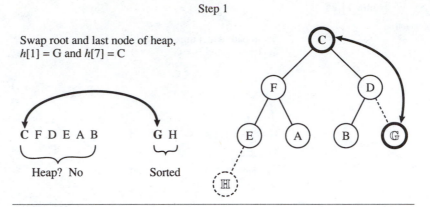

C F D E A B   G H

Heap? No   Sorted

Step 2

Swap parent and maximum child,
$h[1] = C$ and $h[2] = F$

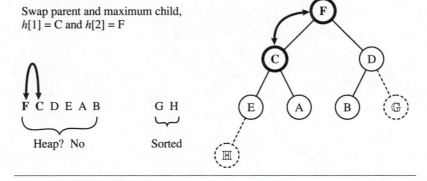

F C D E A B   G H

Heap? No   Sorted

Step 3

Swap parent and maximum child,
$h[2] = C$ and $h[4] = E$

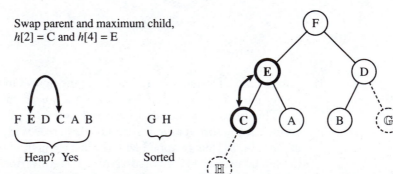

F E D C A B   G H

Heap? Yes   Sorted

Figure 11.27

Placement of F in the sorted subarray, $h[6..8]$, and conversion of sub-array $h[1..5]$ to a heap

Step 1

Swap root and last node of heap, $h[1] = F$ and $h[6] = B$

Heap? No   Sorted

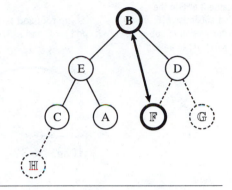

Step 2

Swap parent and maximum child, $h[1] = B$ and $h[2] = E$

Heap? No   Sorted

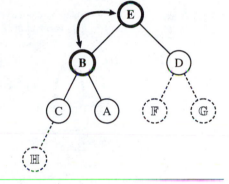

Step 3

Swap parent and maximum child, $h[2] = B$ and $h[4] = C$

Heap? No   Sorted

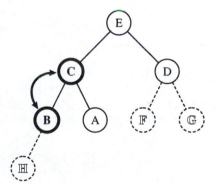

Figure 11.28

Placement of E in the sorted subarray, $h[5..8]$, and conversion of subarray $h[1..4]$ to a heap

Step 1

Swap root and last node of heap, $h[1] = E$ and $h[5] = A$

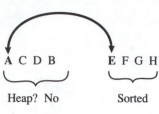

A C D B   E F G H

Heap? No   Sorted

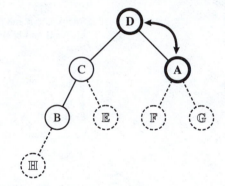

Step 2

Swap parent and maximum child, $h[1] = A$ and $h[3] = D$

D C A B   E F G H

Heap? Yes   Sorted

Figure 11.29

Placement of D in the sorted subarray, $h[4..8]$, and conversion of subarray $h[1..3]$ to a heap

Step 1

Swap root and last node of heap, $h[D] = C$ and $h[4] = B$

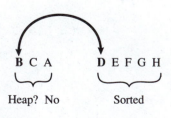

B C A   D E F G H

Heap? No   Sorted

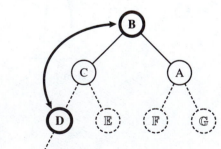

Figure 11.29

continued

Step 2

Swap parent and maximum child,
$h[1] = B$ and $h[2] = C$

C B A   D E F G H

Heap? Yes   Sorted

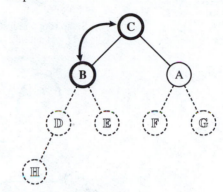

Figure 11.30

Completion of conversion
of h from a heap to a
sorted array

Step 1

Swap root and last node of heap,
$h[1] = C$ and $h[3] = A$

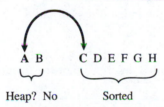

A B   C D E F G H

Heap? No   Sorted

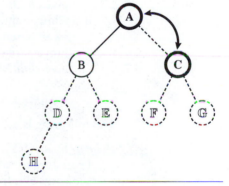

Step 2

Swap parent and maximum child,
$h[1] = A$ and $h[2] = B$

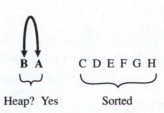

B A   C D E F G H

Heap? Yes   Sorted

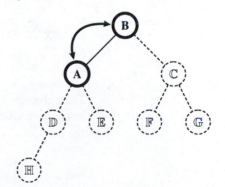

continued on next page

Figure 11.30

continued

Step 3

Swap root and last node of heap,
$h[1] = B$ and $h[2] = A$

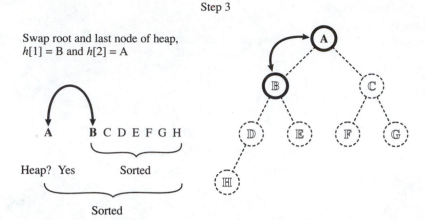

Heap? Yes   Sorted

Sorted

Start parent at the root
Give *childNX* the index of the left child
while (the left subarray is not a heap) and (the left child exists) do
    if the right child exists then
        give *childNX* the index of the larger child.
    if the larger child is greater than the parent
        swap parent and child
        move parent down one level
        give *childNX* the index of its left child
    else
        we have a heap

The following is a detailed description of the procedure *Reheap*:

Reheap(h, sortNX)
    Procedure to reform h so that the complete binary tree stored in the
    subarray $h[1..(sortNX - 1)]$ is a heap; the root in $h[1]$ may be out of
    place.
Input:
    h — array
    sortNX — index of the first element of the sorted subarray
Output:
    h — revised array
Assumptions:
    The subarray $h[1..(sortNX - 1)]$ with $h[sortNX]$ replacing $h[1]$ is a
    heap; *sortNX* is less than or equal to the number of elements in h.

Figure   **Algorithm**

                  parentNX ← 1
                  childNX ← 2 * *parentNX*
                  heap   ← *false*

{11.25}   while (not *heap*) and (*childNX* < *sortNX*) do
                    RchildNX ← *childNX* + 1

                    if *RchildNX* < *sortNX* then
{Step 1}   if *h*[*RchildNX*] > *h*[*childNX*] then
                            childNX ← *RchildNX*
                    if *h*[*childNX*] > *h*[*parentNX*] then
{Step 2}   swap(*h*[*parentNX*], *h*[*childNX*])
                        parentNX ← *childNX*
                        childNX ← 2 ∗ *parentNX*
                else
                        heap ← *true*

The formation of the sorted array is given in the procedure *BuildSortTree*. That operation repeatedly exchanges the root for the last element of the heap and then performs *Reheap* on the resulting smaller subarray.

BuildSortTree(h, n)
    Procedure to sort an array *h* of *n* elements that stores a heap
Input:
    h — array
    n — number of elements in *h*
Output:
    h — revised array
Assumptions:
    Array *h* stores a heap in elements *h*[1] to *h*[*n*]; the index type is a subrange starting at 1 and going to at least *n*.

Figure	**Algorithm**
{11.24–30}	for *sortNX* from *n* downto 2 do
	swap(*h*[1], *h*[*sortNX*])
	Reheap(*h*, *sortNX*)

The entire heapsort process of building a heap and then converting it to a sorted array is as follows:

Heapsort(h, n)
    Procedure to perform a heapsort on the array *h* of *n* elements
Input:
    h — array
    n — number of elements in *h*
Output:
    h — revised array
Assumptions:
    The index type of *h* is a subrange starting at 1 and going to at least *n*; elements *h*[1] through *h*[*n*] have values.

Figure	**Algorithm**
{11.20–30}	*BuildHeap*(*h*, *n*)
	BuildSortTree(*h*, *n*)

The complexity of the heapsort algorithm is $O(n \log_2 n)$, regardless of the original data, random, sorted, or reverse sorted. We process $n - 1$ elements in building the heap. For the addition of an element, in the worst case *PlaceIn-Heap* must move that element through every level of the tree. But in a complete tree the number of levels is $\lceil \log_2(n + 1) \rceil$. Thus, the procedure *BuildHeap* has complexity $O(n \log_2 n)$. With each of the two stages of the *Heapsort* being on the order of $O(n \log_2 n)$ and with $O(2n \log_2 n) = O(n \log_2 n)$, the complexity of *Heapsort* is $O(n \log_2 n)$. Usually, *Heapsort* is slower than *Quicksort* on the average case but is a vast improvement over *Quicksort*'s $O(n^2)$ performance in the sorted and reverse sorted cases.

$\triangledown$

SECTION 11.4 EXERCISES

1. Draw a hierarchy chart for *Heapsort*.

2. Describe with sketches the action of *PlaceInHeap*(*h*, *childNX*) for *childNX* = 5 and *h:* M G A B K.

3. Repeat Exercise 2 for *childNX* = 6 and *h:* P F B C A Z.

4. Repeat Exercise 2 for *childNX* = 18 and *h:* Y P S N L M K H J C F G D F B A E X.

5. Repeat Exercise 2 for *childNX* = 3 and *h:* A_1 A_2 A_3, where $A_1 = A_2 = A_3$.

6. Describe with sketches the action of *BuildHeap*(*h*, *n*) for *n* = 4 and *h:* S U P T.

7. Repeat Exercise 6 for *n* = 5 and *h:* A B C D E.

8. Repeat Exercise 6 for *n* = 5 and *h:* E D C B A.

9. Repeat Exercise 6 for *n* = 3 and *h:* A_1 A_2 A_3, where $A_1 = A_2 = A_3$.

10. Describe with sketches the action of *Reheap*(*h*, *sortNX*) for *sortNX* = 4 and *h:* B E K.

11. Repeat Exercise 10 for *sortNX* = 5 and *h:* D K A C.

12. Repeat Exercise 10 for *sortNX* = 13 and *h:* E P N K M L D C H F G J.

13. Describe with sketches the action of *BuildSortTree*(*h*, *n*) for *n* = 3 and *h:* V T S.

14. Repeat Exercise 13 for *n* = 5 and *h:* X T W R S.

15. Repeat Exercise 13 for *n* = 5 and *h:* E D C B A.

16. Repeat Exercise 13 for the heap you developed in Exercise 6, *h:* U T P S.

17. **a.** Repeat Exercise 13 for the heap you developed in Exercise 9, *h:* A_1 A_2 A_3.
    b. Is *Heapsort* stable?

18. Describe with sketches the action of *Heapsort(h, n)* for $n = 5$ and *h:* E X A C K.

19. Repeat Exercise 18 for $n = 7$ and *h:* M D E A P H G.

20. Code *Heapsort* in Pascal with the actual code for the procedures used in place of procedure calls.

▽

PROGRAMMING PROJECT

1. The operating system of a time-sharing computer assigns a priority to each program that is awaiting execution. The job with the highest priority executes first. If two or more jobs share a priority, the job that has been waiting the longest executes first. A heap can be used to implement this priority queue. Simulate the action of this priority queue of jobs in a fashion similar to the example in Section 6.3.

▽

SECTION 11.5

Mergesort

Mergesort is another $O(n \log_2 n)$ sorting algorithm. This method has the advantage of displaying that performance for all arrangements of the data. In the average case, however, though the complexity is the same, *Quicksort* will usually run faster. Moreover, for an array implementation, room for twice as many elements will be needed to complete the mergesort.

To illustrate the algorithm, again suppose you have dropped your notes and now need to put the numbered pages back in order. One technique is to split the folder of notes in two, sort each half, and then merge the two halves to yield the notes in correct order. But how should we sort each half? We could follow the same procedure, cutting each part in half, sorting, and merging. This process could continue recursively until you arrive at the terminating condition of only one page of notes. We see that *Mergesort*, like *Quicksort*, is a divide and conquer algorithm. Figure 11.31 illustrates the recursive calls to *Mergesort*, repeatedly cutting each subarray in half. Figure 11.32 shows the results of the merges of these adjacent, sorted subarrays. The merge procedure will be considered momentarily, but the main focus of the mergesort procedure is to call itself to sort each half and then to call *merge* to blend the results. The general sketch of the algorithm below mirrors Figures 11.31 and 11.32.

if there is more than one element in the subarray
    mergesort the left half of the subarray
    mergesort the right half of the subarray
    merge the two subarrays

Figure 11.31

Recursive calls to *Merge-sort*

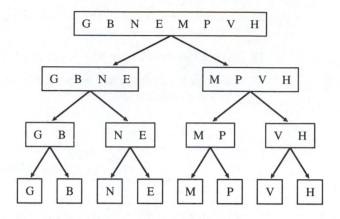

Figure 11.32

Merges of adjacent, sorted subarrays

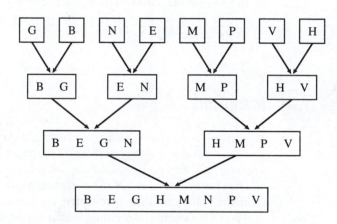

To split the array in two, we must calculate the index of the middle element as we did for the binary search,

$mid \leftarrow (first + last) \ div \ 2$

For example, in the array a of eight elements with indices ranging from 1 to 8,

$mid \leftarrow (1 + 8) \ div \ 2 = 9 \ div \ 2 = 4$

Consequently, the two subarrays are $a[1..4]$ and $a[5..8]$. For an array a of 5 elements,

$mid \leftarrow (1 + 5) \ div \ 2 = 6 \ div \ 2 = 3$

Thus, we consider one subarray containing three elements, $a[1..3]$, and another containing two, $a[4..5]$. A detailed description of the mergesort procedure follows:

Mergesort(a, first, last)

Procedure to perform a mergesort on the subarray of *a* for indices *first* to *last*

Input:

a	— array
first, last	— indices of *a*

Output:

a	— revised array

Assumptions:

The index type of *a* is a subrange of integers; *first* and *last* are in this subrange; *a* is defined for indices from *first* to *last*.

Figure	Algorithm
	if *first* < *last* then
	mid ← (*first* + *last*) *div* 2
{11.31}	*Mergesort(a, first, mid)*
	Mergesort(a, mid + 1, last)
{11.32}	*merge(a, first, mid, last)*

The merging process is illustrated in Figures 11.33−11.35 for adjacent subarrays $a[1..4]$ containing B, E, G, N and $a[5..8]$ with H, M, P, V. A temporary array, *temp*, is needed to store the developing merged array. We compare the first two elements in the subarrays. Whichever is smaller is copied into *temp* with the appropriate indices in the subarray and *temp* being advanced. In Step 2 of Figure 11.33 the element from the subarray $a[1..4]$, $a[1]$ = B, is smaller than the corresponding element from $a[5..8]$, $a[5]$ = H. Thus, we copy the value of $a[1]$ = B into *temp*[1] and increment by 1 the indices of $a[1..4]$ and *temp*, *ndx1* and *i*, respectively. We now repeat the process on subarrays $a[2..4]$ and $a[5..8]$ with the elements indicated by *ndx1* and *ndx2*, respectively. Because E < H and G < H, E and G are copied into *temp* with the first subarray index, *ndx1*, and the index of *temp*, *i*, advanced to 4. (See Step 3 of Figure 11.33 and Step 1 of Figure 11.34.) At this point we must merge the subarrays $a[4..4]$ and $a[5..8]$. We have

$$a[ndx1] = a[4] = N$$

and

$$a[ndx2] = a[5] = H$$

With N > H, *temp*[4] is assigned H and *ndx2* and *i* are incremented (Step 2, Figure 11.34).

This process of sending the smaller of $a[ndx1]$ and $a[ndx2]$ to the *temp* array continues until we have advanced through all the elements of one of the two subarrays. After Step 1 of Figure 11.35 when N is written to *temp*, *ndx1* becomes 5 which is past *last1*, so that the first subarray is empty. Thus, as in Steps 2 and 3, we only need to copy the remaining elements of the other subarray into *temp*. At this point, *temp* contains merged arrays, but *a* does not.

Figure 11.33

Initial action of *merge* (*a*, 1, 4, 8)

Figure 11.33

Initial action of *merge* (*a*, 1, 4, 8)

Step 1

Step 2
B < H

Step 3
E < H

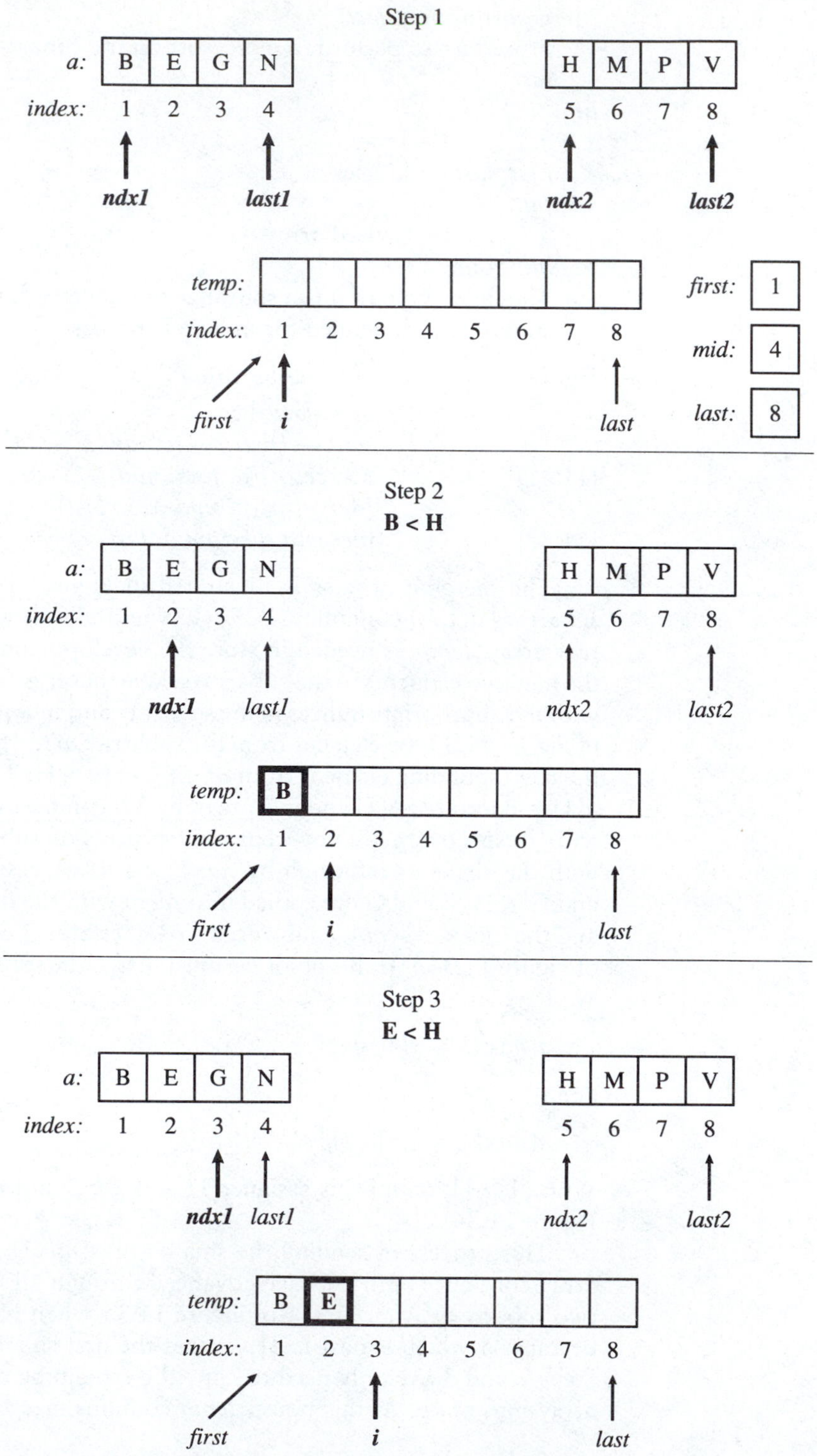

Figure 11.34

Continuation from Figure 11.33 of *merge* (*a*, 1, 4, 8)

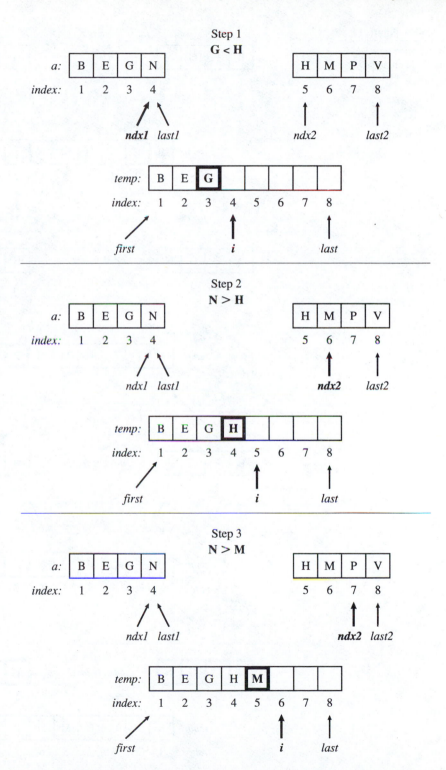

Step 1
G < H

Step 2
N > H

Step 3
N > M

Figure 11.35

Continuation from Figure 11.34 of *merge* (*a*, 1, 4, 8)

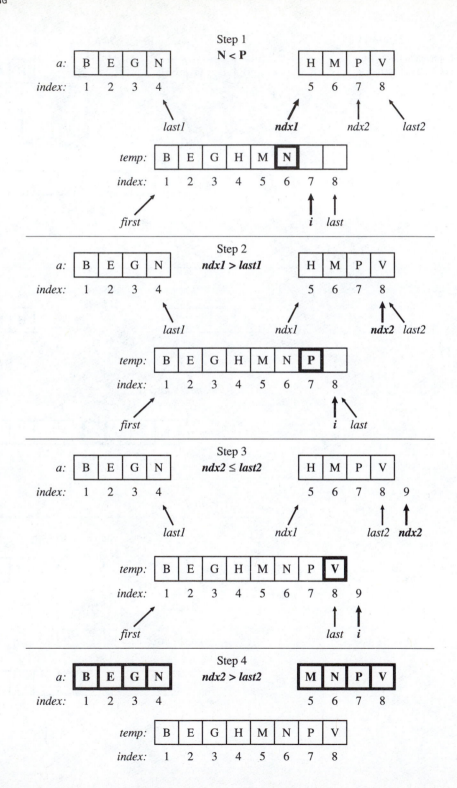

Thus, as Step 4 shows, we complete the procedure by copying the elements of $temp[1..8]$ into $a[1..8]$.

This algorithm would work equally as well for $first = 9$, $mid = 12$, and $last = 16$. In this case we merge subarrays $a[9..12]$ and $a[13..16]$ into $temp[9..16]$ and then copy the result back into $a[9..16]$.

The general outline of the *merge* algorithm follows:

Initialize indices.
While neither subarray is empty do
    Copy the smaller first subarray element into *temp*.
    Advance the indices of *temp* and that subarray.
Copy the rest of the first subarray elements (if any) into *temp*.
Copy the rest of the second subarray elements (if any) into *temp*.
Copy *temp*'s elements into *a*.

When the first *while* loop is complete, one of the subarrays is empty. Consequently, we need to copy elements of either the first subarray or the second into *temp*. A detailed description of the merge procedure follows:

merge(a, first, mid, last)
    Procedure to merge sorted subarrays $a[first..mid]$ and $a[(mid + 1)..last]$
    into a sorted subarray $a[first..last]$
Input:
    a   — array
    first, mid, last — indices of *a*
Output:
    a   — revised array
Assumptions:
    $mid = (first + last)$ *div* 2; $a[first..mid]$ and $a[(mid + 1)..last]$ are each
    sorted.

Figure	**Algorithm**
{11.33}	
{Step 1}	$ndx1 \leftarrow first$
	$last1 \leftarrow mid$
	$ndx2 \leftarrow mid + 1$
	$last2 \leftarrow last$
	$i \quad \leftarrow first$
{11.34}	
	while $(ndx1 \leq last1)$ and $(ndx2 \leq last2)$ do
{Step 1}	if $a[ndx1] \leq a[ndx2]$ then
	$temp[i] \leftarrow a[ndx1]$
	$ndx1 \quad \leftarrow ndx1 + 1$
	$i \quad\quad \leftarrow i + 1$
{Step 2}	else
	$temp[i] \leftarrow a[ndx2]$
	$ndx2 \quad \leftarrow ndx2 + 1$
	$i \quad\quad \leftarrow i + 1$

while $(ndx1 \leq last1)$ do
$\quad temp[i] \leftarrow a[ndx1]$
$\quad ndx1 \quad \leftarrow ndx1 + 1$
$\quad i \qquad \leftarrow i + 1$

{11.35}
{Steps 2–3}   while $(ndx2 \leq last2)$ do
$\quad temp[i] \leftarrow a[ndx2]$
$\quad ndx2 \quad \leftarrow ndx2 + 1$
$\quad i \qquad \leftarrow i + 1$

{Step 3}   for i from *first* to *last* do
$\quad a[i] \leftarrow temp[i]$

The procedure *Mergesort* repeatedly divides the problem in half. Thus, as the tree in Figure 11.36 illustrates, for an array of n elements, there are $\lceil \log_2 n \rceil + 1$ levels of the tree. For our example with eight elements,

$$\lceil \log_2 n \rceil + 1 = \lceil \log_2 2^3 \rceil + 1 = 3 + 1 = 4$$

With nine elements another level would be required with

$$\lceil \log_2 n \rceil + 1 = \lceil \log_2 9 \rceil + 1 = \log_2 2^4 + 1 = 4 + 1 = 5$$

At each level approximately n comparisons are made to accomplish the merge of the two subarrays. Thus, *Mergesort* has a total complexity of $O(n \log_2 n)$. Regardless of the original order of the elements, we do a similar process of the splitting in half with $\lceil \log_2 n \rceil + 1$ levels and about n comparisons at each level. This procedure contrasts with *Quicksort* which in the best situations has $\lceil \log_2 (n + 1) \rceil$ levels, but in the worst situations of originally sorted and reverse sorted data has n levels. Thus, if there is a fairly good chance of a large amount of data being sorted or almost sorted, consider using *Heapsort* or *Mergesort*. Usually, however, *Quicksort* executes faster than those two procedures, and certainly for arrays *Quicksort* does not have the space overhead of the tempo-

Figure 11.36

Mergesort repeatedly divides the problem in half

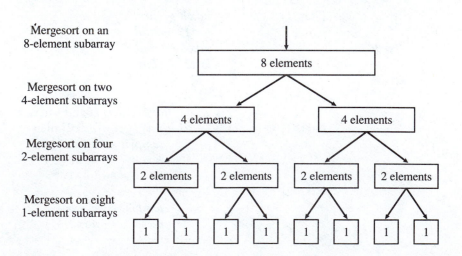

rary array for *Mergesort*. In contrast, *InsertionSort*, *SelectionSort*, *Quicksort*, and *Heapsort* are all **in-place** algorithms, moving elements within the original array and not requiring an additional temporary array.

▽

SECTION 11.5 EXERCISES

1. **a.** With sketches similar to Figures 11.31 and 11.32, describe the action of *Mergesort*(*a*, 1, *n*) for *n* = 4 and *a*: B C A D.
   b. How many levels are in the tree down to subarrays of two elements?

2. Repeat Exercise 1 for *n* = 11 and *a*: M P B T Z X S C F Y W.

3. Repeat Exercise 1 for *n* = 6 and *a*: A B C D E F.

4. Repeat Exercise 1 for *n* = 6 and *a*: F E D C B A.

5. Repeat Exercise 1 for *n* = 4 and *a*: $A_1 B_1 B_2 A_2$, where $A_1 = A_2$ and $B_1 = B_2$.

6. With sketches similar to Figures 11.33–11.35, describe the action of *merge* (*a, first, mid, last*) for *first* = 1, *mid* = 2, *last* = 4, and *a*: E J C F D G A B.

7. Repeat Exercise 6 for *first* = 1, *mid* = 3, *last* = 6, and *a*: C G M B H J.

8. Suppose the number *n* of elements to be sorted is a power of 2: $n = 2^m$ for some nonnegative integer *m*. Let *T*(*n*) be the maximum number of comparisons in a mergesort of *n* elements. Thus, *T*(*n*) is the maximum number of comparisons to sort both halves of *n*/2 elements each plus the maximum number of comparisons to merge the two halves. Complete the recursive definition of *T*.

$$T(1) = \underline{\quad a \quad}$$

$$T(n) = \underline{\quad b \quad} \times \underline{\quad c \quad} + \underline{\quad d \quad} \text{ for } n \geq 2$$

9. Code the *merge* procedure in Pascal.

10. Code the *Mergesort* procedure in Pascal.

11. Implement *merge* using linked lists.

12. Implement *Mergesort* using linked lists.

▽

PROGRAMMING PROJECT

1. Write a program to generate 1000 random integers in the range from 0 to 5000 and to save these numbers in a text file. If your version of Pascal does not have a built-in random number generator, refer to Appendix A.

   Investigate how you can time procedures with your version of Pascal. Then write two other programs to perform and time a quicksort and a mergesort on this file, saving the sorted data in a text file. Do not include input and output procedures in the timing. How do the times of the procedures compare?

Next, edit the sorted file to put a few numbers out of order. Repeat the timing and sorting discussed in the last paragraph, comparing the results.

Note that the timing process for a time-sharing system is probably dependent on the load. In this environment, for the actual timing test submit the programs immediately one after another to obtain a better approximation of the sort times.

SECTION 11.6 Sorting with a Permutation Array

The examples used to demonstrate the five sorting techniques of this chapter all involved arrays of characters. In these methods, the key by which we sort consists of the entire element. Usually, however, the key is a small subfield of a much larger record. The selection sort has a constant number of moves on the order of $O(n)$, but the number of comparisons with complexity $O(n^2)$ is great. Even efficient sorting methods that move the entire record bog down in large arrays with long records. Moreover, techniques such as mergesort that make a copy of the entire array consume a great deal of space. One alternative that avoids movement is to store the records in a linked list. The pointers do, however, consume space, and some processes, such as locating the middle element, are time consuming to implement.

In this section we consider a method that avoids moving the entire record when sorting the elements in an array. With this **sort-by-address** technique we have another array, p, called a **permutation array**, which stores the indices of the sorted array, a, in order. Each $p[i]$ is initialized to be i; instead of moving the element $a[i]$, we move the index $p[i]$. In situations where we normally exchange elements with $swap(a[i], a[j])$, we now switch indices with $swap(p[i], p[j])$. After sorting, $p[1]$ is the index of the smallest array element, so that $a[p[1]]$, instead of $a[1]$, is that least element. Figure 11.37 illustrates an array p before and after sorting.

Figure 11.37

Action of the sort-by-address method

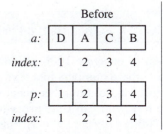
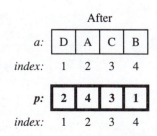

To print this sorted array of $n = 4$ elements in ascending order, we can employ this segment:

```
for i := 1 to n do
    writeln( a[ p[i] ] )
```

Thus, we have the following trace of the execution of this loop:

i	$p[i]$	$a[p[i]]$
1	$p[1] = 2$	$a[2] = $ A
2	$p[2] = 4$	$a[4] = $ B
3	$p[3] = 3$	$a[3] = $ C
4	$p[4] = 1$	$a[1] = $ D

The first element is $a[p[1]] = a[2] = $ A, while the last is $a[p[4]] = a[1] = $ D.

Any of the sorting methods work using sort by address. We must remember to initialize array p, pass this permutation array through the argument/parameter list, and assign values to p instead of a. Below is the insertion sort algorithm without and with sort by address. Differences between the two are in boldface for emphasis.

Insertion Sort

$a[0] \leftarrow$ low sentinel value

for i from 2 to n do
    temp $\leftarrow a[i]$
    loc $\leftarrow i$

    while $a[\textbf{loc} - \textbf{1}] > temp$ *do*
        $\textbf{a}[loc] \leftarrow \textbf{a}[loc - 1]$
        loc $\leftarrow loc - 1$

$\textbf{a}[loc] \leftarrow \textbf{temp}$

Insertion Sort with Sort by Address
for i from 0 to n do
    $p[i] \leftarrow i$
$a[0] \leftarrow$ low sentinel value

for i from 2 to n do
    temp $\leftarrow a[i]$
    loc $\leftarrow i$

    while $a[\textbf{p}[\textbf{loc} - \textbf{1}]] > temp$ *do*
        $\textbf{p}[loc] \leftarrow \textbf{p}[loc - 1]$
        loc $\leftarrow loc - 1$

$\textbf{p}[loc] \leftarrow \textbf{i}$

Because of the initialization of array p, at the beginning of the ith iteration of the *for* loop we have $p[i] = i, p[i + 1] = i + 1, \ldots, p[n] = n$. The values of $p[0], p[1], \ldots, p[i - 1]$, however, may have been permuted from earlier iterations. Since on the ith iteration $p[i]$ and i have the same value, we can say

    temp $\leftarrow a[i]$

instead of

    temp $\leftarrow a[p[i]]$.

Figure 11.38 parallels the insertion sort in Figure 11.1. For the insertion sort with the permutation array, by using *p*, the indices are inserted and the values in *a* are immobile.

A permutation array is useful when it is necessary to access an array of records by each of two different key fields. We can sort the array on the primary key and use a binary search to access a record by that key. With a sort-by-address method we can also sort the array by the secondary key. A permutation

Figure 11.38

Insertion sort as in Figure 11.1 and the corresponding insertion sort using a permutation array

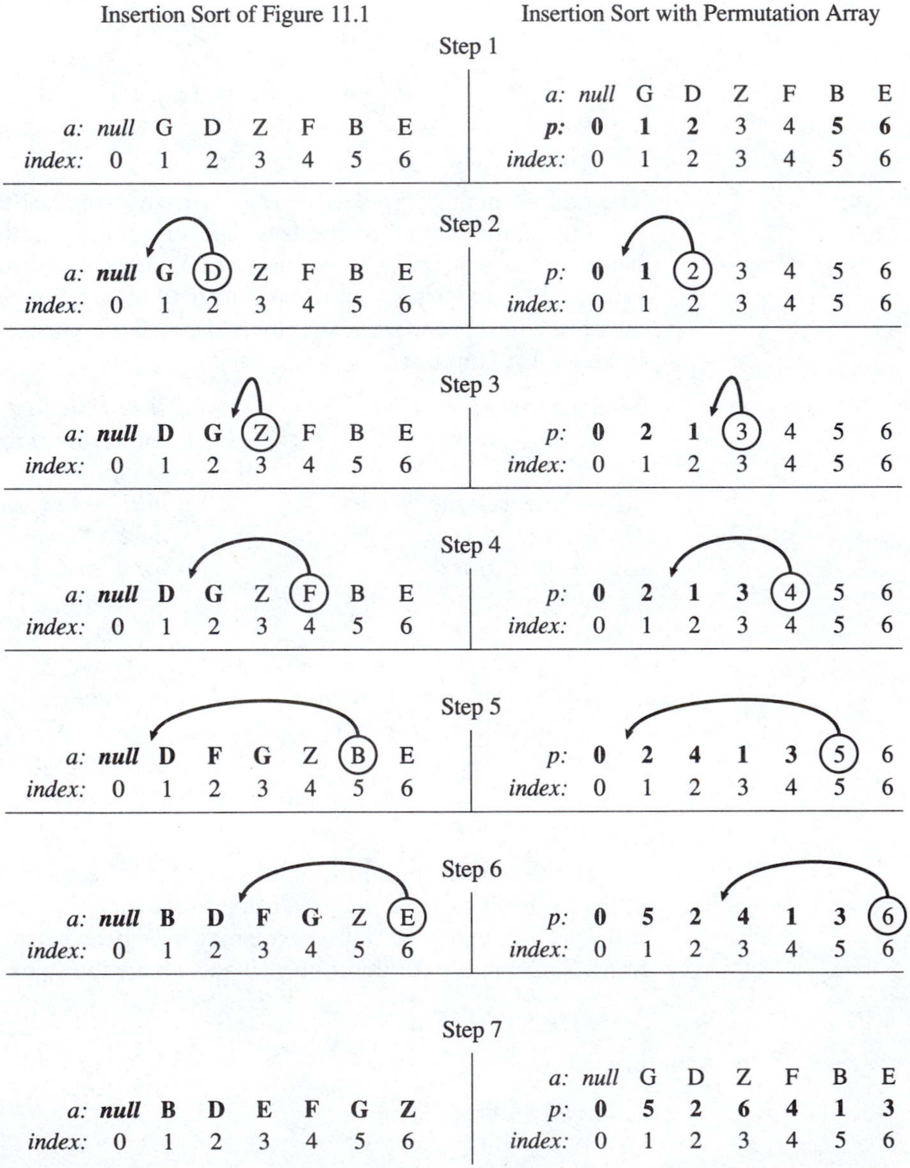

Insertion Sort of Figure 11.1 | Insertion Sort with Permutation Array

Step 1

```
a: null G D Z F B E          a: null G D Z F B E
index: 0 1 2 3 4 5 6         p:  0 1 2 3 4 5 6
                             index: 0 1 2 3 4 5 6
```

Step 2

```
a: null G (D) Z F B E        p:  0 1 (2) 3 4 5 6
index: 0 1 2 3 4 5 6         index: 0 1 2 3 4 5 6
```

Step 3

```
a: null D G (Z) F B E        p:  0 2 1 (3) 4 5 6
index: 0 1 2 3 4 5 6         index: 0 1 2 3 4 5 6
```

Step 4

```
a: null D G Z (F) B E        p:  0 2 1 3 (4) 5 6
index: 0 1 2 3 4 5 6         index: 0 1 2 3 4 5 6
```

Step 5

```
a: null D F G Z (B) E        p:  0 2 4 1 3 (5) 6
index: 0 1 2 3 4 5 6         index: 0 1 2 3 4 5 6
```

Step 6

```
a: null B D F G Z (E)        p:  0 5 2 4 1 3 (6)
index: 0 1 2 3 4 5 6         index: 0 1 2 3 4 5 6
```

Step 7

```
                             a: null G D Z F B E
a: null B D E F G Z          p:  0 5 2 6 4 1 3
index: 0 1 2 3 4 5 6         index: 0 1 2 3 4 5 6
```

array can then provide efficient access to the secondary key, perhaps through a binary search.

When sorting on one key, the permutation array should only be used in situations where an array record is large in comparison to the key and the number of records is about a hundred or more. In this case, time is saved by not having to move the entire record. This advantage is, however, at the sacrifice of room for the permutation array, a more involved algorithm, and computer time in locating $p[i]$ and then $a[p[i]]$. Thus, for a small array with lengthy records and short keys, the selection sort is preferable.

▽
SECTION 11.6 EXERCISES

1. Convert the selection sort algorithm of Section 11.2 to employ a permutation array.

2. Convert the quicksort algorithm of Section 11.3 to employ a permutation array.

3. Convert the quicksort algorithm with the median-of-three method to employ a permutation array.

4. Convert the heapsort algorithm of Section 11.4 to employ a permutation array.

5. Convert the mergesort algorithm of Section 11.5 to employ a permutation array.

6. Convert the bubblesort algorithm of Exercise 13, Section 11.1, to employ a permutation array.

7. Convert the doubly linked list implementation of insertion sort from Exercise 5, Section 11.1, to employ a permutation array of pointers.

▽
PROGRAMMING PROJECT

1. Write a program to read into an array an unordered file of names (last name first) and user-identification numbers (user-ids). Sort the array by the name and then use the sort-by-address technique to sort by user-id. After sorting, interactively ask the user for a name (user-id) and return the corresponding user-id (name). Use efficient sorting and searching techniques.

▽
SECTION 11.7

Comparison of Sorting Techniques

In this section we compare the five sorting techniques of this chapter. Figure 11.39 presents such a comparison relative to the complexity and stability of the

	Average Case	Best Case	Worst Case	Sort In-Place	Stable	Recursive*
Insertion sort	$O(n^2)$	$O(n^2)$	$O(n^2)$	Y	Y	N
Selection sort	$O(n^2)$	$O(n^2)$	$O(n^2)$	Y	N	N
Quicksort	$O(n \log_2 n)$	$O(n \log_2 n)$	$O(n^2)$	Y	N	Y
Quicksort with median of three	$O(n \log_2 n)$	$O(n \log_2 n)$	$O(n \log_2 n)$	Y	N	Y
Heapsort	$O(n \log_2 n)$	$O(n \log_2 n)$	$O(n \log_2 n)$	Y	N	N
Mergesort	$O(n \log_2 n)$	$O(n \log_2 n)$	$O(n \log_2 n)$	N	Y	Y

Figure 11.39

A comparison of the complexity and stability of sorting techniques

*Recursive version of procedure presented in the text.

methods. Notice that in the average case the insertion sort has complexity $O(n^2)$, while the quicksort is of order $O(n \log_2 n)$. Thus, the former executes with a speed less than or equal to $c \cdot n^2$ for some constant of proportionality, c. Similarly, for some constant of proportionality, d, the speed of quicksort is less than or equal to $d \cdot n \cdot \log_2 n$. These constants depend on many factors, including the particular machine on which the sort is being performed and the time for recursive procedure calls. In fact, for some values of these constants of proportionality and some smaller values of n, we can have $c \cdot n^2$ less than $d \cdot n \cdot \log_2 n$. For example, suppose $c = 1$ and $d = 5$. If there are $n = 16$ array elements,

$$c \cdot n^2 = 1 \cdot 16^2 = 256$$

while

$$d \cdot n \cdot \log_2 n = 5 \cdot 16 \cdot \log_2 16 = 5 \cdot 16 \cdot \log_2 2^4 = 5 \cdot 16 \cdot 4 = 320.$$

In this case, the insertion sort would be a better technique than the quicksort. In general, when there are less than about 20 elements to be sorted, the insertion sort with its straightforward algorithm is an excellent choice. Moreover, the insertion sort is stable and has complexity $O(n)$ for already sorted data, which give this technique distinct advantages over the selection sort.

The algorithm *Quicksort* is fast in part because the inner *repeat* loops of the partition are extremely fast. When data is almost sorted or reverse sorted, however, *Quicksort* degenerates to an order of $O(n^2)$. Augmented with the median-of-three technique, the complexity of $O(n \log_2 n)$ is restored but at the expense of computation of the medians.

The *Quicksort* procedure in Section 11.3 is recursive, so there is a danger of stack overflow with a large array. In this case, we can use a quicksort until the subarrays are of size 15 or 20 and complete the process on the almost sorted array with insertion sort; or we can convert to a nonrecursive version of quicksort.

When a quicksort is performed on a key and then on another key, we lose the first sort. Thus, when stability is important, we should use another technique or alter the keys. One method involves attaching progressively larger values at the end of each key. For example, we can augment array a,

a: Z X X Y X

with the letters of the alphabet as

aug: ZA XB XC YD XE

With every key unique and with XB < XC < XE, quicksort yields the sorted array

aug: XB XC XE YD ZA

Stripping off the additional key, we have a sorted array that is stable:

a: X X X Y Z.

Heapsort is a sound alternative when stability is not important and when almost sorted data is a strong possibility. Also, since the version presented in Section 11.4 is not recursive, we do not have the concern with stack overflow and time-consuming procedure calls. Because of the time spent building the heap and then building the sort tree, however, heapsort does usually execute slower than quicksort.

The version of mergesort from Section 11.5 is recursive. We can, however, avoid stack overflow problems with some of the same solutions mentioned for quicksort. For example, we can use mergesort to obtain arrays of about size 15 or 20 and then use insertion sort on each subarray. Because of the partitioning with quicksort, all the elements in a subarray are less than or equal to all the elements that follow in the array. Thus, after employing quicksort, we perform the insertion sort on the entire array. With mergesort values are still dispersed even after the array is split into subarrays. Consequently, we must use insertion sort on each small subarray before merging. Because this method chops the array into smaller subarrays and we merge two subarrays at a time, mergesort is an excellent technique for sorting an external file that is too large to be stored in the computer at one time.

The choice of sorting techniques depends on the data, the computer, and the desired results. It has been proven, however, that a method that employs comparisons of keys cannot be faster than $O(n \log_2 n)$. Analysis of the performance of existing sorting algorithms and development of additional ones are active areas of computer science research.

SECTION 11.7 EXERCISES

1. For each situation give the best sorting technique(s) to use.

   a. The array has 500 records. Each record is 700 characters with a 9-character key.

   b. The array has 18 real numbers.

   c. An array of 2000 records contains fall registration information, which will be sorted twice to produce a report of students enrolled in each class.

     d. The array has 14 records. Each record is 1000 characters with an integer key.

     e. An array of 1000 employee records is probably sorted by name.

2. Consider array *a:* $A_1 A_2 A_3$, where $A_1 = A_2 = A_3$.

     a. Attach an extra character in sequence on the right of each element and perform a quicksort partition of the array. Then strip off the extra character.

     b. Was the result of Part a stable?

3. For the array *StudentRec* in Section 1.2, code in Pascal a version of quicksort that will be stable by attaching two extra characters on the end of each name.

4. Suppose a table is implemented as a linked list with each key being a three-digit number. The **radix** or **distribution sort** splits the nodes into 10 buckets or linked lists based on the least significant digit of the key. Every linked list has a head and tail pointer. Each time a node is placed in a bucket, the node is inserted at the tail. Thus, when the node with key 387 is processed, that node is placed at the rear of the linked list with head and tail indicated by *head*[7] and *tail*[7], respectively. The buckets are concatenated into one linked list, and the process is repeated using the second digit. After concatenation, the nodes are distributed to the 10 buckets based on the most significant digit. The final concatenation yields a sorted linked list.

     a. Perform the radix sort by hand on the following set of keys: 387, 690, 913, 744, 327, 431 213, 161, 065, 979, 625, 521, 517, 415, 875, 750, 946, 269, 368, 814.

     b. What data structure best describes each bucket?

     c. Write a nonrecursive radix sort procedure.

     d. How many times is the inner loop executed for a table with *n* elements?

5. One way to place items into an array *a* so that *a* will eventually be ordered is with a **linear probing sort**. A **linear interpolation function** is used to estimate the position *i* of an item *x* in *a*. If *a*[*i*] is empty, *x* is inserted. If a collision occurs and *x* is smaller than *a*[*i*], values are swapped. After the collision and possible exchange, position $i + 1$ is examined in the same fashion. The process continues until *x* can be inserted. When all the records are in the array, nonempty elements are compressed to the beginning of the array. Because the search for an available location can carry the element well beyond the original probing index, the interpolation function should not return values close to the end of the table. For example, in an array with indices from 0 to 99, the function might return indices between 0 and 74 with the locations 75 through 99 used for overflow. Design a program to perform the linear probing sort where data is read from a binary file. (See Exercise 17 of Section 3.2 for a similar linear interpolation formula used in an interpolation search where keys are fairly uniformly distributed throughout the array.)

6. Suppose you need to work with sets of integers in the range from 1 to n, where n is very large. Probably the version of Pascal you are using will not be able to store such a set using the built-in type *set*. One possibility is to implement a set as a packed array of boolean values as described in Project 1 of Section 3.5. If, however, each set contains few elements, this solution wastes an excessive amount of space. For example, suppose a set is expected to hold at most $m = 50$ integers in the range from 1 to $n = 1,000,000$. Assuming 8 bits to a byte, each set, implemented as a boolean array of one million elements, would consume over 122 K of memory (1K = 1024 bytes) with all but about 6 bytes wasted.

   One alternative is to store the integers in an array of 100 elements using the linear probing sort of Exercise 5. If 4 bytes can contain an integer, such an arrangement would only use about 0.4 K. For $n = 1,000,000$ and $m = 50$, the linear interpolation function should map each integer to an index from 0 to 49 with the second half of the array used for overflow. For fairly uniformly distributed integers, we can calculate the initial probe position by multiplying the number by 50/1,000,000 = 0.00005 and taking the integer part. For example, to insert 326,059, we compute $\lfloor 326,000 \cdot 50/1,000,000 \rfloor$ = 16 and attempt an insertion into the array element with index 16.

   Implement the ADT set operations using this linear probing technique for sets of at most m elements in the range from 1 to n.

PROGRAMMING PROJECTS

1. Write a program to read a file of unique integers in the range from 1 to 27,000 and sort these values. For example, each number could be the index to a precinct in a political district of a state. One fast way of sorting is to initialize each element of a packed boolean array of 27,000 items to be *false*. We read each integer from the file, and in a process called **bit mapping** we change the corresponding array element to be *true*. Afterwards, each integer from 1 to 27,000 with an array value of *true* is written to the file.

   Be sure you handle the errors of the same number appearing twice in the input and of a number being out of range.

   What is the complexity of this algorithm?

2. Write a program to read in a list of words from a file and produce a report of all the anagrams. Anagrams are different words that use the same letters, such as "below," bowel," and "elbow." If your computer system has a dictionary you can access, use part of that as your file of words. To find the anagrams assign to each letter a different prime number. Then calculate the product of the corresponding primes for each word in your list. For example, the number associated with "below" is $3 \times 11 \times 37 \times 47 \times 83 = 4,763,121$. The Fundamental Theorem of Arithmetic tells us that each positive integer factors in exactly one way (other than different possible orders) into a product of primes. Consequently, the only factors of 4,763,121 are 3, 11, 37, 47,

and 83; and only anagrams to "below," such as "bowel" and "elbow," have the same associated number. After pairing each word with its number, sort the list into ascending order by the number. All the anagrams for each word will be clustered with the word since they are all paired with the same number.

To avoid overflow, use words that are five letters or less in length and have real number products. Recall that we cannot accurately test if two real numbers x and y are equal using the expression $(x = y)$. Because we are only multiplying integers, however, we can claim that x and y are equal if they are within 0.25 of each other,

$$|x - y| < 0.25$$

12

Graphs and Networks

Introduction

In Section 10.1 we defined a graph, g, as a set of nodes, N, and a set of edges, E, connecting pairs of nodes. For example, a tree is a particular type of graph. Graphs help us understand and represent structures in computer science and aid our application of computer science to other fields, such as business and the sciences. In this chapter we present the abstract data type graph along with two kinds of implementations and several applications.

SECTION 12.1

ADT Graph

We denote an edge e connecting two nodes of a graph, u and v, as a pair (u, v) or (v, u). The graph in Figure 12.1 contains five nodes and four edges. This graph certainly is not a graph of a function like those you would encounter in calculus.

Figure 12.1

A graph

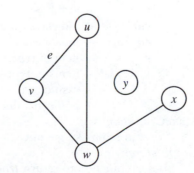

In a graph a **path** from node v_0 to v_n is a sequence of nodes

$$v_0, v_1, v_2, \ldots, v_{n-1}, v_n$$

where there is an edge connecting pairs of vertices, (v_0, v_1), (v_1, v_2), ..., (v_{n-1}, v_n). Thus, in Figure 12.1 one path from x to u is x, w, v, u. The **length** of a path is the number of nodes along the path, so that this path from x to u with its four nodes has length 4. (Some texts define the length of a path as the number of edges along the path.) As every path does, this path has one more node than edge. A path is a **cycle** if it begins and ends at the same point ($v_0 = v_n$) and no edge or vertex, except the first, is repeated. We see that Figure 12.1 contains the cycle u, v, w, u.

This figure is not a connected graph since it is in two parts. In a **connected** graph there is a path from any vertex to any other vertex. In Chapter 10 we discussed trees, which are connected graphs with no cycles.

Nodes w and x in Figure 12.1 are **adjacent** or are **neighbors** because there exists an edge, $(w, x) = (x, w)$, connecting them. Edge e is **incident** to vertices u and v since u and v are endpoints of e. The **degree** of node w, $deg(w)$, is 3, the number of times w is an endpoint of an edge. Since $deg(y) = 0$, y is an **isolated node**. Without node y we have a connected subgraph; s is a **subgraph** of graph g if s is a graph and every node and edge of s is in g.

Figure 12.2 presents the definition of the ADT graph, and examples that follow develop additional operations. As with entries in the ADT table and the ADT binary tree, each node in the ADT graph has a key. For simplicity, instead of referring to "the node with key k" we often say "the node k." Similarly, one notation for the edge connecting nodes with keys $k1$ and $k2$ is $(k1, k2)$.

Figure 12.2.

Formal definition of ADT graph

ADT Graph

Objects: A graph structure of nodes and edges. Each node has a key that identifies the entry and that is the entire entry or a subfield.

Operations:
Notation:

elType	— type of the element portion of a node
keyType	— type of the key portion of the element
infoType	— type of the information portion of the element
g	— graph
curNode	— indicates a node
curEdge	— indicates an edge
e	— item of type *elType*
k, k1, k2	— items of type *keyType*
x	— item of type *infoType*
b	— boolean value

MakeGraphEmpty(g)
Procedure to make g empty

GraphIsEmpty(g) → b
Boolean function to return *true* if g is empty

Figure 12.2

continued

GraphIsFull(*g*) → *b*
> Boolean function to return *true* if *g* is full

KeyGraphEl(*e*) → *k*
> Function to return *e*'s key

KeyFoundGraph(*g, k*) → *b*
> Boolean function to return *true* if a node with key *k* is found in *g*

ToNode(*g, k, curNode*)
> Procedure to make *curNode* point to the node in *g* with key *k*; assume such a node exists

ToEdge(*g, k1, k2, curEdge*)
> Procedure to make *curEdge* point to the edge in *g* that connects nodes with keys *k1* and *k2*; assume such nodes exist; if the edge does not exist, *curEdge* becomes empty

EdgeIsEmpty(*g, CurEdge*) → *b*
> Boolean function to return *true* if the edge indicated by *curEdge* is empty

InsertNode(*g, e*)
> Procedure to insert a node containing *e* into *g* as an isolated node; assume before insertion a node containing the key of *e* is not in *g*

InsertEdge(*g, k1, k2*)
> Procedure to insert an edge in *g* incident to nodes with keys *k1* and *k2*; assume such nodes exist; assume edge (*k1, k2*) does not exist before insertion

DeleteNode(*g, curNode*)
> Procedure to delete from *g* the node indicated by *curNode* along with all incident edges; assume before deletion that such a node exists

DeleteEdge(*g, curEdge*)
> Procedure to delete from *g* the edge indicated by *curEdge*; assume before deletion that such an edge exists

UpdateNode(*g, curNode, x*)
> Procedure to place *x*'s value in the information portion of the node indicated by *curNode* in graph *g*; assume *curNode* indicates a node

RetrieveNode(*g, curNode*) → *e*
> Function to return the value in the node indicated by *curNode* in graph *g*; assume *curNode* indicates a node

TraverseGraph(*g, Visit*(*ArgumentList*))
> Procedure to traverse *g*, executing *Visit*(*ArgumentList*) for every element in *g*, where *Visit* is a user-specified procedure and *ArgumentList* is a list of arguments

---

Example 12.1.

▼ In this example we will design a boolean function *IsAdjacent*(*g, k1, k2*) to return *true* if graph *g* contains an edge (*k1, k2*) connecting nodes with keys *k1* and *k2*.

We have a boolean function, *KeyFoundGraph*, to detect the presence of a node containing a key. Consequently, we can test if nodes *k1* and *k2* are in *g*. If they are, we use the procedure *ToEdge*. If the edge (*k1, k2*) exists, *ToEdge* forces *curEdge* to point to that edge; if not, *curEdge* becomes empty. Afterwards *EdgeIsEmpty* can test whether *curEdge* is empty or actually does point to the edge (*k1, k2*). The algorithm follows:

IsAdjacent(g, k1, k2) → b
>   Boolean function to return *true* if graph *g* contains an edge (*k1, k2*)
>   connecting nodes with keys *k1* and *k2*

Input:
>   g   — graph
>   k1, k2 — keys

Output:
>   b   — boolean value

Assumption:
>   g exists.

Algorithm:
>   if *KeyFoundGraph*(g, k1) and *KeyFoundGraph*(g, k2) then
>   *ToEdge*(g, k1, k2, curEdge)
>   *IsAdjacent* ← not *EdgeIsEmpty*(g, curEdge)
>   else
>   *IsAdjacent* ← *false*

Example 12.2.

For this example we develop a procedure to form a queue of the keys from nodes adjacent to a node with key *k*.

After initializing the queue, we use the *TraverseGraph* procedure to process all the nodes of the graph. The visit procedure consists of checking with *IsAdjacent* of Example 12.1 to see if an edge exists between the current node and the node with key *k*. If so, the key value for the current node is enqueued. The visit procedure, *AdjToQueue*, is as follows:

AdjToQueue(q, g, k1, k2)
>   Procedure to enqueue *k2* into *q* provided the nodes with keys *k1* and *k2*
>   are adjacent in graph *g*

Input:
>   q   — queue
>   g   — graph
>   k1, k2 — keys

Output:
>   q   — revised queue

Assumptions:
>   q exists; k1 and k2 are keys of nodes in the graph g.

Algorithm:
>   if *IsAdjacent*(g, k1, k2) then
>   *EnQueue*(q, k2)

On our traversal of the graph we use *KeyGraphEl(e)* to obtain the key for each node. Thus, we call the above visit procedure with

   AdjToQueue(q, g, k, KeyGraphEl(e))

The entire *AdjacentQueue* procedure is:

AdjacentQueue(q, g, k)
   Procedure to build a queue *q* of keys from nodes adjacent to a node *k* in graph *g*
Input:
   g — graph
   k — key
Output:
   q — queue
Assumptions:
   g is defined; there exists a node with key *k*.
Algorithm:
   MakeQueueEmpty(q)
   TraverseGraph(g, AdjToQueue(q, g, k, KeyGraphEl(e)))

▲

SECTION 12.1 EXERCISES

1. Answer the following questions concerning the graph in Figure 12.3.

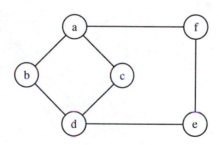

Figure 12.3

Graph for Exercise 1

   a. List every path from *a* to *e* that does not repeat an edge, and give the length of each of these paths.
   b. Give all the cycles starting with *a*.
   c. Draw three subgraphs that are trees.
   d. Draw two subgraphs that are not connected.
   e. Draw three subgraphs that are connected but are not trees.

2. For Figure 12.1 find all the nodes adjacent to

   a. *u*   **b.** *v*   **c.** *w*   **d.** *x*   **e.** *y*

3. For Figure 12.1 find

   a. *deg(u)*   **b.** *deg(v)*   **c.** *deg(w)*
   d. *deg(x)*   **e.** *deg(y)*
   f. The sum of the degrees of all the vertices.
   g. The number of edges.
   h. What is the relation between Parts f and g?
   i. Why is the sum of all the degrees twice the number of edges?

4. For the graph in Figure 12.1 draw all

   a. the subgraphs of exactly one node.
   b. the subgraphs of two nodes and an edge.
   c. the cycles.
   d. trees containing four points that are subgraphs.

5. Draw four trees that are subgraphs and that contain every node in Figure 12.3.

6. In a connected graph an **articulation point** is a node whose removal, along with the elimination of all incident edges, causes the graph to become disconnected. Find the articulation points, if any, in

   a. Figure 10.1   **b.** Figure 12.3   **c.** Figure 12.4

Figure 12.4

Graph for Exercises 6 and 9–13

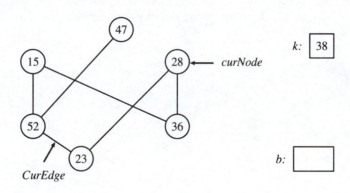

7. A graph is **complete** if exactly one edge connects each pair of distinct nodes. Draw a complete graph with the following number of nodes and give the degree of each vertex in such a graph.

   a. 1   **b.** 2   **c.** 3   **d.** 4   **e.** 5

8. Let *g* be a complete graph of *n* nodes. (See Exercise 7.)

   a. What is the degree of each node?
   b. What is the sum of the degrees of all the nodes?
   c. Using Part b of this exercise and Part i of Exercise 3, develop a formula for the number of edges in a complete graph.

For the graph g in Figure 12.4 suppose the number presented in the node is a key and that the key is the entire element stored in the node. Moreover, cur-Node indicates a node and curEdge *points to an edge. Variable* k *is of type* keyType = elType. *Starting with that figure in Exercises 9–13, draw the results of each sequence of ADT graph operations.*

9. *DeleteNode*(*g, curNode*)
   DeleteEdge(*g, curEdge*)

10. *InsertNode*(*g, k*)
    TraverseGraph(*g, InsertEdge*(*g, e, k*))

11. if not *IsAdjacent*(*g*, 47, 23)
    then *InsertEdge*(*g*, 47, 23)

12. *ToEdge*(*g*, 15, 52, *curEdge*)
    b ← EdgeIsEmpty(*curEdge*)

13. *InsertEdge*(*g*, 52, *RetrieveNode*(*curNode*))
    ToNode(*g*, 52, *curNode*)

Use pseudocode and ADT graph operations to define the routines in Exercises 14–33.

14. Procedure *DeleteGraphValue*(*g, f*) to read each value *k* of type *keyType* from a binary file *f* and, if in *g*, delete the corresponding node from *g*.

15. Procedure *GraphTwo*(*g, e1, e2*) to create a graph *g* with two adjacent nodes containing *e1* and *e2*.

16. Boolean function *IsEdge*(*g, k1, k2, curEdge*) to return *true* if the node indicated by *curEdge* is (*k1, k2*).

17. Procedure *PrintGraph* to print all the values stored in a graph.

18. Function *NumNodes* that returns the number of nodes in a graph.

19. Function *deg* to return the degree of a node.

20. Boolean function *IsIsolated* to return *true* if a node is isolated; use *deg* from Exercise 19.

21. Procedure *PrintAdjacents* to print the key of each node and the keys of all adjacent nodes in a graph.

22. Procedure *FileToGraph* to read information from a text file into a graph. On one line is the key and information for a node and on the next line are the keys of all adjacent nodes. Thus, node data are on every other line and edge data are on alternate lines.

23. Function *SumDegrees* to return the sum of the degrees of all nodes in a graph.

24. Function *NumEdges* that returns the number of edges in a graph; use *Sum-Degrees* from Exercise 23.

25. Function *AddGraph* to return the sum of all the keys in a graph where each key is a number.

26. Function *MinInGraph* to return the minimum key held in a graph; assume the graph is not empty.

27. Procedure *DeleteGraph* to delete every node in a graph.

28. Procedure *ToAdjacent*(*g, curNode*) that makes *curNode* indicate a node adjacent to the one to which it presently points. If there is no adjacent node, *curNode* becomes empty; assume *curNode* is pointing to a node initially.

29. Procedure *InsertConnectAll*(*g, e*) to insert a node containing *e* into *g* and make that node adjacent to every other node in *g*; assume *g* exists.

30. Procedure *BuildCompleteGraph*(*g, f*) to read information from a file *f* and build a complete graph *g*. Initialize *g*; then insert each item read, *e*, into *g* and make that node adjacent to every other node. Thus, a complete graph is built with information from *f*. Use *InsertConnectAll* from Exercise 29.

31. Boolean function *Subgraph*(*s, g*) to return *true* if *s* is a subgraph of *g*.

32. Boolean function *EqualGraph*(*s, g*) to return *true* if graphs *s* and *g* are identical; use *Subgraph* from Exercise 31.

33. Procedure *CopyGraph*(*s, g*) that makes a copy *s* of a graph *g*.

▽
SECTION 12.2   ## Adjacency Matrix Implementation of Graph

There are two major implementation techniques of graphs, one involving arrays, the other linked lists. In the array method, a one-dimensional array stores the values in the nodes of a graph, while a two-dimensional array represents the edges. The latter, called an **adjacency matrix**, is a two-dimensional boolean array, where the *ij* element is *true* if and only if there exists an edge between nodes *i* and *j*. The graph in Figure 12.5 has the node array, *node*, and the adja-

Figure 12.5

Graph represented by a count of the number of nodes, *count*; a node array, *node*; and an adjacency matrix, *edge*

$$count = 4$$

$$node = \begin{bmatrix} \overset{1}{a} & \overset{2}{b} & \overset{3}{c} & \overset{4}{d} \end{bmatrix}$$

$$edge = \begin{matrix} 1 \\ 2 \\ 3 \\ 4 \end{matrix} \begin{bmatrix} 0 & 0 & 1 & 1 \\ 0 & 0 & 0 & 1 \\ 1 & 0 & 0 & 1 \\ 1 & 1 & 1 & 0 \end{bmatrix}$$

cency matrix, *edge*, along with a count, *count*, of the number of nodes. The one-dimensional array *node* stores the values *a, b, c,* and *d* in elements 1, 2, 3, and 4, respectively. The array *edge* shows 1 representing *true* and 0, *false*. Since *node*[1] = *a* is adjacent to both *node*[3] = *c* and *node*[4] = *d*, *edge*[1, 3] = 1 and *edge*[1, 4] = 1. By symmetry, the edges (*a, c*) = (*c, a*) and (*a, d*) = (*d, a*), so we must also have *edge*[3, 1] = 1 and *edge*[4, 1] = 1.

Below are type definitions and variable declarations to create a graph *g*. Notice that besides storing the values in the nodes and the existence of the edges, a count field indicates the number of nodes in the graph. Moreover, *cur-Node* points to a node by storing that node's index in the array *node*. An edge must be represented by a pair of indices in *curEdge*, one index from *node* for each end point.

```
const
    NumNodes      = . . . . . . . . . . . . . ;
type
    keyType       = . . . . . . . . . . . . . ;
    infoType      = . . . . . . . . . . . . . ;
    elType        = record
        key       :  keyType;
        info      :  infoType
    end;

    countType     = 0..NumNodes;
    indexType     = 1..NumNodes;
    elArrayType   = array [indexType] of elType;
    adjType       = array [indexType, indexType] of boolean;

    graph         = record
        count     :  countType;
        node      :  elArrayType;
        edge      :  adjType
    end;

    edgeType      = record
        row,
        col       :  countType
    end;

var
    g             :  graph;
    k,
    k1,
    k2            :  keyType;
    e             :  elType;
    curNode       :  indexType;
    curEdge       :  edgeType;
```

As with tables and binary trees, the key can hold all the information in a node. In that situation *elType* = *keyType*. Sometimes no information at all is stored in the nodes, and only the number of the nodes along with the connection between them needs to be represented. In this case, *node* can be of type *indexType*.

MakeGraphEmpty, GraphIsEmpty, GraphIsFull, along with *InsertNode* and *DeleteNode*, all reference the count of the number of nodes in the graph, *g.count*. The information in the node array can be ordered or unordered. If ordered, a binary search of the array can be used to locate a key for *KeyFoundGraph* or *ToNode*. Otherwise, we employ a sequential search. *KeyFoundGraph* only indicates whether or not the key is present, while *ToNode(g, k, curNode)* assigns the corresponding *node* index of *k* to *curNode*. *ToEdge(g, k1, k2, curEdge)* behaves in a similar fashion, returning the *node* index of *k1* in *curEdge.row* and that of *k2* in *curEdge.col*.

Inserting a node also depends on the organization of the data. If unordered, we increment *g.count* and store *e*'s value in *g.node[g.count]*. As Figure 12.6 shows, we must also indicate that this new node is isolated by making *g.edge[i, j] false* in *g.count* row and *g.count* column of the adjacency matrix. This procedure follows:

```
{  Insert an isolated node containing e into a graph g of
   unordered data }


procedure InsertNode (var g: graph; e: elType);
var
    i, j : indexType;
begin
    with g do
        begin
            {*** Place e in a new node ***}
            count       : = count + 1;
            node[count]: = e;

            {*** In array g.edge indicate no edges ***}
            {*** incident to node[count]= e          ***}
            for i : = 1 to count do
                edge[i, count] : = false;

            for j : = 1 to count do
                edge[count, j] : = false

        end    { with }
end;
```

Should data be ordered in the node array, the proper insertion point must first be located; then, by movement of elements within both the arrays *node* and *edge*, we must make room for the node.

Figure 12.6

Variable *count*, arrays *node* and *edge*, and graph from Figure 12.5 after addition of a node

count = 5

	1	2	3	4	5
node = [	*a*	*b*	*c*	*d*	*e*]

		1	2	3	4	5
	1	0	0	1	1	0
	2	0	0	0	1	0
edge =	3	1	0	0	1	0
	4	1	1	1	0	0
	5	0	0	0	0	0

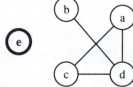

Similarly, when the node with index *curNode* is deleted, we must move values in arrays *node* and *edge*. Figure 12.7 illustrates the *DeleteNode* procedure below. With *curNode* = 2 in that figure, *b* and incident edge (*b*, *d*) are deleted. Since the data in array *node* is unordered, we can copy the value from the last element of *node* into the second, so that *node*[2] gets the value of *node*[4] = *d*. For consistency and to remove edges incident to *b*, we also copy the last row and column of *edge* into the second row and column, respectively; then, we decrement *count*. If *node* is sorted, however, to maintain the ordering,

Figure 12.7

Variable *count*, arrays *node* and *edge*, and the graph from Figure 12.5 after deletion of the node containing *b*, that is, the node whose index is *curNode* = 2

curNode = 2

	1	2	3
node = [	*a*	*d*	*c*]

		1	2	3
	1	0	1	1
edge =	2	1	1	0
	3	1	0	1

count = 3

we must move all values beyond *node*[*curNode*] and beyond the *curNode*-row and *curNode*-column of *edge*.

```
{ Procedure to delete the node with index curNode from a
  graph g of unordered data }

procedure DeleteNode (var g: graph; curNode: indexType);
var
   i, j: indexType;
begin
   with g do
      begin

            {*** Delete node from array g.node     ***}
               node[curNode] := node[count];

            {*** Delete incident edges             ***}
            {*** Copy row count into row curNode   ***}
            {*** from array g.edge                 ***}
               for j := 1 to count do
                  edge[curNode, j] := edge[count, j];

            {*** Copy column count into column curNode ***}
            {*** from array g.edge                     ***}
               for i := 1 to count do
                  edge[i, curNode] := edge[i, count];

            {*** The graph now contains one less node ***}
               count := count - 1
      end   { with }
end;
```

As Figure 12.8 shows, however, deletion of an edge between *node*[*i*] and *node*[*j*] involves changing *g.edge*[*i, j*], and symmetrically *g.edge*[*j, i*], to *false*. In that example we wish to delete the edge incident to *node*[2] = *b* and *node*[4] = *d*,(*b, d*) = (*d, b*), from the graph in Figure 12.5. Thus, we assign *false* to *g.edge*[2, 4] and to *g.edge*[4, 2]. When an edge is removed, nodes are not deleted, so that *g.count* and *g.node* are not changed.

```
{ Procedure to delete an edge from a graph g }

procedure DeleteEdge (var g: graph; curEdge: edgeType);
begin
   g.edge [curEdge.row, curEdge.col] := false;
   g.edge [curEdge.col, curEdge.row] := false
end;
```

Figure 12.8

Array *edge* and graph *g* from Figure 12.5 after deletion of the edge connecting nodes *b* and *d*, that is, the edge whose end points are indicated by *curEdge* = (2, 4)

curEdge = (2, 4)

$$
edge = \begin{array}{c} \\ 1 \\ 2 \\ 3 \\ 4 \end{array}
\begin{array}{cccc}
1 & 2 & 3 & 4 \\
\left[\begin{array}{cccc}
0 & 0 & 1 & 1 \\
0 & 0 & 0 & \mathbf{0} \\
1 & 0 & 0 & 1 \\
1 & \mathbf{0} & 1 & 0
\end{array}\right]
\end{array}
$$

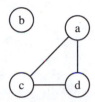

There are two major orders of traversing the nodes of a graph—depth-first and breadth-first. Both these techniques are examined in detail in Section 12.4. Implementation of the other ADT graph operations is covered in the exercises.

▽

SECTION 12.2 EXERCISES

1. Give the node array and adjacency matrix for the graph in Figure 12.1.

2. Give the node array and adjacency matrix for the graph in Figure 12.3.

Using the definitions and declarations associated with graph *at the beginning of this section, code the ADT graph operations in Exercises 3–10.*

3. *MakeGraphEmpty*

4. *GraphIsEmpty*

5. *GraphIsFull*

6. *EdgeIsEmpty,* where a pair of zeros in *curEdge* indicate an empty edge

7. *KeyGraphEl*

8. *InsertEdge*

9. *RetrieveNode,* implemented as a procedure for a composite *elType*

10. *UpdateNode*

Using an unordered node array implementation, code the ADT graph operations in Exercises 11–13.

11. *KeyFoundGraph*

12. *ToNode*

13. *ToEdge*

Using an ordered node array implementation, code the ADT graph operations in Exercises 14–18.

14. *KeyFoundGraph*

15. *ToNode*

16. *ToEdge*

17. *InsertNode*

18. *DeleteNode*

19. As in Figure 12.7, show the action of *DeleteNode*(*g*, 3) on the graph in Figure 12.5.

Using the implementation of this section, in Exercises 20–31 code in Pascal the routines from Section 12.1.

20. Boolean function *IsAdjacent* of Example 12.1 to return *true* if graph *g* contains an edge (*k1, k2*).

21. Procedure *AdjToQueue*(*q, g, k1, k2*) of Example 12.2 to enqueue *k2* into queue *q* provided nodes with keys *k1* and *k2* are adjacent in graph *g*.

22. Procedure *DeleteGraphValue*(*g, f*) from Exercise 14 to read each value *k* of type *keyType* from a binary file *f* and, if in *g*, delete the corresponding node from *g*.

23. Procedure *GraphTwo*(*g, e1, e2*) from Exercise 15 to create a graph *g* with two adjacent nodes containing *e1* and *e2*.

24. Boolean function *IsEdge*(*g, k1, k2, curEdge*) from Exercise 16 to return *true* if the node indicated by *curEdge* is (*k1, k2*).

25. Procedure *PrintGraph* from Exercise 17 to print all the values stored in a graph.

26. Boolean function *IsIsolated* from Exercise 20 to return *true* if a node is isolated.

27. Procedure *PrintAdjacents* from Exercise 21 to print the key of each node and the keys of all adjacent nodes in a graph.

28. Procedure *FileToGraph* from Exercise 22 to read information from a text file into a graph.

29. Function *NumEdges* from Exercise 24 that returns the number of edges in a graph.

30. Procedure *BuildCompleteGraph*(*g, f*) from Exercise 30 to read information from a file *f* and build a complete graph *g*.

31. Boolean function *EqualGraph*(*s*, *g*) from Exercise 32 to return *true* if graphs *s* and *g* are identical.

Give the complexity of the array implementation of operations in Exercises 32–41.

32. *MakeGraphEmpty*

33. *KeyGraphEl*

34. *KeyFoundGraph* for *g.node* being

   a. ordered
   b. unordered

35. *ToNode* for *g.node* being

   a. ordered
   b. unordered

36. *ToEdge* for *g.node* being

   a. ordered
   b. unordered

37. *InsertEdge* for *g.node* being

   a. ordered
   b. unordered

38. *DeleteNode*

   a. ordered
   b. unordered

39. *DeleteEdge*

40. *UpdateNode*

41. *RetrieveNode*

42. Assume vertices of a graph are numbered from 1 to *n*. Also, suppose no information is held in those vertices so that we say the key and element of a node are equal to the number of the node. In this case the graph can be implemented with an adjacency matrix only.

   a. Give the creation of the ADT graph for this structure.
   b. Implement all the ADT graph operations for this structure.

▽

PROGRAMMING PROJECTS

1. A graph and adjacency matrix are presented in Figure 12.9.

A **reachability matrix** has 1 (*true*) in the *ij* position if and only if it is possible to start at node *i* and reach node *j* along a path of length greater than

Figure 12.9

Graph for Project 1

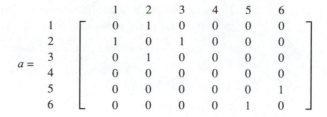

$$a = \begin{array}{c} \\ 1 \\ 2 \\ 3 \\ 4 \\ 5 \\ 6 \end{array} \begin{array}{cccccc} 1 & 2 & 3 & 4 & 5 & 6 \\ \begin{bmatrix} 0 & 1 & 0 & 0 & 0 & 0 \\ 1 & 0 & 1 & 0 & 0 & 0 \\ 0 & 1 & 0 & 0 & 0 & 0 \\ 0 & 0 & 0 & 0 & 0 & 0 \\ 0 & 0 & 0 & 0 & 0 & 1 \\ 0 & 0 & 0 & 0 & 1 & 0 \end{bmatrix} \end{array}$$

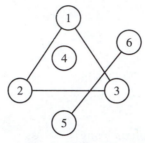

one. As the graph and adjacency matrix in Figure 12.9 indicate, there exists an edge connecting nodes 1 and 2. Since it is possible to get from node 1 to 2, any vertex reachable from 2 is reachable from 1. Thus, we can replace row 1 with the boolean algebra sum of rows 1 and 2.

$$\begin{array}{ccccccc} & 0 & 1 & 0 & 0 & 0 & 0 \\ + & 1 & 0 & 1 & 0 & 0 & 0 \\ \hline & 1 & 1 & 1 & 0 & 0 & 0 \end{array}$$

As we saw in Section 3.5, the boolean algebra addition corresponds to the Pascal *or*. Thus, $1 + 0 = 1$ corresponds to *true or false = true*; $0 + 0 = 0$ means *false or false = false*; and $1 + 1 = 1$ indicates *true or true = true*. **Warshall's algorithm** to obtain a reachability matrix says that for every *ij* element of the adjacency matrix that is *true* (1), replace the *i*th row with the boolean algebra sum (*or*) of corresponding elements from the *i*th and *j*th rows. Following this algorithm we see that the reachability matrix for the above adjacency matrix is as follows:

$$a = \begin{array}{c} \\ 1 \\ 2 \\ 3 \\ 4 \\ 5 \\ 6 \end{array} \begin{array}{cccccc} 1 & 2 & 3 & 4 & 5 & 6 \\ \begin{bmatrix} 1 & 1 & 1 & 0 & 0 & 0 \\ 1 & 1 & 1 & 0 & 0 & 0 \\ 1 & 1 & 1 & 0 & 0 & 0 \\ 0 & 0 & 0 & 0 & 0 & 0 \\ 0 & 0 & 0 & 0 & 1 & 1 \\ 0 & 0 & 0 & 0 & 1 & 1 \end{bmatrix} \end{array}$$

We can reach nodes 1, 2, or 3 from 1; we can only reach nodes 5 and 6 starting at 5 or 6; and node 4 is not reachable from any node using a path of length greater than 1.

Suppose a graph has nodes numbered from 1 to *n* and the nodes contain no other information. Read *n* and the edges as pairs of integers from a file. Create the adjacency matrix and using Warshall's algorithm, generate the reachability matrix. For each node in the graph print a list of every node that can be reached following some path from that node.

Auxiliary questions:

a. Give the adjacency matrix for Figure 12.1.
b. Give the reachability matrix for Figure 12.1.

SECTION 12.3

Adjacency List Implementation of Graph

There are several forms of the linked structure that can implement the ADT graph. If information is contained in the nodes, both nodes and edges must be stored regardless of the structure. Consider the graph in Figure 12.10, where the elements in the nodes are key values. Were we just to store the values in the nodes we might use a linked list structure called a **node list**, as in Figure 12.11.

Figure 12.10

A graph

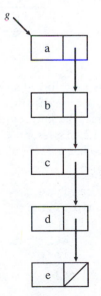

Figure 12.11

Node list to represent the graph of Figure 12.10

But we also must record the edges. One technique is to form an edge list for each node. An **edge list** is a linked list of all the nodes adjacent to a given node. Thus, since *a* is adjacent only to *c, c* will be the single element on *a*'s edge list. Node *c*, however, is adjacent to nodes *a, e,* and *d*, so three items will appear on *c*'s edge list. Recall that edge (*a, c*) can also be represented as (*c, a*). Consequently, *a* is in *c*'s edge list and *c* is in *a*'s. Figure 12.12 presents the complete **adjacency list** structure for the graph in Figure 12.10. In this structure we have a linked structure of the values in the nodes, called a node list, and for each node an edge list or a linked list of keys of adjacent nodes. Note that an element in the node list must contain two pointers, one to the next node and one to the present node's edge list.

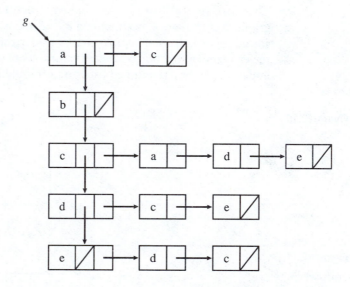

This multilinked structure is created in Pascal below. Note that the entire value at a vertex is stored in the node list; only its key appears in an edge list. Of course, the key could be the entire value with *elType = keyType*. Figures 12.13–12.15 present schematics with labels of some of this structure. In the first sketch, *curEdge* points to the edge (*a, c*) and *curNode* points to node *d*.

```
type
    keyType      = ............;
    infoType     = ............;
    elType       = record
        key      :  keyType;
        info     :  infoType
    end;
```

```
    PtrAdj      = ^Adj;
    Adj         = record
       keyAdj   : keyType;
       nextAdj  : PtrAdj
    end;

    graph       = ^Node;
    Node        = record
       el       : elType;
       nextNode : graph;
       headAdj  : PtrAdj
    end;

    edgeType    = record
       v1,
       v2       : graph
    end;

var
    g,
    curNode : graph;
    curEdge : edgeType;
    k,
    k1,
    k2      : keyType;
    e       : elType;
```

Figure 12.13

Schematic of *curEdge* pointing to edge(*a, c*) and *curNode* pointing to node *d*

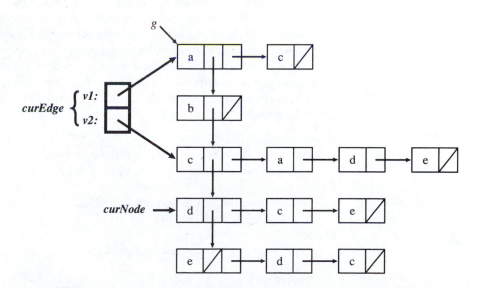

Figure 12.14

Schematic of *Node* from the node list in Figure 12.13

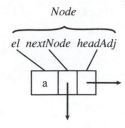

Figure 12.15

Schematic of node *Adj* from an edge list in Figure 12.13

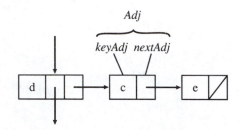

Under this structure, we use sequential searches of the node list for *Key-FoundGraph, ToNode,* and *ToEdge.* Insertion of a new node is easiest at the beginning of the node list. *InsertEdge(g, k1, k2)* involves inserting *k1* into the edge list for *k2* and vice versa. Again, we can rapidly insert each at the beginning of the proper linked list.

Deletion of an edge pointed to by *curEdge* requires the removal of two nodes from two different edge lists. As the example in Figure 12.13 shows, *curEdge* contains two pointers, *v1* and *v2*, to nodes in the node list. Taking the key value from these nodes, we delete those values from each other's edge lists. For example, to delete the edge *(a, c)* = *(c, a)* we take *a* from the edge list of *c* and remove *c* from *a*'s edge list. Since the process of removing a value from an edge list is executed twice, we first define a procedure *DeleteEdgeEnd(head, k)* to delete the node containing *k* from the edge list pointed to by *head.* This procedure is a straightforward deletion from a linked list as Figure 12.16 and the following design using ADT linked list operations demonstrate.

DeleteEdgeEnd(head, k)
   Procedure to delete the node containing *k* from a linked list pointed to by *head*; assume such a node is in the list initially
Input:
   head — pointer to a linked list
   k   — value stored in a linked list
Output:
   head — pointer to a revised linked list
Assumption:
   The value *k* is in the linked list.

Figure 12.16

Action of *DeleteEdge-End*(*head, a*)

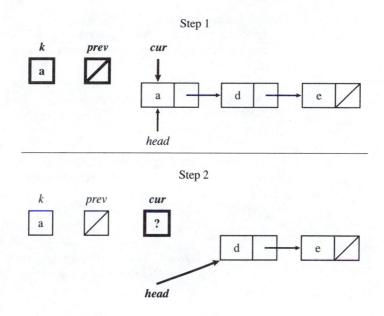

Step 1

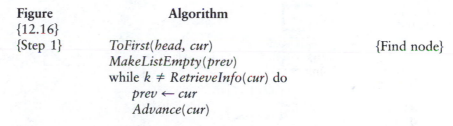

Step 2

Figure	Algorithm	
{12.16}		
{Step 1}	*ToFirst*(*head, cur*)	{Find node}
	MakeListEmpty(*prev*)	
	while $k \neq RetrieveInfo(cur)$ do	
	prev ← *cur*	
	Advance(*cur*)	
{Step 2}	*Delete*(*head, prev*)	{Remove node}

We call this procedure twice in *DeleteEdge*. Since the entire record is held in an element of the node list, we retrieve that record and separate out the key with the ADT graph function reference *KeyGraphEl*(*RetrieveNode*(*cur-Edge.v1*)). A node in the edge list only contains the key as information; thus, the ADT linked list reference *RetrieveInfo*(*cur*) is sufficient to access a key in the *DeleteEdgeEnd* procedure. Because of a Pascal restriction, if the node element is of a composite type *elType*, we must implement *RetrieveNode* as a procedure. Since *RetrieveInfo* returns a key, however, we can code this operation as a function provided *keyType* is a scalar type.

An element of the node list contains two pointer fields, one link to the rest of the node list and another, *headAdj*, to the first element of the edge list. Therefore, to avoid ambiguity we do not use the ADT linked list operation *RetrieveNext* in the description of the procedure *DeleteEdge*. Instead, the pointer *curEdge.v1* indicates an element of the node list, so we use *curEdge.v1^.headAdj* as the head of the corresponding edge list. Figure 12.17 traces the steps of the following design of *DeleteEdge*:

DeleteEdge(g, curEdge)
>   Procedure to delete the edge pointed to by *curEdge* from the graph *g*;
>   assume before deletion that such an edge exists

Input:
>   *g*   — graph
>   *curEdge* — pointer to an edge

Output:
>   *g*   — revised graph

Assumption:
>   The variable *curEdge* points to an edge in *g*.

Figure	Algorithm
{12.17}	{Find keys for end points}
{Step 1}	$k1 \leftarrow KeyGraphEl(RetrieveNode(curEdge.v1))$
	$k2 \leftarrow KeyGraphEl(RetrieveNode(curEdge.v2))$
	{Remove nodes from edge lists}
{Step 2}	$DeleteEdgeEnd(curEdge.v1\char94.headAdj, k2)$
	$DeleteEdgeEnd(curEdge.v2\char94.headAdj, k1)$

Figure 12.17

Deletion of edge (*c*, *a*) =
(*a*, *c*) using *Delete-
Edge*(*g*, *curEdge*)

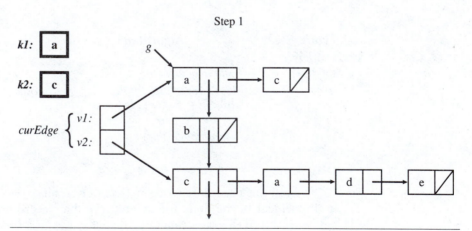

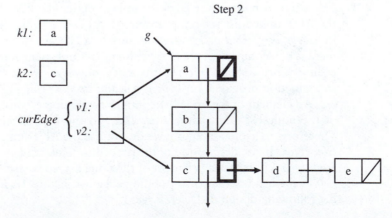

For *DeleteNode* we must be careful not only to make the appropriate deletion from the node list but first to remove all edges incident to that node. Moreover, removal of an edge (u, v) requires removal of a node containing u and one containing v from two different edge lists. We use the ADT linked list operations *DeleteFirst* and *DeleteLater* as well as the just-defined *DeleteEdgeEnd* operation to accomplish the actual removal of nodes. The formal definition of *DeleteNode* appears after the pseudocode description below, and Figures 12.18–12.21 illustrate the action of the operation:

Get the key, *k1*, of the vertex to be deleted.
While there are elements in its edge list do the following:
> Obtain the key, *k2*, of the first element in the edge list.
> Delete the edge $(k1, k2)$ by deleting *k2* from *k1*'s edge list and *k1* from
>> *k2*'s edge list.
Delete the node containing *k1* from the node list.

DeleteNode(g, curNode)
> Procedure to delete the node pointed to by *curNode* in graph *g*
Input:
> *g*   — graph
> *curNode* — pointer to a node of *g*
Output:
> *g*   — revised graph
Assumptions:
> Graph *g* is not empty, and *curNode* points to a node of *g*.

Figure	Algorithm
{12.18}	{Find key of node to be deleted}
{Step 1}	$k1 \leftarrow KeyGraphEl(RetrieveNode(curNode))$
	{Remove incident edges}
	{*ListIsEmpty*, *RetrieveInfo*, and *DeleteFirst* are ADT linked list operations}
	while not *ListIsEmpty*(*curNode*^.*headAdj*) do
	$\quad k2 \leftarrow RetrieveInfo(curNode\text{^}.headAdj)$
{Step 2}	$\quad DeleteFirst(curNode\text{^}.headAdj)$
	$\quad ToNode(g, k2, curNode2)$
{12.19}	$\quad DeleteEdgeEnd(curNode2\text{^}.headAdj, k1)$
	{Remove node}
	if *curNode* = *g* then {Remove first node}
	$\quad g \leftarrow g\text{^}.nextNode$
	$\quad Dispose(curNode)$
{12.21}	else
{Step 1}	$\quad prev \leftarrow g$ {Point *prev* to the node before *curNode*'s}
	$\quad$ while $prev\text{^}.nextNode \neq curNode$ do
	$\quad\quad prev \leftarrow prev\text{^}.nextNode$
	{Remove later node}
{Step 2}	$\quad prev\text{^}.nextNode \leftarrow curNode\text{^}.nextNode$
	$\quad Dispose(curNode)$

Figure 12.18

Initial action of *Delete-Node*(*g*, *curNode*) to delete edge (*d*, *c*) = (*c*, *d*) by removing *c* from the edge list of *d* and pointing *curNode2* to node *c*

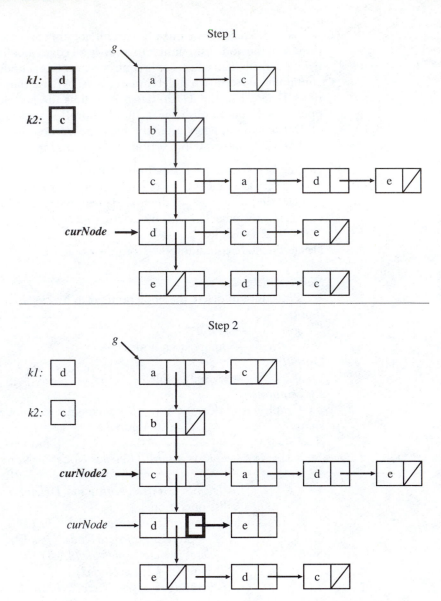

The implementations of ADT graph presented in this section and Section 12.2 each have applications for which they are best suited. When *n* graph vertices store no information except a number from 1 to *n*, the adjacency matrix reference *g.edge*[*i, j*] indicates immediately the existence of an edge between vertices *i* and *j* or not. In other situations where the key is not of type *indexType*, we can arrange the data in the array *g.node* to facilitate a binary search.

Figure 12.19

Action of *DeleteNode*(*g,
curNode*) continued from
Figure 12.18 to remove *d*
from the edge list of *c*;
graph inset

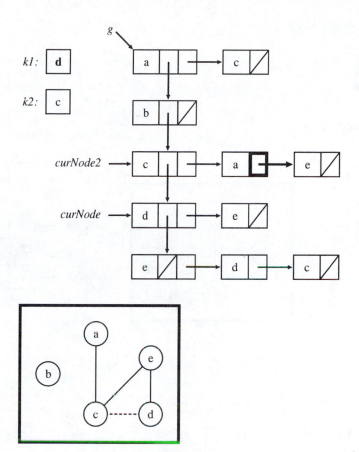

Figure 12.20

Action of *DeleteNode*(*g,
curNode*) continued from
Figure 12.19; delete edge
(*d, e*) = (*e, d*);
graph inset

continued on next page

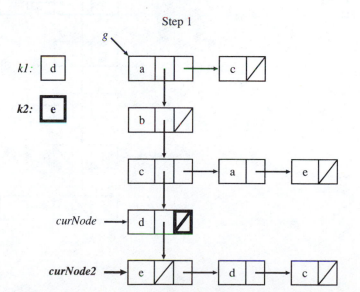

Figure 12.20

continued

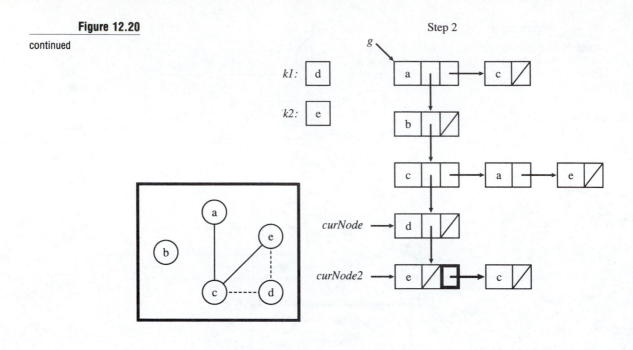

Figure 12.21

Action of *DeleteNode*(*g*, *curNode*) continued from Figure 12.20; delete node *d*; graph inset

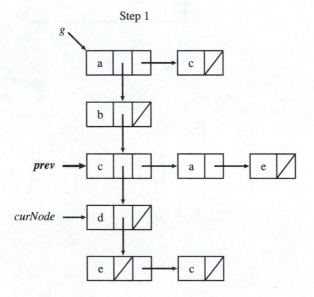

Figure 12.21

continued

Step 2

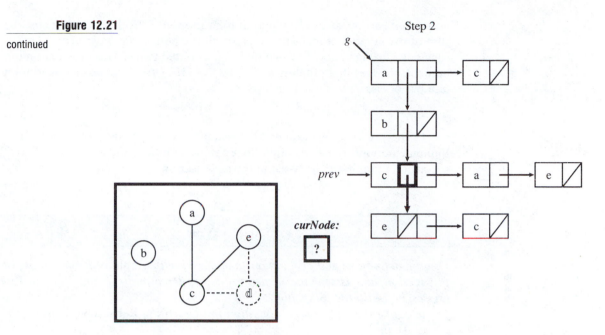

As discussed, however, with implementation of other structures such as tables, stacks, and queues, an array is of a fixed size requiring prior knowledge of the maximum number of vertices in the graph. Moreover, insertion into and deletion from the middle of an ordered array involves movement of a number of elements. With the linked structure, enquiries about all the incident edges to a vertex can be rapidly answered through examination of the edge list. For a graph with many vertices but few edges, a check of a particular row of the adjacency matrix is slower.

Storage requirements between the two implementations vary as well. Suppose the number of vertices in graph g is n and the number of edges is e. For the array implementation, the adjacency matrix is an $n \times n$ matrix so that the total storage for the nodes and vertices of a graph is proportional to $n + n^2$. For a graph with many nodes but relatively few edges, much space is wasted. With the linked representation shown in this section, each vertex appears once in the node list and each edge (u, v) consumes two nodes in the edge lists, one for u and one for v. Thus, the storage for the adjacency list is proportional to $n + 2e$. For example, suppose the number of vertices is $n = 100$ and the number of edges is $e = 25$. Then the space for the array representation of a graph is on the order of $n + n^2 = 100 + 100^2 = 10,100$, while storage for the linked representation is on the order of $n + 2e = 100 + 2 \cdot 25 = 150$. Of course, the pointers themselves often consume a great deal of room, but only actual edges are represented in the adjacency list. As developed in Exercises 7 and 8 of Section 12.1, the maximum number of edges in a graph of n nodes is $n(n - 1)/2$. There are n

nodes and each node can be adjacent to at most $n - 1$ other nodes. Thus, the sum of the number of incident edges for all the nodes is at most $n(n - 1)$. But each edge, being incident to two nodes, is counted twice. Thus, the maximum number of edges in a graph is $n(n - 1)/2 = (1/2)(n^2 - n)$ and the maximum number of elements in the edge lists is

$$2e = n^2 - n < n^2$$

In the exercises, we examine the complexity of various graph operations. Implementations as well as other linked representations are also covered. Traversals of a graph are discussed in the next section.

▽

SECTION 12.3 EXERCISES

Use the definitions and declarations associated with graph *at the beginning of this section, and assume the elements are unordered in the linked lists. For Exercises 1–14 do the following:*

  a. *Code the ADT graph operation implementing* RetrieveNode *as a procedure.*
  b. *Give its worst case complexity.*

1. *MakeGraphEmpty*   **2.** *GraphIsEmpty*   **3.** *GraphIsFull*

4. *KeyGraphEl*   **5.** *KeyFoundGraph*   **6.** *ToNode*

7. *ToEdge*   **8.** *EdgeIsEmpty*   **9.** *InsertNode*

10. *InsertEdge*   **11.** *DeleteNode*   **12.** *DeleteEdge*

13. *UpdateNode*   **14.** *RetrieveNode*

15. As in Figures 12.18–12.21, draw the action of *DeleteNode* in deleting node *a* from the graph in Figure 12.10.

16. Another approach to an adjacency list is to store the node list in an array of records with fields for information and a pointer to an edge list that is a linked list.

   a. Give the definitions and declarations to define this structure.
   b. Draw this structure for the graph in Figure 12.10.
   c. Give the advantages and disadvantages of this structure.

17. Another approach to an adjacency list is to store each edge list in a binary search tree. Suppose the node list is in an array of records with fields for information and a pointer to an edge list.

   a. Give the definitions and declarations to define this structure.
   b. Draw this structure for the graph in Figure 12.10.
   c. Give the advantages and disadvantages of this structure.

    d. Give the advantages and disadvantages of the node list also being in a binary search tree.

18. Another approach to an adjacency list is to store each edge list in a hash table. Suppose the key ranges from 0 to 9999. Suppose the node list is also in a hash table that is statically implemented. Repeat Parts a and c of Exercise 16 for this structure.

19. Another approach to an adjacency list is to store each edge list in a doubly linked list. Suppose the node list is in a singly linked list. Repeat Parts a and c of Exercise 16 for this structure.

Consider the implementation of ADT graph where both node list and edge lists are
    a. linked lists
    b. binary search trees
    c. hash tables
and where
    d. the node list is an ordered array and the edge lists are linked lists
For each implementation give the complexity of the operation in Exercises 20–28.

20. *MakeGraphEmpty*   **21.** *KeyGraphEl*   **22.** *ToEdge*

23. *InsertNode*   **24.** *InsertEdge*   **25.** *DeleteNode*

26. *DeleteEdge*   **27.** *UpdateNode*   **28.** *RetrieveNode*

Using the implementation of this section, in Exercises 29–40 code in Pascal the routines from Section 12.1.

29. Boolean function *IsAdjacent* of Example 12.1 to return *true* if graph g contains an edge ($k1$, $k2$).

30. Procedure *AdjToQueue*(q, g, $k1$, $k2$) of Example 12.2 to enqueue $k2$ into queue q provided nodes with keys $k1$ and $k2$ are adjacent in graph g.

31. Procedure *DeleteGraphValue*(g, f) from Exercise 14 to read each value k of type *keyType* from a binary file f and if in g, delete the corresponding node from g.

32. Procedure *GraphTwo*(g, $e1$, $e2$) from Exercise 15 to create a graph g with two adjacent nodes containing $e1$ and $e2$.

33. Boolean function *IsEdge*(g, $k1$, $k2$, $curEdge$) from Exercise 16 to return *true* if the node indicated by *curEdge* is ($k1$, $k2$).

34. Procedure *PrintGraph* from Exercise 17 to print all the values stored in a graph.

35. Boolean function *IsIsolated* from Exercise 20 to return *true* if a node is isolated.

36. Procedure *PrintAdjacents* from Exercise 21 to print the key of each node and the keys of all adjacent nodes in a graph.

37. Procedure *FileToGraph* from Exercise 22 to read information from a text file into a graph.

38. Function *NumEdges* from Exercise 24 that returns the number of edges in a graph.

39. Procedure *BuildCompleteGraph(g, f)* from Exercise 30 to read information from a file *f* and build a complete graph *g*.

40. Boolean function *EqualGraph(s, g)* from Exercise 32 to return *true* if graphs *s* and *g* are identical.

41. A rooted general tree can be implemented with an adjacency list. Since a direction is implied for edges, the edge list of a vertex contains only the children of a node.

   a. Draw the adjacency list for the tree in Figure 12.22.
   b. Design a procedure to read a text file where each line contains a vertex and its children, and to build the adjacency list structure for the tree.

Figure 12.22

Rooted general tree for
Exercise 41

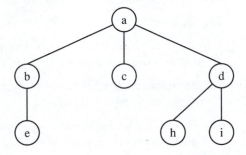

42. Sometimes it is useful to convert a rooted general tree to a rooted binary tree. The process of conversion is as follows: For each node *v* make its left-most child *f* (the first element in its edge list) its left child in the binary tree. Then have the remainder of *v*'s children go off to the right of *f*. Figure 12.23 illustrates the conversion.

   a. Convert Figure 12.22 to a binary tree.
   b. Write a recursive procedure to convert a rooted general tree, implemented with an adjacency list, to a rooted binary tree. Assume the root is the first element in the node list and all the children in an edge list are linked in order from left to right.

Figure 12.23

Rooted general tree converted to a rooted binary tree

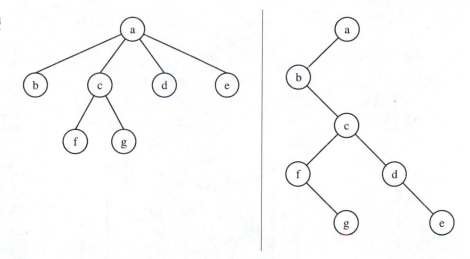

Graph Traversal

In this section we discuss the graph traversal operation. There are two major methods of traversal, depth first and breadth first. We will see how these techniques of visiting every node can be implemented with the adjacency matrix and adjacency list of Sections 12.2 and 12.3, respectively.

The name **depth-first order** is descriptive of the traversal process as we follow a path in the graph as deeply as we can go. When there are no adjacent, unprocessed nodes, we **backtrack** to the last place we had a choice of an adjacent node and repeat the process. Thus, we examine the depths of the graph first. A stack with its last in, first out structure is used to store vertices so that we can backtrack to the last visited node.

For a depth-first traversal of the graph in Figure 12.24, we initially visit node 1, mark that we have visited that vertex, and push 1 onto the stack. (See Step 1 of Figure 12.24.) Either of the adjacent vertices, 2 or 3, could be visited next. If we visit 2, we also mark and push node 2. From 2 we can proceed to node 4 or 5. If we process node 4, we then have a choice of visiting node 6 or 7. Picking 6, node 9 must follow. But node 9 has no unprocessed neighbors, so as shown in Step 2 of Figure 12.24, we pop 9. Does the top vertex, 6, have adjacent, unprocessed nodes? No, so we pop 6 (Step 3, Figure 12.24). But the new top, 4, is adjacent to node 7, which has not been visited. We process node 7 by visiting and placing 7 on the top of the stack. (See Step 1 of Figure 12.25.) Since nodes 7 and 4 have no adjacent, unvisited nodes, we pop both and backtrack to vertex 2, where we did have a choice (Steps 2 and 3, Figure 12.25). Taking the only remaining choice, we traverse the graph to node 5. (See Step 1 of Figure 12.26.) After pushing 5, we do have a choice of nodes 8 or 3. Suppose we take the path to node 8 (Step 2, Figure 12.26). We visit and push 8, but node 8 has no

Figure 12.24

Initial action of a depth-first traversal of a graph

Step 1

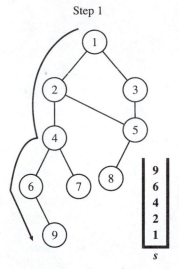

Push 1, 2, 4, 6, 9
Visit 1, 2, 4, 6, 9

Step 2

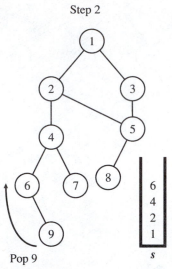

Pop 9
No unprocessed
adjacent nodes

Step 3

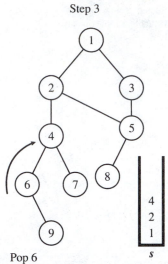

Pop 6
No unprocessed
adjacent nodes

Figure 12.25

Continuation of depth-first traversal of graph from Figure 12.24

Step 1

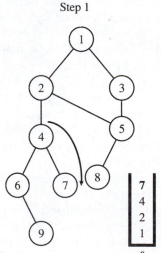

Pop 4
Push 4 and adjacent 7
Visit 7

Step 2

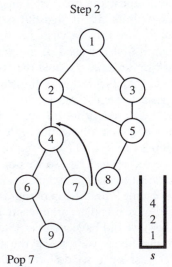

Pop 7
No unprocessed
adjacent nodes

Step 3

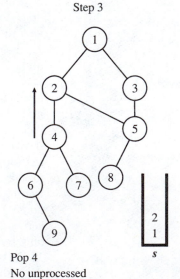

Pop 4
No unprocessed
adjacent nodes

Step 1

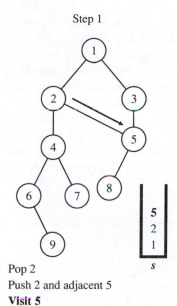

Pop 2
Push 2 and adjacent 5
Visit 5

Step 2

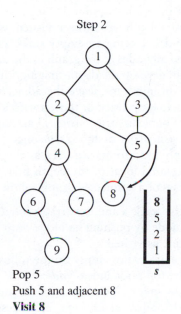

Pop 5
Push 5 and adjacent 8
Visit 8

Step 3

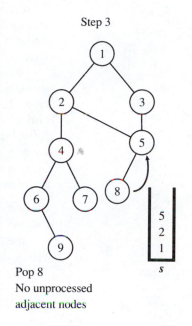

Pop 8
No unprocessed adjacent nodes

Step 1

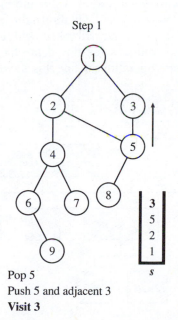

Pop 5
Push 5 and adjacent 3
Visit 3

Step 2

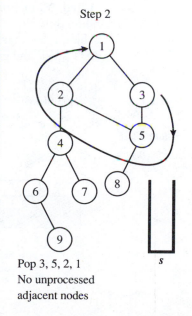

Pop 3, 5, 2, 1
No unprocessed adjacent nodes

527

unprocessed nodes, so we immediately pop 8 (Step 3, Figure 12.26). From node 5 we take the path to point 3. (See Step 1 of Figure 12.27.) But since 3 has no neighbors that have not been visited, we pop 3. For the same reason we pop nodes 5 and 1, leaving an empty stack as in Step 2 of Figure 12.27. Now, we have visited all nodes of the graph in the following order: 1, 2, 4, 6, 9, 7, 5, 8, 3.

We will develop the depth-first algorithm with the adjacency matrix implementation in mind and leave the adjacency list implementation for the exercises. To help keep track of those vertices that have been visited, we will maintain a local boolean array, *visited*. Each element of this array is initialized to be *false*, but *visited*[i] is assigned *true* once *g.node*[i] has been visited. This *visited* array is only used to mark nodes as they are processed for the traversal and, thus, is declared local to the depth-first procedure. The general algorithm of this traversal of a connected graph follows:

Initialize the stack s and the array *visited*
Process a node by pushing its index onto s, visiting the node, and marking
     the node as visited
While the stack is not empty do the following:
     Pop the top node index (*index*).
     Find the index (*NextIndex*) of an adjacent, unprocessed node.
     If there is such an adjacent, unprocessed node then
          Push *index* onto s.
          Process the adjacent node by pushing its index, *NextIndex*, onto s,
               visiting the node, and marking the node as visited.

Several routines can aid the top-down design. An *InitializeDFT* procedure can establish s and *visited*. A *ProcessDFT* procedure can push the index onto s, visit the vertex with the procedure *Visit*, and mark that node as having been visited. A function *NextAdjacent* will return the index of an adjacent, unvisited node. If no such node exists, *NextAdjacent* will return 0. Figure 12.28 presents a hierarchy chart of routines for this depth-first traversal. Pseudocode and ADT stack and graph operations define this traversal as follows:

Figure 12.28

Hierarchy chart for *Depth-FirstTraversal*

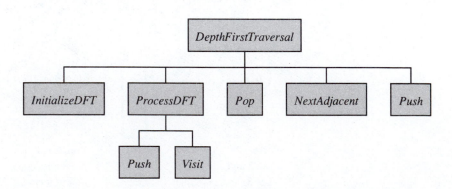

DepthFirstTraversal(g, Visit(ArgumentList))
>   Procedure to perform a depth-first traversal of graph g using the
>   procedure *Visit*

Input:
> g — *graph*

Output:
>   Dependent upon the procedure *Visit*

Assumptions:
>   Graph g is implemented with an array of nodes, *g.node*, an adjacency
>   matrix, *g.edge*, and a count of the number of nodes, *g.count*. The indices
>   of the actual nodes range from 1 to n. Assume g is connected with at
>   least one node.

Figure	**Algorithm**
{12.24}	
	InitializeDFT(s, visited, g.count)
{Step 1}	*ProcessDFT(s, visited, 1)*
{12.25}	while not *StackIsEmpty(s)* do
{Step 1}	*Pop(s, index)*
	NextIndex ← *NextAdjacent(g, visited, index)*
	if *NextIndex* > 0 then
	Push(s, index)
	ProcessDFT(s, visited, NextIndex)

The initialization creates an empty stack and gives values of *false* to each
visited[i].

InitializeDFT(s, visited, n)
>   Procedure to initialize s and *visited* for the procedure *DepthFirstTraversal*

Input:
> n — number of elements in *visited* to be initialized

Output:
> s — stack
>   *visited* — boolean array

Assumption:
> n is a nonnegative integer.

Algorithm:
>   *MakeStackEmpty(s)*
>   for i from 1 to n do
>   *visited*[i] ← *false*

When we process the index, *ndx*, of a node, we push that index onto the
stack, visit the corresponding node, and mark that node as having been visited by changing *visited*[*ndx*] to *true*. The procedure *Visit* is user specified and
may require as an argument the index (*ndx*) of the node, the value of the node
(*g.node* [*ndx*]), or the key (*g.node*[*ndx*].*key*). The particular application dictates the definition of *Visit*.

ProcessDFT(s, visited, ndx)

Procedure called by *DepthFirstTraversal* to process an index, *ndx*, of a node. *ProcessDFT* calls *Visit*.

Input:

s — stack
visited — boolean array
ndx — index of a node

Output:

s — revised stack
visited — revised boolean array

Algorithm:

Push(*s, ndx*)
Visit(*ArgumentList*)
visited[*ndx*] ← *true*

The function *NextAdjacent* returns the index of an unprocessed node that is adjacent to vertex *g.node*[*ndx*] or returns zero if no such node exists. We increment *i* through the elements in the *ndx* row of the adjacency matrix of the graph to find a value of *i* where an edge exists between the *ndx* and *i* nodes. If such an edge exists, the *ndx-i* element of the adjacency matrix, *g.edge*[*ndx, i*], will be *true*. We must also check the *visited* array to see if the *i*th node has been processed. The value of *visited*[*i*] is *false* for an unprocessed *i*th node. Thus, we seek the smallest index *i* where *g.edge*[*ndx, i*] is *true* and *visited*[*i*] is *false*. If no such *i* exists from 1 to *g.count*, we return 0.

NextAdjacent(g, visited, ndx) → *NextIndex*

Function called by *DepthFirstTraversal* to return the index of an adjacent, unprocessed node or 0 if no such node exists.

Input:

g — graph
visited — boolean array
ndx — index of a node

Output:

NextIndex — index of an adjacent, unprocessed node

Algorithm:

continue ← *true*
$i \leftarrow 1$
while ($i <= g.count$) and *continue* do
    if *g.edge*[*ndx, i*] and (not *visited*[*i*]) then
        continue ← *false*
    else
        $i \leftarrow i + 1$

if *continue* then
    NextAdjacent ← 0
else
    NextAdjacent ← *i*

The **breadth-first traversal** takes a different approach. Instead of plunging as deeply as possible into the graph, we examine nodes across the breadth of the graph before advancing to the next level. With the depth-first technique we use a stack, pushing the index of each vertex as visited. Moreover, the next node we visit is an adjacent, unprocessed one. If there is no such adjacent node, we backtrack to the most recently visited node that has an unprocessed neighbor. Thus, the last in, first out stack structure provides ready access to the most recently processed nodes. For a breadth-first traversal we use a queue. In this method we pick a node to visit first and enqueue its unprocessed neighbors. Then we repeatedly dequeue an element from the front. If that front element is unprocessed, we visit the vertex and enqueue at the rear all of its adjacent, unprocessed nodes.

Figures 12.29–12.32 demonstrate a breadth-first traversal of the graph considered earlier in this section. In this traversal we visit the nodes in the order 1, 2, 3, 4, 5, 6, 7, 8, and 9. For the implementation involving an adjacency matrix, we again employ a local *visited* array. The general algorithm for this traversal of a connected graph follows:

Initialize the queue q and the array *visited*.
Process the root by enqueuing indices of all unprocessed neighbors, visiting
    the root, and marking the root as visited.
While the queue is not empty do the following:
    Dequeue the front node index.
    If that node has not been processed then
        Process the node by enqueueing indices of all unprocessed
           neighbors, visiting the node, and marking the node as visited.

Figure 12.29

Initial action of breadth-first traversal of a graph

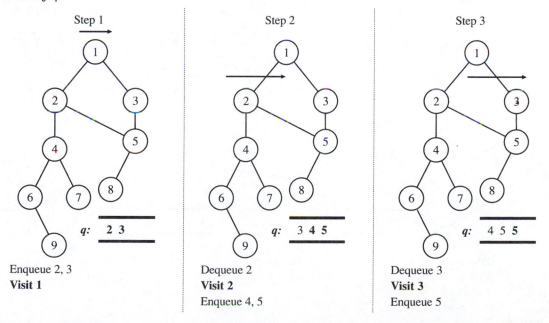

Step 1
q: 2 3
Enqueue 2, 3
Visit 1

Step 2
q: 3 4 5
Dequeue 2
Visit 2
Enqueue 4, 5

Step 3
q: 4 5 5
Dequeue 3
Visit 3
Enqueue 5

Figure 12.30

Continuation of breadth-
first traversal of graph
from Figure 12.29

Step 1

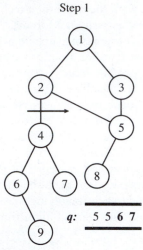

q: 5 5 **6 7**

Dequeue 4
Visit 4
Enqueue 6, 7

Step 2

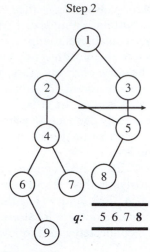

q: 5 6 7 **8**

Dequeue 5
Visit 5
Enqueue 8

Step 3

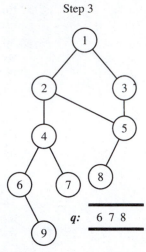

q: 6 7 8

Dequeue 5
Already visited

Figure 12.31

Continuation of breadth-
first traversal of graph
from Figure 12.30

Step 1

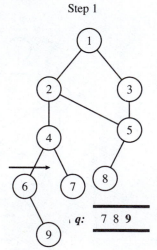

q: 7 8 **9**

Dequeue 6
Visit 6
Enqueue 9

Step 2

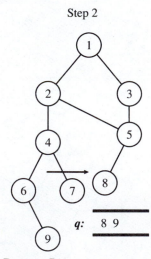

q: 8 9

Dequeue 7
Visit 7

Step 3

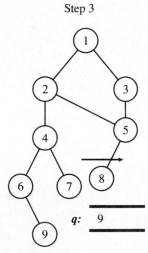

q: 9

Dequeue 8
Visit 8

Figure 12.32

Continuation of breadth-first traversal of graph from Figure 12.30

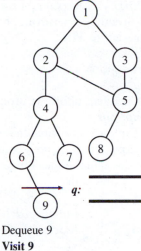

Dequeue 9
Visit 9

Notice that with the depth-first traversal we visit a node as we are placing it *into* the stack. With breadth-first traversal, however, we visit a node as we are taking it *from* the queue. With the former the index of the *node* itself is pushed; with the latter, the indices of the *neighbors* of the node are enqueued.

The hierarchy chart for breadth-first traversal appears in Figure 12.33; its formal definition is below. The subroutine *InitializeBFT* initializes the queue *q* and the array *visited*. Nodes are processed by the procedure *ProcessBFT* that calls a routine, *AllAdjacent*, which enqueues all adjacent, as yet unvisited nodes.

Figure 12.33

Hierarchy chart for breadth-first traversal

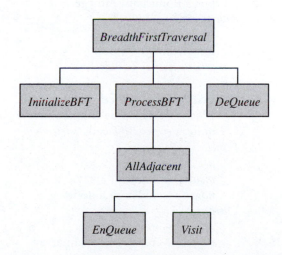

BreadthFirstTraversal(g, Visit(ArgumentList))
>   Procedure to perform a breadth-first traversal of graph g using the procedure *Visit*

Input:
> g — graph

Output:
>   Dependent upon the procedure *Visit*

Assumptions:
>   Graph g is implemented with an array of nodes, *g.node*, an adjacency matrix, *g.edge*, and a count of the number of nodes, *g.count*. The indices of the actual nodes range from 1 to n. Assume g is connected with at least one node.

Figure	Algorithm
{12.29}	*InitializeBFT(q, visited, g.count)*
{Step 1}	*ProcessBFT(q, g, visited, 1)*
	while not *QueueIsEmpty(q)* do
{Step 2}	*Dequeue(q, index)*
	if not *visited[index]* then
	ProcessBFT(q, g, visited, index)

InitializeBFT(q, visited, n)
>   Procedure to initialize q and *visited* for the procedure *BreadthFirstTraversal*

Input:
> n — number of elements in *visited* to be initialized

Output:
> q — queue
>   *visited* — boolean array

Assumption:
> n is a nonnegative integer.

Algorithm:
>   *MakeQueueEmpty(q)*
>   for i from 1 to n do
>   *visited[i]* ← *false*

ProcessBFT(q, g, visited, ndx)
>   Procedure called by *BreadthFirstTraversal* to process an index, *ndx*, of a node. *ProcessBFT* calls *Visit*.

Input:
> q — queue
>   *visited* — boolean array
>   *ndx*   — index of a node

Output:
> q — revised queue
>   *visited* — revised boolean array

Algorithm:
> *AllAdjacent(q, g, visited, ndx)*
> *Visit(ArgumentList)*
> *visited[ndx] ← true*

AllAdjacent(q, g, visited, ndx)
> Procedure called by *BreadthFirstTraversal* to enqueue the indices of all adjacent, unvisited nodes to the vertex with index *ndx*

Input:
> *q*   — queue
> *g*   — graph
> *visited* — boolean array
> *ndx*   — index of a node

Output:
> *q*   — revised queue

Algorithm:
> for *i* from 1 to *g.count* do
>   if *g.edge[ndx, i]* and (not *visited[i]*) then
>   *Enqueue(q, i)*

SECTION 12.4 EXERCISES

1. Give three different depth-first traversals of the graph in Figure 12.34. Start with node 1 each time.

2. Repeat Exercise 1 for the graph in Figure 12.35.

Figure 12.34

Graph for Exercise 1

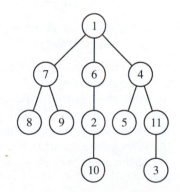

Figure 12.35

Graph for Exercise 2

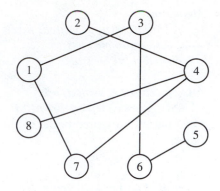

3. For Figure 12.36 give all depth-first traversals of the graph starting with node

    a. 1   **b.** 2   **c.** 3   **d.** 4

Figure 12.36

Graph for Exercise 3

4. Code in Pascal the procedure *DepthFirstTraversal* and all subroutines.

5. The algorithm for depth-first traversal presented in the text assumes the graph is connected.

    a. For the graph in Figure 12.37 show how the algorithm does not process the entire graph.

    b. Alter the *DepthFirstTraversal* algorithm to process all graphs, even unconnected ones. Use a loop to contain all but the initialization.

    c. Show how your algorithm from Part b works on Figure 12.37.

    d. Alter your algorithm of Part b to return the number of connected parts of the graph. For example, Figure 12.37 has two connected parts.

Figure 12.37

Graph for Exercise 5

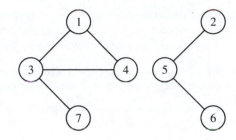

6. Design and code a depth-first traversal of a connected graph implemented with an adjacent list.

7. What is the complexity of the depth-first traversal?

8. Write a recursive version of *DepthFirstTraversal*.

For Exercises 9–16 repeat the requested exercise for breadth-first traversal.

9. Exercise 1	**10.** Exercise 2	**11.** Exercise 3
12. Exercise 4	**13.** Exercise 5	**14.** Exercise 6
15. Exercise 7	**16.** Exercise 8	

In Exercises 17–27 code in Pascal the routines from Section 12.1 using
  a. *depth-first traversal with an adjacency matrix*
  b. *depth-first traversal with an adjacency list*
  c. *breadth-first traversal with an adjacency matrix*
  d. *breadth-first traversal with an adjacency list*

17. Procedure *PrintGraph* from Exercise 17 to print all the values stored in a graph.

18. Function *NumNodes* from Exercise 18 that returns the number of nodes in a graph.

19. Function *deg* from Exercise 19 to return the degree of a node.

20. Procedure *PrintAdjacents* from Exercise 21 to print the key of each node and the keys of all adjacent nodes in a graph.

21. Function *SumDegrees* from Exercise 23 to return the sum of the degrees of all nodes in a graph.

22. Function *AddGraph* from Exercise 25 to return the sum of all the keys in a graph where each key is a number.

23. Function *MinInGraph* from Exercise 26 to return the minimum key held in a graph; assume the graph is not empty.

24. Procedure *ToAdjacent*(*g, curNode*) from Exercise 28 that makes *curNode* indicate a node adjacent to the one to which it presently points; if there is no adjacent node, *curNode* becomes empty.

25. Procedure *InsertConnectAll*(*g, e*) from Exercise 29 to insert a node containing *e* into *g* and make that node adjacent to every other node in *g*.

26. Boolean function *Subgraph*(*s, g*) from Exercise 31 to return *true* if *s* is a subgraph of *g*.

27. Procedure *CopyGraph*(*s, g*) from Exercise 33 that makes a copy *s* of a graph *g*.

28. Code procedure *DeleteGraph* from Exercise 27 to delete every node in a graph; use a breadth-first traversal.

29. The following appeared in the sample questions of the *1984 AP Computer Science Examination**:

A rectangular array is used to represent a maze. Cells containing ones represent walls; cells containing zeros represent rooms that can be entered from neighboring rooms; i.e., from cells that adjoin them horizontally or vertically (but not diagonally). The cell at the upper left and the cell at the lower right each contain a zero. Which of the following describe(s) a correct method of determining whether there is a path through the maze from the upper left to the lower right?

I. Place a two in the upper left cell. Then repeatedly place a two in each cell that contains a zero and adjoins a cell containing a two. If a two ever appears in the lower right cell, then a path exists through the maze.

II. Move horizontally from the cell in the upper left corner of the maze until a wall or the edge of the array is reached. Then turn right and move until another wall or another edge is reached. Continue in this fashion, turning right each time an obstruction is reached, until either the lower right cell is reached (in which case there is a path through the maze) or the upper left cell is again reached (in which case there is not).

III. Consider separately the one or two moves that are possible from the, upper left cell (if no moves are possible, there is no path). In each case, reduce the size of the array by eliminating the row and column of the cell just left. Apply this method recursively until no moves are possible or until the lower right cell is reached.

(A) I only
(B) II only
(C) III only
(D) I and II
(E) II and III

*AP question selected from *AP Computer Science Examination*, 1984. Reprinted by permission of Educational Testing Service, the copyright owner of the sample questions.

▽

PROGRAMMING PROJECT

1. Write a Pascal program to read a maze represented by a rectangular array as described in Exercise 29 and to indicate if a path exists through the maze or not. Use Algorithm I of Exercise 29, to define a boolean function to return *true* if there is a path through the maze and to return *false* otherwise.

SECTION 12.5

Graph Applications

Computer implementations of graphs can be used to solve complicated problems, such as those found in game theory, telephone networking, scheduling interrelated tasks for a job, and routing from one location to another. Some applications involve **directed graphs** or **digraphs** where the edges are arrows. Others are modeled by networks where values are associated with edges as well as nodes. One technique using networks for dealing with the scheduling problem was developed by the U.S. Navy and used to complete the Polaris missile program in five years instead of the estimated seven.

Example 12.3

Maze.

Suppose we want the computer to find a path through a maze, such as the one in Figure 12.38. This maze is obviously very simple, but our approach to this problem can apply to more complicated mazes.

Figure 12.38

Maze for Example 12.3

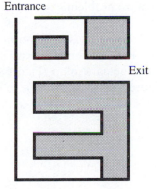

Entrance

Exit

We will use a graph to model the maze. Every right angle intersection, dead end, entrance, or exit will be represented as a node, and the straight lengths will be edges. Therefore, this maze can be pictured schematically by the graph in Figure 12.39. By shifting the sketch slightly, we see that this graph is identical to the one in Figure 12.24, with the same nodes and adjacencies. We are searching for a path from the entrance, node 1, to the exit, node 8.

Figure 12.39

Graph for maze in Figure 12.38

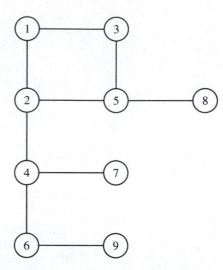

If you were walking a maze yourself, undoubtedly you would go as far as possible on a path until finding the exit or a dead end. If you encounter a dead end, you might backtrack to the last intersection. Then you could follow the alternative as far as possible, repeating the process of backtracking if necessary. But this technique is just a depth-first traversal that may suddenly halt should you find the exit. In fact, notice the traversal of this graph in Figures 12.24– 12.27. When you visit node 8, the stack from top to bottom contains 8, 5, 2, and 1, a sequence that is one of the paths from node 1 to node 8 in reverse order. Thus, with an ADT graph implementation a depth-first search can solve the maze problem.

A **network** is a graph or digraph having a number associated with each edge. Perhaps the numbers, called **weights**, represent distances between cities on a schematic map (Figure 12.40) or the cost of flying between these cities (Figure 12.41) or the time in minutes of a flight (Figure 12.42).

Figure 12.40

Network of distances between cities

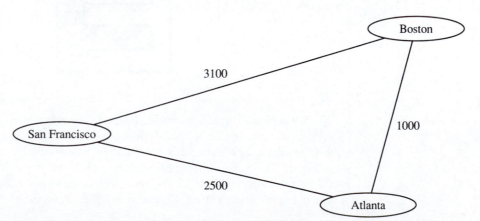

Figure 12.41

Network of cost of flying
between cities

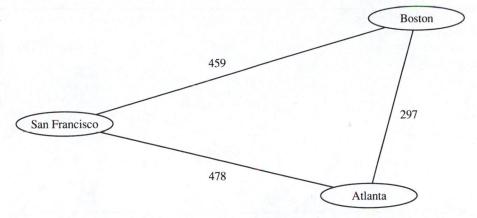

Figure 12.42

Network of time in min-
utes of flights between
cities

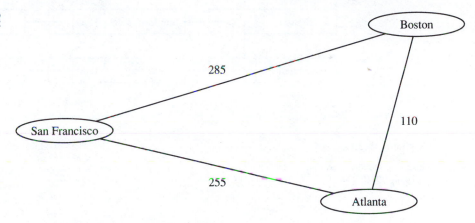

The ADT graph definition can be extended to define the ADT network graph. We describe the objects as a network graph structure of nodes and edges and we include two additional operations, *StoreEdge* and *RetrieveEdge*, to store and retrieve values associated with an edge, respectively. The implementation of the ADT graph from Section 12.2, too, can be extended for networks. Instead of having the adjacency matrix be a two-dimensional boolean array, we declare the matrix to be a two-dimensional array of some appropriate range of numbers. Then the *ij* entry will be the value associated with the *ij* edge. The arrays of Figure 12.43 store the nodes and edges of the map in Figure 12.40.

Similarly, in the adjacency list implementation of Section 12.3, for each element in the edge lists we can have a value field as well as key and link fields. Figure 12.44 illustrates the adjacency list representation of the map in Figure 12.40. Of course, in other applications elements of the node list could contain far more information.

Figure 12.43.

Arrays to store the nodes and edges of the map in Figure 12.40

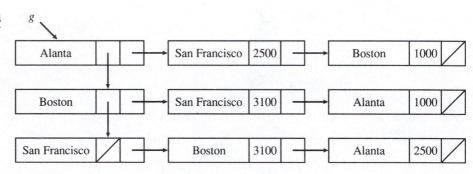

$$count = 3$$

$$node = \begin{matrix} 1 & 2 & 3 \\ [\text{Atlanta,} & \text{Boston,} & \text{San Francisco}] \end{matrix}$$

$$edge = \begin{matrix} & 1 & 2 & 3 \\ 1 & \begin{bmatrix} 0 & 1000 & 2500 \\ 2 & 1000 & 0 & 3100 \\ 3 & 2500 & 3100 & 0 \end{bmatrix} \end{matrix}$$

Figure 12.44

Adjacency list representation of the map in Figure 12.40

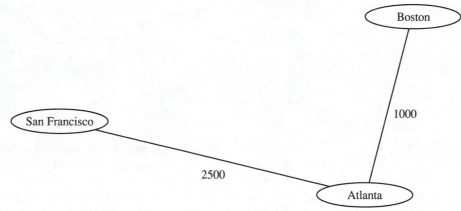

Figure 12.45

Minimal spanning tree for the map in Figure 12.40

Some applications require finding a spanning tree of a connected graph. A **spanning tree** of a graph *g* is a subgraph that is a tree containing all the nodes of *g*. In the case of a connected network we may want to find a **minimal spanning tree,** a spanning tree with the smallest possible sum of edge values. For example, connecting many computer centers in an international computer network, we might want to find the best routing through the system in order to achieve the least possible delay in message relay. Figure 12.45 gives the minimal spanning tree for the map of Figure 12.40.

| **Example 12.4** | **Minimal Spanning Tree.** |

▼ **Kruskal's algorithm** below can be applied to network g of n vertices to find a minimal spanning tree t:

Select for t an edge of g that has the smallest number associated with it.
Repeat the following until there are $n - 1$ edges in t:

> Select for t an edge of g that is not already in t; that is adjacent to a node of t; that has the smallest number associated with it; and whose addition to t will not form a cycle.

Kruskal's method is an example of a class called **greedy algorithms**. At each intermediate step we are greedy to take what obviously appears to be the best choice. For a greedy algorithm, these opportunistic short-term selections do yield the desired result. Not all algorithms can boast that picking the locally obvious choices will produce the best overall solution.

To illustrate Kruskal's algorithm, suppose we wish to find a minimal spanning tree for the network in Figure 12.46. We start by picking for t the edge with the smallest weight, (a, e), of weight 2. Thus, t has two nodes, a and e, and one edge. (See Step 1 of Figure 12.47.) We then form a queue of all edges incident to a or e. But the queue must be ordered by weight from smallest to largest. (Such priority queues were discussed in Exercise 7 of Section 6.3 and Programming Project 1 of Section 11.4.) Dequeuing edge (a, c) to add to the tree, t now has two edges and three nodes, a, e, and c. With the addition of node c we place incident edge (c, d) with weight 4 into an ordered location in the priority queue. (See Step 2 of Figure 12.47.)

When we dequeue edge (e, c), however, we detect a problem. Addition of this edge would only complete a cycle, which is not allowed in a tree. Therefore, nothing is done with (e, c). The next queue element, (e, f), can legally be added to the tree. Moreover, we place edges incident to f, (f, d) with weight 5 and (f, g) with weight 9, into the priority queue. (See Step 1 of Figure 12.48.) Then, as Step 2 of Figure 12.48 shows, the new front element, (e, g), is inserted into the tree. Since edge $(g, f) = (f, g)$ is incident to node f of the tree as well as

Figure 12.46

Network for Example 12.4

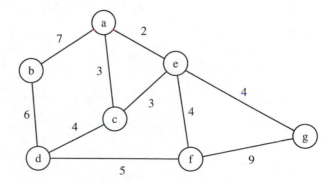

Figure 12.47

Initial action of Kruskal's algorithm to find a minimal spanning tree for the network in Figure 12.46

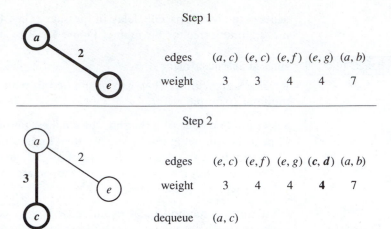

Step 1

edges	(a, c)	(e, c)	(e, f)	(e, g)	(a, b)
weight	3	3	4	4	7

Step 2

edges	(e, c)	(e, f)	(e, g)	(c, d)	(a, b)
weight	3	4	4	**4**	7

dequeue	(a, c)

Figure 12.48

Continuation of Kruskal's algorithm on the graph from Figure 12.47

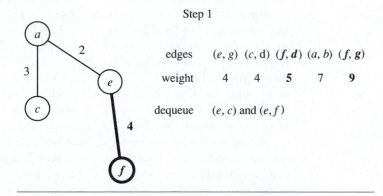

Step 1

edges	(e, g)	(c, d)	(f, d)	(a, b)	(f, g)
weight	4	4	**5**	7	**9**

dequeue	(e, c) and (e, f)

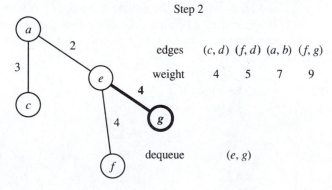

Step 2

edges	(c, d)	(f, d)	(a, b)	(f, g)
weight	4	5	7	9

dequeue	(e, g)

node g, we do not place the edge in the queue. In fact, that edge (f, g) is already in the queue.

Edge (c, d) becomes the latest addition to the developing minimal spanning tree. Consequently, edge (b, d) with weight 6 being incident to d is placed in the priority queue. (See Step 1 of Figure 12.49.) Edge (f, d), the next front queue element, would complete a cycle in t. Thus, we reject (f, d) and examine the next edge, (b, d). Node b is not in the tree t, so as Step 2 of Figure 12.49 shows, we insert that node and edge into t. Now t contains six edges and all seven nodes of g and Kruskal's algorithm for finding a minimal spanning tree for a network is complete.

Figure 12.49

Completion of Kruskal's algorithm on the graph from Figure 12.48

Step 1

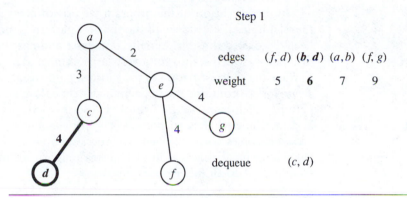

edges	(f, d)	$(\boldsymbol{b}, \boldsymbol{d})$	(a, b)	(f, g)
weight	5	**6**	7	9

dequeue (c, d)

Step 2

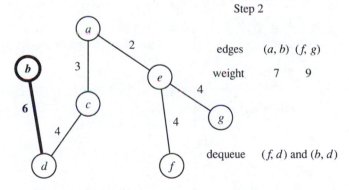

edges	(a, b)	(f, g)
weight	7	9

dequeue (f, d) and (b, d)

Example 12.5.

Shortest Path.

Dijkstra's algorithm presents a method for finding the shortest path from one point in the graph and any other. Such a path may not cover every node in the graph and, therefore, is not necessarily a spanning tree. Like Kruskal's technique, however, Dijkstra's is a greedy algorithm.

For simplicity suppose the vertices of the graph are numbered from 1 to n and that a path will start at node 1. The idea is to process all the other nodes one at a time. Each time, we greedily take the unprocessed vertex, *IndexMin*, which has the smallest computed distance to node 1. Then, for any unprocessed vertex j that is adjacent to node *IndexMin* we see if the path from 1 to *IndexMin* and then directly to j is shorter than the previous distance we had computed from 1 to j. If that new path is shorter, we change the distance from 1 to j to that new path length. We also record in a *fromNode* array that to get to node j it is best to go through vertex *IndexMin*. When we have processed all the vertices, the distance associated with each node will be the optimum path length from 1. Moreover, using the *fromNode* array we can trace backwards from the destination to discover the path.

In the execution of the program we use an array *distance*, such that *distance*[j] holds the distance of the shortest path from node 1 to node j that has been discovered thus far. Initially, if nodes 1 and j are not adjacent, we call this distance ∞, which stands for a very large number. The array *fromNode* is used to trace the shortest path. On the shortest path from 1 to j discovered thus far, *fromNode*[j] contains the node immediately before node j. Thus, that shortest path proceeds from vertex 1 through a series of vertices to point *fromNode*[j] and then immediately to point j. The jth element of the boolean array *processed* becomes *true*(1) if we have processed node j.

The general description of Dijkstra's algorithm to find the shortest path from node 1 to all other nodes follows:

Initialize arrays:

$$distance[i] \leftarrow \begin{cases} 0 \text{ if } i = 1 \\ \text{length of arc between nodes 1 and } i \text{ if adjacent} \\ \infty, \text{ otherwise} \end{cases}$$

$$fromNode[i] \leftarrow \begin{cases} 1 \text{ if nodes 1 and } i \text{ are adjacent} \\ 0 \text{ otherwise} \end{cases}$$

$$processed[i] \leftarrow \begin{cases} true(1) \text{ if } i = 1 \\ false(0) \text{ otherwise} \end{cases}$$

For $n - 1$ times do the following:
    IndexMin ← the index of the unprocessed node that is closest to vertex 1.
    Mark that node as having been processed.
    For each node j from 2 to n do the following:
        If node j has not been processed
            and nodes j and *IndexMin* are adjacent then
          If shorter to go through node *IndexMin* to get to node j then
            Change *distance*[j] to that distance.
            fromNode[j] ← *IndexMin*.
                    {Path to j goes through *IndexMin* }

Using the implementation where *g.edge* is the adjacency matrix, the length of the path from node 1 to *j* through node *IndexMin* is

$$distance[IndexMin] + g.edge[IndexMin, j]$$

the distance from 1 to *IndexMin* plus the length of the arc from *IndexMin* to *j*.

Figures 12.50 and 12.51 detail the steps of the algorithm for a particular network. Suppose we wish to discover the shortest path between nodes 1 and 7.

Figure 12.50

Initialization of *processed*, *fromNode*, and *distance* for and beginning steps of Dijkstra's algorithm

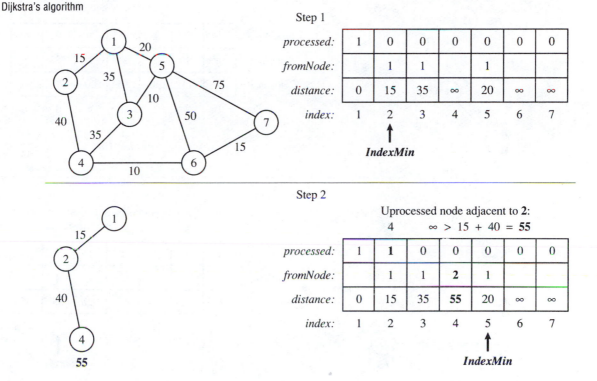

Step 1

processed:	1	0	0	0	0	0	0
fromNode:		1	1		1		
distance:	0	15	35	∞	20	∞	∞
index:	1	2	3	4	5	6	7

↑
IndexMin

Step 2

Uprocessed node adjacent to **2**:
  4   ∞ > 15 + 40 = **55**

processed:	1	**1**	0	0	0	0	0
fromNode:		1	1	**2**	1		
distance:	0	15	35	**55**	20	∞	∞
index:	1	2	3	4	5	6	7

↑
IndexMin

Step 2

Uprocessed nodes adjacent to **5**:
  3   35 > 20 + 10 = **30**
  6   ∞ > 20 + 50 = **70**
  7   ∞ > 20 + 75 = **95**

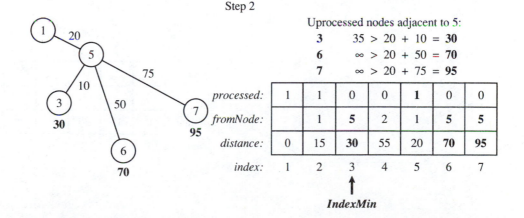

processed:	1	1	0	0	1	0	0
fromNode:		1	5	2	1	5	5
distance:	0	15	30	55	20	70	95
index:	1	2	3	4	5	6	7

↑
IndexMin

Figure 12.51

Continuation of Dijkstra's algorithm from Figure 12.50

Step 1

Unprocessed node adjacent to 3:

4        $55 \leq 30 + 35 = 65$

No change in arrays
distance and *fromNode*

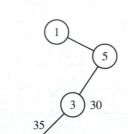

processed:	1	1	**1**	0	1	0	0
fromNode:		1	5	2	1	5	5
distance:	0	15	30	55	20	70	95
index:	1	2	3	4	5	6	7

IndexMin

Step 2

Unprocessed node adjacent to **4**:

6        $70 > 55 + 10 = 65$

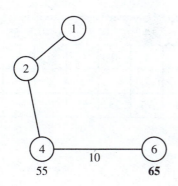

processed:	1	1	1	**1**	1	0	0
fromNode:		1	5	2	1	**4**	5
distance:	0	15	30	55	20	**65**	95
index:	1	2	3	4	5	6	7

IndexMin

Step 3

Unprocessed node adjacent to **6**:

7        $95 > 65 + 15 = 80$

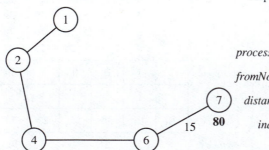

processed:	1	1	1	1	1	**1**	0
fromNode:		1	5	2	1	4	**6**
distance:	0	15	30	55	20	65	**80**
index:	1	2	3	4	5	6	7

IndexMin

The last step tells us the length of the path is *distance*[7] = 80. Moreover, to get to 7 we come from node *fromNode*[7] = 6. Tracing backwards, *fromNode*[6] = 4 tells us we came through node 4. Before that vertex, we traveled through *fromNode*[4] = 2, and the node before 2 was *fromNode*[2] = 1. Thus, the shortest path from 1 to 7 is 1, 2, 4, 6, 7. Actually, as we will explore in the exercises, upon completion of the algorithm, the *fromNode* array indicates all ▲ the shortest paths from node 1 to other nodes.

SECTION 12.5 EXERCISES

1. **a.** Draw a graph corresponding to the maze in Figure 12.52.
   b. Perform a search for the path through the maze as described in Example 12.3.

Figure 12.52

Maze for Exercise 1

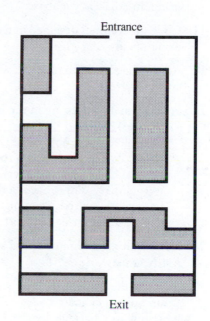

Figure 12.53

Network for Exercises 3, 5, and 7

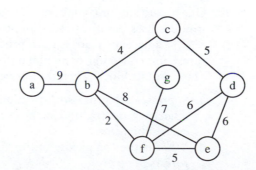

2. Give the node and adjacency matrix representation for the graph in Figure 12.46.

3. Repeat Exercise 2 for Figure 12.53.

4. Give the adjacency list representation for the network in Figure 12.46.

5. Repeat Exercise 4 for Figure 12.53.

6. Give all the minimal spanning trees of the network in Figure 12.46.

7. Repeat Exercise 6 for Figure 12.53.

8. a. Construct a hierarchy chart of routines for Kruskal's algorithm.
   b. Design all the routines with pseudocode and ADT operations.

9. Give the complexity of Kruskal's algorithm.

10. Code the routines designed in Exercise 8 when the network is implemented using an adjacency matrix.

11. Code the routines designed in Exercise 8 when the network is implemented using an adjacency list.

12. Adjust the algorithm of Exercise 8 to return the total weight of the minimal spanning tree.

13. a. How many edges are in the minimal spanning tree of seven nodes from Figure 12.46?
   Complete the proof of the theorem that a tree t of n nodes has $n - 1$ edges: Pick any vertex as a root and direct all edges away from this root. Only __**b**__ (give number) node(s) has (have) no arrows pointing into it (them). (**c.** Why?) Each of the remaining __**d**__ (give number) nodes has exactly one edge coming into it. (**e.** Why?) Thus, there are exactly $n - 1$ edges in a tree of n vertices.

14. Design an algorithm to find a spanning tree for a graph. The graph need not be a network.

15. a. Code the routine of Exercise 14 where the graph is implemented using an adjacency matrix.
   b. Using an adjacency list.

16. One algorithm for computing the minimum spanning tree of a graph with n nodes uses parallel processing with p computers and partitions of the $n \times n$ adjacency matrix. Each processor evaluates the **minimal spanning forest,** or collection of minimal spanning trees for the connected subgraphs, of its block. Then the answers are merged.

   a. Suppose each processor works on the same size square submatrix of the adjacency matrix, and suppose p divides n. How many entries are in each submatrix?
   b. What is the complexity of the operation to find the minimal spanning forests?

    c. Suppose the merge operation is on the order of

$$O(n/p + n + (n/\sqrt{p} + p)\log_2 n).$$

    What is the complexity of the entire minimal spanning tree procedure?

17. a. How would we alter the definition of the ADT graph to define the ADT digraph?

    b. For Figure 12.54, draw a picture of the node array and adjacency matrix to model the digraph.

    c. The adjacency matrix for a graph is symmetric; that is, the *ij* element is the same as the *ji* element. Is the adjacency matrix for a digraph symmetric?

    d. For Figure 12.54 draw a picture of the adjacency list to model the digraph.

    e. Using the implementation in the text for Section 12.3, for an edge $(a, c) = (c, a)$ in a graph, we need a node for *c* in *a*'s edge list and a node for *a* in *c*'s edge list. Are these two nodes needed to represent an edge of a digraph? What is needed?

Figure 12.54

Digraph for Exercise 17

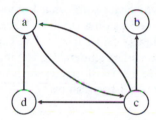

18. For each vertex in the network of Figures 12.50–12.51 give the shortest path from node 1 to that vertex. Also, give the length of each such path.

19. a. Perform Dijkstra's algorithm on the graph in Figure 12.55, tracing the steps as in Figures 12.50–12.51.

    b. For each vertex in the network give the shortest path from node 1 to that vertex. Also, give the length of each such path.

Figure 12.55

Network for Exercise 19

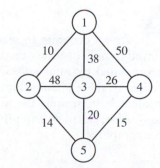

20. a. Construct a hierarchy chart of routines for Dijkstra's algorithm.
b. Design all routines.

21. Code the routines designed in Exercise 20, where the network is implemented using an adjacency matrix.

22. Alter Dijkstra's algorithm to compute the shortest paths from node 1 to every other node, where the length of the path is the number of nodes in that path. You will not need to access any numbers associated with the edges.

23. Give the complexity of Dijkstra's algorithm.

▽
PROGRAMMING PROJECTS

1. Write a program to read a maze as pairs of adjacent nodes, to read the starting point and the destination, and then to find and print a path through the maze from the entrance to the exit.

2. Sometimes data is analyzed using graphs or digraphs to discover **clusters**, which are somewhat homogeneous groups. For example, suppose we ask students on a small college campus to list the names of other students that they consider friends. We can represent the results by a digraph. If student i considers student k a friend, we draw an arrow from node i to node k. Figure 12.56 illustrates such a graph. Cluster analysis can be used to detect mutual friendships.

Figure 12.56

Digraph for Project 2 where an arrow from node i to node k means student i considers student k a friend

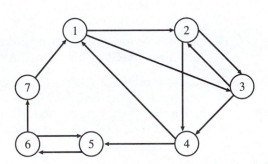

Write a program to read each student (represented by a number) followed by a list of the other students that he or she considers friends (also represented by numbers). Construct and print an adjacency matrix A to represent these relationships, where a_{ik} is *true* if and only if student i likes student k. In printing the adjacency matrix, record each *true* as 1 and *false* as 0. Also, calculate and print the similarity matrix as described in the next paragraph.

A **similarity matrix, C,** indicates the closeness of two students based on the number of mutual friends and mutual non-friends. Evaluate c_{ik} as the number of values in common between rows i and k of the adjacency matrix divided by the number of nodes. For example, rows 1 and 2 of the adjacency matrix for Figure 12.56 are

0 1 1 0 0 0 0
0 0 1 1 0 0 0

Consequently, $c_{12} = 5/7$ since they share four zeros and one 1 in the same position and since the number of nodes is 7. The similarity matrix is symmetric with $c_{ii} = 1$ for all i. Thus, we only need to store C as a triangular matrix.

a. Give the adjacency matrix A for Figure 12.56.
b. Give the similarity matrix C for Figure 12.56.

RANDOM NUMBER GENERATOR

There are many different random number generators, but one of the best kinds is a **multiplicative linear congruential generator,** which generates a sequence of random integers:

$$random_n = \begin{cases} seed & \text{if } n = 0 \\ (multiplier * random_{n-1}) \bmod modulus & \text{if } n > 0 \end{cases}$$

To get a real number we divide the result by *modulus.*

Much research has been performed to discover good choices for *multiplier* and *modulus.* The random number generator presented in this appendix can be implemented on any computer where the mantissa of a real number is at least 32 bits long; that is, the mantissa can store all the digits of $2^{31} - 1 = 2,147,483,647$. Most systems, including most microcomputers, can hold such a mantissa. Because many microcomputers have a *maxint* of 32,767, however, we will declare all variables to be real.

In the main program we have the declaration of a global variable, *seed*:

```
var
    seed : real;
```

Also, in the main program we assign to *seed* some integer between 1 and $2^{31} - 1 = 2,147,483,647$, expressed as a real number. For example, we could assign a Social Security number to *seed*:

```
seed := 348217659.0
```

The function *Random* below returns a real number x with $0 < x < 1$. For each invocation of *Random*, the last value of *seed* is used to generate a new value for *seed* and a new random number. The function implements the definition above with precautions to prevent overflow:

```
{ *** Random number generator to return the real number
        multiplier * seed mod modulus
  without overflow in a machine that has:
    1. at least a 32-bit mantissa for a real number
    2. a maxint of at least 32767                          *** }

function Random : real;
const
   multiplier = 16807.0;
   modulus    = 2147483647.0;   { 2^31 - 1 }
   quotient   = 127773.0;       { modulus div multiplier }
   remainder  = 2836.0;         { modulus mod multiplier }
var
   low,
   high,
   PossibleSeed : real;
begin
   high := trunc(seed/quotient);
   low := seed - quotient * high;
   PossibleSeed := multiplier * low - remainder * high;
   if PossibleSeed < 0.0 then   { modulus + 1 < PossibleSeed < 0 }
      seed := PossibleSeed + modulus
   else                         { 0 < PossibleSeed < modulus }
      seed := PossibleSeed;
   Random := seed / modulus
end; { Random }
```

To generate a random integer in the set $\{\,0, 1, 2, \ldots, n-1\,\}$, we can use the following function with the appropriate definition of *NonNeg*:

```
type
   NonNeg = 0..maxint;
   .
{ *** Function to return a random integer
   in the range from 0 to n - 1 *** }

function RandomInteger ( n : NonNeg) : NonNeg;
begin
   RandomInteger := trunc ( n * Random )
end; { RandomInteger }
```

For a more complete discussion of random number generators along with other alternatives refer to Stephen K. Park and Keith W. Miller, "Random Number Generators: Good Ones Are Hard to Find," *Communications of the ACM*, vol. 31, no. 10 (Oct. 1988), pp. 1192–1201.

TURBO PASCAL AND UCSD PASCAL: EXTENSIONS AND VARIATIONS

This appendix contains some of the commonly used extensions and variations of Borland International's Turbo Pascal 5.0 for the IBM PC and UCSD Pascal, which was developed at the University of California at San Diego. Topics include encapsulation, files, graphics, random number generator, sets, and strings.

Encapsulation

TURBO PASCAL

```
uses UnitName;
```

Separately compiled unit *UnitName* made available. Place *uses* statement after program statement.

```
unit UnitName;
    interface
        {Place public information here:
            uses clauses,
            constant and type definitions,
            variable declarations, and
            procedure and function headings}
    implementation
        {Place private information here:
            uses clauses,
            constant and type definitions,
            variable declarations, and
            procedure and function definitions—
                For those declared in the interface,
                have "procedure" or "function" followed
                by the routine's name (no parameters
                listed) and body}
end.
```

Compile unit separately.

Files

TURBO PASCAL

```
assign(FileVariable, 'ActualFileName');
```

Opens file and associates the name of the permanent file, *ActualFileName*, with the file identifier, *FileVariable*, for the program. Statement must be used before *reset* or *rewrite*.

```
close(FileVariable)
```

Statement should be used to close a file.

put, *get*, and associated buffer variable *FileVariable*^ are not available.

UCSD PASCAL

```
reset(FileVariable, 'ActualFileName');
```

Opens file for input and associates the name of the permanent file, *ActualFileName*, with the file identifier, *FileVariable*, for the program.

```
rewrite(FileVariable, 'ActualFileName');
```

Opens file for output and associates the name of the permanent file, *ActualFileName*, with the file identifier, *FileVariable*, for the program.

```
close(FileVariable, lock)
```

Close a permanent file.

```
close(FileVariable, purge)
```

Close a temporary file.

Graphics

TURBO PASCAL

```
uses graph;
```

Makes available graphics unit. Place statement after program statement.

```
GraphDrive := Detect;        {built-in constant}
InitGraph(GraphDriver, GraphMode, '')
```

Procedure to initialize graphics system and put hardware in graphics mode.

```
color := GetMaxColor
```

Function reference returns the highest color.

```
PutPixel (x, y, color)
```

Plots pixel (x, y) using color *color*. Pixel (0,0) is in the upper left corner.

`CloseGraph;`

Close graphics system.

Several additional graphics routines are available that include drawing, attribute selection, text output, and fill routines.

Random Number Generator

TURBO PASCAL

`Randomize`

Procedure to initialize the random number generator's seed, *Rand-Seed*, with a random value. To obtain the same sequence of random numbers each time, do not call *Randomize* but assign a value to *Rand-Seed*. Call *Randomize* or assign a value to *RandSeed* before invoking *Random*.

`x : = Random`

Function reference that returns a random real number x, $0 \leq x < 1$.

`m : = Random(n)`

Function reference that returns a random integer m, $0 \leq m < n$, where n is a positive integer.

Sets

TURBO PASCAL

Maximum number of elements is 256.

Strings

Notation:
   s, u, sub, s1, s2, . . . , sn — strings
   n, p, lng   — nonnegative integers

TURBO PASCAL AND UCSD PASCAL

`string[n]`

Type of a string of n characters, $1 \leq n \leq 255$.

```
string
      Typestring[255]
```

Strings may be read, written, assigned, and compared.

Strings of length 1 and characters are compatible.

```
lng := length(s)
```

Function reference to return the length of *s*; implementation of the ADT string operation *LengthString(s)*.

```
p := pos(sub, s)
```

Function reference to return the position of *sub* in *s*; 0 if not found; implementation of the ADT string operation *Position(sub, s)*.

```
u := concat(s1, s2,..., sn)
```

or

```
u := s1 + s2 + · · · + sn
```

Function reference or operation to return the concatenation of *s1, s2, . . . , sn*; implementation of the ADT string operation *Concat*.

```
u := copy(s, p, lng)
```

Function reference to return the substring from *s* starting at position *p* for *lng* characters; implementation of the ADT string operation *CopySubstring(u, s, p, lng)*.

```
delete(s, p, lng)
```

Procedure call to delete from *s* the substring starting at position *p* for *lng* characters; implementation of the ADT string operation *DeleteString(s, p, lng)*.

```
insert(sub, s, p)
```

Procedure call to insert *sub* into *s* at position *p*; implementation of the ADT string operation *InsertString(sub, s, p)*.

ABRIDGED ASCII AND EBCDIC TABLES

Decimal	Hexadecimal	ASCII	EBCDIC
0	0	NUL	NUL
.	.	.	.
.	.	.	.
.	.	.	.
32	20	space	
.	.	.	
.	.	.	
.	.	.	
46	2E	.	
47	2F	/	
48	30	0	
49	31	1	
50	32	2	
51	33	3	
52	34	4	
53	35	5	
54	36	6	
55	37	7	
56	38	8	
57	39	9	
.	.	.	
.	.	.	
.	.	.	
64	40	@	blank
65	41	A	
66	42	B	
67	43	C	
68	44	D	
69	45	E	

Decimal	Hexadecimal	ASCII	EBCDIC
70	46	F	
71	47	G	
72	48	H	
73	49	I	
74	4A	J	¢
75	4B	K	.
76	4C	L	<
77	4D	M	(
78	4E	N	+
79	4F	O	|
80	50	P	&
81	51	Q	
82	52	R	
83	53	S	
84	54	T	
85	55	U	
86	56	V	
87	57	W	
88	58	X	
89	59	Y	
90	5A	Z	!
.	.	.	.
.	.	.	.
.	.	.	.
97	61	a	/
98	62	b	
99	63	c	
100	64	d	
101	65	e	
102	66	f	
103	67	g	
104	68	h	
105	69	i	
106	6A	j	
107	6B	k	,
108	6C	l	%
109	6D	m	—
110	6E	n	>
111	6F	o	?
112	70	p	
113	71	q	
114	72	r	
115	73	s	
116	74	t	
117	75	u	
118	76	v	

Decimal	Hexadecimal	ASCII	EBCDIC
119	77	w	
120	78	x	
121	79	y	
122	7A	z	:
.	.	.	.
.	.	.	.
.	.	.	.
129	81		a
130	82		b
131	83		c
132	84		d
133	85		e
134	86		f
135	87		g
136	88		h
137	89		i
.	.		.
.	.		.
.	.		.
145	91		j
146	92		k
147	93		l
148	94		m
149	95		n
150	96		o
151	97		p
152	98		q
153	99		r
.	.		.
.	.		.
.	.		.
162	A2		s
163	A3		t
164	A4		u
165	A5		v
166	A6		w
167	A7		x
168	A8		y
169	A9		z
.	.		.
.	.		.
.	.		.
193	C1		A
194	C2		B
195	C3		C
196	C4		D

Decimal	Hexadecimal	ASCII	EBCDIC
197	C5		E
198	C6		F
199	C7		G
200	C8		H
201	C9		I
.	.		.
.	.		.
.	.		.
209	D1		J
210	D2		K
211	D3		L
212	D4		M
213	D5		N
214	D6		O
215	D7		P
216	D8		Q
217	D9		R
.	.		.
.	.		.
.	.		.
226	E2		S
227	E3		T
228	E4		U
229	E5		V
230	E6		W
231	E7		X
232	E8		Y
233	E9		Z
.	.		.
.	.		.
.	.		.
240	F0		0
241	F1		1
242	F2		2
243	F3		3
244	F4		4
245	F5		5
246	F6		6
247	F7		7
248	F8		8
249	F9		9
.	.		
.	.		
.	.		
255	FF		

ANSWERS TO SELECTED EXERCISES

Chapter 1

SECTION 1.1

1. Read students' names and grades
Calculate the test average
Print report of those above average

2. $NumStu \leftarrow 0$
Prompt for a name and grade; '*', 0 to stop
ReadStr(DataString)
While *DataString* is not '*' do the following:
    Increment *NumStu* by 1
    Copy name into name field of array element with index *NumStu*
    Read grade into grade field of array element with index *NumStu*
    Prompt for a name and grade
    ReadStr(DataString)
Read end-of-line marker

3. Calculate total of the test scores
Calculate the average
Print the average

4. $TotalOfGrades \leftarrow 0$
for *i* from 1 to *NumStu* do
    $TotalOfGrades \leftarrow TotalOfGrades +$ Grade of *i*th student

5. If $NumStu = 0$ then
    $CalculateAverage \leftarrow 0$
else
    $CalculateAverage \leftarrow TotalOfGrades / NumStu$

6. print headings
    for *i* from 1 to *NumStu* do
        if the grade of *i*th student is greater than the average then
            print that student's name

7. for *i* from 1 to *length* do
    print *i*th character in string

8.

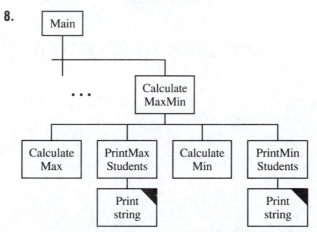

9. *CalculateMaxMin*
    if NumStu > 0 then
        Calculate the maximum grade
        Print the names of all students with that grade
        Calculate the minimum grade
        Print the names of all students with that grade

CalculateMax
    MaxGrade ← first student's grade
    for *i* from 2 to *NumStu* do
        if *i*th grade is larger than *MaxGrade* then
            MaxGrade ← *i*th grade
    CalculateMax ← *MaxGrade*

PrintMaxStudents
    for *i* from 1 to *NumStu* do
        if *i*th grade is *MaxGrade* then
            print the name of the *i*th student

For the minimum, make the following changes:
    "maximum" becomes "minimum";
    Max becomes *Min*;
    "larger" becomes "smaller"

10. *Merge(**outfile, infile1, infile2**)*
   reset (*infile1*)
   reset (*infile2*)
   rewrite (*outfile*)
   CompareFiles(*outfile, infile1, infile2*)
   EchoPrint(*outfile, infile1*)
   EchoPrint(*outfile, infile2*)

  *CompareFiles(**outfile, infile1, infile2**)*
   if (not eof (*infile1*)) and (not eof(*infile2*)) then
    done1 ← false
    done2 ← false
    readln (*infile1, X1*)
    readln (*infile2, X2*)
    while (not *done1*) and (not *done2*) do
     if *X1 > X2* then
      writeln (*outfile, X1*)
      if not eof (*infile1*) then
       readln (*infile1, X1*)
      else
       done1 ← true
     else
      writeln (*outfile, X2*)
      if not eof (*infile2*) then
       readln (*infile2, X2*)
      else
       done2 ← true
    if not *done1* then
     writeln (*outfile, X1*)
    else if not *done2* then
     writeln (*outfile, X2*)

  *EchoPrint(**outfile, infile**)*
   while not eof (*infile*) do
    readln (*infile, X*)
    writeln (*outfile, X*)

SECTION 1.2

1.
```
begin {AboveAverage}
    ReadData(StudentRec, NumStu);
    writeln;
    Calculate(StudentRec, NumStu, average);
    writeln;
    PrintAboveAverage(StudentRec, NumStu, average)
end.
```

2.

```
{*** Procedure to read data into array of student records ***}

procedure ReadData(var StudentRec: ArrayType;
                   var NumStu: NumStuType);
var
   DataString : StringType;
begin
   NumStu := 0;
   write ('Type name, grade; *, 0 to stop: ');
   ReadStr (DataString);
   while DataString.name.str[1] <> '*' do
     begin
        NumStu := NumStu + 1;
        StudentRec[NumStu].Name := DataString;
        readln(StudentRec[NumStu].Grade);
        write('Type name, grade; *, 0 to stop: ');
        ReadStr (DataString)
     end; {while}
   readln    {read eoln marker}
end; {ReadData}
```

3.

```
{*** Procedure to calculate total and average of grades ***}

procedure Calculate(var StudentRec: ArrayType;
                    NumStu: NumStuType; var average: real);
var
   TotalOfGrades: real;
begin
   TotalOfGrades := CalculateTotal(StudentRec, NumStu);
   average       := CalculateAverage(NumStu, TotalOfGrades);
   writeln('The average of the grades for ', NumStu:3,
           'students is ', average:5:2)
end; {Calculate}
```

4.

```
{*** Function to return total of grades ***}

function CalculateTotal(var StudentRec: ArrayType;
                        NumStu: NumStuType): real;
var
   TotalOfGrades   :   real;
   i               :   NumStuType;
```

```
begin
   TotalOfGrades := 0;
   for i := 1 to NumStu do
      TotalOfGrades := TotalOfGrades + StudentRec[i].Grade;
   CalculateTotal := TotalOfGrades
end;   {CalculateTotal}
```

5.
```
   {*** Function to return average of grades ***}

   function CalculateAverage(NumStu: NumStuType;
                             TotalOfGrades: real): real;
   begin
      if NumStu = 0 then
         CalculateAverage := 0
      else
         CalculateAverage := TotalOfGrades / NumStu
   end;   {CalculateAverage}
```

6.
```
{**Procedure to print names and scores of those above average**}

procedure PrintAboveAverage(var StudentRec: ArrayType;
              NumStu: NumStuType; average: real);
var
   i : NumStuType;
begin
   writeln('Students and grades with scores above average:');
   for i := 1 to NumStu do
      if StudentRec[i].Grade > average then
         begin
            PrintString(StudentRec[i].Name);
            writeln(StudentRec[i].Grade:4)
         end {if}
end;   {PrintAboveAverage}
```

7.
```
   {*** Procedure to print name ***}

   procedure PrintString(var NameString: StringType);
   var
      i : lengthType;
   begin
      for i := 1 to NameString.length do
         write(NameString.str[i])
   end;   {PrintString}
```

8.

```
{**Procedure to find maximum and minimum scores and who made them**}

procedure CalculateMaxMin (var StudentRec: ArrayType;
                              NumStu: NumStuType);
var
   MaxGrade,
   MinGrade   :   GradeType;
begin
   if NumStu > 0 then
      begin
         MaxGrade := CalculateMax (StudentRec, NumStu);
         PrintMaxStudents (StudentRec, NumStu, MaxGrade);
         writeln;
         MinGrade := CalculateMin (StudentRec, NumStu);
         PrintMinStudents (StudentRec, NumStu, MinGrade)
      end {if}
end;   {CalculateMaxMin}

{*** Function to return maximum score ***}

function CalculateMax (var StudentRec: ArrayType;
                         NumStu: NumStuType): GradeType;
var
   MaxGrade   :   GradeType;
   i          :   NumStuType;
begin
   MaxGrade := StudentRec[1].Grade;
   for i := 2 to NumStu do
      if StudentRec[i].Grade > MaxGrade then
         MaxGrade := StudentRec[i].Grade;
   CalculateMax := MaxGrade
end;   {CalculateMax}

{*** Procedure to print students who made maximum score ***}

procedure PrintMaxStudents (var StudentRec: ArrayType;
                  NumStu: NumStuType; MaxGrade: GradeType);
var
   i : NumStuType;
```

```
begin
    writeln('Students with the Maximum Grade of ', MaxGrade, ':');
    for i := 1 to NumStu do
        if StudentRec[i].Grade = MaxGrade then
            begin
                PrintString(StudentRec[i].Name);
                writeln
            end {if}
end;    {PrintMaxStudents}
```

CalculateMin and *PrintMinStudents* are like *CalculateMax* and *PrintMaxStudents*, respectively, with *MinGrade* substituted for *MaxGrade*, *CalculateMin* for *CalculateMax*, and < for >.

10. {*** Procedure to swap the values in X and Y ***}

```
procedure swap(var X, Y: elType);
var
    temp    : elType;
begin
    temp   := X;
    X      := Y;
    Y      := temp
end;    {swap}
```

11.
{*** Procedure to handle error situations ***}

```
procedure ErrorHandler(ErrorCode: ErrorCodeType);
begin
    case ErrorCode of
        DivisionByZero    :    writeln('Division by zero');
        NoData            :    writeln('File empty');
        IndexOutOfRange   :    writeln('Index out of range');
        NoGrade           :    writeln('Missing grade');
        NegativeGrade     :    writeln('Negative grade');
        Over100Grade      :    writeln('Grade over 100');
        NameTooLong       :    writeln('Name too long')
    end;
    goto 99    {Halt program. Last statement is "99 end."}
end;    {ErrorHandler}
```

SECTION 1.3

4.
```
procedure sort(var StudentRec: ArrayType;
                   NumStu: NumStuType);
begin
    writeln('***Sort procedure executed***')
end; {sort}
```

SECTION 1.4

2. *f*   **6.** *g*   **8.** equal   **10.** *f*   **14.** $O(n^{3/2})$ **16.** $O(n)$

18. $O(n\ X)$

22. *f*

24. *g*

27. $O(n)$ **29.** $O(1)$ **33. a.** 6 nsec   **36. a.** $O(n/4) = O(n)$

37. b. $O(1)$ **e.** $\log_2(8) = 3$

Chapter 2

SECTION 2.1

2. a. $3, 7, 15, 31, 63$

b.
```
function f (n : NonNeg): NonNeg;
begin
    if n = 0 then
        f := 3
    else
        f := 2 * f (n−1) + 1
end; {f}
```

5. b.
```
function Amount (P, R: real; n: NonNeg): real;
    begin
        if n = 0 then
            Amount := P
        else
            Amount := Amount (P, R, n − 1) * (1 + R)
    end; {Amount}
```

11.
```
function SumArray (var a: ArrayType; n: IndexType): real;
begin
    if n = 1 then
        SumArray := a[1]
    else
        SumArray := SumArray (a, n − 1) + a[n]
end; {SumArray}
```

13. a. IndexType   **b.** real   **c.** a   **d.** n − 1   **e.** a[n]

18. a. 1 followed by any number (including none) of zeros.

   c. n = 1   **d.** false   **e.** InLang (a, n − 1)

21. a. 1   **b.** 1

SECTION 2.2

3.
```
function NRf (n: NonNeg): NonNeg;
var
    i,                        {index}
    FunctionValue : NonNeg;   {ongoing value of function}
begin
    FunctionValue := 3;
    for i := 1 to n do
        FunctionValue := 2 * FunctionValue + 1;
    NRf := FunctionValue
end; {NRf}
```

4.
```
function NRAmount (P, R: real; n: NonNeg): real;
    var
        year        : NonNeg;   {index}
        AmountValue : real;     {accumulated amount}
    begin
        AmountValue := P;
        for year := 1 to n do
            AmountValue := AmountValue * (1 + R);
        NRAmount := AmountValue
    end; {NRAmount}
```

9.

```
function NRMaxa (var a: ArrayType; n: IndexType): real;
var
    Max : real;              {ongoing maximum}
    i   : IndexType;         {index}
begin
    Max := a[1];
    for i := 2 to n do
        if a[i] > Max then
            Max := a[i];
    NRMaxa := Max
end; {NRMaxa}
```

12.

```
function NRInLang (var a: ArrayType; n: Positive): boolean;
var
    StillInLang : boolean;    {test if string is still in language}
    i           : Positive;   {index}
begin
    StillInLang := a[1] = '1';
    i := 1;
    while StillInLang and (i < n) do
        begin
            i := i + 1;
            if a[i] <> '0' then
                StillInLang := false
        end; {while}
    NRInLang := StillInLang
end; {NRInLang}
```

19. a.

```
function NRna (n: NonNeg; a: real): real;
var
    i         : NonNeg;   {index}
    NRnaValue: real;      {accumulated value of function}
begin
    NRnaValue := 0;
    for i := 1 to n do
        NRnaValue := NRnaValue + a;
    NRna := NRnaValue
end; {NRna}
```

SECTION 2.3

1. Statement $P(n)$ is "*factorial*(n) returns $n!$"
  Prove $P(0)$ or "*factorial*(0) returns $0!$"
    If $n = 0$, then *factorial* $\leftarrow 1 = 0!$
  Assume $P(k)$ or "*factorial*(k) returns $k!$"
  Prove $P(k + 1)$ or "*factorial*($k + 1$) returns $(k + 1)!$"
    Since $k + 1 \neq 0$,
      factorial $\leftarrow (k + 1) * factorial((k + 1) - 1)$
    or
      factorial $\leftarrow (k + 1) * k! = (k + 1)!$
  by the induction hypothesis and the definition of $(k + 1)!$

4. a. $A = P(1 + R)^n$

10. a. $2^N - 1$

13. a. $0 \leq i \leq n$ and *factorial* is the product of the integers from n down to $(i + 1)$.

15. a. $1 \leq year \leq n + 1$ and *AmountValue* $= P(1 + R)^{year-1}$
  b. (1) Show the loop invariant is initially true: The loop index *year* is initialized to be 1, which satisfies $1 \leq year \leq n + 1$ for n ≥ 0. Moreover, before the loop is executed, *AmountValue* is initialized to P, which is $P(1 + R)^0 = P(1 + R)^{year-1}$.
  (2) Show the invariant is true after each iteration. Assume the invariant holds after the kth iteration where $1 \leq k < n$ and $year = year_k$. In the $(k + 1)$ iteration, $year_k$ is incremented by 1 so that the value of *year* after the $(k + 1)$ iteration is $year_{k+1} = year_k + 1$. Thus, $1 \leq year_{k+1} \leq n + 1$. During the $(k + 1)$ iteration *AmountValue* is also multiplied by $(1 + R)$ so that after this iteration the value of *Amount-Value* is *AmountValue*$_{k+1}$ = *AmountValue*$_k (1 + R)$. But *Amount-Value*$_k$ is assumed to be $P(1 + R)^{year_k-1}$ so that

$$AmountValue_{k+1} = P(1 + R)^{year_k-1}(1 + R)$$
$$= P(1 + R)^{year_k}$$
$$= P(1 + R)^{year_{k+1}-1}$$

  (3) Show that when the loop terminates, we have the desired result of *AmountValue* being $P(1 + R)^n$. When the loop terminates, $year = n + 1$ and the invariant reads $1 \leq n + 1 \leq n + 1$ and *AmountValue* $= P(1 + R)^{(n+1)-1} = P(1 + R)^n$.
  (4) The loop will eventually terminate because all *for* loops do terminate when the control variable exceeds the final value; i.e., $i = n + 1$.

SECTION 2.4

3. *GreaterThan*(i, j) $\rightarrow b$
  Input: i, j — integers; *Output*: b — boolean value
  Algorithm:
    GreaterThan $\leftarrow$ *GreaterThanZero*(*IntegerSubtraction*(i, j))

6. *UnitsDigit(i)* → *d*
  Input : *i* — integer; *Output*: *d* — digit
  Algorithm:
    UnitsDigit ← *Remainder(i, 10)*

17. *Nand(b1, b2)* → *b3*
  Input: *b1, b2* — boolean values; *Output*: *b3* — boolean value
  Algorithm:
    Nand ← *Not(And(b1, b2))*

21. *GreaterOrEqualZero(i)* → *b*
  Input: *i* — integer; *Output*: *b* — boolean value
  Algorithm:
    GreaterOrEqualZero ← *Or(EqualZero(i), GreaterThanZero(i))*

26. *pred(c1)* → *c2*
  Input: *c1* — character; *Output*: *c2* — character
  Algorithm:
    pred(c1) ← *chr(IntegerSubtraction(ord(c1), 1))*

30. *EqualEnumeration(e1, e2)* → *b*
  Input: *e1, e2* — enumeration values; *Output*: *b* — boolean value
  Algorithm:
    EqualEnumeration ← *Equal(ord(e1), ord(e2))*

Chapter 3

SECTION 3.1

1. b.
```
const
    MaxNumEls    =   500;
type
    salaryType   =   array [1..MaxNumEls] of real;
var
    salary       :   salaryType;
```

8. 565   **12.** 581   **16.** 553   **20.** 549   **28. a.** *ColIndex*   **b.** *RowType*

34. a. 182   **b.** 182 words   **c.** 517   **50. b.** 7503

SECTION 3.2

3. a. 4, 2   **6. a.** when *a* has one element

10. a. 10,571 μsec   **b.** 1533 μsec

16. a. Write a *SeqSearchNext* function that performs a sequential search similar to *SeqSearch*. *SeqSearchNext* returns the final value of *i*, regardless if *x* = a[*i*] or not. Thus if *x* cannot be found, *i* will be the index of the first array element larger than *x* or *i* will be *n*.

```
        procedure SeqRange (var a: ArrayType; n: IndexType;
                             LowGrade, HighGrade: integer;
                             var LowIndex, HighIndex: IndexType);
        begin
           LowIndex := SeqSearchNext (a, n, LowGrade);
           HighIndex := SeqSearchNext (a, n, HighGrade);
           { Find the last array element with a value <= HighGrade }
           if a[ HighIndex ] > HighGrade then
              HighIndex := HighIndex - 1
        end;
```

SECTION 3.3

1. a.
```
        StockType  =  record
             Code    :  char;
             Cost    :  real;
             Number  :  integer
           end;
        var
           Stock   :  StockType;
```

b.
```
        with Stock do
           begin
              Code   := 'X';
              Cost   := 346.59;
              Number := 10
           end {with}
```

c.
```
        with stock do
           writeln ('code: ', Code,' cost: ', cost:7:2,
                    ' Number: ', Number)
```

5.
```
procedure DisplayRec(vStudent: elType);
var
   i: GradeIndexType;    {index}
begin
   with vStudent do
      begin
         write (Name);
         case RecCode of
            header : writeln (' Semester = ', semester : 2,
                              ' Year = ', year : 2);
            withdraw : writeln;
```

```
              undergrad,
              grad           : begin
                                writeln;
                                write ('Grades: ');
                                for i := 1 to MaxNumGrades do
                                  write (Grade[i]: 4);
                                writeln;
                                writeln(' Average = ', Average :8:2,
                                          ' CourseGrade = ', CourseGrade )
                              end {undergrad, grad}
           end {case}
        end {with}
  end;    {DisplayRec}
```

SECTION 3.4

1. c.

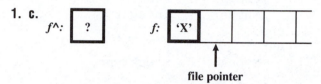

file pointer

2. c. File, buffer, and file pointer unchanged; output to standard display: D.

7. a.

```
procedure CopyFile (var InFile, OutFile: FileType);
var
    x : elType;
begin
    reset (InFile);
    rewrite (OutFile);
    while not eof (InFile) do
        begin
            read (InFile, x);
            write(OutFile, x)
        end {while}
end; {CopyFile}
```

b. The file pointer for *InFile* points to a location in that file, which is in input mode. The file pointer for *OutFile* points to a corresponding location in that file, which is in output mode. From the first of the files up to the locations before those indicated by the file pointers, the files are identical.

SECTION 3.5

1. [1, 3, 4, 5, 6, 7]   **2.** [3, 7]   **3.** [1]   **13.** *true*   **15.** *true*

24.
```
type
    letters          = 'A'..'Z';
    SetLettersType   = set of letters;
var
    vowels, consonants : SetLettersType;
begin
    vowels     := ['A','E','I','O','U'];
    consonants := ['A'..'Z'] − vowels
```

25.
```
procedure RemoveX (var S: SetType; x: elType);
begin
    S:= S − [x]
end;  {RemoveX}
```

Chapter 4

SECTION 4.1

2. $n \leftarrow 7$ **5.** $v \leftarrow$ 'ANT'   **8.** $u \leftarrow$ 'TLNT'

12. *AppendAsterisks(s)*
Input: s — string; *Output: s* — string
Algorithm:
  for *i* from 1 to 20 − *LengthString(s)* do
   AppendChar(s, '*')

SECTION 4.2

1.
```
procedure MakeStringEmpty (var s: StringType);
begin
    s.length := 0
end;
```

11. a.
```
procedure InitBoyerMoore (var dist : distType; sub : StringType);
var
    c : 'A'..'Z';
    i : IndexType;
begin
    for c := 'A' to 'Z' do
        dist[c] := sub.length;
    for i := 1 to sub.length − 1 do
        dist[sub.el[i]] := sub.length − i
end;
```

15.

```
procedure AppendAsterisks (var s: StringType);
const
    asterisk        = '*';
    MaxNumAsterisks = 20;
var
    i,
    NumAsterisks : 0..MaxNumAsterisks;
begin
    NumAsterisks := MaxNumAsterisks - LengthString(s);
    for i := 1 to NumAsterisks do
        AppendChar(s, asterisk)
end;   {AppendAsterisk}
```

SECTION 4.3

2.

```
function InAlphaOrder (var Name: StringArrayType; n: range): boolean;
var
    AlphaOrder : boolean;
    i          : range;
begin
    AlphaOrder := true;
    i := 1;
    while (i < n) and AlphaOrder do
        if LessOrEqualString (Name[i], Name[i + 1]) then
            i := i + 1
        else
            AlphaOrder := false;
    InAlphaOrder := AlphaOrder
end; { InAlphaOrder }
```

Chapter 5

SECTION 5.1

9. b. *Push*(*s*, next input = 1)
Pop(*s*, *e*) and write (*e* = 1)
Push(*s*, next input = 2)
Push(*s*, next input = 3)
Pop(*s*, *e*) and write (*e* = 3)
Pop(*s*, *e*) and write (*e* = 2)

10. *SwapStack(s)*
   Input: *s* — stack   *Output: s* — stack
   Algorithm:
       if not *StackIsEmpty(s)* then
           Pop(s, first)
           if not (*StackIsEmpty(s)*) then
               Pop(s, second)
               Push(s, first)
               Push(s, second)
           else
               Push(s, first)

18. *Append(s, u)*
   Input: *s, u* — stacks   *Output: s, u* — stacks
   Algorithm:
       if not *StackIsEmpty(u)* then
           Pop(u, e)
           Append(s, u)
           if *StackIsFull(s)* then
               StackIsFullError(e)
           else
               Push(s, e)

SECTION 5.2

```
3. procedure SwapStack (var s: stack);
   var
       first,
       second : elType;
   begin
       if not StackIsEmpty (s) then
           begin
               Pop (s, first);
               if not StackIsEmpty (s) then
                   begin
                       Pop (s, second);
                       Push (s, first);
                       Push (s, second)
                   end { if }
               else
                   Push (s, first)
           end { if }
   end; { SwapStack }
```

11. {*** Error procedure for full stack ***}

```
procedure StackIsFullError (e : elType);
   begin
      writeln ('Stack is full.');
      writeln ('Not enough room to push ', e);
      goto 99 {halt}
   end; { StackIsFullError }

procedure Append (var s, u: stack);
var
   e : elType;
begin   { Append }
   if not StackIsEmpty (u) then
      begin
         Pop (u, e);
         Append (s, u);
         if StackIsFull (s) then
            StackIsFullError (e)
         else
            Push (s, e)
      end { if }
end; { Append }
```

SECTION 5.3

1.

```
procedure SimRecProc (n : integer);
var
   s : stack;
begin
   { Build stack of values of n }
   MakeStackEmpty(s);
   while (not TerminalCondition(n)) and (not StackIsFull(s)) do
      begin
         PreStatements(n);
         Push(s, n);
         n := f(n)
      end; { while }
   if not TerminalCondition(n) then
      StackOverflowError
```

```
    else
        begin
            { Terminal Case }
            TerminalCase(n);
            { Build value of procedure from stack }
            while not StackIsEmpty(s) do
                begin
                    Pop(s, n);
                    PostStatements(n)
                end { while }
        end { else }
end;
```

8. a. *7*   **12.** *A B C* ∗ +

Chapter 6

SECTION 6.1

8. *AddQueue*(*q*) → *n*
Input: q — queue   *Output: n* — number
Algorithm:
    MakeQueueEmpty(*p*)
    sum ← 0
    while not *QueueIsEmpty*(*q*) do
        DeQueue(*q, e*)
        EnQueue(*p, e*)
        sum ← *sum* + *e*
    AddQueue ← *sum*
    AppendQueue(*q, p*)   {restore *q*}

15. a. *Reverse*(*q*)
Input: q — queue   *Output: q* — queue
Algorithm:
    if not *QueueIsEmpty*(*q*) then
        DeQueue(*q, e*)
        Reverse(*q*)
        Enqueue(*q, e*)

b. *NRReverse*(*q*)
Algorithm:
    MakeStackEmpty(*s*)
    while not *QueueIsEmpty*(*q*) do
        DeQueue(*q, e*)
        Push(*s, e*)
    while not *StackIsEmpty*(*s*) do
        Pop(*s, e*)
        EnQueue(*q, e*)

SECTION 6.2

3.
```
function Addqueue (var q: queue): real;
var
    p    :    queue;
    e,
    sum  :    real;
begin
    MakeQueueEmpty (p);
    sum := 0;
    while not QueueIsEmpty (q) do
       begin
           Dequeue (q, e);
           Enqueue (p, e);
           sum := sum + e
       end; { while }
    AddQueue := sum;
    AppendQueue (q, p)
end; { AddQueue }
```

10. **a.**
```
procedure Reverse (var q: queue);
var
    e    : elType;
begin
    if not QueueIsEmpty (q) then
       begin
           Dequeue (q, e);
           Reverse (q);
           Enqueue (q, e)
       end { if }
end; { Reverse }
```

b.
```
procedure NRReverse (var q: queue);
var
    s    : stack;
    e    : elType;
begin
    MakeStackEmpty(s);
    while not QueueIsEmpty(q) do
       begin
           DeQueue (q, e);
           Push (s, e)
       end;    { while }
    while not StackIsEmpty (s) do
       begin
           Pop (s, e);
           EnQueue (q, e)
       end    { while }
end;    { NRReverse }
```

SECTION 6.3

4.

```
program TestPostOfficeSimulation (input, output);
var
    ans : char;
procedure PostOfficeSimulation;
    . . .
begin
    repeat
        PostOfficeSimulation;
        repeat;
            write('Do you want to perform another simulation? (Y/N) ');
            readln (ans)
        until ans in [ 'Y', 'y', 'N', 'n']
    until (ans = 'N') or (ans = 'n')
end.
```

Chapter 7

SECTION 7.1

3.

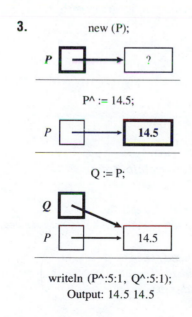

new (P);

P^ := 14.5;

Q := P;

writeln (P^:5:1, Q^:5:1);
Output: 14.5 14.5

8.

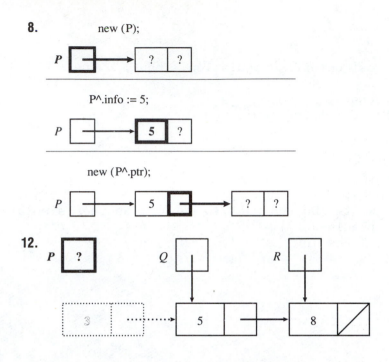

new (P);

P^.info := 5;

new (P^.ptr);

12.

SECTION 7.2

4. Current node's information is greater than or equal to target node's information.

6. b. *NumNames* = 0

SECTION 7.3

1. *SwapInfo(cur, prev)*
   Input: cur, prev — pointers
   Algorithm:
   $\quad$ *e* ← *RetrieveInfo(cur)*
   $\quad$ *StoreInfo(cur, RetrieveInfo(prev))*
   $\quad$ *StoreInfo(prev, e)*

4. *InsertTailList(head, tail, Target)*
   Input: head, tail, Target — pointers   *Output: head, tail — pointers*
   Algorithm:
   $\quad$ if *ListIsEmpty(head)* then
   $\quad\quad$ *InsertFirst(head, Target)*
   $\quad\quad$ *ToFirst(head, tail)*
   $\quad$ else
   $\quad\quad$ *InsertLater(tail, Target)*
   $\quad\quad$ *Advance(tail)*

7. b. *RPrintList*(**head**)
Input: *head* — pointer
Output: information stored in linked list printed
Algorithm:
       if not *ListIsEmpty*(*head*) do
          print *RetrieveInfo*(*head*)
          RPrintList(*RetrieveNext*(*head*))

SECTION 7.4

1. b. 7   **6. a.** 5, 4, 2, 6, 7   **7. b.** 0

20. i.
```
procedure SwapInfo (cur, prev: pointer);
var
    e: InfoType;
begin
    e := RetrieveInfo (cur);
    StoreInfo (cur, RetrieveInfo (prev));
    StoreInfo (prev, e)
end;
```

ii.
```
procedure SwapInfo (cur, prev: IndexType);
{Procedure body identical to body of Part i.}
{Array A for linked list declared globally. }
```

26. b i.
```
procedure RPrintList (head: pointer);
begin
    if not ListIsEmpty (head) then
        begin
            writeln (RetrieveInfo (head));
            RPrintList (RetrieveNext (head))
        end { if }
end; { RPrintList }
```

SECTION 7.5

10.
```
procedure MakeMatEmpty (var A: pointer);
begin
    new (A);
    A^.row     := MaxRow;
    A^.column  := MaxCol;
    A^.right   := nil;
    A^.down    := nil
end; { MakeMatEmpty }
```

14.
```
function AtEndRow (P: pointer): boolean;
begin
    AtEndRow := (P^.right = nil)
end;
```

34. *ToRow(A, i, cur)*

    Input: A — pointer; *i* — row number   *Output: cur* — pointer
    Algorithm:

        ToFirstMat(A, cur)   { Find *i*th row }
        if *AtEndCol(cur)* then
           cur ← null
      else
        AdvanceDown(cur)
        while (*RetrieveRow(cur) < i*) and (not *AtEndCol(cur)*) do
           AdvanceDown(cur)
        if *RetrieveRow(cur) ≠ i* then
           cur ← null

Chapter 8

SECTION 8.1

8.

```
function InfIntegerToReal (num: pointer): real;
begin
   if ListIsEmpty (num) then
      InfIntegerToReal := 0.0
   else
      InfIntegerToReal := 10.0 * InfIntegerToReal (RetrieveNext (num))
                     + RetrieveInfo (num)
end; { InfIntegerToReal }
```

10. c. *ElimDuplicates(P)*

    Input: P — pointer
    Algorithm:

        ToFirst(P, prev)
        while not *AtEnd(prev)* do
           if *RetrieveInfo(P) = RetrieveInfo(RetrieveNext(prev))* then
               DeleteLater(prev)
           else
               Advance(prev)

11. c.

```
procedure ElimDuplicates (P: pointer);
var
   prev :  pointer;
begin
   ToFirst (P, prev);
   while not ListIsEmpty (RetrieveNext (prev)) do
      if RetrieveInfo (P) = RetrieveInfo (RetrieveNext (prev)) then
         DeleteLater (prev)
      else
         Advance (prev)
end; { ElimDuplicates }
```

24. $car(G) = (a, b)$; $cdr(G) = ((c) (e (f g)) (\ ) h)$

27.
```
function atomP (L: GeneralizedList): boolean;
begin
    atomP := L^.atom
end;   { atomP }
```

SECTION 8.2

6. a.
PointDeleteWord(s, p)
Input: s, p — pointers   *Output: s* — pointer
Algorithm:
    InWord ← true
    if *ListIsEmpty(p)* then
        while (not *ListIsEmpty(s)*) and *InWord* do
            if *RetrieveInfo(s)* in (['A'..'Z'] + ['a'..'z']) then
                DeleteFirst(s)
            else
                InWord ← false
    else
        while not *AtEnd(p)* and *InWord* do
            if *RetrieveInfo(RetrieveNext(p))* in (['A'..'Z'] + ['a'..'z']) then
                DeleteLater(p)
            else
                InWord ← false

SECTION 8.3

3. Answer identical to that of Exercise 3, Section 5.2. Use linked list stack package.

11. Answer identical to that of Exercise 11, Section 5.2; use linked list stack package. Or because *StackIsFull(s)* is always *false* in this package, we can use the following implementation without a *StackIsFullError* procedure:

```
{*** Procedure to append stack u on the
        top of stack s ***}

procedure Append (var s, u: stack);
var
    e: elType;
begin
    if not StackIsEmpty (u) then
        begin
            Pop (u, e);
            Append (s, u);
            Push (s, e)
        end { if }
end; { Append }
```

SECTION 8.4

4.
```
procedure EnQueue (var q: queue; e: elType);
var
    p: pointer;
begin
    AddNode (p, e);
    if ListIsEmpty (q.front) then
        begin
            InsertFirst (q.front, p);
            ToFirst (q.front, q.rear)
        end { if }
    else
        begin
            InsertLater (q.rear, p);
            Advance (q.rear)
        end { else }
end; { EnQueue }
```

9. Answer identical to that of Exercise 3, Section 6.2, except that it is unnecessary for *q* to be a variable parameter. Use linked list queue package.

Chapter 9

SECTION 9.1

7. *DeleteTable*(*t*, 'Jordan, Ann')

8. *VisitFreshman*(*e*)
   Procedure called by a traversal of the table in Figure 9.1 to print *e* if *e* is the record of a freshman (*e.year* = 1).

   Input: e — record from table in Figure 9.1   *Output:* possibly printed *e*
   Algorithm:
       if *e.year* = 1 then
           print *e*

   FreshmanRpt(*t*)
   Input: t — table from Figure 9.1   *Output:* printed report of freshmen
   Algorithm:
       print title and headings
       Traverse(*t*, *VisitFreshman*(*e*))

13. *SubTable(s, t) → b*
   Input: s, t — tables   Output: b — boolean value
   Algorithm:
       IsInTable ← true   { Initialize in case *s* is empty }
                               {Abort traversal if IsInTable becomes false}
       Traverse(s, TestInTable(e, t, IsInTable))
       SubTable ← IsInTable   { Last value of *IsInTable*}

SECTION 9.2

1.
```
const
    NumEls      = 200;
type
    IndexType   = 1..NumEls;
    range    ·  = 0..NumEls;
    KeyType     = packed array [1..24] of char;
    elType      = record
       Name     : KeyType;
       Year     : 1..4;
       GPA      : real
    end;
    TableType   = array [ IndexType ] of elType;
    table       = record
       count    : range;
       el       : TableType
    end;
var
    t    : table;
    e    : elType;
```

4.
```
procedure VisitFreshman (e: elType);
begin
    with e do
        if year = 1 then
            writeln (Name:32, Year:6, GPA:9:2)
end; { VisitFreshman }

procedure FreshmanRpt (var t: table);
var
    i: IndexType;
begin
    writeln ('Report on Freshmen': 39);
    writeln ('Name': 12, 'Year': 26, 'GPA': 9)
    for i := 1 to t.count do
        VisitFreshman (t.el[i])
end; { FreshmanRpt }
```

13. a.
```
const
    NumEls        =    ........;
type
    IndexType     =    1..NumEls;
    range         =    0..NumEls;
    KeyType       =    .........;
    elType        =    record
        key       :    KeyType;

             :
    end;
    TableType     =    array [ IndexType ] of elType;
    table         =    record
        count     :    range;
        el        :    TableType
    end;

procedure Update (var t: table; e: elType);
var
    i : range;
begin
    { Search for a match of the key fields of e and
        table entry }
    i := BiSearch (t.el, 1, t.count, e.key);
    if i = 0 then
        NotInTableError (e)
    else
        t.el[i] := e
end;
```

b. Change first executable line in Part a to:

```
i := UnorderedSeqSearch (t.el, 1, t.count, e.key)
```

In the unordered sequential search, only finding the key or coming to the end of the array will stop the search.

c.
```
type
         :
    table   =   ^Node;
    Node    =   record
        info : elType;
        next : table
    end;
```

```
procedure Update (var t:table; e: elType);
var
    p : table;
begin
    p := OrderedSeqSearch (t, e.key);
    if TableIsEmpty (p) then
        NotInTableError (e)
    else
        p^.info := e
end; { Update }
```

In this ordered sequential search, the search stops as soon as the key for the current table entry is greater than or equal to *e.key* or we reach the end of the table.

d. Substitute an unordered sequential search for the ordered one in Part c. The search only stops when the current key equals *e.key* or we reach the end of the table.

SECTION 9.3

1. b.
```
function h (key : NonNeg): NonNeg;
begin
    key := key div 100;
    h   := key mod 10
end;
```

2. a. 8

14.
```
function LinearProbe (var t: table; k: KeyType;
                          h: IndexType): IndexType;
var
    j : integer;
begin
    j := 0;
    h := (h + 1) mod TableSize;
    while (t[h].key > 1) and (t[h].key <> k)
            and (j < MaxNum) do
        begin
            j := j + 1
            h := (h + 1) mod TableSize;
        end;
    LinearProbe := h
end; { LinearProbe }
```

21. 77

36.
```
{ Assume key in table. }

procedure DeleteTable (var t: table; k: KeyType);
var
   cur, prev   : pointer;
   n           : IndexType;
begin
   Probe(t, k, cur, prev);
   if not ListIsEmpty(prev) and not ListIsEmpty(cur) then
      DeleteLater(prev)
   else if not ListIsEmpty(cur) then
      DeleteFirst(t[hash(k)])
end; { DeleteTable }
```

Chapter 10

SECTION 10.1

1. n. g e a b f c d   **o.** a e b g c f d

  p. a b e c d f g   **6. d.** 8   **8. d.** 15

SECTION 10.2

15.

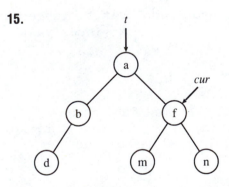

16. a. *InsertRoot(t, e)*
  b. *TreeIsEmpty(RetrieveRight(cur))*
  c. *InsertRight(cur, e)*
  d. *continue ← false*
  e. *ToRight(cur)*

17. *LeftIsEmpty(t)* → *b*
   Input: t — tree   *Output: b* — boolean value
   Algorithm: LeftIsEmpty ← TreeIsEmpty(RetrieveLeft(t))

21. *LeafCountVisit(t, count)*
　　　Visit procedure for *LeafCount*
　　Input: t — points to current node in tree; *count* — nonnegative integer
　　Output: count — nonnegative integer
　　Algorithm:
　　　　if *IsLeaf(t)* then
　　　　　　count ← count + 1

　　LeafCount(t) → *count*
　　Input: t — tree　　　*Output: count* — nonnegative integer
　　Algorithm:
　　　　count ← 0
　　　　　　{ Ellipsis indicates any traversal permissible }
　　　　. . . *Traverse(t, LeafCountVisit(t, count))*
　　　　LeafCount ← count

SECTION 10.3

4.
```
function LeftIsEmpty (t: BinaryTree): boolean;
begin
    LeftIsEmpty := TreeIsEmpty(RetrieveLeft(t))
end;
```

8.
```
procedure LeafCountVisit (t: BinaryTree; var count: Nonneg);
begin
    if IsLeaf(t) then
        count := count + 1
end;

function LeafCount (t: BinaryTree): NonNeg;
var
    count: NonNeg; {Number of leaves}
begin
    count := 0;
    InOrderTraverse (t, count); {Visit procedure is LeafCountVisit}
    LeafCount := count
end;
```

20. a. i. 0　　**ii.** *level*　　**iii.** *RecSumofLevels(RetrieveRight(t), level + 1)*

　　iv. *RecSumofLevels(t, 1)*

SECTION 10.4

8.
```
procedure InsertRight (t: BinaryTree; e: elType);
var
    cur,                        { pointer to new node }
    successor: BinaryTree;      { pointer to inorder successor }
begin
    successor   := t^.right; { hold successor }
    new (t^.right);            { new node to right }
    t^.thread   := false;
    cur         := t^.right; { point to new node }
    cur^.el     := e;          { fill new node }
    cur^.left   := nil;
    cur^.right  := successor;
    cur^.thread := true
end;                            { InsertRight }
```

17.
```
function RightIsEmpty (t: BinaryTree): boolean;
begin
    RightIsEmpty := t^.thread
end;    { RightIsEmpty }
```

SECTION 10.5

2. f. 2

l.

8.
```
function KeyFoundBST (t: BinaryTree; k: KeyType): boolean;
var
    cur: BinaryTree;
begin
    SearchBST (t, cur, k);
    KeyFoundBST := cur <> nil
end;    { KeyFoundBST }
```

14. g. $2^m - 1$ **j.** 1, m

SECTION 10.6

1. i, ii, iv, vii

6. right rotation

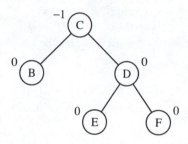

12. a. *LeftRightRotation(t)*
       ToRoot(t, cur)
       ToLeft(t)
       ToRoot(t, prev)
       ToRight(t)
       StoreRight(prev, RetrieveLeft(t))
       StoreLeft(t, prev)
       StoreLeft(cur, RetrieveRight(t))
       StoreRight(t, cur)

SECTION 10.7

1.

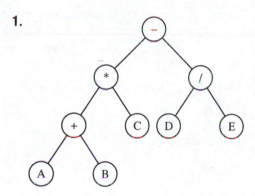

6. a. From left to right, level 3: 9, 7, 3, 8; level 2: 7, 3; level 1: 7.

10. a. no

Chapter 11

SECTION 11.1

1. a. **null** M S   C R T F P   **b.** 16   **c.** 22
       null C M S R T F P
       null C M R S T F P
       null C M R S T F P
       null C F M R S T P
       null C F M P R S T

8. a. *InsertTable(a[0. .m], **temp**)*
   Assumptions: $a[0] = null$; $m <$ the number of elements in a,
        excluding $a[0]$
   Algorithm:
        if $a[m] \leq temp$ then
            $a[m + 1] \leftarrow temp$
        else
            $a[m + 1] \leftarrow a[m]$
            InsertTable(a[0. .(m − 1)], temp)

SECTION 11.2

1. a. C S M R T F P
        C F M R T S P
        C F M R T S P
        C F M P T S R
        C F M P R S T
        C F M P R S T

   b. 21   **c.** 18

7. a. *MinIndex* is the index of the minimum element in the subarray
        $a[i. .(j − 1)]$
   c. The subarray $a[1. .(i − 1)]$ is sorted, and every element of $a[i. .n]$ is
        greater than or equal to every element of $a[1. .(i − 1)]$.

SECTION 11.3

1. a. 1024; 1,048,576; 10,240

3. a. M A D H R E C P N
        M A D H C E R P N
        E A D H C M R P N

9. a. M

SECTION 11.4

2.

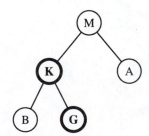

6.

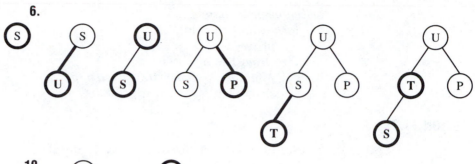

10.

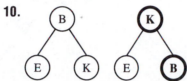

13.

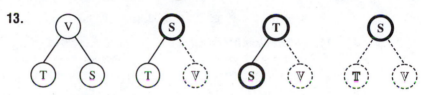

SECTION 11.5

1. a.

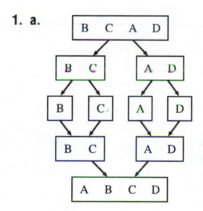

8. a. 0   **b.** 2   **c.** $T(n/2)$ **d.** $n-1$

SECTION 11.6

1. *IndexOfMin(a, i, n, p) → MinIndex*
      MinIndex ← i
      for *j* from *i* + 1 to *n* do
            if *a[p[j]]* < *a[p[MinIndex]]* then
                  MinIndex ← j
      IndexOfMin ← MinIndex

$$
\begin{aligned}
&SelectionSort(a, n, p) \\
&\quad \text{for } i \text{ from } 1 \text{ to } n \text{ do} \\
&\quad\quad p[i] \leftarrow i \\
&\quad \text{for } i \text{ from } 1 \text{ to } n - 1 \text{ do} \\
&\quad\quad MinIndex \leftarrow IndexOfMin(a, i, n, p) \\
&\quad\quad swap(p[i], p[MinIndex])
\end{aligned}
$$

SECTION 11.7

1. d. selection sort   **e.** heapsort   **4. b.** queue

Chapter 12

SECTION 12.1

2. e. none   **3. a.** 2   **8. a.** $n - 1$

14. *DeleteGraphValue(g, f)*
  Input: g — graph; *f* — file   *Output: g* — graph
  Algorithm:
      reset(f)
      while not *EOF(f)* do
          read(*f, k*)
          if *KeyFoundGraph(g, k)* then
              ToNode(g, k, curNode)
              DeleteNode(g, curNode)

SECTION 12.2

1. *node* = [u v w x y]

$$
edge = \begin{bmatrix}
0 & 1 & 1 & 0 & 0 \\
1 & 0 & 1 & 0 & 0 \\
1 & 1 & 0 & 1 & 0 \\
0 & 0 & 1 & 0 & 0 \\
0 & 0 & 0 & 0 & 0
\end{bmatrix}
$$

8.
```
procedure InsertEdge (var g: graph; k1, k2: keyType);
var
    curNode1,
    curNode2    :    indexType;
begin
    ToNode (g, k1, curNode1);
    ToNode (g, k2, curNode2);
    g.edge[curNode1, curNode2] := true;
    g.edge[curNode2, curNode1] := true
end;
```

22.

```
procedure DeleteGraphValue (var g: graph; var f: FileType);
var
    curNode :    indexType;
    k       :    keyType;
begin
    reset (f);
    while not eof (f) do
        begin
            read (f, k);
            if KeyFoundGraph (g, k) then
                begin
                    ToNode (g, k, curnode);
                    DeleteNode (g, curnode)
                end {if}
        end {while}
end;  {DeleteGraphValue}
```

SECTION 12.3

6. a.
```
procedure ToNode(g: graph; k: keyType; var curNode: graph);
begin
    curNode := g;
    while curNode^.el.key <> k do    {key of current node is not k}
        curNode := curNode^.nextNode {advance curNode in node list}
end;
```

b. n

22. a. n **b.** $\log_2 n$ **c.** 1   **d.** $\log_2 n$

SECTION 12.4

1. 1, 7, 8, 9, 6, 2, 10, 4, 5, 11, 3;
1, 7, 9, 8, 6, 2, 10, 4, 5, 11, 3;
1, 4, 5, 11, 3, 7, 8, 9, 6, 2, 10;
several other possibilities

9. 1, 7, 6, 4, 8, 9, 2, 5, 11, 10, 3;
1, 7, 6, 4, 9, 8, 2, 5, 11, 3, 10;
1, 4, 6, 7, 11, 5, 2, 9, 8, 3, 10;
several other possibilities

SECTION 12.5

13. a. 6   **b.** 1   **c.** definition of root   **d.** $n - 1$
e. A tree has no cycles.

Index